Introduction to Computers Using the IBM® and MS-DOS® PCs
WITH BASIC

SECOND EDITION

Popular Commercial Software Version

Introduction to Computers Using the IBM® and MS-DOS® PCs
WITH BASIC

STEVEN L. MANDELL ■ SECOND EDITION

Popular Commercial Software Version for:

WordStar® 2000
WordPerfect®
Lotus® 1-2-3®
dBase® III

Includes the following software:

WestSoft™ 1.0
Student File Disk

WEST PUBLISHING COMPANY
St. Paul   New York   San Francisco   Los Angeles

COPYRIGHT © 1985 By WEST PUBLISHING COMPANY

COPYRIGHT © 1987 By WEST PUBLISHING COMPANY
50 W. Kellogg Boulevard
P.O. Box 64526
St. Paul, MN 55164-1003

All rights reserved
Printed in the United States of America
94 93 92 91 90 89 88   8 7 6 5 4 3 2

Library of Congress Cataloging-in-Publication Data

Mandell, Steven L.
  Introduction to computers using the IBM and MS-DOS PCs with BASIC/popular commercial software.

  Second ed. of: Introduction to computers using the IBM PC.
  Includes index.
  1. Computers.   2. Microcomputers   3. BASIC (Computer program language)   4. Computer programs.
  I. Mandell, Steven L.   Introduction to computers using the IBM PC.   II. Title.
QA76.M27478   1987   004   87-2000
ISBN 0-314-32171-3

IBM® is the registered trademark of International Business Machines Corporation.
MS-DOS® is the registered trademark of Microsoft Corporation.
WordStar® 2000 is the registered trademark of the MicroPro International Corporation.
WordPerfect® is the registered trademark of the WordPerfect Corporation.
Lotus® 1-2-3® is the registered trademark of the Lotus Development Corporation.
dBase®II, dBase® III, and dBase® Plus are the registered trademarks of Ashton-Tate Corporation.
CorrectStar® is the registered trademark of MicroPro International Corporation.

Copyright © 1987, M & M Productions, Rawhide Software™

Cover Photo: Walter Urei Photography. Photo by Walter Urei.
Composition: Parkwood Composition Service, Inc.
Copy Editor: Joan Compton
Artwork: Carlisle Graphics

Part and Chapter Opening Photos

Part One Courtesy of International Business Machines, Inc., **Chapter 1** Courtesy of Shell Oil Company, **Chapter 2** Photo by Walter Urei, **Chapter 3** Courtesy of Electro Scientific Corporation, **Chapter 4** Courtesy of Hewlett-Packard, **Chapter 5** Courtesy of Blyth Software, **Chapter 6** Courtesy of Apple Computer, Inc., **Chapter 7** Courtesy of U.S. Postal Service, **Part Two** Courtesy of Crown Zellerbach, **Chapter 8** Courtesy of WordPerfect Corporation, **Chapter 9** Courtesy of Compugraphic, **Chapter 10** Courtesy of Union College, **Chapter 11** Courtesy of Hewlett-Packard, **Chapter 12** Courtesy of Lotus Development Corporation, **Chapter 13** Courtesy of Los Alamos National Laboratory, **Chapter 14** Courtesy of Texas Instruments, **Chapter 15** Courtesy of Concurrent Computer Corporation, **BASIC Supplement** Courtesy of Dow Chemical U.S.A., **Chapter 16** Courtesy of Virginia Tech, **Chapter 17** Courtesy of National Computer Camps, **Chapter 18** Courtesy of International Business Machines, Inc., **Chapter 19** Courtesy of International Business Machines, Inc., **Chapter 20** Courtesy of Honeywell, Inc., **Chapter 21** Courtesy of Sperry Corporation, **Chapter 22** Courtesy of New England Digital

Intext Photo Credits

Fig. 1-1 Courtesy of Chrysler Corporation, **Fig. 1-2a** Courtesy of AT&T Bell Laboratories, **Fig. 1-2b** Courtesy of AT&T Bell Laboratories, **Fig. 1-3** Courtesy of Bethlehem Steel Corporation, **Fig. 1-4** Courtesy of Santa Fe Southern Pacific Corporation, **Fig. 1-5** Photo Courtesy of Best Western International, Inc., **Fig. 1-6** Courtesy of Ohio Citizen's Bank, **Fig. 1-7** Courtesy of Brooks Shoe, Inc., **Fig. 1-8** Courtesy of N.Y. Yankees Magazine, **Fig. 1-9** Photograph by John Morgan, **Fig. 1-10** Courtesy of Whirlpool Corporation, **Fig. 1-11** Courtesy of Toshiba's Information Systems Division, Tustin, CA, **Fig. 1-15a** Courtesy of International Business Machines Corporation, **Fig. 1-15b** Courtesy of International Business Machines Corporation, **Fig. 1-16** Crown Copyright, Science Museum, London, **Fig. 1-17a** Courtesy of International Business Machines Corporation, **Fig. 1-17b** Courtesy of International Business Machines Corporation, **Fig. 1-19** Courtesy of Sperry Corporation, **Fig. 1-20** Courtesy of Sperry Corporation, **Fig. 1-21** Courtesy of International Business Machines Corporation, **Fig. 1-22** Photo Courtesy of Digital Equipment Corporation, **Fig. 1-23** Courtesy of International Business Machines Corporation, **Fig. 1-24** Courtesy of AT&T Bell Laboratories, **Fig. 2-1** Courtesy of International Business Machines Corporation, **Fig. 2-2** Photo by Walter Urei, **Fig. 2-3** Photo by Walter Urei, **Fig. 2-4** Photo by Walter Urei, **Fig. 2-5** Photo by Walter Urei, **Fig. 2-6** Photo by Walter Urei, **Fig. 2-7** Photo by Walter Urei, **Fig. 2-8** Photo by Walter Urei, **Fig. 2-9** Photo by Walter Urei, **Fig. 2-10** Photo by Walter Urei, **Fig. 2-11** Photo by Walter Urei, **Fig. 2-12** Photo by Walter Urei, **Fig. 3-1** Courtesy of International Business Machines Corporation, **Fig. 3-2** Photo Courtesy of Wang Laboratories, Inc., **Fig. 3-3** Courtesy of Honeywell Information Systems, **Fig. 3-4** Courtesy of Cray Research, Inc., **Fig. 3-8** Courtesy of Motorola Inc., **Fig. 3-11** Courtesy of Verbatim Corporation, **Fig. 3-14** Courtesy of Anacomp, Inc., **Fig. 3-15** Photo courtesy of 3M Office Systems Division, **Fig. 3-16** Courtesy of International Business Machines Corporation, **Fig. 3-17** Courtesy of AT&T Bell Laboratories, **Fig. 3-19** Photo Courtesy of Wang Laboratories, Inc., **Fig. 3-21a** Courtesy of International Business Machines Corporation, **Fig. 3-21b** Courtesy of Albertson's Inc., **Fig. 3-22** Courtesy of Sperry Corporation, **Fig. 3-23** Photo supplied by New Image Technology, Inc., **Fig. 3-24** Courtesy of AT&T Bell Laboratories, **Fig. 3-25** Courtesy of Texas Instruments, **Fig. 3-27** Courtesy of Dataproducts Corp., **Fig. 3-28** Courtesy of Blyth Software, **Fig. 3-29** Photo courtesy of Hewlett-Packard Company, **Fig. 5-1** Reproduced with permission of AT&T Corporate Archive, **Fig. 5-2** Courtesy of Apple Computer, Inc., **Fig. 5-4** Photo courtesy of Hewlett-Packard Company, **Fig. 5-5** Courtesy of Corona Data Systems, Inc.,

   Credits are continued following the index.

CONTENTS-IN-BRIEF

Preface xxi

PART ONE   COMPUTER LITERACY 1

Chapter 1
Computers in Our World 3

Chapter 2
Getting to Know Your IBM 33

Chapter 3
Hardware 63

Chapter 4
Software Development 97

Chapter 5
Microcomputers 129

Chapter 6
Computers' Impact on Society 151

Chapter 7
Issues of Concern 187

PART TWO   APPLICATIONS SOFTWARE: USING WORDSTAR 2000, WORDPERFECT, LOTUS 1-2-3, AND DBASE III 209

Chapter 8
Introduction to Word Processing and WordStar 2000 211

Chapter 9
Advanced WordStar 2000 245

Chapter 10
Introduction to Word Processing and WordPerfect 277

Chapter 11
Advanced WordPerfect 313

Chapter 12
Introduction to Spreadsheets and Lotus 1-2-3 345

Chapter 13
Advanced Lotus 1-2-3 387

Chapter 14
Introduction to Data Managers and dBase III 421

Chapter 15
Advanced dBase III 461

Appendix
Installation Procedures A-1

PART THREE   BASIC SUPPLEMENT B-1

Section I
Introduction to BASIC B-3

Section II
Getting started with BASIC B-19

Section III
Input and Output B-39

Section IV
Control Statements and Subroutines B-65

Section V
Looping B-91

Section VI
Arrays B-117

Section VII
Graphics and Sound B-147

BASIC Glossary B-165

BASIC Index B-169

Glossary G-1

Index I-1

CONTENTS

Preface xxi

PART ONE	COMPUTER LITERACY	1

CHAPTER 1	Computers In Our World	3

Introduction	4
Daily Encounters	6
The Computer's Role In Data Processing	9
Analog and Digital Computers	10
The Computer Advantage	10
LEARNING CHECK	12
Stages of Data Processing	13
Types of Data Processing	16
LEARNING CHECK	17
Computers Yesterday and Today	17
Early Developments	18
HIGHLIGHT: Ada Lovelace	19
HIGHLIGHT: John Vincent Atanasoff	22
LEARNING CHECK	23
The First Generation: 1951–1958	24
The Second Generation: 1959–1964	26
The Third Generation: 1965–1970	27
The Fourth Generation: 1971–Today	29
LEARNING CHECK	30
Summary Points	31
Review Questions	32

CHAPTER 2	Getting to Know Your IBM	33

Introduction	34
IBM Hardware	34
The Monitor	34
The Keyboard	36
The Disk Drive	37
Caring for Your Computer	39
LEARNING CHECK	40
Getting Started	40

HIGHLIGHT: A Tale of Two Bugs	44
Initializing a Disk	45
Disk Operating System Commands	47
Using WestSoft™ 1.0	48
Loading WestSoft	49
WestSoft Home Banking System	49
WestSoft Personality Traits Program	52
WestSoft Ticket-Office Manager	53
HIGHLIGHT: Winning With Antonia Stone	55
WestSoft Information Network	55
WestSoft Dental Office Manager	57
Summary Points	58
Review Questions	59
Review Exercises	60

CHAPTER 3

Hardware   63

Introduction	64
Computer Classifications	64
Mainframes	64
Minicomputers	65
Microcomputers	66
Supercomputers	66
LEARNING CHECK	68
The Central Processing Unit	68
Control Unit	68
Arithmetic/Logic Unit	69
Primary Memory	69
HIGHLIGHT: The Connection Machine	70
Registers	70
LEARNING CHECK	72
Secondary Storage	73
Sequential-Access Media	73
Direct-Access Media	74
Other Storage Media	78
LEARNING CHECK	80
Hardware for Input and Output	80
Input Methods	81
Printers	86
Specialized Output Devices	89
HIGHLIGHT: Ray Kurzweil and His Amazing Machines	90
LEARNING CHECK	91
Data Representation	91
Binary Representation	91
Computer Codes	93

	Code Checking	93
	LEARNING CHECK	94
Summary Points		95
Review Questions		96

CHAPTER 4

Software Development — 97

Introduction		98
Solving Problems with the Computer		98
	Define the Problem	98
	Design the Solution	100
	Write the Program	102
	Compile, Debug, and Test the Program	102
	LEARNING CHECK	104
Structured Problem Solving		104
	Top-Down Design	106
	HIGHLIGHT: Software Prices Dropping?	107
	Documentation	107
	Program Testing	108
	The Programming Team	109
	LEARNING CHECK	109
Types of Programs		109
	HIGHLIGHT: Programs As Models of the Real World	110
Operating Systems		110
	LEARNING CHECK	112
Programming Languages		112
	Low-Level Languages	112
	High-Level Languages	113
	Natural Languages	125
	LEARNING CHECK	126
Summary Points		126
Review Questions		128

CHAPTER 5

Microcomputers — 129

Introduction		130
Microcomputers: An Overview		130
	The New Technology	130
	The Machines Themselves	131
	HIGHLIGHT: Please! Count Your Eggs Before They Hatch!	135
	LEARNING CHECK	135
Understanding the Microchips		136
	The Microprocessor's Speed	136

Memory	136
Operating Systems	137
Compatibility	138
LEARNING CHECK	139
Using Microcomputers	139
Input Devices	139
Output Devices	140
Online Storage	143
Add-Ons	145
Software Packages	146
HIGHLIGHT: Jonathan Rotenberg and the Boston Computer Society	147
Users' Groups	148
LEARNING CHECK	149
Summary Points	149
Review Questions	150

CHAPTER 6

Computers' Impact on Society — 151

Introduction	152
Telecommunications	152
Message Transmission	152
Software for Transmission	154
Communication Networks	156
LEARNING CHECK	158
Automation	158
The Electronic Office	158
Automation in Manufacturing	161
HIGHLIGHT: Desktop Publishing	162
LEARNING CHECK	164
Electronic Monitoring	164
Monitoring in Science Laboratories	164
Monitoring the Human Body	166
The Automated Home	168
HIGHLIGHT: Nan Davis's New Venture	169
LEARNING CHECK	169
Number Crunching	170
Simulation and Modeling	170
Weather Predictions	171
Business Forecasting	172
Graphics	172
Pictures of Our Earth	172
Graphic Computer-Assisted Diagnosis	173
CAD/CAM	175
Business Graphics	176
Graphics for Analyzing Motion	176
Education	177
Computer Literacy	178
Programming	178

CONTENTS xi

Computer-Assisted Instruction	179
Interactive Video	180
Networks	181
Computers on Campus	181
LEARNING CHECK	182
Summary Points	182
Review Questions	184

CHAPTER 7

Issues of Concern — 187

Introduction	188
Privacy	188
Databases	188
Privacy Legislation	190
LEARNING CHECK	192
Crime and Security	192
Computer Crime	192
HIGHLIGHT: Monitoring in the Workplace	193
Security	195
Computer Mistakes: Who Is Responsible?	196
LEARNING CHECK	197
Computer Ethics	199
LEARNING CHECK	201
Identification of Computer and Security Needs	201
Artificial Intelligence and Automation	203
Artificial Intelligence Applied	203
Questions and (No) Answers	204
HIGHLIGHT: Seymour Cray	205
LEARNING CHECK	206
Summary Points	206
Review Questions	207

PART TWO

APPLICATIONS SOFTWARE: USING WORDSTAR 2000, WORDPERFECT, LOTUS 1-2-3, AND dBASE III — 209

CHAPTER 8

Introduction to Word Processing and WordStar 2000 — 211

Introduction	212
Definitions	212
Uses of Word Processors	213
LEARNING CHECK	213
Guide to WordStar 2000	216
Getting Started with WordStar 2000	216
Getting Help with WordStar 2000	217
Creating a New Document	218

Naming a File	219
Choosing a Document's Format	220
Recording a Document's History	221
Entering Text	222
Saving a Document	224
LEARNING CHECK	225
Editing a Document	226
Copying a Document	227
Moving the Cursor	227
Removing Text	228
Moving Blocks of Text	231
Correcting Spelling Mistakes	232
Printing	235
LEARNING CHECK	236
Summary of Frequently Used WordStar 2000 Menus	237
Summary Points	242
WordStar 2000 Exercises	242
WordStar 2000 Problems	244

CHAPTER 9

Advanced WordStar 2000 — 245

Introduction	246
Formatting a Document	246
Setting Tabs and Margins	246
The Options Menu	248
Viewing Command Tags	248
Print Enhancements	255
LEARNING CHECK	262
More Advanced Features	262
Headers and Footers	262
Footnotes	264
Locate and Replace	265
Changing a Format Design	270
LEARNING CHECK	271
Summary Points	273
WordStar 2000 Exercises	274
WordStar 2000 Problems	275

CHAPTER 10

Introduction to Word Processing and WordPerfect — 277

Introduction	278
Definitions	278
Uses of Word Processors	279
Guide to WordPerfect	279
LEARNING CHECK	282
Getting Started with WordPerfect	284
Getting Help with WordPerfect	286
LEARNING CHECK	287
Creating a New Document	288

Entering Text	288
Saving a Document	290
Retrieving a Document	292
LEARNING CHECK	294
Editing a Document	294
Moving the Cursor	294
Removing Text	296
Moving Blocks of Text	299
Correcting Spelling Mistakes	301
Printing	306
Summary Points	308
LEARNING CHECK	309
WordPerfect Exercises	309
WordPerfect Problems	311

CHAPTER 11

Advanced WordPerfect — 313

Introduction	314
Formatting A Document	314
Print Format	314
Line Format	315
Indenting Paragraphs	318
LEARNING CHECK	319
Character Enhancements	324
Viewing Command Codes	324
More Advanced Features	331
Page Format	331
Footnotes and Endnotes	333
Search	333
LEARNING CHECK	341
Summary Points	341
WordPerfect Exercises	341
WordPerfect Problems	343

CHAPTER 12

Introduction to Spreadsheets and Lotus 1-2-3 — 345

Introduction	346
Definitions	346
Uses of Spreadsheets	347
LEARNING CHECK	348
Guide To Lotus 1-2-3	349
Identifying Parts of the Worksheet	349
LEARNING CHECK	351
Getting Started With Lotus 1-2-3	351
Moving Around the Worksheet	352
Menus and Menu Options	354

Saving and Retrieving Files	356
Saving An Amended File	358
Getting Help With Lotus 1-2-3	359
Quitting a File and Quitting the Access System	361
Creating A Worksheet	362
LEARNING CHECK	362
Entering Labels	363
Entering Values	365
Ranges	366
Entering Formulas	369
Formatting Cells	372
Erasing A Cell	374
LEARNING CHECK	374
Changing the Appearance of a Worksheet	375
Aligning Labels	375
Adjusting Column Widths	376
Inserting and Deleting Rows and Columns	377
Printing A Worksheet	378
LEARNING CHECK	380
Summary Points	381
Lotus 1-2-3 Exercises	382
Lotus 1-2-3 Problems	383

CHAPTER 13

Advanced Lotus 1-2-3   387

Introduction	388
Copy and Move	388
The Difference Between Global and Range Commands	390
Functions	391
Copying Formulas	393
Freezing Titles	394
Order of Precedence	397
Spreadsheet Analysis	400
LEARNING CHECK	401
Graphics	401
Bar Graphs and Pie Charts	402
Creating a Bar Graph and Pie Chart	403
Printing a Graph	408
LEARNING CHECK	410
Summary Points	411
Lotus 1-2-3 Exercises	412
Lotus 1-2-3 Problems	418

CHAPTER 14

Introduction to Data Managers and dBase III — 421

Introduction	422
Definitions	422
Uses of Data Managers	424
LEARNING CHECK	425
Guide to dBase III	425
Getting Started with dBase III	426
Creating a Database File	427
Entering Records	433
Using dBase III Commands	435
QUIT	436
USE	436
HELP	437
DISPLAY	438
DISPLAY FOR	440
DISPLAY STRUCTURE	442
MODIFY STRUCTURE	442
LIST	443
LEARNING CHECK	444
APPEND	445
BROWSE	445
PACK	447
EDIT	448
DELETE and RECALL	450
GOTO	452
GO TOP and GO BOTTOM	452
dBase III Summary Commands	453
COUNT	453
SUM	454
AVERAGE	455
Printing a dBase III File	455
LEARNING CHECK	456
Summary Points	457
dBase III Exercises	457
dBase III Problems	459

CHAPTER 15

Advanced dBase III — 461

Introduction	462
SORT TO	462
Conditional Sort	464
INDEX ON	465
Indexing on Multiple Fields	468
FIND	469
LEARNING CHECK	470
Creating a Report with dBase III	471

CREATE REPORT	471
Filling in the Report Headings Screen	472
Defining Report Columns	474
MODIFY REPORT	477
Printing a Report	479
Using Multiple Database Files	480
SELECT	480
LEARNING CHECK	484
Joining Two Files	484
Summary of dBase III Commands	487
Creating Files	487
Using a Database File	488
Modifying Files	488
Manipulating Files	488
Displaying Data	489
Editing Records	489
Deleting Records	490
Creating Reports	490
Printing	490
Selecting Specific Records	490
Summary Points	491
dBase III Exercises	491
dBase III Problems	495

APPENDIX	**Installation Procedures**	**A-1**

PART THREE	**BASIC SUPPLEMENT**	**B-1**

SECTION I	**Introduction to BASIC**	**B-3**

Introduction	B-4
Background on BASIC	B-4
The Programming Process	B-4
Defining the Problem	B-5
Designing a Solution	B-5
Writing the Program	B-6
Submitting the Program to the Computer	B-6
Getting Started	B-8
LEARNING CHECK	B-9
DOS Commands	B-10
BASIC Commands	B-11
NEW	B-12
RUN	B-12
SAVE	B-13
LOAD	B-14
LIST	B-14

FILES and KILL	B-15
LEARNING CHECK	B-16
Summary Points	B-16
Review Questions	B-17

SECTION II

Getting Started with BASIC — B-19

Introduction	B-20
Data Types	B-20
Constants	B-20
Numeric Constants	B-20
Character String Constants	B-21
Variables	B-21
Numeric Variables	B-22
Character String Variables	B-22
Reserved Words	B-22
Line Numbers	B-22
LEARNING CHECK	B-25
Elementary BASIC Statements	B-25
The REM Statement	B-25
The Assignment Statement	B-26
The PRINT Statement	B-29
The END Statement	B-31
Comprehensive Programming Problem	B-31
Problem Definition	B-31
LEARNING CHECK	B-32
Solution Design	B-32
The Program	B-34
Summary Points	B-34
Review Questions	B-36
Debugging Exercises	B-36
Additional Programming Problems	B-37

SECTION III

Input and Output — B-39

Introduction	B-40
The INPUT Statement	B-40
Printing Prompts for the User	B-42
The READ and DATA Statements	B-44
The RESTORE Statement	B-45
Comparison of the Two Data Entry Methods	B-46
LEARNING CHECK	B-47
Clearing the Screen	B-47

Printing Results	B-47
Print Zones and Commas	B-47
Using Semicolons	B-49
The TAB Function	B-50
SPC	B-53
LOCATE	B-53
The PRINT USING Statement	B-55
LEARNING CHECK	B-58
Comprehensive Programming Problem	B-58
Problem Definition	B-58
Solution Design	B-59
The Program	B-59
Summary Points	B-60
Review Questions	B-63
Debugging Exercises	B-63
Additional Programming Problems	B-63

SECTION IV

Control Statements and Subroutines   B-65

Introduction	B-66
The GOTO Statement: Unconditional Transfer	B-66
The IF Statement: Conditional Transfer	B-67
Single Alternative: IF/THEN	B-68
Double Alternative: IF/THEN/ELSE	B-69
Nested IF Statements	B-70
AND/OR	B-71
The ON/GOTO Statement	B-71
LEARNING CHECK	B-73
Menus	B-74
Subroutines: Structured Programming	B-76
The GOSUB Statement	B-76
The RETURN Statement	B-77
Example of Subroutine Usage	B-77
The STOP Statement	B-77
The ON/GOSUB Statement	B-78
LEARNING CHECK	B-81
Comprehensive Programming Problem	B-81
The Problem	B-81
Solution Design	B-81
The Program	B-84
Summary Points	B-84
Review Questions	B-87
Debugging Exercises	B-87
Additional Programming Problems	B-88

CONTENTS

SECTION V

Looping — B-91

Introduction	B-92
Looping Methods	B-92
Trailer Values	B-93
Counters	B-94
Elements of Looping	B-96
Rules for Using the FOR/NEXT Loop	B-98
Flowcharting the FOR/NEXT Loop	B-100
Advantages of Using the FOR/NEXT Loop	B-100
Nested FOR/NEXT Loops	B-100
LEARNING CHECK	B-104
The WHILE/WEND Loop	B-106
Comprehensive Programming Problem	B-108
Problem Definition	B-108
Solution Design	B-108
The Program	B-109
Summary Points	B-109
Review Questions	B-112
Debugging Exercises	B-113
Additional Programming Problems	B-113

SECTION VI

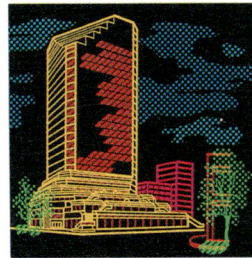

Arrays — B-117

Introduction	B-118
Subscripts	B-118
The DIM Statement	B-119
LEARNING CHECK	B-120
One-Dimensional Arrays	B-121
Reading Data to an Array	B-121
Displaying the Contents of an Array	B-122
Computations on Array Elements	B-123
LEARNING CHECK	B-124
Two-Dimensional Arrays	B-124
Reading and Displaying Two-Dimensional Arrays	B-126
Computations on Array Elements	B-128
LEARNING CHECK	B-130
Manipulating Arrays	B-131
Sorting Arrays—The Bubble Sort	B-131
Merging	B-135
Searching	B-137
LEARNING CHECK	B-138
Comprehensive Programming Problem	B-138
Problem Definition	B-138
Solution Design	B-139

The Program	B-140
Summary Points	B-140
Review Questions	B-140
Debugging Exercises	B-143
Additional Programming Problems	B-143

SECTION VII

Graphics and Sound — B-147

Introduction	B-148
Display Modes	B-148
Medium-Resolution Graphics Mode	B-148
Color Graphics	B-149
The PSET and PRESET Statements	B-150
The LINE Statement	B-151
LEARNING CHECK	B-153
High-Resolution Graphics Mode	B-154
The CIRCLE Statement	B-156
Graphics and Text	B-156
LEARNING CHECK	B-157
Sound on the PC	B-157
The BEEP Statement	B-157
The SOUND Statement	B-157
The PLAY Statement	B-158
Comprehensive Programming Problem	B-160
The Problem	B-160
LEARNING CHECK	B-161
Solution Design	B-161
The Program	B-161
Summary Points	B-162
Review Questions	B-162
Debugging Exercises	B-163
Additional Programming Problems	B-163

BASIC Glossary — B-165
BASIC Index — B-169
Glossary — G-1
Index — I-1

PREFACE

The goal for books in the first edition of this series was to combine computer concepts, application packages and BASIC programming in each textbook. Three versions were offered in the first edition series—one for use with the IBM, Apple and TRS 80 microcomputers. Because of the tremendous proliferation in applications software, and in order to give adoptors a wide range of choices, three second edition texts now focus on the IBM PC and MS-DOS computers, while the fourth text is for use with Apple II computers.

In addition to *Introduction to Computers Using The IBM and MS-DOS PCs with BASIC, Second Edition, Popular Commercial Software Version*, the following texts are available for use with IBM and MS-DOS PCs:

- West 2.5 version (with WestWord™, WestCalc™, WestGraph™, WestSoft™ 1.0 and Student File Disk)
- Educate-Ability 1.1 Version, an integrated software package (with WestSoft™ 1.0 and Student File Disk)

The fourth text in the series is *Introduction to Computers Using The Apple II with BASIC, Second Edition, West 2.5 Version* (with WestWord™, WestCalc™, WestGraph™, WestData™, WestSoft™ 1.0 and Student File Disk).

Each second edition text retains the strengths of those in the first edition—combining computer concepts with hands-on applications and BASIC programming. The second edition series, however, is improved in structure and substance, thanks to the excellent feedback from instructors who served as reviewers.

New Features

Like books from the first edition, second edition texts are divided into three sections: The first part focuses on fundamental computer concepts, the second section on applications software, and the final section presents BASIC programming. Although the basic format of the first and second editions is the same, readers familiar with the first edition will notice several changes, including the following for the IBM versions:

- The chapter on "Getting to Know Your IBM" has been moved from Part Two of the book to Part One. WestSoft™ 1.0, a program containing simulations of a home banking system, personality traits test, ticket office manager, information network, and dental office manager, has been incorporated into the chapter. Moving this chapter to the front of the book enables students to become familiar with the computer right at the start of the course.
- All the chapters in Part One have been updated and revised.
- Part Two of the book for the Popular Commercial Software Version, the hands-on application software section, focuses on the most popular versions of professional software. Included in Part Two are introductory and advanced chapters on WordStar 2000, WordPerfect, Lotus 1-2-3, and dBase III.
- In addition to WestSoft™ 1.0, a Student File Disk is included with each book. This disk contains permanent files to be used with problems at the end of each chapter in Part Two, and permanent files to be used with additional problems included in the Instructor's Manual.
- The entire BASIC section has been rewritten to emphasize structured programming.

In the last few years, there has been an explosion in the number of students taking introductory courses on computers. The content of these courses is undergoing constant rethinking and revision. A current trend seems to be to expose students to state-of-the-art professional software—the software they will encounter when they enter the workplace. The Popular Commercial Software Version introduces students to professional software packages in a logical and uncluttered manner. My hope is that students using the text will gain an increased awareness of the usefulness of application packages and acquire the necessary skills to successfully run these professional packages on their own.

Color coding has been used in the applications software examples and the BASIC programming examples throughout the text to assist the reader. The legend for this coding is shown below:

| Light Blue Shading | Computer Output |
| Blue | User Response or Input |

Supplementary Educational Material

A complete instructor's resource package has been designed to reduce administrative efforts. The classroom support for each chapter of the first section includes a detailed Lecture Outline, Answers to Review Questions, and Additional Questions. For the Application Software section, Answers to Exercises in Text and Additional Problems (with answers) are included. The BASIC Programming section includes Answers to Review Questions in Text, Additional Questions, Answers to Debugging Exercises in Text, Answers to Programming Problems in Text and three Additional Programming Exercises per section. All the Answers to Programming Problems in Text are accompanied by a flowchart and an actual printout of the program. A Test Bank with more than 550 multiple choice questions is also included in the Instructor's Manual. Answers to questions follow each chapter test. In addition, there are more than fifty Transparency Masters provided in the Instructor's Manual.

WestTutor™ is a computer-assisted instruction package to be used to support the BASIC Programming section. Instructions are provided at the bottom of each screen to direct the student through the tutorial. At the end of a section, checkpoint questions are included to test the student's understanding of the material. The student reads each question and selects an answer. The program indicates whether the correct answer was selected and gives an explanation concerning the correct answer.

Acknowledgments

I was very fortunate to have had several outstanding college educators serve as reviewers for this book. I would like to thank the following people for their invaluable comments:

David Allen
San Antonio College

Clark B. Archer
Winthrop College, South Carolina

Ellis Blanton
University of South Florida

W. Joseph Cochran
University of Southern California

Stanley P. Franklin
Memphis State University

Dwight Graham
Prairie State College, Illinois

Janet Bard Hanson
University of South Florida

Berni Hopper
Clark College, Washington

George Kelley
Erie Community College, City Campus, New York

Beverly Oswalt
University of Central Arkansas

Thomas A. Parkinson
Oakland Community College, Michigan

E. Raydean Richmond
Tarrant County Jr. College, South Campus, Texas

Douglas F. Robertson
University of Minnesota

Lee Tangedahl
University of Montana

Numerous corporations and government agencies supplied the color photographs for this book. Many professionals provided the assistance required for completion of a textbook of this magnitude: Michelle Westlund and Susan Moran on manuscript development; Sarah Basinger on Part One Computer Literacy; Meredith Flynn and Alan Johnson on Part Two Applications Software; Sue Baumann, Irene Bulas, and Sara Fetterman on the BASIC Programming Section; Christine Custer on photographs; Shannan Benschoter, Linda Cupp and Kathleen Shields on manuscript preparation; and Robert Slocum on the index.

The design of the book is a tribute to the many talents and great patience of John Orr. One final acknowledgment goes to my publisher and valued friend, Clyde Perlee, Jr. If it were not for his constant encouragement, this project would never have been completed.

Steven L. Mandell

PART ONE

Computer Literacy

CHAPTER 1

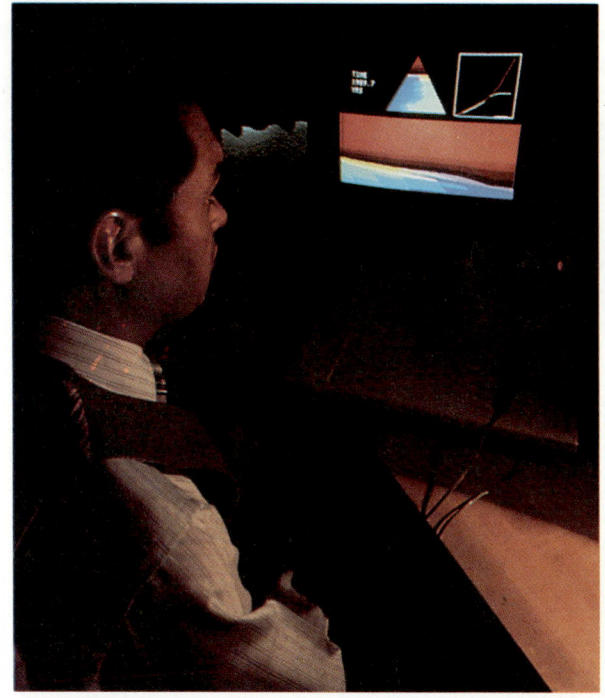

Computers in Our World

Outline

Introduction
Daily Encounters
The Computer's Role in Data
 Processing
  Analog and Digital Computers
  The Computer Advantage
Learning Check
Stages of Data Processing
  Types of Data Processing
Learning Check
Computers Yesterday and Today
  Early Developments
Highlight: Ada Lovelace
Highlight: John Vincent
  Atanasoff
Learning Check
  The First Generation: 1951–
   1958
  The Second Generation: 1959–
   1964
  The Third Generation: 1965–
   1970
  The Fourth Generation: 1971–
   Today
Learning Check
Summary Points
Review Questions

4   PART ONE: COMPUTER LITERACY

Introduction

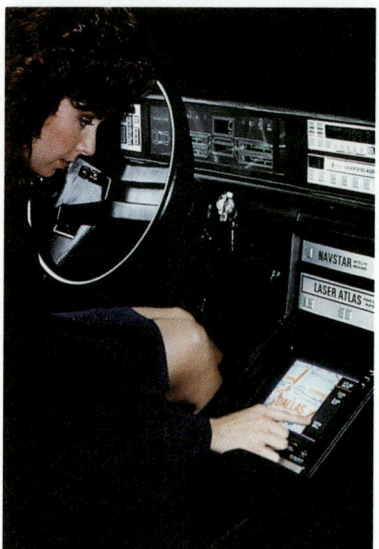

Figure 1-1
Car With Electronic Map

Forty-five years ago, scientists began to use computers for research, mathematics, and technology. When computers became available commercially, only the largest businesses acquired them, often just for the prestige of owning one. The uses of computers were quite limited in those days. Today, however, it would be hard to name areas in which computers are not being used. Computers have entered almost every aspect of the average American's life.

Think of the many household items that contain some type of computer. Televisions, video recorders, stereos, microwave ovens, and even coffee makers are computer-controlled. Computerized telephones can store and dial up to 100 telephone numbers. Some houses have computers that regulate temperature and energy use. Our cars, too, contain computer devices that govern fuel mixture, control emissions from the car's exhaust system, and tell us to buckle up or take the keys out of the ignition. Some cars even contain electronic maps that help the driver navigate through unfamiliar territory (see Figure 1-1).

More and more American families are buying personal computers for home use. Many people use their personal computers for playing games, but home computer use goes far beyond entertainment. People are realizing the tremendous potential of home computers in gathering information. Using the telephone lines and specially equipped computers, subscribers can call a commercial database such as CompuServe (see Figure 1-2) for information about the stock market, current

Figure 1-2
Commercial Database Menu Screen
With a subscription to a commercial database, personal computer users have the world at their fingertips. These women are checking the week's best-selling fiction books.

CHAPTER 1: COMPUTERS IN OUR WORLD 5

Figure 1-3 Computer-Aided Manufacturing
The entire steel-rolling operation of this Bethlehem Steel mill is supervised and monitored from this computerized control center.

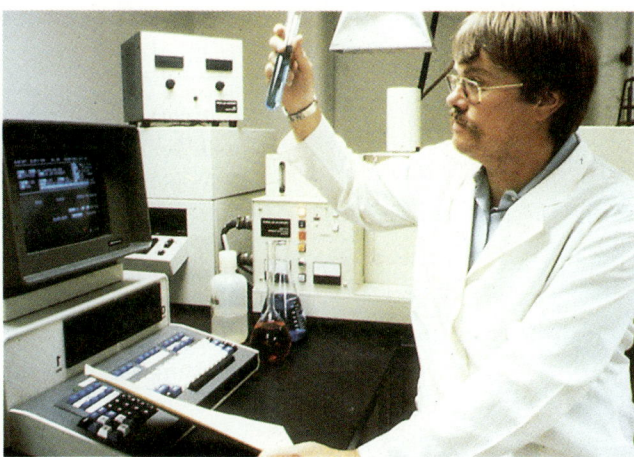

Figure 1-4 Laboratory Testing
A laboratory technician uses computers to aid in research and development.

WORD PROCESSING
The use of computer equipment in preparing text; involves writing, editing, and printing.

COMPUTER
General-purpose electronic machine with applications limited only by the creativity of the humans who use it. Its power is derived from its speed, accuracy and memory.

events, and sports information. In addition, they can do their banking by computer, shop via an electronic catalog, or enroll in accredited college courses through electronic communications systems such as TeleLearning's Electronic University. Other popular home uses include **word processing,** filing, financial planning, and educational games.

In the workplace, computers have made financial analysis, bookkeeping, manufacturing processes, and other functions faster and more efficient. Company executives use personal computers as aids in decision making. Clerks and secretaries use personal computers for preparing documents and keeping records. Manufacturers use computers in designing machines and products, controlling robots, and regulating manufacturing processes (see Figure 1-3).

Scientists build computer models of airplane crashes in order to determine the crash behavior of airplanes. This information helps aircraft designers plan safer seats and windows, and fabrics that decrease fire hazards during a crash. Ecologists use computers for monitoring problems such as acid rain and suggesting solutions for environmental management. Educators use computers in the classroom for performing chemistry experiments that might otherwise be dangerous. Computers are used by medical researchers in testing drugs; by meteorologists for predicting the weather; by musicians for synthesizing and reproducing sounds; by artists for producing graphics; and by students for learning basic skills (see Figure 1-4). Moviegoers may notice an increased sophistication in special effects, thanks to computer scene simulation. Even the farmer of the 1980s benefits from such computer applications as bookkeeping, maintaining animal health and production records, and devising economical feed programs.

This chapter discusses additional examples of computers in our daily lives, and provides introductory material to help you understand the machine we call the **computer.**

Daily Encounters

Businesses, governments, research laboratories, and many other organizations deal with so much information every day that it would be difficult to operate without computers. Most businesses lend themselves to computerization. Historically, the types of jobs most easily computerized have been routine, repetitive jobs. These simple tasks can be performed quickly and accurately by a computer. A good example is the preparation of a company's payroll. The preparer finds each employee's net pay by multiplying the pay rate by the number of hours worked, then subtracting taxes and other deductions. When given accurate data and instructions, the computer can produce paychecks for hundreds of employees quickly and with little error.

Although some organizations use computers only in simplifying their accounting activities, others have benefited from using computers in making decisions. For example, computers can calculate sales forecasts using any number of variables or combinations of variables. A computer can quickly determine how changes in price, inventory level, volumn of advertising, or coupon offers are likely to affect sales.

Some decision-making aspects of a business are not easily computerized. These processes are not routine and are hard to define, so it is difficult to write instructions for the computer. Many businesses are now computerizing risk analysis, one important aspect of business decision making. Risk analysis determines whether a business investment will be profitable. The largest users of computerized risk analysis to date have been oil and utility companies. Utility companies generally use the technique for determining locations for nuclear power stations, and oil companies use it in placing offshore oil-drilling rigs.

Many businesses link their computers by communication lines so that several computers can share data and programs. Connecting computers eliminates the need for duplicating the data stored by each computer. The data is more easily kept up to date, because all changes made to the data on any computer are immediately accessible from the other computers.

Just as computers improve business people's performance, they improve the services offered to consumers. Computers affect the way many businesses, from banks to restaurants to grocery stores, deal with their customers. Airlines, travel agencies, and hotels use extensive networks of computer equipment for scheduling reservations (see Figure 1-5). Some large shopping malls contain computers that act as electronic directories. Through computer use, banks have been able to offer more services to their customers. These services include direct deposit of payments, automatic teller machines, and banking from home (see Figure 1-6).

Manufacturers make extensive use of computers, too. Engineers use computers in drawing plans for products, for machines to build those products, and for machines to build the machines to make the products. During the manufacturing process, computers are used in controlling the operation of machinery. Computers also are helpful in testing prototypes of products. Among the items we use every day that may have been designed by computer are car seats, lenses in sunglasses, sport shoes, and other sports equipment (see Figure 1-7).

The federal government is the largest user of computers in the United States. This fact is not surprising when one considers the many government agencies that

CHAPTER 1: COMPUTERS IN OUR WORLD   7

Figure 1-5
A Hotel Reservation Network
Reservation sales agents utilize Best Western International's worldwide computerized network to book room reservations.

Figure 1-6
Automatic Teller Machine
This customer of Ohio Citizen's Bank can use the bank's automatic teller machine at any time of day that is convenient for him.

Figure 1-7
Computer-Aided Design In Sport Shoes A final shoe design is shown on the terminal screen.

collect, process, and store information. Typical examples include the U.S. census taken every ten years; the millions of income tax returns processed every year; the huge databases maintained in the Library of Congress and Federal Bureau of Investigation; and the public assistance and social security systems.

In science and medicine, as in business, computers are used for routine clerical functions. More importantly, computers can make calculations and perform design testing functions in seconds which human beings could not otherwise complete in months. Data analyzed by computers can be collected by satellites for military intelligence and environmental planning; by seismographs for earthquake prediction; by CAT scans for medical diagnosis; and by sensors for determination of toxicity levels.

Educators also are becoming more involved in computer use. A frequently asked question in the past ten years has been: "Will the computer replace the teacher?" The answer, of course, is no. In fact, the opposite is true, because computers can help teachers and students with their work. Computers become private tutors for students who need extra help or additional challenges. Computers are used in helping students learn programming languages such as Pascal or BASIC. Videodisks combined with computers offer a learning aid that includes motion and sound. Using videodisk lessons, students can watch reenactments of the early colonists preparing for the Revolutionary War or the Wright brothers trying out their first airplane. They can interact with lessons on current events and watch news footage from old newscasts.

Computers play important roles in sports, too. In baseball, computers are used to calculate statistics such as batting averages and runs batted in, and to evaluate how pitchers and hitters work together. A computer analyzes the statistics collected during a game so that a manager can predict the most likely moves in a certain situation (see Figure 1-8). For example, a Chicago White Sox coach once determined that a certain left-handed batter for an opposing team almost always got a hit when a left-handed pitcher threw a breaking ball. Bits of information like that can help a team win. In fact, teams are finding computers so successful in analyzing statistics that many maintain secrecy as to how they use the machines.

In professional football, computers are being used in scouting and evaluating other teams and college players. Olympic cyclists wear helmets designed with the aid of computers for efficient aerodynamics. These athletes may also improve their performance after a computer indicates that their pedaling motions are inefficient. Olympic pole vaulters are using the technology to record movements with high-speed video cameras and store the results, in digitized form, in a computer. They can then view their movements on the screen by watching a computerized stick figure (see Figure 1-9).

We have seen how computers can be powerful tools in both large-scale applications and everyday functions of our lives. By knowing how computers work,

Figure 1-8
Collecting Baseball Data
A team manager uses an Apple Computer at the Yankee Stadium to record pitches, hits, and runs of the New York Yankees.

Figure 1-9
Computer Analysis in Pole Vaulting

what they can do, and what their limitations and benefits are, we can use computers to their best advantage.

The Computer's Role In Data Processing

DATA PROCESSING
A set of procedures for collecting, manipulating, and disseminating data to achieve specified objectives.

ELECTRONIC DATA PROCESSING (EDP)
Data processing performed by electronic equipment, such as computers, rather than by manual or mechanical means.

DATA
Facts, the raw material of information.

INFORMATION
Data that has been organized and processed so it is meaningful.

Data processing is nothing new. People have processed data ever since they have had things to count. **Data processing** refers to collecting, manipulating, and distributing data in order to achieve certain goals. Using computers for data processing is called **electronic data processing (EDP),** although EDP usually is known simply as data processing.

The objective of all data processing, whether manual or electronic, is the conversion of data into useful information. The words data and information often are used interchangeably, but in the context of data processing they have different meanings. **Data** refers to raw facts collected from various sources, but not organized or perhaps even defined. Data cannot be used in making meaningful decisions. For example, a bank manager may have little use for a daily list of the amounts of all checks and deposit slips from the branch offices. The manager could, however, use a summary that gives the dollar value and total number of deposits and withdrawals at each branch. Such a summary provides **information,** which is processed data that increases understanding and helps people make intelligent decisions. Information must be accurate, timely, complete, concise, and relevant. It must be delivered to the right person at the right time in the right place. If information fails to meet these requirements, it fails to meet the needs of those who use it and is of little value.

**Figure 1-10
Analog Computer**

ANALOG COMPUTER
A computer that measures changes in continuous electrical or physical conditions rather than counting data.

DIGITAL COMPUTER
A computer that operates on distinct data by performing arithmetic and logic processes on specific data units.

CHARACTER
A single letter, digit, or special sign (such as $, #, or *).

BIT
Short for *binary digit*, the smallest unit of data which the computer can handle.

HARDWARE
Physical components that make up a computer system.

SOFTWARE
Program or programs used to direct the computer in solving problems and overseeing operations.

PROGRAM
A series of step-by-step instructions which tells the computer exactly what to do.

Analog and Digital Computers

There are two types of computers: analog and digital. **Analog computers** measure changes in continuous physical or electrical states, such as pressure, temperature, voltage, length, number of shaft rotations, or volume (see Figure 1-10). A gasoline pump uses a simple analog device that measures the quantity of gasoline pumped to the nearest tenth of a gallon. More complex analog devices are used in testing and adjusting the performance of electronic equipment.

Digital computers, by contrast, represent data by discrete "on" and "off" (conducting/nonconducting or yes/no) states of the computer's electronic circuitry. **Characters** (numbers, letters, and symbols) are stored in binary notation, a code based on the binary number system, which consists of two digits: 1 (on) and 0 (off). Each 1 or 0 is called a **bit,** short for *bi*nary dig*it*, the smallest unit of data a computer can handle. The binary number system is well suited to the on/off states of electric current. A digital computer must convert all data to binary form in order to process it.

The electronic and electrical parts of a digital computer—that is, the tangible parts of a computer system—are called **hardware.** Examples of hardware are the computer itself, monitors used for viewing data, keyboards, and printers (see Figure 1-11). Hardware is useless without **software,** the instructions or **programs** that direct the equipment in performing various tasks. The hardware and software discussed in this book apply to digital computers.

The Computer Advantage

A computer pulls data from storage, acts on it, and stores it again under the direction of programs that determine the yes/no, conducting/nonconducting, or

**Figure 1-11
Computer Hardware**

on/off operations of its circuits. It must be given exact, step-by-step instructions for any task it performs. Within the limitations of its circuits, a computer can carry out three basic functions.

1. Arithmetic operations (addition, subtraction, multiplication, and division).
2. Logical comparisons of relationships among values (greater than, less than, or equal to).
3. Storage and retrieval operations.

INSTRUCTION SET
The fundamental logical and arithmetic procedures that the computer can perform, such as addition and comparison.

The manufacturer builds into the computer a basic set of instructions—the **instruction set**—which performs these three tasks. By working with the instruction set, people can direct the computer to perform many tasks. The computer can perform these tasks quickly and reliably and can store vast amounts of data.

Speed Modern computers can perform millions of calculations in one second. Computer speed describes the time required to perform one operation, and is measured in terms of nanoseconds or other small units (see Figure 1-12). A nanosecond is one-billionth of a second. In one nanosecond, electricity can travel 11.8 inches. The smaller the distances in the electronic circuitry of a computer, the shorter the time needed for the computer to perform a task. In the past, the time required for performing one addition ranged from 200 nanoseconds to 4

**Figure 1-12
Divisions of a Second**

Unit	Symbol	Divisions of a Second — Fractions of a Second
Millisecond	ms	one-thousandth (1/1,000)
Microsecond	µs	one-millionth (1/1,000,000)
Nanosecond	ns	one-billionth (1/1,000,000,000)
Picosecond	ps	one-trillionth (1/1,000,000,000,000)

microseconds. In the future, it may be 200 to 1,000 times faster. This means that computers can do certain jobs hundreds of thousands of times faster than humans can.

Accuracy The accuracy of a computer refers to the inherent reliability of its electronic components. The same type of current passed through the same circuits should yield the same results each time. We take advantage of this aspect of circuitry every time we switch on an electric device. When we turn on a light switch, we expect the light to go on, not the radio or a fan. The computer is reliable for the same reason. Its circuitry is reliable. A computer can run for hours, days, and weeks at a time, giving accurate results for millions of activities. Of course, if the data or programs submitted to the computer are faulty, the computer will not produce correct results. The output will be useless and meaningless, illustrating the human error involved. This is called the garbage in–garbage out (GIGO) principle and is fundamental in understanding computer "mistakes."

PRIMARY MEMORY
The section of the computer which holds instructions, data, and intermediate and final results during processing.

Storage Besides being very fast and reliable, computers can store large amounts of data. Some data is held in **primary memory** for use during immediate operations. The amount of data held in primary memory varies among computers. Some small computers hold as few as 16,000 characters, and large computers can

---

Learning Check

1. Many of the jobs that are easily computerized are ____.
   a. decision-making tasks
   b. routine and repetitive
   c. hard to define
   d. used in risk analysis

2. In the context of data processing, what is the difference between data and information?

3. One of the three functions digital computers can perform is ____.
   a. measuring continuous physical and electrical states
   b. manipulating a half bit
   c. providing accurate information
   d. storing and retrieving information

4. When you inquire about machines and programs at a computer store, you might use the terms ____ and ____ respectively.

5. We know that information resulting from EDP is not always accurate. Why, then, is accuracy considered one of the features of using computers?

Answers

1. b 2. The term *data* means raw, unorganized facts. The term *information* means processed data that increases understanding and aids in making decisions. 3. d 4. hardware, software 5. Accuracy refers to the reliability of electrical currents, not to the reliability of human programmers and data entry personnel.

SECONDARY STORAGE
Storage that supplements primary memory and is external to the computer; data is accessed at slower speeds than with primary storage.

hold billions of characters. Data also can be recorded on magnetic disks or tapes; this **secondary storage** makes a computer's "memory" almost limitless. Secondary storage holds data that is not immediately needed by the computer.

Electronic data storage requires considerably less space and less retrieval time than manual methods. Vast quantities of data stored in paper files are extremely bulky and require substantial storage space. Further, the job of manually extracting data from such files becomes more tedious and time consuming as the size of the files increases.

The ability to store, retrieve, and process data, all without human intervention, separates the computer from a simple calculator and accounts for its power and appeal. Whereas humans can perform the same functions as computers, the difference is that the computer can execute millions of instructions reliably in a second and store the results in an almost unlimited memory.

Stages of Data Processing

All data processing follows the same basic data flow: input, processing and output (see Figure 1-13). These stages are described in the following paragraphs.

INPUT
Data submitted to the computer for processing.

Input **Input** means capturing data and putting it in a form that the computer can understand. Input of data can involve entering new data, changing old data, or deleting data. It involves three steps:

- **Collecting** raw data and assembling it at one location.
- **Verifying,** or checking, the accuracy and completeness of data, including both the facts and the programs. This step is very important, since most computer errors result from human error.
- **Coding** the data into a machine-readable form for processing.

ONLINE
In direct communication with the computer.

OFFLINE
Not in direct communication with the computer.

Data can be entered either online or offline. **Online** entry occurs when the input device used is connected directly to the computer. Some examples are typing on a keyboard, using a scanning device (such as the wand found in a department store or the scanner found in grocery stores), or speaking into a microphone connected to the computer. Some processing and output usually occur during online data entry. **Offline** entry occurs when a device not connected directly to the computer is used for recording data onto tapes, disks, or other storage media. Later, the data is read in batches by another machine directly connected to the computer for processing. Chapter 3 discusses input devices in detail.

PROCESS
To transform data into useful information by classifying, sorting, calculating, summarizing, and/or storing.

CENTRAL PROCESSING UNIT (CPU)
The "brain" of the computer, composed of three sections: arithmetic/logic unit (ALU), control unit, and primary storage unit.

ACCESS
To get or retrieve data from a computer system.

Processing Once the data has been input, it can be processed. **Processing** occurs in the part of the computer called the **central processing unit (CPU),** which is examined in Chapter 3. The CPU includes the circuitry needed for performing arithmetic and logical operations and holding data in primary memory. Once an instruction or data is stored in primary memory, it stays there until new data or instructions are written over it. The same data can be **accessed** repeatedly during processing, or the same instructions can be used repeatedly while processing many different pieces of data.

**Figure 1-13
The Data Flow**

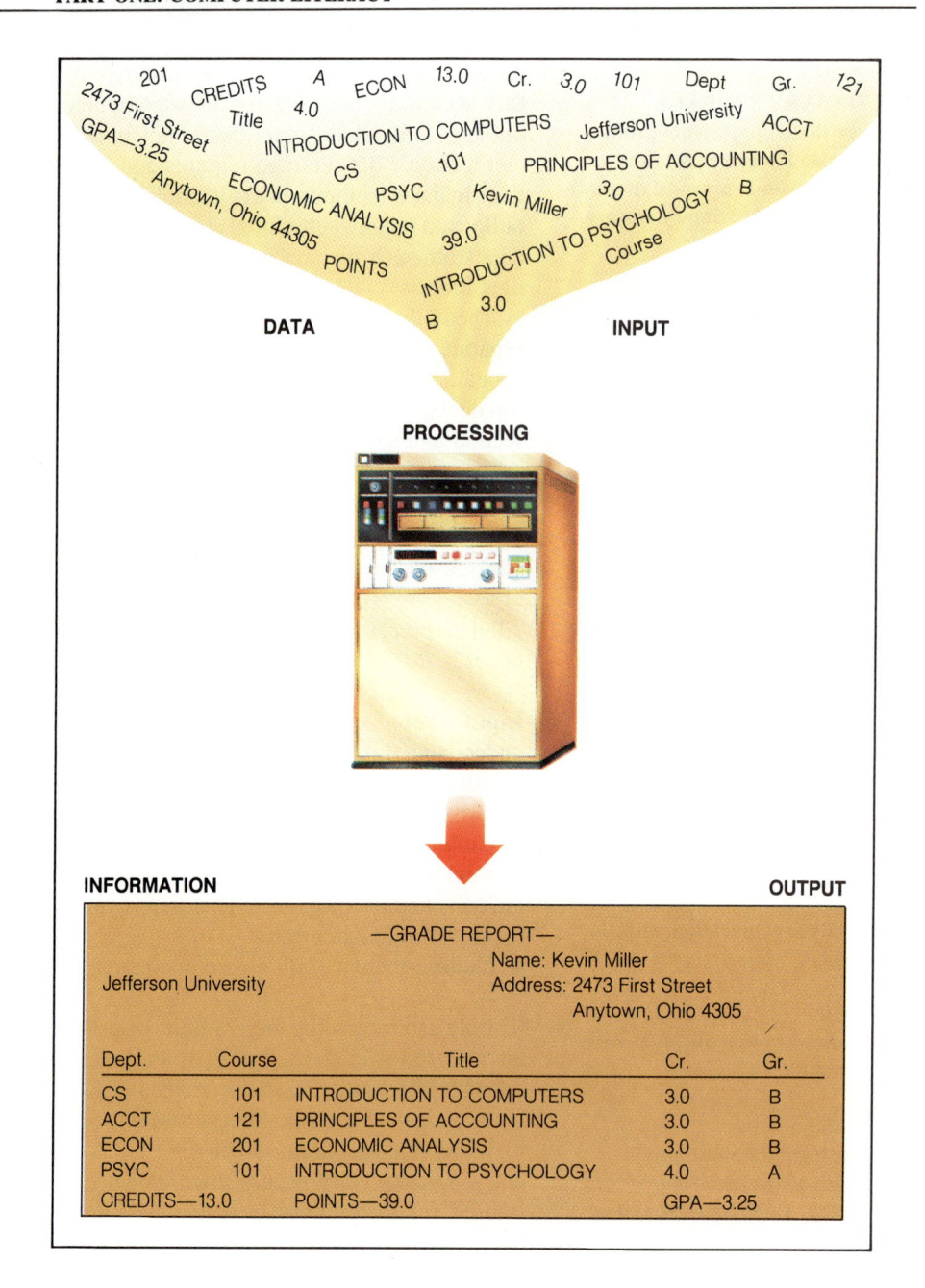

Processing entails several kinds of manipulations (see Figure 1-14):

- **Classifying,** or categorizing, data according to certain characteristics. For example, sales data can be grouped by salesperson, product, or customer.
- **Sorting** or arranging the data alphabetically or numerically. An employee file can be sorted by social security number or by last name.
- **Calculating** results arithmetically or logically, such as computing grade-point averages, bank balances, and payrolls.

**Figure 1-14
Processing Functions**

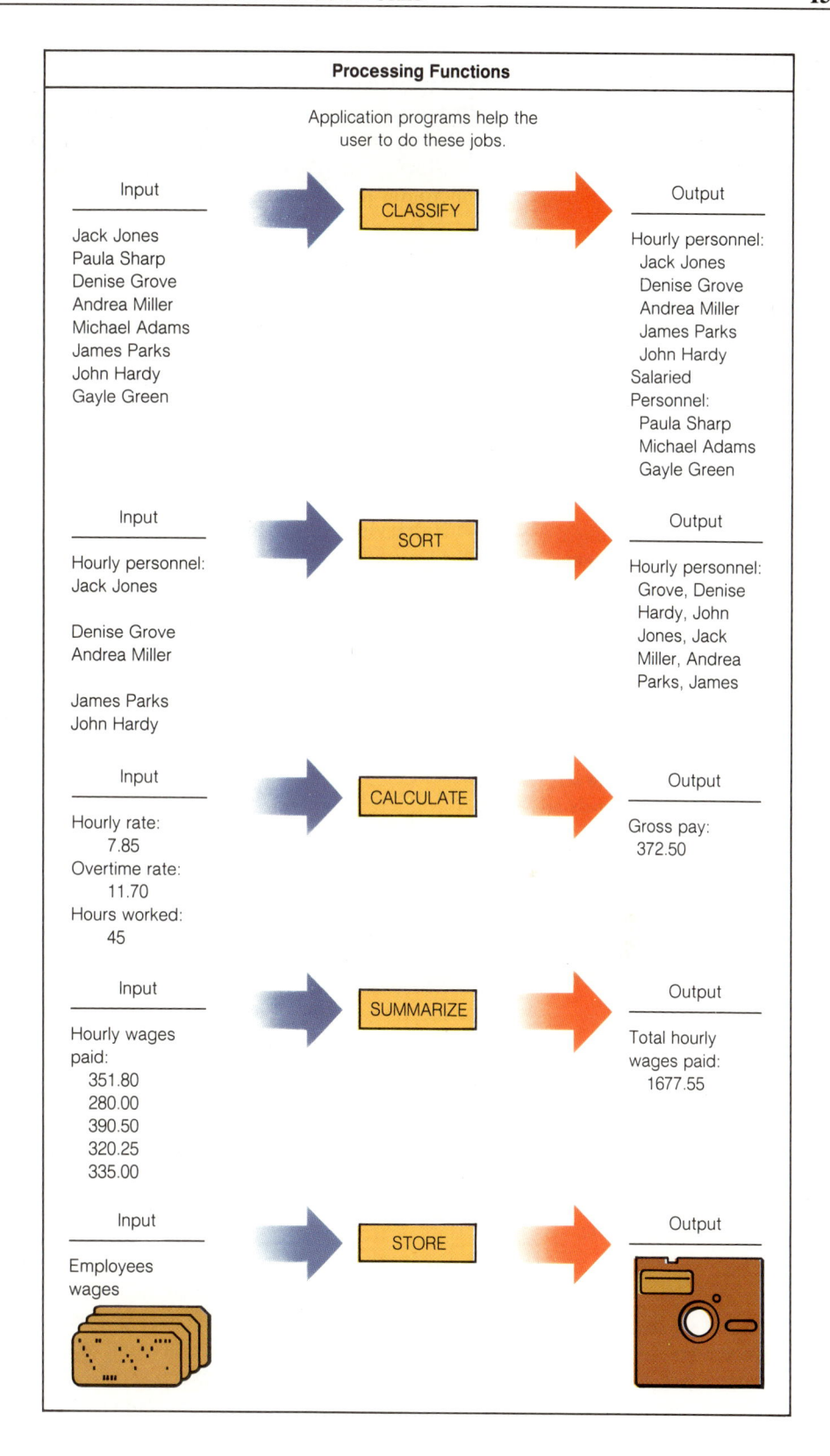

Processing Functions

Application programs help the user to do these jobs.

Input

Jack Jones
Paula Sharp
Denise Grove
Andrea Miller
Michael Adams
James Parks
John Hardy
Gayle Green

→ CLASSIFY →

Output

Hourly personnel:
  Jack Jones
  Denise Grove
  Andrea Miller
  James Parks
  John Hardy
Salaried
Personnel:
  Paula Sharp
  Michael Adams
  Gayle Green

Input

Hourly personnel:
Jack Jones

Denise Grove
Andrea Miller

James Parks
John Hardy

→ SORT →

Output

Hourly personnel:
  Grove, Denise
  Hardy, John
  Jones, Jack
  Miller, Andrea
  Parks, James

Input

Hourly rate:
  7.85
Overtime rate:
  11.70
Hours worked:
  45

→ CALCULATE →

Output

Gross pay:
  372.50

Input

Hourly wages paid:
  351.80
  280.00
  390.50
  320.25
  335.00

→ SUMMARIZE →

Output

Total hourly wages paid:
  1677.55

Input

Employees wages

→ STORE →

Output

OUTPUT
Information that comes from the computer as a result of processing into a form that can be used by people.

SOFT COPY
A temporary, or nonpermanent, record of machine output; for example, a CRT display.

HARD COPY
Output that is printed on some permanent medium, such as paper.

FEEDBACK
A check within a system to see whether predetermined goals are being met.

BATCH PROCESSING
A method of processing data in which data items are collected and forwarded to the computer in a group.

INTERACTIVE PROCESSING
A data processing method by which the user inputs data from the keyboard during processing.

REAL TIME
Descriptive of a system's capability to receive and process data and provide output fast enough to control the outcome of an activity.

■ **Summarizing** data, or reducing it to concise, usable form. Grade-point averages can be scanned in order to compare the performance of this year's senior class to that of last year's senior class. Sales figures can be summarized in order to compare sales in various outlets of the same department store.
■ **Storing,** or retaining, data on storage media such as magnetic disks, tapes, or microfilm for later retrieval and processing.

Output   After data has been processed according to some or all of the preceding steps, information can be distributed to the users. There are two types of **output:** soft copy and hard copy. **Soft copy** is information that appears on a television-like screen or monitor attached to the computer. As soon as the monitor is turned off or new information is required, the old information vanishes. **Hard copy** is output printed in a tangible form, such as paper or microfilm. It can be read without using the computer and can be carried around conveniently, written on, or passed to other readers. Printers and plotters produce hard copy, as discussed in Chapter 3.

Three steps are necessary in the output phase of data flow:

■ **Retrieving,** or pulling, data from storage.
■ **Converting,** or translating, data into a form that humans can understand and use (words or pictures displayed on a computer screen or printed on paper).
■ **Communicating,** or providing information to the proper users at the proper time and place, in an intelligible form.

User requirements for information may change over time. The output is evaluated periodically and the input or processing steps are adjusted in order to ensure that processing results in good information. This procedure is called **feedback.**

Types of Data Processing

There are two general types of computer processing. One type is **batch processing,** in which data items are collected over time and processed all at once. In a bank, transactions—deposits, withdrawals, loans, or loan payments—are entered into the computer system as they occur. A summary of the number and dollar amounts of all transactions for one day is processed by batch at night when the bank is closed.

Many computer applications, however, require immediate feedback. If the computer is being used for preparing documents or for learning a skill, the user wants to see the results of processing as he or she works. This feedback occurs during **interactive processing.** For example, the user can type a memo, see the words on a screen, and make any necessary corrections. Interactive processing usually occurs online.

Interactive processing often is used for transactions. A person making a plane reservation wants to know immediately what flight is available and at what cost. The computer system also must record the transaction immediately, or a travel agent in another office may sell the same seat to another customer. A bank customer putting money into a savings account wants the amount entered in a passbook now, not tomorrow or next week. Such transactions occur in **real time**—that is, they provide results fast enough to affect the outcome of an activity.

Learning Check

1. Define the term online, with reference to data input, and name its opposite.
2. What input step can help prevent GIGO?
3. Name five kinds of manipulations which can occur during computer processing.
4. Summarizing an entire day's sales at several branch stores often involves batch processing, whereas playing a computer game requires _____ processing.
5. Evaluating data by computer during a rocket launch must occur in _____ time.

Answers

1. *Online* describes data entry via a device directly connected to the computer used to process the data. Its opposite is *offline*. 2. Verification 3. Classifying, sorting, calculating, summarizing, storing 4. Interactive 5. Real

Computers Yesterday and Today

By now, we take the computer for granted. We make our plane reservations, use automatic teller machines, and listen to synthesized music, forgetting that true electronic computers are only about 45 years old. The first mechanical calculator was invented just a few hundred years ago.

People have always had ways to figure, sort, compile, store, and classify data. They tied knots in rope to keep track of livestock and carved marks on clay or stone tablets to record transactions. Later, they added and subtracted with an abacus, a device made of beads strung on wires. The abacus, along with hand calculations, was adequate for computation until the early 1600s. Then John Napier designed a portable multiplication tool called Napier's Bones or Rods. The user slid the ivory rods up and down against each other, matching the numbers printed on the rods to figure multiplication and division problems. Napier's idea led to the invention of the slide rule in the mid-1600s.

These tools were useful, but they were anything but automatic. As business became more complex and tax systems expanded, people needed faster, more accurate aids for computation and record-keeping. The idea for the first mechanical calculating machine grew out of the many tedious hours a father and his son spent preparing tax reports. Once this machine was introduced, the way opened for better machines as inventors built upon each succeeding development.

As we trace the history of computers, we see that the concepts of input, processing, and output have not changed. Only the method of entering data, the speed of processing, and the media and display devices for output have advanced.

Early Developments

In the mid-1600s, Blaise Pascal, a mathematician and philosopher, and his father, a tax official, were compiling tax reports for the French government in Paris. As they agonized over the columns of figures, Pascal decided to build a machine that would do the job much faster and more accurately. His machine, the Pascaline, could add and subtract (see Figure 1-15). Much as an odometer keeps track of a car's mileage, the Pascaline functioned by a series of eight rotating gears. Although it had limited uses, it was an improvement over knots, beads, and bones. Yet a market for the Pascaline never grew. Clerks and accountants would not use it. They were afraid it might replace them at their jobs and thought it could be rigged, like a scale or roulette wheel.

About 50 years later, in 1694, the German mathematician Gottfried Wilhelm von Leibniz designed the Stepped Reckoner that could add, subtract, multiply, divide, and figure square roots. Although the machine was not widely used, almost every mechanical calculator during the next 150 years was based on it.

The first signs of automation benefited France's weaving industry when Joseph Marie Jacquard built a loom controlled by **punched cards** (see Figure 1-16). Heavy paper cards linked in a series passed over a set of rods on the loom. The pattern of holes in the cards determined which rods were engaged, thereby adjusting the color and pattern of the product. Prior to Jacquard's invention, a loom operator adjusted the loom settings by hand before each glide of the shuttle, a tedious and time-consuming job.

Jacquard's loom emphasized three concepts important in computer theory. One was that information could be coded on punched cards. A second was that cards could be linked in a series of instructions—essentially a program—thus allowing

PUNCHED CARDS
Heavy paper storage medium in which data is represented by holes punched according to a specific coding scheme.

Figure 1-15
Blaise Pascal and the Pascaline
The Pascaline worked very well for addition, but subtraction was performed by a roundabout adding method.

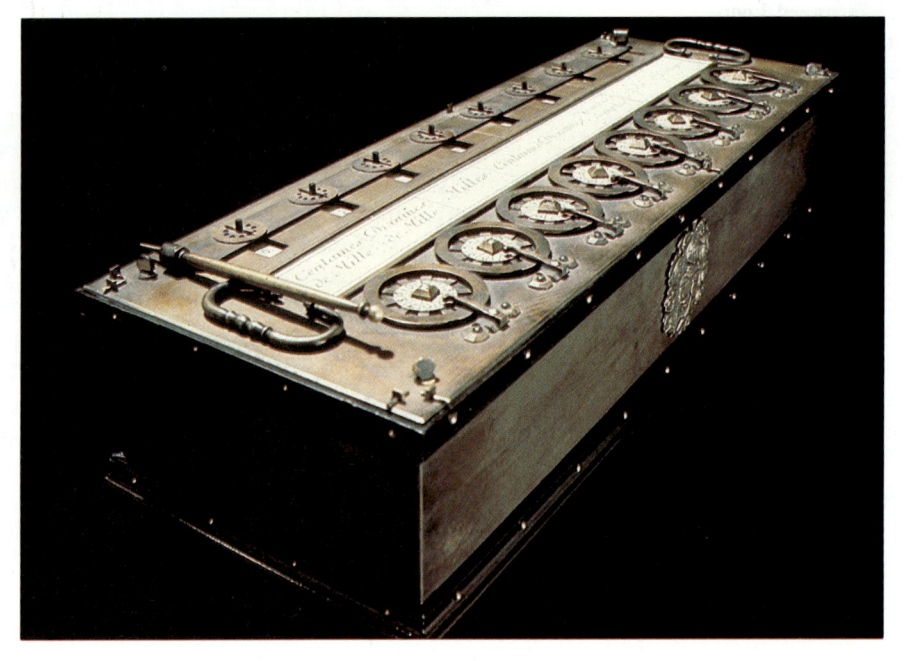

HIGHLIGHT

Ada Lovelace

Ada Augusta Byron, Countess of Lovelace, did not lead the kind of life typical of most aristocratic English women during the early 1800s. The daughter of the romantic English poet Lord Byron, Lady Lovelace contributed significantly to modern-day programming concepts.

Lady Lovelace first became involved with the theoretical concepts of computers when she translated a paper on Charles Babbage's analytical engine, a device designed to perform mathematical calculations from coded card instructions. In 1842, at the age of 27, Lady Lovelace began working with Babbage. Several of her ideas were incorporated into the design of the analytical engine.

The most significant of Lady Lovelace's ideas was what is now called the loop. In her studies, Lovelace noticed that the same sequence of instructions often had to be repeated in performing a single calculation. She concluded that only one set of instruction cards was needed if there was a way to loop back to those instructions. A calculation then could be made with only a fraction of the original effort. Lady Lovelace also suggested that Babbage use the binary number system in coding his machine.

Lovelace is now considered to be the first programmer because of her insight into the programming process. In honor of her achievements, a high-level programming language used mostly by the U.S. government was named Ada.

Figure 1-16
The Jacquard Loom
Although other weavers already had designed looms that used punched cards, Jacquard refined the idea and he is credited with the invention.

a machine to do its work without human intervention. A third concept was that such programs could automate jobs.

The first person to use these concepts in a computing machine was Charles Babbage, a professor at Cambridge University in England. As a mathematician, Babbage needed an accurate method for computing and printing tables of the properties of numbers (squares, square roots, logarithms, and so on). Existing tables contained too many mistakes, the results of miscalculations and printing errors. So Babbage designed the Difference Engine, a machine that would compute and print the tables. A model of the machine worked well, but the technology of the day was too primitive for manufacturing metal parts precise enough for a full-sized version.

Later, Babbage envisioned a new machine, the Analytical Engine, for performing any calculation according to instructions coded on cards. The idea for this steam-powered machine was amazingly similar to the design of computers. It had four parts: a "mill" for calculating; a "store" for holding instructions and intermediate and final results; and "operator" or system for carrying out instructions; and a device for "reading" and "writing" data on punched cards. Although Babbage died before he could construct the machine, his son built a working model from Babbage's notes and drawings. Because of the ideas he introduced, Babbage is known as the father of computers.

Punched cards played an important role in the next advance toward automatic machines, a machine used for tabulating census data. Totals from the 1880 census were not completed until 1888; by then the data had little meaning, being so out of date. Therefore, the U.S. Census Bureau asked Dr. Herman Hollerith, a statistician, to develop a faster method of tabulating the data. Hollerith invented a

Figure 1-17
Herman Hollerith and the Tabulating Machine
Once data was punched onto the cards, a tabulator read the cards as they passed over tiny brushes. Each time a brush found a hole, it completed an electrical circuit and caused special counting dials to increment the data. The cards then were sorted into 24 compartments by the sorting component of the machine.

Tabulating Machine that read and compiled data from punched cards (see Figure 1-17). These cards were the forerunners of today's standard computer card (see Figure 1-18). Thanks to Hollerith's invention, the time needed to process the 1890 census data was reduced to two and one-half years, despite the fact that the population increased by thirteen million people in the intervening ten years.

Encouraged by his success, Hollerith formed the Tabulating Machine Company in 1896 to supply equipment to census takers in western Europe and Canada. In 1911, Hollerith sold his company, which later combined with twelve others as the Computing-Tabulating-Recording Company (CTR). Thomas J. Watson, Sr., became president of CTR in 1924, and changed the name to International Business Machines Corporation (IBM). The IBM machines made extensive use of punched cards. After Congress set up the Social Security System in 1935, Watson won for IBM the contract to provide machines needed for this massive accounting and payment distribution system. The U.S. Census Bureau also bought IBM equipment.

During the late 1920s and early 1930s, accounting machines evolved which could perform many record-keeping and accounting functions. Although they handled the U.S. business data processing load well into the 1950s, they did little more than manipulate vast quantities of punched cards. These machines were limited in speed, physical size, and versatility.

The first real advance toward modern computing came in 1944, when Howard Aiken's team at Harvard University began designing the Mark I. This machine, the first automatic calculator, used Hollerith's punched card concept and was controlled by instructions coded on punched paper tapes. The U.S. Navy used the Mark I for designing weapons and calculating trajectories until the end of World War II.

Regardless of its role in computer history, the Mark I was outdated before it was finished. Only two years after work on it was begun, John Mauchly and

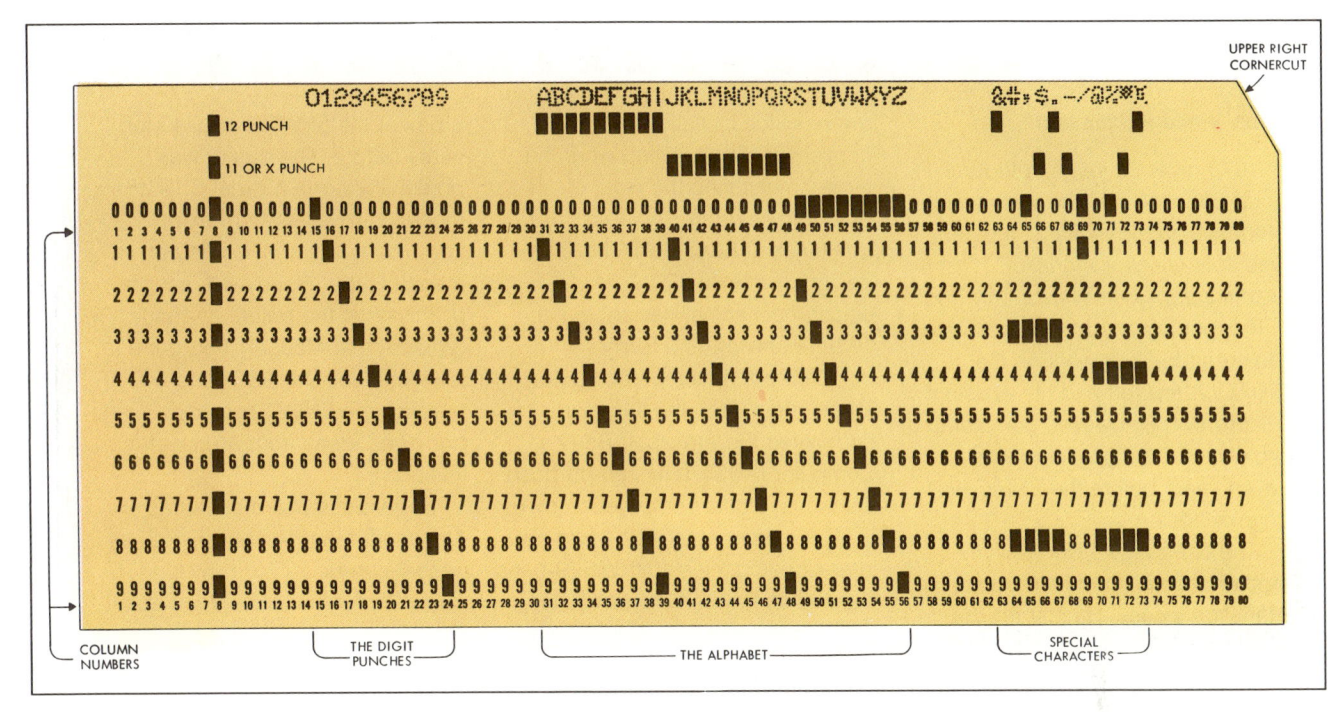

Figure 1-18
A Computer Card

J. Presper Eckert, Jr., introduced the first electronic computer for large-scale, general use at the University of Pennsylvania Moore School of Engineering. This machine was called the ENIAC, short for Electronic Numerical Integrator and Calculator (see Figure 1-19). Although it was invented because of a need for faster ways to calculate artillery trajectories during World War II, ENIAC was finished after the war ended, and was used instead for studying weather, cosmic rays, and

Figure 1-19 The ENIAC
The ENIAC's first job was calculating the feasibility of a proposed design for the hydrogen bomb. The computer also was used for studying weather and cosmic rays.

HIGHLIGHT ▲▲▲▲▲▲▲▲▲▲▲▲▲▲▲▲▲▲▲▲

John Vincent Atanasoff

In 1973, after 32 years, a federal court declared that the true inventor of the electronic digital computer was John Vincent Atanasoff. Traditionally, John W. Mauchly and J. Presper Eckert, Jr., had received the credit for their work on the ENIAC. Atanasoff and his assistant Clifford Berry, however, completed a prototype of a digital computer seven years before the ENIAC was developed.

The old adage, "Necessity is the mother of invention," held true in Atanasoff's case. He first felt the need for a computing machine while working on his doctorate in math and physics. After Atanasoff completed his degree, he accepted a teaching position at Iowa State University. He became even more aware of the limitations of conventional calculating when he began monitoring the work of graduate students.

Atanasoff began working on the design of a binary electromechanical device. In late 1939, Atanasoff and Berry completed a prototype computer. Three years later, the two men completed the Atanasoff-Berry Computer (ABC), a limited-purpose electronic digital computer.

At the time, Atanasoff could not interest companies such as IBM and Remington Rand in the computer. Even more disturbing, he failed to obtain patent rights for the invention. This issue came to court as a dispute over patents. Sperry Rand had purchased the rights to Eckert and Mauchly's design and received a patent the two had applied for years before. The patent was potentially worth a great deal of money in royalties from other companies. Another computer manufacturer, Honeywell, sought dismissal at the patent on the grounds that Mauchly had gone to Iowa to study the ABC before building the ENIAC and had borrowed ideas from Atanasoff's invention.

Regardless of the outcome, Atanasoff, Mauchly, and Eckert all deserve credit for their work. Atanasoff for his initial ideas about using vacuum tubes and binary code and Mauchly and Eckert for having built the first true large-scale general-purpose computer.

STORED-PROGRAM CONCEPT The idea that program instructions can be stored in primary memory in electronic form so that no human intervention is required during processing.

nuclear energy. It represented the shift from mechanical/electromechanical devices that used wheels, gears, and relays for computing to devices that depended upon electronic parts, such as vacuum tubes and electrical circuitry.

The ENIAC was a huge machine; its 18,000 vacuum tubes took up a space 8 feet high and 80 feet long. It weighed 30 tons and consumed 174,000 watts of power. In 20 seconds, ENIAC performed a mathematical calculation that would have required 40 hours for one person to complete using manual techniques. At the time, the ENIAC seemed so fast that scientists predicted that seven computers like it could handle all the calculations the world would ever need.

The ENIAC had one major limitation: Operating instructions had to be fed into it manually by setting switches and connecting wires on control panels called plugboards. This was a tedious, time-consuming, and error-prone task. In the mid-1940s, the mathematician John von Neumann proposed a way to overcome this difficulty. The solution was the **stored-program concept** (discussed further in Chapter 3). Von Neumann believed that both instructions and data could be written in binary notation and stored in the computer's primary memory. This advance decreased the number of manual operations needed in switching programs and other computer operations. Eckert and Mauchly actually conceived the stored-program concept long before von Neumann did, but they did not outline a plan for its use and therefore did not profit from their ideas.

Table 1-1
Summary of Early Calculating Developments

Person	Motivation	Machine
Pascal	Needed a faster, more accurate way to compute tax reports	Pascaline
von Leibniz	Wanted a faster method for computing	Stepped Reckoner
Jacquard	Thought changing loom settings by hand was tiresome and time-consuming	Loom automated by punched cards
Babbage	Needed accurate mathematics tables	Difference engine, Analytical engine
Hollerith	Worked on a project to finish tabulating the 1890 census faster	Tabulating Machine
Aiken	Helped in designing a machine that aided in calculating artillery trajectories	Mark I
Eckert, Mauchly	Designed a machine meant to be used in calculating artillery trajectories	ENIAC
von Neumann	Recognized the problem with setting computer instructions by moving switches and wires	EDVAC

Von Neumann's principles spurred the development of the first stored-program computer in the United States, the EDVAC (Electronic Discrete Variable Automatic Computer). This development marked the beginning of the modern computer era and the so-called information society. Subsequent refinements of the stored-program concept have focused on speed, size, and cost. (See Table 1-1 for a summary of early developments.)

Learning Check

1. What was Pascal's contribution to the development of computers?
2. In what three ways was Jacquard's loom important to the development of computers?
3. Who is known as the father of computers?
4. What did the federal government want Herman Hollerith to invent in time for the 1890 census?
5. What need spurred the development of the Mark I and the ENIAC?
6. What was von Neumann's contribution to computer development?

Answers

1. A mechanical calculator, the Pascaline 2. Information could be coded on punched cards; punched cards could be linked to form a "program;" and such programs and machines could automate jobs. 3. Charles Babbage 4. A faster method for tabulating census data 5. The need for faster ways to calculate artillery trajectories 6. The stored-program concept

Table 1-2
Hardware Benchmarks
Vacuum tubes gave way to transistors and transistors gave way to chips in the effort to reduce the size of computer components.

Vacuum Tubes	
Mauchly, Eckert, and ENIAC	First electronic digital computer
von Neumann and EDVAC	First stored-program computer
Mauchly, Eckert, and UNIVAC	First general-purpose, large-scale computer used for commercial purposes
Transistors and Magnetic Cores	
Bell Laboratories	Developed first transistor
U.S. Navy and Whirlwind I	First computer used for real-time functions
Integrated Circuits	
Jack S. Kilby	Developed integrated circuit
Robert Noyce	Developed integrated circuit
Ted Hoff and microprocessor	Led to development of microcomputers

The First Generation: 1951–1958

Improvements in computer capabilities are grouped into generations, based upon the electronic technology available at the time. (See Tables 1-2 and 1-3 for reviews of hardware benchmarks and characteristics of the generations.) There is some disagreement among professionals about the exact dates associated with each computer generation. The dates given in this chapter are approximations. The first generation of computers—based upon the designs of the ENIAC and EDVAC—began with the sale of the first commercial electronic computer (see Figure 1-20). This machine, called the UNIVAC I, was developed by Mauchly and Eckert, who had approached Remington Rand for financing. Remington Rand (today Sperry Corporation) bought Mauchly and Eckert's company and entered the computer age with a product that was years ahead of the machines produced by competitors. In 1951, the first UNIVAC I replaced IBM equipment at the U.S. Census Bureau.

Figure 1-20
The UNIVAC I
The most popular business uses for the UNIVAC I were payroll and billing.

Table 1-3
Chracteristics of the Four Generations

Period	Characteristics
First Generation 1951–1958	Vacuum tubes for internal operations. Magnetic drums for primary memory. Limited primary memory. Heat and maintenance problems. Punched cards for input and output. Slow input, processing, and output. Low-level symbolic languages for programming.
Second Generation 1959–1964	Transistors for internal operations. Magnetic cores for primary memory. Increased primary memory capacity. Magnetic tapes and disks for secondary storage. Reductions in size and heat generation. Increase in processing speed and reliability. Increased use of high-level languages.
Third Generation 1965–1970	Integrated circuits on silicon chips for internal operations. Increased primary memory capacity. Common use of minicomputers. Emergence of software industry. Reduction in size and cost. Increase in speed and reliability.
Fourth Generation 1971–Today	Large-scale and very large-scale integration for internal operations. Development of the microprocessor. Introduction of microcomputers and supercomputers. Greater versatility in software. Increase in speed, power, and storage capacity. Parallel processing. Artificial intelligence and expert systems. Robotics.

MACHINE LANGUAGE
The only language the computer can execute directly; designates the computer's electrical states as combinations of 0's and 1's.

ASSEMBLY LANGUAGE
Lower-level, symbolic programming language that uses abbreviations rather than groupings of 0's and 1's.

Another UNIVAC was installed at General Electric's Appliance Park in Louisville, Kentucky. For the first time, business firms saw the potential of computer data processing.

The UNIVAC I and other first-generation computers were huge, costly to buy, expensive to power, and often unreliable. They were slow compared to today's computers, and primary memory was limited. They depended upon the first-generation technology of vacuum tubes for internal operations. The masses of vacuum tubes took up a lot of space and required an air-conditioned environment to dissipate the considerable heat they generated. When a tube burned out, too much time was wasted hunting for it.

Punched cards were used to enter data into the machines. Internal storage consisted of magnetic drums, cylinders coated with magnetizable material. A drum rotated at high speeds, while a device poised just above it either wrote on the drum by magnetizing small spots, or read from it by detecting spots already magnetized. Then the results of processing were punched on blank cards.

Early first-generation computers were given instructions coded in **machine language.** Preparing the program or instructions was extremely tedious, and errors were common. In order to overcome this difficulty, **assembly languages** were developed. Assembly languages consist of mnemonic symbols. For example, ADD might stand for addition. These symbols were easier for people to use than the strings of 0s and 1s of machine language. Special programs were developed to translate the assembly language into machine language, the only language computers can understand. Commodore Grace Murray Hopper of the U.S. Navy worked with a team that developed the first of these programs.

The public was not yet aware of the amazing computing machines, but this situation changed with the 1952 presidential election. After analyzing only 5 percent of the tallied vote, a UNIVAC I computer predicted that Dwight David Eisenhower would defeat Adlai E. Stevenson. CBS doubted the accuracy of the prediction and did not release the information to the public until the election results were confirmed by actual votes. The electronic prediction became the first in a burgeoning trend that has culminated in today's controversy about predicting election results from East Coast tallies before polls are closed on the West Coast.

Business acceptance of computers grew quickly. In 1953, Remington Rand and IBM led the infant industry, having placed a grand total of nine installations. By the late 1950s, IBM alone had leased 1,000 of its first-generation computers.

The Second Generation: 1959–1964

Four hardware advances in the 1940s and 1950s characterized the second-generation computers: the transistor, magnetic core storage, magnetic tapes, and magnetic disks. Transistors, developed by Bell Laboratories, replaced the vacuum tubes of first-generation machines. A transistor is a small component made of solid material which acts like a vacuum tube in controlling the flow of electric current. Using transistors in computers resulted in smaller, faster, and more reliable machines that used less electricity and generated much less heat than the first-generation computers.

Just as transistors replaced vacuum tubes as primary electronic components, magnetic cores replaced magnetic drums as internal storage units. Magnetic cores consisted of tiny rings of magnetic material strung on fine wires (see Figure 1-21). Each magnetic core was placed at the intersection of a vertical and a horizontal wire. To turn on a core, half the electricity needed was run through each wire. Thus, only at the intersection of specific wires would a core become charged. In this way, groups of cores stored instructions and data.

The development of magnetic cores resulted from the U.S. Navy's need for a more advanced, reliable high-speed flight trainer. Known as Whirlwind I, the Navy project was one of the most innovative and influential projects in the history of the computer. Because of the high speed with which instructions and data could be located and retrieved using magnetic cores (a few millionths of a second), the Whirlwind allowed the real-time processing necessary in flight simulation. The development led to other real-time functions such as air traffic control, factory management, and battle simulations.

This new type of internal storage was supplemented by external storage on **magnetic tapes** and **disks.** During World War II, huge, heavy steel tapes were used for sound recording. Plastic magnetic tapes eventually replaced the metal tapes and were used later for recording computer output, recorded as magnetized spots on the tape's surface. Another byproduct of sound recording, the phonograph record, led to the introduction of the magnetic disk, which allows direct access to

MAGNETIC TAPE
A sequential storage medium consisting of a narrow strip of material upon which spots are magnetized to represent data.

MAGNETIC DISK
A direct-access storage medium consisting of a metal or plastic platter upon which data can be stored as magnetized spots.

Figure 1-21
A Frame of Magnetic Cores
An assembled core unit looked much like a window screen.

data. Both disks and tapes greatly increased the speed of processing and storage capacities, and eventually replaced punched cards for storage.

During this period, more sophisticated, English-like computer languages such as COBOL and FORTRAN were commonly used.

The Third Generation: 1965–1970

INTEGRATED CIRCUIT
An electronic circuit etched on a small silicon chip less than one-quarter inch square.

SILICON CHIP
Solid-state logic circuitry on a small piece of silicon.

LARGE-SCALE INTEGRATION (LSI)
Method by which circuits containing thousands of electronic components are densely packed on a single chip.

At the same time that transistors were replacing vacuum tubes, Jack S. Kilby of Texas Instruments and Robert Noyce at Fairchild Semiconductor were separately developing the **integrated circuit (IC)**. Using their own methods, they discovered that the components of electronic circuits could be placed together—or integrated—onto small chips. Soon, a single **silicon chip** less than one-eighth inch square could hold sixty-four complete circuits. This seems crude to us, since today's chips can contain as many as 500,000 transistors.

The chips marked the third generation of computers, which used less power, cost less, and were smaller and much more reliable than previous machines. Although computers were smaller, their internal memories were larger due to the placement of memory on chips. In early third-generation computers, the density with which components were integrated was known as medium-scale integration (MSI). **Large-scale integration (LSI)** soon followed, which put thousands of components on a silicon chip.

Figure 1-22
A Third-Generation Minicomputer
The development of minicomputers enabled many small businesses to acquire computer power, because the costs were much less than for mainframes.

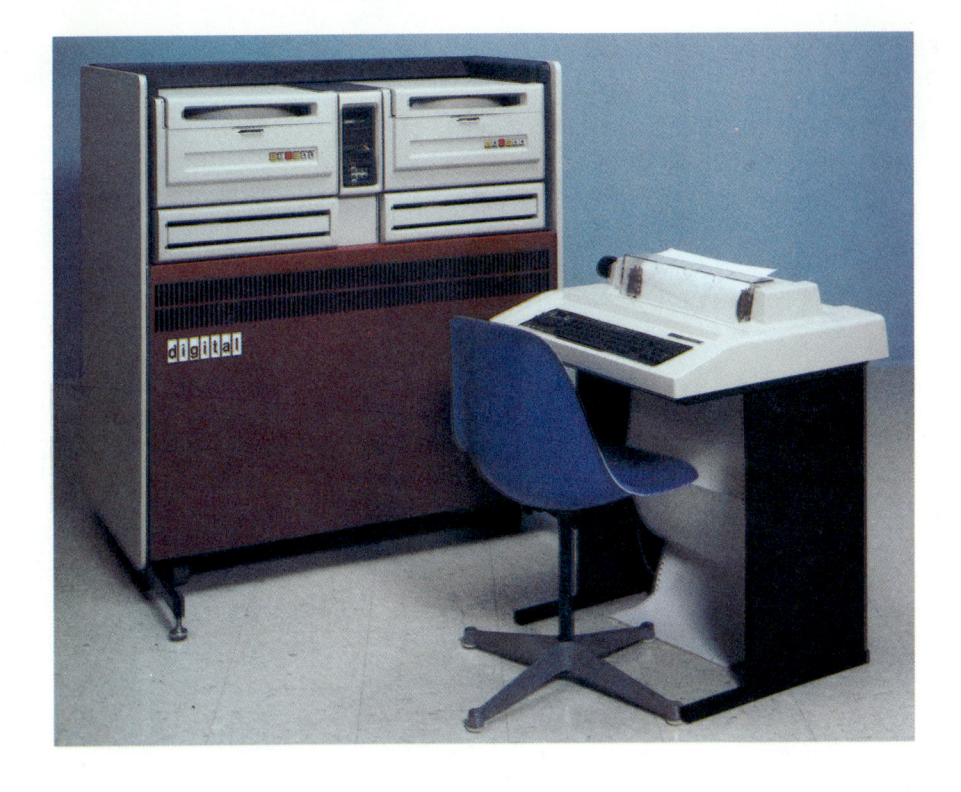

A major innovation resulted when IBM realized its company was turning out too many incompatible products. The company responded to the problem by designing the System/360 computers, which offered both scientific and business applications and introduced the family concept of computers. The first series consisted of six computers designed to run the same programs and use the same input, output, and storage equipment. Each computer offered a different memory capacity. For the first time, a company could buy a computer and feel that its investment in programs and peripheral equipment would not be wasted when the time came to move to a machine with a larger memory. Other manufacturers followed IBM's lead, and before long, over 25,000 similar computer systems were installed in the United States.

MINICOMPUTER
A type of computer with the components of a full-sized system but with smaller primary memory.

Minicomputers, developed during the second generation, were commonly used in the 1960s (see Figure 1-22). Although these machines had many of the same capabilities as large computers, they were much smaller, had less storage space, and cost less. Use of remote terminals also became common. Remote terminals are computer terminals located some distance away from a main computer and linked to it through cables such as telephone lines. Thus it is not necessary to be in the same room, or even the same building, in order to use the computer.

The software industry also began to emerge in the 1960s. Programs to perform payroll, billing, and other business tasks became available at fairly low cost. Yet software rarely was free of "bugs," or errors. The computer industry experienced growing pains as the software industry lagged behind advances in hardware technology. The rapid advancements in hardware meant that old programs had to be rewritten to suit the circuitry of the new machines, and programmers skilled enough

Figure 1-23
An IBM Microcomputer

MICROPROCESSOR
A programmable processing unit (placed on a silicon chip) containing arithmetic, logic, and control circuitry.

MICROCOMPUTER
A small, low-priced computer used in homes, schools, and businesses; also called a personal computer.

VERY LARGE-SCALE INTEGRATION (VLSI)
Method by which circuits containing hundreds of thousands of components are packed on a single chip even more densely than with LSI.

SUPERCOMPUTER
Currently the largest, fastest, most expensive type of computer; can perform millions of calculations per second and process enormous amounts of data.

Figure 1-24
A Computer Chip
This 32-bit chip contains almost 150,000 transistors and offers processing power comparable to that of today's minicomputers.

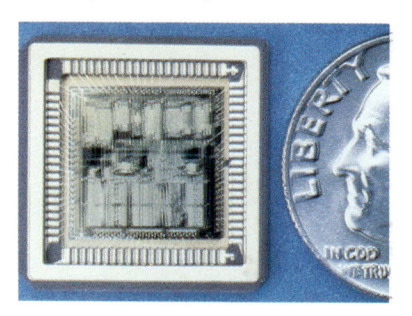

to do this were scarce. Software problems led to computer horror stories, such as a $200,000 water bill or $80,000 worth of duplicate welfare checks.

The Fourth Generation: 1971–Today

Although the dividing lines between the first three generations of computers are clearly marked by major technological advances, historians are not so clear as to when the fourth generation began. They do agree that, in fourth-generation computers, magnetic cores had replaced memory on silicon chips. Even today, however, programmers often refer to main memory as "core."

Engineers continued to cram more circuits onto a single chip in LSI, thus shortening the distance electricity had to travel during data processing. The functions that could be performed with a chip, however, were permanently fixed during the production process. Ted Hoff, an engineer at Intel Corporation, introduced an idea that resulted in a single programmable unit: the **microprocessor** or "computer on a chip." In 1969, working with a team at Intel, Hoff packed the arithmetic and logic circuitry needed for computations onto one microprocessor chip, which could be made to act like any kind of calculator or computer desired. Other functions, such as input, output, and memory, were placed on separate chips. The development of the microprocessor led to a boom in computer manufacturing which gave computing power to homes and schools in the form of **microcomputers** (see Figure 1-23).

As microcomputers became more popular, many companies began producing software that could be run on the smaller machines. Most early programs were games. Later, instructional programs began to appear. One important software development was the first electronic spreadsheet for microcomputers: *VisiCalc*, introduced in 1979. *VisiCalc* vastly increased the possibilities for using microcomputers in the business world. Today, a wide variety of software exists for microcomputer applications in business, school, and personal use.

Currently, **very large-scale integration (VLSI)** has replaced large-scale integration. In VLSI, as many as 500,000 electronic components can be placed on a single silicon chip (see Figure 1-24). This further miniaturization of integrated circuits offers even greater improvements in price, performance, and size of computers. A microprocessor based on VSLI is more powerful than a roomful of 1950s computer circuitry.

Trends in miniaturization led ironically to the development of the largest and most powerful of computers: the **supercomputers.** By reducing the size of circuitry

PARALLEL PROCESSING
A type of processing in which instructions and data are handled simultaneously by two or more processing units.

and changing the design of the chips, companies that manufacture supercomputers were able to create computers powerful enough with memories large enough to perform the complex calculations required in aircraft design, weather forecasting, nuclear research, and energy conservation. Supercomputers process data differently than other computers. Traditional processing occurs serially—that is, all the data is handled bit by bit. Supercomputers, on the other hand, use **parallel processing.** In parallel processing, two or more CPUs or microprocessors work simultaneously on parts of the same problem, so that more than one bit is handled at one time. Computer speed is increased without further miniaturizing the circuits and encountering problems that result when circuits are packed too densely. The technique shows great potential for tackling very large problems with multiple variables. Parallel processing aids further development of speech recognition, interpretation of data from sensing devices, navigation uses, expert systems, artificial intelligence, and new generations of robots. (See Chapters 6 and 7 for more information about robots, expert systems, and artificial intelligence.)

Today's trends in chip design, supercomputers, and computer languages anticipate a fifth generation of computer development. In the effort to increase processing speed and develop ultra-large-scale integration needed in supercomputers, scientists are working on a new generation of chips that can perform more than a million calculations in a single second. Experts predict that, by 1990, a single chip may contain as many as 16 million components. Materials such as gallium arsenide, which achieves speeds five to seven times that of the fastest silicon chips, may be used in developing these new chips.

Some scientists believe that tiny computer circuits can be grown from the proteins and enzymes of living material, such as *E. coli* bacteria. Like other life forms, these "biochips" would require oxygen, and the signals they would send would be similar to those sent and received by our brains. Since biochips would be made from living material, they could repair and reproduce themselves. They would be 10 million times as powerful as today's most advanced computers.

Learning Check

1. What was the distinction given UNIVAC I?
2. What electronic technology characterized each of the four generations of computers?
3. Why was the magnetic core an important development?
4. Name one problem of software during the third generation.
5. What development led to microcomputers?
6. What is the advantage of parallel processing?

Answers

1. It was the first commercial computer. 2. Vacuum tubes, transistors, integrated circuits, and very large-scale integration respectively. 3. It allowed real-time processing. 4. All software had to be rewritten for the new technology. 5. Microprocessors 6. Since it processes more than one bit at a time, it allows faster processing without further miniaturization of circuits.

CHAPTER 1: COMPUTERS IN OUR WORLD

Biochips might first be used to sense odors that indicate unusual or dangerous conditions. Such chips also could be implanted in a blind person's brain and linked to a visual sensor like a miniature camera, thus enabling the person to see. Some biochips placed in the human bloodstream could monitor and correct chemical imbalances. Although the idea of biochips may seem farfetched at present, scientists continue to experiment.

It is no wonder that writers describe computer chips in terms of angels dancing on the heads of pins and house-by-house maps of the largest cities etched on postage stamps. With the breakneck pace of chip development in the past few years, nothing seems surprising now.

Summary Points

- Computers are powerful tools in many areas such as business, manufacturing, banking, government, education, and personal use. Most of today's transactions and procedures involve computers.
- Electronic data processing involves the use of computers in collecting, manipulating, and distributing data to achieve goals.
- Data refers to unorganized, raw facts. Information is data that has been organized and processed so that it can be used in making intelligent decisions.
- Analog computers measure changes in continuous physical or electric states, whereas digital computers count data in the form of yes/no, conducting/nonconducting, on/off states of electronic circuitry. The digital computer must convert all data to binary form, which is based on the binary number system of two digits, 0 and 1.
- The terms *hardware* and *software* describe the physical components of a computer and the instructions or programs respectively.
- The computer performs three basic functions: arithmetic operations, logic comparisons, and storage and retrieval operations.
- A computer's internal memory is called primary storage. Media used to hold data outside the computer constitute secondary storage, which makes the computer's memory almost limitless.
- Converting data into information includes three steps: input, processing, and output.
- The two types of processing are batch, in which data are collected and forwarded to the computer in groups, and interactive, in which the user communicates with the computer during processing.
- The first programmable machine was a weaving loom. The same punched-card principle was used later by Hollerith in processing census data.
- Charles Babbage is called the father of computers because his plans for an analytical engine outlined some ideas important in the design of computers.
- The Mark I, the first automatic calculator, was the first real advance toward modern computers, although it was out of date by the time it was finished.
- ENIAC was the first general-purpose electronic computer put to large-scale practical use, but it had no internal memory. A later machine, EDVAC, used internal memory and stored program instructions.

- First-generation computers used vacuum tubes to control operations. These machines were large and unreliable, and they generated much heat.
- Second-generation computers used transistors to control operations. Transistors are smaller, more reliable, and faster than vacuum tubes. During this period, computers had magnetic core storage and magnetic tapes and disks for secondary storage.
- Third-generation computers used integrated circuits to control operations. Integrated circuits are smaller, faster, and more reliable than transistors. Some third-generation computers used large-scale integration (LSI). The third generation also was characterized by the use of minicomputers, remote terminals, and families of computers. The software industry was beginning to emerge.
- Fourth-generation computers continue to become smaller, faster, and less costly; they are characterized by very large-scale integration (VLSI). The refinement of the microprocessor led to the development of microcomputers.
- Faster chips and parallel processing will increase the capabilities of computers. Some experts believe that a single chip may contain as many as 16 million components by 1990. Others believe that circuits will be grown into biochips from protein and enzyme material. Parallel processing improves processing speed by allowing one computer to handle more than one bit simultaneously.

Review Questions

1. Name some ways that computers affect you in your job or school today. Relate these examples to applications discussed in the first section of this chapter.
2. Distinguish between data and information in the context of data processing. Give some examples.
3. Define data processing. Why is it often referred to as EDP?
4. Using data that a store might collect when you purchase groceries, describe the five types of manipulations that may occur in the processing stage of EDP.
5. Although computer processing is essentially error-free, mistakes can and do occur. What is meant by the "garbage in–garbage out" principle? Name two procedures mentioned in the data flow discussion which could prevent GIGO.
6. Describe two types of storage involved in data processing. Why is the computer's memory almost limitless?
7. From the material in this chapter, name and describe at least two terms that would characterize the computer processing involved in buying tickets to the Olympic Games.
8. Describe how the use of punched cards affected the advance of automation, beginning with the invention of Jacquard.
9. Describe the stored-program concept and explain how it changed computer processing.
10. Based on the material in the text, name at least three factors that usually indicate a new generation of computers.
11. Why has the development of the integrated circuit and large-scale integration made such an impact on the computer industry?
12. How will further development of parallel processing affect use of computers?

CHAPTER 2

Getting to Know Your IBM

Outline

Introduction
IBM Hardware
  The Monitor
  The Keyboard
  The Disk Drive
Caring for Your Computer
Learning Check
Getting Started
Initializing a Disk
Highlight: A Tale of Two Bugs
Your Turn
Disk Operating System Commands

Using WestSoft™ 1.0
  Loading West Soft
  WestSoft Home Banking
    System
Your Turn
Your Turn
  WestSoft Personality Traits
    Program
Your Turn
Your Turn
Your Turn
  WestSoft Ticket-Office Manager

Your Turn
Highlight: Winning With Antonia Stone
  WestSoft Information Network
Your Turn
  WestSoft Dental Office
    Manager
Your Turn
Your Turn
Summary Points
Review Questions
Review Exercises

Introduction

IBM microcomputers are popular for business applications and for writing and editing. They are powerful enough, yet inexpensive enough, for small businesses to use for financial management, bookkeeping, billing, and professional-looking document preparation. Large businesses also are buying IBM microcomputers for linking to mainframe systems. Workers can use these microcomputers as independent machines for tasks that do not need the power of a mainframe. They can access data from the mainframe system through communication lines. This solution keeps the data in one central location, thus facilitating data integrity by reducing the number of places where the same data must be updated. It also reserves the mainframe for tasks that require its greater capacity.

IBM microcomputers are also popular in schools and homes. A wide variety of software is available for educational, recreational, and home-management purposes.

IBM microcomputers come in several models, including the IBM PC, PC jr. (no longer manufactured), IBM PC/XT, IBM PC/AT, and the IBM PC Convertible. This chapter explains how to begin using the IBM PC and how to care for your computer and disks.

IBM Hardware

DISK DRIVE
The mechanical device used to rotate a disk, floppy disk, or disk pack past a read/write head during data transmission.

MONITOR
A video display device or screen used for showing computer output.

PRINTER
A machine that prints characters or other images on paper.

KILOBYTE (K)
1,024 (2^{10}) storage units, or bytes; often rounded to 1,000.

PRIMARY MEMORY
The section of the computer which holds instructions, data, and intermediate and final results during processing.

In order to run software on an IBM PC, you need three standard pieces of equipment (see Figure 2-1). The main part of an IBM PC is the system unit (see the back of a system unit in Figure 2-2), which holds the computer itself and one or more **disk drives.** A **monitor** and a keyboard also are needed. If you want paper copies of your work, a fourth piece of hardware, the **printer,** will do the job.

The basic IBM PC has 256 **K (kilobytes)** of **primary memory,** but it can be upgraded to 640 k which will allow it to handle almost any type of software. The amount of memory a computer can handle is important because each program requires a specific amount of memory. The software package lists the amount of memory needed, so be sure to check the requirements before buying a program. More memory can be added to an IBM PC by installing additional memory chips or expansion boards containing memory chips (see Figure 2-3). An IBM dealer can give you details about adding memory.

The Monitor

The monitor displays output on a screen that is similar to a television screen. Without it, you could not see what you have typed. IBM PCs usually are equipped with a monochrome monitor or color monitor. A monochrome monitor displays a single color on a black or gray background. Color monitors require a special graphics circuit card that is installed in the computer. Television sets can be used, too, but they display a poorer quality of text than monitors designed for computer use. The type of monitor depends on the purposes for which the computer will be used. (More information about monitors appears in Chapter 5, Microcomputers.)

CHAPTER 2: GETTING TO KNOW YOUR IBM   35

Figure 2-1
IBM PC Microcomputer

Figure 2-2
Back View of an IBM PC

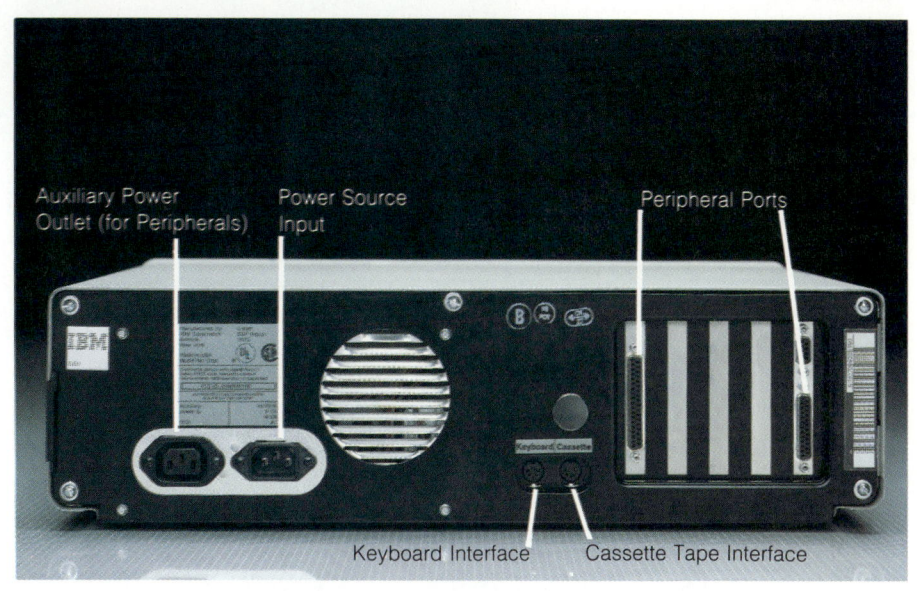

CURSOR
A character (square, vertical bar, or arrow) on a screen which shows where the next typed character will appear; the cursor may flash.

The Cursor You see your location on the screen by looking for the **cursor.** The cursor for many programs on IBM computers is a tiny horizontal bar (see Figure 2-4). As you type, the cursor moves ahead of each typed character that appears on the screen.

Figure 2-3
A Card of Memory Chips

Figure 2-4
The Cursor

PROMPT
A message or cue that guides the user during computer processing.

Changing Screen Width When in the DOS mode (DOS is explained later in this chapter), the IBM PC shows 80 columns on the screen. The computer is in DOS mode when you see the A> **prompt.** (Depending on which disk drive you are using, the prompt may be B> or C> instead.) If you are using a color/graphics monitor, you can type the following command to change the screen width from 80 columns to 40 columns:

```
MODE BW40
```

Similarly, you can type the following command to change the screen width from 40 columns to 80 columns:

```
MODE BW80
```

The Keyboard

Before using your IBM computer, you should become familiar with its keyboard. The IBM PC, IBM PC/XT, and older IBM PC/AT keyboards are similar. Each keyboard has the same keys as a regular typewriter (see Figure 2-5). The letter and number keys work the same as a typewriter's keys. Pressing the shift key (marked ⇧) with a letter key produces a capital letter. Pressing the shift key with a number or special character key produces the character shown on the top half of the key. When any key is held down, the character is repeated until the key is

Figure 2-5
The IBM PC Keyboard

released. Because of this feature, be sure that you press keys just long enough for the character to appear on the screen or for the computer to receive the command.

On the left side of the keyboard is a set of ten numbered function keys. The function that each key performs is determined by the software being used. (On the new IBM PC/AT keyboards, these function keys are the top row of keys.)

The keyboard has a numeric keypad on the right side, similar to a calculator's keypad, which also is used for editing purposes. When the Num Lock key in the top row of keys is pressed, the keypad can be to enter numbers 0–9.

Arrow keys for controlling the cursor are located within the numeric keypad. They can be used to move the cursor up, down, to the left, or to the right on the screen. The left arrow key is the same key as the 4, the right arrow key is the same key as the 6, the up arrow key is the same key as the 8, and the down arrow key is the same as the 2. If you make a typing mistake, these keys help you move the cursor to it. Then you can correct the mistake. Mistakes also can be corrected by moving the cursor to the left using the backspace key, which is located in the top row of keys and marked with an arrow pointing left.

The key marked with the ← ↑ symbol, located just to the left of the numeric keypad, is referred to as either the Enter Key or the Return Key. It moves the cursor down to the beginning of the next line. The line of data just typed is entered into the computer's memory.

Other special keys on IBM keyboards are listed in Table 2-1. When two keys are used together, hold down the first one while typing the second. Then release both keys immediately. Do not continue holding them down. The functions of some key combinations vary depending on the software being used. Always read the software documentation to find out the functions of the keys.

FLOPPY DISK
A low-cost, direct-access form of secondary storage made of flexible plastic; also called a flexible disk or diskette.

The Disk Drive

Disk drives can be double-sided or single-sided. A double-sided disk drive can write data to and read data from both sides of a **floppy disk** without the user

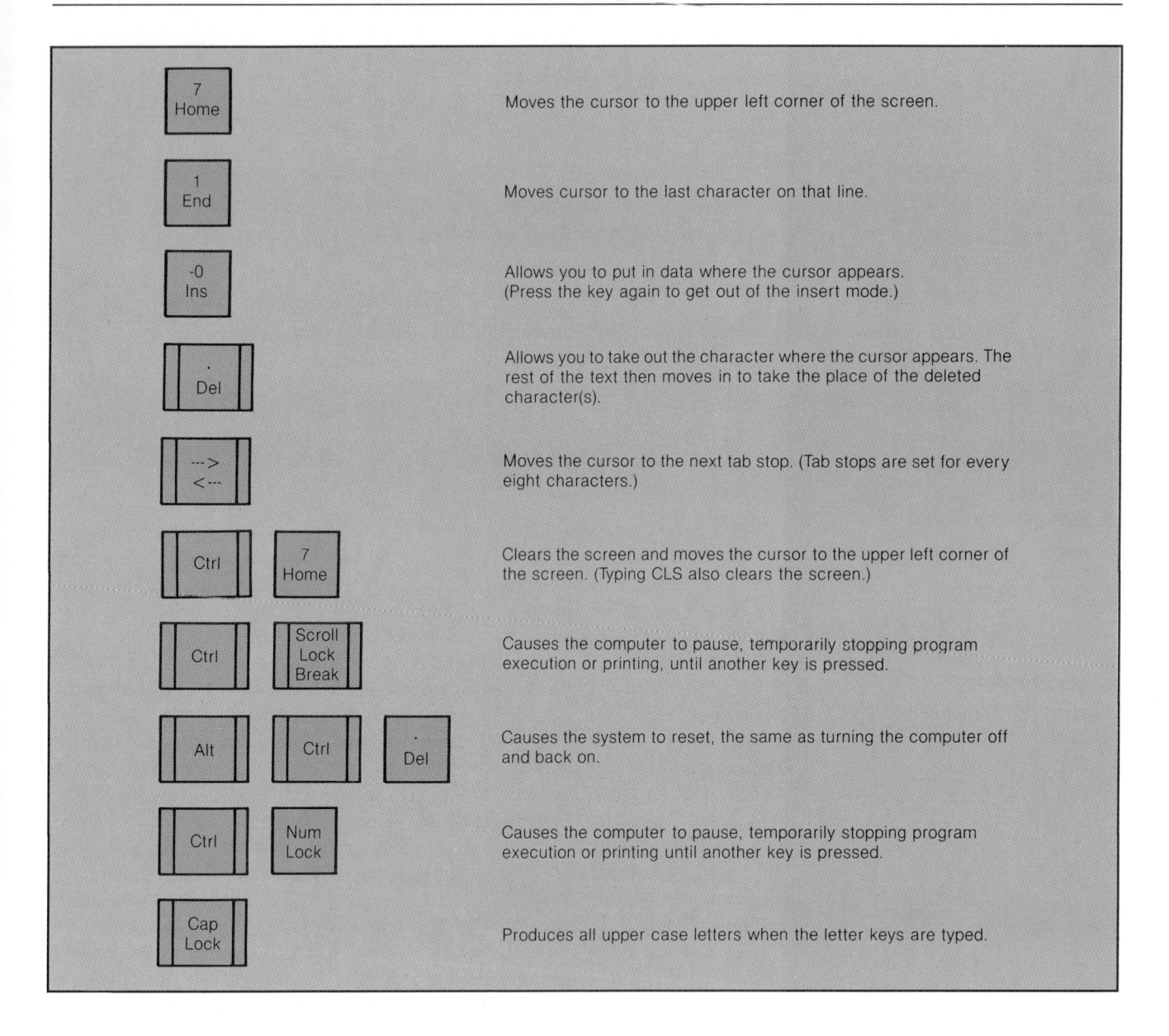

Key	Function
7 Home	Moves the cursor to the upper left corner of the screen.
1 End	Moves cursor to the last character on that line.
-0 Ins	Allows you to put in data where the cursor appears. (Press the key again to get out of the insert mode.)
. Del	Allows you to take out the character where the cursor appears. The rest of the text then moves in to take the place of the deleted character(s).
---> <---	Moves the cursor to the next tab stop. (Tab stops are set for every eight characters.)
Ctrl + 7 Home	Clears the screen and moves the cursor to the upper left corner of the screen. (Typing CLS also clears the screen.)
Ctrl + Scroll Lock Break	Causes the computer to pause, temporarily stopping program execution or printing, until another key is pressed.
Alt + Ctrl + . Del	Causes the system to reset, the same as turning the computer off and back on.
Ctrl + Num Lock	Causes the computer to pause, temporarily stopping program execution or printing until another key is pressed.
Cap Lock	Produces all upper case letters when the letter keys are typed.

Table 2-1
Special Keys and Their Functions

flipping the disk. (See Figure 2-6 for a graphic description of a floppy disk.) A single-sided disk drive can write data to and read data from only one side of the floppy disk at a time. The standard IBM disk drive is a double-sided drive. A diskette drive adapter card must be installed in the system unit for the disk drive to operate. The card can control up to four disk drives.

When two floppy disk drives are used, one drive is called Drive A and the other is called Drive B. Drive A is the drive on the left. A disk should be inserted in Drive A before one is inserted in Drive B. When only one drive is present, it is Drive A.

Figure 2-6
Floppy Disk

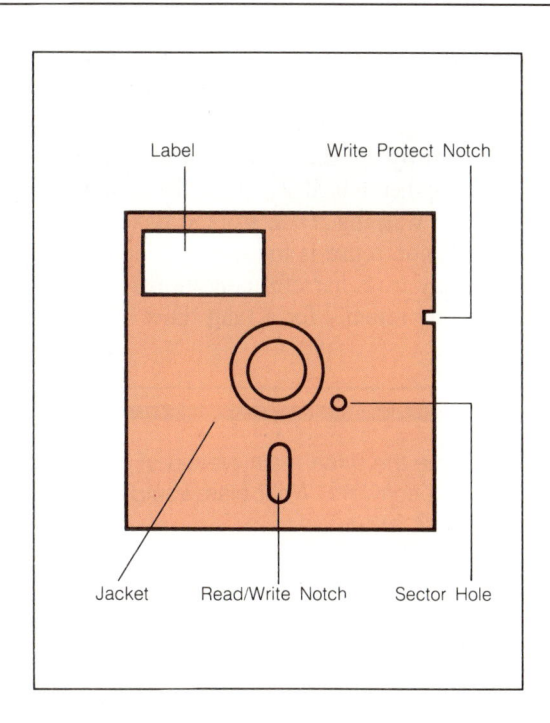

Label — Write Protect Notch

Jacket — Read/Write Notch — Sector Hole

Caring for Your Computer

Taking good care of your IBM computer will help keep it working properly. The computer should be set on a sturdy desk or table. The room should be clean and dry, but not too dry. When the humidity in a room is very low, static electricity may be created, which can destroy the data stored on floppy disks. Extreme heat and cold also may harm the computer. Keep the machine away from direct sunlight. Never set the computer or any hardware on appliances that get hot, such as televisions, and keep hardware away from heating ducts and air conditioners.

Eating and drinking should be avoided near the computer. Crumbs and spilled drinks can make the keyboard keys stick. Dust and dirt from the air can harm the keyboard or cause static. It is a good idea to keep the computer and hardware devices covered with anti-static covers when they are not being used.

When the computer is on, be careful not to move it or jolt it, including the desk or table where it is placed. If the electrical plug is disconnected accidentally, data that has not been recorded on a disk is lost.

Your computer is only as reliable as the data storage medium. Floppy disks always should be handled with care. Never touch the exposed surface of the disk. Hold disks by their labels. Floppy disks can be ruined by extreme temperatures, dust, and eraser crumbs. For example, disks should not be left in a car when it is hot or cold outside. Avoid setting disks near magnets or telephones or on top of computers, disk drives, or television sets. Magnets and electrical devices can destroy data stored on disks.

Always prepare the disk label before affixing it to the disk. If you must write on a label that is already on the disk, use a felt-tip or nylon-tip marker and press very lightly. Pressure caused by writing on the label with a pencil or ballpoint pen may destroy the data stored on the disk.

Do not bend the disk. Store disks, in their paper envelopes, in an upright position to avoid warping. Disk storage boxes are available for this purpose.

Common sense is the key to proper computer care. Keep the equipment clean and away from harmful conditions. Taking good care of the computer will keep it running reliably for a long time.

Learning Check

1. Name the three main pieces of hardware an IBM computer needs to run most software. What else would you need for making paper copies of your work?

2. Explain why the amount of internal memory is an important factor.

3. What key on an IBM keyboard must be pressed to get capital letters? To move the cursor to the next line without typing to the end of the current line?

4. What keys can be used to move the cursor to a mistake for correction? Where are they located?

5. When an IBM computer uses two floppy-disk drives, what names are used to designate them? Into which drive should a disk always be inserted first?

6. Name three things that can harm a computer or its hardware devices.

7. Describe how floppy disks should be handled so that data stored on them remains reliable.

Answers

1. System unit (computer and disk drives), monitor, and keyboard; printer. 2. It determines which software can be used. 3. Shift; Enter. 4. The arrow keys on the numeric keypad, or the backspace key in the top row of keys. 5. Drive A and Drive B; Drive A. 6. Static, heat, spilled food. 7. Hold them by the labels. Never touch the exposed surface of the disk. Use only felt-tip or nylon-tip pens for writing on a label already attached to the disk. Put the disks in their protective paper envelopes and then rest them vertically for storage. Keep them away from extreme heat and cold and magnetic or electrical devices. Keep dust and eraser crumbs away from them.

Getting Started

LOAD
To put a program into a computer's primary memory from a disk or other medium.

Before you can use software with your IBM computer, you need to know how to **load** it. To load a program means to put it into the computer's primary memory. The method used to load software differs from one package to another, so you should read the directions accompanying the software.

CHAPTER 2: GETTING TO KNOW YOUR IBM   41

Figure 2-7
Removing the Disk from Its Envelope

OPERATING SYSTEM (OS)
A collection of programs used by the computer to manage its own operations.

Many software packages require that some type of operating system software be loaded first. IBM PC DOS 3.10 is one version of the **operating system** that comes with IBM microcomputers. An operating system consists of programs that allow the computer to manage itself. Disk operating system (DOS) is a name given to an operating system that resides on a disk. One of the programs in a DOS, for example, governs the transfer of data to and from disks.

When loading DOS, use Drive A if there are two drives. Hold the disk with your thumb on the label and take it out of its envelope (see Figure 2-7). Gently slide the disk into the slot (see Figure 2-8) on the drive. The oval cutout (read/

Figure 2-8
Inserting the Disk into the Disk Drive

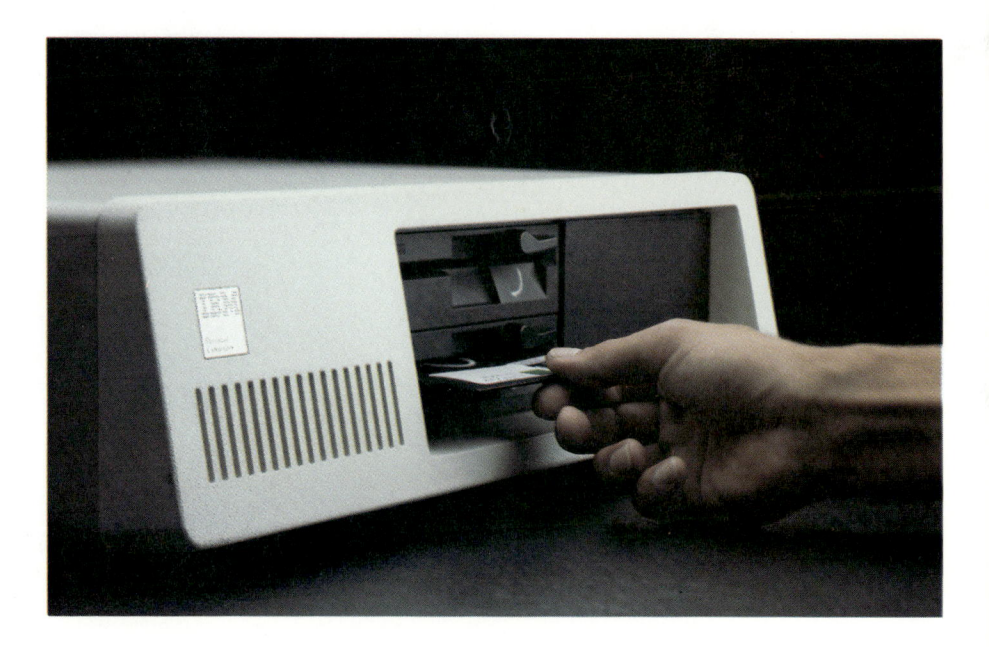

**Figure 2-9
Closing the Disk Drive Door**

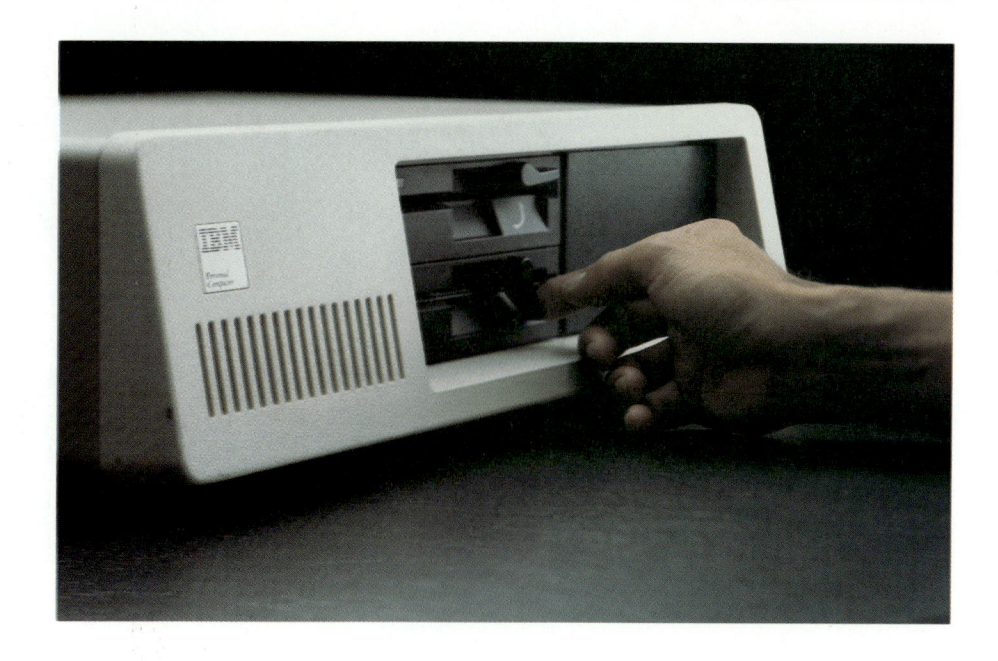

write notch) goes in first. Do not bend or force the disk. When the disk is in all the way, lock the diskette into place by pressing down on the knob to the right of the slot (see Figure 2-9).

Note that IBM also manufactures a diskette drive which has a disk-drive door which you open first and then insert the diskette. Once you insert the diskette, the door must be closed. See Fig. 2-10.

**Figure 2-10
Opening the Disk Drive Door**

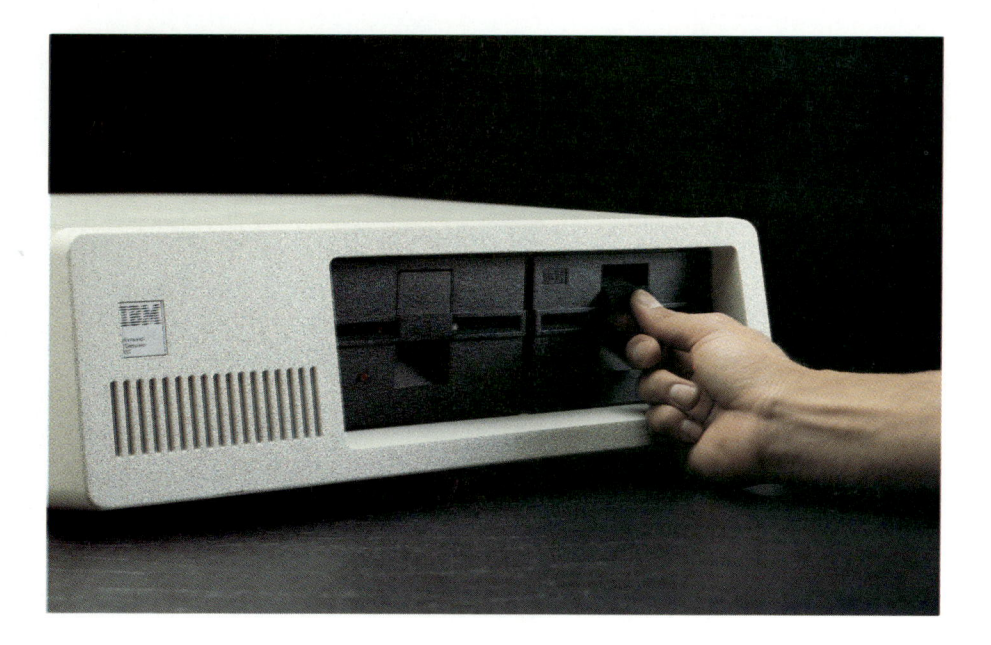

CHAPTER 2: GETTING TO KNOW YOUR IBM 43

Figure 2-11
Turning on the Power

Now turn on the computer and the monitor. Reach to the right rear side of the computer to find and turn on the power switch (see Figure 2-11).

Switches for most monitors are on the front right-hand side of the monitor. Turn or pull the ON switch of the monitor to the ''on'' position (see Figure 2-12). Then adjust the brightness control knob. Turning the knob to the left usually makes the screen darker. Turning the knob to the right usually brightens the screen.

Figure 2-12
Turning on the Monitor

HIGHLIGHT ▲▲▲▲▲▲▲▲▲▲▲▲▲▲▲▲▲▲▲▲▲▲

A Tale of Two Bugs

The story of the first computer bug has become a legend. In the summer of 1945, something went wrong with the Mark II, a large electromechanical machine used by the Department of Defense. Although the machine was not working properly, the operating personnel could find no obvious problems. A continued search revealed a large moth beaten to death by one of the electromechanical relays. The moth was pulled out with tweezers and taped to a log book (now exhibited in the Naval Museum at the Naval Surface Weapons Center, Dahlgren, Virginia). "From then on," said Rear Admiral Grace Hopper, one of the people working with the machine, "when the officer came in to ask if we were accomplishing anything, we told him we were 'debugging' the computer." So the expressions "bugs in the program" and "debugging the program" became popular in describing programming errors.

Few people realize, however, that the use of the word bug to mean an error is at least 100 years old. Thomas Alva Edison introduced the word in a letter to Theodore Puskas, Edison's representative in France, on November 13, 1878. He wrote:

I have the right principle and am on the right track, but time, hard work, and some good luck are necessary too. It has been just so in all of my inventions. The first step is an intuition, and comes with a burst, then difficulties arise—this thing gives out and then that—"bugs"—as such little faults and difficulties are called—show themselves and months of intense watching, study and labor are requisite before commercial success—or failure—is certainly reached.

So now you have it—A Tale of Two Bugs.

When the computer is turned on, the power indicator on the keyboard and the small light on the front of Drive A both light. The disk drive makes a whirring noise as it reads the disk. After a few seconds, the noise stops and the disk-drive light goes off. *Never remove the disk or press any keys when the disk drive light is on.*

The opening display for your version of IBM PC DOS appears on the screen, as shown in Figure 2-13. First, the computer asks you to input today's date and time. Press the Enter key after you respond to each of these prompts. If you do not want to enter the date and time, press the Enter key twice instead. When the A> prompt appears, you can take out the DOS disk and insert the program disk. At this point, you probably need to type the name of the program in order to access the software. Read the software directions completely and follow them carefully.

Some software disks contain DOS in addition to the program, so it is not necessary to load DOS first. Just insert the disk into Drive A, and then turn on the computer and monitor.

When you are ready to remove a disk from the disk drive, make sure the light on the drive is off and that no noise is coming from the drive. Open the door and gently pull on the disk. Put the disk in its envelope. Turn off the computer and monitor if you are finished using the computer.

Figure 2-13
Opening Display for IBM PC DOS

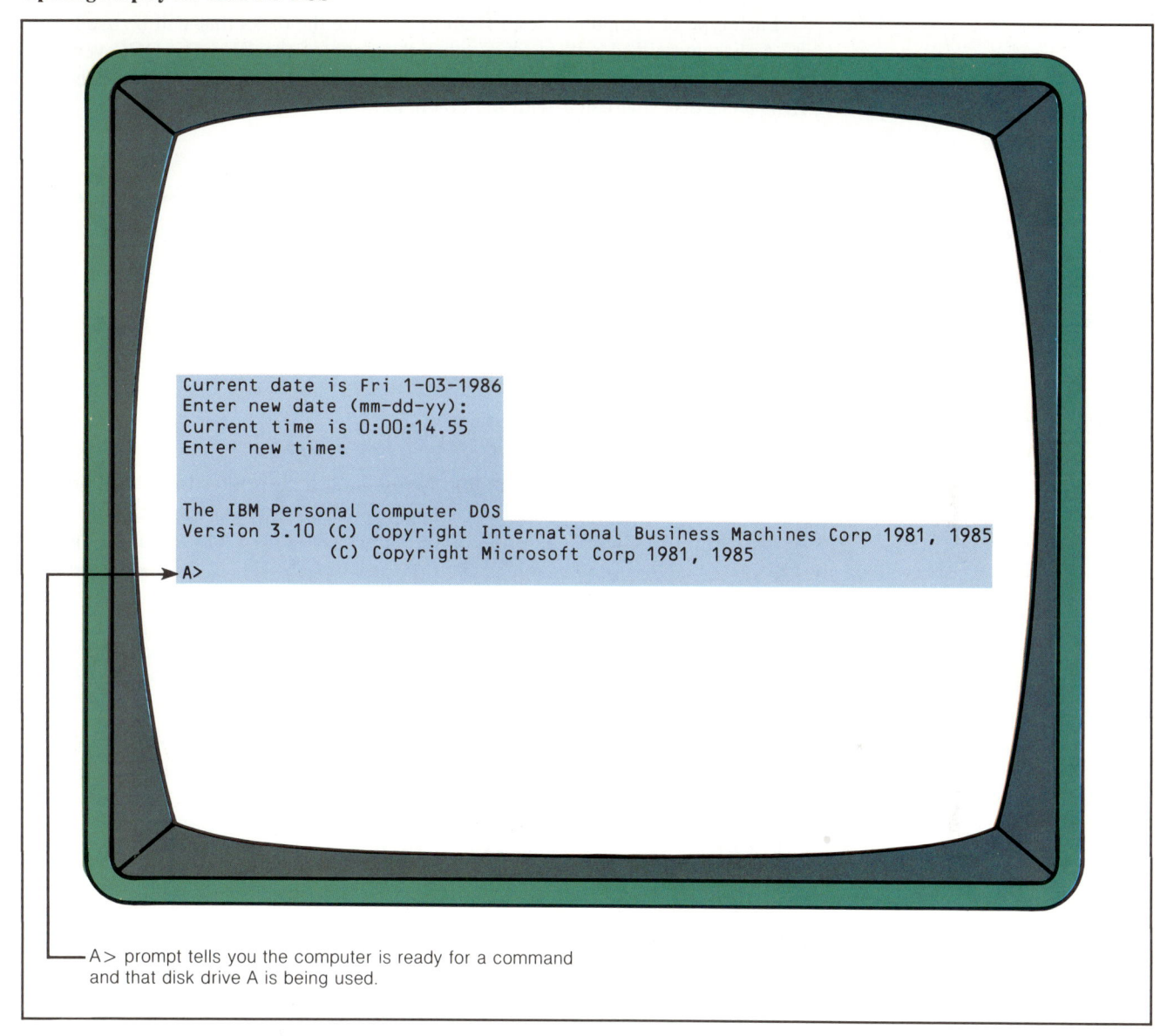

```
Current date is Fri 1-03-1986
Enter new date (mm-dd-yy):
Current time is 0:00:14.55
Enter new time:


The IBM Personal Computer DOS
Version 3.10 (C) Copyright International Business Machines Corp 1981, 1985
         (C) Copyright Microsoft Corp 1981, 1985
A>
```

A> prompt tells you the computer is ready for a command and that disk drive A is being used.

Initializing a Disk

INITIALIZE (FORMAT)
To prepare a disk so that data and programs can be stored on it.

Before a blank disk can be used for storing data, you must **initialize** or **format** it. Initializing prepares the disk so that data and programs can be stored on it, according to the specifications of the DOS. When a used disk is initialized, everything stored on the disk is erased so that the disk can be used for new data and programs. Never initialize a disk with data stored on it unless you are sure you no longer need the data.

Each type of computer uses a DOS to initialize the disks that will be used with it. A disk initialized with a DOS other than one of the IBM PC DOS versions may not work on an IBM PC. To initialize a disk for an IBM PC, you need the IBM DOS disk that came with the computer and a blank disk.

YOUR TURN

1. Insert the IBM PC DOS disk into the disk drive. Use Drive A if there are two drives. Close the disk-drive door and turn on the computer and the monitor.

2. When the system prompt A> appears, type the following command:

FORMAT B:/S (for a two-drive system)
or
FORMAT A:/S (for a one-drive system)

Press the Enter key. (The B that you type tells the computer that the blank disk is in Drive B. The A tells the computer that only one drive is being used. The /S, which is optional, copies three operating system files to the disk.

3. The following message appears:

```
Insert new diskette for drive B: (A for one drive)
and strike ENTER when ready
```

Insert the blank diskette in Drive B (or remove the DOS disk and insert the blank disk in Drive A) and close the door. Then press the Enter key. You should see the following message:

```
Formatting . . . Format complete
System transferred
```

along with some information about the byte space available. Remember, never remove a disk while the red light on the drive is still on.

4. The system asks if you need to format another disk. Type a Y if you do, or an N if you are finished.

5. Make a label for the disk. The label should state what the disk will be used for. Remove the disk from the drive, and put the label on the disk.

Initialize a disk using the steps listed above. You will need the IBM PC DOS disk and a blank disk. Be sure to put a label on the disk and put the disk back into its envelope when you are finished. The initialized disk can be used as a backup disk for the programs you will write in Section III of this text.

Disk Operating System Commands

The operating system contains the programs that control the computer (see Chapters 3 and 5). The few operating system instructions held permanently in primary memory do not contain all the programs needed for controlling operations. The remainder of the operating system is stored on a disk, and is loaded into primary memory as described in the last section. Part of this DOS is copied onto a blank disk when the blank disk is initialized using the /S option.

When you type the DOS commands, DOS programs tell the computer what to do. Some of these commands tell the computer to copy the contents of a disk onto another disk, rename a **file,** or erase a file. These commands are explained in Tables 2-2 and 2-3. Table 2-2 lists the steps involved in copying a disk. The DISKCOPY command is useful when you want to create backup disks of the programs you write while working on Section III of this text. The commands in Table 2-3 allow you to work with files stored on the disk.

FILE
A group of related records stored together; a specific unit of data stored on a disk, tape, or other medium.

**Table 2-2
Copy a Disk**

You should make copies of the disks that hold your files and programs as a precaution in case the originals are damaged or lost. Keep these backup disks in a place where they will not be damaged, and update them each time you update the original files or programs.

Insert the DOS disk into Drive A. Turn on the computer and monitor. Take out the DOS disk and insert the disk to be copied in Drive A and the disk to be copied to in Drive B. Then follow these steps:

1. The command for copying a disk is as follows:

```
DISKCOPY source drive: target drive:
```

You must specify the letter of the source drive (drive containing the disk to be copied) and the letter of the target drive (drive containing the disk to be copied to). For example, to copy the contents of the disk in Drive A onto the disk in Drive B, type the following command and press the Enter key:

```
DISKCOPY A: B:
```

For a system with only one disk drive, specify only one drive as shown. (The program will tell you when to switch disks during the copying process.)

```
DISKCOPY A:
```

2. After copying, the following message appears:

```
COPY ANOTHER (Y/N)?
```

Type Y to continue copying disks on the same drives indicated, or type N if you are finished.

3. When the copying process is completed, use the following command, which checks to see if the disks are identical:

```
DISKCOMP source drive: target drive:
```

To specify drives, follow the same examples that were shown for the DISKCOPY command. The disk in the first drive specified will be compared to the disk in the second drive. Again, for a one-drive system, specify only one drive. (You will have to switch disks again.) If there are any errors, a message indicates the location of the error. Check your user's manual if an error occurs.

Table 2-3
Operating System Commands

The operating system commands appear in uppercase letters in this chart. Do not type the word *filename.ext*; instead, type a name of your own choosing, as shown in the examples. Files sorted using Microsoft IBM DOS are typed with extensions. After the filename, type a period (.) and then an extension such as BAS for programs written in the BASIC programming language, TXT for text files, or DOC for document files. Press the Enter key after typing the complete command. The Enter key signals to the computer that it is time to execute the command.

Command	Example	Job Performed
DIR	DIR	Stands for DIRECTORY; shows the names of all the files stored on the disk.
ERASE *filename.ext* or DEL *filename.ext*	ERASE GRADES. TXT DEL GRADES. TXT	Erases or deletes a program on the disk.
RENAME *drive: old filename.ext new filename.ext*	RENAME A: GRADES.BAS SCORES.BAS	Changes a file's name. The old filename must be typed exactly as in the directory.
COPY *source drive: filename.ext target drive:*	WRONG COMMAND	Makes a copy of one file onto another disk. The file indicated is copied from the source disk to the target disk.

Using WestSoft™ 1.0

SIMULATION
A computer program that imitates a real-life event.

The WestSoft software contains simulations of popular computer applications. A computer **simulation** is a program that imitates a real-life event. Thus a simulated program lets the user learn how to do a certain task or how to use a computerized service, such as an information network or home banking service.

The WestSoft programs demonstrate typical steps involved in using a home banking service, taking a personality survey, ordering tickets through a ticket agency, calling an information network, and using an office management system. The home banking system and information network are similar to services offered to people with microcomputers in their homes or offices. Both types of services require that the user have a **modem,** but the WestSoft programs are only simulations, so you do not need a modem.

MODEM
A device that modulates and demodulates signals transmitted over communication lines; allows linkage with another computer.

Four of the programs demonstrate the use of a menu-driven program. That means that you select the next operation from a **menu,** or list of options. In the case of WestSoft, you tell the computer which selection you have chosen by typing the number that appears to the left of the selection. Once you have typed the number, the program automatically goes to that operation. You do not need to press the Enter key after typing menu selections. The same is true for responses to most prompts such as WOULD YOU LIKE INSTRUCTIONS? or ARE YOU SURE? The answer to such prompts is a simple N for no or Y for yes. Other

MENU
A list of choices or options shown on the display screen, from which the user selects commands or data for entry into the computer.

instructions tell you to press the Enter key or Space Bar in order to advance to the next step in a program.

After typing data during a simulation, you must press the Enter key, which tells the computer to process your input. If you make a mistake while typing data, use the backspace key to space back to the error. Make the correction and then finish typing the data.

If you type something that does not follow the rules of the program, you will see a message explaining the mistake. Usually the program does nothing if you type a mistake. If the program does not seem to be doing what you expect, stop and read the directions and then continue. If all else fails, you can restart the WestSoft software, or simply restart the project by pressing the Esc key and returning to the MAIN MENU, where you can select the program again. Pressing the Esc key usually returns the program to the previous menu. This operation and other directions are listed in the help area that appears at the bottom of many screens.

The WestSoft simulations can be used on a IBM PC or compatible with 128K or more of primary memory, using DOS 2.0 or higher.

Loading WestSoft

In order to use the programs, you must first boot the IBM DOS disk unless you are using a self-booting disk. (To create a self-booting disk, you format the disk using the /S option.) Insert the DOS disk into Drive A and turn on the computer and monitor. Press the Enter key in response to the time and date prompts. When the A> prompt appears, remove the DOS disk. Insert the disk labeled *WestSoft* into the disk drive and close the door. Type WESTSOFT after the A> prompt and press the Enter key.

Read the information that appears on the screen, pressing the Space Bar as needed. Soon the WestSoft MAIN MENU appears, as shown in Figure 2-14. (The Information Network and Dental Office programs are on side 2 of the disk. Directions for accessing these two programs appear on the screen when you make your selection from the MAIN MENU on side 1.)

The directions for each WestSoft program assume that you are loading the software for the first time. You may wish to run more than one program during your session at the computer. In that case, when you finish a program, select the EXIT option that appears at the end of that simulation's menu. The software returns to the WestSoft MAIN MENU, so that you can choose another simulation without going through the beginning information again. (The Personality Traits program automatically returns to the MAIN MENU when you are finished with the test.)

When you are ready to exit the WestSoft programs, choose option 6 from the MAIN MENU. Remove the disk from the disk drive, turn off the computer and monitor, and put the disk in its envelope.

WestSoft Home Banking System

The WestSoft Home Banking System simulates a system that enables you to perform some banking tasks using a microcomputer, modem, and telephone lines.

Figure 2-14
WestSoft MAIN MENU

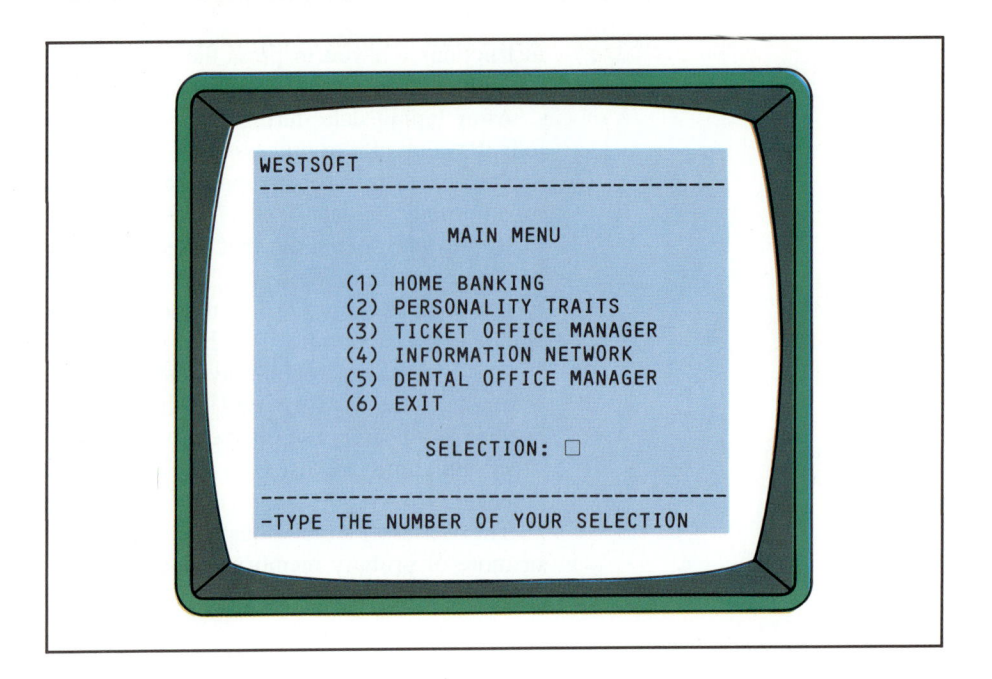

```
WESTSOFT
----------------------------------------
                MAIN MENU

         (1) HOME BANKING
         (2) PERSONALITY TRAITS
         (3) TICKET OFFICE MANAGER
         (4) INFORMATION NETWORK
         (5) DENTAL OFFICE MANAGER
         (6) EXIT

         SELECTION: ☐

----------------------------------------
-TYPE THE NUMBER OF YOUR SELECTION
```

A home banking system does not allow you to withdraw or deposit money directly, but you can move money from one account to another, check the current balance of your account, and pay your bills. Whereas most home banking systems allow an unlimited number of transactions per month, this demonstration allows eight new transactions before you must restart the program. This means that a total of eight money transfers and bill payments can be done each time the program is used. You can check an account's balance or print account statements as many times as you want.

To experiment with home banking, load the WestSoft program into your computer. Read the beginning screens as they appear. When the WestSoft MAIN MENU appears, type 1 for the home banking simulation. The program asks for a telephone number. The number 352-1616 connects your computer to the bank's computer. Type 352-1616 and press the Enter key.

When the telephone number has been entered correctly, the program asks for your password, which gives you access to your account. Type the password ABC and press the Enter key. If the password is typed correctly, the BANK MENU appears (see Figure 2-15).

The following exercises guide you through some typical home banking transactions.

YOUR TURN

You believe that you have charged too much on your credit card. In order to make sure that the funds in your credit-card account cover the charges, transfer $300 from your savings account to your credit card account.

CHAPTER 2: GETTING TO KNOW YOUR IBM   51

**Figure 2-15
BANK MENU**

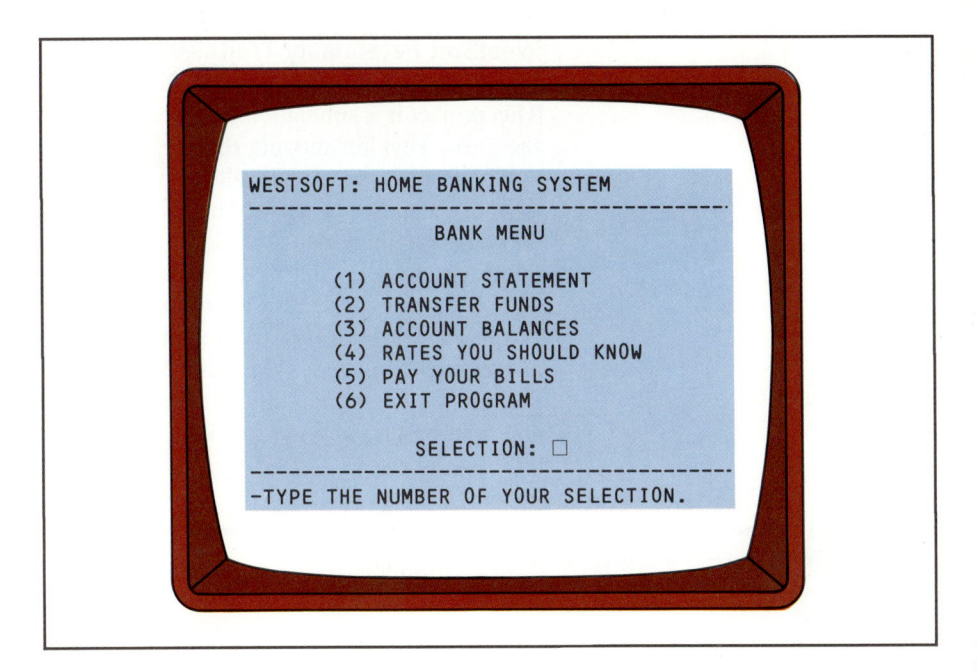

```
WESTSOFT: HOME BANKING SYSTEM
------------------------------------
              BANK MENU

     (1) ACCOUNT STATEMENT
     (2) TRANSFER FUNDS
     (3) ACCOUNT BALANCES
     (4) RATES YOU SHOULD KNOW
     (5) PAY YOUR BILLS
     (6) EXIT PROGRAM

         SELECTION: ☐
------------------------------------
-TYPE THE NUMBER OF YOUR SELECTION.
```

1. Type 2 in order to choose TRANSFER FUNDS from the BANK MENU.
2. The source of the money is the SAVINGS account. Type 2 for SAVINGS.
3. You will put the money in your charge account. Type 3 for CHARGE.
4. The amount you want moved is $300. Type 300, and press the Enter key.
5. A summary of the transaction appears. If it is correct, type Y for yes. The program returns to the BANK MENU. If it is not correct, type N for no and repeat steps 2 through 5. Does the summary tell you the balance in the charge account?

YOUR TURN

You now want to print the charge account statement so that you can refer to it later. Follow these steps for making a paper copy.

1. Make sure that the printer is properly connected to the computer and that there is enough paper. Turn on the printer.
2. Choose ACCOUNT STATEMENT from the BANK MENU by typing 1.
3. You want a statement of the charge account. Type 3 for CHARGE.
4. Type Y when the program asks whether you want to print the statement. If the printer is not properly connected, the program will display an error message.
5. When the printing is finished, what step(s) are needed to return to the WestSoft MAIN MENU?

WestSoft Personality Traits Program*

This project is a simulation of a personality traits test. In this simulation, you use the arrow keys for moving the cursor on the screen.

The test compares the traits you see in yourself with the program's evaluation of your responses to particular situations. In the introductory part of the test, you choose traits that you think describe yourself. Then you answer multiple-choice questions. Finally, during assessment, the test calculates and displays the most significant traits based on your answers to the questions.

Load the WestSoft software into your computer. Read the beginning screens as they are displayed. When the WestSoft MAIN MENU appears, type 2 for the Personality Traits program. The program tells you that the test can be stopped at any time by pressing the Esc key. Now try the following exercises.

YOUR TURN Choose the traits that you believe describe yourself.

1. Type your name. If you make a mistake, use the Backspace key to go back to the error. Then type the data correctly. Press the Enter key to continue.
2. Read the next two screens, which describe the test. Press the Enter key again.
3. A new screen asks you to examine the way you see yourself. In order to mark your responses, you need to move the cursor using the arrow keys. Type X next to each personality trait that you think describes your strongest characteristics. Choose as many traits as you think apply. For example, the cursor first appears in front of the word PATIENT. If patience is one of your more predominant traits, then type the letter X. If not, use the cursor movement commands in order to move to another trait. What key do you press if you want to delete an X?
4. Put the cursor in front of the word PATIENT. What happens if you press a letter other than X?
5. Finish making your selections and press the Enter key.
6. The screen now lists the selections you made. You can edit the list or continue with the test.

YOUR TURN You are now ready for the question/answer part of the test.

1. The screen that you see gives a brief description of this stage. Then press the Enter key to begin this stage of the survey.

---

* *Note:* The material presented in this simulation was not prepared by a psychologist and is not intended to be an accurate assessment of individual personalities. The simulation is structured to acquaint you with the procedures used in many surveys conducted by computer.

2. For each question that appears, choose the answer that most closely describes your actions or feelings by typing the letter that corresponds to your selection. Your response appears on the screen, and the program asks if you are sure. Press Y for yes, or, if you wish to change your response, press N for no and make a new selection. Go one to step 3 before answering all fifteen of the questions.

3. What happens if you press something other than one of the selection letters when the screen displays TYPE SELECTION LETTER.>>?

4. Answer all fifteen questions.

YOUR TURN

1. When you finish the test, a screen appears which reminds you of the upcoming assessments. Press the Enter key to obtain the first page, or screen, of results.

2. This screen displays two columns. The column on the left, labeled TEST SELECTIONS, lists the traits the survey determined to be the most significant in your personality. Your trait selections are listed in the right column. Compare the test results with your perception of yourself. Press the Enter key to continue.

3. The next screen shows four columns. The first column contains a list of the twelve traits evaluated in this survey. The second contains the number of points you acquired for each trait during the test. The third lists the total number of points possible for each trait. The fourth displays your percentage of points out of those possible.

4. Press the Enter key when you are finished reading the results. The next screen displays an option to print the results. Check to see that the printer is properly connected to the computer and that there is enough paper. Turn on the printer and then press Y for a printout. What happens when printing is finished?

WestSoft Ticket-Office Manager

The WestSoft Ticket-Office Manager simulates a type of software used in a ticket office. A ticket-office manager program keeps track of the seats sold, the seats available, and the ticket prices for various events. It also prints the ticket with the event, date, time, seat number, and price of the event. This program does not have all the features available in most real ticket-office software packages, but it will show you how to use a menu, choose ticket options, and print the tickets.

Imagine that you are working at a local ticket office, and customers are inquiring about tickets for several events. Before handling any customer requests, load the WestSoft disk. Read the beginning screens as they are displayed. When the WestSoft MAIN MENU appears, type 3 for the ticket-office manager program. The program then displays the TICKET MENU (see Figure 2-16).

**Figure 2-16
TICKET MENU**

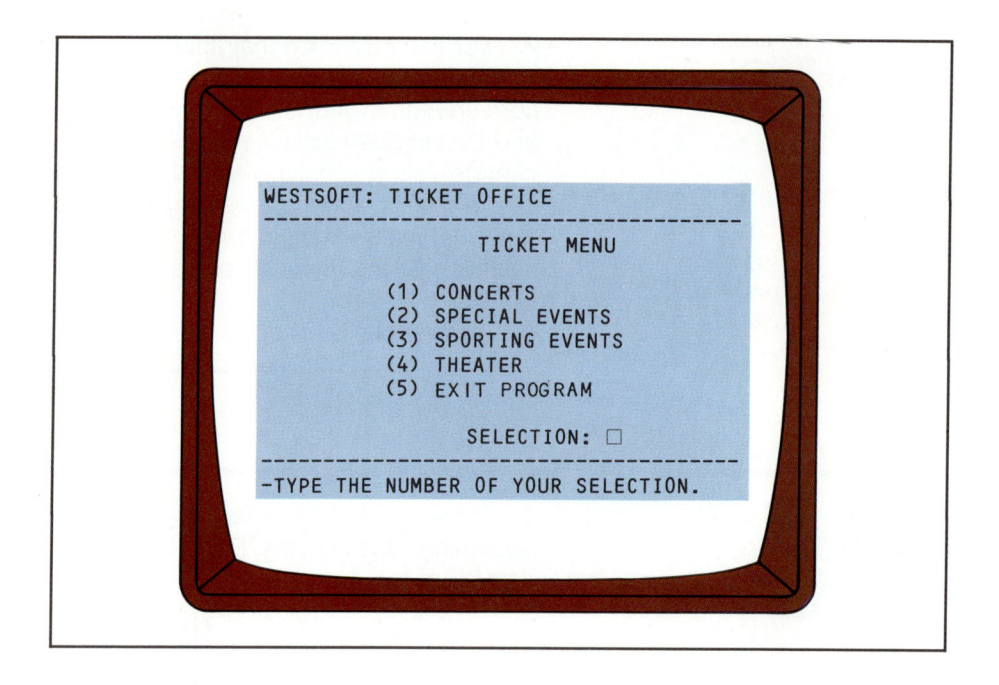

```
WESTSOFT: TICKET OFFICE
----------------------------------------
                TICKET MENU

            (1) CONCERTS
            (2) SPECIAL EVENTS
            (3) SPORTING EVENTS
            (4) THEATER
            (5) EXIT PROGRAM

            SELECTION: ☐
----------------------------------------
-TYPE THE NUMBER OF YOUR SELECTION.
```

The following exercises guide you through some typical ticket requests.

YOUR TURN

Your first customer would like four tickets to the September 15 matinee showing of *Annie*. Because *Annie* is a play, choose the THEATER option from the TICKET MENU by typing 4. After you have selected the THEATER menu, follow these steps:

1. Choose the option entitled *Annie* from the THEATER MENU by typing 3.
2. The time and date are listed on the screen for five showings of *Annie*. Press M to see more dates. (In this simulation, ten showings are listed for each event.)
3. To select the September 15 matinee showing, you must move the cursor (the highlighted bar) to this date and showing. Use the up arrow key to move the cursor up, and the down arrow key to move the cursor down. Once you have moved the cursor to the September 15 matinee showing, press the Enter key to enter the request.
4. A screen appears with the name of the play, the date, and the time. Now you can enter the section, row, and seat numbers the customer wants. The customer wants section 45, row 26, and seats 12–15. Type the numbers at the appropriate prompts, pressing the Enter key after each.
5. The next screen asks you to enter the number of seats wanted. Type 4 and press the Enter key.

HIGHLIGHT ▲▲▲▲▲▲▲▲▲▲▲▲▲▲▲▲▲▲▲▲

Winning With Antonia Stone

People in prisons, halfway houses, and housing-project community centers are "playing to win" by using microcomputers as learning tools, all because of the efforts of Antonia Stone.

Antonia Stone spent 25 years teaching in public and private schools in New Jersey and New York. As she watched children spend hours playing arcade video games, Stone wondered how she could use computers to motivate culturally disadvantaged students. She believed that computers also would benefit prisoners, who could use their incarceration time for learning useful skills that would give them a better chance in the world upon their release.

As she researched the needs of students and prisoners, she began to develop the concepts behind Playing To Win. Playing To Win is a nonprofit organization dedicated to promoting computer use for the education of minorities, inmates of correctional institutions, juvenile delinquents, and other socially disadvantaged people. Through the organization, Stone helped set up programs at the Fortune Society, a non-residential counseling center in New York City serving ex-offenders and young people in trouble with the law. She also designed programs for the Playing To Win Computer Center in the East Harlem area of New York City, the Massachusetts Department of Corrections, the New York Public Library's Computer Outreach Project, and the Spofford Juvenile Detention Center in New York City.

Part of Stone's success results from the fact that she hasn't just "dropped" computers into detention centers and prisons. She has studied the situation, set up the proper equipment, trained the teachers and tutors to run the computers and help the students, and changed the programs as needed. By her intense involvement in Playing To Win, she has given many people the core of a new lease on life and a feeling that they can learn skills for a technological age.

---

6. The program tells you to get the printer ready. make sure the printer has enough paper and is connected to the computer. Then turn on the printer. You may press the Esc key at this time to stop the print operation. Otherwise, press the Space Bar to print the tickets.

7. When printing is complete, you are returned to the THEATER MENU. What steps are needed to return to the WestSoft MAIN MENU?

WestSoft Information Network

An information network, or information service, makes a wide variety of information available to microcomputer users. The microcomputer user pays a fee to subscribe to such a system. Subscribers can access world or national news, sports news, weather reports, current facts, and much more. The computer must be connected to a modem so it can get information over telephone lines. (Modems and information services are described in more detail in Chapter 6.) Some of these services, called buyer's services, are electronic mail-order catalogs. Subscribers to these services can order products shown on the screens of their computers.

The WestSoft Information Network is a simulation of a system that contains useful information and shows products available for ordering. Because this is only a simulation, it does not contain nearly as much information as the popular information services.

To see how an information service works, load the WestSoft disk. Read the beginning screens as they are displayed. When the WestSoft MAIN MENU appears, type 4 in order to choose the INFORMATION NETWORK.

The program asks for a telephone number. The number 352-1616 will connect your computer with the information service computer. Type 352-1616 and press the Enter key.

Once you have typed the number correctly, you are asked for your host name, identification number, and password. These codes tell the system, for billing purposes, who is using the service. The codes also ensure that someone else does not access the service through your account, thereby billing the time to you.

When the program asks for your host name (a name supplied by the service), type WIS and press the Enter key. Next, you are asked for your user ID number. Type 7411 and press the Enter key. Finally, you are asked for your password. Type ABC and press the Enter key. When these codes are typed correctly, the NETWORK MENU appears on the screen (see Figure 2-17). You need to go through these same steps every time you want to use the service.

The following exercises give you an idea of how to use an information network and how to make selections from a program that is menu-driven.

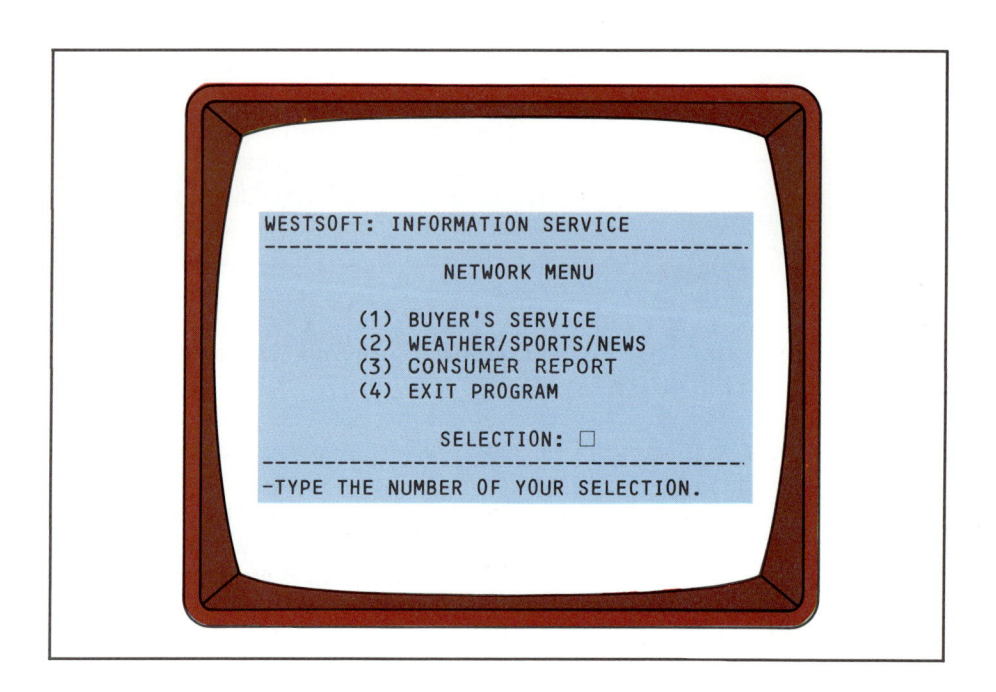

Figure 2-17
NETWORK MENU

CHAPTER 2: GETTING TO KNOW YOUR IBM 57

YOUR TURN

You would like to see what products can be ordered through the Buyer's Service this month. To do this, follow these steps:

1. From the NETWORK MENU, type 1 for the Buyer's Service. Read the screen that appears and press the Enter key.
2. The BUYER'S SERVICE MENU appears on the screen. It displays the types of items available. Type the number next to the item in which you are interested.
3. The screen now displays a list of specific brands of the product you choose. The service asks if you want to buy something. If you want to buy, type Y for yes. If not, type N for no. Typing N returns you to the BUYER'S SERVICE MENU.
4. Once you have decided to buy something, type the invoice number and discount price of the item you would like. If you do not make a mistake while typing, you are asked for mailing and billing information (for example, your name and address).
5. Next, the program shows a summary of the order. It asks for information about your method of payment. Respond accordingly. Then you can print a summary of the transaction for your records. Make sure that the printer is connected to the computer and that there is enough paper. Turn on the printer. Type Y to indicate that you want to print the summary, then press the Space Bar to print or the Esc key to stop the PRINT function. When printing is completed, the program returns to the BUYER'S SERVICE MENU.

WestSoft Dental Office Manager

As personal computers have become cheaper and easier to use, many offices that could not afford a larger computer system have computerized their record-keeping systems. Computerization has enabled them to store all the records that formerly occupied an entire filing cabinet on a few disks, and to gain access easily to any of these records. The WestSoft Dental Office Manager uses a dental office as an example, but a similar system could be used in any type of office. This kind of software can be used to maintain records such as client payments and records, personnel files, and accounting files.

Load the WestSoft software into your computer. Read the beginning screens as they are displayed. When the WestSoft MAIN MENU appears, type 5 in order to choose the DENTAL OFFICE MANAGER. The DENTAL MENU appears.

The following exercises demonstrate how to use an office manager program. use today's date when asked to enter the date of a transaction. This version of the dental office manager allows two charges per patient.

YOUR TURN

Chris Allen enters the office to have a tooth filled. The filling costs $40. Enter the charge into his account, using the following steps:

1. Type 1 from the DENTAL MENU to enter a charge into Chris's account.
2. Type the patient's last name and press the Enter key.
3. Type the appropriate data concerning the new charge—the date, type of service, and amount, pressing the Enter key after each entry. *Do not type a dollar sign ($).*
4. The program asks if the information is correct. If the information you typed is correct as displayed, type Y for yes. Otherwise, type N and make the corrections.
5. Return to the DENTAL MENU by pressing the Escape key.

YOUR TURN

Greg Allgair and Jody Katzner both have written to the office requesting copies of their insurance forms. Make the copies using the DISPLAY AN INSURANCE FORM option from the DENTAL MENU.

1. Type 5 from the DENTAL MENU for the insurance form option.
2. Type the last name of the first patient and press the Enter key.
3. When the information appears on the screen, press the F1 function key to print it.
4. When the printer is done, use the left and right arrow keys to move through the list of patients until you find the file for Jody Katzner.
5. When the file appears on the screen, print the form as directed in step 3.
6. Return to the DENTAL MENU.

Summary Points

- The IBM microcomputers are popular with businesses for performing routine tasks and for linking with larger computers. They are also popular in homes and schools for a variety of educational, recreational, and home-management purposes.
- The standard parts of an IBM PC microcomputer are the system unit, monitor, and keyboard. The system unit holds the computer itself and the disk drive(s).
- The number of columns displayed on the color/graphics screen can be changed from 80 to 40 columns and back again while the IBM PC is in the DOS mode by typing the commands MODE BW40 and MODE BW80.
- The letter and number keys on any IBM computer work the same as a typewriter's keys. Computer-specific keys let you move the cursor (a symbol that

shows your current location on the screen) and perform other functions by entering keystroke commands.

■ In a two-drive IBM PC, the drives are called Drive A and Drive B. A disk should be inserted in Drive A before one is inserted in Drive B. When only one drive is installed, it is Drive A.

■ The best place for a computer is on a sturdy desk or table in a clean, dry room. Keep food, dust, and dirt away from equipment and disks, and avoid creating static electricity around the equipment.

■ Computer equipment should be kept out of direct sunlight, off appliances that get hot, and away from heating ducts and air conditioning units.

■ Floppy disks should be handled with care so they will remain reliable storage devices. Store them vertically in their envelopes, away from heat or cold.

■ Programs are loaded into the computer's memory in several ways. If operating system files are on the disk, you can insert it into the disk drive and turn on the computer. Otherwise, the operating system software must be loaded first.

■ Disks must be initialized (formatted) according to the specifications of the operating system you are using before they can be used to store data.

■ The operating system contains the programs that control the computer. Disk operating system (DOS) programs reside on a disk and are loaded from the disk drive.

■ A program that imitates a real-life event is called a simulation. The purpose of a program simulation is to teach the user how to do a task, or how to use a computerized service such as an information network.

■ Services such as home banking or information networks require modems. A modem is a hardware device that connects one computer to another over telephone lines.

■ A menu is a list of choices or options displayed on the screen. Prompts are messages or cues that guide you as you use the software.

■ Home banking is a service that lets you perform banking tasks using a microcomputer, modem, and telephone lines.

■ Some ticket offices use ticket-office manager software that keeps track of the seats sold, the seats available, and the ticket prices for various events. This software can print tickets with the event, date, time, seat number, and price.

■ An information service or information network makes a wide variety of information available to microcomputer users, such as world or national news, sports news, weather conditions, current facts, and much more.

■ A dental office manager program facilitates the record-keeping, accounting, and billing that occur in a dentist's office. Similar software is used in other offices.

Review Questions

1. What does the symbol K represent?
2. What is the character called which shows your location on the screen?
3. What two things happen when the Return key is pressed?
4. Why would you not continue to hold down the keys that you press to relay a command to the computer, or that you use for typing data?

5. In a two-drive system, how are the drives differentiated and how do you use them?
6. Describe the ideal environment for a microcomputer.
7. Name at least three things to remember in caring for disks.
8. What does the term *load* mean in computer usage?
9. Why is the disk drive light important?
10. What is the purpose of formatting, or initializing, a disk?
11. List the steps involved in formatting a disk.
12. Two features that make programs easier to use are menus and prompts. Describe each, and tell why they make using computers easier.

Review Exercises

1. WestSoft HOME BANKING Exercises

Your telephone bill for April was $112.37. You want to pay the bill from your checking account, but you are not sure there is enough money in the account. Determine the balance of your checking account, transfer more money to the account if necessary, and pay the telephone bill. (The telephone number to call is 352-1616, and the password is ABC.)
   a. What steps did you take to check the balance in the checking account?
   b. What two steps should you perform to return to the BANK MENU?
   c. What did you do to transfer money to your checking account, if you did so?
   d. What four steps did you take to pay the telephone bill?

Last month you wrote check #831 to a friend. The check was not cashed, according to last month's bank statement. You want to know whether the check has been cashed since then.
   a. What two steps did you take to see the checking-account statement? Was the check cashed?
   b. How can you return to the BANK MENU?
   c. Transfer $50 from your savings account to your checking account in order to have enough funds to cover expenses you anticipate in the next couple of weeks. List the steps required to perform the task.

2. WestSoft TICKET OFFICE MANAGER Exercises

A customer would like tickets for the October 25 game of the Philadelphia Minutemen hockey team, or the September 16 Detroit Bengals game.
   a. What steps would you take to get tickets to the game, once the TICKET MENU is on the screen?
   b. Describe what happens when you try to get tickets for the game.
   c. What happens when you try to print a ticket for section 45, row 11, and seat 10, for the September 16 Detroit Bengals game?

One customer calls to ask about performances by the Boston Pops.
    a. Who appears with the Boston Pops on September 20?
    b. Who appears with the Boston Pops on September 27?
    c. On what dates and at what times does Thomas Klein appear with the Boston Pops?
    d. What happens when you try to get tickets for the Washington Philharmonic Orchestra?

3. WestSoft INFORMATION SERVICE Exercises

You are planning a party based on trivia questions, and you need to write questions and answers on cards. Find the answers to these questions, and then write three more questions with their answers based on information provided in this information network. (The telephone number is 352-1616, the host name is WIS, the user ID number is 7411, and the password is ABC.)
    a. Who hold the baseball world-series record for the most home runs? How many home runs did he have?
    b. By what two names was baseball known in the United States before it became baseball?
    c. Which two teams played in the 1934 NFL championship game, and who won?
    d. Which two swimmers tied for the gold medal in the women's 100-meter freestyle at the 1984 Olympics?
    e. According to the surgeon general's report, what are the three long-term health risks of smoking?

4. WestSoft DENTAL OFFICE MANAGER Exercises

Mark Steiner has mailed a partial payment to the office. The check is for $50. Enter this payment into his account. (This version of the Dental Office Manager allows two payments per patient.) List the steps required to make the payment and return to the DENTAL MENU.

Dave Biesiada drops by the office to tell you that his insurance company will be covering the remainder of his bill. He wants to know how much that is. Write his balance. The money from Dave's insurance company arrives later that day. Enter the new payment and make sure that Dave's new balance is zero.

Tim Newman enters the office for a checkup. The charge is $24, but Tim has only $10.50 in his pocket. He gives you the $10.50 and owes the rest. Enter the new charge and the payment. What is Tim's new balance?

The office manager decides that too many patients have neglected paying their bills. The manager wants to know which patients owe money and how much each owes. List the patients currently in debt and the amount each owes. Begin the search with Christopher Allen's account.

CHAPTER 3

Hardware

Outline

Introduction
Computer Classifications
   Mainframes
   Minicomputers
   Microcomputers
   Supercomputers
Learning Check
The Central Processing Unit
   Control Unit
   Arithmetic/Logic Unit
   Primary Memory

Highlight: The Connection
   Machine
   Registers
Learning Check
Secondary Storage
   Sequential-Access Media
   Direct-Access Media
   Other Storage Media
Learning Check
Hardware for Input and Output
   Input Methods
   Printers
   Specialized Output Devices

Highlight: Ray Kurzweil and His
   Amazing Machines
Learning Check
Data Representation
   Binary Representation
   Computer Codes
   Code Checking
Learning Check
Summary Points
Review Questions

Introduction

Computer hardware consists of the physical devices that constitute a computer system. This chapter discusses the classifications of computer systems and the hardware components of a computer system: the central processing unit, the input devices, the output devices, and the storage devices. It also describes the codes in which data are handled during computer operations.

Computer Classifications

Computers are grouped by their amount of memory, capability, price range, and speed of operation. The four major groups of computers are mainframes, minicomputers, microcomputers, and supercomputers.

Defining the point at which one classification ends and the next begins is difficult, because the capabilities of computers in one classification overlap those of computers in the next category. Computers at the low end of the scale have increasingly larger primary memories and can handle an increasing number of **peripheral devices,** such as printers and secondary storage devices.

PERIPHERAL DEVICE
A device that attaches to the central processing unit, such as a secondary storage device, input device, or output device.

Mainframes

During the 1960s, the term mainframe was synonymous with CPU. Today, the word refers simply to a group of computers intermediate in capacity between the minicomputer and the supercomputer.

MAINFRAME
A type of large, full-scale computer capable of supporting many peripheral devices.

Mainframes operate at very high speeds and support many input and output devices, which also operate at very high speeds. They can be subdivided into small, medium, and large mainframe systems. Most mainframes are manufactured as "families" of computers. A family consists of several mainframe models that differ in size and power. An organization can purchase or lease a small system and, if processing needs expand, upgrade to a medium or large system, while retaining the existing software and peripheral devices. Purchase prices range from $200,000 to several million dollars for a large mainframe with peripherals. Mainframes are used chiefly by large businesses, hospitals, universities, and banks with large data processing needs (see Figure 3-1).

A mainframe creates a fair amount of heat, so it requires cooling systems. It cannot be plugged into a standard electrical outlet, and therefore it needs special electrical wiring. It may rest on a special platform so that its wires and cables can be housed beneath it. Because a mainframe operates day and night and provides access to a large amount of data, access to it must be controlled for security reasons. These factors add to its cost.

Because of their sophistication and size, mainframe computers require a great deal of support from the vendor, who may invest considerable time and money in helping a customer select and install the system. The vendor spends additional effort training the customer's employees to use the system, servicing and repairing

CHAPTER 3: HARDWARE 65

Figure 3-1
IBM System/370/158 Mainframe

Figure 3-2
Wang Laboratories' VS85 Minicomputer
A minicomputer system for a small firm may consist of the computer, a visual display terminal, a disk storage unit, and a printer. A large system may consist of hundreds of minicomputers and peripherals tied together by communication channels to meet the needs of a geographically dispersed organization.

the mainframe, and solving any questions and problems. Some major mainframe manufacturers are IBM, Burroughs, Honeywell, NCR, and Sperry.

Minicomputers

Minicomputers were developed in the 1960s to perform specialized tasks. They were smaller, less powerful, and less expensive than the mainframes available at that time, thus offering computer capabilities to organizations that did not need or could not afford mainframe systems. As minicomputers became more sophisticated, their capabilities, memory size, and overall performance overlapped those of mainframes. The more powerful minicomputers are called superminis.

Minicomputers are easier to install and operate than mainframe computers. They take up less floor space than mainframes; they may fit on a desk, or they may be as large as a file cabinet (see Figure 3-2). Minicomputers require few special environmental conditions. They can be plugged into standard electrical outlets and often do not require facilities such as air conditioning or special platforms. Prices for minicomputers range from a few thousand dollars to two or three hundred thousand dollars.

Minicomputers are used in multi-user applications, numerical control of machine tools, industrial automation, and word processing. They are also used in conjunction with communication facilities for sharing data and peripherals or for serving a geographically dispersed organization.

A minicomputer system can easily be enlarged to meet the needs of a growing organization, because it can be implemented in a modular fashion. For example, a hospital might install one minicomputer in its outpatient department for record keeping and another in the pharmacy or laboratory. As additional minicomputers are installed, they can be connected to existing ones to share common data.

In the late 1970s and early 1980s, the minicomputer industry grew at a rate of 35 to 40 percent annually. Today, the market for minicomputers is weakening. The increased capabilities and improved software of **microcomputers** has led to the increased use of microcomputers in traditional minicomputer markets. Many companies now link microcomputers with mainframes or existing minicomputers to hold down equipment investment costs and still meet processing needs. This practice, however, creates new security problems for many corporations, because more people have access to data.

Some major manufacturers of minicomputers include Digital Equipment Corporation (DEC), Hewlett-Packard, Data General, Honeywell, General Automation, Burroughs, Texas Instruments, Wang Laboratories, Prime Computer Inc., and IBM.

Microcomputers

Figure 3-3
Honeywell PC DP

When technology advanced to the point at which many circuits could be etched onto a single chip, the microprocessor was developed. A microprocessor is a chip that contains the portions of the CPU that control the computer and perform arithmetic and logic operations. It may also contain some primary storage. The microprocessor became the foundation for the microcomputer, also called the personal computer.

Microcomputers are the most popular type of computer today. They may fit on a desktop or in a briefcase (see Figure 3-3). Some microcomputers designed for home use cost as little as $100, but users can spend many thousands of dollars for state-of-the-art microcomputers and peripherals. Most microcomputers are single-user systems.

One important aspect of microcomputer design involves the development of user-friendly hardware and software, that is, equipment and programs that are easy to use and easy to learn to use. The concern for user friendliness has overflowed into the development of other categories of computers.

Microcomputers are available in computer stores, office supply stores, and department stores. In some cases they are sold in the same way as an appliance, such as a television or video cassette recorder. Packaged software for microcomputers is available, but many users like the challenge of developing their own, and many businesses need custom software.

Chapter 5 provides a detailed discussion of microcomputers.

Supercomputers

Supercomputers are the largest, fastest, most expensive computers currently made (see Figure 3-4). They process data at speeds exceeding 400,000,000 to 600,000,000 operations per second. The Cray-2, for example, operates at speeds of 1.2 billion flops (floating-point operations per second, a measure of optimum computer efficiency). It can perform calculations in one minute which a personal computer could perform in three weeks. By 1992, U.S. supercomputer industries hope to

Figure 3-4
The Cray X-MP Supercomputer

build computers that will reach speeds of 1,000 gigaflops (billions of flops per second).

Research in supercomputer development has become a heated race between the United States and Japan. Whoever develops and commercializes improved supercomputer technology will have the competitive edge in all computer-related industries, an important consideration for both economics and national defense. Some major companies developing supercomputers include Cray Research, Fujitsu, and ETA Systems, Inc.

Only a few supercomputers currently are produced each year, because the manufacturing cost is high and the market is limited. Each machine costs several million dollars to develop and install. In addition, software development for supercomputers is much more complex and expensive, because the design of the machines is so much different from that of less powerful computers. To justify costs this high, an organization must be very large and must need to process millions of instructions very quickly or maintain large databases. Despite these facts, demand for supercomputers is increasing. In 1980, there were only 21 supercomputers in the world. As of 1986, about 150 supercomputers are busy crunching numbers, and the demand for them seems insatiable. Even universities are beginning to install supercomputers for their extensive research projects.

Supercomputers are used to perform lengthy and complex calculations. Scientists use them in weather forecasting, oil exploration, energy conservation, seismology, nuclear reactor safety analysis, and cryptography. In addition, supercomputers are used for simulations in nuclear energy research and for stress tests in automotive and aircraft design.

All categories of computers process data by the same three stages discussed in Chapter 1: input, processing, and output. All computers have a CPU, primary memory, secondary storage devices and media, input devices, and output devices. The following sections discuss these aspects of hardware in general terms.

Learning Check

1. How can mainframe "families" benefit businesses?
2. Why might a business choose a minicomputer rather than a mainframe?
3. What effect have today's microcomputers had on the minicomputer market?
4. Why is supercomputer research of national importance?

Answers

1. Businesses can upgrade easily and still use existing software and peripherals. 2. Mainframes are more expensive and require the added expense of air conditioning, special platforms, and special electrical wiring. Minicomputers can be added in modular form to an organization's existing system. 3. They have weakened the minicomputer market. 4. Whoever leads in supercomputer development will lead in all computer-related industries. In addition, supercomputers are used for research in areas important to national defense.

The Central Processing Unit

CENTRAL PROCESSING UNIT (CPU)
Acts as the "brain" of the computer; composed of three sections—the arithmetic/logic unit (ALU), control unit, and primary memory.

CONTROL UNIT
The section of the CPU which directs the sequence of operations and governs the actions of the various units that make up the computer.

ARITHMETIC/LOGIC UNIT (ALU)
The section of the processor, or CPU, which handles arithmetic computations and logical operations.

A computer stores data temporarily and acts on it. The component that is responsible for this operation is the **central processing unit (CPU)**. The CPU is often called the "brain" of the computer. It is a complex collection of electronic circuitry which directs electrical signals to all parts of a computer system. The CPU decides what to do with the instructions that the programmer gives the computer, and ensures that assigned tasks are carried out properly.

The CPU consists of three parts that function together as a unit. These parts are the **control unit,** the **arithmetic/logic unit (ALU),** and primary memory (see Figure 3-5). The CPU is located inside the computer, so primary memory is also called internal storage, primary storage, or main memory. The control unit and the arithmetic/logic unit often are referred to collectively as the processor.

A processor may contain many chips, each with special functions. In a large computer, the processor may be built on several circuit boards in box-like structures or frames, hence the term mainframe. In a microcomputer, the processor is reduced in size to fit onto a single plug-in chip and is referred to as a microprocessor. A microcomputer may contain more than one microprocessor for performing various functions. Whereas primary memory is part of the CPU, typically it is located on separate circuit boards.

Control Unit

The control unit, as the name implies, maintains order and controls the activity that occurs in the CPU. It does not process or store data, but directs the sequence

CHAPTER 3: HARDWARE

of operations. It interprets instructions and produces signals that act as commands for the execution of instructions. The control unit communicates with and directs input equipment and keeps track of the instructions that have been executed. It also sends the results of processing to the designated locations.

Arithmetic/Logic Unit

The ALU manipulates data. It does not store data, but performs arithmetic computations and logical operations. Arithmetic computations performed in the ALU include addition and subtraction, whereas logical operations involve comparisons. The computer makes a comparison and then performs some action based on the result of the comparison. There are six possible results in all: equal to, not equal to, greater than, less than, equal to or greater than, and equal to or less than. For example, a computer might have to deal with the following logic statement: "If the total is not equal to 100, then read more data."

Primary Memory

Memory is a major factor in computer power. The more powerful computers store more data and operate on it in larger amounts. Data in primary memory can be accessed quickly. It is stored as "on" and "off" electrical states. Primary memory is in charge of storing data and programs temporarily in the computer's internal memory. When a program resides in primary memory, it is called a **stored program.** In order for data to be processed, the computer must be able to locate the programs and data in memory. Each piece of data in memory has an address which is a unique, built-in number that identifies its location. The address helps the computer locate the data, just as a post office box number identifies the proper box for depositing letters (see Figure 3-6).

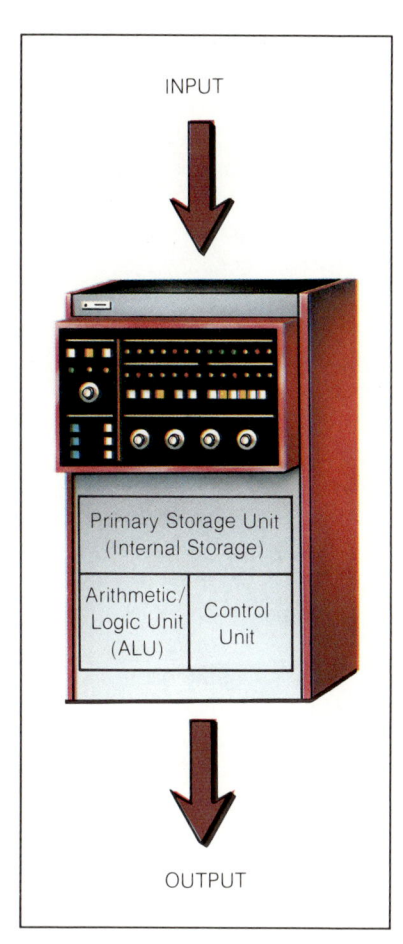

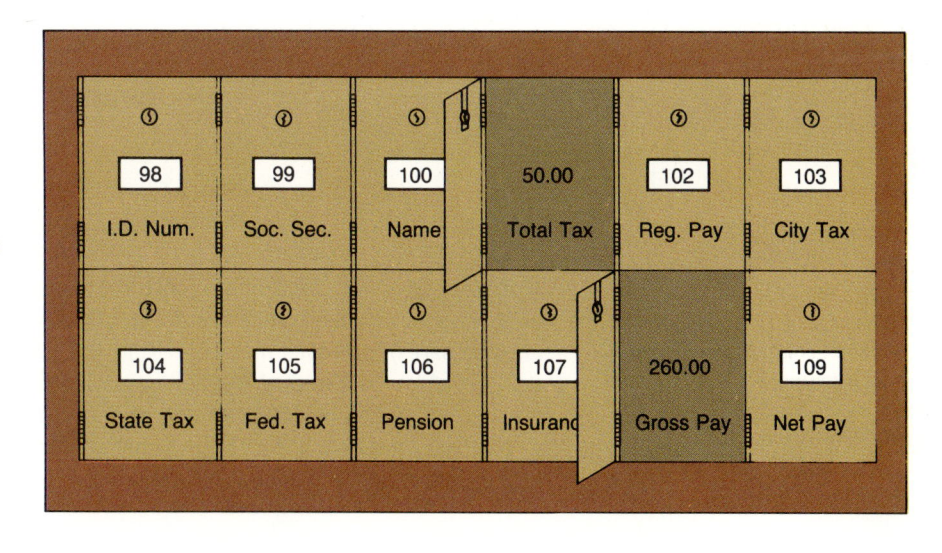

Figure 3-5
Parts of the CPU

Figure 3-6
Mailbox Representation of Storage
If a programmer specifies that the value in TOTAL TAX is to be subtracted from the value in GROSS PAY, the computer uses its own addressing system to find the proper locations of the data, just as you look under a box number to find the "data" in the post office box that is designated for your mail.

HIGHLIGHT ▲▲▲▲▲▲▲▲▲▲▲▲▲▲▲▲▲▲▲

The Connection Machine

It resides inside a 5-foot Lexon plastic cube. It contains 65,536 processors. When the initial kinks are worked out, it will operate at speeds in excess of 1 billion instructions per second—about the power of a Cray X-MP supercomputer. And it costs only one-fourth as much as the Cray X-MP. It is the Connection Machine, brainchild of Daniel Hillis, co-founder of Thinking Machines Corp. of Cambridge, Massachusetts.

This computer not only looks different from most mainframe computers; it *is* different. Packed in a much smaller machine than mainframes and supercomputers, it is to a conventional mainframe what a supersonic jet is to a bicycle, says Hillis. It scanned three months of Reuters news stories—16,000 articles—in 1/20 of a second. In 3 minutes, it laid out the circuitry for a computer chip containing 4,000 transistors.

The Connection Machine reaches its remarkable speed because of two factors. The first is the thousands of processors that act in parallel, or in concert. Mainframes operate serially (one instruction at a time). The second factor is the manner in which the processors are connected. Each processor is directly or indirectly connected to every other one, in a manner similar to a miniature telephone system. The links contain 4,096 switching stations and 24,576 trunk lines that can be programmed and reprogrammed without changing the computer's wiring. These connections give the computer its name. Programming such a machine, however, calls for complex instructions that even computer scientists find difficult to write.

Regardless of the difficulties, the Connection Machine offers hope of solving problems in machine vision and artificial intelligence which even today's supercomputers cannot solve. It signals the wave of the future in computer architecture, mimicking the action of the billions of neurons in the human brain.

SOURCE: *Time*, June 9, 1986, p. 64.

STORED PROGRAM
A program held in primary memory in electronic form, which can be executed repeatedly during processing.

Once an instruction or piece of data is stored at a particular location, it stays there until new data or instructions are written over it. The same data can be accessed repeatedly by a single program. In addition, the same instructions can be used repeatedly to process many different pieces of data. Storing programs in this manner—the stored-program concept—enables the computer to call upon the programs instantly and to operate at top speed, with minimal human intervention.

Primary memory holds the program that is being executed, the program's input and output, and the intermediate results of any calculations. When a program is entered into the computer, the control unit sends the program to primary memory. The control unit then retrieves one instruction at a time from the primary memory unit (see Figure 3-7).

Registers

REGISTER
An internal computer component used as a temporary holding area for an instruction or data item during processing.

During data processing, data or instructions may be placed in temporary storage areas known as **registers.** Even though registers are used for holding data, they are not part of primary memory. Registers receive data, hold it, and transfer it very quickly, as directed by the control unit of the CPU. The computer uses registers in all the calculations and manipulations it performs.

Registers perform specific functions and are named according to the functions they perform. An accumulator is a register that accumulates the results of com-

CHAPTER 3: HARDWARE

Step A:
Instruction and data from the input device are stored in primary storage under direction of the control unit.

Step B:
The control unit examines one instruction and interprets it.

Step C:
The control unit sends appropriate electronic signals to the ALU and to primary storage.

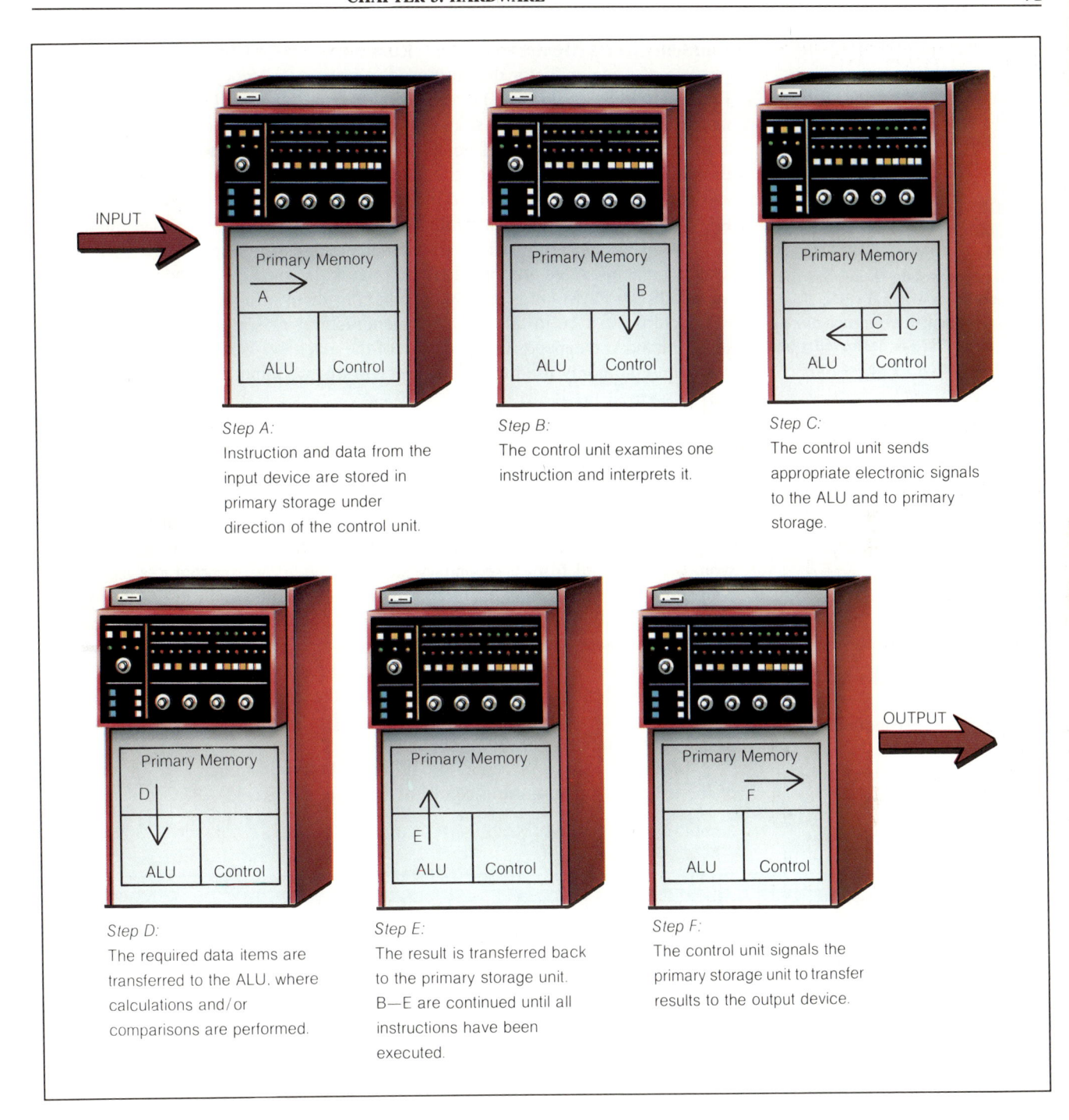

Step D:
The required data items are transferred to the ALU, where calculations and/or comparisons are performed.

Step E:
The result is transferred back to the primary storage unit. B—E are continued until all instructions have been executed.

Step F:
The control unit signals the primary storage unit to transfer results to the output device.

**Figure 3-7
Computer Operations**

putations. A storage register holds data being sent to or taken from primary memory. During program execution, each instruction is transferred to an instruction register, where it is decoded by the control unit. The address of a data item called for by an instruction is kept in an address register. General-purpose registers can be used for both arithmetic and addressing functions.

RANDOM-ACCESS MEMORY (RAM)
A form of primary memory in which the contents can be changed many times during processing; volatile or temporary memory.

NONDESTRUCTIVE READ/ DESTRUCTIVE WRITE
The feature of computer memory which permits data to be read and retained in its original state, thus allowing repeated reference during processing. Data is destroyed when it is overwritten by new data.

READ-ONLY MEMORY (ROM)
The part of computer hardware which contains instructions built into the circuitry; it cannot be deleted or altered by stored-program instructions.

PROGRAMMABLE READ-ONLY MEMORY (PROM)
Read-only memory that can be programmed once by the manufacturer or user in order to meet unique requirements.

Random-Access Memory (RAM) Random-access memory (RAM) is the major type of semiconductor memory used in primary memory. The items stored in RAM can be accessed (read) over and over again without destroying them. New instructions or data can be stored (written) over existing ones, however, thus destroying or erasing the old items. This feature is called **nondestructive read/destructive write.** RAM is volatile, or nonpermanent. It relies on electric current, and if the power fails or is turned off, the contents of RAM are lost. As the name RAM suggests, data and instructions stored in RAM can be accessed randomly.

RAM memory can be added to a computer by installing RAM chips, which usually come mounted on printed circuit boards. In some cases, the user can install the additional RAM chips simply by plugging them into the circuit board. Other RAM chips must be installed by the manufacturer or service personnel. The installation method depends on the design of the machine. Boards, or cards, of RAM chips are commonly used to add memory to microcomputers. (See Chapter 5 for a discussion of the RAM disk.)

Read-Only Memory (ROM) Read-Only Memory (ROM) cannot be changed or deleted by stored-program instructions. ROM instructions are hardwired, or permanently built into circuitry. The only way to change the contents of ROM is to alter the physical construction of the circuits. A microprogram is a sequence of instructions built into read-only memory for carrying out functions that otherwise would be accessed from a secondary storage device. Microprograms usually are supplied by computer manufacturers and cannot be altered by users, but microprogramming allows the basic operations of the computer to be tailored to meet the needs of users. If all instructions that a computer can execute are located in ROM, a complete new set of instructions can be obtained by changing the ROM chip. When selecting a computer, users can get the standard features of the machine plus their choice of the optional features available through microprogramming. Many microcomputers use programs stored in ROM.

A version of ROM that can be programmed before installation to suit the needs of the user is **programmable read-only memory (PROM).** PROM can be pro-

---

Learning Check

1. What do the letters CPU stand for?
2. Which part of the CPU handles mathematical operations?
3. Which part of the CPU interprets instructions and directs the other parts?
4. How is RAM different from ROM?
5. What does the phrase nondestructive read/destructive write mean?

Answers

1. Central processing unit. 2. Arithmetic/logic unit (ALU). 3. Control unit. 4. RAM is volatile; ROM is hard-wired. 5. It means that data can be read repeatedly without destroying or erasing it, but once new data is written over the old data, the old data is destroyed.

Figure 3-8
8-Bit Microprocessor with EPROM

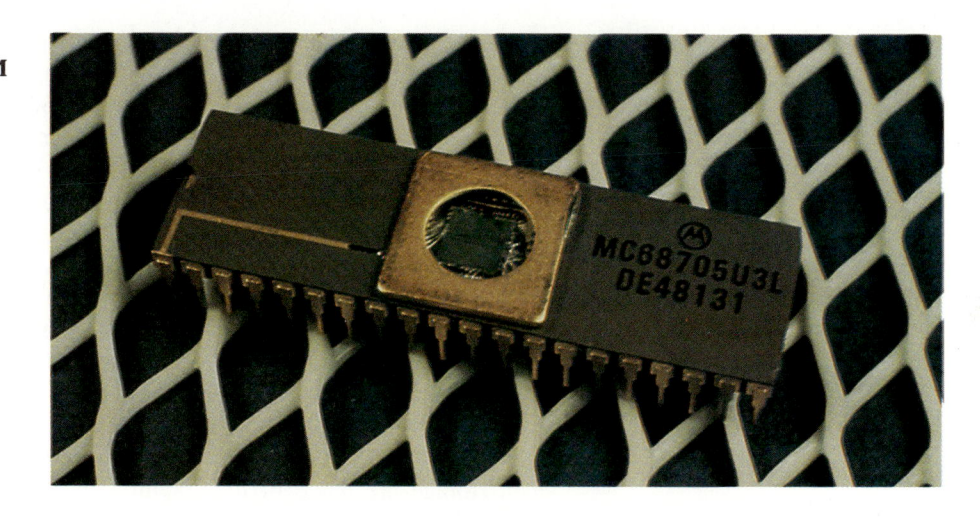

grammed by the manufacturer, or it can be shipped blank for the end user to program. Once programmed, however, its contents are unalterable. PROM gives the end user the advantages of ROM plus the flexibility to meet special needs. PROM technology has one drawback, however: mistakes programmed into the unit cannot be corrected. In order to overcome this drawback, **erasable programmable read-only memory (EPROM)** has been developed. This type of memory unit can be erased, but only by being submitted to a special process, such as being bathed in ultraviolet light (see Figure 3-8).

ERASABLE PROGRAMMABLE READ-ONLY MEMORY (EPROM)
A form of read-only memory which can be reprogrammed by a special process.

Secondary Storage

Secondary storage, also called auxiliary storage, is storage outside the CPU. It is used for storing large amounts of data at low cost. Access to data in secondary storage can be either direct or sequential, depending on the medium used.

Magnetic tapes provide **sequential-access storage.** This means that the computer must start at the beginning of the tape and read what is stored until it comes to the needed data. In contrast, storage media such as magnetic disks and magnetic drums do not have to be read sequentially; data can be accessed directly. Therefore, these media are called **direct-access storage** media. Direct-access media allow faster retrieval than sequential-access media.

SEQUENTIAL-ACCESS STORAGE
Secondary storage from which data items must be read one after another from the beginning until the needed data is located.

DIRECT-ACCESS STORAGE (RANDOM-ACCESS STORAGE)
Secondary storage from which data can be located and retrieved directly, without reading all preceding data.

Sequential-Access Media

A **magnetic tape** is a continuous strip of coated plastic tape, wound onto a reel quite similar to that used in reel-to-reel audio recorders. The magnetic tape's plastic base is treated with a magnetizable coating, usually iron oxide. Typically, the tape is one-half inch wide and 400 to 3,200 feet long. Tapes are inexpensive and easy to store. They hold a very large amount of data in a small amount of space, and they can be erased and reused.

MAGNETIC TAPE
A sequential-access storage medium, consisting of a narrow strip of material upon which data can be recorded as magnetized spots.

Data is recorded on magnetic tape by magnetizing small spots of the iron oxide coating on the tape. Although these spots can be read by the computer, they are invisible to the human eye. Large volumes of information can be recorded on a single tape. Densities of 1,600 characters per inch are common, and some tapes can hold up to 6,250 characters per inch.

When a program calls for the information that a tape contains, the tape is mounted onto a **tape drive** (see Figure 3-9). The drive has a **read/write head** that creates or reads the magnetized spots as the tape moves past it (see Figure 3-10). When it is reading, the head detects the magnetized areas and converts them into electrical pulses that are sent to the CPU. When writing, the head magnetizes the appropriate spots on the tape, while erasing any previously stored data.

Magnetic tape also is available in cassettes. This form of magnetic tape usually is used with microcomputers for backing up data. Tape cassettes look like those used in audio recording—and some can be used that way—but those made for data storage are made of high-quality, high-density digital recording tape (see Figure 3-11). They are popular with microcomputer users because they can be used with an ordinary cassette player.

Direct-Access Media

The **magnetic disk** is a metal platter, usually 14 inches in diameter, coated on both sides with a magnetizable material like iron oxide. Data is stored on the surface of the disk as magnetized spots. In many respects, a magnetic disk resembles a phonograph record, but it has a smooth surface instead of a record's characteristic grooves. A disk drive stores and retrieves data in much the same way as a phonograph. The disk is rotated while a read/write head is positioned above its magnetic surface. Instead of spiraling into the center of the disk like a phonograph needle, however, the read/write head stores and retrieves data in concentric circles called **tracks.** The tracks are concentric, that is, one track never touches another. A typical disk has from 200 to 500 tracks per surface (see Figure 3-12).

TAPE DRIVE
A device that moves tape past a read/write head.

READ/WRITE HEAD
The electromagnet of a tape drive or disk drive. In reading, it detects magnetized spots; in writing, it magnetizes appropriate areas.

MAGNETIC DISK
A direct-access storage medium consisting of a metal platter upon which data can be recorded as magnetized spots.

TRACK
One of a series of concentric circles on the surface of a magnetic disk.

Figure 3-9
Magnetic Tape Drive
A computer operator mounts tapes on tape drives and pushes the proper button for entry of stored data into the computer.

CHAPTER 3: HARDWARE

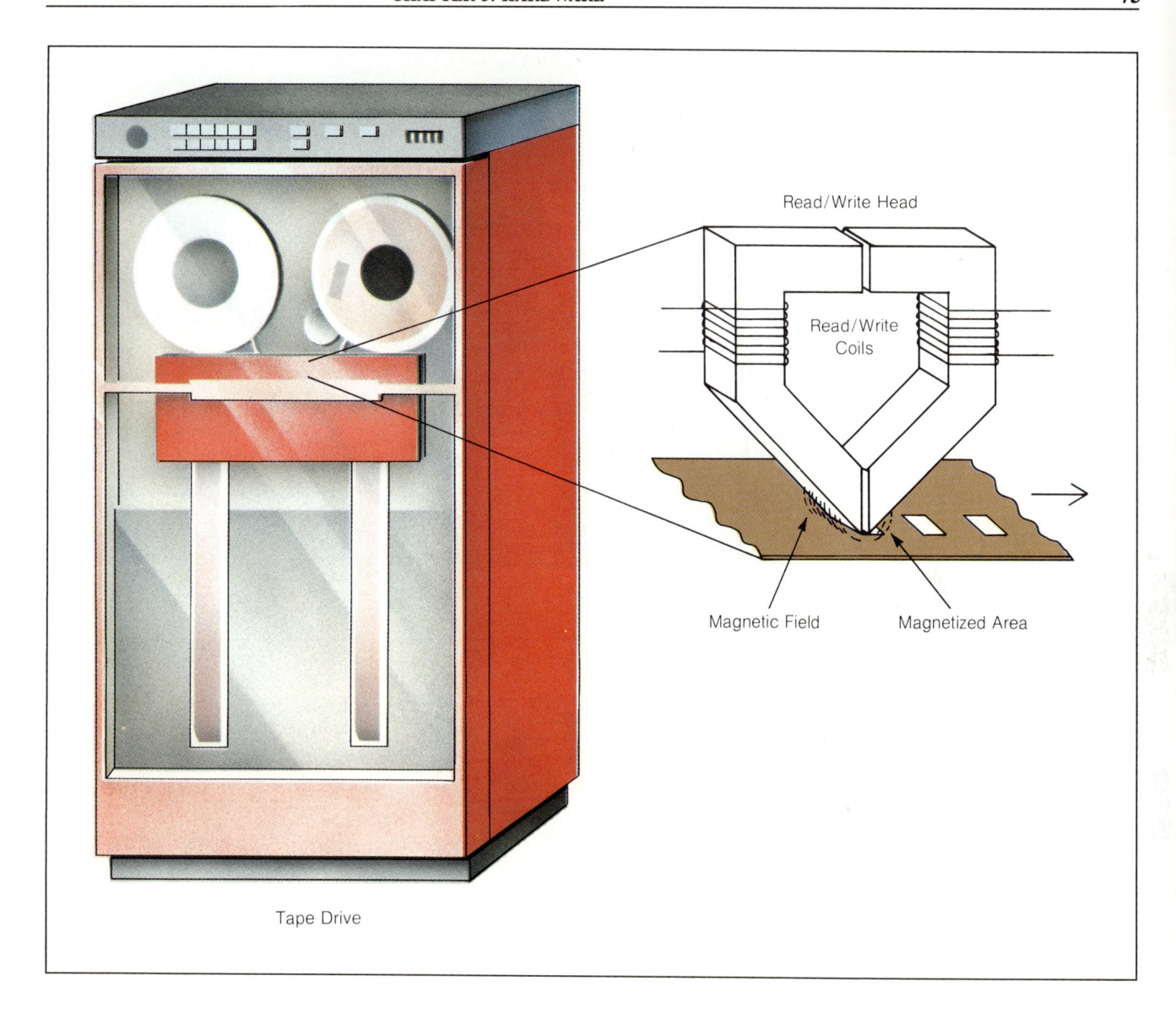

Figure 3-10
Read/Write Head
In recording on magnetic media, the read/write head creates a magnetic field for either writing or reading data.

The fast access time offered by magnetic-disk storage allows data files to be changed immediately. In addition, response to inquiries occurs in seconds. Because disks provide direct access, they are routinely used to store data about which frequent inquiries are made. Depending upon the type of drive, transfer rates of up to 850,000 characters per second are possible.

Several disks can be mounted on a center shaft and encased in plastic units. When assembled in this manner, the unit is called a disk pack. The individual disks are spaced on the shaft, allowing room for read/write mechanisms to move between them. The disk pack in Figure 3-13 has eleven disks and provides twenty usable recording surfaces. The extreme top and bottom surfaces are not used for storing data because they are likely to become nicked or scratched. A disk pack may contain five to 100 disks.

76 PART ONE: COMPUTER LITERACY

Figure 3-11
Cassette Tapes

Figure 3-12
Top View of Disk Surface

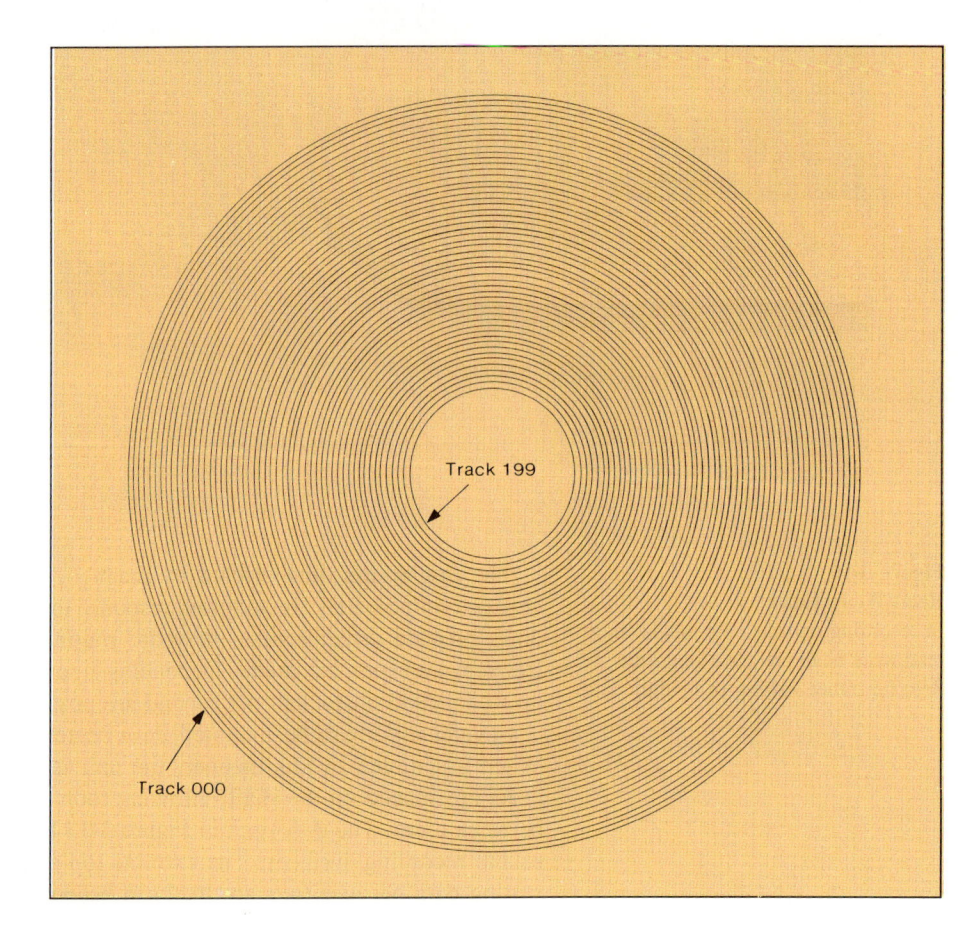

Figure 3-13
Disk Pack Showing Read/Write Heads on Access Arms

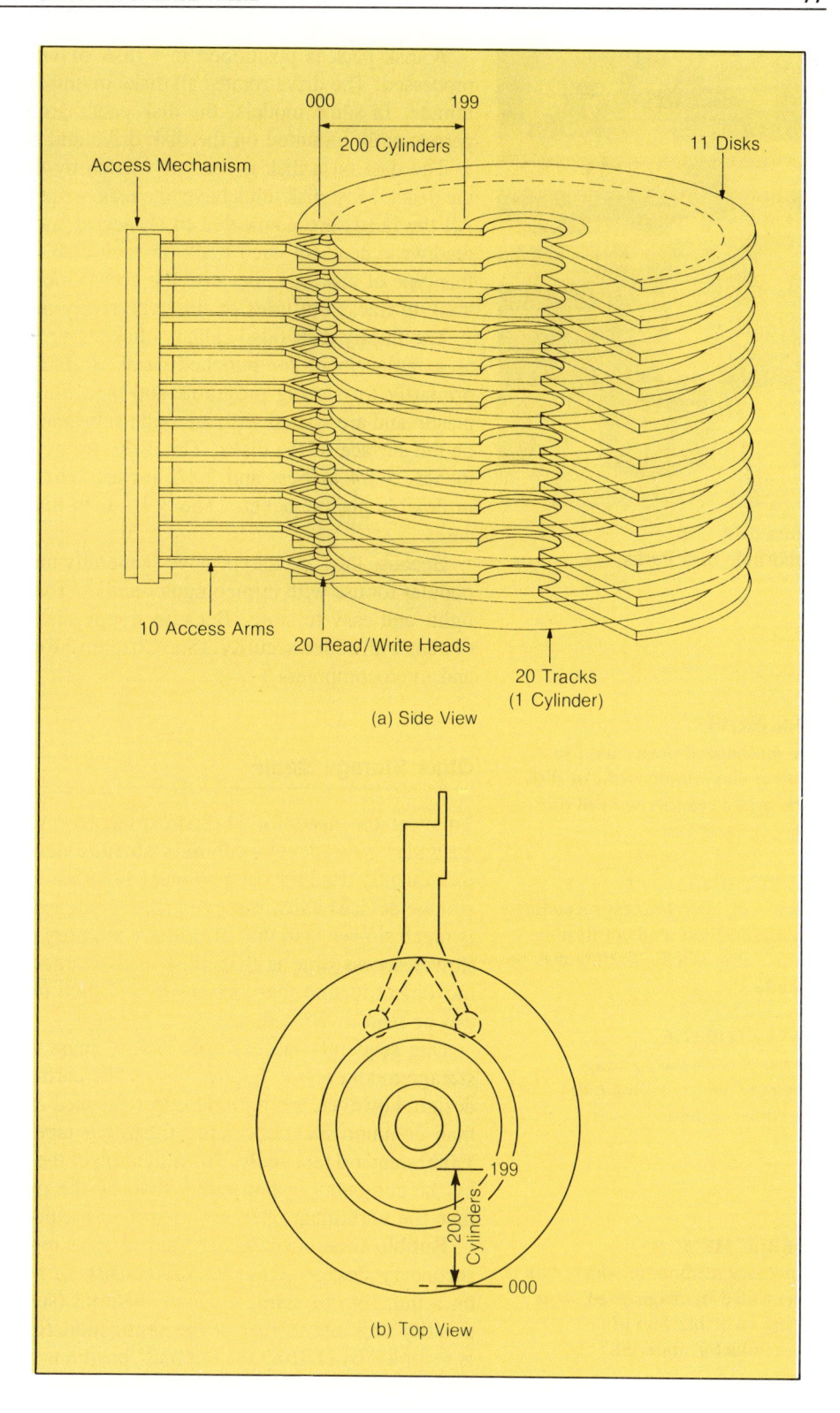

(a) Side View

(b) Top View

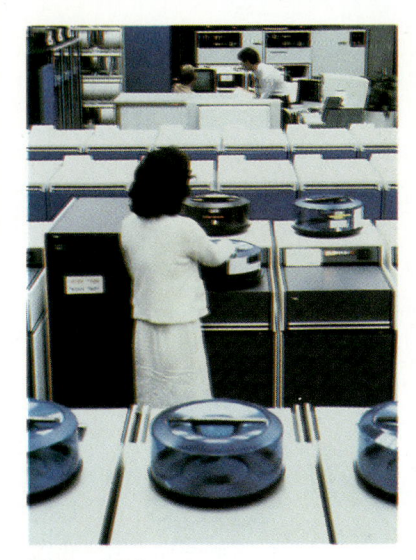

Figure 3-14
Removable Disk Packs

DISK DRIVE
The mechanical device used to rotate a disk, floppy disk, or disk pack past a read/write head during data transmission.

FLOPPY DISK
A low-cost, direct-access secondary storage medium made of flexible plastic; also called a flexible disk or diskette.

MASS STORAGE
A type of secondary storage developed for recording huge quantities of data.

BUBBLE MEMORY
A memory medium in which data is represented by magnetized spots resting on a thin film of semiconductor material.

A disk pack is positioned in a **disk drive** when the data on the pack is to be processed. The drive rotates all disks in unison speeds up to 3,600 revolutions per minute. In some models, the disk packs are removable; in others, the disks are permanently mounted on the disk drive and sealed (see Figure 3-14).

The data on a disk is read or written by the read/write heads located between the disks. Most disk units have one read/write head for each disk recording surface. All the heads are connected to an access mechanism. Some disk units have one read/write head for each track on each disk. The access time is much faster with this type of disk unit, because the access mechanism does not need to move from track to track, but units of this type rarely are used because of their high cost.

The **floppy disk** (also called a diskette or flexible disk) was introduced in 1973 as a replacement for punched cards in data entry. Today these disks are used primarily for storing programs and data files. Floppy disks are made of flexible plastic and are coated with an oxide substance. Data is stored as magnetized spots on the surface of the disks. The disks are available in three standard diameters: 8 inches, 5 1/4 inches, and 3 1/2 inches. The larger disks are permanently sealed in flexible plastic jackets. The 3 1/2 inch disks are enclosed in thin, hard plastic cases.

Because they are inexpensive (generally under $2 apiece), floppy disks are very popular for use with minicomputer and microcomputer systems. They are reusable, light, and easy to store. Because floppy disks can be removed, they provide the system with added security. (See Chapter 5 for more information about disk storage and microcomputers.)

Other Storage Media

To meet the need for cheaper storage of very large amounts of data, system designers have developed **mass storage** devices. Large files, backup files, and infrequently used files can be placed in mass storage at a relatively low cost. Mass storage devices allow rapid, usually direct access to data, although the access time is much slower than that of primary memory or magnetic disk. The reason for the slower access time is that most mass storage devices require extensive physical movement to find the correct file and then to mount it mechanically before data can be read or written.

One sequential access approach to mass storage uses a cartridge tape as the storage medium (see Figure 3-15). The cartridges are similar to cassette tapes in design; however, the high-density tape used requires 90 percent less storage space than common magnetic tape. Cartridge tapes can hold the equivalent of up to 1,000 standard tape reels. The mounting of the cartridges is controlled and executed by the computer system rather than by the operator (Figure 3-16), so it is faster than the traditional operator-controlled method.

Bubble memory was introduced as a replacement medium for primary and secondary storage. This memory consists of magnetized spots, or bubbles, resting on a thin film of semiconductor material (see Figure 3-17). The bubbles have a polarity opposite to that of the semiconductor material on which they rest. Data is recorded by shifting the bubbles' positions on the surface of the material. When data is read, the presence of a bubble indicates a 0 bit. The bubbles retain their magnetism indefinitely. Bubble memory can store huge amounts of data. A bubble

CHAPTER 3: HARDWARE 79

**Figure 3-15
Cartridge Tapes**

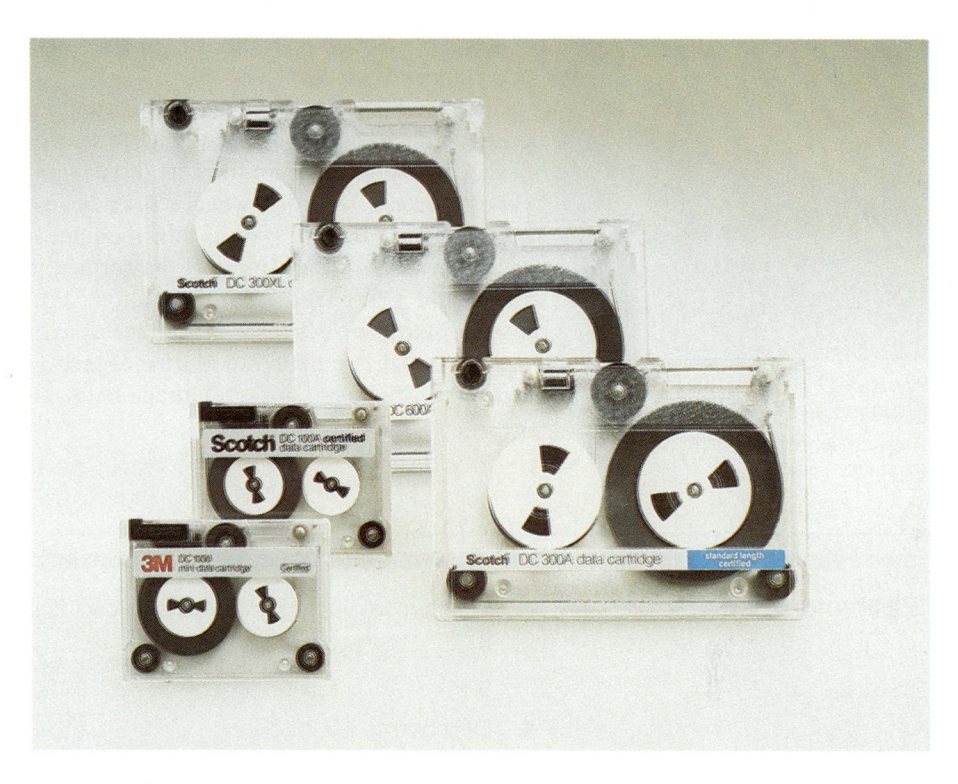

memory slightly larger than a quarter can store 20,000 characters of data. Bubble memory is nonvolatile, that is, data is preserved even if the electric power fails.

Many portable computers contain bubble memory. A more common use of bubble memory is for limited storage capabilities in input or output devices. High

Figure 3-16 Mass Storage
A mechanical arm removes a cartridge from its cell when the data stored on it is needed for processing. Because these data cartridges are stored in slots resembling a honeycomb, this type of mass storage sometimes is called honeycomb storage.

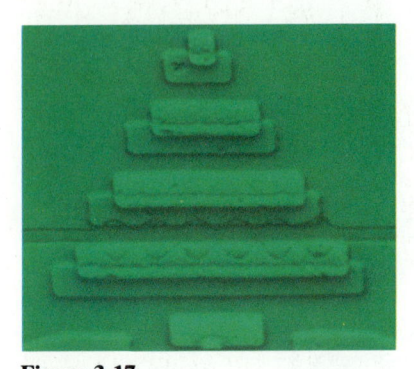

Figure 3-17
Bubble Memory
This bubble memory section is magnified 1,500 times.

cost and production difficulties have been major factors limiting industry and user acceptance of bubbles.

Laser technology provides an opportunity to store massive quantities of data at greatly reduced costs. A laser storage system can store nearly 128 billion characters of data at about one-tenth the cost of standard magnetic media. In a laser storage system, data is recorded when a laser beam forms patterns on the surface of a polyester sheet coated with a thin rhodium metal layer. To read data from this sheet, the laser reflects light off the surface, reconstructing the data into a digital bit stream. Laser data resists alteration; any attempt to alter it can be detected readily, so it provides a secure storage system. Laser storage does not deteriorate over time and is immune to electromagnetic radiation. Chapters 5 and 6 discuss another development in laser storage technology: the optical disk, or laser disk.

Learning Check

1. Which medium, tapes or disks, allows faster access to data, and why?
2. What is the device that detects and/or puts magnetized spots on tape or disk?
3. Describe a disk pack.
4. What advantages might removable disk packs have over permanent ones?
5. Name three other approaches to secondary storage.

Answers

1. Disks, because they allow direct access to data. Tapes require that data be read from the beginning of the tape, no matter where the needed data is located. 2. The read/write head. 3. A disk pack is a series of hard disks mounted on a center shaft. It contains access arms that hold read/write heads in the proper position for each disk side. Usually it is enclosed in a plastic unit. 4. Removable disk packs allow more data to be accessed by one drive, thereby cutting down on the number of drives needed. The disk packs can be locked away when not in use. 5. Mass storage; bubble memory; laser storage systems.

Hardware for Input and Output

A computer system includes more than just a central processing unit (CPU). Data must be provided to the computer in a form it can recognize, and output must be translated into a form humans can understand. Input and output are important activities in any computer system, because they are the communication links between people and machines. If the interfaces between people and machines are weak, the overall performance of the computer system suffers.

CHAPTER 3: HARDWARE

Input Methods

In order to enter data into the computer—to write instructions, select an operation, ask a question, or update data—you must use an input device. The one with which you are most familiar is the keyboard. The layout of a keyboard is much like that of a typewriter keyboard, except that there are additional keys for specific computer functions. Other data input methods are discussed in the following sections.

Punched Cards Traditionally, data from documents such as time cards, bills, invoices, and checks was transferred onto punched cards and then read into the computer. Today, a few of these documents are still punched cards themselves, because data is keyed directly onto the cards at their source. The most common example is the utility bill. These cards can be read directly into the computer, thus saving time and eliminating errors that can result from retyping the data.

The standard punched card has 80 vertical columns and 12 horizontal rows. Data is recorded as a set of holes punched in a particular column to represent a given character (see Figure 3-18).

Usually, an operator transcribes data from a source document onto cards by pressing keys on a keyboard that resembles an ordinary typewriter. The keypunch machine automatically feeds, positions, and stacks the cards. The data on the cards then is read into the computer by a card reader. Most card readers are photoelectric readers—that is, they detect the positions of the holes in the cards by passing light over them. Even with these automatic functions, keypunching is costly in both time and personnel. For these reasons, punched cards and keypunches are limited in use today.

Figure 3-18 Punched Card

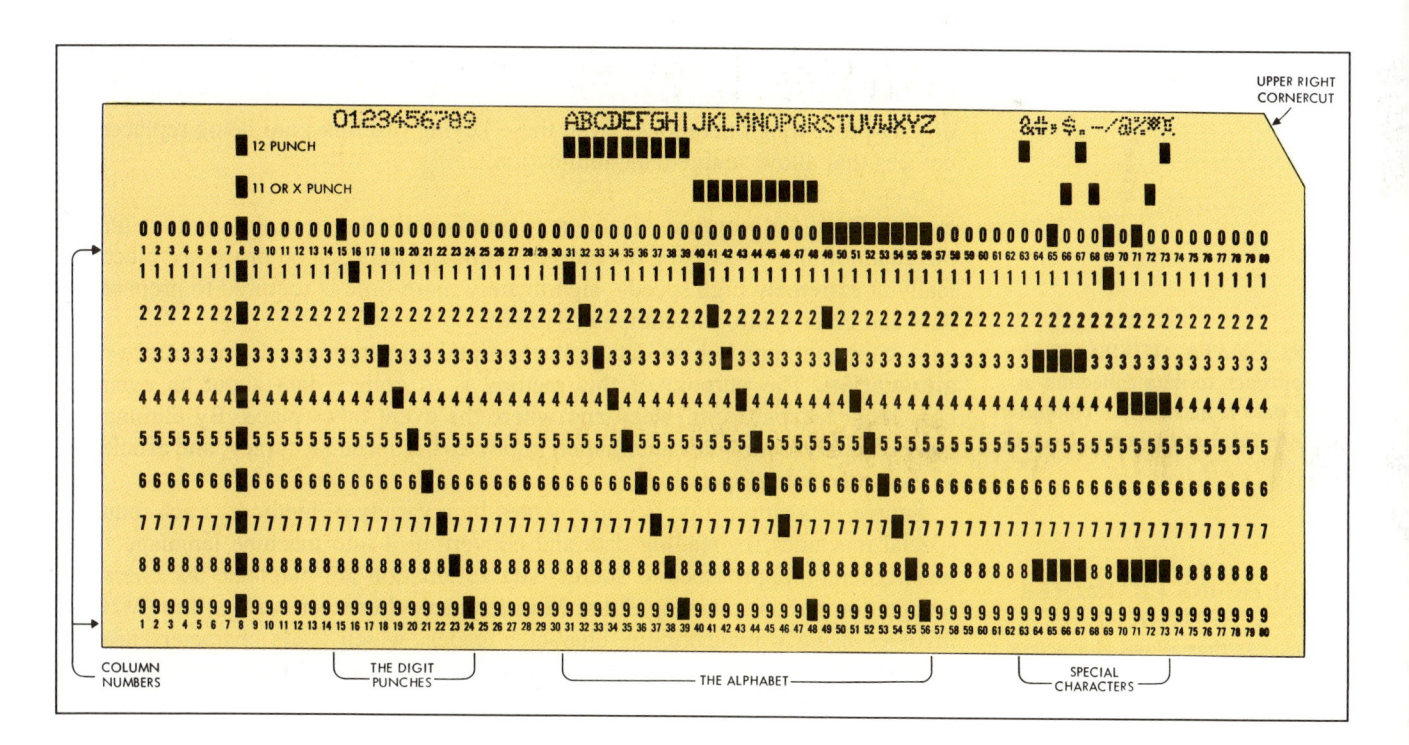

Figure 3-19
Key-to-Disk System

Key-to-Magnetic Media Key-to-tape and key-to-disk systems were developed for recording data on magnetic media, after it became obvious that magnetic media would soon replace punched cards (see Figure 3-19). With these systems, data is entered from the keyboard and stored as magnetized spots on the surface of a tape of disk. Because the spots retain their magnetism, the data can be stored and used indefinitely. Unlike punched cards, which cannot be repunched, old data on tape and disks can be replaced with new data. Tape and disks also can store much more data than cards, and in a much smaller space. In addition, data stored on tape or disk can be read into the CPU hundreds of times faster than data on cards. Therefore, the use of magnetic tape or disk storage significantly increases the efficiency of data-processing operations. Even these keying machines are being replaced by devices that allow source-data automation.

Source-Data Automation Data entry traditionally has been the weakest link in the chain of data-processing operations. Although data can be processed electronically at extremely high speeds, significantly more time is required to prepare the data and enter it into the computer system.

A common approach to data collection and preparation today is **source-data automation.** The purpose of this method is to collect data about an event in computer-readable form, when and where the event takes place. By eliminating manual input, source-data automation improves the speed, accuracy, and efficiency of data-processing operations.

Source-data automation is implemented by a variety of methods. Each requires special machines for reading data and converting it into machine language. The most common approaches to source-data automation are magnetic-ink character recognition and optical recognition. **Magnetic-ink character recognition (MICR)** involves using a magnetic-ink character reader, which reads characters printed with ink that contains magnetized particles of iron oxide. Check processing is a major application of MICR. The magnetic-ink characters are printed at the bottom of checks, as shown in Figure 3-20, and can be read by both humans and the

SOURCE-DATA AUTOMATION
An approach to data collection in which data is gathered in computer-readable form at its point of origin.

MAGNETIC-INK CHARACTER RECOGNITION (MICR)
The process that allows characters printed with magnetized ink to be read by a magnetic-ink character reader.

CHAPTER 3: HARDWARE   83

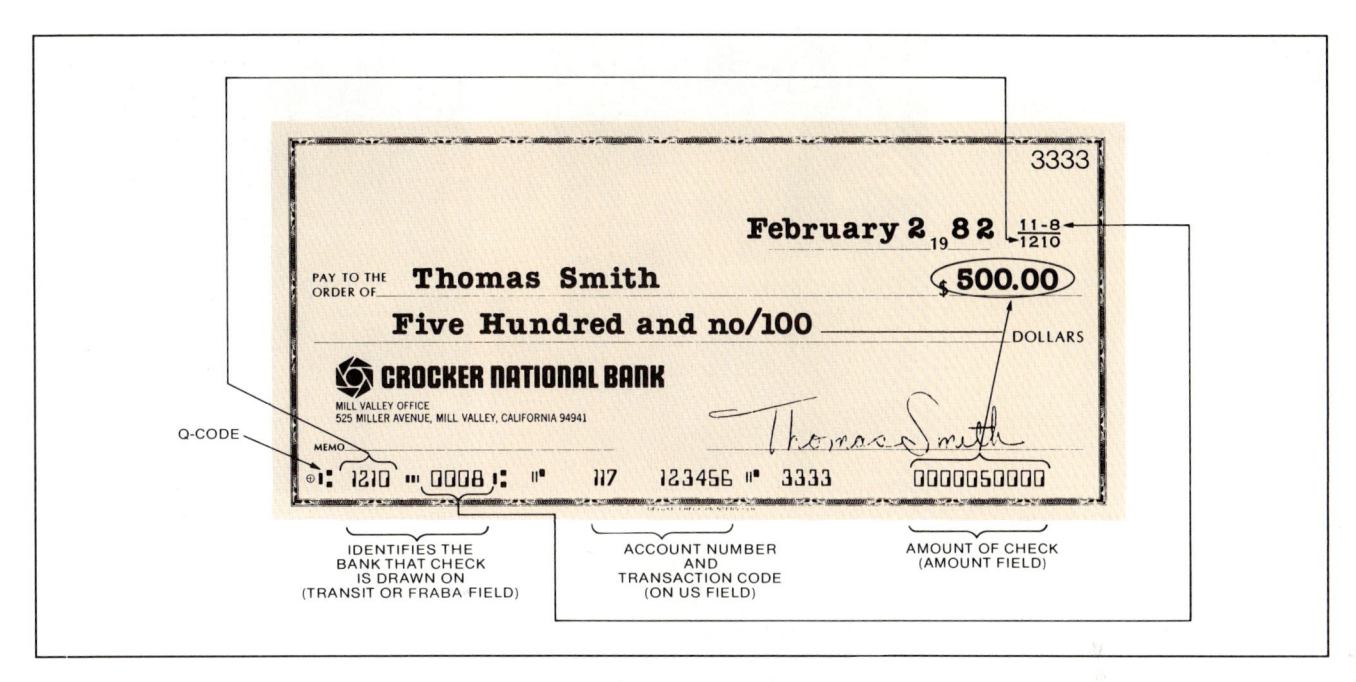

Figure 3-20
Sample Check with Magnetic Ink Characters

OPTICAL RECOGNITION
A method of electronic scanning which reads marks, bars, or characters and converts the optical images into appropriate electrical signals.

BAR CODE
A machine-readable code made up of bars and spaces of varying widths; often used on packaging of merchandise and read by optical scanning devices.

REMOTE TERMINAL
A terminal that is placed at a location distant from the central computer.

POINT-OF-SALE (POS) TERMINAL
A terminal that serves as a cash register, but also records data for such tasks as inventory control and accounting at the location where goods are sold.

character reader. Between 750 and 1,500 checks per minute can be read and sorted by an MICR device.

Optical recognition uses devices to read marks or symbols coded on paper documents and to convert them into electrical pulses. These pulses then are transmitted directly to the CPU or stored on magnetic tape for input at a later time. Optical character recognition is used extensively in mail sorting, credit card billing, utility billing, and inventory control.

There are several types of optical recognition, but one type we see frequently interprets **bar codes** (see Figure 3-21). A bar code is a pattern of lines which appears on products in grocery and department stores. The code for each product is a unique combination of vertical bars of varying widths and varying spaces between them. The bars represent data such as the product name and manufacturer.

Remote terminals often are used in conjunction with optical recognition. Remote terminals collect data at its source and transmit it to a central computer for processing. Remote terminals that function as cash registers and also capture sales data are called **point-of-sale (POS) terminals.** These terminals have a keyboard for data entry, a panel that displays the price, a cash drawer, and a printer that provides a cash receipt. Some POS terminals have a scanner that reads the bar code stamped on an item. Many supermarkets are equipped with this type of terminal. Other POS terminals are used with wands that read characters from a price tag or other document on clothing and other goods (see Figure 3-22). By using POS terminals and other forms of source-data automation, retailers can update inventory and sales information almost immediately. In many cases, the resulting data source can be read by both humans and machines.

Specialized Input Devices   Traditional input devices, such as those used in source-data automation or with key-to-magnetic media, do not meet the needs of every

84   PART ONE: COMPUTER LITERACY

Figure 3-21
Bar Code A clerk passes the merchandise over a scanner, which reads a bar code printed on the packages.

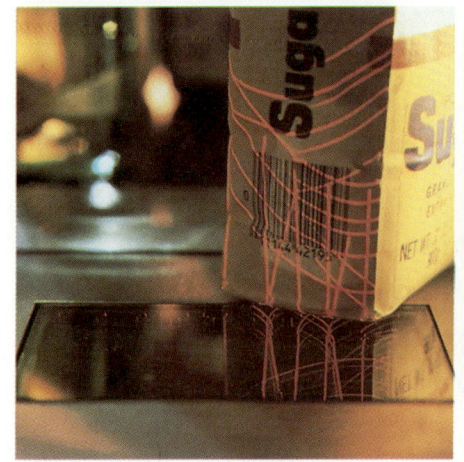

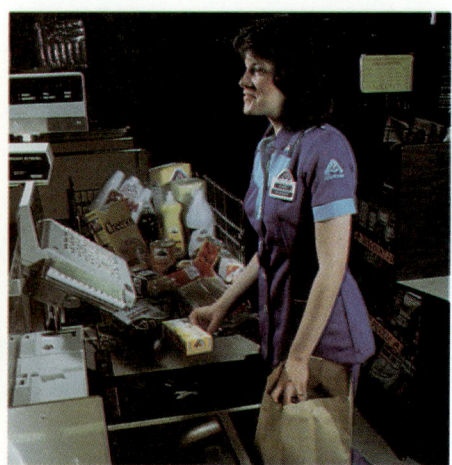

Figure 3-22
Optical Recognition with a Wand Scanner Some methods of optical recognition reads specially shaped characters much as the ones shown below.

CHAPTER 3: HARDWARE 85

Figure 3-23
Spatial Digitizer

SPATIAL DIGITIZER
An input device that can reconstruct a three-dimensional object graphically on a computer's display screen.

TOUCH SCREEN
A computer screen equipped for detecting the point at which it is touched by the user, thus enabling the user to bypass the keyboard.

Figure 3-24
Touch Screen

situation. Special input devices may be required, such as spatial digitizers, touch screens, and voice recognition systems. Other specialized input devices are discussed in conjunction with microcomputers in Chapter 5.

Three-dimensional graphics can be created on a display screen with the use of a **spatial digitizer** (see Figure 3-23). A spatial digitizer allows a user to trace an object with the digitizer's arm or pointer for reproduction on the display screen. The precise measurements are taken electronically, and the object is reconstructed graphically on the screen.

A **touch screen** looks like a normal computer screen, but it can detect a user's touch and can identify the point at which the user actually touches the screen (see Figure 3-24). The touch screen is especially useful when the user has a list of

Figure 3-25
Voice Recognition System

VOICE RECOGNITION SYSTEM
An input system that recognizes certain speech and voice patterns; the user is limited to the patterns that the system is programmed to recognize.

IMPACT PRINTER
A printer that forms characters by physically striking the ribbon, paper, and embossed character together.

NONIMPACT PRINTER
A printer that uses heat, laser, or photographic methods for producing images.

alternatives from which to choose. When the user touches the desired alternative, the computer registers the choice made and continues processing accordingly.

Remote terminals that use audio input, **voice recognition systems,** are suitable for low-volume, highly formal input. Because of the limitations of current technology, voice recognition is best used with short-answer data. The user must speak in short, clearly enunciated words because the computer is programmed to recognize specific voice and speech patterns. In industry, workers can use a voice recognition unit for entering data about inventory or quality control, thus leaving their hands free for sorting products (see Figure 3-25). Research in voice recognition focuses on improving three areas: amount of recognized vocabulary, ability to recognize different voices, and ability to interpret continuous or flowing speech.

Printers

Once data have been fed into the computer by card, tape, disk, or other method, it is processed and output in the way that best suits the user's needs. Output may appear as soft copy on a computer screen, or it may be printed as hard copy, the standard term for permanent printed copy. (Monitors for microcomputers are discussed in Chapter 5.) The type of output device is determined by the needs of the user. In most cases, however, when we refer to output we mean hard copy that has been produced by a printer. There are two general types of printers: **impact printers** and **nonimpact printers.**

Impact Printers This type of printer uses a striking motion. A hammer mechanism strikes together an inked ribbon, the paper, and the character embossed on a plastic or metal part. Impact printers come in a variety of sizes and shapes.

Figure 3-26
Dot-Matrix Character Set

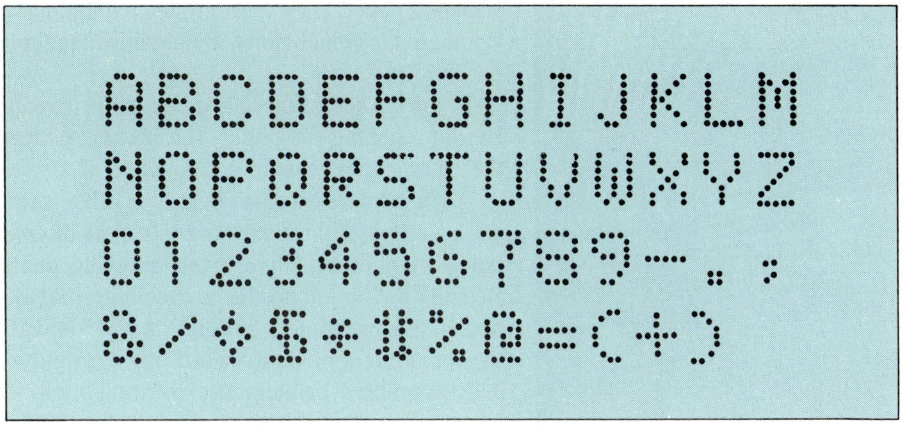

DOT-MATRIX PRINTER
An impact printer that forms characters from a matrix of pins arranged in a rectangular shape. Only the pins necessary for forming a particular character are selected from the matrix.

DAISY-WHEEL PRINTER
An impact printer whose print element is a removable flat wheel of spokes, each with a character embossed at its tip.

Some print one character at a time, whereas others print a line at a time. Printers in the first category include dot-matrix and daisy-wheel printers.

Dot-Matrix (also called wire-matrix) **printers** operate by striking pins in a print element against the ribbon and paper. The pins are arranged in a rectangular matrix, usually seven pins high and five pins wide. Combinations of pins are activated to represent various characters. The dot combinations used to represent numbers, letters, and special characters are shown in Figure 3-26. High-quality, or near–letter-quality, dot matrix images are produced when the matrix contains more pins for the same amount of space or when each character is struck twice. Dot-matrix printers typically can print 100 to 200 characters per second.

Daisy-wheel printers are solid-font printing devices that create a character like a typed character. They use a flat disk or wheel with petal-like projections, each with a single character embossed at the tip (see Figure 3-27). The wheel rotates to bring the desired character into position and is then struck by a hammer mechanism to form an image on paper. Daisy wheels come in several type fonts that can be interchanged quickly. The daisy-wheel printer often is used in word processing systems to give output a typewriter-quality (or "letter-quality") appearance. Daisy-wheel printers can print between 15 and 55 characters per second.

Devices that print one line at a time include print-wheel printers, chain printers, drum printers, and band printers. All have multiple sets of characters, so they can print all the characters on a line at once or in very fast succession. These printers are used primarily with mainframes and minicomputers.

Nonimpact Printers Nonimpact printers do not print characters by means of a mechanical printing element that strikes the paper. Instead, heat, laser, or photographic methods are used in producing the image. Electrostatic, thermal, ink-jet, laser, and xerographic printers are discussed here.

An electrostatic printer forms an image of a character on special paper, using a dot matrix of charged wires or pins. The paper is moved through a solution containing ink particles that have a charge opposite to that of the pattern. The ink particles adhere to each charged pattern on the paper and form visible characters.

Thermal printers generate characters by using heat and heat-sensitive paper. Rods are heated in a matrix. As the ends of the selected rods touch the heat-

Figure 3-27
Daisy Wheel
The daisy wheel produces solid-font characters.

Figure 3-28
Apple Laser Writer
Laser printers are becoming inexpensive enough for small offices and individuals to buy.

sensitive paper, they create images. Neither the electrothermal nor the electrostatic printer makes much noise in operation, and most produce at least 40 to 80 characters per second.

In an ink-jet printer, nozzles shoot streams of charged ink toward the paper. Before reaching the paper, the ink passes through an electrical field that arranges the charged particles into characters at a rate of up to 220 characters per second.

Laser printers use laser beams in image production. The laser beams are reflected off a rotating disk containing a full set of characters or a grid of thousands of tiny holes. A photosensitive drum picks up the images and transfers them to paper. Because the output produces excellent images, the process often is used for printing books. Laser printers produce 8 to 10 pages per minute and are replacing the slower printers of many word processing systems (see Figure 3-28).

Xerographic printers use printing methods like those employed in common photocopying machines. For example, Xerox, the pioneer in this type of printing, has one model that prints on single 8 1/2 × 11-inch sheets of plain paper. Xerographic printers can turn out 4,000 lines per minute.

New printing systems now on the market combine many features of the printing process into one machine, including stacking, routing, hole punching, blanking out of priority information, and perforating. Some printers produce both text and graphic images on plain paper, thus reducing or eliminating the need for preprinted forms.

**Figure 3-29
Flatbed Plotter**

Specialized Output Devices

PLOTTER
An output device that typically uses pens to produce hard-copy graphic output, such as drawings, charts, maps, and other images.

Plotters A **plotter** uses pens to produce hard copies of graphic images, such as bar charts, graphs, organizational charts, engineering drawings, maps, trend lines, supply and demand curves, and other useful graphics.

The two types of plotters are the flatbed plotter and the drum plotter. A flatbed plotter looks like a table with pens mounted on a track (see Figure 3-29). On some plotters, the pens move; on others, the table holding the paper moves. Drum plotters draw on paper that is rolled on a cylinder.

Many plotters operate with a variety of pens—filter-tip, ballpoint, liquid roller, and nylon-tip. For high-quality output, fine drafting pens are used. Output can be produced in four, six, or eight colors. Some plotters can position the pen at as many as 45,000 different points within each square inch of paper.

COMPUTER-OUTPUT MICROFILM (COM)
A form of computer output in which information from a printer or magnetic tape is placed on microfilm or microfiche.

Computer-Output Microfilm Sometimes large amounts of information must be printed and stored for future reference. Printing the output on conventional-sized paper would quickly create both a storage and an access problem. A technique that solves this problem is **computer output microfilm (COM).** In this method, photographed images are produced in miniature by the computer. Sometimes the

HIGHLIGHT ▲▲▲▲▲▲▲▲▲▲▲▲▲▲▲▲▲▲▲▲

Ray Kurzweil and His Amazing Machines

Ray Kurzweil likes to make things. He has made the Kurzweil Reading Machine and the Kurzweil 250, a keyboard that sounds much like a concert grand piano, and he is working on perfecting a voice-activated typewriter. Not the sorts of things most people who like to make things make.

Kurzweil had an early start. When he was 12, he developed a software package that was distributed by IBM. As a high school student he won the prestigious International Science Fair, with a computer program that analyzed musical patterns and used them to generate what he now calls second-rate Mozart. At age 28, he introduced the world's first optical character recognition technology for reading a wide variety of type fonts. The Kurzweil Reading Machine, widely used today in helping visually impaired people read printed matter, uses this technology.

Another popular Kurzweil product is the Kurzweil 250, a digital music synthesizer. The 250 creates a complex model of an acoustic piano sound—rather than an electronic sound—as well as sounds of other musical instruments and human voices. (If you want to know how successful the 250 is, ask Stevie Wonder, whose desire for better acoustic sound imitation in electronic music prompted the development of the machine.)

Kurzweil's current project centers on voice-activated typewriter (VAT) technology. If Kurzweil's VAT machines are successful, people won't have to hunt and peck at the typewriter, and deaf people will be able to use the telephone with complete freedom and flexibility.

---

output is first recorded on magnetic tape and then transferred to 35-millimeter microfilm rolls or to 4 × 6-inch microfiche cards.

The COM system can store graphics as well as characters, and records at a rate 25 to 50 times that of traditional printing. Another advantage is that it costs relatively little to produce additional microfilm copies.

VOICE RESPONSE UNIT
A device through which the computer "speaks" by arranging half-second records of phonemes, or voice sounds.

VOICE SYNTHESIZER
The output portion of a voice communication system; used to provide verbal output from the computer system to the user.

Voice Output Computer audio output, or **voice response units,** "speak" by arranging half-second records of voice sounds (phonemes) or prerecorded words. This approach is being used in the banking industry for reporting customer account balances, and in supermarkets for informing customers of the amount of each purchase. Audio output is well suited to situations that require short, formal messages.

Some audio systems use **voice synthesizers,** which use a mathematical model of the human voice to create the output. Many people with special needs are using voice synthesizers to improve the quality of their lives. The Kurzweil Reading Machine, designed by Ray Kurzweil to aid the blind, scans a printed page and reads aloud. Other synthesizers are connected to microcomputers and synthesize speech for those who cannot speak.

As of 1986, the quality of speech produced by many voice synthesizers is poor. Continuing research and development efforts will improve both the range of words and quality of speech produced by these devices. Someday, listeners may be unable to tell that audio output and synthesized voices are coming from computers.

CHAPTER 3: HARDWARE

Learning Check

1. What approach to data collection involves collecting data at its source at the time an event occurs, in computer-readable form?
2. What is a POS terminal?
3. Why might a touch screen be easy to use?
4. In what three ways must voice recognition be improved?
5. Differentiate between an impact printer and a nonimpact printer.
6. What type of output do plotters primarily produce?
7. Of what advantage is COM?

Answers

1. Source-data automation. 2. Point-of-sale terminal. 3. The user does not have to type or learn special key sequences in order to use the computer. 4. Recognized vocabulary must be expanded, different voices must be able to use the system, and people must be able to talk in continuous speech. 5. An impact printer uses a striking motion in producing an image, whereas a nonimpact printer uses heat, laser, or photographic methods of producing the image. 6. Graphic output. 7. It is cheap and takes up little space.

Data Representation

MACHINE LANGUAGE
The only language the computer can execute directly; a code that designates the computer's electrical states as combinations of 0s and 1s.

When data is entered into a computer through an input device such as a keyboard, it is not in a form that the computer can interpret. Computers cannot understand the complex symbols that humans use. They recognize only a code composed of 0s and 1s, known as **machine language.** Machine language suits the computer because electronic components and storage media represent two states: on/off, conducting/nonconducting, or present/absent. Before the computer can execute the English-like statements of most programming languages, these statements must be translated by special programs into machine language. Machine language uses binary code or one of several other codes based on it.

Binary Representation

BINARY NUMBER SYSTEM
The base 2 number system, which uses the digits 0 and 1; convenient for use in computer coding because it corresponds to the two states in machine circuitry.

BINARY REPRESENTATION
Use of a two-state, or binary, system for representing data.

Because data is represented in the computer by the electrical states of its circuitry, data representation is easily accomplished by using the **binary number system.** In the binary or base 2 number system, there are only two digits: 1 and 0. Using binary numbers to represent data is called **binary representation.**

The binary system is similar to the decimal (base 10) number system that we use every day. Both represent the values of digits as powers of the base, and in both, the digits farther to the left represent larger powers than the digits to the right. For example, the decimal number 3,568 can be analyzed like this:

**Figure 3-30
Decimal Place Values**

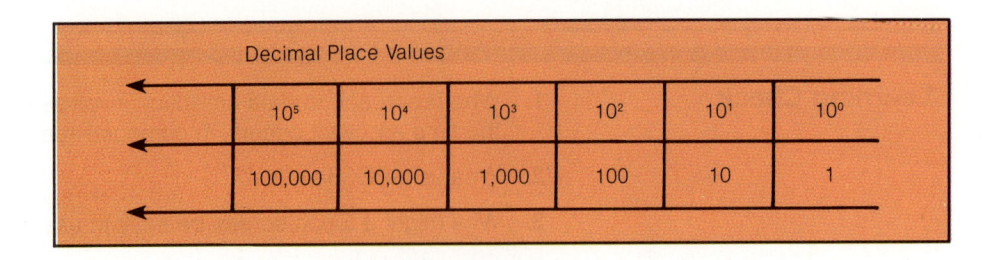

Decimal Place Values					
10^5	10^4	10^3	10^2	10^1	10^0
100,000	10,000	1,000	100	10	1

$$8 \times 10^0 = 8 \times 1 \text{ or } 8$$
$$6 \times 10^1 = 6 \times 10 \text{ or } 60$$
$$5 \times 10^2 = 5 \times 100 \text{ or } 500$$
$$3 \times 10^3 = 3 \times 1,000 \text{ or } 3,000$$
$$\overline{3,568}_{\text{base 10}}$$

Each position represents a power of the base 10. The progression of power is from right to left—that is, digits farther to the left in a decimal number represent larger powers of the base 10 (see Figure 3-30).

The same principle holds for binary representation. The difference is that, in binary representation, each position in the number represents a power of 2 (see Figure 3-31). For example, consider the decimal number 11. In binary, the value equivalent to 11 is written as follows:

$$1 \quad 0 \quad 1 \quad 1_{\text{base 2}}$$
$$1 \times 2^0 = 1 \times 1 \text{ or } 1$$
$$1 \times 2^1 = 1 \times 2 \text{ or } 2$$
$$0 \times 2^2 = 1 \times 4 \text{ or } 0$$
$$1 \times 2^3 = 1 \times 8 \text{ or } 8$$
$$\overline{11}_{\text{base 10}}$$

Each digit position in a binary number is called a bit. A 1 in a bit position indicates the presence of a specific power of 2; a 0 indicates the absence of a specific power. As in the decimal number system, the progression of powers is from right to left.

**Figure 3-31
Binary Place Values**

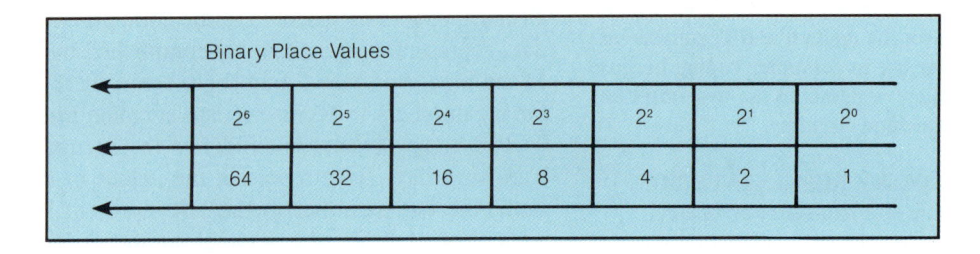

Binary Place Values						
2^6	2^5	2^4	2^3	2^2	2^1	2^0
64	32	16	8	4	2	1

Computer Codes

A single binary digit (0 or 1) cannot represent a number of letter. By using combinations of the two digits, however, computer scientists have developed codes that represent the alphanumeric characters. Many computers use coding schemes that group the bits in order to represent characters.

A fixed number of adjacent bits operated on as a unit is called a **byte.** Bytes usually are eight bits long. The number of possible combinations of 0s and 1s in eight bits is enough to represent all the characters. For example, one standard coding system codes an upper-case letter B as follows:

$$\underset{\text{byte}}{1\ 1\ 0\ 0\ \ 0\ 0\overset{\overset{\text{bit}}{\downarrow}}{1}\ 0} = B$$

BYTE
A fixed number of adjacent bits, usually eight, operated as a unit.

Other combinations of 0s and 1s represent the other letters, numbers, and special characters. There are 256 possible bit combinations in an eight-bit code.

One eight-bit code is known as **Extended Binary Coded Decimal Interchange Code (EBCDIC,** pronounced EP-see-DICK). The 256 (2^8) possible bit combinations in EBCDIC are used to represent uppercase and lowercase letters and additional special characters, such as the cent sign and the quotation mark.

The **American Standard Code for Information Interchange (ASCII,** pronounced ASK-ee) is a seven-bit code developed cooperatively by several computer manufacturers in order to establish a standard code for all computers (see Figure 3-33). Because certain machines are designed to accept eight-bit rather than seven-bit code patterns, an eight-bit version of ASCII, called ASCII-8, was also created. ASCII and EBCDIC are similar. The key difference is in the bit patterns used to represent certain characters.

EXTENDED BINARY CODED DECIMAL INTERCHANGE CODE (EBCDIC)
An eight-bit code for character representation.

AMERICAN STANDARD CODE FOR INFORMATION INTERCHANGE (ASCII)
A seven-bit standard code used for information interchange among data-processing systems, communications systems, and associated equipment.

Code Checking

Computers do not always function without errors. When errors occur, they must be detected immediately to keep data from being changed. Most computers include an extra bit at each storage location to check for certain kinds of internal errors. This extra bit is called a **parity bit.** Computers can be set to either odd parity or even parity. If a computer is set for odd parity, each character is represented by an odd number of 1 bits. The parity bit is set to 0 if the number of 1 bits in the character is already odd. If the number of 1 bits is even, the parity bit is set to 1, making the total number of 1 bits odd. With even parity, the parity bit is set to either 0 or 1 so that the total number of 1 bits is even.

PARITY BIT
A bit added to a byte to detect incorrect transmission of data within a computer system.

When the computer checks each character for errors, it checks for the proper number of 1 bits. For example, a computer set for even parity checks for an even number of 1 bits and detects an error in any character that has an odd number of 1 bits.

Figure 3-32
ASCII Code and ASCII Values
The ASCII values in decimal form often are used in programming. These are only some of the ASCII representations, 0–9 and A–Z.

Character	ASCII Code	Decimal Value	Character	ASCII Code	Decimal Value
0	0110000	48	I	1001001	73
1	0110001	49	J	1001010	74
2	0110010	50	K	1001011	75
3	0110011	51	L	1001100	76
4	0110100	52	M	1001101	77
5	0110101	53	N	1001110	78
6	0110110	54	O	1001111	79
7	0110111	55	P	1010000	80
8	0111000	56	Q	1010001	81
9	0111001	57	R	1010010	82
A	1000001	65	S	1010011	83
B	1000010	66	T	1010100	84
C	1000011	67	U	1010101	85
D	1000100	68	V	1010110	86
E	1000101	69	W	1010111	87
F	1000110	70	X	1011000	88
G	1000111	71	Y	1011001	89
H	1001000	72	Z	1011010	90

If an error is detected, the computer may try to repeat the operation in which the error occurred. If the error remains, the computer informs the operator. The computer cannot correct these errors; it can only detect them.

Learning Check

1. What is the number system suited to represent the states of computer circuitry?
2. What does the binary number 11010 stand for in decimal representation?
3. In $1100\underline{0}10_{\text{base 2}}$, the underlined digit stands for what power of 2? What place is it in?
4. Two binary-based codes used for representing letters, numbers, and special characters are _____ and _____.
5. The extra bit used as a check for some internal errors is called a _____ bit.

Answers

1. Binary number system. 2. 26. 3. 2^3 (2 to the third power); eights. 4. EBCDIC and ASCII. 5. Parity.

Summary Points

- Computers are categorized by memory capacity, capability, price range, and speed of operation. The four classifications are supercomputer, mainframe, minicomputer, and microcomputer.
- Advances in technology have blurred the distinctions between these classifications of computers.
- The component that is responsible for temporarily storing data and acting on it is the central processing unit (CPU). The CPU is made up of the control unit, which maintains order and controls what is happening in the CPU; the arithmetic/logic unit (ALU), which performs arithmetic and logical operations; and primary memory, which holds all data and instructions necessary for processing.
- Each location in primary memory has a unique address, which allows stored-program instructions and data items to be located by the control unit as it directs processing operations.
- Random-access memory (RAM) is the major type of primary memory. The nondestructive read/destructive write characteristic of RAM allows a program to be executed as many times as needed, since the program remains intact until another is stored over it.
- Read-only memory (ROM) is hardwired primary memory. It stores microprograms or other data in a form that cannot be changed. ROM that can be programmed once is called programmable read-only memory (PROM). ROM that can be reprogrammed is called erasable programmable read-only memory (EPROM).
- Storage located outside the computer is called secondary storage. There are two types of secondary storage: sequential-access and direct-access. Sequential-access storage media must be read from and written to sequentially—that is, from the beginning and in order. Examples are magnetic tapes and tape cassettes. Direct-access storage media allow the user to access data directly at any point. Examples are magnetic disks and floppy disks.
- Other types of storage include mass storage devices for storing large amounts of data at low cost; nonvolatile bubble memory, in which data are stored as magnetized spots or bubbles on a thin film of semiconductor material; and laser storage, which resists alteration.
- Traditional input methods include punched cards and key-to-magnetic media systems. These forms of input require an intermediate step, in which data is recorded manually by keypunching or typing from the original source of data.
- Source-data automation is a technique that allows data to be collected at the source in computer-readable form. Most source-data automation systems use some type of mark or character recognition device, such as the bar code.
- Remote terminals often are used in conjunction with source-data automation; point-of-sale terminals function as cash registers and capture sales data at the same time.
- Spatial digitizers, touch screens, and voice recognition systems are 3 devices for specialized input.
- Traditional output devices produce either hard or soft copy. Hard-copy output is printed on paper, whereas soft-copy output appears on a computer screen.
- The most common output device is the printer. Printers come in two types:

impact and nonimpact. Impact printers press the print elements against the paper and ribbon. Common impact printers are dot-matrix printers and daisy-wheel printers. Nonimpact printers use a variety of means to create their images, but the print element never touches the paper. Nonimpact printers include electrostatic printers, thermal printers, ink-jet printers, laser printers, and xerographic printers.

■ Other types of output devices include plotters, which produce graphic images with pens; computer output microfilm (COM), in which output is produced on microfilm rather than paper; and voice response units, which "speak" by arranging half-second records of voice sounds (phonemes) or prerecorded words. Some audio systems use voice synthesizers, which use a mathematical model of the human voice to create the output.

■ Data representation in the computer is based on a two-state system or binary number system. This system suits the computer because it matches the on/off, conducting/nonconducting, present/absent states of computer hardware and storage.

■ A bit is one position in a binary number. A byte is a specified number of adjacent bits (usually eight), and a parity bit is used to detect errors in data transmission. Check digits are used to determine the correctness of data entry.

■ Because numeric representation in binary is tedious, coding schemes have been devised which offer shorthand methods of representing binary. Two coding schemes are Extended Binary Coded Decimal Interchange Code (EBCDIC) and American Standard Code for Information Interchange (ASCII).

Review Questions

1. For what purposes might you use a supercomputer? Have you heard of any uses other than the ones mentioned in the text? What are they?

2. What market trend currently is affecting sales of minicomputers?

3. Name the parts of the central processing unit and discuss the functions of each.

4. Relate RAM, the stored-program concept, and nondestructive read/destructive write.

5. Explain the concept of ROM and how it might help prevent unauthorized copying of software.

6. Explain the difference between sequential-access storage and direct-access storage, and give examples of each.

7. What is source-data automation, and how would it benefit a retail store owner? Describe some instances of source-data automation which you have encountered.

8. Differentiate between impact printers and nonimpact printers, and give some examples of each. What factors would you take into consideration when deciding which printer to buy?

9. Describe how computer-output microfilm (COM) might be useful to a large bank.

10. How are characters represented in binary coding methods?

CHAPTER 4

Software Development

Outline

Introduction
Solving Problems with the Computer
  Define the Problem
  Design the Solution
  Write the Program
  Compile, Debug, and Test the Program
Learning Check
Structured Problem Solving
  Top-Down Design
Highlight: Software Prices Dropping
  Documentation
  Program Testing
  The Programming Team
Learning Check
Types of Programs
Highlight: Programs As Models of the Real World
Operating Systems
Learning Check
Programming Languages
  Low-Level Languages
  High-Level Languages
  Natural Languages
Learning Check
Summary Points
Review Questions

Introduction

PROGRAMMING
The process of writing the step-by-step instructions that direct a computer in performing a task.

Computers are capable of performing all kinds of tasks that sometimes seem magical. In order to perform even the simplest task, however, computers need directions from people. **Programming** is the process of giving step-to-step instructions to computers so that the machines will execute the desired tasks.

The earliest computers were programmed by arranging wires and switches within the computer components. Up to 6,000 switches could be set on ENIAC for executing one program. When a new program was to be run, the switches had to be reset. EDSAC, the first stored-program computer, allowed instructions to be entered into primary memory without rewiring or resetting the switches. Instructions were written in codes based on the binary number system. This method of coding was tedious and error-prone. The development of assembly language and high-level, English-like languages has simplified and streamlined the programming process and has increased the variety of problems that can be solved using computers.

This chapter describes the programming process, one part of which is writing the program in a suitable programming language. Also discussed are structured programming techniques, the types of computer programs, and some popular programming languages.

Solving Problems with the Computer

PROGRAMMER
A person who writes the instructions that tell a computer what to do.

Every day you solve problems, many of which have several solutions. Often you solve them without consciously thinking of all the steps involved. For example, traveling from your home to a friend's house involves deciding when to leave and what route to take. When you arrive at your friend's door, any of a number of different decisions could have helped you get there safely.

Computer problem solving is similar. Many solutions exist for a single problem. Some are more efficient than others. In order to develop a good solution to a problem, a **programmer** follows four steps, known as the programming process (see Figure 4-1):

1. Define the problem.
2. Design the solution.
3. Write the program.
4. Compile, debug, and test the program.

Define the Problem

This step is built upon the answers to a number of questions: Who needs information? What kind is needed? What data is needed to yield the information, and where can it be found? Must the data be accumulated in a certain order? In what form should the data be given to the computer, once it has been gathered? In what

CHAPTER 4: SOFTWARE DEVELOPMENT 99

Figure 4-1
The Programming Process
Each step of the programming process must be carefully documented.

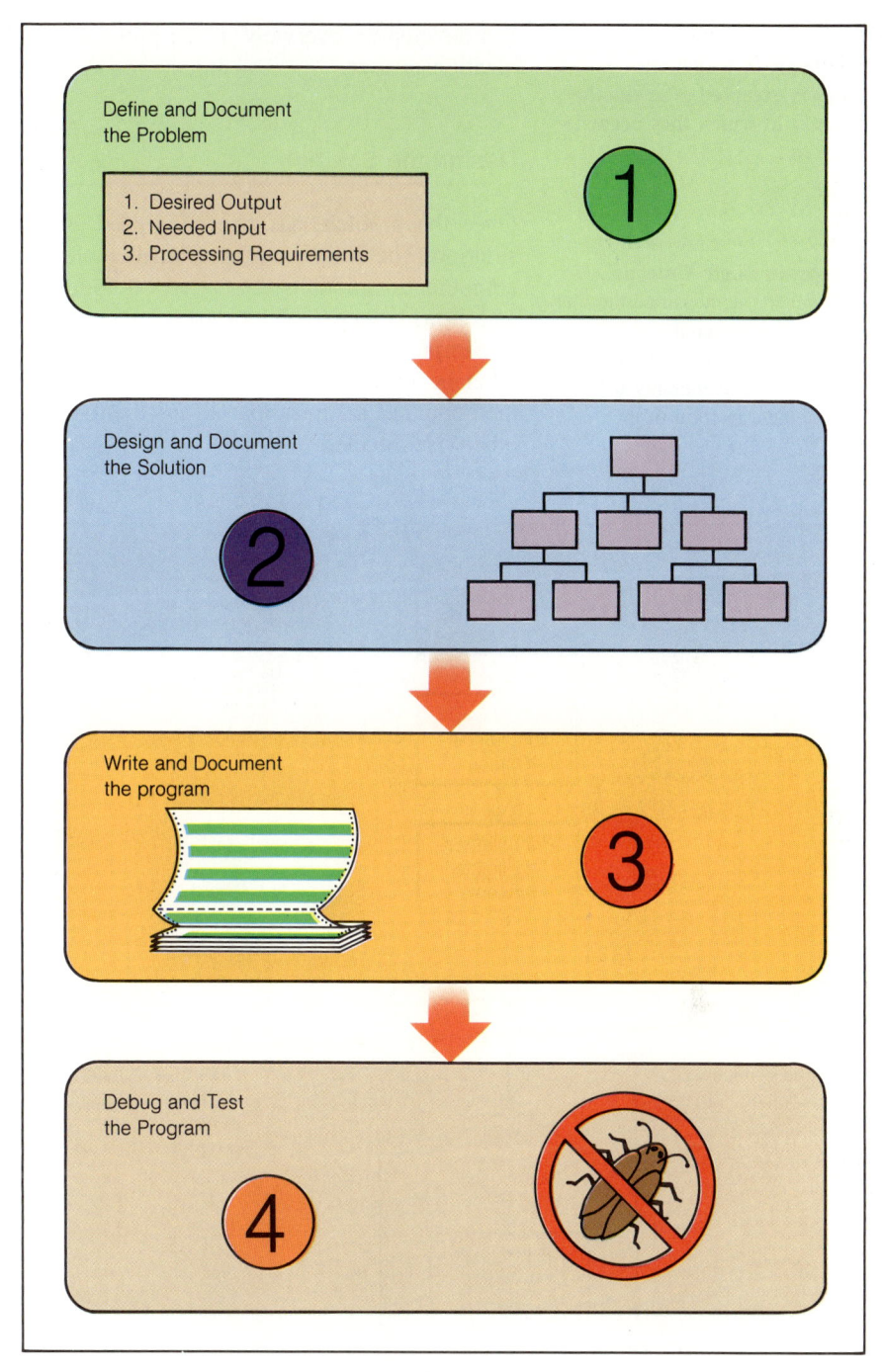

Define and Document the Problem
1. Desired Output
2. Needed Input
3. Processing Requirements
①

Design and Document the Solution
②

Write and Document the program
③

Debug and Test the Program
④

SYSTEM ANALYST
A person who is the communication link or interface between users and technical persons; responsible for designing software.

form will the information be most useful to the intended users? The answers to such questions provide the desired output, the needed input, and the processing requirements for solving the problem.

Not all of these questions can be answered by the programmer. Some guidance often is needed from management. An information specialist, the **system analyst**,

SIMPLE SEQUENCE
Program logic in which one statement is executed after another, in the order in which they occur in the program.

Figure 4-2
Four Program Logic Patterns
These flowcharts demonstrate the four logic patterns. Structured programming languages use only the first three. BASIC commonly uses the GOTO statement, a form of the branch.

can develop an overview of the problem and how its solution can help an organization or user.

Design the Solution

Once the problem has been analyzed, the programmer can begin designing a solution. The design requires considerable creativity from the programmer, but all computer instructions are based on four basic logic patterns: simple sequence, selection, branch, and loop (see Figure 4-2).

Simple sequence logic involves executing instructions one statement after another in consecutive order. It is the simplest and most often used pattern. In fact, the computer assumes that all instructions are to be executed in this order unless otherwise directed.

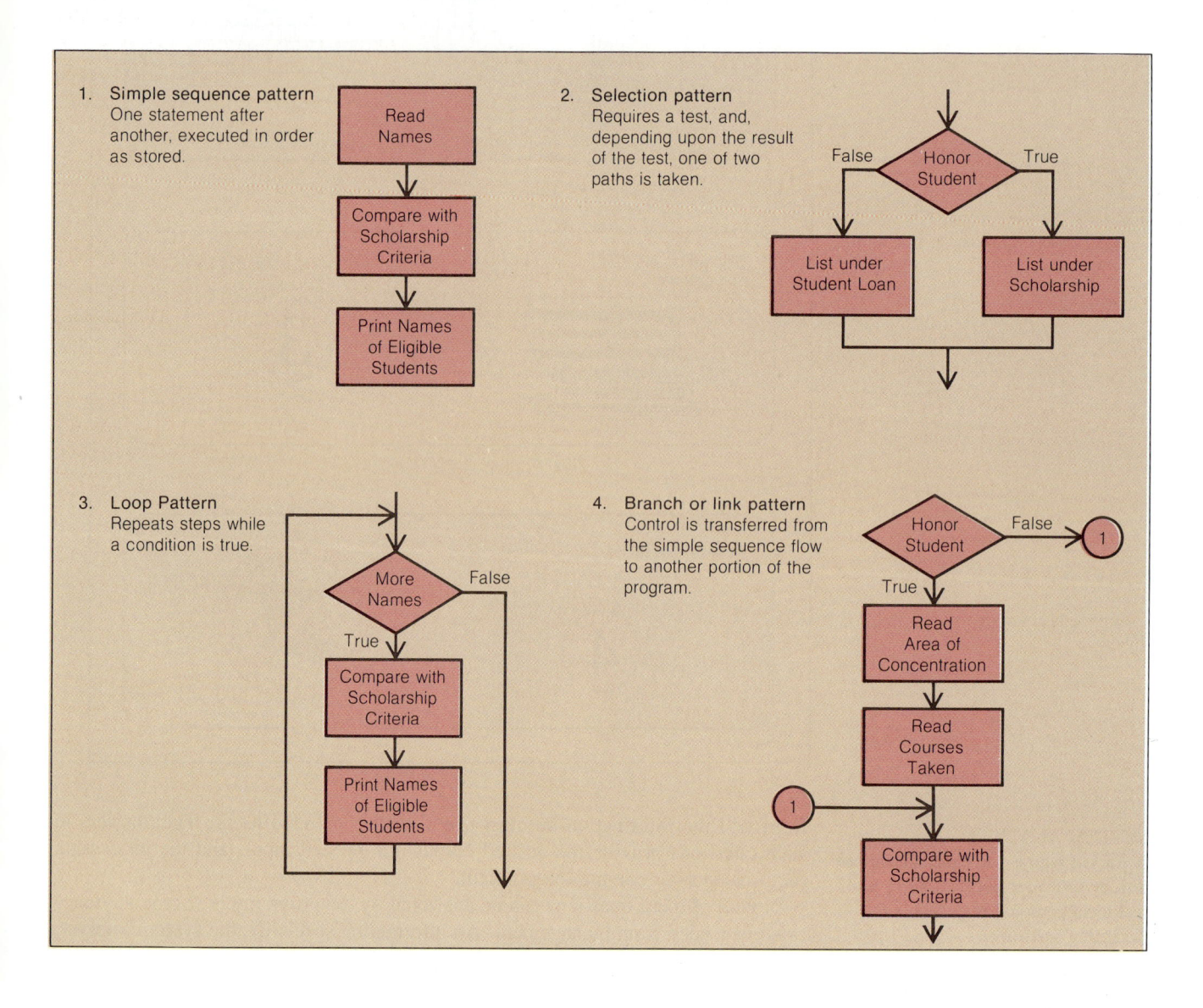

1. **Simple sequence pattern**
   One statement after another, executed in order as stored.

2. **Selection pattern**
   Requires a test, and, depending upon the result of the test, one of two paths is taken.

3. **Loop Pattern**
   Repeats steps while a condition is true.

4. **Branch or link pattern**
   Control is transferred from the simple sequence flow to another portion of the program.

CHAPTER 4: SOFTWARE DEVELOPMENT

SELECTION
Program logic that requires the computer to make a comparison; the result of the comparison determines which execution path will be taken next.

BRANCH
Program logic used to bypass or alter the normal flow of program execution.

LOOP
Program logic that allows a specified sequence of instructions to be executed repeatedly, as long as stated conditions are met.

ALGORITHM
A set of well-defined instructions that outline the solution of a problem in a finite number of steps.

PSEUDOCODE
An informal, narrative language used for representing the logic of a programming problem solution.

FLOWCHART
A graphic representation in which symbols represent the flow of operations, logic, data, and equipment of a program or system.

The **selection** pattern requires the computer to choose from two or more items. Each choice is based on one of the three comparisons a computer can make: equal to, less than, or greater than. When complex selections must be made, several comparisons can be combined. For example, the computer can select employees who have worked for a company for ten years or longer, or determine whether your checking account is overdrawn.

A variation of selection is the **branch.** The branch pattern allows the computer to skip statements in a program, based on the answer to a question. The branch often is signaled with the command GOTO. Frequent use of branching results in a program that is inefficient and difficult for other programmers to follow. According to many experts, few or no GOTO statements are needed in a well-planned program.

A **loop** pattern directs the computer to loop back through previous instructions in the program. A given set of statements can be performed as many times as needed. By looping, a programmer avoids writing the same set of instructions over and over. For example, a loop might be used in figuring weekly pay for 500 employees or in calculating your telephone bill. Because the loop and selection patterns pass control to another part of a program, statements that signal those patterns are known as control statements or control structures.

In order to avoid writing and using faulty programs, programmers must carefully formulate an outline of the logic used to solve the problem. This outline is called an **algorithm.** An algorithm outlines the desired sequence and details of instructions so they can be checked for errors. Two popular ways of representing algorithms are with pseudocode and flowcharts.

Pseudocode is a brief set of instructions written in prose form in the order that the instructions will appear in the actual program (see Figure 4-3). Pseudocode allows the program planner to focus on the steps required for performing a particular task rather than on the rules of a particular programming language. Pseudocoding is similar to writing an outline or a rough draft for a term paper.

Like pseudocode, the **flowchart** is a skeleton of the program. It is a diagram of the necessary steps, rather than a prose statement. Other names for flowcharts are block diagrams, logic diagrams, and logic charts. Accurate flowcharts, both in their original and updated forms, are good visible records of programs and how they were designed. When drawing flowcharts, programmers should use the stan-

Figure 4-3
Pseudocode for a Payroll Processing Example

```
Begin
Begin loop; perform until no more records
        Read employee's name, hours
        worked, and hourly wage
        Calculate gross pay
        Calculate withholdings
        Calculate net pay
        Print check
End loop
Generate summary reports
End
```

CODING
The process of writing a programming problem solution in a programming language.

MACHINE LANGUAGE
A code that the computer can execute directly, and that designates electrical states in the computer as combinations of 0s and 1s.

ASSEMBLY LANGUAGE
A low-level programming language that uses abbreviations called mnemonics, rather than the groupings of 0s and 1s used in machine language.

HIGH-LEVEL LANGUAGE
A language that is oriented more toward the user than the computer system (contrast with low-level language).

LANGUAGE-TRANSLATOR PROGRAM
A system program that translates programming languages other than machine language into machine-executable code.

SOURCE PROGRAM
A program written in a language other than machine language, which must be translated into machine language before execution can occur.

OBJECT PROGRAM
A sequence of machine-executable instructions generated by a language translator program from source program statements.

ASSEMBLER PROGRAM
The translator program for an assembly language program; produces a machine language program that can be executed.

INTERPRETER PROGRAM
A high-level language translator that evaluates and translates a program one statement at a time.

dard flowchart symbols established by the American National Standards Institute (ANSI) and keep the flowcharts complete, up to date, and legible (see Figures 4-4 and 4-5).

Write the Program

Writing the program involves translating the algorithm or flowchart into a programming language. This process is also known as **coding.** The language chosen depends upon what the program is expected to do and what facilities are available to the programmer. A well-written program should be:

- Easy to read and understand. The program should be written so that another programmer can see quickly what the program does.
- Reliable. The program should consistently produce the right output.
- Workable under all conditions. Even when incorrect or inappropriate input data is entered, the program's internal logic should cause it to operate correctly.
- Easy to modify and update. Programs should be constructed in independent, structured segments, so that a change in one segment does not mandate a change in others. (Structured programming is discussed later in this chapter.)
- Portable. A program should be usable on other computers with little or no modification.
- Efficient. Programs should execute as quickly as possible.

Compile, Debug, and Test the Program

After a program has been written, it is submitted to the computer for translation into **machine language. Assembly** and **high-level languages** are used by programmers much more widely than machine language, but these languages cannot be executed directly by computers, so they are converted into machine-executable form by a **language-translator program.** The instructions written by the programmer (the **source program**) are transformed by the language-translator program into machine language (the **object program**).

The translator program for assembly language is an **assembler program,** and a high-level language translator is either an **interpreter program** or a **compiler program.** (Many high-level languages are available in both compiled and interpreted versions.) Translator programs are designed for specific machines and languages. A compiler that translates a program written in FORTRAN into machine language cannot translate COBOL statements, for example.

During the compilation process, the object program is generated and the programmer receives a listing that indicates any errors detected during translation. Compilers translate the source program all at once. Interpreters, on the other hand, translate the source program one instruction at a time. The interpreter reads a program statement by statement—first checking for errors, then translating the statement, and finally executing the statement before proceeding to the next one.

Once the program (or statement, in the case of an interpreted language) has been translated, the programmer must locate and correct any errors before the program will run correctly. This is part of the debugging process. In general,

**Figure 4-4
Flowchart Symbols**

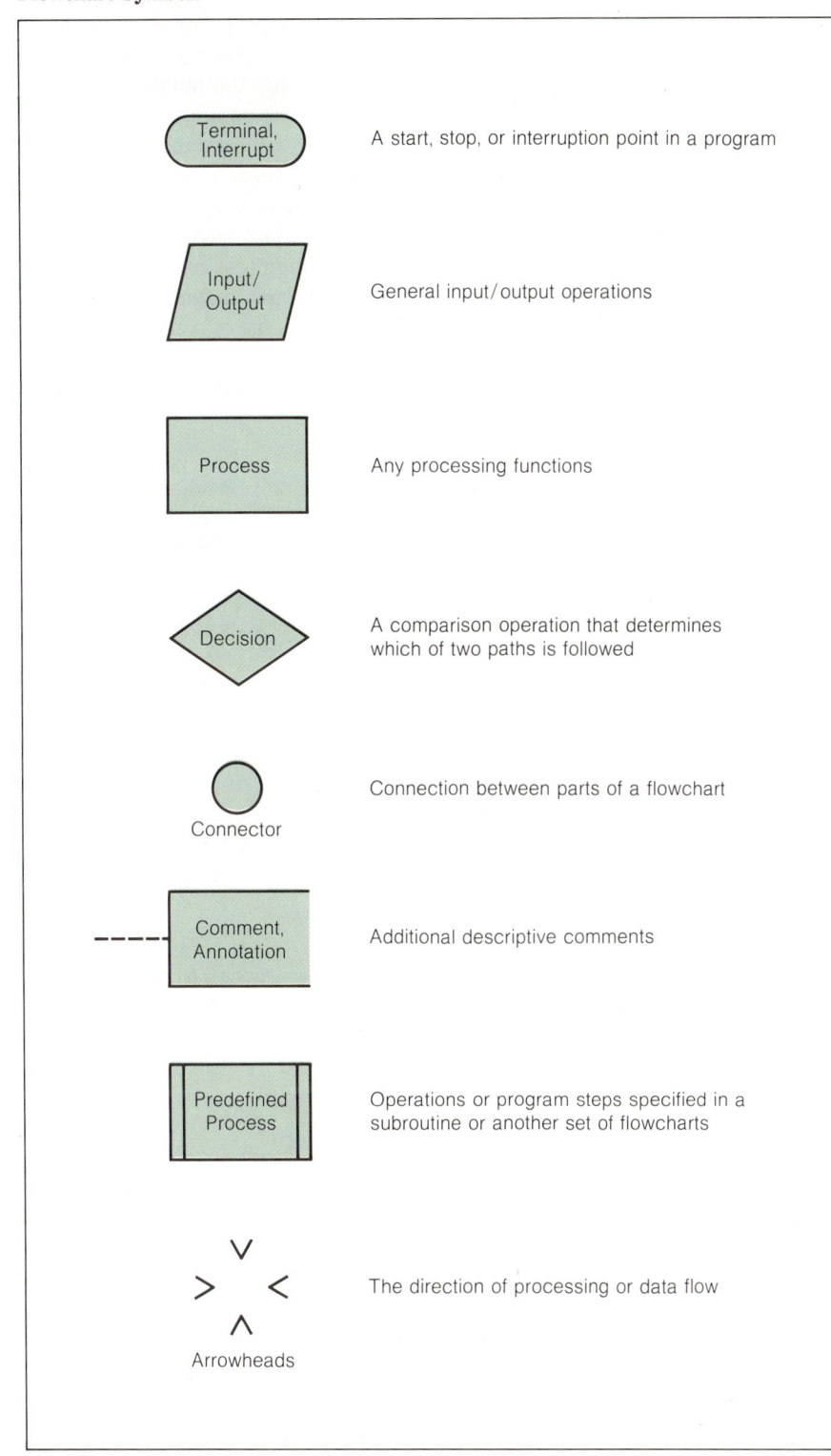

Symbol	Name	Description
(oval)	Terminal, Interrupt	A start, stop, or interruption point in a program
(parallelogram)	Input/Output	General input/output operations
(rectangle)	Process	Any processing functions
(diamond)	Decision	A comparison operation that determines which of two paths is followed
(circle)	Connector	Connection between parts of a flowchart
(rectangle with dashed line)	Comment, Annotation	Additional descriptive comments
(rectangle with double sides)	Predefined Process	Operations or program steps specified in a subroutine or another set of flowcharts
> < ∨ ∧	Arrowheads	The direction of processing or data flow

**Figure 4-5
Flowchart Example**

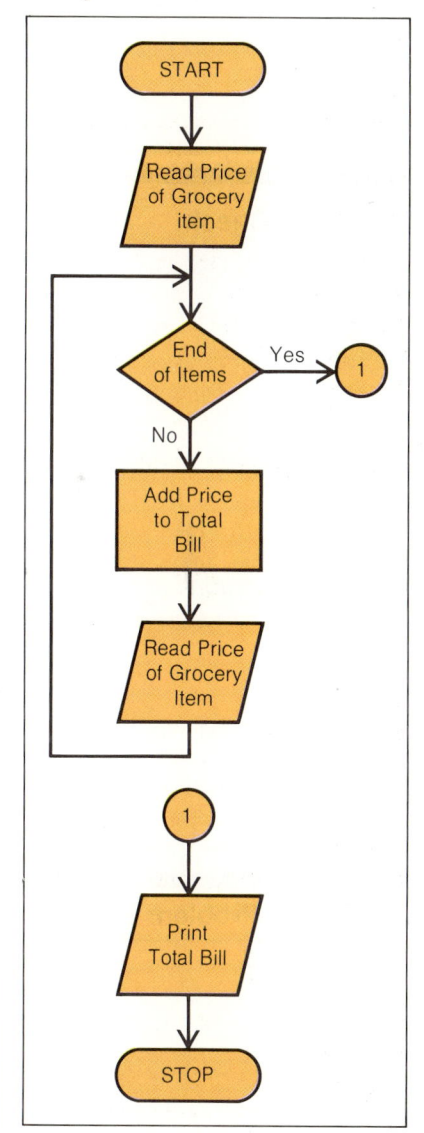

START → Read Price of Grocery item → End of Items? — Yes → (1)
No ↓
Add Price to Total Bill → Read Price of Grocery Item → (loop back to End of Items)

(1) → Print Total Bill → STOP

there are three types of computer errors: syntax errors, run-time errors, and logic errors.

Syntax errors violate the rules of grammar of a particular programming language. Run-time errors occur when the programmer tells the computer to do something it cannot do. For example, if you told the computer to add ten numbers but only gave it nine numbers, a run-time error would occur as the computer tried to read missing data. Logic errors are the worst type of errors, because they produce no error messages. A program with a logic error compiles and executes as if everything were working fine, but the computer returns the wrong answer. When a program does not perform as expected after the syntax and run-time errors are corrected, the logic probably is faulty. See Figure 4-6 for a debugging session using a BASIC interpreter. Notice that the computer stops processing when a syntax or run-time error is detected. Then look at Figure 4-7 for a portion of a list of compiler-detected errors.

Testing should occur at every stage of program development. To learn more about testing, read Program Testing in the next section.

Learning Check

1. List the four steps in the programming process.
2. Which logic pattern is illustrated when a professor repeats the same process to calculate a grade for each student in a class?
3. Which logic pattern is illustrated when you decide you have enough money to buy a personal computer?
4. Name two ways in which you can illustrate an algorithm.
5. If you were shopping for a programming language that would translate a program line by line and give you error messages at appropriate spots within the program, what word would you use to describe this language?

Answers

1. Define the problem, design the solution, write the program, and compile, debug, and test the program. 2. The loop. 3. Selection (if MONEY = X, then buy computer). 4. Pseudocode; flowchart. 5. Interpreter.

Structured Problem Solving

In the early days of software development, there were no standards or concrete rules. A programmer's objective was to develop a program that executed properly, without regard for how this was accomplished or who else might read the program. This approach created programs that were unreliable, difficult to follow, and expensive to maintain. Furthermore, without standard design procedures, a pro-

Figure 4-6 A Debugging Session Using an Interpreter

```
100 REM *** THIS PROGRAM WILL ADD FIVE GRADES, ***
110 REM *** CALCULATE THE AVERAGE, AND DETERMINE ***
120 REM *** A FINAL LETTER GRADE FOR EACH STUDENT ***
130 REM
140 REM *** PRINT HEADINGS ***
150 PRINT
160 PRNT TAB( 35);"FINAL"
170 PRINT  TAB( 8);"NAME"; TAB( 25);"AVERAGE"; TAB( 35);"GRADE"
180 PRINT
190 FOR J = 1 TO 5
200 REM *** READ DATA ***
210 READ N,G1,G2,G3,G4,G5
220 REM *** AVERAGE GRADES ***
230 LET T = G1 + G2 + G3 + G4 + G5
240 LET A = T / 5
250 REM *** DETERMINE LETTER GRADE ***
260 IF A > = 90 THEN F$ = A
270 IF A > = 80 AND A < 90 THEN F$ = "B"
280 IF A > = 70 AND A < 80 THEN F$ = "C"
290 IF A > = 60 AND A < 70 THEN F$ = "D"
300 IF A < 60F$ = "F"
310 REM *** PRINT DATA ***
320 PRINT N$; TAB( 27);A; TAB( 37);F$
330 REM
340 REM *** DATA ***
350 DATA "FRED J. SMITH",70,65,24,100,98
360 DATA "JASON JACKSON",97,96,59,78,60
370 DATA "JOHN S. LAWSON",90,94,88,98,96
380 DATA "SUSAN EAKINS",83,76,87,89,95
390 DATA "MARY Q. JOHNSON",66,79,83,75,70
999 END
```

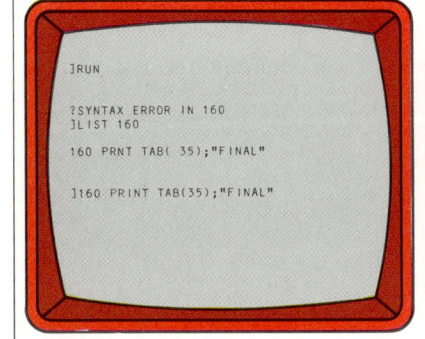

Error 1:

```
]RUN

?SYNTAX ERROR IN 160
]LIST 160

160 PRNT TAB( 35);"FINAL"

]160 PRINT TAB(35);"FINAL"
```

The syntax error is that PRINT is spelled PRNT. When that error is corrected, the program will run until another error is detected.

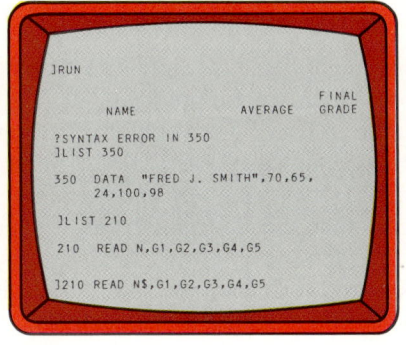

Error 2:

```
]RUN

                            FINAL
        NAME       AVERAGE  GRADE
?SYNTAX ERROR IN 350
]LIST 350

350  DATA "FRED J. SMITH",70,65,
     24,100,98

]LIST 210

210  READ N,G1,G2,G3,G4,G5

]210 READ N$,G1,G2,G3,G4,G5
```

The computer indicates an error in line 350, but when 350 is listed, we see that it is typed correctly. A review of the program reveals that the error is in line 210, where the variable N should have been typed N$ to show that the variable values are words rather than numbers.

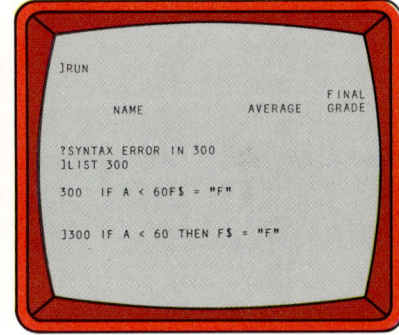

Error 3:

```
]RUN

                            FINAL
        NAME       AVERAGE  GRADE
?SYNTAX ERROR IN 300
]LIST 300

300  IF A < 60F$ = "F"

]300 IF A < 60 THEN F$ = "F"
```

The syntax error in line 300 is the omission of the word THEN.

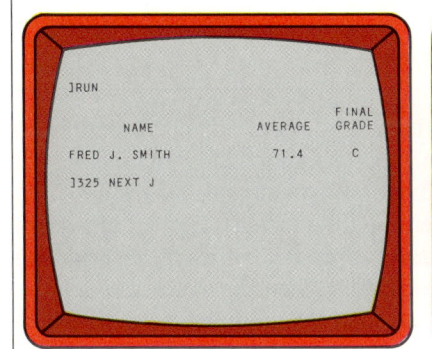

Error 4:

```
]RUN

                            FINAL
        NAME       AVERAGE  GRADE

FRED J. SMITH       71.4     C

]325 NEXT J
```

The program runs, but for only one name. Since we know there are five names typed in the DATA list, there must be an error. The NEXT statement has been omitted.

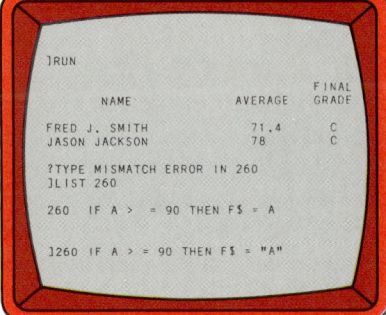

Error 5:

```
]RUN

                            FINAL
        NAME       AVERAGE  GRADE
FRED J. SMITH       71.4     C
JASON JACKSON       78       C
?TYPE MISMATCH ERROR IN 260
]LIST 260

260  IF A > = 90 THEN F$ = A

]260 IF A > = 90 THEN F$ = "A"
```

A "TYPE MISMATCH ERROR" is indicated for line 260. Upon examination, we see that the variable name does not match the variable value. Therefore, we change F$ = A to F$ = "A" to show that the variable value is a string.

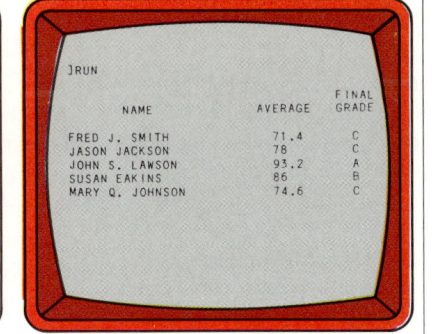

The program runs correctly

```
]RUN

                            FINAL
        NAME       AVERAGE  GRADE
FRED J. SMITH       71.4     C
JASON JACKSON       78       C
JOHN S. LAWSON      93.2     A
SUSAN EAKINS        86       B
MARY Q. JOHNSON     74.6     C
```

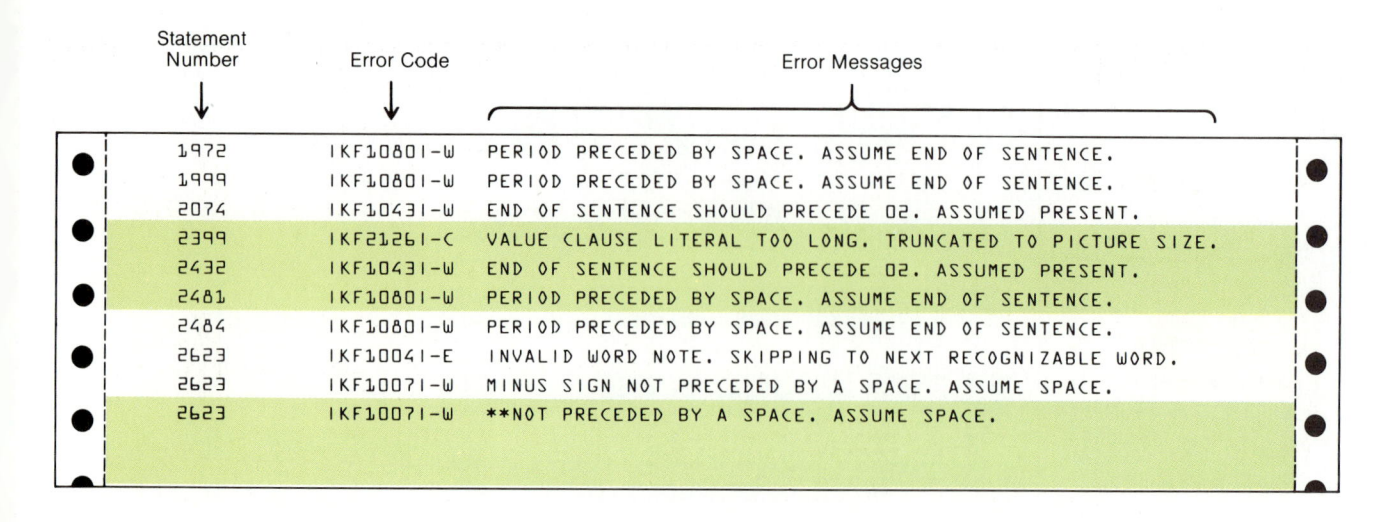

```
Statement
 Number       Error Code                       Error Messages

  1972        IKF1080I-W    PERIOD PRECEDED BY SPACE. ASSUME END OF SENTENCE.
  1999        IKF1080I-W    PERIOD PRECEDED BY SPACE. ASSUME END OF SENTENCE.
  2074        IKF1043I-W    END OF SENTENCE SHOULD PRECEDE 02. ASSUMED PRESENT.
  2399        IKF2126I-C    VALUE CLAUSE LITERAL TOO LONG. TRUNCATED TO PICTURE SIZE.
  2432        IKF1043I-W    END OF SENTENCE SHOULD PRECEDE 02. ASSUMED PRESENT.
  2481        IKF1080I-W    PERIOD PRECEDED BY SPACE. ASSUME END OF SENTENCE.
  2484        IKF1080I-W    PERIOD PRECEDED BY SPACE. ASSUME END OF SENTENCE.
  2623        IKF1004I-E    INVALID WORD NOTE. SKIPPING TO NEXT RECOGNIZABLE WORD.
  2623        IKF1007I-W    MINUS SIGN NOT PRECEDED BY A SPACE. ASSUME SPACE.
  2623        IKF1007I-W    **NOT PRECEDED BY A SPACE. ASSUME SPACE.
```

Figure 4-7
Compiler-Detected Errors
A programmer receives a list of errors after the entire program has been translated. Once the errors are corrected, the program must be recompiled before it can be executed.

grammer might spend far more time than necessary in determining an appropriate solution and writing the program.

In order to offset these tendencies, programmers defined structured programming techniques in the early 1970s. **Structured programming** encourages programmers to think about the problem first, rather than spending an unreasonable amount of time on debugging later. Structured programming has four goals:

1. Reducing time and costs associated with program development.
2. Increasing programmer productivity.
3. Increasing clarity by reducing complexity.
4. Decreasing time and effort required to maintain a program once it is implemented.

STRUCTURED PROGRAMMING
A collection of techniques that encourage the development of well-designed, less error-prone programs with easy-to-follow logic.

Four methodologies characterize structured programming: top-down design, program documentation, program testing during all states of the problem-solving process, and use of a programming team.

TOP-DOWN DESIGN
A method of defining a solution in terms of major functions to be performed, and breaking down the major functions into subfunctions.

Top-Down Design

The most difficult part of programming is learning how to organize solutions in a clear, concise way. One method of organizing a solution is to define the major steps or functions first and then expand the functions into more detailed steps later. This method, which proceeds from the general to the specific, is called **top-down design.** Top-down design employs the **modular approach,** which means breaking a problem into smaller and smaller subproblems. When the actual program is written, these subproblems can be written as separate **modules,** each of which performs a specific task.

MODULAR APPROACH
A method of simplifying a programming project by breaking it into segments or subunits referred to as modules.

MODULE
A program segment that performs one specified task in a program.

The most general level of organization is the main control module. This overall definition of the solution is critical to the success of the program. Modules at this level contain broad descriptions of the steps in the solution process. These steps are further detailed in several lower-level modules. Depending on the complexity

HIGHLIGHT ▲▲▲▲▲▲▲▲▲▲▲▲▲▲▲▲▲▲▲▲▲

Software Prices Dropping?

Back in 1981, Adam Osborne pioneered the concept of inexpensive transportable computers by shipping the first Osborne 1. Now he's at it again. No longer with Osborne Computer Corporation, Adam Osborne is selling inexpensive software primarily through bookstores. His company, Paperback Software International, reflects his philosophy: If people pay a lot of money for software packages, they don't buy many of them. If the packages are less expensive, they buy a lot more.

Osborne believes the same thing will happen with software as happened with hardware: Inexpensive—and perhaps better—clones of expensive, well-known brands will edge into the market.

Many of the new software packages do not have the perceived value necessary for people to pay hundreds of dollar per package out of idle curiosity. Customers want to be reassured that software will be useful to them. If a program costs only $50, they may try it without worrying too much about long-term usefulness. When software prices drop, people will realize that low-cost software can be good—and they will buy lots of it. Software essentially will be bought like books, at $25 to $50 per program. So now we will wait and see if Adam Osborne is right.

STRUCTURE CHART
A graphic representation of the results of the top-down design process, displaying the modules and their relationships to one another.

of the problem, several levels of modules may be required, with the lowest-level modules containing the greatest amount of detail. Figure 4-8 shows a diagram of a top-down design for inventory control. The diagram, called a **structure chart,** illustrates the various modules and their relationships to one another. When the program is coded, each box in the structure chart is written as a separate module performing a specific task.

When writing a program in modular form, the programmer uses only three of the four logic patterns: the simple sequence, selection, and loop. The branch pattern (including the GOTO statement) is avoided, thus limiting the amount of jumping around that can occur otherwise. The modules should be small in order to make programming and debugging easier. Each module should have only one entry point and one exit point, so that a programmer can follow the flow of instructions easily. A program whose modules have only one entrance and one exit is called a **proper program.** Programs developed in this manner tend to have fewer errors than unstructured programs, because the logic is readily apparent.

PROPER PROGRAM
A structured program in which each individual segment or module has only one entrance and one exit.

Documentation

DOCUMENTATION
Written material that accompanies a program and includes definitions, explanations, charts, tests, and records of changes to the program.

Documentation is text that explains the program. Sometimes it is listed as a separate programming step, but in fact it should occur during each of the four programming steps. Documentation begins with the initial request for a program and continues throughout the problem-solving process and into program maintenance. It describes what the program should do, what data is needed, how data is identified in the program statements, and how the output is formatted.

In top-down design, documentation describes the modules as well, explaining their individual functions and their relationship to the entire program. Documentation also includes the flowcharts or pseudocode produced during program design, the tests and data used to check the program, and any changes made to the program.

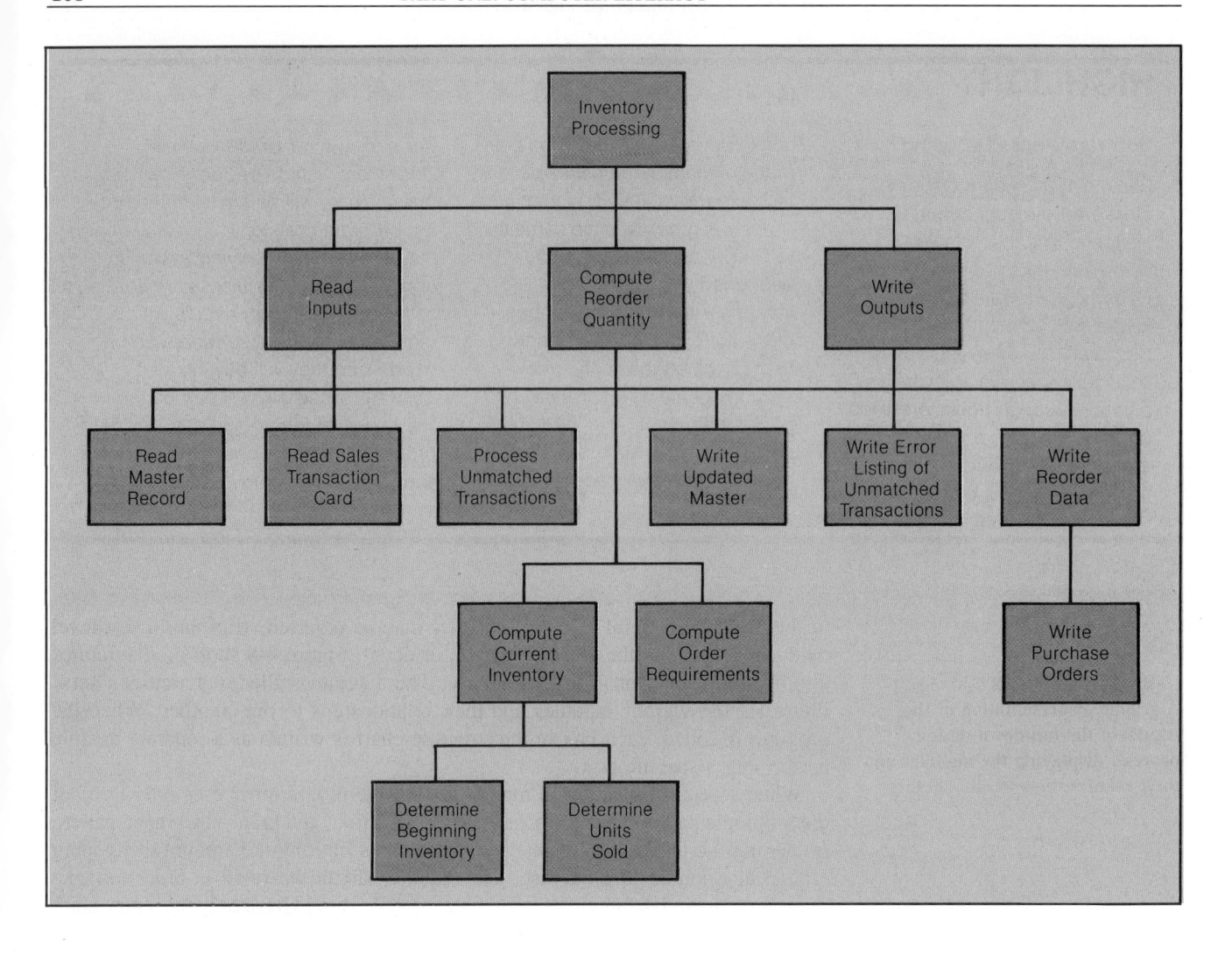

Figure 4-8
Structure Chart for Inventory Control

Other important documentation provides instructions to program users and lists hardware requirements for running the program. A paper copy of the actual computer program is a part of documentation.

An example of documentation is a user's manual that explains how to use a program or piece of computer hardware. You also use documentation when you follow program instructions that appear on a computer monitor. If you read a copy of the actual computer program, you might also see documentation interspersed throughout.

Program Testing

At each step during the problem-solving process, the program should be tested before going on to the next step. This approach often was ignored during the early years of programming, and testing occurred after an entire program was completed. Corrections were made in a haphazard manner, and major errors often were discovered after the programs were implemented. Software buyers commonly were discouraged by programs that did not work correctly. Today, software developers test their programs more thoroughly, yet errors still occur. Clearly, testing is an important step in developing reliable software.

Testing involves executing the program with input data that is either a representative sample of actual data or a facsimile of it. Even incorrect data can be entered, in order to see how the program reacts. The results should be compared with correct results determined by the programmer. Testing cannot prove that the program will work in all situations, but it decreases the likelihood of problems. Each time a program is modified during testing and debugging, the documentation must be rewritten to reflect the changes.

The Programming Team

CHIEF PROGRAMMER TEAM (CPT)
A method of organization in which a chief programmer supervises the development and testing of software.

A popular method of organizing and managing system projects involves the use of a **chief programmer team (CPT).** The purpose of a CPT is to facilitate the goals of structured programming. Team members review one another's work and the accompanying documentation at each stage of development, making suggestions for changes and improvements. The CPT usually includes a chief programmer (often a system analyst), who is responsible for the overall coordination and development of the project. Depending on the size and complexity of the project, the team may also have a number of regular programmers, each working on a different module, and a librarian who updates the documentation and performs other clerical tasks.

Learning Check

1. The goals of structured programming include reducing the _____ and _____ associated with program development while increasing _____.

2. Top-down design involves breaking a problem into subproblems that can be written as separate _____, each performing a particular task.

3. Name at least one other characteristic of structured programming.

Answers

1. Time; costs; productivity. 2. Modules. 3. Documentation; limited jumping within the program; adequate program testing; the chief programmer team.

Types of Programs

The programming methods we have described are used in generating the two basic types of programs: **system programs,** which coordinate the operation of the computer, and **application programs,** which solve user problems.

HIGHLIGHT ▲▲▲▲▲▲▲▲▲▲▲▲▲▲▲▲▲▲▲▲▲

Programs As Models of the Real World

Computer scientists often try to create programs that resemble or reflect real-life situations. In other words, they attempt to produce programs that correspond closely with the processes they are controlling and which can act, in a sense, as models of the real world.

An article in *Science Digest,* December 1985, reports on the work of Peter Oppenheimer, a research scientist at the New York Institute of Technology Computer Graphics Laboratory. After studying the crystalline structure of snowflakes, Oppenheimer decided to generate computer images of them. He started with a tiny "seed image." Then he designed a computer algorithm that modified the seed pattern to make a new image, which in turn served as the basis for a new modification. He was able to do this because of a property found in nature, called self-similarity. Self-similarity means that if a small part of an image is magnified, it resembles the geometric structure of the whole.

Using a mathematical definition of self-similarity, computer scientists have been able to construct graphic images that resemble natural phenomena such as Oppenheimer's snowflake images. Oppenheimer says that the logic of the computer scientist reflects the logic of life. In this sense the program is the model, and its output, the images produced, is the test. If the image looks right, then the model must be in some sense a valid image of the real world.

SYSTEM PROGRAM
Instructions written for coordinating the operation of computer circuitry and helping the computer run quickly and efficiently.

APPLICATION PROGRAM
A sequence of instructions written for solving a specific user problem.

System programs directly affect the operation of the computer. They are designed for efficient and fast use of the hardware. System software includes a variety of programs such as operating systems, utility programs, and language translators. A system program may, for example, allocate storage for data being entered into the system. The programs vary from computer to computer and cannot be used without modification on different machines. System programming normally is provided by the computer manufacturer or by a specialized programming firm.

Application programs perform specific data processing or computational tasks for solving an organization's information needs, or help an individual with personal or educational tasks. They can be developed by the user or purchased from software firms. Typical examples of application programs include those used by businesses for inventory control and accounting, and by banks for updates in customer accounts. Application programs also help in preparing documents, drawing graphs, learning new skills, and filing data. Several types of application programs are discussed in Part II of this text.

Operating Systems

OPERATING SYSTEM (OS)
A collection of system programs used by the computer for managing its own operations.

When computer systems were in their infancy, human operators monitored computer operations, decided the order in which the programs would run, and handled input and output devices. Although the processing speeds of CPUs increased, the speed of human operators stayed the same. This situation created time delays and errors. **Operating systems,** developed in the 1960s, eased the problem. An operating system is a collection of programs that the computer uses to manage its own operations at computer speeds. An operating system provides the interface between the user and the applications programs and computer hardware (see Figure 4-9).

Each program in an operating system performs a specific duty. Because all operating system programs work as a "team," idle CPU time is avoided and use of computer facilities is increased. Operating system programs usually are stored on a secondary storage medium (magnetic tape or disk) and are called into primary storage when needed.

Two types of programs make up the operating system: control programs and processing programs. Control programs oversee system operations and perform tasks such as communicating with input/output devices, scheduling tasks, and communicating with the computer operator or programmers. One type of control program, the supervisor program, is the major component of the operating system. It coordinates the activities of all other parts of the operating system. When the computer is first put into use, the supervisor is the first program to be transferred into primary storage from the system residence device. The supervisor schedules input/output operations and allocates channels to various input/output devices. It also sends message to the computer operator, indicating the status of particular jobs, error conditions, and so forth.

Processing programs are executed under the supervision of control programs. Their purpose is to simplify program preparation for the computer system. The principal processing programs are language translators, library programs, and utility programs. The language translator program translates the source programs written by humans into object programs of machine-language instructions. A library program maintains a directory of programs in secondary storage and contains procedures for adding and deleting programs. Utility programs perform specialized functions, such as transferring data from tape to disk, or from tape to printer.

Figure 4-9
Operating System As Interface

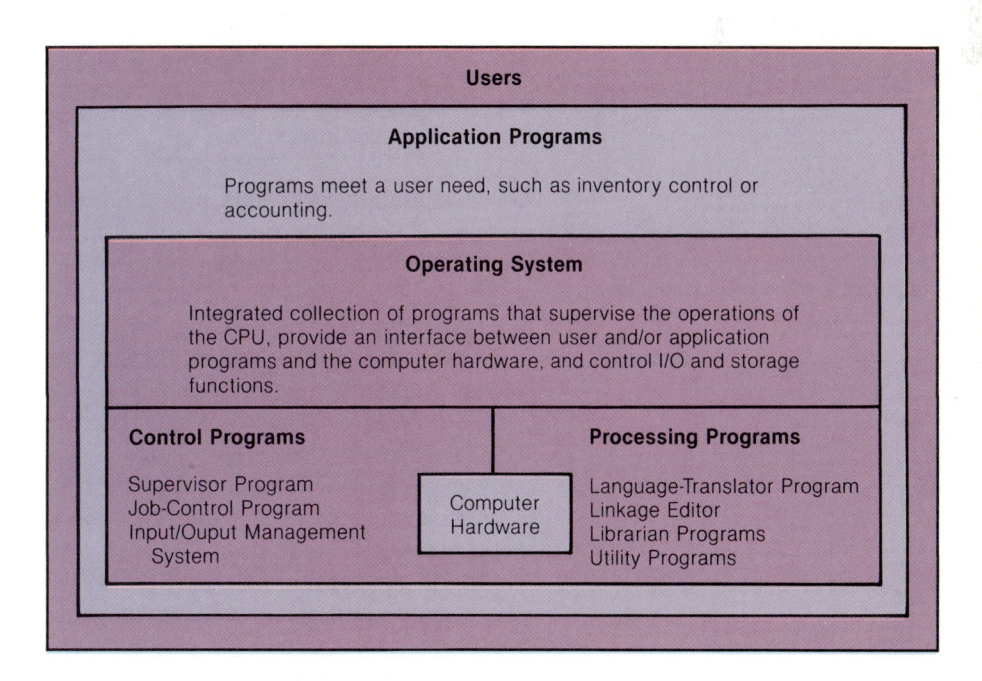

Users

Application Programs

Programs meet a user need, such as inventory control or accounting.

Operating System

Integrated collection of programs that supervise the operations of the CPU, provide an interface between user and/or application programs and the computer hardware, and control I/O and storage functions.

Control Programs

Supervisor Program
Job-Control Program
Input/Ouput Management System

Computer Hardware

Processing Programs

Language-Translator Program
Linkage Editor
Librarian Programs
Utility Programs

Learning Check

1. A program that translates a high-level language into machine language and a program that communicates with a disk drive are examples of _____ programs.
2. Why were operating systems developed?
3. What does the supervisor program do?
4. Besides the type of program mentioned in question 1, what other type of program is there? Give a general or specific example of one.

Answers

1. System. 2. To allow the computer to handle its own operations at its own speed (human operators were too slow). 3. It coordinates the activities of all other parts of the operating system; schedules input/output operations, allocates channels to various hardware devices, and communicates with the computer user. 4. Application program; software used for outlining a paper (for example, ThinkTank).

Programming Languages

SYNTAX
The grammatical rules of a language.

Programming languages are used during the coding stage of the programming process. Like the languages we use for everyday speech, programming languages have their own rules. This group of rules governing a language is called **syntax.** A computer program with incorrect syntax cannot run. Some languages are suited for scientific uses, some for business uses, some for artificial intelligence, and so on. Several languages are described in the following paragraphs.

Low-Level Languages

LOW-LEVEL LANGUAGE
A machine-oriented language; machine language and assembly languages are low-level languages.

Low-level languages give the programmer direct control over details of computer hardware. They enable the programmer to specify memory locations, direct input and output operations, and govern the use of registers. Each type of computer has its own low-level languages, which are not transferable to other types of computers. Each instruction in a low-level language must state not only the operation required, but also the storage locations of the data items. For this reason, the programmer must know exactly how the specific computer works.

The lowest-level language is **machine language,** which designates the on/off electrical states of the digital computer. Being so closely linked to computer operations, it is the only language that the computer can execute directly. Programs written in any other language must be translated into machine language before the computer can execute them.

Machine language is the most efficient language in terms of storage area use and execution speed. It allows the programmer to use all of the computer's potential for processing data. Coding a program in machine language, however, is very tedious, time-consuming, and error-prone.

MNEMONICS
Symbolic names or memory aids; used in assembly and high-level programming languages.

Assembly languages were developed in order to alleviate many of the disadvantages of machine-language programming. When programming in an assembly language, the programmer uses **mnemonics** (symbolic names) to specify machine operations; thus, coding in 0s and 1s is not required. Mnemonics are alphabetic abbreviations for the machine language instructions. For example, STB might stand for *store in register B,* and LDA might stand for *load register A.* Assembly language programs are highly efficient in terms of storage space and processing. Assembly language often is chosen when fast execution is essential, for example, for writing operating systems. In general, one assembly-language instruction is translated into one machine-language instruction. This one-to-one relationship makes it easier—and therefore faster—for the computer to translate the program into machine language than to translate a high-level language into machine language. (See Figure 4-10 for a comparison of machine instructions and assembly instructions.)

High-Level Languages

High-level languages enable the programmer to focus on problem solving rather than on the details of computer operations. They are easier to understand than low-level languages, because they use meaningful words such as READ and PRINT and common mathematical terms and symbols. Although one assembly language statement generally is equivalent to one machine language statement, a single high-level language statement can represent several machine language statements. These features reduce the time needed for writing a program and make programs easier to correct and modify.

During the past 40 years, approximately 400 computer languages have been developed. Many are highly specialized. Their names often are colorful—CLIP,

Figure 4-10
Examples of Assembly Language and Machine Language Codes for Computer Operations

Operation	Typical Assembly Language Codes for Operations	Typical Binary (Machine Language) Codes for Operations
Add memory to register	A	01011010
Add (decimal) memory to register	AP	11111010
Multiply register by memory	M	01011100
Multiply (decimal) register by memory	MP	11111100
Subtract memory from register	S	01011011
Subtract (decimal) memory from register	SP	11111011
Move (numeric) from register to memory	MVN	11010001
Compare memory to register	C	01011001
Compare (decimal) memory to register	CP	11111001
Zero register and add (decimal) memory to register	ZAP	11111000

FLAP, SOAP, SNOBOL, LISP, and TREE, to name a few. Some languages are widely used and have played an important role in the development of the computer industry. Some of the more commonly-used languages are FORTRAN, COBOL, BASIC, Pascal, APL, RPG, C, Ada, Modula-2, FORTH, LISP, and Logo, which are discussed in the following sections.

FORTRAN (FORmula Translator)
The oldest surviving high-level programming language; used primarily for mathematical or scientific operations.

FORTRAN FORTRAN (FORmula TRANslator) is the oldest surviving commercial high-level programming language. It was introduced in the mid-1950s because programmers needed a language that resembled English.

As the language became accepted, several manufacturers offered variations of FORTRAN which could be used only with their own brands of computers. In response to this problem, ANSI laid the groundwork for a standardized FORTRAN. In 1966, two standard versions of FORTRAN were recognized: ANSI FORTRAN and Basic FORTRAN. A more recent version, FORTRAN 77, enhances the language's usefulness and supports structured programming. In spite of these attempts to standardize FORTRAN, however, most computer manufacturers have continued to offer their own extensions of the language. Therefore, compatibility of FORTRAN programs remains a problem.

In 1957, when the language was first released, computers were used primarily by engineers, scientists, and mathematicians. FORTRAN was designed to meet their needs, and this purpose has remained unchanged. FORTRAN provides extraordinary mathematical capabilities and is executed quickly. FORTRAN is not often used for business purposes, because its capabilities are not well suited to programs involving file maintenance, editing of data, or production of documents. Use of FORTRAN is increasing, however, for business applications that require complex mathematics formulas, such as feasibility studies, forecasting, and production scheduling. FORTRAN does not resemble English as closely as do many high-level languages; therefore, the programs must be well documented so that they are understandable. Figure 4-11 contains a simple FORTRAN program that calculates a payroll.

COBOL (COmmon Business-Oriented Language)
A high-level programming language generally used for business applications.

COBOL COBOL (COmmon Business-Oriented Language) is the most popular business programming language. Its specifications were established in 1960 by the Conference of Data Systems Languages (CODASYL) Committee, and the first commercial versions of the language were offered that year. One of the objectives of the CODASYL group was to establish a language that could be used on any computer. When several manufacturers began offering their own modifications and extentions of COBOL, the need for standardization became apparent.

In 1968, ANSI established and published guidelines for a standardized version of COBOL that became known as ANSI COBOL. ANSI has revised these standards twice. The 1974 standards are widely accepted, but new ANSI standards for COBOL were published in 1985. These new standards made many changes to the language, including the addition of structured programming facilities. It will be several years before we know how widely accepted and implemented this new COBOL will be.

COBOL is well suited for handling large amounts of data. It is often used in businesses for storing customer or employee information. Since COBOL is standardized, a firm can switch computer systems with little or no rewriting of existing programs.

Figure 4-11
Payroll Program in FORTRAN

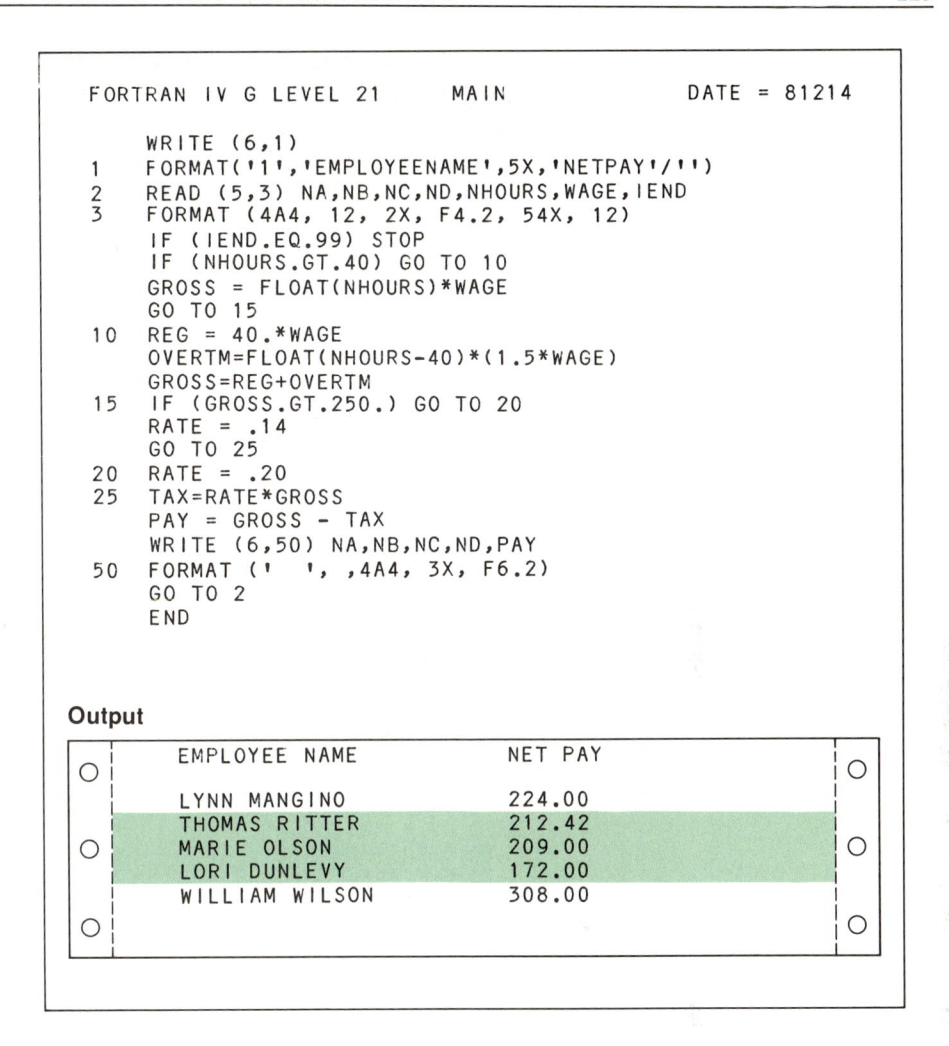

```
FORTRAN IV G LEVEL 21       MAIN            DATE = 81214
       WRITE (6,1)
1      FORMAT('1','EMPLOYEENAME',5X,'NETPAY'/'')
2      READ (5,3) NA,NB,NC,ND,NHOURS,WAGE,IEND
3      FORMAT (4A4, 12, 2X, F4.2, 54X, 12)
       IF (IEND.EQ.99) STOP
       IF (NHOURS.GT.40) GO TO 10
       GROSS = FLOAT(NHOURS)*WAGE
       GO TO 15
10     REG = 40.*WAGE
       OVERTM=FLOAT(NHOURS-40)*(1.5*WAGE)
       GROSS=REG+OVERTM
15     IF (GROSS.GT.250.) GO TO 20
       RATE = .14
       GO TO 25
20     RATE = .20
25     TAX=RATE*GROSS
       PAY = GROSS - TAX
       WRITE (6,50) NA,NB,NC,ND,PAY
50     FORMAT (' ', ,4A4, 3X, F6.2)
       GO TO 2
       END
```

Output

EMPLOYEE NAME	NET PAY
LYNN MANGINO	224.00
THOMAS RITTER	212.42
MARIE OLSON	209.00
LORI DUNLEVY	172.00
WILLIAM WILSON	308.00

Well-written COBOL programs tend to be self-explanatory. This feature makes programs easier to maintain and modify, an important feature because business programs are often expanded and changed. In addition, programmers other than the authors can read COBOL programs, and quickly discern what they do. You can judge the clarity of a COBOL program by looking at the COBOL-coded application in Figure 4-12.

BASIC (Beginners' All-purpose Symbolic Instruction Code)
A high-level programming language commonly available with interpreter programs; often taught to beginning programmers.

BASIC **BASIC,** an acronym for Beginner's All-purpose Symbolic Instruction Code, was developed in the mid-1960s at Dartmouth College to help students learn how to program. Most computer manufacturers offer BASIC support on their computers, and many companies have adapted BASIC for their data processing needs.

Among BASIC's most attractive features are its simplicity and flexibility. Because BASIC is easy to learn, it can be used by people with little or no programming experience. BASIC can be used for solving a wide variety of problems. A BASIC program is shown in Figure 4-13.

Figure 4-12
Payroll Program in COBOL

```
        IDENTIFICATION DIVISION.
        PROGRAM-ID. PAYROLL.
        INPUT-OUTPUT SECTION.
        FILE-CONTROL.
            SELECT CARD-FILE ASIGN TO UR-S-SYSIN.
            SELECT PRINT-FILE ASSIGN TO UR-S-OUTPUT.

        DATA DIVISION.
        FILE SECTION.
        FD  CARD-FILE
            LABEL RECORDS ARE OMITTED
            RECORD CONTAINS 80 CHARACTERS
            DATA RECORD IS PAY-RECORD.
        01  PAY-RECORD.
            03   EMPLOYEE-NAME       PIC A(16).
            03   HOURS-WORKED        PIC 99.
            03   WAGE-PER-HOUR       PIC 99V99.
            03   FILLER              PIC X(58).

        FD  PRINT-FILE
            LABEL RECORDS ARE OMITTED
            RECORD CONTAINS 132 CHARACTERS
            DATA RECORD IS PRINT-RECORD.
        01  PRINT-RECORD             PIC X(132).

        WORKING-STORAGE SECTION.
        77  GROSS-PAY                PIC 9(3)V99.
        77  REGULAR-PAY              PIC 9(3)V99.
        77  OVERTIME-PAY             PIC 9(3)V99.
        77  NET-PAY                  PIC 9(3)V99.
        77  TAX                      PIC 9(3)V99.
        77  OVERTIME-HOURS           PIC 99.
        77  OVERTIME-RATE            PIC 9(3)V999.
        77  EOF-FLAG                 PIC X(3)        VALUE 'NO'.

        01  HEADING-LINE.
            03 FILLER                PIC X           VALUE SPACES.
            03 FILLER                PIC X(21)       VALUE
                'EMPLOYEE NAME'.
            03 FILLER                PIC X(7)        VALUE
                'NET PAY'.

        01  OUTPUT-RECORD.
            03 FILLER                PIC X           VALUE SPACES.
            03 NAME                  PIC A(16).
            03 FILLER                PIC X(5)        VALUE SPACES.
            03 AMOUNT                PIC $$$$.99.
            03 FILLER                PIC X(103)      VALUE SPACES.

        PROCEDURE DIVISION.
        MAIN-LOGIC.
            OPEN INPUT CARD-FILE
                 OUTPUT PRINT-FILE.
            PERFORM HEADING-ROUTINE.
            READ CARD-FILE AT END MOVE 'YES' TO EOF-FLAG.
            PERFORM WORK-LOOP UNTIL EOF-FLAG = 'YES'.
            CLOSE CARD-FILE
                  PRINT-FILE.
            STOP RUN.

        HEADING-ROUTINE.
            WRITE PRINT-RECORD FROM HEADING-LINE
                  BEFORE ADVANCING 2 LINES.
```

Figure 4-12 (continued)

```
WORK-LOOP.
    IF HOURS-WORKED IS GREATER THEN 40
        THEN
            PERFORM OVERTIME-ROUTINE
        ELSE
            MULTIPLY HOURS-WORKED BY WAGE-PER-HOUR
                GIVING GROSS-PAY.
    PERFORM TAX-COMPUTATION.
    PERFORM OUTPUT-ROUTINE.
    READ CARD-FILE AT END MOVE 'YES' TO EOF-FLAG.

OVERTIME-ROUTINE.
    MULTIPLY WAGE-PER-HOUR BY 40 GIVING REGULAR-PAY.
    SUBTRACT 40 FROM HOURS-WORKED GIVING OVERTIME-HOURS.
    MULTIPLY OVERTIME-HOURS BY 1.5 GIVING OVERTIME-RATE.
    MULTIPLY OVERTIME-HOURS BY OVERTIME-RATE
        GIVING OVERTIME-PAY.
    ADD REGULAR-PAY, OVERTIME-PAY GIVING GROSS-PAY.

TAX-COMPUTATION.
    IF GROSS-PAY IS GREATER THEN 250
        THEN
            MULTIPLY GROSS-PAY BY 0.20 GIVING TAX
        ELSE
            MULTIPLY GROSS-PAY BY 0.14 GIVING TAX.
    SUBTRACT TAX FROM GROSS-PAY GIVING NET-PAY.

OUTPUT-ROUTINE.
    MOVE EMPLOYEE-NAME TO NAME.
    MOVE NET-PAY TO AMOUNT.
    WRITE PRINT-RECORD FROM OUTPUT-RECORD
        BEFORE ADVANCING 1 LINES.
```

Output

EMPLOYEE NAME	NET PAY
LYNN MANGINO	224.00
THOMAS RITTER	212.42
MARIE OLSON	209.00
LORI DUNLEVY	172.00
WILLIAM WILSON	308.00

The main criticism of BASIC focuses on the fact that traditionally it has not been a structured programming language. Many popular versions of BASIC do not encourage dividing the program into modules, nor do they contain adequate control statements. Many implementations of BASIC require the use of unconditional branches, commonly signaled by GOTO statements, which can cause program logic to be convoluted and difficult to follow.

Some newer versions of BASIC support the development of structured programs. One of these is True BASIC, which was developed by the original writers of BASIC, John Kemeny and Thomas Kurtz. True BASIC is an economical language that uses English-like commands, yet it provides options that enable programmers to develop properly structured programs. The format of the new BASIC looks

Figure 4-13
Payroll Program in BASIC

```
10 REM THIS PROGRAM CALCULATES A WEEKLY
20 REM PAYROLL FOR FIVE EMPLOYEES
30 PRINT "EMPLOYEE NAME",,"NET PAY"
40 PRINT
50 READ N$,H,W
60 IF N$ = "END OF DATA" THEN 270
70 IF H > 40 THEN 100
80 LET G = H * W
90 GOTO 130
100 LET R = 40 * W
110 LET O = (H - 40) * (1.5 * W)
120 LET G = R + O
130 IF G > 250 THEN 160
140 LET T = .14
150 GOTO 170
160 LET T = .2
170 LET T2 = T * G
180 LET P = G - T2
190 PRINT N$,P
200 GOTO 50
210 DATA "LYNN MANGINO  ",35,8.00
220 DATA "THOMAS RITTER ",48,4.75
230 DATA "MARIE OLSON   ",45,5.50
240 DATA "LORI DUNLEVY  ",40,5.00
250 DATA "WILLIAM WILSON",50,7.00
260 DATA "END OF DATA",0,0
270 END
```

Output

```
         RUN
         EMPLOYEE NAME          NET PAY

         LYNN MANGINO           224.00
         THOMAS RITTER          212.42
         MARIE OLSON            209.00
         LORI DUNLEVY           172.00
         WILLIAM WILSON         308.00
```

much like that of Pascal, a language noted for its structure. In addition, ANSI is in the process of adopting new standards for a structured BASIC.

PASCAL
A high-level structured programming language, developed for instructional purposes, but now commonly used in a wide variety of applications.

Pascal **Pascal** was the first major programming language to implement the ideas and methodology of structured programming. Niklaus Wirth, a Swiss computer scientist, developed Pascal between 1969 and 1970. The first Pascal compiler became available in 1971, and in 1982 ANSI adopted a standard for Pascal. Wirth named the language after the French philosopher and mathematician Blaise Pascal, inventor of the first mechanical adding machine.

Like BASIC, Pascal was developed for teaching programming concepts to students. Often it is the first programming language taught to college-level students; at present, it is the introductory programming course for computer science students at 80 percent of all universities. Pascal is relatively easy to learn, and it is a powerful language capable of performing a wide variety of tasks, including sophisticated mathematical operations. It supports structured programming concepts, such as modular programming and structured methods for controlling loops and selection patterns. These features encourage students to develop good programming habits. Figure 4-14 contains a short program written in Pascal.

Figure 4-14
Payroll Program in Pascal

```
PROGRAM PAYROLL (INPUT,OUTPUT);
VAR HOURS,REGULAR,WAGE,OVERTIME,GROSS,TAX,NETPAY : REAL;
NAME : ARRAY (.1..17.) OF CHAR;
I : INTEGER;
BEGIN
WRITELN('1','EMPLOYEE NAME','              NET PAY');
WRITELN(' ');
WHILE NOT EOF DO
    BEGIN
    FOR I:=1 TO 17 DO
        READ (NAME(.I.));
        READLN (HOURS,WAGE);
    IF HOURS>40
        THEN BEGIN
            REGULAR:=40*WAGE;
            OVERTIME:=(HOURS-40)*(1.5*WAGE);
            GROSS:=REGULAR + OVERTIME
            END
        ELSE BEGIN
            GROSS:=HOURS*WAGE
            END;
    IF GROSS>250
        THEN BEGIN
            TAX:=0.20*GROSS;
            NETPAY:=GROSS-TAX

        ELSE BEGIN
            TAX:=0.14*GROSS;
            NETPAY:=GROSS-TAX
            END;
    WRITE (' ');
FOR I :=1 TO 17 DO
    WRITE(NAME(.I.);
    WRITELN(NETPAY:12:12);
    END
END.
```

Output

```
       EMPLOYEE NAME          NET PAY

       LYNN MANGINO           224.00
       THOMAS RITTER          212.42
       MARIE OLSON            209.00
       LORI DUNLEVY           172.00
       WILLIAM WILSON         308.00
```

At first Pascal's availability was limited, but more computer manufacturers now are offering Pascal compilers for their machines. Some compilers developed for microcomputers, such as TURBO Pascal, are inexpensive and versatile. Many of these compilers can create intricate, detailed graphics on properly equipped display terminals. This feature is attractive to scientists as well as to business personnel. Many people believe that Pascal has poor input/output capabilities, however, a limitation that makes it less than ideal for applications involving manipulation of large data files.

RPG (Report Program Generator)
A high-level language designed for producing business reports. RPG requires the programmer to record data and operations on specification forms.

RPG RPG (Report Program Generator) was designed in the late 1960s for producing business reports. A programmer using RPG must describe the kind of report desired, but need not specify much of the logic involved. Acting upon this description, a generator program builds a program that produces the report. Instead of coding statements, the programmer completes specification forms, such as those shown in Figure 4-15. The data on these forms is entered into the computer. The RPG generator program then builds an object program that the computer executes.

IBM introduced a new version, RPGII, in the 1970s for use with its IBM System/3 computers. This version has replaced the original RPG. A third version introduced in 1979, RPGIII, provides the capability of processing data stored in a database.

RPG is easy to learn and use. It provides an efficient means for generating reports requiring simple logic and calculations. It is commonly used for processing files for accounts receivable, accounts payable, general ledgers, and inventory. Because RPG requires little main storage space, it is one of the primary languages of microcomputers and minicomputers.

The language has shortcomings, however, among them its limited computational capabilities. Also, RPG is not standardized. RPG programs written for one computer may require significant changes before they can be used on another computer.

C
A high-level structured programming language that includes low-level language instructions; popular because it is portable and is implemented on a wide variety of computer systems.

PORTABLE
Describes a program that can be run on many different computers with minimal changes.

C Developed in 1972, C is rapidly becoming popular for both system and application programming. It has some capabilities similar to those of assembly languages; for example, it can manipulate individual bits and bytes in storage locations. Yet it also offers many high-level language features, such as a wide variety of useful control structures. Therefore, it is sometimes referred to as a middle-level language.

C is popular for several reasons. First, it is independent of machine architecture, so that C programs are **portable.** This means the same program can be run on different computers. Second, C can be implemented on a wide variety of systems, from eight-bit microcomputers to supercomputers such as the Cray-1. Third, it includes many of the structured programming features found in languages like Pascal. Fourth, the compilers are simple and compact. C, however, is a language intended for experienced programmers. Figure 4-16 shows a payroll program written in C.

C was designed by Dennis Ritchie at Bell Laboratories. One of its first uses was in the rewriting of Bell Laboratories' Unix operating system. Unix and its utilities include over 300,000 lines of C source code, a very ambitious programming project. Today, many major microcomputer manufacturers and software developers use C for system programs, utility programs, and graphics applications. C is also useful for text processing and database programs.

CHAPTER 4: SOFTWARE DEVELOPMENT

Figure 4-15
RPG Program Specification Forms

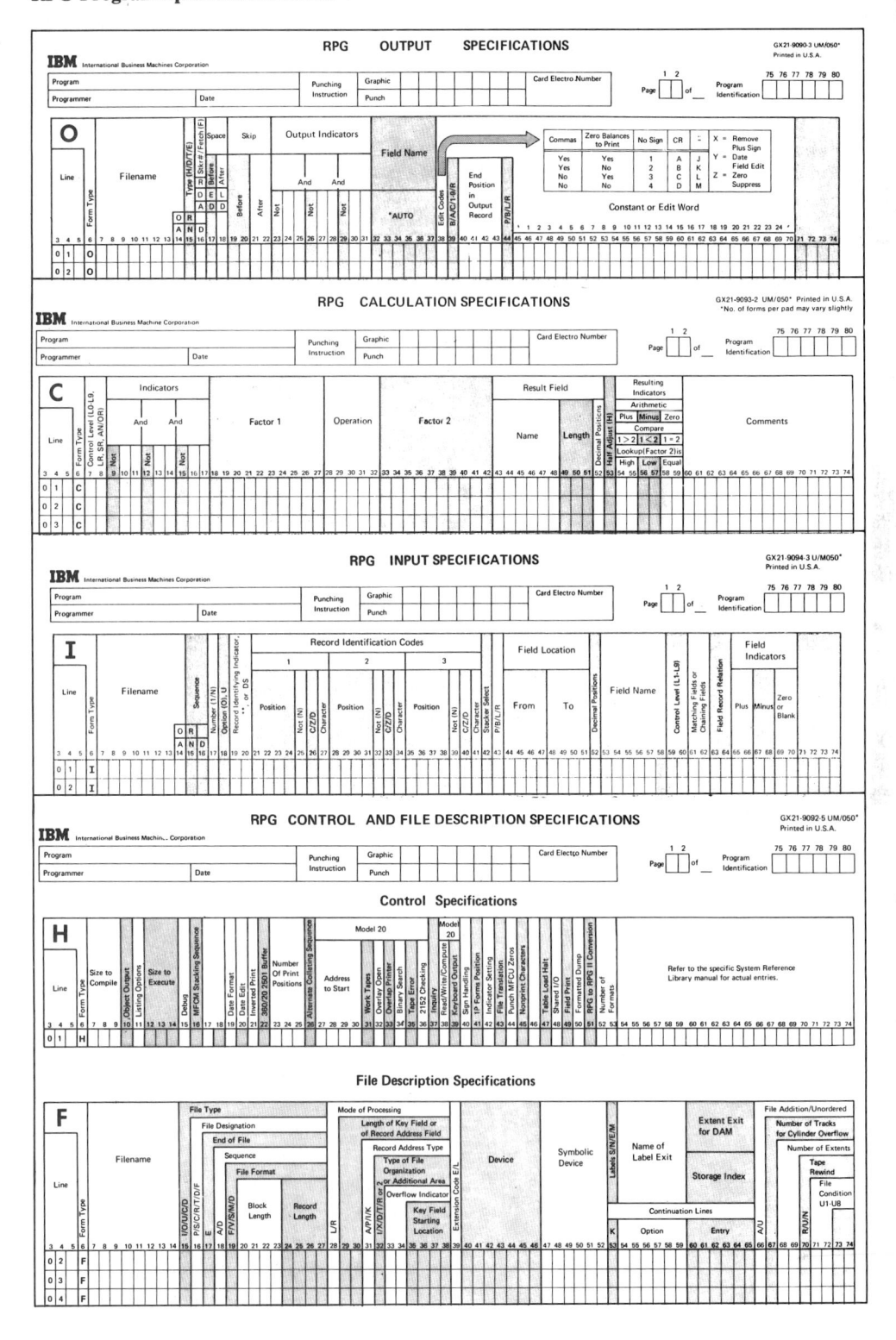

Figure 4-16
Payroll Program in C

```
        main()
        {
        /*********************************************
                This program calculates a weekly payroll.
        *********************************************/
                double atof();
                float wage, hours, grosspay, tax, netpay;
                char *chwage, *chhours, *name;

                flag = 0;
                printf ("EMPLOYEE NAME            NETPAY \n");
                emplfile = fopen("payroll","r");
                while (1) {
        /*********************************************
                        procedure read data
        *********************************************/
                    readname(name);
                    if (flag)
                            break;
                    readname(chhours);
                    readname(chwage);

        /*********************************************
                        Calculate gross pay
        *********************************************/
                    wage = atof(chwage);             /* convert the string  */
                    hours = atof(chhours);           /* to a float value    */
                    if (hours <= 40)
                            grosspay = hours * wage;
                    else
                            grosspay = hours * wage + (hours - 40.0) * wage * 0.5;

        /*********************************************
                        Calculate net pay
        *********************************************/
                    if (grosspay > 250)
                        tax = 0.2 * grosspay;
                    else
                        tax = 0.14 * grosspay;
                    netpay = grosspay - tax;
```

ADA
A high-level structured programming language developed for use by the U.S. Department of Defense.

Ada Ada is a relatively new programming language developed by the United States Department of Defense (DOD). It is derived from Pascal and is also a structured language. Ada is named in honor of the first programmer, Augusta Ada Byron, Countess of Lovelace and daughter of the poet Lord Byron (see Chapter 1).

The need for a language such as Ada was determined by a DOD study conducted in 1974, which found that in 1973 over $7 billion was spent on software that did not meet the needs of the department. Through further study, the DOD found that no current high-level language met its needs for reliability and portability, and concluded that a new language would have to be developed. In 1980 the DOD approved the initial Ada standard, and in 1983 ANSI approved it.

Ada has the sophistication and reliability (that is, the ability to obtain correct results consistently) that are necessary for programming in critical areas such as defense, weather forecasting, and oil exploration. It is not a beginner's language,

Figure 4-16 (continued)

```
/*****************************************************
                Print the results
*****************************************************/
        printf("%-24s  %7.2f\n",name,netpay);
        } /* while loop closing bracket */
        fclose(emplfile);
} /* main closing bracket */

/*****************************************************
                Subroutine readname
*****************************************************/
readname(ts)
char *ts;
{
        int cc;
        char *cs;

        cs = ts;
        while ((cc = getc(emplfile)) != EOF)   /*look for EOF */
                {
                if (cc == 13)                   /* return if CR is seen */
                        break;
                if (cc != 10)                   /* do not process LF */
                        *cs++ = cc;             /* build the string */
                }
        if (cc == EOF) flag = 1;                /* IF EOF we are done */
        *cs = '\0';                             /* make sure we terminate
                                                   a string value */
}
```

Output

```
    EMPLOYEE NAME               NETPAY
    LYNN MANGIN                 224.00
    THOMAS RITTER               212.42
    MARIE OLSON                 209.00
    LORI SANCHEZ                172.00
    WILLIAM LUOMA               308.00
```

however, and a skilled programmer may take six months to become proficient in the language.

MODULA-2
A high-level structured programming language that is a descendent of Pascal; incorporates low-level language commands.

Modula-2 Modula-2 is a descendant of Pascal. Designed by the creator of Pascal, Niklaus Wirth, Modula-2 contains all aspects of Pascal and is learned easily by Pascal programmers.

As Pascal became widely implemented during the 1970s, it became evident that certain improvements in the language were possible. Wirth proposed the creation of a single, high-level language that also had low-level capabilities for interacting more closely with hardware. In this respect, Modula-2 is similar to C and FORTH.

Modula-2 is a structured language that is easy to modularize and has a wide variety of useful control structures. Because Modula-2 is a new programming language, it remains to be seen how widely implemented it will be.

FORTH

FORTH
A high-level programming language that includes low-level language instructions; used at many astronomical observatories worldwide.

FORTH Working at Kitt Peak National Observatory, Charles Moore developed FORTH in response to a need for an adequate programming language for use in satellite tracking and astronomy. Like C and Modula-2, FORTH often is categorized as a middle-level language. FORTH can be modeled to meet the programmer's particular needs, and it is a very portable language. In FORTH, a programmer can build up a dictionary of programs that can be called up by name for many uses.

FORTH is used at many astronomical observatories around the world. It is also used for guiding automated movie cameras, running portable heart monitors, and simulating radar for the Air Force. In addition, it is being used increasingly for less glamorous tasks such as database management and word processing.

The simplicity of FORTH makes it fast and efficient. Because FORTH systems are interpreted rather than compiled, the programmer can write one word (procedure) at a time and test it thoroughly before writing the next word. FORTH is a strange-looking language, however, and it is hard to read. It also lacks many of the safety features built into other languages, so finding program errors is difficult.

LISP (LISt Processing)
A high-level programming language commonly used in artificial intelligence research and in the processing of lists of elements.

LISP LISP (or LISt Processing) is the language commonly associated with artificial intelligence. Using concepts of lambda calculus (a branch of mathematics) and a new idea in computing called list processing, John McCarthy developed the language in 1960 at the Massachusetts Institute of Technology (MIT). LISP aids in the manipulation of nonnumeric data that change considerably in length and structure during execution of a program. Essentially, LISP performs built-in or user-defined functions on lists.

These lists can contain collections of functions (for example, finding the square or cube of a number), sentences, mathematical formulas, logic theorems, or even complete computer programs. This capability makes LISP a powerful tool in applications such as the generation of mathematical proofs and simulations of human problem-solving techniques. To beginning programmers in LISP, however, the tangle of parentheses used in writing the lists can be confusing.

LOGO
An education-oriented programming language designed to allow anyone to begin programming and communicating with computers quickly.

Logo LOGO was designed originally as a teaching tool by Seymour Papert and the MIT Logo group in the late 1960s. Logo's main attraction is that it enables both children and adults to begin programming and communicating with the computer in a short period of time. Logo enables the user to draw images, animate them, and color them using simple instructions. Some instructions involve commanding a triangular object called a turtle, which leaves a graphic trail in its path. The user commands the turtle to draw straight lines, squares, or other objects, which can be combined to form images. Figure 4-17 contains Logo statements that draw a triangular figure inside a square.

The strength of Logo lies in its ability to help the inexperienced user learn logic and programming. Because it is a structured language, it encourages the beginning programmer to develop good programming habits.

Although Logo can help young children learn geometry and programming, it is a powerful language, and learning every aspect of Logo can be difficult. Because Logo is derived from LISP, it handles list processing with ease. Its large memory and file-handling capabilities make it appropriate for advanced applications, such

Figure 4-17
Logo Program for Drawing a Square with a Triangular Design

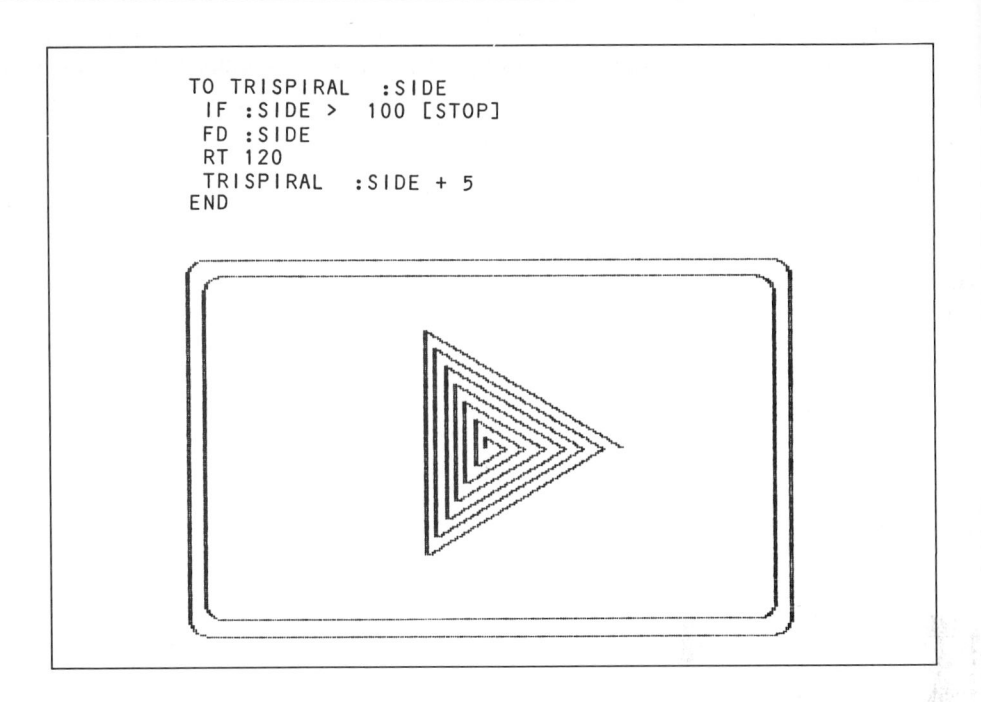

```
TO TRISPIRAL   :SIDE
  IF :SIDE > 100 [STOP]
  FD :SIDE
  RT 120
  TRISPIRAL   :SIDE + 5
END
```

as creating music, performing sophisticated mathematics functions based on trigonometry and logarithms, and studying physics.

Natural Languages

Computer scientists have long realized that computers cannot achieve their full potential if only a few people know how to use them. Programmers have developed user-friendly software that uses menus and other devices that make computers easier to use. In addition, they are developing ways for people to interact with computers by using natural English, the English used in everyday speech.

Natural languages, or **query languages** as they sometimes are called, are programming languages that enable the user to state queries in English-like sentences. They are used most frequently in conjunction with **databases.** For example, a member of a personnel department might ask, *"How many women hold a position at level 10 or above?"* in order to gain information for reporting purposes. The question then is translated into a form that the computer can use in searching a database for the correct answer. If the natural language processor does not fully understand the inquiry, it may request further information from the user.

Most natural language processors are designed to be used with a vocabulary of words and definitions which allows the processor to translate the English-like sentences into machine-executable form. Currently, natural language sentences are typed at the keyboard; in the future, however, the combination of voice recognition technology and natural languages could result in a very powerful tool for computer users. The ability to interface natural language systems with graphic software also provides a valuable decision making tool for managers. Although limited to mainframe computers in the past, natural language systems are being developed for minicomputer and microcomputer systems.

NATURAL LANGUAGE (QUERY LANGUAGE)
A language designed primarily for novice computer users which allows use of statements very much like everyday speech, usually for the purpose of accessing data in a database.

DATABASE
A collection of data items that are commonly defined and consistently organized to fit the information needs of a wide variety of users in an organization.

Learning Check

1. Explain the advantages of low-level languages.
2. In what circumstance might a programmer choose assembly language rather than a high-level language?
3. In what cases might programs written in FORTRAN be useful to a business organization?
4. Name three languages widely used in teaching beginning programmers, and tell why each is popular for that use.
5. State one major use each for Ada, C, FORTH, and LISP.
6. What type of language is the most English-like? What is the primary use of this type of language?

Answers

1. Low-level languages give the programmer direct control of hardware details. Also they are efficient in terms of memory and execution speed. 2. Assembly language may be chosen when fast execution is essential, but coding directly in machine language is too time-consuming. 3. FORTRAN can be used for business applications that require complex calculations, such as feasibility studies, forecasting, and production scheduling. 4. BASIC is easy to learn, and Pascal and Logo are structured languages that encourage the development of good programming habits. 5. Ada is used in defense-related programming, C is used for writing operating systems, FORTH is used at astronomical observatories, and LISP is used in artificial intelligence studies. 6. Natural or query languages are the most English-like, and they are used in accessing databases.

Summary Points

■ A computer program should be developed using these four steps: define the problem, design the solution, write the program, and compile, debug, and test the program.

■ Defining the problem involves defining the desired output, the needed input, and the processing required for solving the problem.

■ Designing a solution to a problem may require considerable creativity and one or more of four basic logic patterns: simple sequence, selection, loop, or branch.

■ To guard against writing and using faulty programs, programmers use an outline of the program logic called an algorithm. Algorithms can be represented by pseudocode or flowcharts.

■ Writing the program involves coding—writing the algorithm in a programming language. A program should be easy to read, reliable, workable under all conditions, easy to modify and update, portable, and efficient.

■ Compiling, debugging, and testing are the final steps of program development. Compiling means using a special program that translates the program to machine language. Debugging means locating and correcting any errors in the program. Testing means running the program with a wide variety of data in order to see if it performs correctly.

■ Structured programming is characterized by top-down design, good documentation, program testing at all stages of the problem-solving process, and use of a programming team to develop the software.

■ In the top-down approach, a program is broken down into functional modules that follow a hierarchy from general to specific.

■ Program documentation should occur at all programming stages. It facilitates testing and review of programs at the development stages, and simplifies modification and updating of existing programs.

■ Program testing should occur at all programming stages in order to isolate errors early in the process, thereby reducing time and costs.

■ A chief programmer team (CPT) should reduce the time and costs associated with program development, increase programmer productivity, increase program clarity, and decrease time and effort in maintaining a program once it is implemented.

■ The two basic types of programs are system programs, which coordinate the operation of the computer circuitry, and application programs, which solve user problems.

■ An operating system is a collection of programs designed to enable a computer system to manage its own operations. It allocates computer resources among the users, keeps track of the data, and establishes job priorities.

■ Low-level languages, including machine language and assembly language, are machine-oriented and require extensive knowledge of computer circuitry. Machine language is the only language the computer can execute directly. Assembly language uses symbolic names for machine operations, thus making programming less tedious and time-consuming than when machine language is used.

■ High-level languages are user-oriented and allow the programmer to focus on problem solving rather than on details of computer operation. They use meaningful words such as READ and PRINT and common mathematical terms and symbols.

■ Examples of high-level languages are FORTRAN, used for scientific applications; COBOL, the most popular business programming language; RPG, designed for producing business reports; LISP, used in artificial intelligence programming and research; and Ada, a new language developed by the Department of Defense.

■ Languages commonly used in education are BASIC, a language widely implemented on microcomputers, and Pascal and Logo, both structured languages that develop good programming habits.

■ C, Modula-2, and FORTH are high-level languages that contain low-level language capabilities, thereby allowing the programmer to interact closely with the computer's hardware.

■ Natural languages (or query languages) are designed to enable the novice computer user to access the computer's capabilities more easily. English-like sentences are easy to write and understand; they enable the user to access information in a database, for example.

Review Questions

1. List the four steps in the software development process.
2. Discuss some important qualities that make one program better than another.
3. Why should the system analyst consult with the potential program user(s) when developing software?
4. Is is important for a system analyst to have a specific programming language in mind when performing the first two steps of the software development process? Why?
5. What are the four basic logic patterns that the computer is capable of executing? Which of these patterns is avoided in structured programming? Why?
6. What is meant by the term top-down design, and how are structure charts used in this design methodology?
7. At what point in the programming process should documentation be written? What should it include?
8. Contrast the compiler program and the interpreter program.
9. Give several reasons why a programmer might choose a low-level language rather than a high-level language.
10. Name two or three high-level languages that would fulfill the requirements listed in the answer to question 9.
11. Describe some of the key advantages associated with the Pascal language and with the C language.
12. What is the purpose of natural languages? For what type of user are they best suited?

CHAPTER 5

Microcomputers

Outline

Introduction
Microcomputers: An Overview
   The New Technology
   The Machines Themselves
Highlight: Please! Count Your
   Eggs Before They Hatch
Learning Check
Understanding the Microchips
   The Microprocessor's Speed
   Operating Systems

Compatibility
Learning Check
Using Microcomputers
   Input Devices
   Output Devices
   Online Storage
   Add-Ons
   Software Packages

Highlight: Jonathan Rotenberg
   and the Boston Computer
   Society
   Users' Groups
Learning Check
Summary Points
Review Questions

Introduction

Few technological changes equal the recent impact of microcomputers. In just one decade, microcomputers have evolved from primitive toys for hobbyists to sophisticated machines that far surpass the early mainframe computers in both speed and capabilities. The small machines have become so common that they now appear in every area of our lives, from work to play. This chapter examines the terms and hardware associated with microcomputers and describes some of their unique aspects.

Microcomputers: An Overview

Microcomputers, also called personal computers or home computers, are the smallest computers. They are smaller and less expensive than minicomputers and mainframes. Although they cannot perform as many complex functions as the large computers, their capabilities in terms of speed and memory are rapidly expanding. In fact, a clear distinction no longer exists between the capabilities of some microcomputers and those of the next class of computers, minicomputers. Microcomputers have come a long way since the first commercial microcomputer kit was introduced in 1975.

The New Technology

The invention of the microprocessor ushered in the fourth generation of computers in 1971. The microprocessor is a single chip containing the **instruction set,** that is, the fundamental logic and arithmetic circuitry as well as control capability for memory and input/output access (see Figure 5-1). It controls the arithmetic and logic operations and the sequence in which they are performed. It also controls the storage of data, instructions, and intermediate and final results of processing, much as the CPU of a mainframe computer does. A mainframe's CPU contains a series of integrated circuits, however, and is much more complex than the microprocessor.

BIT
Acronym for Binary digiT; the smallest unit of data than can be represented in binary notation; a bit can be either a 0 or a 1.

The first microprocessor, the Intel 4004, was developed for use in a calculator. It had a very limited instruction set, could not perform many functions, and could handle only four **bits** of data at a time. By 1974, however, microprocessors were faster; they could handle eight bits of data at a time. Early eight-bit chips still in use today are the Zilog Z-80, Intel 8080, MOS 6402, and Motorola 6809. These eight-bit microprocessors were used in the first microcomputers. The number of orders received for the first commercial microcomputer kit, the MITS Altair 8800, indicated that the market for microcomputers was well worth pursuing. Companies such as Apple Computer, Commodore, Atari, and Tandy/Radio Shack began offering preassembled microcomputers for home use.

Microprocessors quickly increased in power while they decreased in size. This combination of power and miniaturization paved the way for microcomputers as

Figure 5-1 Microprocessor
This microprocessor from Bell Labs has as much processing power as some minicomputers.

Figure 5-2 Microcomputer
Microcomputers, the least expensive category of computers, are general-purpose machines used in homes, schools, and offices. This Apple IIe is found frequently in schools.

they exist today. In 1981, IBM introduced the IBM PC with a 16-bit microprocessor. The success of the IBM PC for business uses prompted other microcomputer manufacturers to develop 16-bit microcomputers. Established manufacturers of larger computer and communications systems, such as DEC, WANG, Hewlett-Packard, AT&T, and NCR, entered the microcomputer market. Soon customers expected even more powerful machines, containing 16-bit microprocessors with 32-bit capabilities (Zilog Z8000, Intel 80286, and Motorola MC68000).

Today, the true 32-bit microprocessor offers faster processing, multi-user capability, minicomputer and mainframe compatibility, and the ability to tackle enormous tasks such as voice recognition. The Intel 80386 and Motorola MC68020 are examples of these popular chips. Perhaps there will never be a point at which microcomputers have reached their full potential.

The Machines Themselves

Most microcomputers today are desk-top models (see Figure 5-2). They are small enough to place entirely on a desk, but too large to carry around easily. A fairly versatile system includes the computer, a keyboard for input, a disk drive or two as storage devices, and a monitor and a printer for output. Other **peripheral devices** can be added to most systems.

Inside the computer is a main system board, often called the motherboard, which holds the microprocessor, other circuits, and memory chips. The system board may contain slots for plugging in cards (smaller, add-on circuit boards) that expand the capabilities of the computer. For example, you can insert cards that add memory, change the number of characters per line on the monitor, or interface with printers, modems, voice recognition units, music synthesizers, and bar code

Figure 5-3 Ports
The places where peripheral equipment can be connected to the computer are called ports.

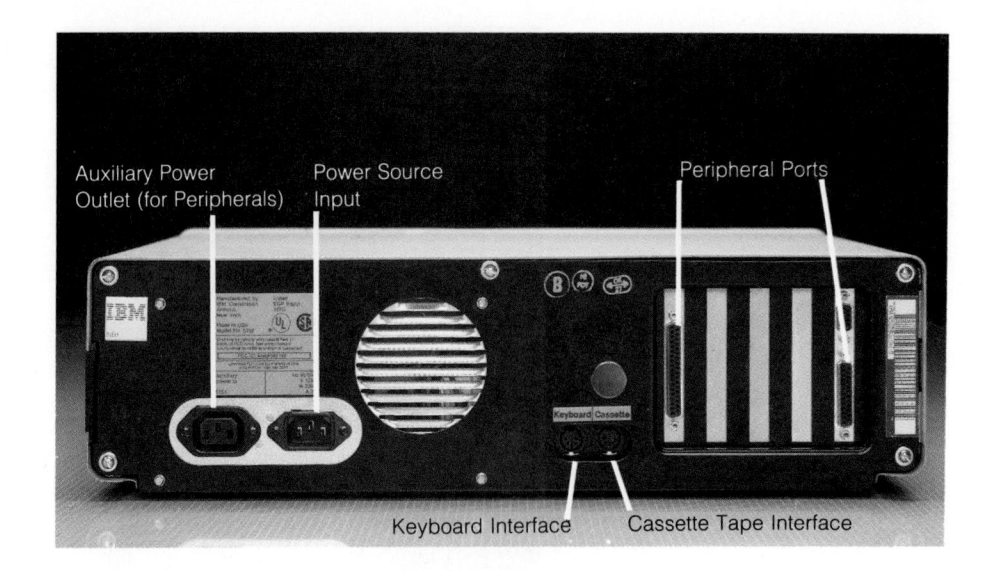

readers. Of course, there is a limit to the number of cards that can be added at once.

Microcomputers also have ports used for plugging in peripherals (see Figure 5-3). A port may be designed for serial communication, in which the bits are transferred one at a time, much as people pass through a turnstyle; or for parallel communication, in which the bits are transferred eight at a time, much as cars drive down a multi-lane expressway. Cables for telephone connections and some printers require serial ports, but parallel ports also are used for communicating with printers. "Closed systems"—those that cannot easily be opened for access to the system board—depend almost entirely on ports for expanding the capabilities of the system.

Although most microcomputers are desktop models, there are three other classifications of microcomputers: portables, transportables, and supermicrocomputers.

PORTABLE
A small microcomputer that is light enough to be carried easily and does not need an external source of power.

Portables and Transportables The smallest microcomputers available are **portables.** Portables are light enough to be carried and do not need an external source of power. They are powered by rechargeable or replaceable batteries. Their flat display screens allow them to be slim and therefore easy to carry. Portables usually need some form of direct-access storage medium, such as floppy disks.

Portables can be divided further by size into briefcase and notebook portables. The Hewlett-Packard 110 is a briefcase computer and is noted for being very fast (see Figure 5-4). Radio Shack's TRS-80 Model 100 and Model 200 are even smaller; they are called notebook computers and are used mostly for word processing.

Some portables are capable of performance almost equal to that of small desktop microcomputers as reflected by their prices—from $3000 to $8000. Other portables carry a much lower price tag, between $500 and $2,000.

Each portable has different features, so users must evaluate their particular needs before selecting a portable. Some useful features include built-in **modems** and software for transmitting and receiving data by telephone. Some portables

Figure 5-4
Hewlett-Packard 110 Portable Computer This computer can fit in a briefcase, which makes carrying it on business trips easy.

TRANSPORTABLE
A class of microcomputer smaller than the desktop models for easier carrying, but larger than the portables and therefore bulkier to carry.

have ports for connecting floppy disk drives, cassette recorders, or bar code readers. Most portables have built-in software such as a word processor, spreadsheet, or database manager (see the section on software later in this chapter). Built-in programming languages such as BASIC may also be included.

Portables are especially useful for reporters, businesspeople, and students. For example, a salesperson might use a portable to compose reports that are sent to the main office via telephone lines. Journalists use portables in similar ways. A reporter can cover an event 2,000 miles from the newspaper's headquarters, write the story using a word processor and a portable computer, and use a modem for sending the article over telephone lines to the editor's desk. Students carry briefcase or notebook computers to classes in order to take decipherable lecture notes and prepare assignments.

Portables should be distinguished from another class of small microcomputers, the **transportables.** Transportables generally are larger than portables but are still small enough to be carried easily. They differ from portables because they require an external power source (see Figure 5-5).

Supermicrocomputers Some microcomputers are so powerful that they can compete with low-end minicomputers. These **supermicrocomputers** usually are built around powerful 32-bit microprocessors, and can handle large amounts of data and support more than one user (see Figure 5-6). Because microprocessors are inexpensive compared to the CPUs of minicomputers, supermicrocomputers offer a significant price edge over minicomputers. In fact, the minicomputer market

134 PART ONE: COMPUTER LITERACY

Figure 5-5
A Transportable Computer

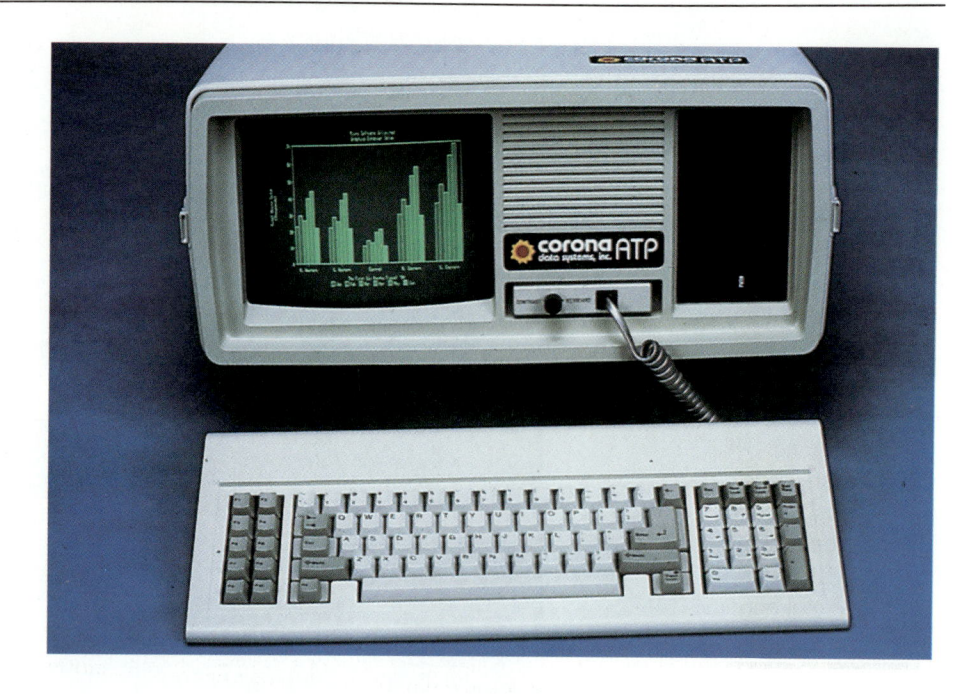

already is weakening as more customers upgrade their systems by linking supermicrocomputers to existing minicomputers or mainframes.

Supermicrocomputers must be able to store large amounts of data. Hard disks can store much more data than the floppy disks often used with microcomputers.

Figure 5-6
Supermicrocomputer
The Tower 1632 Supermicrocomputer from NCR

CHAPTER 5: MICROCOMPUTERS　　　　　　　　　　　　　　　　135

HIGHLIGHT ▲▲▲▲▲▲▲▲▲▲▲▲▲▲▲▲▲▲▲▲

Please! Count Your Eggs Before They Hatch!

An egg counter? You've got to be kidding.

On second thought, when you're faced with counting 700,000 eggs daily, an egg counter would be handy.

Stephen Herbruck of Poultry Management Systems (Saranac, Michigan) developed an egg-counting system about six years ago. The systems use as many as 1,500 photodetectors to record the passage of eggs on conveyors (deposited there, of course, by obliging hens). The count is transferred to an IBM PC, which records and displays the count. The system saves hiring the one or two persons needed for the full-time job of counting eggs.

This year, Herbruck is testing an extension of his egg counters on his own egg-laying hens (about 1 million of them). The new system is called NOAH (Natural On-Line Animal Housing). NOAH controls all aspects of egg production, including as many as 2,000 devices: water-flow meters, feed-weighing devices, variable-speed ventilating fan motors, and thermostats. NOAH is outgrowing the IBM PC, so Herbruck probably will switch to the IBM PC/AT. Herbruck can even check the feeding system from a remote NOAH terminal in his home before going to bed.

Now he has to sell the system to other egg production centers—no easy hendeavor.

SOURCE: "Automating America's Heartland," Raeburn, Paul, *High Technology*, December 1985, p. 51.

The prices of hard disk drives have fallen in recent years, making them ideal storage devices for supermicrocomputers.

One problem hindering full-scale implementation of supermicrocomputers is the limited amount of available software. As they gain in popularity, however, there will be more interest in developing software for these machines, just as a great deal of software has been developed for traditional microcomputers.

Learning Check

1. Compare microcomputers with minicomputers and mainframes in terms of size, cost, and capabilities.
2. What event prompted many manufacturers to enter the microcomputer market?
3. What basic equipment makes up a fairly versatile microcomputer system?
4. What features make portable computers useful to salespersons?
5. How are some customers using supermicrocomputers?

Answers

1. They are smaller, less expensive, and have lesser capabilities, although some approach minicomputers in capabilities. 2. IBM introduced the 16-bit IBM PC. 3. A computer, keyboard, monitor, one or two disk drives, and a printer. 4. They are lightweight, flat, easy to carry, and do not need an external source of electricity. 5. They are upgrading their systems by linking microcomputers to existing minicomputers and mainframes.

Understanding the Microchips

In Chapter 1, you learned that a computer's power is derived from its speed and memory and the accuracy of its electronic circuits. This section explains two of those factors—speed and memory—as related to microprocessors. It also discusses the programs that integrate the workings of a microcomputer's circuitry.

The Microprocessor's Speed

The speed with which the microprocessor can execute instructions affects the speed of the microcomputer. Speed depends on several factors, including word size and clock speed.

Word size is the number of bits that can be manipulated at one time. An eight-bit microprocessor, for example, manipulates data in clusters of eight bits (each of which is called a byte). A 16-bit microprocessor can handle 16 bits—two eight-bit bytes of data—at a time. Therefore, a 16-bit microprocessor can manipulate twice as much data as an eight-bit microprocessor in approximately the same amount of time. This does not necessarily mean that there is a direct relationship between word size and speed. A 16-bit microprocessor may not be twice as fast as an eight-bit microprocessor. It may be more than twice as fast in performing some operations, but less than twice as fast in performing others. Generally speaking, however, a 32-bit microprocessor is faster than a 16-bit microprocessor and a 16-bit microprocessor is faster than an eight-bit microprocessor.

The 16- and 32-bit microprocessors are appropriate for business users for two reasons. First, in business, several users often use the same software and data in a system of linked microcomputers. Second, business users often work on several programs at one time and therefore need a large amount of primary memory, which can be handled by the 16- and 32-bit microprocessors. Nonetheless, many eight-bit machines are used. Applications and operating systems (see the section on operating systems) for eight-bit systems are well established, and most users do not require a lot of speed. In addition, eight-bit machines are cheaper.

The **clock speed** of a microprocessor is the number of electronic pulses the chip can produce each second. Clock speed is built into a microprocessor and is measured in **megahertz (MHz).** (*Mega* means million and *hertz* means times per second, so one megahertz is one million times per second.) The electronic pulses affect the speed with which program instructions are executed, because instructions are executed at predetermined intervals that are timed by these pulses.

As an illustration of this concept, assume that one instruction is executed every 100 pulses. A 4 MHz microprocessor, then can process 40,000 instructions per second (4 million pulses divided by 100 pulses). An 8 MHz microprocessor can process 80,000 instructions, or twice as many as a 4 MHz microprocessor. Thus, the more pulses produced per second, the faster the instructions can be executed. Most microcomputers have clock speeds between 2 MHz and 8 MHz.

Memory

Primary memory is important in microcomputer speed because the more memory directly accessible by the CPU, the faster the machine. In addition, a computer

---

WORD SIZE
The number of bits than can be manipulated at one time; for instance, an eight-bit microprocessor can manipulate eight bits (one byte) of data at a time.

CLOCK SPEED
The number of electronic pulses a microprocessor can produce each second.

MEGAHERTZ (MHz)
One million times per second; the unit of measurement for clock speed.

with more memory can use more complex programs. Primary memory consists of thousands of on/off devices, each of which holds one bit. Primary memory consists of RAM and ROM.

RAM The primary memory that holds the data and programs for immediate processing is a form of semiconductor memory called **random-access memory (RAM).** RAM is the working area of the computer. Because RAM is volatile or nonpermanent, data and programs are erased when the electric power to a computer is turned off or disrupted in some other way. When any changes or results are to be saved, they must be saved on an external form of storage, such as magnetic disks or tapes.

The size of RAM memory is stated in bytes. The most common sizes in microcomputers are 64K (kilobytes), 128K, 256K, 512K and 640K. The sizes are related to the word sizes of microprocessors, in that each microprocessor can access directly only a certain number of bytes of data in primary memory. As the word size increases, so does the amount of RAM that can be handled. Typically, an eight-bit microprocessor can directly access 64K bytes of data and a 16-bit microprocessor can directly access 256K. Many 8- and 16-bit machines are available with more RAM than their microprocessors can directly access. The extra RAM is additional "indexed" memory that can be accessed indirectly at a slightly slower speed than RAM. Just as 16-bit and 32-bit microcomputers are appropriate for business uses, 256K and 512K RAMs are appropriate for holding the increased amount of data and programs that a business user needs to access.

ROM When functions are built into the hardware of a microcomputer, they are placed in **read-only memory (ROM).** Read-only memory instructions cannot be changed or deleted by other stored-program instructions. Because ROM is permanent, it cannot be occupied by instructions or data read from a disk or tape. ROM and versions—PROM and EPROM—are available for microcomputers. See Chapter 3 for a complete discussion of these chips. ROM programs are also available on cartridges that can be inserted into special slots built into the computer. Programs built into ROM chips or cartridges often are called firmware.

Operating Systems

Without an **operating system,** a computer cannot recognize that a key has been pressed, much less what it means. Several operating systems have been designed for use with microcomputers (see Table 5-1).

Most operating systems are loaded into a computer's RAM from floppy disks, a process called **booting.** The word boot derives from the expression "lift yourself up by your own bootstraps," which essentially is what a computer does. In order to read and write data residing on a disk, the disk operating system must be loaded into memory from the disk where it is kept. The computer has a small program built into ROM which starts the process of reading the operating system code from a disk.

BOOT
To start or restart a computer by reading a small amount of code from a storage device into the computer's memory.

	CP/M	MS DOS	Apple DOS	Unix
Manufacturer	• Digital Research	• Microsoft	• Apple Computer	• Bell Laboratories
Microprocessor	• Intel 8080 • Intel 8085 • Zilog Z-80	• Intel 8088 • Intel 8086 • Intel 8286	• MOS 6502	• Not built around a single family of microprocessors
Features	• First OS for micros • For 8-bit mmicroprocessors • Not easy for beginners to use, but succeeding versions easier • Concurrent DOS new version for 16-bit microprocessors; runs programs written for MS-DOS and 8-bit CP/M	• First licensed for use on the IBM PC • Quickly became most popular for 16-bit machines • Over 100 commputers using it • Not easy for beginners to use	• Designed to be used by nonprofessional computer users • Easy to learn and easy to use • Limited utilities and file usage • Closely tied to Apple's version of BASIC • Apple ProDOS overcomes its problems; ProDOS can be used with hard disks	• First used on minicomputers • Easily adapted for different types of computers • Used on various classifications of computers (micros, minis, mainframes) • Handles multiple usage • Handles several tasks from one terminal • Many utility programs • Not all versions compatible • Few applications for home users

Table 5-1
Operating Systems for Microcomputers

Generally, a person uses the operating system by typing keystroke combinations that direct the computer to copy data, save data, delete data, or get a list of items kept on disks.

Compatibility

The owner of a microcomputer can enhance its capabilities by adding peripheral equipment to the system, such as a disk drive, color monitor, printer, or modem. It is not always necessary to choose peripherals made by the same manufacturer as the microcomputer. Another manufacturer's equipment may have the same or better capabilities at a better price. The peripherals do have to be **compatible**, though. Software also must be compatible. Programs designed for one operating system cannot be used on computers with different operating systems. Compatibility in software includes the ability to read and write data on the same diskette and to use common data files. If one manufacturer's equipment or software can be used with another manufacturer's equipment or software, the two are said to be compatible.

Compatibility can be extended by adding a **coprocessor** to a computer. The coprocessor makes the computer compatible with another operating system. It is a microprocessor that can be plugged into the original computer to replace or work with the original microprocessor. The coprocessor usually comes on a plug-in board or card, along with other chips necessary for it to run. For example, adding a Z-80 board to the main system board makes an Apple IIe compatible with the CP/M operating system. The original microprocessor and the coprocessor share the computer's disk drives, keyboard, and other peripherals.

COMPATIBLE
Descriptive of hardware and/or software that can work together.

COPROCESSOR
A microprocessor that can be plugged into a microprocessor to replace or work with the micrcomputer's original microprocessor.

Learning Check

1. What does it mean to define a microprocessor in terms of the number of bits—eight or 16, for example?
2. How are word size and RAM related?
3. How can a computer be started if the disk operating system is on a disk, but the computer needs it in primary memory in order to read and write data residing on a disk?
4. What characteristic must you look for when buying peripheral equipment or software for use with a certain type of computer?

Answers

1. This refers to the word size—the number of bits which can be handled in one cluster. 2. As word size increases, so does the amount of RAM that can be handled directly. An eight-bit microprocessor can directly access 64K bytes of data, and a 16-bit microprocessor can directly access 256K. 3. A small program is built into ROM which starts the process of reading the operating system code from the disk. 4. Compatibility.

Using Microcomputers

Microcomputers are designed to perform a variety of tasks. The people who buy and use microcomputers are a diverse group—businesspeople, teachers, students, doctors, lawyers, and farmers—and their computing needs are just as diverse. This section describes some of the many equipment and software options available for microcomputers.

Input Devices

The increased use of microcomputers has promoted the popularity of a variety of input and output devices, many of which have become essential for easy use of microcomputers.

The most common input device is indispensable: the keyboard. Most computer keyboards resemble typewriter keyboards in the layout of keys for letters, numbers, and symbols. They also include computer-specific keys, such as control keys, arrow keys, and function keys. Typing combinations of these keys sends commands to the CPU for performing specific tasks, such as moving the **cursor,** printing a document, inserting a sentence, or removing some data. Some keyboards contain a numeric keypad, which enables the user to enter numbers in a manner similar to using an adding machine (see Figure 5-7).

Keyboard entry is too slow or inconvenient for some applications. Devices that allow the user to bypass the keyboard in moving the cursor and in entering data or commands include joysticks, game paddles, mice, graphics tablets, and light pens. See Figure 5-8 for pictures and descriptions of these devices.

Figure 5-7
The Mac+ Keyboard

MONOCHROME MONITOR
A monitor that displays a single color, such as white, green, or amber, against a darker background.

COMPOSITE COLOR MONITOR
A color monitor that displays a composite of colors received in a single video signal.

RGB MONITOR
A monitor that receives three separate color signals, one for each of three colors—red, green, and blue.

Other input devices formerly used only with minicomputers and mainframes are being adapted for use with microcomputers. These include the voice input devices and scanning equipment discussed in Chapter 3.

Output Devices

The most common output device is the monitor. This device enables users to view information before sending it to the microprocessor for processing, as well as to view information sent from the microprocessor. The information displayed on the monitor can be in either character or graphic form.

A monitor is one of the essential peripherals of a microcomputer system. Monitors generally are divided into three categories: (1) monochrome, (2) composite color, and (3) RGB (red-green-blue).

Monochrome monitors display a single color, such as white, green, or amber, against a dark background. They display text clearly and are inexpensive, ranging from $100 to $300. Most monochrome monitors are composite monitors, so-called for their single video signal.

Composite color monitors display a composite of colors received in a single video signal, and are slightly more expensive than monochrome monitors. They deliver less clarity in displaying text, however, than monochrome monitors. On some, in fact, text is almost unreadable in the 80-column mode. Images on a composite color monitor are less crisp than images on RGB monitors.

RGB monitors receive three separate color signals, one for each of three colors: red, green, and blue (see Figure 5-9). Commonly used for high-quality graphic displays, they display sharper images than the composite color monitors, but they produce fuzzier text than monochrome monitors. They are more expensive than

CHAPTER 5: MICROCOMPUTERS 141

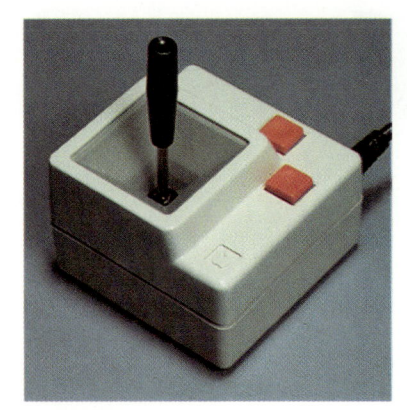

(a) Joystick

(b) Mouse

(c) Graphic Tablets

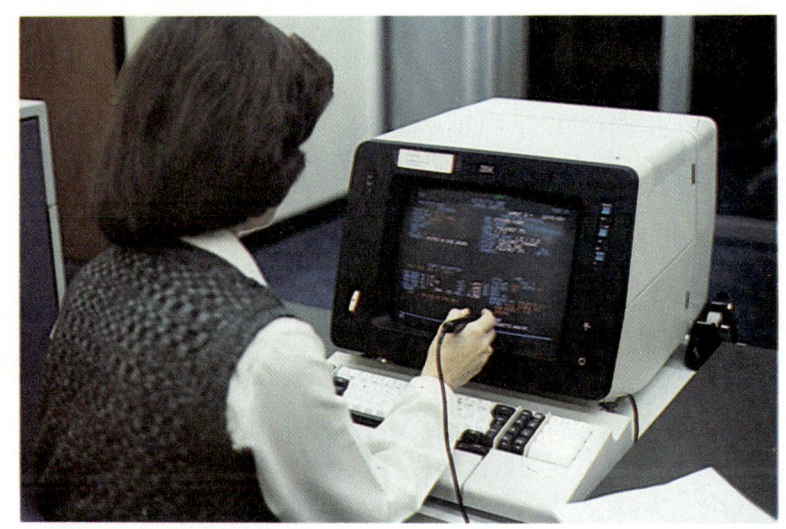

(d) Light Pen

Figure 5-8
Special Input Devices
(a) Joysticks generally are used with game and graphics applications. They allow very fast, multidirectional cursor control. (b) The mouse is a hand-movable input device about the size of a Jell-O box. On the bottom is a small ball like a roller bearing. On top is a pushbutton or two for activating a command. When the mouse is rolled across a flat surface, it sends electronic signals through an input cord to the computer, and the cursor moves accordingly. Using the mouse eliminates a considerable amount of typing. (c) Graphics tablets are flat, boardlike surfaces upon which the user draws, using a pencil-like device. The image is then transmitted to the screen. (d) A light pen is a pen-shaped object with a light-sensitive cell at its end. A person uses the device by touching the light pen to the screen.

**Figure 5-9
RGB Monitor**

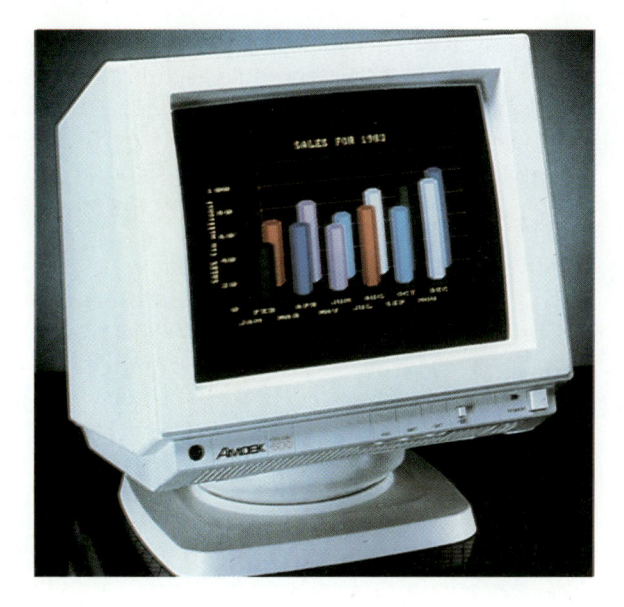

composite color monitors, generally from $500 to $900. An add-on display card is necessary for using RGB monitors with most computers.

Also available are RF modulators, which allow television sets to be used as monitors. Television sets deliver less resolution than any of the other types of monitors discussed here.

Flat panel displays are available for portable computers (see Figure 5-10). They are less bulky and require less power than the cathode ray tubes used in most

**Figure 5-10
Flat Panel Display**

from an angle or in direct lighting makes the image appear faint or even invisible. Two common types of flat panel display technologies are liquid crystal display (LCD) and electroluminescence. LCDs generally show poor contrast and visibility, although new technology is improving them. The electroluminescent panel shows a better display and a wider viewing angle, but also costs more than the LCD. In the future, it is expected that electroluminescent panels will display full color and be readable even in sunlight.

Other common output devices for microcomputers are printers and plotters. The same types of printers and plotters discussed in Chapter 3 are available for use with microcomputers. In fact, the high-quality reproduction, versatile type sizes and styles, and graphics capabilities of laser printers used with microcomputers have fostered a new aspect of computing: desktop publishing (Chapter 6).

Online Storage

The storage media commonly used with microcomputers are cassette tapes and floppy disks. These tapes and disks are inexpensive and small, so they are ideal for microcomputer data storage. They are not suitable for storing large amounts of data, however. Hard disks are more expensive than floppy disks, but they can hold over ten times as much data.

Cassette tapes are popular with microcomputer users because they are inexpensive, easy to store, and in most instances, can be used with a regular cassette player (see Figure 5-11). Data access with cassette tapes is sequential and very slow, so cassettes are used mostly for backing up data held on disks.

**Figure 5-11
Cassette Tapes**

144 PART ONE: COMPUTER LITERACY

Figure 5-12
Floppy Disks
Floppy disks are of three sizes: 8-inch, 5 1/4-inch, and 3 1/2-inch. The 3 1/2-inch disks are enclosed in hard plastic for protection.

Figure 5-13
Hard Disk Unit

Floppy disks (also called diskettes) offer direct data access, so they are much faster than cassette tapes. These disks come in three sizes and are reusable, lightweight, easy to store, and safe to mail (see Figure 5-12). They are accessed by disk drives, which are either built into the computer or separate units connected to the computer. A 5 1/4-inch floppy disk can hold as much as 1.2 Mb (megabytes) of data. Most microcomputers use 5 1/4-inch or 3 1/2-inch disks. Eight-inch disks also are available.

Hard disks are the most expensive form of storage, but they allow very rapid access to data (see Figure 5-13). They can be shared by more than one microcomputer and offer more flexibility than other media. Hard disks hold more data than cassette tapes or floppy disks. Common capacities range from 5 Mb to 80 Mb, although some very expensive hard disks for special purposes hold over 400 Mb. Data access is faster with hard disks than with floppy disks. Hard disks act more like RAM than secondary storage.

There are two varieties of hard disks: fixed and removable. A fixed disk is a sealed unit that the user cannot open, so it is well protected from dust and other environmental factors. Often the disk drive unit comes installed in the computer. It may contain one or more polished aluminum platters covered with a high-quality magnetic coating. Fixed disks are reliable and hold a large amount of data. A removable disk enables the user to change disks. Each disk is enclosed in a cartridge that is inserted into the hard disk drive. This feature provides security, because the disks can be removed and locked away from the computer. Removable disks are not as popular as fixed disks, however, because most have less capacity than fixed disks.

No matter what type of hard disk is used, a backup system such as floppy disks or tape is necessary. The nature of the copy protection on some software prevents convenient use with hard disks.

The development of optical disks will change the way microcomputers are used in the future. With such tremendous storage capacity (550 Mb on a single 5 1/4-inch disk), they make possible a wide range of training and instructional capabilities

CHAPTER 5: MICROCOMPUTERS   145

for businesses. Combined with computer data, the video images stored on one optical disk can provide instruction similar to that given in films, yet enable the user to interact through the computer rather than watch passively. The optical disks commercially available today cannot be erased or recorded on, but that situation is expected to change by 1987 or 1988.

Add-Ons

Add-ons are printed circuit boards or expansion boards containing chips that can increase the capabilities of a microcomputer (see Figure 5-14). They are inserted into a slot on the main system board of a microcomputer. Here are some examples

- Changing the number of characters displayed across the width of the screen (usually from 40 characters to 80 characters).
- Adding graphics capabilities to the computer.
- Adding a coprocessor to the computer so that software for a different operating system can be run.
- Adding memory.
- Providing interfaces for input and output devices, such as printers, graphics tablets, joysticks, or mice.
- Acting as a hard disk drive.

Some software and hardware requires the use of one or more add-ons. Some computers are sold with interfaces for RGB monitors and graphics, for example, whereas others need additional boards.

Figure 5-14 Add-ons
A connected speech recognition board.

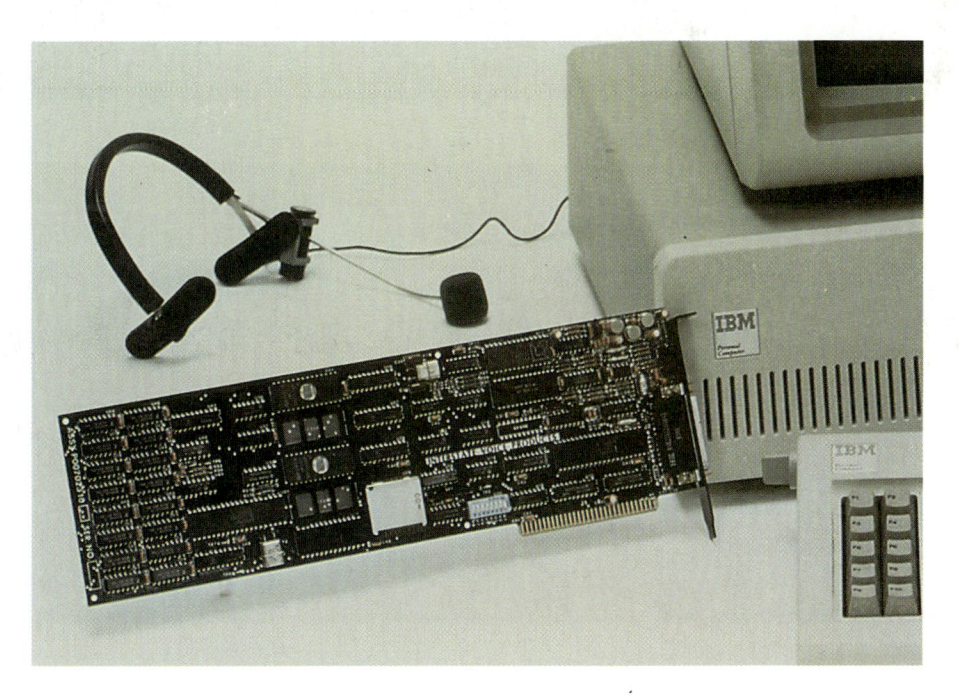

Software Packages

SOFTWARE PACKAGE
A set of standardized computer programs, procedures, and related documentation needed for a particular application.

Figure 5-15
Software Packages
The screens demonstrate the type of display you might see if you were using a similar application. (a) Word Processing (b) Electronic Spreadsheet (c) Business Graphics (d) Data Base

A **software package** is a set of standardized computer programs, procedures, and related documentation necessary for solving problems of a specific application. A wide variety of software is available for managing finances and data, preparing documents, creating art, and learning new skills. Among the popular packages are word processors, data managers, spreadsheets, and business graphics (see Figure 5-15).

Word processing software enables the user to write, edit, format, and print text. Electronic spreadsheets are used for preparing financial data for summaries. Most spreadsheets look like tables, with data and formulas arranged in columns and rows. As the data is changed, the results of the calculations in the formulas change. Data can be filed using data management programs, some of which imitate traditional filing methods: Material is filed by category, and the same data can appear in several files. Other programs provide databases, which allow entry of thousands

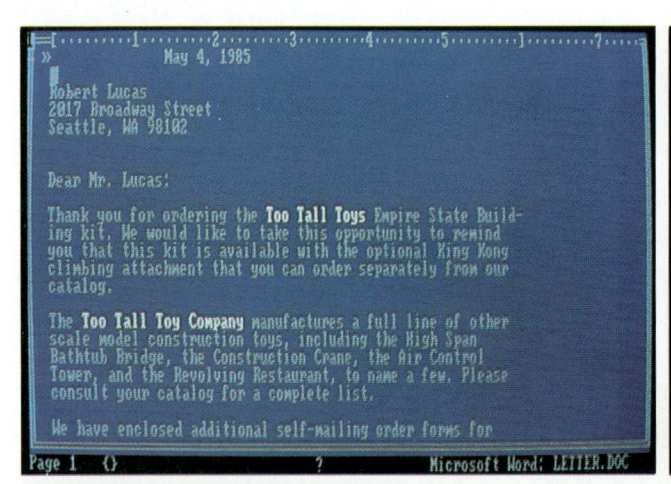

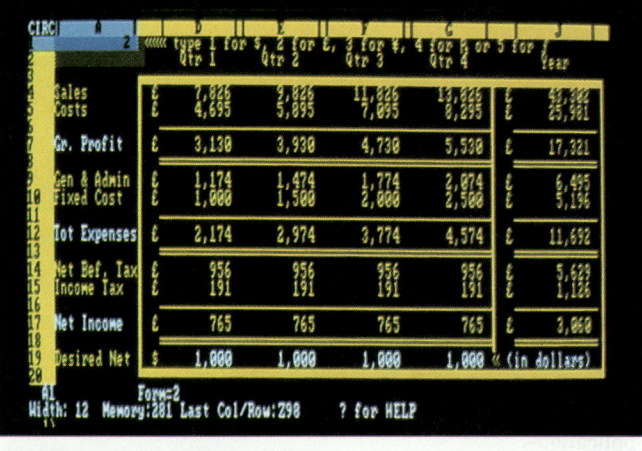

(a) Word processing software

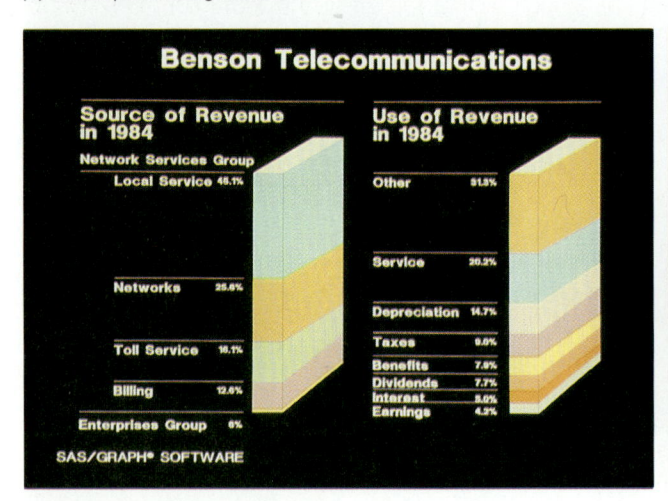

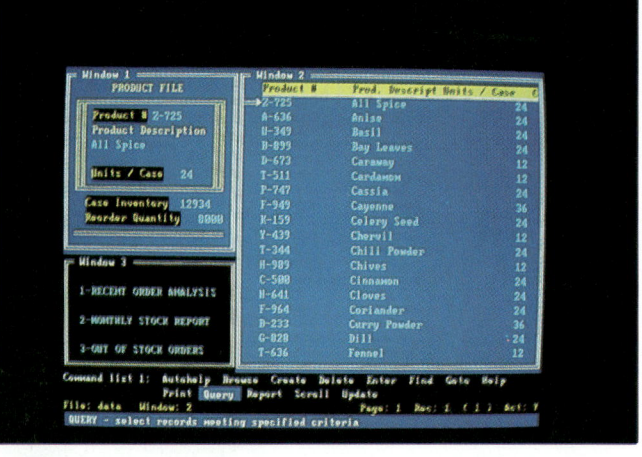

(b) Electronic spreadsheet software

(c) Business graphics software

(d) Data base software

HIGHLIGHT ▲▲▲▲▲▲▲▲▲▲▲▲▲▲▲▲▲▲▲▲▲

Jonathan Rotenberg and the Boston Computer Society

At age 21, he received up to $1500 per consultation as a consultant to computer companies. Earlier, he had organized "Softcon," a huge computer software show at the New Orleans Superdome which attracted more than 1,400 software companies to exhibit their products. And at the tender age of 13, he founded the Boston Computer Society. He's Jonathan Rotenberg, and he's been interested in computers ever since his prep school bought an Altair computer kit and he helped assemble it.

Jonathan and a friend decided to form the Society because they wondered why more people weren't involved in learning how to make use of computers. No one showed up at the first meeting, however, and Jonathan's friend lost interest and quit. Undaunted, Jonathan began publishing a newsletter about new computer products and upcoming computer shows in the Boston area. A few months later, he called another meeting. This time, fifty-seven people showed up.

Gradually, the Boston Computer Society began to gain members and respect. Today, the Society has become the largest, most active, and influential computer group in the world, and sponsors over twenty-two users' groups. Today, in society meetings, Jonathan talks with top management about databases and systems for business. Quite a change from those early meetings in 1975, where discussion focused on computer kits and solder.

---

of records that can be accessed in many ways. Graphics software packages are designed for displaying data as charts, such as bar charts, line graphs, and pie charts. These four types of software are described in Part II of this text, along with exercises for practicing the skills that these programs require.

INTEGRATED SOFTWARE
Two or more application programs that work together, allowing easy movement of data between the applications.

Integrated Software Integration suggests the blending of two or more parts into a whole. When the term integration is used in conjunction with software, it means that two or more types of software are blended into one application package. **Integrated software** generally conforms to three standards:

1. The software consists of several programs that would otherwise be separate application packages.
2. The software allows for easy movement of data among the applications.
3. A common group of commands is used for all the applications in the package.

An integrated package may result when several applications are combined into one. For example, a data manager, spreadsheet, and graphics package could be combined to share data and pass data to another application. Integration also can occur when one type of software is enhanced. An example would be the addition of a spelling program, thesaurus, or grammar program to a word processing program.

Utilities and Other Functions Software can be used for many functions that an office employee or businessperson encounters every day. Some programs provide a calendar for entering appointments and business functions. Others set alarm clocks, dial telephone numbers, or act as calculators and notepads. There are utility programs for programming functions into single keystrokes in order to save time while typing. Such a function may produce a string of characters, such as an often-used sentence or phrase, or a string of commands which performs a task such as backing up or accessing data. Other programs check spelling and grammar and offer alternate word choices.

Utility software may involve a concept called the **RAM disk.** The RAM disk uses a predefined section of computer memory to act as a disk drive. Usually the intent is not to get more storage space, but rather to accelerate access to data. Accessing data on disks is slow compared with accessing data from primary memory. The RAM disk approximates the speed of the microprocessor, therefore increasing the speed of data access.

The setup process is simple: All that is needed is some spare RAM and RAM disk utility software. Typically a RAM disk uses memory in add-on cards, but it may also allocate part of the original primary memory of a computer. The RAM utility software is available on newer versions of some operating systems (MS DOS 3.0 and Apple ProDOS, for example), but it can be purchased separately instead. The RAM disk is commonly used for holding the utility programs described in the previous paragraph which operate compatibly with word processors or other major application programs. When utility programs are used in this manner, sometimes they are referred to as RAM-resident programs.

RAM DISK
A portion of RAM memory that acts temporarily as a disk drive, but approximates the speed of the microprocessor.

Users' Groups

Where can a new microcomputer owner go for help in operating the machine? When a $150 software package will not run, who can identify the problem? Which word-processing package priced under $200 works best on a certain microcomputer?

Questions such as these often baffle the proud new owner of a microcomputer. One answer is a **users' group.** A users' group is a relatively informal group of owners of a particular microcomputer model or software package, who meet or communicate by modem to exchange information about hardware, software, service, and support. Users' groups also may form around applications and related topics, such as real estate, medicine, telecommunications, education, and computer-aided publishing.

The value of users' groups comes from the accumulation of knowledge and experience ready to be shared by members. The best evaluation of hardware and software comes from one who has actually purchased and tried it. As software becomes more sophisticated and more hardware becomes available for enhancing microcomputers, users' groups will become even more valuable.

Users' groups also may be beneficial to small companies whose internal computing experience is limited. Top management may join users' groups to learn about new technology and how it can be used in maintaining a competitive position in a particular business field. Individual businesspeople may be interested in improving their individual productivity.

Since users' groups normally do not have telephones or office space, finding a local group is not always easy. Dealers who sell a given microcomputer usually know how to contact users' groups, and groups often post notices and flyers in computer stores. Information on national groups sometimes is included in a microcomputer package when it is sold. Contacting the manufacturer directly also may yield the name of the person to contact about a local group.

USERS' GROUP
An informal group of computer users who meet to exchange information about hardware, software, service, and support.

CHAPTER 5: MICROCOMPUTERS

Learning Check

1. Describe computer hardware and software that you might use for producing a high-quality bar chart to present a new idea to your boss.
2. Why might flat panel displays be hard to look at for long periods of time?
3. What type of microcomputer storage would you buy to enable two users to access the storage at once.?
4. How are add-ons different from peripherals such as printers, keyboards, and monitors?
5. How does a RAM disk save time?

Answers

1. Computer, RGB monitor, graphics add-on, interface for RGB monitor, keyboard, and color plotter (which also might need an interface). 2. Looking at a flat panel display from an angle or in direct lighting makes the image appear faint or even invisible. 3. Hard disk. 4. They are on circuit boards that are inserted into slots inside the computer. The other peripherals are plugged into a port. 5. It allows faster access to data than a disk drive does.

Summary Points

- Microcomputers are the smallest and least expensive computers. The distinctions between microcomputers and minicomputers are fading as microcomputers become more powerful.
- The increased power and miniaturization of microprocessors paved the way for the development of microcomputers.
- The first microprocessors could manipulate four bits of data at a time. Most microprocessors today handle data clusters of eight, 16, or 32 bits.
- Portable computers can be classified in size as briefcase or notebook. Both types are light enough to be carried and do not need an external power source. Transportables are larger than portables, but still are light enough to be carried. They require an external power source.
- Supermicrocomputers are less expensive than minicomputers and provide users with high performance at a relatively low cost.
- The speed of microcomputers depends on word size and clock speed. Word size refers to the number of bits that can be manipulated at one time. Clock speed is the number of electronic pulses the microprocessor can produce each second.
- Primary memory consists of random-access memory (RAM) and read-only memory (ROM). The amount of RAM is related to the word size of a microprocessor, in that each microprocessor can directly access only a certain amount of data in primary memory.
- An operating system is a collection of programs used by the computer for managing its own operations. Microcomputers with different operating systems are not compatible.

■ Some popular input and output devices used with microcomputers include joysticks, mice, graphics tablets, light pens, printers, and plotters. Keyboards and monitors are among the essential peripherals for microcomputers.

■ Cassette tapes and floppy disks are the storage media commonly used with microcomputers. Hard magnetic disks are used when large amounts of data must be stored and shared. Optical disks are becoming a popular storage medium for use with microcomputers, although they cannot yet be erased and reused.

■ Add-ons are boards containing chips and printed circuits which are inserted into slots on the main system board for the purpose of adding memory, graphics capabilities, coprocessors, or other capabilities to the computer.

■ Popular software includes programs for word processing, electronic spreadsheets, data management, and graphics. Combinations of programs—such as a data manager, spreadsheet, and graphics package, or a word processor and a spelling program—are called integrated software.

■ Users' groups offer owners advice and information about machines, programs, and topics of special interest such as electronic publishing or telecommunication.

Review Questions

1. What differentiates microcomputers from larger computers?

2. Discuss why a closed system microcomputer might be less flexible than a system that you can open easily. Gain access to a microcomputer at home or at school and tell which type it is.

3. Differentiate between portables, supermicrocomputers, and the desktop models of microcomputers.

4. Explain the role of the microprocessor in the operation of a microcomputer. How is it related to RAM?

5. Explain how word size and clock speed affect the speed of a microcomputer.

6. What is meant by microcomputer compatibility, and how is it determined?

7. Name some input devices that allow you to bypass the keyboard, thus reducing the amount of typing needed.

8. Name three disk concepts or technologies that offer greater capabilities than floppy disks. What is special about each?

9. How can an add-on enhance a microcomputer system?

10. Describe the benefits of joining a users' group.

11. Look through computer magazines and find one specific brand name or picture representing each of the following terms: portable computer, flat panel display, RGB monitor, dot matrix printer, keyboard, graphics tablet, floppy disk, word processor, electronic spreadsheet, database, integrated software, utility program for defining keystrokes, and add-on (for any purpose). To make the project more difficult, find products that are compatible with one another.

CHAPTER 6

Computers' Impact on Society

Outline

Introduction
Telecommunications
   Message Transmission
   Software for Transmission
   Communication Networks
Learning Check
Automation
   The Electronic Office
   Automation in Manufacturing
Highlight: Desktop Publishing
Learning Check
Electronic Monitoring
   Monitoring in Science
     Laboratories
   Monitoring the Human Body

The Automated Home
Highlight: Nan Davis's New
   Venture
Learning Check
Number Crunching
   Simulation and Modeling
   Weather Predictions
   Business Forecasting
Graphics
   Pictures of Our Earth
   Graphic Computer-Assisted
     Diagnosis
   CAD/CAM
   Business Graphics
   Graphics for Analyzing Motion

Education
   Computer Literacy
   Programming
   Computer-Assisted Instruction
   Interactive Video
   Networks
   Computers on Campus
Learning Check
Summary Points
Review Questions

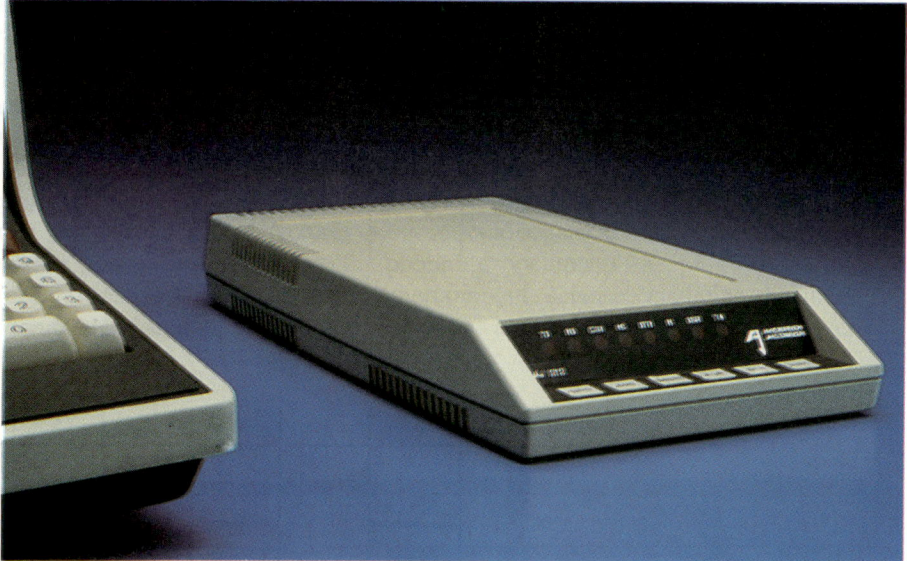

Figure 6-2
Types of Modems

BAUD
A unit of measurement for transmission speed.

BANDWIDTH
The range of frequencies available for transmission on a given channel; also known as grade.

Modes of Transmission Modems handle the actual transmission of the data in one of three basic modes: simplex, half-duplex, or full-duplex (see Figure 6-3). Simplex transmission is unidirectional, or one-way: Data can be sent or received, but not both. Half-duplex transmission occurs in both directions, but only one way at a time. Full-duplex transmission occurs when data is both sent and received simultaneously.

Speeds of Transmission The speed at which data is transmitted is referred to as **baud.** Baud is commonly identified as the number of bits per second that can be transmitted over a communication line. Baud rates vary. The most common speeds used with microcomputers are 300 baud and 1,200 baud. A 2,400-baud modem is available for use with microcomputers, but at that speed, poor telephone lines can rob the signal of its strength or introduce noise that distorts the message. Baud rates higher than 2,400 are used only in specialized data transmission.

The grade or **bandwidth** of a channel determines the rate at which the channel can transmit data. A narrow bandwidth channel, such as a telegraph line, transmits data at rates of 45 to 90 baud. Telephone lines have a wider frequency range and fall into the classification of voice-grade channels. They carry data at 300 to 9,600 baud. For high-speed transmission of large volumes of data, broad-band channels transmit data at rates of up to 120,000 baud. Coaxial cables, microwaves, and fiber optic cables (see Figure 6-4) belong in this category.

Software for Transmission

Communication software also is required for data transmission. For example, communication software helps a microcomputer become temporarily a part of the remote computer system with which it is communicating. In effect, the software "tricks" the microcomputer into acting as a part of the remote system. In larger

CHAPTER 6: COMPUTERS' IMPACT ON SOCIETY 155

**Figure 6-3
Transmission Modes**

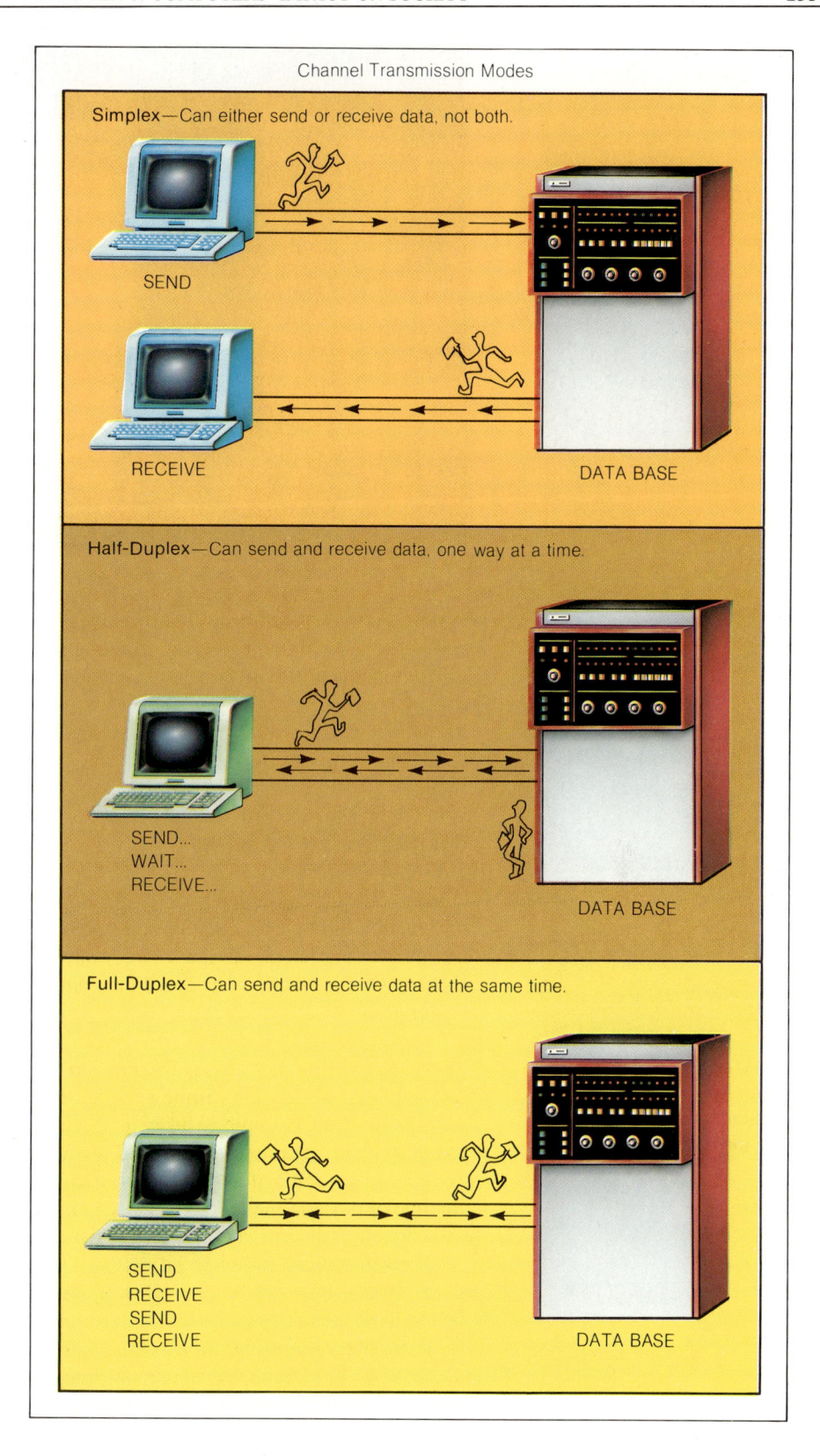

Channel Transmission Modes

Simplex—Can either send or receive data, not both.

SEND

RECEIVE

DATA BASE

Half-Duplex—Can send and receive data, one way at a time.

SEND...
WAIT...
RECEIVE...

DATA BASE

Full-Duplex—Can send and receive data at the same time.

SEND
RECEIVE
SEND
RECEIVE

DATA BASE

Figure 6-4
Cross Section of a Fiber Optic Cable

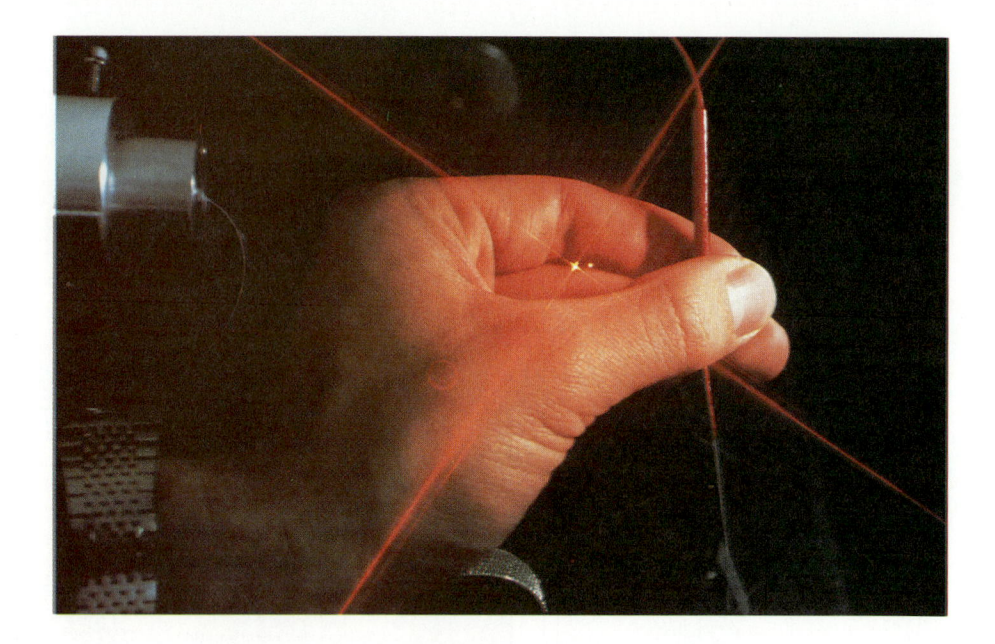

systems, communication software manages the communication between the central computer and remote terminals, microcomputers, and other equipment.

Communication software for microcomputers should be able to transmit data in ASCII (American Standard Code for Information Interchange) form. Most information services send their data in ASCII form, and personal computers store their data in this form.

Communication Networks

One of the most popular uses of personal computers is sharing resources and information through the use of commmunication networks. Networks can connect a computer via telephone lines to commercial information services or electronic bulletin boards. They can also link computers within a building or complex, forming a local area network.

INFORMATION SERVICE
A commercial service that offers information over communication lines to paying subscribers.

Information Services An **information service** gives the user access to vast databases of information. Some services even enable users to communicate with one another; for example, a user in Rochester, New York, might compete in a computer game against a player in Phoenix, Arizona. Most services require the payment of an initial fee. All services charge an hourly rate, which varies with the time of day and the type of service being used. Passwords and/or identification numbers are issued to subscribers to ensure legitimate access to the service.

There are several commercial network services available to subscribers. Three of the largest are The Source, Dow Jones/Retrieval Service, and CompuServe, Inc. Individuals and businesses subscribe to these and other information services to fill a variety of information needs. They can receive video versions of major newspapers, stock market reports, airline and hotel reservation services, sports news, movie and book reviews, gourmet recipes, foreign language drills, and video catalogs for shopping by computer. Students, researchers, businesses, and private investors all can benefit from using an information service. As the information needs of our society increase, information services will play an important role in fulfilling those needs.

ELECTRONIC BULLETIN BOARD
A smaller, user-run version of the commercial information services, offered at little or no cost to users.

Electronic Bulletin Boards Computer users also can access **electronic bulletin boards,** which are operated by computer enthusiasts and can be accessed at little or no cost. The thousands of bulletin boards in operation across the United States are used primarily for the exchange of information or programs. People who call a bulletin board may want to try one of the many programs stored on the system. They can also post messages for other users. This option is helpful for finding buyers and sellers for hardware, locating user groups in other communities, and getting evaluations of new software packages.

A bulletin board can be started by practically anyone who has a telephone, a microcomputer, a modem, and communications software. Electronic bulletin boards often are set up for users of a particular computer system, for example, IBM computers. Some bulletin boards are set up for users with special interests rather than for owners of particular computers. For example, there are bulletin boards for writers, lawyers, and pilots. Others have been created to help people research events or to conduct informal polls on political issues.

LOCAL AREA NETWORK
A specialized network of computers and peripherals which operates within a limited geographic area, such as a building or complex of buildings.

Local Area Networks Local area networks (LANs) link computers in the same general area for the purpose of sharing information and hardware (see Figure 6-5). Usually the computers are within 1,000 feet of each other, because they must be connected by a cable hookup, which can be expensive. People at the work stations in a LAN gain more capabilities in word processing, data processing, information retrieval, and communication without duplication of equipment, databases, and activities. LANs are just starting to become popular. Many businesses are installing LANs in order to improve the efficiency of office functions and to facilitate office automation.

Figure 6-5
Local Area Network
Local area networks will continue to gain popularity because of the explosion in microcomputer use in businesses. Portable microcomputers with LAN capability may represent the wave of the future.

Learning Check

1. Name some common communication channels.
2. What function do modems perform, and in what two ways must they conform to the party being accessed?
3. What four items are needed for telecommunications applications?
4. How do information services and bulletin boards differ?
5. What is a LAN, and what purpose does it serve?

Answers

1. Telegraph lines, telephone lines, microwave links, coaxial cables, communication satellites, fiber optic cables. 2. Modems prepare signals for analog transmission. They must be in the same mode and speed as the connecting party. 3. Computer, telephone or telephone lines, communication software. 4. Information services are commercial and charge a fee; they contain large databases. Bulletin boards are usually free and offer specialized information. 5. Local area network; lets users in the same general area share data and hardware.

Automation

Just mentioning the word automation often is enough to start a group of people arguing about the impact of office automation and robotics on jobs. The current availability of robots and electronic office machines makes the argument seem mere rhetoric; automation is here to stay. Automation, with appropriate human intervention, has helped improve operations in offices and manufacturing plants.

The Electronic Office

The office environment is changing rapidly due to developments in communications, information storage and retrieval, and software. Organizations realize that computer technology is efficient, cost effective, and necessary to handle the information revolution. The increasing amount of reporting required by governmental agencies in particular lends itself to computer technology in the office.

Nearly every office function—typing, bookkeeping, billing, filing, and communications—can be done electronically. Among the specific applications are word processing, electronic mail, teleconferencing, telecommuting, and information retrieval. The term applied to the processes that integrate computer and communication technology with traditional office procedures is **office automation** (see Figure 6-6).

OFFICE AUTOMATION
Integration of computer and communication technology with traditional office procedures in order to increase productivity and efficiency in the office.

WORD PROCESSING
The use of computer equipment in preparing text; involves typing, writing, editing, and/or printing.

Word Processing The most widely adopted office automation technology is **word processing.** An estimated 75 percent of U.S. companies employ some form of word processing, which provides a mechanism for preparing text and bypasses

Figure 6-6
Typical Environment of an Automated Office

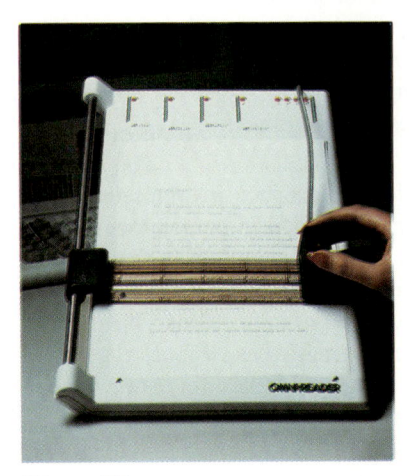

Figure 6-7
Optical Character Recognition Used for Text Input

OPTICAL CHARACTER RECOGNITION (OCR)
A method of electronic scanning which reads numbers, letters, and other characters and then converts the optical images into appropriate electrical signals.

the shortcomings of traditional writing and typing. Like data processing, word processing relieves workers of time-consuming and routine tasks, thereby increasing standards of productivity and quality. It is estimated that, depending on how much typing a secretary does, his or her productivity can be increased by 25 to 200 percent using word processing.

A typical word processing system consists of a computer, keyboard, a visual display device, a storage unit, a printer, and word processing software. A word processing program produces finished copy quickly, in a form that is readable and attractive. The user can edit, rearrange, insert, and delete material electronically until the text is exactly as it should be. Then the text is stored on tape or disk and later printed using a high-quality daisy-wheel printer, laser printer, or draft quality dot-matrix printer. If many form letters must be produced, the secretary has only to type the letter once. When the letter is merged with a file containing names and addresses, an original and personalized letter can be sent to each recipient. Word processing is discussed further in Part II of this text.

The efficiency of a word-processing system can be increased with the addition of an **optical character recognition (OCR)** device (see Figure 6-7). With an OCR scanner, typewritten pages can be read into the computer—a process that saves considerable input time compared to manual retyping. The average operator types text at a rate of 60 words per minute of prepared copy, whereas an OCR can input the same prepared copy at more than 1,000 words per minute. Only the editing needs to be done at the processor's keyboard. OCR scanning relieves a company of some of the expense involved in training operators to use a word processor.

Electronic Mail In large corporations, many messages are exchanged among the members of the organization. Many businesses are using **electronic mail** in order to speed up delivery of the messages and to reduce telephone, paper, and

ELECTRONIC MAIL
Transmission of messages at high speeds over communication channels.

duplicating costs. Electronic mail is the transmission of text at high speeds over telecommunication facilities. It is often used for intercompany communication, and can occur over the company's own communication system or via commercial electronic mail services such as Western Union (EasyLink) and GTE Telenet (Telemail).

The simplest form of computer-based mail system allows one user of the service to send a message to another by placing it in a special storage area in the electronic system. The second user, at his or her own convenience, retrieves the message by printing it on paper or on his or her display screen. The mail can be duplicated, revised, incorporated into other documents, passed along to new recipients, or filed like any other document in the system.

Teleconferencing Office communications can be facilitated by another development in electronic technology—**teleconferencing.** Teleconferencing enables people in different geographical locations to participate in a meeting (see Figure 6-8). Satellite technology has enabled corporations with offices in different countries to take advantage of teleconferencing. Businesses can benefit from reduction in travel time and travel costs.

TELECONFERENCE
A meeting that occurs via telephone, electronic, and/or image-producing facilities, thereby eliminating the need for travel.

The most basic form of conducting electronic meetings, audio conferencing, consists of a conference call linking three or more people. Ideal for impromptu meetings, audio conferencing requires no major equipment investment, but it is limited to voice communication. Other forms of teleconferencing allow the transmission of graphics onto visual display screens, or one-way and two-way full-motion video involving cameras or picture phones. Teleconferences using video are expensive, and few organizations are willing or able to spend the millions of dollars required to install and upgrade the necessary equipment.

TELECOMMUTE
To work at home and communicate with the office or send data to the office via electronic machines and telecommunications facilities.

Telecommuting An exciting aspect of the electronic office involves **telecommuting**—commuting to the office by computer rather than in person (see Figure 6-9). Telecommuting offers advantages in cities where office rent is high and mass transit systems or parking facilities are inadequate, and in businesses that do not require frequent face-to-face meetings among office workers. It also has appeal for people with special needs: disabled employees, employees temporarily homebound with injuries or illnesses, parents of young children, pregnant women, retirees who want to remain involved in the work world, and anyone tired of fighting traffic and dressing for success. Many people who telecommute spend one or two days a week at the office to take care of details that require a personal appearance.

Figure 6-8 Videoconference
A videoconference can often save money for corporations that depend on frequent meetings between people at distant branches.

Salespeople and journalists, who are often away from their offices, have already successfully used telecommuting. They type their assignments on portable computers equipped with modems, and then send information over telephone lines to the office. Some companies, such as Blue Cross and Blue Shield of Columbia, South Carolina, have experimented with telecommuting by hiring workers who process claims at home on personal computers. The data then is transmitted to the company's central computers.

Being such a radical departure from past practices, telecommuting is not universally approved. Many employees are not sure they have the discipline to work as well at home as they do in office surroundings. They miss the social interaction of the office and wonder if they will lose out on promotions. Managers fear they

CHAPTER 6: COMPUTERS' IMPACT ON SOCIETY 161

Figure 6-9 Telecommuting
One futurist, Jack M. Nilles, Director of Interdisciplinary Programs at the University of Southern California, estimates that by 1990, 15 to 20 percent of American workers will work from their homes by telecommuting.

will lose control over employees who are out of sight. In addition, labor unions oppose telecommuting; they say telecommuting will trigger an age of electronic sweatshops, with clerical workers receiving piecework wages without any benefits. They also object to "farming out" electronic data entry to workers in countries where labor costs are low, a practice that results in fewer jobs in the United States.

Information Retrieval The final but integral aspect of office automation is information retrieval—getting stored information to users in a form they can understand. In the past, users often had to look through entire reports to locate the information they needed. Now they can use an electronic file management system and avoid this expensive and time-consuming chore. Database management and text management systems allow direct access to company information. The information may be in the form of data, text, images, or voice. The user specifies key words and asks the computer to search for these words in large volumes of text. The computer produces lists telling where the key words appear, and the user assembles the appropriate information in a form he or she can use.

Information retrieval is not limited to sources or files inside a company. Companies also may subscribe to commercial information services, such as CompuServe Inc. or the Dow Jones/Retrieval Service in order to keep up to date on marketing trends, technology, and other important information. Access to commercial services allows workers to obtain information quickly.

Automation in Manufacturing

The computer revolution has done much to increase productivity in industry. Manufacturing, which involves designing and building products, requires extensive planning and scheduling. Computers can help manufacturers handle the routine

HIGHLIGHT

Desktop Publishing

Is your organization still putting out the same old tired mimeographed in-house newsletter? Well, groan no more. With the use of special software and the new less-expensive laser printers, your organization can produce a snappy, professional-looking newsletter. (That's assuming, of course, that the artist laying out the pages has a good sense of graphic design.)

Arthur Young, one of the "Big Eight" accounting firms, is one company that is taking advantage of desktop publishing. Pamela Davidson, editor of the company's *Micro Newsletter*, has spiffed up the publication by using products such as the Macintosh microcomputer, Apple LaserWriter, and Aldus Corporation's PageMaker software. She no longer shells out $79 a page for typesetting and additional charges for pasteup, but instead completes writing and layout in her office. Once the pages are printed on the LaserWriter, they are sent to a commercial printer to be reproduced in quantity.

Although the LaserWriter produces only 300 dots to the inch compared to the 2,000 dots per inch of professional typesetting equipment, it sure looks a lot better than mimeographed copy. And with the proper software, an editor can design a classy banner for the newsletter, use different fonts and type sizes, right-justify text, lay out multiple columns on one page, and print art on the same page as text. She can even use scanning equipment to digitize photographs for reproduction. Take that, you old mimeographed rag, you!

SOURCE: "New Flash for the Company Newsletter," Michael Antonoff, *Personal Computing*, October, pp. 52–61.

MATERIALS REQUIREMENT PLANNING (MRP)
A computerized method of inventory control which involves entering data into a computer and receiving a report based on the data.

COMPUTER-INTEGRATED MANUFACTURING (CIM)
An arrangement that links departments within an organization to a central database for greater efficiency in the manufacturing process.

scheduling of inventory, machinery, and labor, and they can automate the assembly line.

Materials Requirement Planning Inventory control can be handled by a complex system called **materials requirement planning (MRP).** This system consists of programs that enable the manufacturer to enter projected demands and other data into a computer, and to receive reports that list the manufacturing schedule and raw materials needed to make a product that meets those demands. When the blocks of programs are tied together with purchasing and financial applications, such as cost accounting and accounts receivable, they enable a manufacturer to control the entire plant operation.

Computer-Integrated Manufacturing For great savings and efficient operations, manufacturers can tie together design, manufacturing, scheduling, and monitoring functions in a process called **computer-integrated manufacturing (CIM).** CIM is an attempt to connect various departments within a company into a central database. The CIM database can help management run a more coordinated, efficient operation, from raw materials to completed product.

In the United States, no plants currently have a company-wide CIM program. Some operations do employ the CIM concept in certain areas, however. To be successful, CIM requires a long-term commitment from management. Companies experimenting with CIM include Boeing, General Motors, and General Electric. Boeing has saved $2.8 million annually by using CIM to link certain design and manufacturing operations, and GE has found that CIM is most successful when implemented in a step-by-step plan.

ROBOTICS
The science dealing with the construction, capabilities, and applications of robots.

Robotics A new class of workers is being called upon to perform undesirable work in businesses all over the world. During the 1960s, these workers were assigned simple jobs such as spot welding and spray painting. By the 1980s, their duties were much more complex. They began handling nuclear wastes, moving materials, and mining for coal. These workers are the steel-collar workers, better known as robots.

Robotics is the science that deals with robots, including their construction, capabilities, and applications. Most robots are used for performing tedious, dangerous, or otherwise undesirable work in factories. A typical robot is anchored to a stationary base on the factory floor (see Figure 6-10). It consists of a mobile arm ending in some sort of viselike grip, claw, or other tool that performs the desired task. A second generation of robots possesses tactile sense and crude vision. These robots can "feel" how tightly they are gripping an object and "see" whether there are obstacles in their path. The combination of touch-sensitive grippers and computerized vision has created a robot capable of reaching into a bin of mixed parts, finding a certain object, and picking it up. These actions may sound simple, but they involve a complex series of judgments and movements. Collectively, these robots are called bin-picking robots.

American factories have over 6,000 robots at work; the auto industry is the largest single user of robots in this country. The number of robots in factories is expected to increase rapidly, reaching 150,000 by 1990. General Motors, General Electric, and Westinghouse currently are three leading users of industrial robots. They use steel-collar workers for performing standard jobs such as spot welding and spray painting, as well as more complex jobs such as fitting light bulbs into the dashboards of cars, sorting objects, and assembling electronic parts. Robots also can operate machines, such as stamping mills and electric saws, which otherwise could maim careless workers.

Figure 6-10 Robotics
Robots anchored to the factory floor do routine but often dangerous welding jobs.

Robots operate faster and more efficiently than humans, working around the clock without becoming tired or bored. They do not get hungry or sick or join a union. Robots range in price from $7,500 to $150,000 and have an average lifespan of about eight years. They cost about $5 per hour, whereas human workers might command $20 per hour. Unlike human workers, however, robots lack common sense and may continue making errors that human workers would recognize immediately.

Learning Check

1. What does the term office automation encompass?
2. Name one advantage of word processing.
3. Name two ways of automating communications in an office.
4. What groups of people might need telecommunications?
5. Name two processes that aid in the efficient operation of a manufacturing plant.

Answers

1. It involves using data processing equipment in performing most office functions, including word processing, communications, and information retrieval. 2. It allows a document to be prepared once, personalized for specific circumstances, and printed as an original copy as many times as desired. 3. Electronic mail; teleconferencing. 4. Some examples are disabled employees, parents with small children at home, pregnant women, and retirees who still want some work. 5. Materials requirement planning (MRP); computer-integrated manufacturing (CIM).

Electronic Monitoring

The electronic age has produced many kinds of equipment for use in monitoring chemical and nuclear plants, combustion engine emissions, body functions, air traffic, and many other factors. This section discusses the ways in which computerized monitoring equipment has benefited scientists, physicians, patients, and the general public by maintaining constant vigilance over the changing conditions of our lives.

Monitoring in Science Laboratories

Because of the enormous volumes of data that must be stored and processed for some scientific tasks, scientists use large computers to handle the data and to produce output in a form that is easy to read and interpret. Often these tasks involve monitoring the environment.

CHAPTER 6: COMPUTERS' IMPACT ON SOCIETY

Some monitoring requires instantaneous calculations and results. Because the computer can give results in real time—quickly enough to affect the outcome of a situation—computer technology appears in the chemical industry and in nuclear power plants. Immediate awareness of problems in these areas is crucial. For example, a crisis such as the one that occurred at the Three Mile Island nuclear power plant, where the temperature of the nuclear reactor exceeded safe limits and threatened to melt down the core, may be avoided in the future with emergency management systems. The life-endangering gas leak at the Union Carbide plant in Bhopal, India, might have been prevented with computerized warning systems.

An emergency management system developed by Form & Substance, Inc., of Westlake Village, California, was designed for the chemical industry. It contains information such as the properties of the chemicals manufactured at a particular plant site, evaporation rates of the chemicals, the influence of the surrounding land on wind patterns and flow, and backup plans for possible accident situations. The computerized data bank is constantly updated with information supplied by chemical sensors around the plant. These sensors keep track of temperature, toxin levels, and wind velocity and direction (see Figure 6-11). In the event of an emergency, the system supplies instructions and appropriate emergency telephone numbers. Nearby residents are warned automatically through a prerecorded telephone message. While the residents are being warned by the computer, the necessary plant personnel are free to work with civil defense people and to mobilize resources within the plant itself.

Chemical plants are not the only places where emergency management systems are used. The Federal Nuclear Regulatory Commission now requires such systems in nuclear power plants. Although an emergency management system does not guarantee that a crisis can be resolved, it will make emergency evacuation and response much more efficient.

The use of computerized monitoring equipment enables scientists to spend valuable time conducting experiments rather than overseeing the instruments. For

Figure 6-11
Emergency Management System
The SAFER system (left) is an emergency response system that alerts industrial companies to toxic releases that could pose potential harm to the employees and neighboring area. The system displays actions to take in a variety of emergency situations. The display frame (right) illustrates the essential graphic information helpful in an emergency situation.

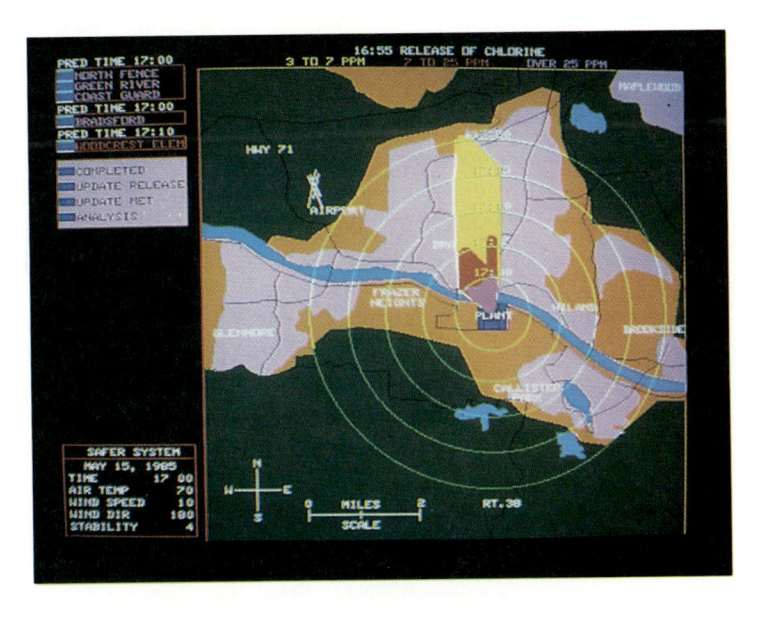

example, computers reduce both the time and cost involved in the study of cells at the California Institute of Technology in Pasadena. Deoxyribonucleic acid (DNA) is a chemical that carries genetic information in human cells. Strands of DNA formerly were synthesized (cloned) by a manual process that took weeks and sometimes months, and cost from $2,000 to $3,000. A computer can perform the same task in less than a day for only $2 to $3! Because the manual procedure involves much repetition, it was easy for technicians to make mistakes. Once the task was turned over to a computer, the mistakes were eliminated and the procedure became more economical.

Another application of scientific instruments involves volcano monitoring. The May 1980 eruption of Mount St. Helens in the state of Washington was predicted by scientists with the help of data analyzed by computers. Devices such as tiltmeters, which show trends in the tilt of the crater floor, and seismometers, which measure harmonic tremors around the volcano, sent data to a laboratory in Vancouver, Washington, every 10 minutes. In the laboratory, computers analyzed the data, thereby helping scientists predict volcanic activity. Because instruments like these are located inside the volcano, volcanic eruptions can be predicted within 30 minutes, so that scientists working near and on the volcano can be evacuated quickly by helicopter. One aspect that cannot yet be predicted, however, is the fury of the eruption and the extent of the mudflow created by the eruption. Mount St. Helens, one of the most extensively monitored volcanos in the world, surprised scientists with the heavy mud flow that followed its eruption.

Monitoring the Human Body

New uses for computers in medicine are emerging daily, while other uses are being improved. Computers have increased the quality of nursing care and the efficiency of monitoring systems. For example, only a few years ago, round-the-clock nursing care was needed for individual critically ill patients. Now computer-controlled machines can monitor life support systems in the intensive care and coronary care units of any hospital. These machines inform doctors and nurses about a patient's vital signs such as heartbeat, blood pressure, respiration, temperature, and pulse. The display for each patient on a monitoring system is shown on a terminal or screen at a nurse's station, so one nurse can oversee many patients rather than just one. When a problem occurs, an alarm is sounded automatically by the computer, and the nurse can initiate appropriate emergency treatment. Besides providing accurate and current information, many of the monitoring systems store data about the patients, which can be retrieved for later study by specialists.

Computer use for intensive care also extends to neonatal units, which specialize in the care of premature and sick newborn babies. In the neonatal unit at New York Hospital, each incubator is equipped with a video screen and keypad. Using the computers, nurses enter and retrieve information needed for treating the infants. Meanwhile, two Hewlett-Packard computers constantly monitor the heartbeat, respiration, and blood pressure of the babies (see Figure 6-12).

Advances in electronic technology have improved implantable monitoring systems for the human body, such as pacemakers. Originally, pacemakers used transistors in controlling the heartbeat. These devices could stimulate the heart only

Figure 6-12
Neonatal Monitoring
Computers are used to monitor infants in neonatal intensive care units.

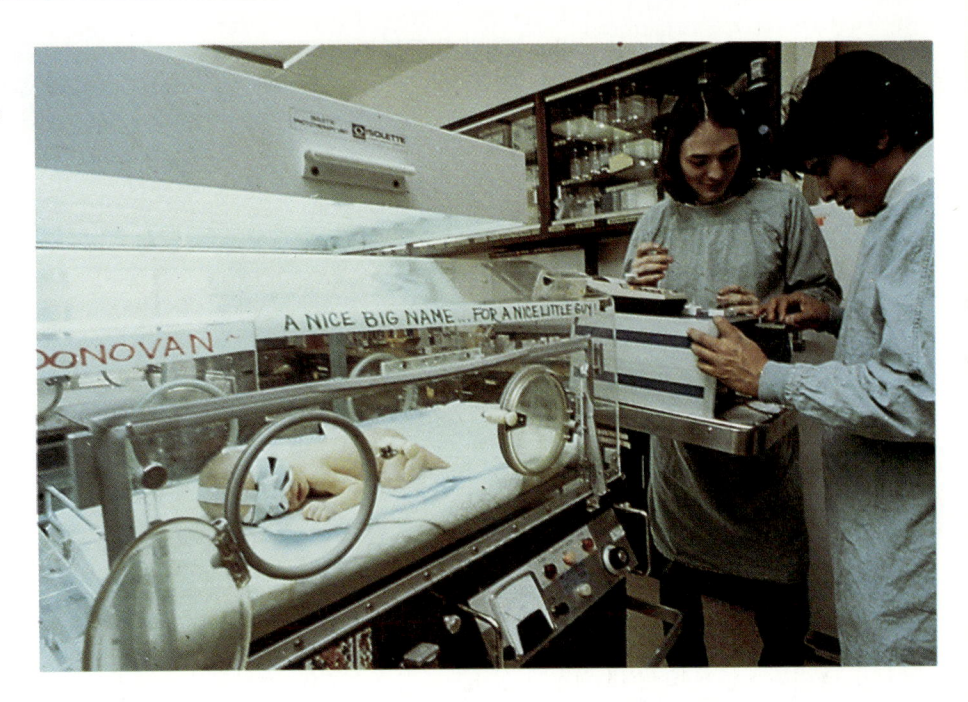

at fixed pulse rates, even though a healthy heart beats at varying rates. In addition, early pacemakers were heavy, weighing almost 7 ounces. Today's contain microprocessors that enable doctors to enter up to thirty separate functions, such as delay between pulses, pulse width, and energy output per pulse. In this way, a pacemaker can be programmed to deal with a patient's particular heart problems. More sophisticated pacemakers can store heart performance data for retrieval by the physician (see Figure 6-13).

Figure 6-13
Symbios Pacemaker System by Medtronics

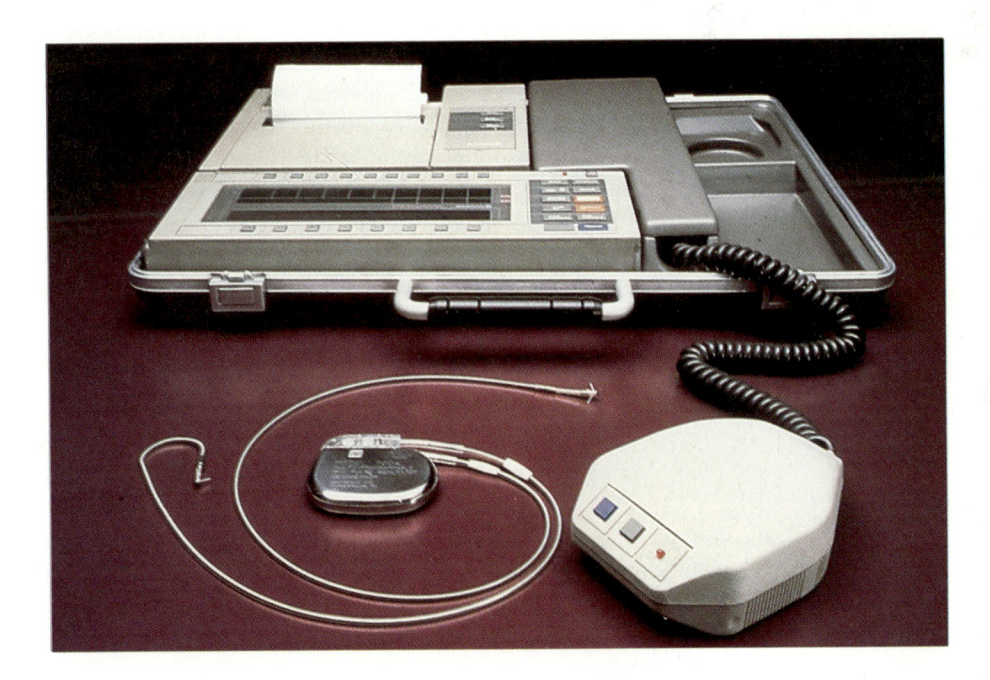

Figure 6-14
The Itrel Spinal Cord Stimulation System This implantable spinal cord stimulator is used for management of chronic, intractable pain. It produces electrical signals that block pain messages traveling to the brain. The stimulator can be programmed at a console or with a hand held programmer.

Another application using microprocessors, still in the experimental stages, involves the controlled release of medication by devices implanted in the body (see Figure 6-14). One device currently undergoing testing is called PIMS (Programmable Implantable Medicine System). PIMS is a 3-inch computer that is programmed to release measured doses of a drug over time. When a drug is taken orally, once or twice a day, it is distributed throughout the whole body; often only a small amount of the drug reaches the correct organ. Also, the amount of the drug present in the bloodstream varies over time as each dose is administered. PIMS and other similar devices are designed to overcome these problems. One experimental device, which is being tested by diabetic patients, dispenses a 40-day supply of insulin from a refillable reservoir using a miniature pump. The reservoir can be refilled with a hypodermic needle. Radiotelemetry and a desktop computer console enable doctors to reprogram the rate at which the pump dispenses medicine. A diabetic's blood sugar level can be monitored closely, and the precise amount of insulin needed can be released into the body. The device has the potential of eliminating some of the life-threatening side effects of diabetes.

The Automated Home

A microcomputer can be dedicated to one particular job, or several microcomputers together can be used for handling many functions in the home. In Arizona, for example, a computer-controlled house has been built as a showcase of home monitoring systems. Called Ahwatukee (a Crow Indian word meaning "house of dreams"), this house is described as the state of the art in technology, ecology, and sociology. Visitors come by the thousands each month to view the house in a half-hour tour.

HIGHLIGHT ▲▲▲▲▲▲▲▲▲▲▲▲▲▲▲▲▲▲▲

Nan Davis's New Venture

You may remember reading about Nan Davis and Dr. Jerrold Petrofsky. Nan Davis is the St. Marys, Ohio, woman who in 1982 was the first paraplegic to walk in Petrofsky's laboratory at Wright State University. Her feat was made possible by a walking system that combined computer-controlled electrical stimulation with a lightweight brace and electrically conductive clothing. Since then, the electronic walking system has been improved by the addition of a mechanical backup, a smaller "power pack," and a reduction in the number of individual wires.

By walking, Nan Davis experiences a reduction in the demineralization of bone and an improvement in circulation, both concerns for people confined to wheelchairs. Davis and Petrofsky are involved in an exercise program at Middletown Regional Hospital for people with spinal cord injuries, and Davis is the administrative director of the program.

The program is the first clinical application of therapy that uses a computer for stimulating muscles, thus enabling paraplegics and quadriplegics to exercise their paralyzed limbs. Participants will exercise on a computerized stationary bicycle about 30 minutes per day, three times a week. At the end of their three- to six-week therapy periods, they will purchase the equipment and continue the program at home. In addition to promoting circulation and bone strength, the exercise promotes aerobic conditioning and muscle development. All these benefits serve to help the patients feel healthier, become more independent, and have a better body image.

Five microcomputers are linked to run the five systems in the house. Heating, cooling, and the opening and shutting of doors and windows are the primary functions of the environmental control system. The security system protects against intruders with the use of television cameras, sensors, and a password-controlled front door. The sensors also watch for fire and sound a warning if necessary. An electrical switching system uses sensors to note people moving through the house

---

Learning Check

1. What is real time, and why is it important to monitoring systems?
2. Name one example of monitoring in science laboratories.
3. Name three uses of monitoring equipment in the medical field.
4. How can monitoring equipment be used in a home?

Answers

1. The term real time describes a situation in which results are received quickly enough to affect the outcome of an event. It is important in monitoring systems because some of these systems are used in situations that could quickly become dangerous to humans and their surroundings. 2. Computer equipment is used for monitoring volcanos. 3. Monitoring life support systems in intensive care units; controlling heart beats; administering correct amounts of medications. 4. To save energy and detect intruders.

and adjusts the lights appropriately. Cost-efficient use of electricity is ensured by the energy management system, and an information storage and retrieval system is provided for personal or home business needs.

Less elaborate systems are available for just about any home user. Among these systems are TomorrowHouse from Compu-Home Systems International in Denver, Colorado; Waldo from Artra Corporation in Arlington, Virginia; and HomeBrain from HyperTeck, Inc., in Whitehouse, New Jersey. Systems such as the ones just named regulate energy consumption, ventilation, and appliance use. Using sensor devices, computers can control the temperatures in all rooms, raise shades, activate switches, and turn on security lights. Some systems are designed to dial the police if a break-in occurs, and turn on a video camera that monitors the area of break-in.

Number Crunching

Computers are very good at number crunching, that is, performing large and complex calculations in a matter of seconds or minutes. Especially in scientific research, weather predictions, and business forecasting, researchers appreciate the number-crunching capabilities of computers. Computers make mathematical calculations and projections in seconds which human beings could not complete unaided in months. Computers gather, compile, and sift statistics to determine similarities and differences that are not apparent to humans. In addition, computers can generate models and make projections without the subjectivity that humans inevitably bring to such tasks. The following sections demonstrate how computers help in making large and complex calculations.

Simulation and Modeling

SIMULATION
Representation of conditions likely to occur in a real-life situation when variables are changed.

MODELING
The process of developing a prototype or mathematical representation of an idea or object in order to design and test it.

EXPERT SYSTEM
Software that uses a base of knowledge in a field of study for decision making and evaluation processes similar to those of human experts in that field.

In science, computers are used for simulating and modeling tasks. The computer is programmed to consider certain facts, which are stored in memory, and then make a decision. The computer makes **simulations** by duplicating the conditions likely to occur when certain variables are changed in a given situation. In the chemistry lab, chemical reactions can be simulated on a computer. One advantage of this type of simulation is that explosive or otherwise dangerous reactions can be discovered without endangering the chemist or destroying the laboratory.

In computer **modeling,** the computer constructs a mathematical model or an image of a prototype of some object on the video screen. Shapes and sizes can be changed easily to alter the model. Computer models are used in many fields, such as astronomy, ecology, engineering, and chemistry. Engineers and designers of airplanes, for example, usually design parts of an aircraft on a computer before building a real model. Many bugs can be worked out on the computer, thus saving considerable time and money.

Some simulations and modeling systems are referred to as **expert systems,** because they plot the best course of action using the same information that experts in a field would use. For example, computer systems programmed to contain the

CHAPTER 6: COMPUTERS' IMPACT ON SOCIETY

knowledge of geological experts are used to assist oil companies. These systems examine geological data and advise the companies where to drill. Usually, an instrument called a dipmeter is dropped down a hole to measure geological conditions. Human specialists qualified to read the dipmeter are scarce; however, computer expert systems can replace the specialist and dipmeter, and have proven to be almost as successful as the traditional method in determining where to drill for oil.

Weather Predictions

The forecasting of weather is one of the most interesting applications of computers. Several variables, such as air pressure, wind velocity, humidity, and temperature, are fed into huge computers that are programmed to solve complex mathematical equations. These equations describe the interaction of these meteorological variables, thus enabling forecasters to predict the weather and study hurricanes and tornadoes.

The world's weather information is collected by the National Weather Service in Maryland from a variety of locations: hundreds of data-collecting programs (DCPs) placed on buoys, ships, weather balloons, and airplanes; about 70 weather stations; and four satellites (see Figure 6-15). Two of the satellites orbit the earth over the poles to send pictures revealing the movement and shape of clouds. The other two satellites are in stationary orbits above the equator.

The Weather Service's "brain" consists of fourteen computers housed at the meteorological center. These computers receive information from some of the DCPs, whose data is beamed up to the two "stationary" satellites above the equator. The computers also receive information from other DCPs; this information

Figure 6-15
Weather Forecasting
This meteorologist is using Centralized Storm Information System to forecast severe weather across the United States.

travels from ground station to ground station. The fourteen computers use all of this incoming data to construct a mathematical description of the atmosphere. These weather reports—2,000 daily—are sent to local weather offices. Manual processing of this amount of data would take so much time that the results would not be available until the weather conditions had already occurred!

Business Forecasting

Although most business computations can be handled by general accounting software, more complex calculations often are needed in order to help businesses make wise investment decisions. Linear algebra often is used in making business forecasts and preparing schedules for production. A computer aids the businessperson in performing these complex mathematical tasks.

Perhaps the most common use of the computer in financial analysis involves the **electronic spreadsheet.** A spreadsheet is a large grid divided into rows and columns. Spreadsheets are used for designing budgets, recording sales, producing profit-and-loss statements, and performing general accounting and bookkeeping. Although electronic spreadsheets are useful in many areas of business, nowhere are they more helpful than in financial analysis, or forecasting, which determines profit margins, sales, and long-term strategies. The reason for the great impact of the electronic spreadsheet in this area is its ability to answer "What if?" questions quickly and accurately. The spreadsheet does this by recalculating all figures when one or two variables are changed.

For example, if the financial analyst for a jeans manufacturer wants to see how a change in the cost of fabric would affect the financial status of the company, he or she could simply enter the expected costs into the computer. Using an electronic spreadsheet, the computer would quickly recalculate all figures that would be affected by the changed costs, such as the cost to manufacture the jeans and the profit. In very little time, the financial analyst could see how profits would go up or down. Spreadsheets are discussed in detail in Part II of this text.

ELECTRONIC SPREADSHEET
An electronic grid, or table, used for storing and manipulating any type of numerical data.

Graphics

Probably the most familiar use of computer graphics is readily seen on television and motion picture screens. Artists use computers for preparing sports logos, commercials, animated cartoons, and science fiction films. There are many other products of computer graphics, however, including pictures generated from data collected by Landsat satellites; pictures of the insides of our bodies used for medical diagnosis; designs for automobiles and airplane wings; business graphics; and graphics that help analyze dance and exercise motions.

Pictures of Our Earth

Landsat satellites launched by NASA orbit the earth and collect approximately 30,000 overlapping pictures to provide a view of the whole earth. These pictures

Figure 6-16 Landsat
From 570 miles above Tokyo, Japan, this computer-generated Landsat picture defines subtle details in surface geology. Urban areas appear in light blue, Tokyo Bay appears in dark blue, and land under cultivation appears in red.

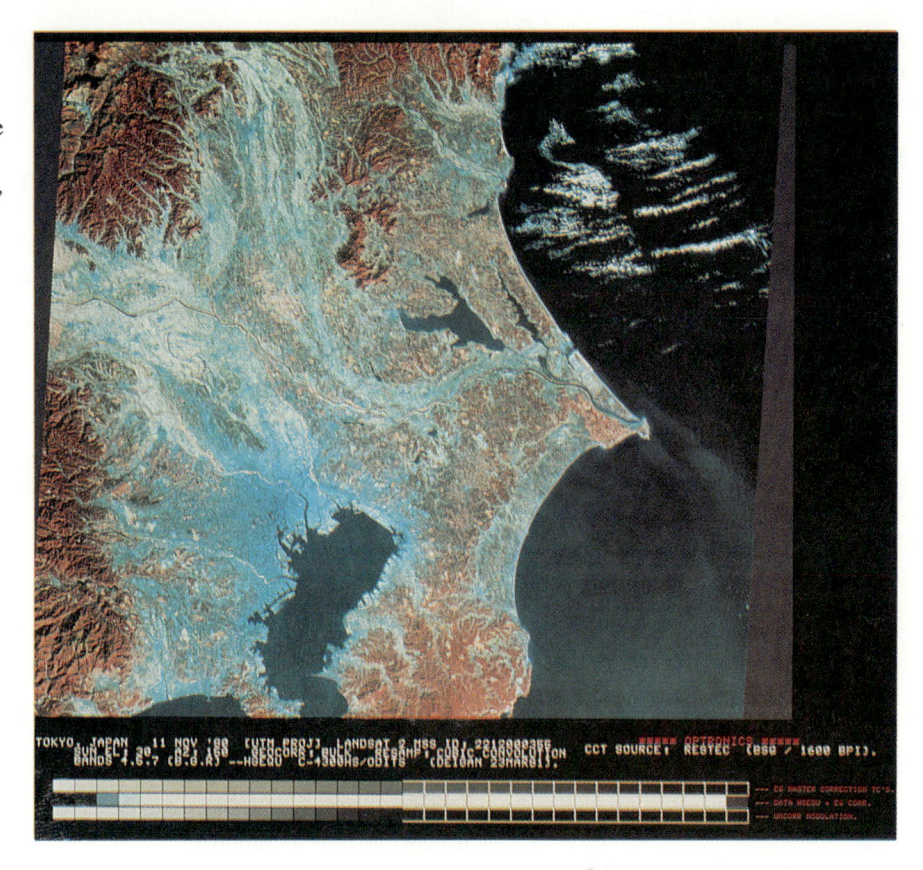

are recorded as digitized electronic pulses, which are broadcast to a ground receiving station. Once received, the data is entered in computer memory and translated into photographs that scientists study (see Figure 6-16). Light patterns and infrared radiation from the sun, which is reflected by the earth, appear on the Landsat pictures and can be detected by the computer. Areas of healthy and sick vegetation can be identified by examining the infrared radiation patterns.

Because the photographs do not show Earth in the same hues that we perceive in our natural environment, they must be enhanced by color. A special color scheme has been adopted: A photograph with red areas indicates healthy vegetation, such as forests and wheat fields, because plants emit high levels of infrared radiation. Areas with a dense human population emit low levels of infrared and are shown as a grayish-blue color. The results of this NASA venture are available to 130 countries. Experts examine the colors and tints to detect mineral deposits, urban areas, and regions of insect infestation or droughts. Landsat photos can even help pick out the best locations for oil drilling.

Graphic Computer-Assisted Diagnosis

Computers often are combined with testing equipment to provide diagnostic tools in hospitals and clinics. Two common diagnostic tools—computerized axial to-

Figure 6-17
CAT Scan Image
A technician studies the image produced by a CAT scan, which will help diagnose a medical problem.

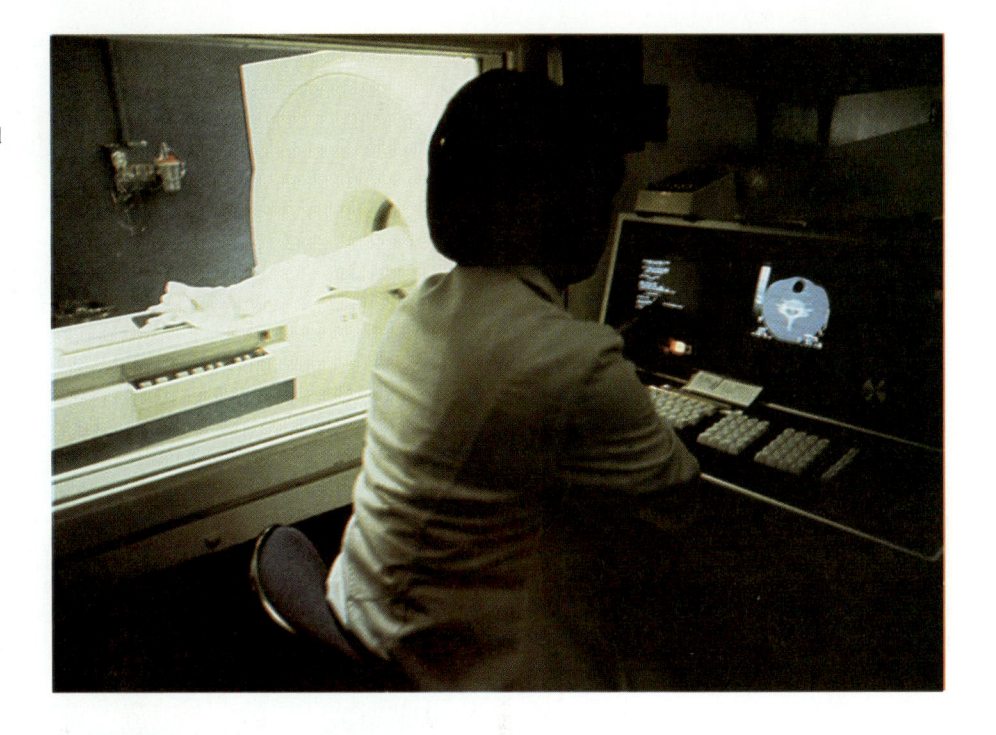

COMPUTERIZED AXIAL TOMOGRAPHY (CT or CAT)
A form of noninvasive physical testing that combines X-ray techniques and computers to aid diagnosis.

NUCLEAR MAGNETIC RESONANCE (NMR) SCANNING
A computerized diagnostic tool that involves sending magnetic pulses through the body in order to identify medical problems.

mography and nuclear magnetic resonance scanning—use graphics in noninvasive (nonsurgical) testing techniques.

Computerized axial tomography (CAP or CT), commonly known as the CAT scan, is a diagnostic aid that joins two tools: X-rays and computerized evaluations of X-ray pictures. A CAT scan can provide clear pictures of cross sections of the body, whereas ordinary X-rays cannot. Using many cross sections together, it is possible for a CAT scan to make a three-dimensional composite of an organ or bone (see Figure 6-17). Computerized axial tomography often is used to assist doctors in reconstructive surgery, because one of the primary concerns in this type of surgery is how the patient will look afterward. Computer-generated pictures can predict the results of reconstructive surgery.

Nuclear magnetic resonance (NMR) scanning may soon replace the CAT scan in hospitals. Unlike X-ray tests or CAT scans, NMR can "see" through thick bones. Moreover, NMR works without radiation. Magnetic pulses sent through the body react differently when they come into contact with different parts of the body. A computer is used to collect the results and to create a detailed picture of the inside of the body. Often NMR scanning is more successful in detecting problems than CAT scanning. Since the procedure does not use radiation, it can be used for testing small children and pregnant women. There are some drawbacks to NMR scanning, however. For example, it does not produce clear images of bones or spot breast cancer.

Both CAT scans and NMR scans enable doctors to conduct tests and make a diagnosis without invading the body through surgery. This approach prevents the patient from having to undergo unnecessary risks associated with surgery, such as infections and fatigue.

CAD/CAM

Before a product can be produced, it must be designed. The actual design process can be quite time-consuming and costly. **Computer-aided design (CAD)** enables the engineer to design, draft, and analyze a new product idea using computer graphics on a video terminal (see Figure 6-18).

The designer, working with full-color three-dimensional graphics, can easily make changes so that the product can be tested before the first prototype is ever built. The model can be turned to expose any side or angle, and cross-sectional cuts show interior details on the display screen. The computer model also detects strengths and weaknesses of a product, such as unwanted vibrations on an airplane wing, before the first sample is ever built. A CAD system in the automobile industry can check the designs of automotive parts for poor tolerance between parts and for stress points. This can save a great deal of money by eliminating defective designs before money is spent on building them.

Computer-aided design often is coupled with **computer-aided manufacturing (CAM),** and the combination is known as CAD/CAM. Using CAD/CAM, an engineer can analyze not only the product but also the entire manufacturing process. Problems can be spotted and adjustments made before manufacturing is begun, thus saving the manufacturer large amounts of time and money.

Although CAD and CAM normally are associated with the design of vehicles, these processes also assist in the design and manufacture of artificial joints for humans. These joints are surgically implanted to replace defective joints. A system developed at New York's Hospital for Special Surgery uses a digital computer to read a patient's X-ray in three dimensions. The computer then creates an image on the computer screen of what the implant will look like. The computer includes in the design variables such as the patient's age, ambulatory (walking) condition, allergies, activity level, and other relevant details of the patient's medical history.

COMPUTER-AIDED DESIGN (CAD)
The process of designing, drafting, and analyzing a prospective product using computer graphics on a video terminal.

COMPUTER-AIDED MANUFACTURING (CAM)
The use of a computer to simulate or monitor the steps of a manufacturing process.

Figure 6-18   CAD

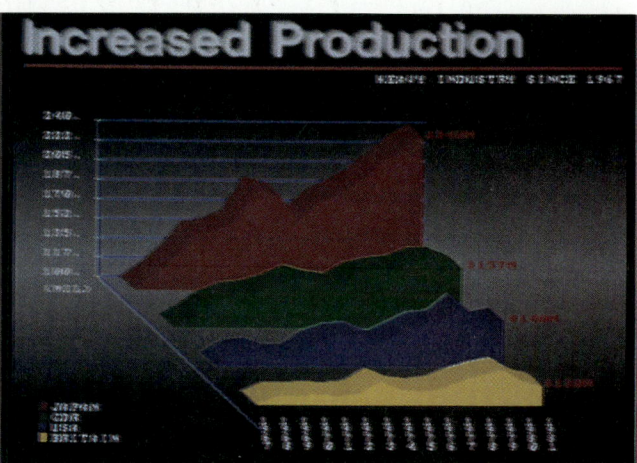

Figure 6-19
Business Graphics
Managers like graphics produced by a computer, such as this pie chart and bar chart, because they summarize information in an easy-to-understand, visual manner.

BIOMECHANICS
The application of engineering methodologies to biological systems.

Business Graphics

Because computers make it so easy to generate and retrieve information, many managers find they suffer from information overload. It is well known in business circles that 80 percent of management decisions are based on 20 percent of the data, but that 20 percent must represent the core data. Finding the right data can be difficult for managers who are flooded with paper. Graphically displayed data helps facilitate decision making. Comparisons, relationships, trends, and essential points can be spotted more easily using graphics.

Business graphics have come a long way from the once-standard black line bar graph. Pie charts, bar graphs, and line and area graphs that are brightly colored and clearly marked can be especially effective in communicating core data (see Figure 6-19). Executives prefer receiving information through graphics because the graphics are attractive and can be understood quickly and easily.

Because these graphs play such a vital role in decision making, many software packages have been developed for use by business managers. The first graphics software package for microcomputers became available in 1979, and the popularity of business graphics software has been growing ever since. Business graphics are discussed in greater detail in Part II of this text.

Graphics for Analyzing Motion

Cameras and computers can be used for analyzing performance in athletics and dance. This process is called **biomechanics.** Sports doctors and biomechanical engineers are creating hardware and software that will help athletes and dancers improve their performance (see Figure 6-20). For example, the Biomechanics and Computer Service Division of the Olympic Training Center, established in 1981, studies sports techniques and bodily stresses during competition. In one procedure, high-speed video cameras record an athlete in competition from two or more angles. The images recorded on video are digitized, and the results are stored in a computer. When these digitized spots are displayed on a computer screen frame by frame,

Figure 6-20 Biomechanics
This equipment in the sports physiology department at the U.S. Olympic Training Center is used to test strength and endurance.

lines connect the dots, creating stick figures that reveal details the human eye cannot see. In gymnastics, for example, the computer reveals exactly how high the athlete leaped, the velocity, and the angle of the arms. Athletes can view the computer screen and see just what they are doing incorrectly. Also, the computer can analyze the data from the digitized images and create graphs showing trends in style. Athletes often find the computer very helpful in improving their performance.

The science of biomechanics also aids dancers, by providing a way of recording dance movements. Traditionally, choreographers have used notation for describing the elaborate dance patterns, but these manual notation methods have not proven adequate and are laborious to perform. A computer graphic system, still in the experimental stage, can record dance by analyzing movements and translating the data into a moving human figure on a computer screen, to be studied and stored for later use. The system allows repetitive steps to be recalled so they do not have to be redrawn each time they are used. Also, the score can be edited instantly.

Education

In the early 1980s, computer experts predicted that there would be millions of microcomputers in schools by the middle of the decade. The experts may have overestimated the numbers somewhat (by the end of 1985 there were about 1,250,000 microcomputers in schools), but there has been steady growth in both the numbers and uses of computers in schools.

Computers also are used for educational purposes outside schools. Businesses and manufacturers are finding that computers help in training their employees, and students can use personal computers for taking college courses at home. In this section, we examine some of the ways computers are helping people to learn new skills and to be successful in school.

Computer Literacy

COMPUTER LITERACY General knowledge about computers; includes technical knowledge, ability to use computers for problem solving, and awareness of how computers affect society.

The appearance of computers in schools is part of an overall educational plan known as **computer literacy.** Not everyone agrees on a definition of computer literacy, but most say computer literacy includes being able to use computers for solving problems and having a basic understanding of computer terminology and technology. Educators believe that computers will play an important part in our lives in the future. If people know how to use computers, they will be better prepared to cope with the changes that technology brings. Educators, parents, and students have seen the computerization of the workplace and realize that there is no turning back. Some form of computer education is necessary for increased chances of success on the job.

One problem with trying to define computer literacy in terms of specific objectives is that the objectives change constantly as the technology changes. Perhaps this point is best illustrated by reviewing the approach to computer literacy in schools during the past ten years. Early attempts at computer literacy focused on computer history, terminology, and internal operations. Although that information is still recognized as important, the focus has changed from how a computer works to how we can use a computer to help solve problems. In other words, the emphasis has moved from theory to applications. Literacy courses also examine the effect of computers on society, and include discussions on computer manners and ethics, in response to some forms of computer abuse.

Just as students need courses in computer literacy, all teachers need to have some computer training. To meet this need, teachers are attending classes, seminars, and workshops to learn about the new technology. In many classrooms, teachers also are learning from their students, to the surprise and delight of both parties.

Perhaps the hardest fact to accept in the area of computer training is that such education is never complete. The technology has not reached a plateau, and one is not expected soon. Whether the students are children, teachers, or business professionals, the learning process is ongoing. As the technology changes, the definition of computer literacy also changes, and the computer literate individual can never stop learning.

Programming

Computer literacy in some schools focuses on programming. In the past, BASIC has been the primary programming language in schools. Its English-like structure and interactive capabilities make it a good language for beginners. You may recall from Chapter 4, however, that some aspects of BASIC seem to encourage sloppy programming and thinking habits. The recent introduction of the version called

CHAPTER 6: COMPUTERS' IMPACT ON SOCIETY

True BASIC offers a more structured style of programming, and one that computer educators find more acceptable for students. The BASIC language does not require the user to be proficient in complex mathematics to be used successfully.

Other popular languages for teaching programming skills are Pascal and Logo. Both emphasize structured programming, and help students develop programming habits encouraged in advanced programming courses in high school and college.

Computer-Assisted Instruction

When computers were first introduced in classrooms in the 1960s, they were used as teaching machines to drill multiplication tables, names of state capitals, and other facts to be memorized. Computers still teach material by repeated question-and-answer presentations of the information, but drills are just one form of **computer-assisted instruction (CAI)** (see Figure 6-21). Included in CAI is a wide selection of software, including the following:

- Drills for quizzing the student. An example is Math Blaster!, which helps students learn arithmetic facts.
- Tutorials for introducing students to new material and quizzing them on their understanding of the material. States and Traits, a program that teaches recognition, placement, and geography of the states in the U.S., is an example of a tutorial.
- Simulations that imitate real-world situations, enabling students to learn through experience and induction without having to take actual risks. An example is Heart Lab, which helps students learn how the heart works.
- Games for learning new concepts and practicing new skills. An example is Archon, an action-strategy chess program that promotes logical and strategic thinking.
- Problem-solving software that encourages exploration and application of pre-

COMPUTER-ASSISTED INSTRUCTION
The use of a computer to instruct or drill students on an individual or small-group basis.

Figure 6-21 CAI

vious knowledge. An example is The King's Rule, which encourages the formation and testing of hypotheses, and recognition of patterns and relationships.

Studies have shown CAI to be a powerful learning tool that is particularly effective when used in certain situations. CAI is quite effective when used with either low- or high-achieving students. It is also an effective teaching tool for specific subjects, such as science, math, and foreign languages. CAI works best when used as a supplement to regular classroom instruction, and has been known to have a positive effect on the behavior and attitudes of students. Using computers, students learn at their own rates, receive immediate feedback, and feel comfortable with their impartial "teacher."

Although many good educational programs exist, much of the software advertised for educational use is unimaginative, poor in quality, and even inaccurate. Too often in the past, educators lacked the knowledge necessary to select appropriate software and to develop a comprehensive plan for its use. In addition, the early software was poorly designed because software publishers hurried to be the first to get their products on the markets, and educators had little choice beyond these inadequate packages.

Fortunately, the educational software picture has improved considerably in the last five years, and there are now some excellent packages on the market which are based on sound educational principles. Among these programs are Gertrude's Puzzles and Rocky's Boots, from The Learning Company; The Factory, a simulation program from Sunburst; The Oregon Trail, from the Minnesota Educational Consortium; In Search of the Most Amazing Thing, from Spinnaker Software; and Where in the World is Carmen Sandiego?, from Broderbund Software. Whatever the software chosen, educators need to spend time assessing their goals before selecting and buying a program.

Interactive Video

INTERACTIVE VIDEO
A multimedia learning concept that merges computer text, sound, and graphics by using a videodisk, videodisk player, microcomputer equipment, and software.

The combination of optical disks and computer programming has created a promising tool called **interactive video.** Some educators believe it will replace the computer, the instructional film, and perhaps even textbooks in many fields. Interactive video merges graphics and sound with computer-generated text by linking an optical disk (videodisk), a videodisk player, a microcomputer with a color monitor and disk drive, and computer software. Using this equipment, a person can watch news footage of historical events, learn about the most recent advances in science, and listen to the music of great composers or the speeches of famous people. The interactive process begins when the user responds to computer-generated questions and forms inquiries to input into the system. The videodisk can be accessed at a chosen point, and motion sequences can be shown in slow motion or still frame for observing critical details.

Videodisk technology will change the way we share information. As a student, you may receive a homework package consisting of software on a floppy disk and graphics on a videodisk to play on your equipment at home. As an employee, you could use the same technology for learning how to demonstrate new cars, trade shares on a stock exchange, or maintain and repair large earth-moving equipment. As a hobbyist, you could purchase a videodisk that contains the latest information about your avocation. Interactive video has become so attractive that some people believe the videodisk player will become the most important peripheral device of this decade. The technology will become even more appealing when disks are developed which can be erased and reused.

Networks

Besides using CAI, some schools allow students to access information utilities. Information services such as CompuServe and The Source provide a range of services from electronic mail to online encyclopedias and additional software. Students are able to access sources that are not found in local libraries and find the most current information on a topic. Using information services teaches new computer skills, too—how to gain access to stored data and transfer that data to the user's disks, for example. Once a communication system is set up, schools can link with other schools, thus enabling students to exchange games, newsletters, and student-written programs.

Special networks or services are available for students through "electronic universities." In 1984, for example, the National Education Corporation (NEC) began offering a system called EdNET, which lets personal computer owners study at home. Over forty courses are available to independent-study participants. Students can correspond with instructional specialists as well as take tests via their home computers. Another company, TeleLearning Systems, Inc. of San Francisco, makes over two hundred courses available to home computer users through its Electronic University. Students enrolled in electronic courses must also purchase textbooks and any other required course materials.

Computers on Campus

In a typical dormitory room on a college or university campus, an observer would expect to find an assortment of books, notebooks, pens, pencils, and other traditional aids to learning. But a survey of college campuses and dormitory rooms in this country might also reveal a relatively new learning tool—the microcomputer (see Figure 6-22). Microcomputers are playing an important role in the college experience, as more and more schools are installing microcomputer laboratories and requiring students to purchase these machines.

New students at Dartmouth College are required to buy Apple Macintosh computers to use as freestanding computers and as terminals linked to the **timesharing** system. Drexel University students also must have access to a Macintosh, which means that most must buy the computers either through the university's purchasing plan or by their own means. Stevens Institute of Technology in Hoboken, New Jersey, requires all students to buy a DEC Pro350 computer with dual floppy disk drives and a 10-megabyte Winchester hard disk, with software, for $2100. Students at Dallas Baptist College in Texas carry 3-pound portable computers around campus for word processing, note taking, and computer literacy classes.

Students and professors are finding dozens of uses for these machines. One of the more popular applications for microcomputers is communication. Many schools are investigating the possibility of implementing campuswide networks, and a few already have networks in operation. A campus network offers students and faculty the opportunity to communicate via electronic mail and bulletin boards. Instructors can help students outside class and receive assignments via computer, and students can access online campus library catalogs from their dormitory rooms.

As students become comfortable with computer use in schools and on college

TIMESHARING
An arrangement in which two or more users can access the same central computer resources and receive apparently simultaneous results.

Figure 6-22
Microcomputers on Campus

campuses, computers will become less of a threat and more of a tool, to be used like a telephone, typewriter, or book.

Learning Check

1. Name three applications that take advantage of the number-crunching abilities of computers.

2. How have computer graphics aided in medical diagnosis?

3. How does CAD benefit an industry?

4. How do graphics overcome the problem of information overload for managers of businesses?

5. Name at least five objectives of computer literacy.

Answers

1. Simulations, weather predictions, business forecasting. 2. They allow testing by nonsurgical methods, such as CAT scans and nuclear magnetic resonance scanning. 3. CAD saves time and money involved in building prototypes of products, by allowing an engineer to design and test a product by computer. 4. They present core material in attractive graphs that are easy to read and understand. 5. Using computers for problem solving; learning about the impact of computers on society; discussing manners and ethics involved in computer use; learning computer terminology; learning how a computer works.

Summary Points

■ Data communication is the electronic transmission of data from one location to another, usually over communication channels such as telephone or telegraph lines, coaxial cables, or microwaves. The combined use of data processing equipment and communication facilities, such as telephone systems, is called telecommunications.

■ Telecommunications applications require the use of a computer, telephone or telephone lines, a modem, and communication software.

■ Modems are required for changing digital signals into signals compatible with the communication facilities. The modem must be able to handle the mode and speed of transmission used by the party or service being accessed.

■ Typical telecommunications applications include using information services and accessing electronic bulletin boards.

■ More and more businesses are linking computers and equipment in local area networks, thus enabling the users to share data and hardware.

■ Most office functions—typing, bookkeeping, billing, filing, and communications—can be performed electronically. Some specific computer applications are word processing, electronic mail, teleconferencing, telecommuting, and information retrieval.

■ Manufacturers can automate several aspects of their operations by using materials requirement planning software, the concept of computer-integrated manufacturing, and robotics.

■ Because the computer can provide instantaneous calculations and results, computer technology appears in areas such as the chemical industry, the environment, nuclear power plants, and medical monitoring, alerting people to problems in these areas.

■ Computers are used in intensive care, coronary care, and neonatal units for monitoring life support systems. Patients also benefit from computer monitoring systems if they must use pacemakers or programmable implantable medicine systems (PIMS).

■ Monitoring systems are also available for home use; they help in energy conservation and alert residents to problems such as break-ins.

■ The number-crunching capabilities of computers help scientists and engineers to create prototypes of ideas or objects, and to simulate conditions likely to occur when certain variables are changed in a given situation.

■ By combining data such as air pressure, wind velocity, humidity, and temperature with mathematical models, forecasters can predict the weather. This is accomplished with the help of fourteen computers at the National Weather Service.

■ Businesspeople benefit from the use of computers in figuring the complex and lengthy calculations required for business forecasting, which includes determination of profit margins, sales, and long-term strategies.

■ Landsat satellites launched by NASA orbit the earth and collect pictures to provide a view of the whole earth. Digitized electronic pulses broadcast to a ground receiving station are entered in computer memory and translated into photographs that scientists study.

■ Computerized axial tomography (CAT or CT), commonly known as the CAT scan, and nuclear magnetic resonance (NMR) scanning are diagnostic aids that use computer graphics to help physicians see the insides of our bodies without surgery.

■ Computer-aided design (CAD) is the process of designing, drafting, and analyzing a prospective product using computer graphics on a video terminal. Computer-aided manufacturing (CAM), often teamed with CAD, is the use of a computer to simulate or monitor the steps of a manufacturing process. These processes are used not only in the automotive and aircraft industries, but also in the design and manufacture of artificial joints.

■ Graphics such as bar charts, line graphs, and pie charts can help businesspeople see core material in an attractive form that is easy to read and understand. These graphics can be created quickly and neatly with the assistance of computer software developed especially for that purpose.

■ Graphics also can be used to analyze the motion of dancers and athletes to help improve performance. The term biomechanics describes the combination of computer graphics and biological systems for this type of analysis.

■ The term computer literacy has come to have many definitions, but generally it refers to a basic understanding of computer terminology, how a computer works, and how to use a computer to help solve problems. The objectives of computer literacy change constantly as the technology changes.

■ Computer-assisted instruction (CAI) is the use of a computer to instruct or drill students on an individual or small-group basis. Generally there are five kinds of CAI: drills, tutorials, simulations, games, and problem-solving software.

■ Students also can use computers with information services, electronic universities, and videodisks, to bring the outside world to their homes or schools.

■ Microcomputers are playing an increasingly important role on college campuses. Many colleges and universities are installing microcomputer laboratories and requiring students to purchase microcomputers. Some of their uses include communications, such as accessing library catalogs or exchanging messages and assignments.

Review Questions

1. Explain the role of each of the four elements required for telecommunications applications.

2. How have electronics and computers enhanced communication within a corporation?

3. Define at least four types of computer applications that help manufacturers deal with inventory, design, and manufacture of products.

4. List some applications in which the instantaneous calculations and results possible with computers can help avert a crisis.

5. Discuss some of the ways in which the emergency management system developed by Form & Substance, Inc., can effectively prevent a disaster. What are some possible problems with using emergency management systems?

6. Describe one application of monitoring equipment which frees scientists from routine tasks and enables them to spend valuable time conducting other experiments.

7. Name and explain five ways computers are being used in the diagnosis and treatment of patients.

8. Discuss how the National Weather Service uses computers to forecast the weather.

9. How are managers victimized by information overload, and how can they deal with this problem?

10. Define the term computer literacy. Why is it so hard to define? What is CAI? List and explain the five types of CAI discussed in this chapter.

11. Discuss some ways in which people can use computers for education in settings other than public schools.

CHAPTER 7

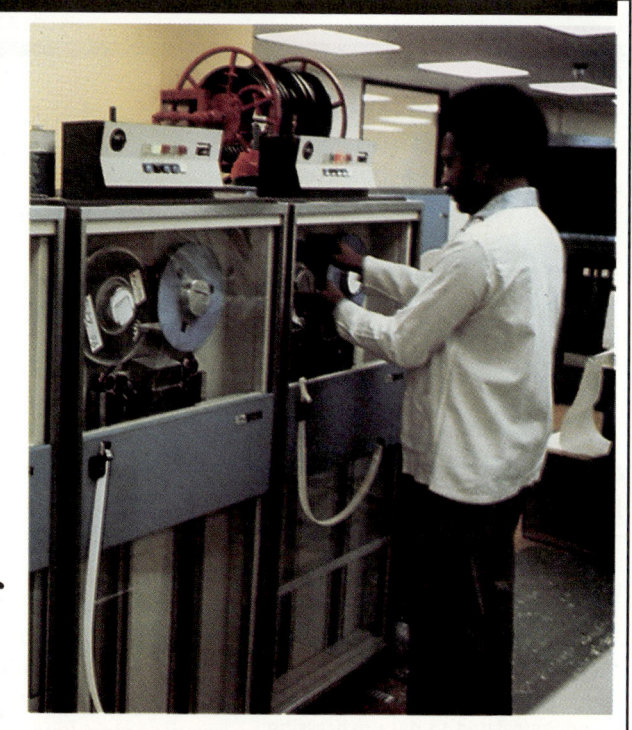

Issues of Concern

Outline

Introduction
Privacy
   Databases
   Privacy Legislation
Learning Check
Crime and Security
   Computer Crime

Highlight: Monitoring in the Workplace
   Security
Learning Check
Computer Mistakes: Who Is Responsible?
Computer Ethics
Learning Check
Identification of Computer and Security Needs

Artificial Intelligence and Automation
   Artificial Intelligence Applied
   Questions and (No) Answers
Highlight: Seymour Cray
Learning Check
Summary Points
Review Questions

Introduction

The impact computers have on our lives goes beyond automated banking, required computer literacy courses, and television commercials. Society itself is rapidly changing as computers become commonplace. Many issues have arisen which are both personal and controversial. No clear-cut answers have been found to questions concerning privacy, computer ethics, and computer crime, for example, but the next few years should bring about more discussion and legislative action on such issues.

Privacy

PRIVACY
The right of an individual to be left alone; as related to data processing, the right of an individual to control various aspects of personal data.

Computers are the main means by which businesses and governments collect and store personal information on credit, employment, taxes, and other aspects of people's lives, and many people have access to this information. Thus, the issue of **privacy** is an important concern. Since the early 1970s in particular, people have worried about the amount of information being gathered about them. As a result, some laws and regulations have been enacted regarding privacy and the use of information about individuals.

Databases

Data regarding the average American appears in thirty-nine federal, state, and local government databases and in forty private-sector files (see Figure 7-1). Computers have made data collection and storage easier; they have also made the exchange of data quick, easy, and inexpensive.

The federal government is the largest collector of such data. Anyone who has served in the armed forces, had a physical or mental disability, committed a crime, received government aid, owned a boat, traveled to foreign countries, or completed an income tax return is listed in the government's databases (see Figure 7-2). The fact that most of these records are accessible by social security number makes it easy for the federal government to sweep the files for matches that indicate a violation of federal regulations. The Internal Revenue Service, for example, is bound by law to share its information with thirty-eight different offices in the government. Social Security and IRS files are scanned for names and addresses of people who have defaulted on student loans or avoided court-ordered child support payments. Other government cross-checks reveal government employees who claim welfare, or match welfare recipients with their bank accounts.

Schools, banks, credit agencies, hospitals, insurance groups, and private businesses also are finding it easier to use computers for storing records. These records probably contain the most comprehensive data maintained about individuals. Information entered into these records may include test scores, periodic performance evaluations, results of physical and psychological examinations, stays in hospitals

Figure 7-1 Databases
Source of data: "How Your Privacy Is Being Stripped Away" *U.S. News and World Report,* April 30, 1984

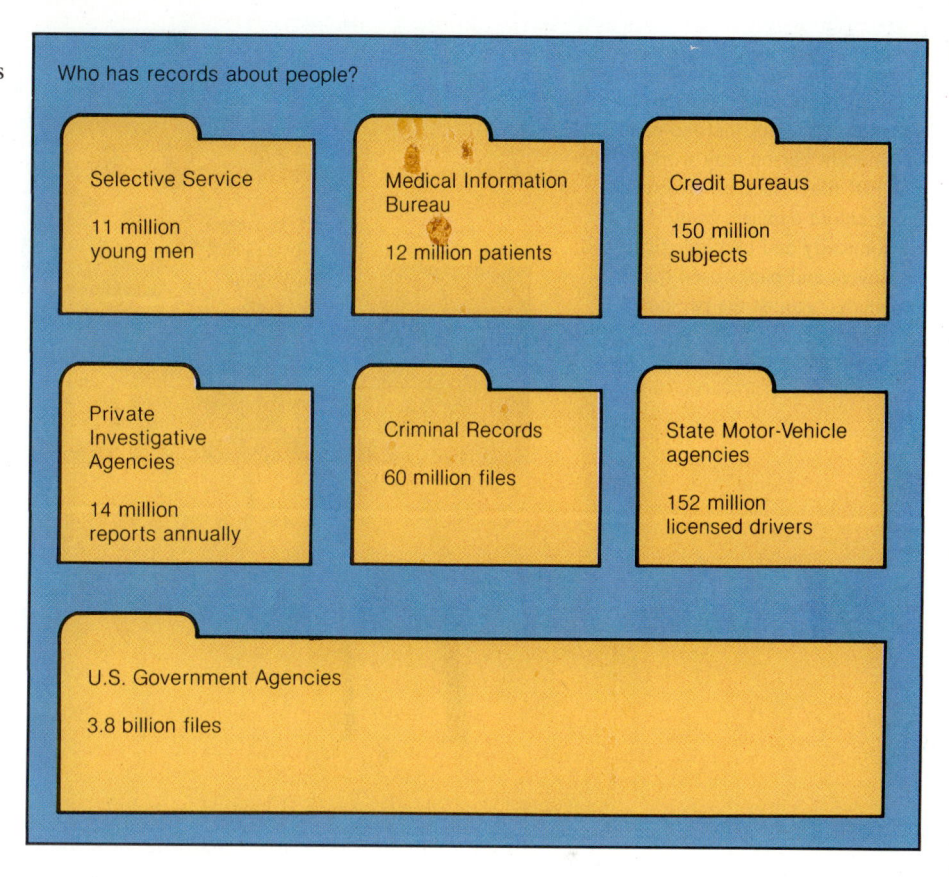

Who has records about people?

Selective Service 11 million young men	Medical Information Bureau 12 million patients	Credit Bureaus 150 million subjects
Private Investigative Agencies 14 million reports annually	Criminal Records 60 million files	State Motor-Vehicle agencies 152 million licensed drivers

U.S. Government Agencies
3.8 billion files

or clinics, transfers and promotions, personal references, salaries, debts, promptness in paying bills, and disciplinary actions.

Release of such information may be embarrassing and may even cause economic or psychological harm to an individual. Yet unauthorized people often see the data, and organizations use the data for unauthorized purposes. The amount of data and the easy access to that data have led to several major concerns about privacy:

■ Too much information about individuals is being collected and stored, and some of it is irrelevant to an organization's goals.
■ Data often is not accurate, complete, or current. Errors are hard to trace, and can be even harder to correct.
■ Organizations make decisions only on the contents of computerized records.
■ Security of the stored data can be a problem.

Despite the problems involved in data collection, organizations need certain data. Businesses need to know a potential employee's background in order to choose the best person for a job. Banks need to know a customer's financial background before granting a loan. Hospitals need data that ensure the proper treatment of patients. Corporations need to know consumer's buying habits in

Figure 7-2
Tapes at the FBI's National Crime Information Center
Some critics worry that the name of an innocent person may work its way into FBI files. Such an error could cause untold damage, both economically and psychologically, if employers and banks used that knowledge against the person.

order to make decisions regarding new products and effective advertising. The government—as seen by the list matching practices—uses data to locate abusers of government services, thus benefiting taxpayers. Using computers in data collection can save time, reduce costs, increase efficiency, alert organizations to risks, and help in decision making by providing the most current information. Therefore, the right balance must be found between an organization's need for information and an individual's right to privacy.

Privacy Legislation

Since the early 1970s, several laws have been enacted which protect privacy by controlling the collection, dissemination, and transmission of personal data. Most of these laws have been passed by the federal government, in order to protect against abuse by the government's own record-keeping agencies (see Figure 7-3). The most sweeping federal legislation is the Privacy Act of 1974, which protects the privacy of individuals about whom the federal government maintains data. Although this act was a step in the right direction, it was criticized for its failure to reach beyond the federal government to abuses by state and private institutions. The act contains the following provisions:

- Individuals must be able to determine what information about them is being recorded and how it will be used.
- Individuals must be able to correct wrong information.

Figure 7-3
Privacy Legislation

Legislation	Provisions
Freedom of Information Act of 1970	Gives individuals access to data about themselves in files collected by federal agencies.
Fair Credit Reporting Act of 1970	Gives individuals the right to access data about themselves.
	Gives individuals the right to challenge and correct erroneous data.
Privacy Act of 1974	Provides individuals with the right to determine what data is recorded by a government agency and how it will be used.
	States that individuals must be provided with a method of correcting or amending incorrect data.
	Requires organizations to ensure the reliability of collected data and take precautions to prevent misuse.
	States that data collected for one purpose may not be used for another without the consent of the individual involved.
Family Education Rights and Privacy Act of 1974	Regulates access to computer-stored records of grades and behavior evaluations in public and private schools.
Right to Financial Privacy Act of 1978	Limits government access to customer records of financial institutions.
	Protects to some degree the confidentiality of personal financial data.
Comprehensive Crime Control Act of 1984	Prohibits individuals from knowingly accessing a computer without authorization to obtain information protected by the Right to Financial Privacy Act of 1978 or information contained in the file of a consumer reporting agency.
	Prohibits individuals from knowingly accessing a government computer and using, modifying, destroying, or disclosing information stored in the computer or preventing the use of the computer.

■ Information collected for one purpose cannot be used for another purpose without the consent of the individual involved.

■ Organizations that create, manipulate, use, or divulge personal information must ensure its reliability and take precautions against its misuse.

Most states also have adopted laws addressing the privacy issue. Unfortunately, relatively few information privacy violation cases have been litigated either on the state or federal level. Because one problem of privacy violation is that information is transferred and disclosed without the knowledge or consent of the subjects, people are not likely to know how their personal records are being used and may not realize they have a claim to take to court. Furthermore, privacy litigation is something of a contradiction in terms: By taking claims to court, litigants may expose private aspects of their lives to a far greater extent than the initial intrusion did.

Learning Check

1. To what aspects of personal data does privacy refer?
2. Name at least ten situations in which data would be collected about a person.
3. Why has the Privacy Act of 1974 been criticized?
4. What is one difficulty of challenging a privacy violation?

Answers

1. The amount collected, the accuracy, the use, and the security of the data. 2. Serving in the armed forces; having a physical or mental disability; committing a crime; traveling under a passport; receiving government aid; filing an income tax return; attending school; being employed; being in the hospital; borrowing money. 3. It fails to extend to abuse of data by state and local agencies. 4. Taking a privacy violation to court may expose private aspects of a person's life to a far greater extent than the initial intrusion did.

Crime and Security

Computers play a role in activities on both sides of the law. They can help in preventing and solving crimes, thus working toward the good of society. Just as easily, they can be used for illegal purposes. Some persons who commit crimes with the aid of computers are computer hobbyists armed only with a home computer, modem, and telephone. Others are programmers who insert hidden instructions into programs, or seemingly respectable employees ranging from data entry clerks to top executives who stumble on a method of increasing their bank accounts by manipulating computerized company data.

Computer crimes are difficult to detect, and the laws protecting victims are few. For this reason, organizations and individuals should investigate methods of securing their hardware, software, and data. Failure to do so can lead to loss or alteration of data, loss of money, and even the ruin of the system.

Computer Crime

Computer-related crime is more of a problem than most people realize. Americans are losing billions of dollars every year to high-technology thieves whose activities go undetected and unpunished. Estimates of losses range from at least $2 billion to more than $40 billion each year. No one really knows how much is being stolen, but the total appears to be increasing rapidly.

What is meant by the term computer crime? Although there is no consensus, a broad but practical view defines computer crime as a criminal act that poses a greater threat to a computer owner than it would to a nonowner or a crime that is accomplished by using a computer. The perpetrator may manipulate input to the computer, change computer programs, or steal data, computer time, and software.

HIGHLIGHT ▲▲▲▲▲▲▲▲▲▲▲▲▲▲▲▲▲▲▲

Monitoring in the Workplace

If you have ever had a heart attack, you're probably thankful that a computer was monitoring your body functions while you were in the hospital. But how would you like to have your work monitored by a computer while you're on the job? Naturally, many employers are enthusiastic about the idea. Knowing that someone is watching you all the time can be unsettling, but computer monitoring is fast becoming an industry standard.

The monitoring system connects workstations to computers to keep tabs on a worker's production. Many employers are using the technique to speed up the work pace and to determine pay raises and promotions. Postal workers are monitored as they key in zip code numbers from each piece of mail. The person who oversees the work watches on a computer monitor that indicates immediately when a zip code is keyed incorrectly. Optical scanners at checkout counters in the Maryland-based Giant Food store chain eliminate pricing guesses by employees and improve inventory control; they also track the workers' speed. In long-haul trucking, on-board computers can track a driver's average speed and number of stops for a freight line employer.

Critics of the monitoring systems maintain that keeping such a close watch over an employee's work habits leads to increased stress, fatigue, and high employee turnover. They also say that the system can easily be abused, citing the case of an 18-year veteran telephone operator who was fired because a computer detected she was taking more than the average 30 seconds per caller. Although she was reinstated the next day due to a top-level protest by the Communication Workers of America, the experience made a deep impression. "To make me responsible for the amount of time customers take is unfair," she said. "What am I supposed to do . . . I can't just cut them off."

Some workers appreciate the discipline imposed by monitoring, however, and mention that computer monitoring is less obtrusive than the constant presence of a supervisor. The tighter control resulted in more accurate data and more prompt completion of work.

Many employers say that computer monitoring is not an issue because they have other ways of measuring output. Traditional monitoring measures the quality of the final product, however, whereas computers monitor measurable work as it is being performed. Experts say that arguments over computer monitoring have just begun. As Michael Smith, professor of industrial engineering at the University of Wisconsin, says: "Nothing frightens people more than if they know that someone is going to be watching them all the time."

SOURCE: "Is Your Friendly Computer Rating You on the Job?" *U.S. News and World Report,* February 18, 1985, p. 66

Sometimes the actual hardware or software is damaged. Because computer crimes often are committed by professional people or office employees—people who have easy access to computer systems and data—they are called white-collar crimes. The four categories of computer crimes are sabotage, theft of services, property crimes, and financial crimes. See Figure 7-4 for definitions and examples of these crimes.

A growing concern is that computer systems will become the targets of terrorists, because of the crucial roles that computers fill in the conducting of a nation's business and military affairs. The awareness that a criminal in one country could tap into computers in another country, in order to switch goods or funds to a third country, is raising questions of law as well as security. In fact, the ease with which computers can transfer data across national borders is creating a security dilemma with a dimension all its own.

**Figure 7-4
Computer Crimes**

Crime	Definition	Examples
Sabotage	Crime directed against hardware or software; physically damages the equipment; requires no special expertise on the part of the criminal.	Flooding the computer room; smashing equipment; damaging stored data or electronic equipment magnetically; planting self-destroying instructions in the software.
Theft of services	Crime that consists of using company computer time, services, or equipment for personal uses.	Acquiring mailing lists or customer lists from a company's computer to use for resale or competitive ventures; using company equipment for freelance work after working hours; using timesharing systems by unauthorized access.
Property crimes	Crime in which computer equipment, software, or company merchandise is stolen.	Stealing computer hardware or making copies of company software for resale or personal use; stealing merchandise by creating dummy accounts to which merchandise is sent, causing checks to be paid out for the receipt of nonexistent merchandise.
Financial crimes	Crime in which computers and software are used to manipulate financial data in the company to the benefit of the perpetrator.	Manipulating the writing of checks, so that multiple checks are sent to the same person or legitimate checks are rerouted to a false address; inserting software instructions that siphon off small amounts from accounts and place them in the perpetrator's account; creating favorable credit ratings for clients.

The unique threat of computer crime is that criminals often use computers to conceal not only their own identities but also the existence of the crimes. Law officers are concerned about the fact that solving computer crimes seems to depend on luck. Many computer crimes are never discovered because company executives do not know enough about computers to detect them. Other crimes are concealed in order to avoid scaring customers and stockholders. It is difficult for a company to admit that its computer systems are not crime-proof.

Perhaps 15 percent of computer thefts are reported to police. Many of these reports do not result in convictions and jail terms, however, because the complexities of data processing mystify most police officials, prosecutors, judges, and jurors. To make matters worse, courts often are lenient in sentencing computer criminals.

The federal government has been slow to pass legislation that deals with computer crime because of disagreements about what computer crime is, how often it occurs, and what to do about it. In 1984, President Ronald Reagan signed into law the Comprehensive Crime Control Act of 1984. This act prohibits individuals from knowingly accessing a computer without authorization in order to obtain information protected by the Right to Financial Privacy Act of 1978 or information contained in the file of a consumer reporting agency. It also prohibits individuals from knowingly accessing a government computer and either using, modifying, destroying, or disclosing information stored in the computer or preventing the use of the computer.

The Comprehensive Crime Control Act follows legislation that many states have enacted regarding a definition of computer crime and penalties for abusing computer use. For example, the Massachusetts state government has passed legislation imposing punishments of up to five years in prison and $20,000 in fines for anyone convicted of damaging computers or software, keeping or destroying software without authorization, entering a computer system with the intent to defraud, or manipulating data to get money, property, or services.

Regardless of the existing laws, it remains largely up to the organization to provide security for its systems and to deal with dishonest or unethical behavior.

Security

Most security problems are caused unintentionally by omission, errors, and accidental destruction. In addition, computer systems, along with data in storage, are vulnerable to hazards such as fire, natural disasters, and environmental problems. Many of these problems would occur less frequently if the proper controls existed. Some problems can be avoided entirely by careful planning, sufficient personnel training, and a well-run computer installation. Other problems, such as computer crime, can be difficult to control completely. Some common security measures are described in the following paragraphs.

■ Organizations should define standards for computer use, with penalties that discourage unethical behavior. Any dishonest or unethical behavior should be dealt with immediately.

■ In order to gain access to company data, authorized users should use special passwords that change periodically.

■ Employees should discontinue careless practices. For example, passwords should not be taped to desks or drawers. Printouts disclosing sensitive financial data or program segments should not be discarded in wastebaskets.

■ Employee responsibilities should be separated. For example, the person who writes orders should not also be the person who authorizes payments.

■ Standards should be established for hiring and training personnel. Persons hired for sensitive computer work should be fully investigated.

■ Data can be translated into a scrambled code, a process called **encryption.** Data transmitted to or from remote terminals is encrypted (scrambled) at one end and decrypted (unscrambled) at the other. Only authorized users can get the data in its unscrambled form.

■ Telephone access to data can be restricted by using a dial-back security measure. Dial-back requires the user to telephone the computer, give a password, and then hang up. If the user and password check out, the computer calls the user back and

ENCRYPTION
The process of encoding data or programs to disguise them from unauthorized personnel.

allows access. This measure ensures that the user is calling from an approved location and that the password corresponds to that location.

■ Backup copies of data should be stored outside the organization's location. Recovery procedures should be established.

In order to deter crime, some organizations have combined several security measures. Access to a computer is granted only after the user passes four tests, which ask for the following:

1. Something the user knows, such as a password.
2. Something the user alone can supply, such as a fingerprint.
3. Something the user alone can do, such as write a signature.
4. Something the user has, such as a magnetic card or electronic key.

Computer security cannot be ignored at home, either. Home computers often contain confidential information that must be protected, such as financial, medical, and insurance information about family members. Also, more business materials will be kept on home computers as more workers participate in telecommuting. Home users also need to employ simple measures that guard against theft and damage to hardware or software.

Just how much security a computer system should have depends on four factors:

■ The value of the hardware.
■ The value of the software and data.
■ The cost of replacing the hardware, software, or data.
■ The cost of the security controls.

Although security precautions reduce the risk of destruction, damage, or theft of computer hardware or software, their cost should be kept within the range that the organization is able and willing to pay.

Computer Mistakes: Who Is Responsible?

We have all heard the story about the man who was declared dead because of a computer error. Social security payments stopped, pension benefits ceased, and the infamous cycle of red tape set in. "So sorry, but if the computer claims you are deceased, you *are* deceased. Computers do not make mistakes . . ."

Of course, computer errors do happen. Some can be humorous, but others are downright annoying. If we have an unhappy experience, we want to know who actually made the mistake and who is responsible for it.

There are several common ways of generating a computer error. By far the most common is using incorrect data. If the data going into the program is wrong, the information coming out will be just as wrong. Incorrect input can come from two sources: (1) the typist mistypes the data, or (2) the person who gathers the data does not check its accuracy. An order from Army officials near Colorado

Learning Check

1. How might a computer crime be committed?
2. What features are included in the Comprehensive Crime Control Act of 1984?
3. Name two inexpensive security measures that could prevent unauthorized persons from obtaining sensitive data.
4. What factors should be considered in deciding just how much security is enough?

Answers

1. By manipulating input to the computer; by changing computer programs; by stealing data, computer time, and software; or by physically damaging the hardware or software. 2. The act prohibits individuals from knowingly accessing a computer without authorization in order to obtain information protected by the Right to Financial Privacy Act of 1978, or information contained in the file of a consumer reporting agency. It also prohibits individuals from knowingly accessing a government computer and using, modifying, destroying, or disclosing information stored in the computer or preventing the use of the computer. 3. Changing passwords often and not taping them to desk drawers or other easily accessible places; being careful about what is discarded in wastebaskets. 4. The factors focus on costs: the value of the hardware; the value of the software and data; the cost of replacing the hardware, software, or data; and the cost of the security controls.

Springs, Colorado, for example, once resulted in the delivery of a ship's anchor to a land-locked U.S. Army base:

The anchor's journey began in early March 1985, when a $6.04 incandescent lamp was requisitioned by computer. Instead of typing the correct order number, 2040-00-368-4972, a clerk at the maintenance unit typed 2040-00-368-4772, the order number for "anchor, marine fluke." Because the order number did correspond to an available item, the computer validated the order. It was shipped from Sharpe Army Depot in Lathrop, California, and arrived at Fort Carson, Colorado, on March 25. Someone astutely observed that it was not a lamp. It was a $28,560 anchor, probably built for use on a destroyer or light cruiser.

Another common cause of computer errors is that the program does not anticipate every possibility. For example, if a program does not take into account the possibility that the current year may be a leap year, a bank's customers could lose one day's interest.

Sometimes this type of error can occur on the system level. That is, rather than an individual program neglecting a possibility, a system might leave out an entire program. A few years ago, the courts faced such a situation:

A North American Van Lines driver drove for over 70 hours in an eight-day period, in violation of an Interstate Commerce Commission rule. The fatigued driver was involved in an accident in which a motorist was killed. The motorist's widow sued North American for negligence, because the company's computer system did not include a program to detect violations of the 70-hour rule. The justices agreed with the motorist's widow, and she was awarded $10 million.

The third type of error occurs when the input is right and the program logic is right—but the answer is wrong. These errors can result if the programmer does not consider the limitations of real and integer arithmetic. Similar errors also can be generated by a power surge. Theoretically, even cosmic rays could interfere with computer operations, but that possibility is very slight.

The fourth type of computer error results from a program designed in such a way that it does not give the same response that a human being would give in the same situation. A prime example involved a stop payment order on a check. A corporate customer of a large bank ordered a stop payment on check number 896, dated February 27, for $1,844.48. The actual amount of the check, however, was $1,844.98. When the computer processed the check, it noted this $.50 difference and did not stop payment. This error resulted in a lawsuit in which the judge ruled that, because a human operator would not have issued payment on the check, the bank was liable for the amount.

A fifth kind of error involves "hackers" who enter a system and change data. Errors can range from altered dosages of drugs or radiation treatments for hospital patients to a few cents siphoned from bank accounts.

Problems and errors also can occur when a new computer system is installed. Consider the case of the Internal Revenue Service and the 1984 income tax returns. The new computer system was scheduled to arrive in the summer of 1984. The IRS twice changed the specifications on the original order, however, requiring more sophisticated equipment each time. As a result, the computers were not ready until November 1984, only a few weeks before the first returns began to arrive. IRS employees scrambled to implement the new system. Equipment malfunctioned, and at the last minute IRS programmers still were rewriting the new software so that it would process data more quickly. As a result, errors occurred, refund checks were late, and many people had to refile their income tax returns. In this situation, the IRS committed a basic mistake of the computer age: It failed to provide sufficient backup during conversion to a new system. The IRS did not have the money or programmers to process tax returns on its old machines in case of emergency.

There is little legal guidance in dealing with computer mistakes. Because the use of computers is relatively new, many states have few, if any, laws pertaining to such errors. Court decisions often are based on Uniform Commercial Code regulations that have to be newly applied—and the rulings are by no means consistent.

As a result, legal responsibility for computer errors may be difficult to determine. Is the programmer personally responsible for errors that are written into the program? Or does the company using the program assume responsibility when it purchases the program? Should the typist be held personally responsible for input errors? Or is it management's responsibility to check the information once it is processed? Can an organization be ruled not responsible for a problem that occurs because a hacker enters its computer system and changes or erases data? Or is it the organization's responsibility to keep backup data and check validity often? And how often is *often?* Can we really expect computers to act as human beings would?

Responsibility is an important issue, because computer errors can be far more serious than most people think. Businesses declare bankruptcy because of computer errors. An insurance company survey showed that 90 percent of all businesses that depend on computers, and that experience a major loss of service due to a computer error, go out of business after that loss.

Computer errors have done more than ruin businesses. Computer errors have endangered people's health, and they have ruined reputations through faulty credit checks. If people, computer systems, and programs are imperfect on a small scale, imagine what could happen when computers have control over much larger aspects of our lives. Imagine what might happen if a computer-controlled space defense shield (Star Wars) system were implemented. Imagine what could happen in a nuclear energy plant run by computers. Under such circumstances, it would be crucial for people to discover errors before the computer does and to determine who is responsible for checking for errors.

Computer Ethics

The issue of computer ethics has become increasingly important as more and more Americans gain access to computers. Any computer user might engage in unethical practices, both at work and at home. For this reason, some code of ethics for computer use is essential.

Violations of ethical behavior range from a minor infringement to the commission of a major crime. As examples, think about the following questions and the ethical issues they involve:

- Should an employee use the company computer for personal use?
- Should an employee look at the records of other employees out of mere curiosity?
- Should a company be allowed to add personal information not related to work performance to an employee's computer records?
- How rigid should a company's policy be regarding monitoring employees by computer, such as keeping track of a typist's speed and mistakes, the number of times people leave their workstations, or the amount of time used in each telephone call at a reservations desk?
- Is is merely unethical to tap online information networks without paying the fees, or is it also a crime?
- What are the legitimate uses (if any) of programs that break copy-protection codes on software?
- If a copy of a program appears on an electronic bulletin board, is it acceptable to download it if the user suspects it is copyrighted software?

These questions and many related ones concern employees, employers, teachers, students, and parents. The answers constitute the standard of moral conduct use, or the degree to which people adhere to computer ethics.

SOFTWARE PIRACY
The unauthorized copying of a copyrighted computer program.

One particular problem in ethics involves **software piracy.** A recent survey by Future Computing Inc. of Dallas revealed that piracy cost vendors $1.3 billion in lost revenues between 1981 and 1984. The firm also predicted lost revenues of $800 million for 1985, and estimated that for every authorized copy of business software for personal computers there is one pirated copy in use. Some experts believe these estimates are conservative.

Most current legal cases regarding copyrights involve illegal bulletin board uses, corporate misuses of software, and pirates who copy popular programs for resale. These cases are heavily prosecuted. In most cases, however, individuals who copy other hobbyists' software for personal use are not taken to court. Their behavior is more a matter of personal ethics, like driving 60 miles per hour when the national speed limit is 55. These people are unlikely to be caught, but they have knowingly violated a law.

Copying software that has been copyrighted is illegal. Software is protected by the U.S. Copyright Act of 1978. Although the creator of an original work is considered to possess the copyright from the moment the work is fixed in some concrete form, he or she gains additional protection by registering the work with the Copyright Office. Registration ensures for the copyright owner the right to bring suit against copyright violators. The creator registers a program by completing Copyright Office registration form TX, paying a ten-dollar fee, and submitting a copy or identifying portion of the program to the Copyright Office.

A copyright notice protects the owner's copyright. In the notice, the symbol ©, the word *Copyright,* or the abbreviation *Copr.* should appear with the name of the copyright owner and the year of the work's first publication. The law makes it illegal to copy a licensed software program except for archival use, which means that one backup copy may be made (see Figure 7-5).

Software vendors have protected their products in other ways besides copyright registration. Many vendors have designed protection codes to make copying disks more difficult. The problem with protecting a disk is that it prevents consumers from making a backup copy, which is legal. It also prevents use of the software with hard disk drives. One trade group is suggesting a hardware device that would be attached to a personal computer. A hard-to-duplicate key purchased with legitimate software would be inserted into the device before the software could be used.

Figure 7-5
Piracy in Other Situations

Object code	Copyright protects the object code, that is, the instructions that actually run the computer. These instructions reside in the operating system, application program, or ROM (read-only memory). A court precedent set in the case of *Apple Computer, Inc. v. Franklin Computer Corporation* extended the copyright protection to the object code. Apple charged Franklin with copyright violations for duplicating the operating system programs contained in the Apple II. Apple was granted an injunction to prevent Franklin from selling the Ace 100, the computer that contained the duplicated operating system.
Databases	With over 2,000 commercial and government databases available for online searching, billions of dollars worth of data now are accessible with a microcomputer and modem. The easy access to the databases and the difficulty in detecting downloading activities makes copyright infringements easy. Whereas downloading data for temporary use or with a downloading license agreement is legitimate, downloading for commercial use or resale is illegal. Copyright infringement cases of databases to date have involved the reproduction of 80 to 100 percent of a program.

CHAPTER 7: ISSUES OF CONCERN

Despite these attempts to discourage software piracy, experts believe the battle will never be won. That prediction probably extends to other matters of ethical behavior, such as unauthorized use of databases and unethical computer-related behavior on the job. For these reasons, computer users need to devise a code of ethics governing their own behavior. Such a code of ethics measures behavior against conscience. After all, the best protection against computer hardware and software abuse is a high standard of personal behavior.

Learning Check

1. What is the most common type of computer error?
2. Name two other ways in which computer errors can occur.
3. How does copyright registration protect the owner of a copyright?
4. What is the meaning of the phrase *computer ethics*?

Answers

1. Using incorrect data. 2. The program may not anticipate every possibility; a program may not give the same response as a human being in the same situation. 3. It gives the owner the right to bring suit against copyright violators. 4. It refers to an individual's standard of behavior regarding computer use.

Identification of Computer and Security Needs

SYSTEM ANALYST
The person who is responsible for the analysis, design, and implementation of computer-based information systems.

Compared to the problematic issues of privacy, computer crime, and errors, concerns about meeting an organization's computing needs seem tame. Yet making the correct decisions regarding computer needs can help an organization overcome difficulties related to these other issues.

In order to identify computer and security needs, a business may employ the services of a **system analyst.** The system analyst deals with the materials, procedures, machines, and people that produce information the corporation needs for making decisions about its business.

To design a system properly, the analyst uses an organized approach called the system approach, which involves five steps: analysis, design, programming, implementation, and audit and review (see Figure 7-6). The analyst performs a detailed investigation of a system which uncovers the objectives of the organization and the best ways for accomplishing these objectives. Some of the factors a system analyst might consider are what types of hardware is needed, whether to develop software in-house or purchase it, and what specific personnel may be needed. The system analyst also guides the organization's decisions about security, procedures for computer use, and policies for access to company data. Once these recommendations are made, the system is designed, the software is prepared, and the system is implemented.

Figure 7-6
The System Approach

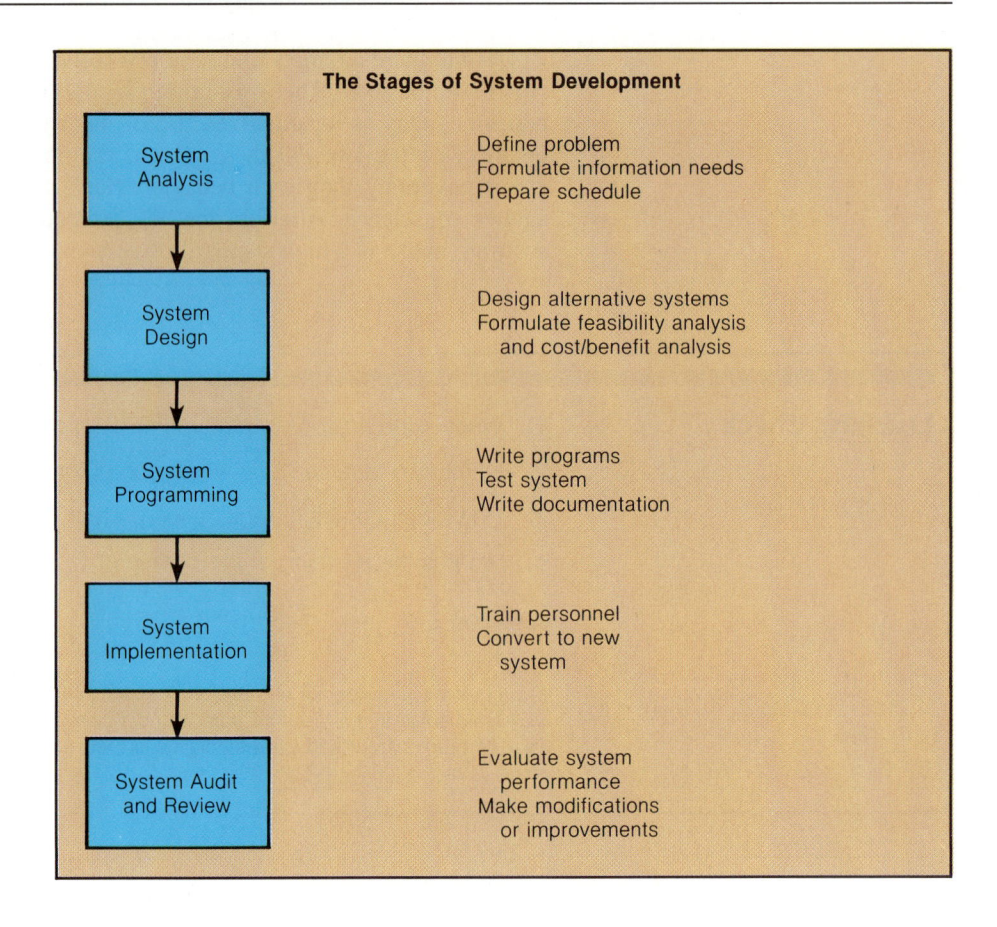

The Stages of System Development

- **System Analysis**
  - Define problem
  - Formulate information needs
  - Prepare schedule

- **System Design**
  - Design alternative systems
  - Formulate feasibility analysis and cost/benefit analysis

- **System Programming**
  - Write programs
  - Test system
  - Write documentation

- **System Implementation**
  - Train personnel
  - Convert to new system

- **System Audit and Review**
  - Evaluate system performance
  - Make modifications or improvements

During the entire process, and after the system is implemented, feedback—audit and review—occurs. The purpose of feedback is to determine whether certain standards have been met within the system. If not, the inputs or processes in the system may need to be changed.

The system analyst may also evaluate a firm's goals, priorities, and general requirements and make suggestions about the kinds of information that could be helpful to its managers. This process is part of establishing a **management information system (MIS),** which uses computers to help managers make better decisions. An MIS differs from a simple data processing system. Simple data processing is used primarily for collecting and manipulating data and producing reports, whereas the purpose of an MIS is to provide managers with useful information that specifically supports their decision-making tasks. To be useful, the MIS must provide relevant information to the appropriate manager at the right time.

Planning a system for an organization is not an easy task, because many factors must be considered. What are the goals of an organization? What are its information needs? Which level of management needs what information? How often are certain types of reports needed? How will the system be implemented so that conversion occurs in a friendly, nonthreatening manner? Will the system require monitoring of employees' work? How will the system meet workers' needs for self-worth,

MANAGEMENT INFORMATION SYSTEM (MIS)
A formal network that uses computers to provide information to support structured managerial decision making.

Artificial Intelligence and Automation

comfort at workstations, and manageable stress levels? Will suggestions from employees at all levels be considered and implemented? Will the benefits of a new system outweigh the costs?

Costs and benefits are primary concerns of managers who are considering implementing devices to improve automation at their companies. The costs and benefits that a manager evaluates, however, may be quite the opposite of the goals of employees. As the technology of automatic devices advances, the rift between management and employees, and between professionals and clients, may widen.

Artificial Intelligence Applied

The term *number crunching* was born in the vacuum tube era of computing, when mathematicians, scientists, and engineers used computers to manipulate huge amounts of numerical data. Even today, number crunching is what most computers do best. As programmers and developers of computer languages become more proficient at designing sophisticated software, however, number crunching will give way to more conceptual applications. Scientists will need faster computers with new designs in order to use the new software ideas. Many people call this new level of computer power the fifth generation.

New computers and languages will only begin to imitate human intelligence at higher levels of abstraction. This type of intelligence exhibited by machines is called **artificial intelligence (AI).** Because human intelligence itself is not clearly understood, current AI programs incorporate just a few aspects of it. The most common AI applications are **expert systems.** These systems are specific to a particular field, and make evaluations, draw conclusions, and recommend action based on a huge database of information in that field (see Figure 7-7).

An example is Dr. Lawrence Weed's medical diagnosis program, called the *Problem-Knowledge Coupler (PKC).* The patient and doctor enter history, symptoms, and test results on the computer. By making cross-references, the computer responds with a list of diseases the patient might have, thus helping the doctor decide on a diagnosis and treatment. Other expert systems include CADUCEUS II, an internal-medicine diagnostic program; ONCOCIN, which advises physicians on the best combination of therapies for cancer patients; PROSPECTOR, an electronic geologist; and a program currently being developed called TRADER'S ASSISTANT, which will help brokers assess the stock market. Many experts in AI contend, however, that expert systems do not qualify as true AI. Intelligence involves coping with change and incorporating new information to improve performance, and expert systems do neither.

Advances in AI will lead to further automation in the workplace. Intelligent computers could be used to read books, newspapers, journals, and magazines and to prepare summaries of the material. They could scan mail and sort all letters but those with the most illegible addresses. Principles of AI also are used in improving **voice recognition** systems so that they can accept larger vocabularies, different

---

ARTIFICIAL INTELLIGENCE (AI)
Intelligence exhibited by a machine or software; a field of research aimed at developing techniques whereby computers can be used for solving problems.

EXPERT SYSTEM
Software that uses a base of knowledge in a field of study for decision-making and evaluation processes similar to those of human experts in that field.

VOICE RECOGNITION
The ability of electronic equipment to recognize speech and voice patterns.

Figure 7-7
MENTOR
The MENTOR system uses artificial intelligence to diagnose maintenance procedures in large central air-conditioning units.

voices, and continuous or flowing speech. Robotics will benefit from AI programming in the areas of robot vision, touch, and mobility. Additional skills will enable robots to take over even more jobs normally performed by human workers.

Questions and (No) Answers

Are people ready for the marvelous machines that AI makes possible? How will people react to expert systems that seem to do jobs better than the experts do? Let's look at medical expert systems as an example.

No human being can be expected to remember every minor symptom of every known disease or ailment, but a computer program can do so easily. It can signal drug incompatibilities and patient allergies, and it can react quickly to changes in a patient's condition. It can help a physician keep up to date on treatments, drugs, and diseases. There may also be negative effects of using expert systems. Some experts fear that medical systems will dehumanize medical practice or become crutches for incompetent physicians. Others ask if the role of physicians will decrease as expert systems are more commonly used. Still others wonder how the use of robots in surgery will affect jobs in medicine.

Manufacturing jobs have been lost due to improved robotics and scanning and voice recognition devices. In 1984 and 1985, two million manufacturing jobs were affected by the use of robots, optical scanners, microchips, and other electronic devices. Of those devices, 17,000 were robots. With unemployment in the United States continuing throughout the 1980s, loss of jobs due to robots remains a problem for workers and management alike.

Can all displaced workers be retrained and relocated? What kinds of jobs will they hold? Most of the new jobs by 1995 will be in retailing and service industries.

HIGHLIGHT

Seymour Cray

Tremendous number crunching capabilities are required for processing scientific data and conducting research in artificial intelligence. It was Seymour Cray's ambition to build a super-fast, super-powerful computer that would meet these needs.

As a young engineer, Cray worked for Engineering Research Associates and then for Remington Rand when it purchased ERA. Later, he was employed by the Univac Division of Sperry Rand Corporation. When William Norris founded Control Data Corporation (CDC) in 1957, Cray left Sperry to become a director at CDC.

Cray's first project at CDC was the 1604 computer. It was so successful in the scientific community that CDC built a private research laboratory for Cray in his hometown of Chippewa Falls, Wisconsin. There Cray continued his work and in 1963 introduced the powerful 6600, a machine that was adopted immediately by the U.S. Weather Bureau and the Atomic Energy Commission.

Cray became well known as a leading designer of large-scale computers. In 1972 he resigned from CDC and founded Cray Research, Inc., to design, develop, manufacture, and market large-capacity, high-speed computers. Cray Research introduced the Cray-1 in 1976. Next came the Cray X-MP. By 1985, over 100 Cray supercomputers were in use around the world, accounting for nearly 70 percent of the supercomputer market.

Seymour Cray was determined to build a supercomputer even faster and more powerful than the Cray-1 or Cray X-MP. He succeeded: In 1985, the Cray-2 was introduced. It is six to twelve times faster than the Cray-1 and has an internal memory of two billion bytes. Currently, Cray is devoting his time to the development of the Cray-3, which will have an eight-billion-byte memory. It is scheduled to be finished in 1988.

Only 11 percent of the 16 million new jobs will be in high technology, and only 6 percent of the 123 million people now currently employed in the U.S. are working in high-technology fields.

Some experts believe, however, that further loss of jobs will be due to attrition rather than layoffs. They argue that even if 2 million jobs are displaced, that accounts for only 2 percent of total employment. They also say that, in some instances, technology has made it possible to keep jobs in the U.S. For example, automating a plant has made it possible to produce a product here for less than it would cost to send the work to Asian countries.

Regardless of which experts we believe, the use of robots, scanning machines, and other devices improved by AI create very real concerns. Just how many jobs can be performed well by machines and software? Will implementation of AI principles in robots, automation, and expert systems eliminate certain skilled occupations? Is the use of automated equipment likely to affect a worker's sense of worth and purpose (see Figure 7-8)? How will automation affect the social aspect of transactions at banks and other institutions? Once such technology is implemented, is it likely to be disbanded in order to restore employment to displaced workers? Could the goals of sophisticated AI software and devices ever conflict with the goals of humans?

AI technology and the changes it creates could eventually improve the quality of life, but not until certain conflicts have been resolved.

**Figure 7-8
Automation**

Learning Check

1. What jobs does a system analyst do?
2. How does an MIS differ from a simple data processing system?
3. How are the principles of artificial intelligence used in automation?
4. What problems does automation present?

Answers

1. Analyzes an organization for data processing needs; suggests a design of equipment, material, people, and procedures for implementing a system. 2. A data processing system is used primarily for collecting and manipulating data and producing reports. An MIS provides managers with useful information that specifically supports their decision-making tasks. 3. They are used in developing expert systems; improving voice recognition systems to include larger vocabularies, a variety of voices, and the use of continuous speech; and improving vision, touch, and mobility of robots. 4. Problems related to automation concern workers being displaced by automation, and uncertainty about changes in the jobs available for humans in the future.

Summary Points

■ Some major concerns about privacy involve the amount of information collected and stored, the accuracy and recency of the information, the security of the stored information, and the uses to which it is put.

- The Privacy Act of 1974 is the major piece of federal legislation passed to protect the privacy of the individual. It addresses these four major concerns on the federal level.
- Computer crime is a growing concern because it is difficult to detect and because it results in loss of money and information. Tighter computer security measures are needed.
- Both computer crime and privacy have been addressed by the Comprehensive Crime Control Act of 1984. This act deals with unauthorized access to computers for illegitimate purposes.
- It is hard to determine who is responsible for computer mistakes. This issue is particularly important in systems that govern sensitive aspects of our lives, such as monitoring nuclear plants.
- Computer ethics refers to an individual's standards of behavior when using computers. It includes such practices as accessing restricted data, copying copyrighted software, using company computers for personal reasons, and downloading data from commercial databases.
- The system analyst can help a company identify security needs and suggest procedures to discourage unethical use of a company's computers. He or she may also recommend equipment, people, materials, and procedures needed to improve the collection, storage, and dissemination of information in the company.
- A management information system (MIS) can help managers make better decisions by providing useful information from the company's databases.
- Artificial intelligence is intelligence exhibited by a machine. It is used in preparing expert systems, improved voice recognition systems, and improved robot vision, mobility, and touch. These uses can affect the quality and number of jobs, because they enable businesses to automate certain functions.

Review Questions

1. Why has the issue of privacy become so important, and how can the problems associated with the storage and use of personal data be resolved?
2. List the organizations, companies, institutions, and government agencies that you think have computer records about you. Does the number make you uncomfortable? Why?
3. What is computer crime? Discuss some ways that computers are related to the perpetration of crimes.
4. What is meant by the phrase computer ethics? Describe some situations in which individuals apply their personal codes of ethics to computer use.
5. Describe some measures that your company or school could impose which would decrease software piracy, computer crime, and unauthorized access to data.
6. Discuss ethical and unethical uses of programs that unlock copy protection codes on licensed software.
7. Discuss some approaches that software developers could use to discourage piracy, other than copy protection programmed onto the disk itself.
8. Name the five major types of computer errors, and give examples that you may have experienced or read about.

9. Data about us is held in many databases, kept by government agencies, schools, employers, and credit bureaus. Sometimes data is traded among these organizations. Discuss the possible implications if one bit of incorrect data enters the trading system.

10. Describe how the protection of software copyright should be extended to other areas of computer use.

11. Explain the types of decisions which a system analyst might help a company make.

12. Describe some applications of artificial intelligence and expert systems, and tell how they might lead to a decrease in jobs.

13. Discuss how much of an obligation management and factory owners have toward workers who have been displaced by robots or other automation.

14. Computer-assisted diagnosis might increase speed and accuracy of medical diagnoses, especially in an emergency situation. It also might pose great threats to the patient's privacy, and might decrease the physician's familiarity with and recall of diagnostic information. All of these factors must be considered before a hospital implements computer-assisted diagnosis. In your opinion, are the advantages or the disadvantages greater? On what information do you base your answer?

PART TWO

Applications Software: Using WordStar 2000, WordPerfect, Lotus 1-2-3, and dBase III

CHAPTER 8

Introduction to Word Processing and WordStar 2000

Outline

Introduction
Definitions
Uses of Word Processors
Learning Check
Guide to WordStar 2000
   Getting Started with WordStar 2000
   Getting Help with WordStar 2000
Creating a New Document
   Naming a File
   Choosing a Document's Format

Recording a Document's
   History
Entering Text
Saving a Document
Learning Check
Editing a Document
   Copying a Document
   Moving the Cursor
   Removing Text

Moving Blocks of Text
Correcting Spelling Mistakes
Printing
Learning Check
Summary of Frequently Used
   WordStar 2000 Menus
Summary Points
WordStar 2000 Exercises
WordStar 2000 Problems

Introduction

Human beings are constantly in search of more efficient and effective methods to accomplish their tasks. The written word has been no exception. The evolution of the writing instrument has progressed from rocks and twigs to what many thought to be the ultimate writing instrument—the typewriter. But the evolution did not stop there; the computer revolution has brought the word processor.

To gain a little perspective, think of the difference between writing with a pen and pad and writing with a typewriter; this comparison approximates the difference between using a typewriter and using a word processor. In terms of speed, power, and capabilities, the word processor is to the pen and pad as the Ferrari is to the Model T.

One of the biggest advantages of word processing is that the words typed are not immediately committed to paper, but rather are displayed on a video screen, where they can easily be manipulated electronically. Word processors have made it simple to insert or delete text and to move text from one place to another, without having to retype or spend hours cutting and pasting. Gone are the days of overflowing wastepaper baskets and irritating correction paper or fluid. A word processor enables the writer to be completely satisfied with what has been written before one word is printed on paper.

This chapter introduces word processing—what it is and what its uses are. In addition, it provides instructions on how to get started using WordStar, one of the most popular word processing packages on the market today.

Definitions

WORD PROCESSOR
A program or set of programs designed to enable you to enter, manipulate, format, print, store, and retrieve text.

WORD PROCESSING
The act of composing and manipulating text electronically.

WORD PROCESSING SYSTEM
The hardware and software used for word processing.

DEDICATED SYSTEM
A computer equipped to handle only one function, such as word processing.

A **word processor** is a program (software) or set of programs which enables a computer user to write, edit, format, and print text. As characters are typed on a keyboard, they appear on the computer screen. Mistakes can be corrected easily because the text has not yet been put on paper. Words, sentences, and even entire paragraphs can be moved by special commands. Nothing is printed on paper until the user is satisfied with the results.

Word processing refers to the actual act of composing and editing text. The words are composed and rearranged in the user's mind; the word processor and the hardware simply provide a convenient way to display, store, edit and recall the work that has been done.

A **word processing system** includes the hardware and software used for the purpose of word processing. There are two general types of word processing systems: (1) **dedicated systems,** which are basically microcomputers equipped to handle only word processing; and (2) multipurpose microcomputers, which are equipped to handle a wide variety of processing tasks, including word processing. In the early days of word processing, the serious user's only choice was a dedicated system. With the development of faster and more sophisticated microcomputers, however, came the development of microcomputer-compatible word processors such as WordStar. Today most, if not all, multipurpose microcomputers on the market have at least one word processor available for them.

Although a word processor is actually a program or programs, many people refer to the combination of both software and hardware as a word processor. Table 8-1 provides a quick reference to other terms often used in connection with word processors.

Uses of Word Processors

Word processors are used in homes, businesses, schools, and many other places. At home, they can be used to write school reports, letters, or the minutes from a meeting. Most word processors for home use are easier to use and have fewer features than those designed for business use.

In offices, word processors take over much of the paperwork involved in running a business. They produce reports, letters, brochures, legal papers, and other important documents. A word processor can print a letter many times, with different names and addresses inserted to make the letter more personal.

Word processors have revolutionized the publishing industry. Books, newspapers, and magazines can be produced faster and with fewer mistakes. Sometimes these documents are not printed on paper until they are ready to be distributed. Writers enter text at computer terminals, and editors review the work at their terminals. Then designers lay out the pages electronically, choosing the type style, size, and column width. Finally, the document is printed for the first and only time.

Learning Check

1. A ____ is a program (software) or set of programs designed to allow a user to enter, manipulate, format, print, store, and retrieve text.
   a. word processor
   b. word processing
   c. word processing system
   d. dedicated system

2. The two general types of word processing systems are ____ and ____.

3. A ____ is the hardware and software that enable a user to write, edit, format and print text on a computer.
   a. word processor
   b. word processing
   c. word processing system
   d. dedicated system

4. Word processing is the act of ____ and ____ text on a computer.

5. A dedicated system handles a wide range of processing tasks, including word processing. (True or False?)

Answers

1. a. 2. dedicated systems; multipurpose microcomputers. 3. c. 4. composing; editing. 5. False

Table 8-1
Frequently Encountered Word Processing Terms

Term	Definition
Automatic pagination	A feature that enables a word processor to number the pages of the printed copy automatically.
Block	A group of characters, such as a sentence or paragraph.
Block movement	A feature that allows the user to define a block of text and then perform a specific operation on the entire block. Common block operations include block move, block copy, block save, and block delete.
Boldface	Heavy type, for example, **this is boldface.**
Character	A letter, number, or symbol.
Character enhancement	Underlining, boldfacing, subscripting, and superscripting.
Control character	A coded character that does not print but is part of the command sequence in a word processor.
Cursor	The marker on the display screen indicating where the next character can be displayed.
Default setting	A value used by the word processor when it is not instructed to use any other.
Deletion	A feature by which a character, word, sentence, or larger block of text can be removed from the existing text.
Document-oriented word processor	A word processor that operates on a text file as one long document.
Editing	The act of changing or amending text.
Format	The layout of a page; for example, the number of lines, margin settings, and so on.
Global	An instruction that will be carried out throughout an entire document, for example, global search and replace.
Header	A piece of text that is stored separately from the text and printed at the top of each page.
Incremental spacing	A method by which the printer inserts spaces between words and letters to produce justified margins; also called *microspacing*.
Insertion	A feature in which a character, word, sentence, or larger block of text is added to the existing text.
Justification	A feature for making lines of text even at the margins.
Line editor	The type of editor that allows the user to edit only one line at a time.
Memory-only word processor	A word processor that cannot exchange text between internal memory and disk during the editing process.
Menu	A list of commands or prompts on the display screen.

Table continued on next page

Table 8-1 Continued

Term	Definition
Page-oriented word processor	A word processor that operates on a text file as a series of pages.
Print formatting	The function of a word processor which communicates with the printer to tell it how to print the text on paper.
Print preview	A feature that enables the user to view a general representation on the screen of how the document will look when printed.
Screen editor	The type of editor that enables the user to edit an entire screen at a time.
Screen formatting	A function of a word processor which controls how the text will appear on the screen.
Scrolling	Moving a line of text onto or off the screen.
Search and find	A routine that searches for, and places the cursor at, a specified string of characters.
Search and replace	A routine that searches for a specified character string and replaces it with the specified replacement string.
Status line	A message line above or below the text area on a display screen which gives format and system information.
Subscript	A character that prints below the usual text baseline.
Superscript	A character that prints above the usual text baseline.
Text buffer	An area set aside in memory to hold text temporarily.
Text editing	The function of a word processor that enables the user to enter and edit text.
Text file	A file that contains text, as opposed to a program.
Virtual representation	An approach to screen formatting which enables the user to see on the screen exactly how the printed output will look.
Word wrap	The feature in which a word is moved automatically to the beginning of the next line if it goes past the right margin.

Schools also are increasing their use of word processors. Students can write essays or reports on the computers in their classrooms. Teachers can format tests and worksheets on a computer much faster than on a typewriter. Of course, school secretaries can use word processors to prepare school reports and letters.

No matter how word processors are used, they enable the writer to think more about organizing ideas than about the mechanics of writing. A word processor makes it easy for a person to revise a document before it is printed.

Guide to WordStar 2000

The remainder of this chapter focuses on how to use WordStar 2000. WordStar 2000, a state-of-the-art word processing program from MicroPro International, is extremely powerful yet easy to use. Memos, letters, reports, and term papers can be created with WordStar 2000.

Some of the directions for using WordStar vary depending on whether the computer has two floppy disk drives or a hard disk drive. The directions in this chapter are written for computers with two floppy disk drives. Differences for computers with a hard disk drive are written in difference boxes.

Each of the following sections introduces one or more features of WordStar 2000. At the end of each section there is a hands-on activity marked YOUR TURN. Do not try the hands-on activity until after you have carefully read the section preceding it.

WordStar 2000 refers to the key marked ↵ as the <Return> key. Throughout this chapter, when instructed to press the <Return> key, press the key marked ↵.

The following symbols and typefaces appear throughout the chapter. This is what they mean:

Type **b:**.	The information in boldface indicates a command that should be typed to the screen.
Press **^C**.	The ^ symbol represents the <Ctrl> key.
Press the <Return> key.	The angle brackets (<>) are used to signify a specific key on the keyboard. Press the key whose name is enclosed by the angle brackets.
WS Tip:	This phrase introduces important information needed to run WordStar successfully.
DOCUMENT TO EDIT OR CREATE?	All capital letters indicate phrases that appear on the computer screen.
Type `Job Opening`	Typewriter font indicates text that is to be entered into a document.

Getting Started with WordStar 2000

BOOT
To load an operating system into a computer's main memory.

To **boot** the computer and start WordStar 2000, you need a special DOS disk, a WordStar 2000 disk, and a blank formatted disk that is your data disk. All the files you create are saved on your data disk. Follow these steps to boot the computer and start WordStar 2000:

1. Insert the DOS disk into drive A. Close the disk drive door. Turn on the computer.
2. When asked to type the date and time, press the <Return> key.
3. When the system prompt (A>) appears on the screen, remove the DOS disk from Drive A. Insert a copy of the WordStar 2000 Program Disk into drive A and close the disk drive door. (WordStar 2000 must have been installed on your system previously.)
4. Insert your data disk into drive B. Close the disk drive door.
5. Type **ws2** and press the <Return> key.

> *Hard Disk Differences:* Turn on your computer. When you see the system prompt (C>), type **ws2** and press the <Return> key.

YOUR TURN Turn on and boot your computer, and start WordStar 2000.

Getting Help with WordStar 2000

After **ws2** is typed and the <Return> key pressed, WordStar's Opening Menu appears on the screen (see Figure 8-1). Depending on the type of monitor, some of the letters may appear brighter than others. If none of the letters appears brighter, try adjusting the brightness knob on the monitor. Some monitors, however, are not capable of highlighting these letters. On a color monitor, some of the letters are a color different from the majority of the letters on the screen.

Usually, the key pressed to activate a command is related to the command so that it is easier to remember. For example, look at Figure 8-1. To **E**dit or create a file, **E** is pressed. To **P**rint a file, **P** is pressed. To **C**opy a file, **C** is pressed. If the monitor being used is capable of highlighting letters, the letter or letters pressed to activate a particular command are highlighted. On a color monitor, these letters are a different color.

The box in the right corner of the Opening Menu contains the command **G**, which stands for **G**et Help. Every WordStar menu includes a Get Help option. This command does exactly what it says: It provides help if you are confused or unsure about what you are doing. When performing the exercises in this chapter, always use the G command to obtain further help. Follow these steps to use the G command:

1. Type **G.** Read the information on the screen.
2. Some of the Get Help menus have more than one screen. For example, at the

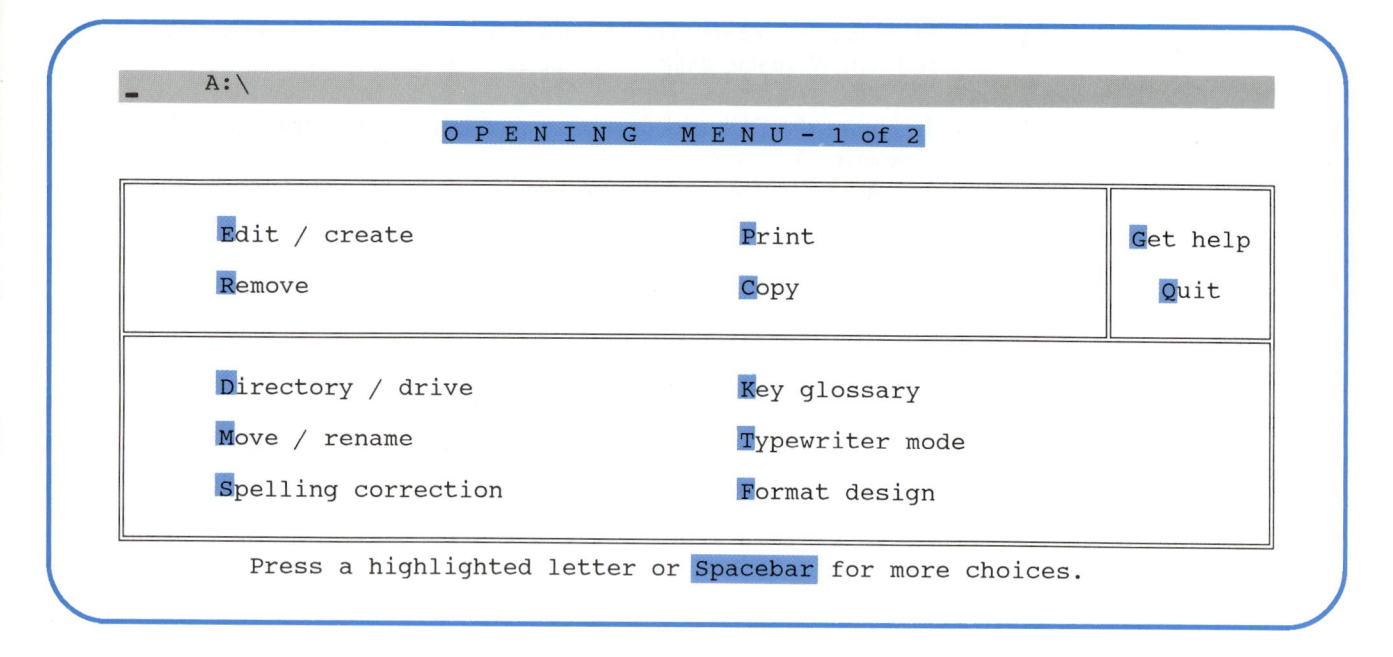

```
     A:\
              O P E N I N G   M E N U - 1 of 2

    Edit / create            Print              Get help
    Remove                   Copy               Quit


    Directory / drive        Key glossary
    Move / rename            Typewriter mode
    Spelling correction      Format design

     Press a highlighted letter or Spacebar for more choices.
```

Figure 8-1
WordStar 2000 Opening Menu

top of the Get Help menu for the Opening Menu, it says HELP-OPENING MENU-1 of 2. This means that this screen is the first of two screens. In order to see the second screen, you must press the Spacebar.

3. To return to the Opening Menu, press the <Esc> key.

YOUR TURN — Use the command that enables you to Get Help with the Opening Menu. Read the information on both screens. Return to the Opening Menu.

Creating a New Document

The files created with WordStar are similar to files in a file cabinet—each file is a unit of storage. Files can be used to store memos, letters, and term papers. For example, when a memo or letter is completed, that file is saved to a disk. Once saved, that file can be reentered in order to revise, edit, or print its contents.

If a two–disk-drive system is used, all the files created must be saved on your data disk in drive B. There is not enough space on the Program Disk in drive A to save documents. To change to drive B, press **D** for **D**irectory/**D**rive. The question CHANGE DIRECTORY OR DISK DRIVE TO? appears on the screen. Type **b:** and press the <Return> key. Every time WordStar 2000 is loaded, the disk drive should be switched immediately to drive B.

To begin using WordStar 2000, you either create a new document or edit an existing one. The exercises in this section go step by step through the process of creating a new document and editing it. For the remaining Your Turn exercises in this chapter, check the following before beginning the exercise:

1. Make sure the data disk—a formatted disk onto which your files will be saved—is in drive B.
2. Make sure the disk drive currently being accessed is drive B. Check this by looking in the upper-left corner when the Opening Menu is on the screen. If B:\ is in the upper-left corner, disk drive B is being accessed. If A:\ is in the upper-left corner, the drives need to be switched.

Naming a File

The first step in creating a new file is to name it. Follow these steps to name a file:

1. Press **E** at the Opening menu. The Choose a Name screen appears (see Figure 8-2). The ^ symbol stands for the <Ctrl> key. For example, to get help with choosing a name, the <Ctrl> key is held down while G is pressed.
2. The question DOCUMENT TO EDIT OR CREATE? appears on the screen. The program is asking for the name of the document to reenter for editing, or the name of a new document to be created.
3. At the bottom of the screen are names of files that have already been stored on the data disk. To edit an existing file, select that file from the list. To create a new file, type the name of the new file and press the <Return> key.

WS TIP: When naming a file, remember the following rules:

1. The name can be from 1 to 8 characters long, with no spaces.
2. The characters in a filename can be the letters of the alphabet, the numbers 0 through 9, or the special characters $#@!()-{}__.
3. An optional extension can be used following the filename. The extension can have from 1 to 3 characters with no spaces, and is separated from the filename by a period (.).
4. Try to give the file a name that will remind you of what it contains.

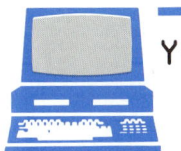

YOUR TURN

Change the disk drive to drive B.
Open a new file and name it JOB.MEM. If you make a mistake typing, for now use the <←> key located in the upper right corner, next to the <Num Lock> key, to delete the mistake. To avoid confusion with the left arrow key located in the numeric keypad, we will refer to this key used for deletion as the <Backspace> key.

```
         B:\
                    C H O O S E   A   N A M E
  ┌─────────────────────────────────────────────────────┐         
  │ Type or highlight name.   Press Return.             │  ^Get help
  │    Move highlighting with cursor keys.              │
  │    Erase errors with Backspace.                     │  Escape
  │    Transfer highlighted letters to answer line with ^T.│
  └─────────────────────────────────────────────────────┘
                ^G means hold down Ctrl key and press G.


  Document to edit or create?_




  JUSTIFY.FRM        MEMOFORM.FRM        MSCRIPT.FRM         NORMAL.FRM
  RAGGED.FRM         UNFORM.FRM          WS2.KEY
```

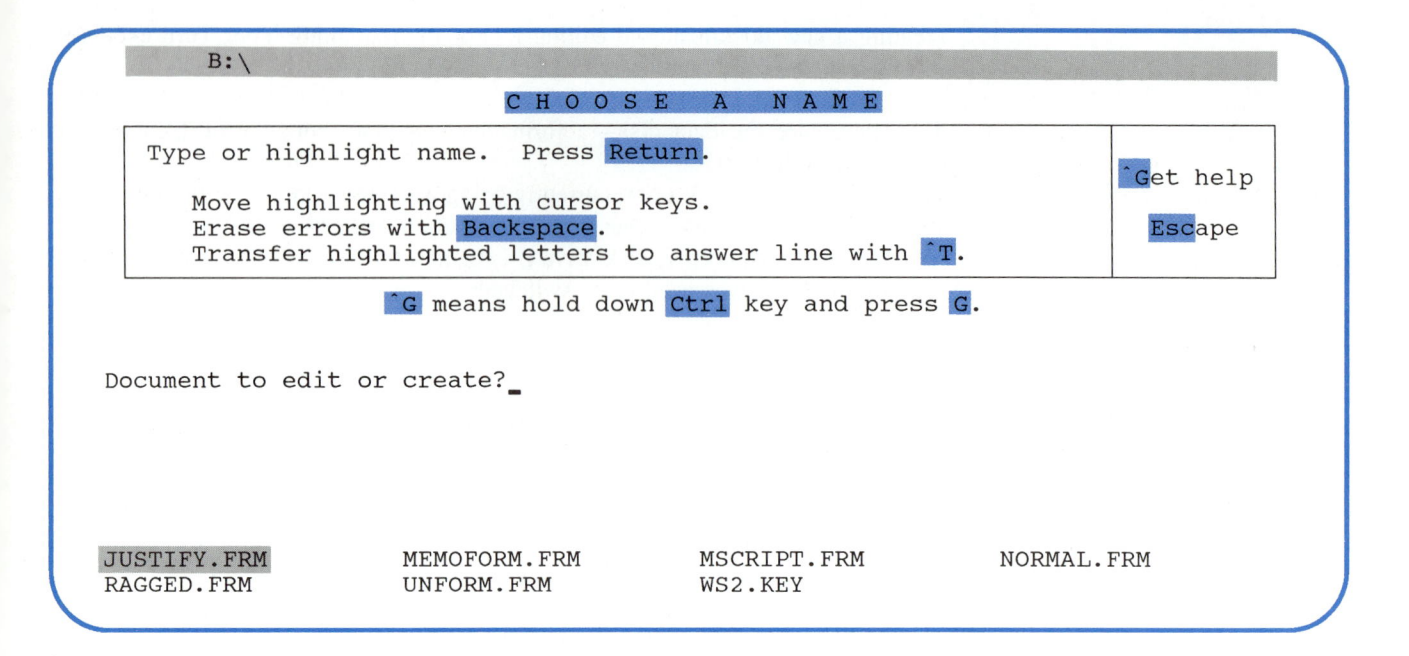

Figure 8-2
Choose a Name Screen

Hard Disk Differences: Omit changing the disk drive.

Choosing a Document's Format

Whenever a new document is created on WordStar 2000, a format must be chosen. A format determines how the document looks on the page. For example, the document can be single-spaced or double-spaced. The top margin can be 1 inch wide or 3 inches wide. The right margin can be ragged or justified. If it is ragged, the lines of text at the right margin are not even; if it is **justified,** the lines of text are even at the right margin.

WordStar 2000 has standard formats already stored in its memory (see Table 8-2 for examples of these formats). Choosing one of these prepared formats eliminates the need to set margins, line spacing, page number location, and other features each time a document is entered or edited.

Follow these steps to select a format:

1. After a new document is named and the <Return> key pressed, the question FORMAT TO USE? appears on the screen. The names of all the formats from which the user can select are listed at the bottom of the screen.

2. In order to select the NORMAL format, press <Return>. If a format other than NORMAL is to be selected, the user can either type the name of the format and press <Return> or the cursor-control keys can be used to select the format. The cursor-control keys are the four arrow keys located on the numeric keypad to the right of the keyboard. The up arrow key, <↑>, moves the cursor one line up; the down arrow key, <↓>, moves the cursor one line down; the left arrow key, <←>, moves the cursor one space to the left; and the right arrow key,

JUSTIFICATION
A feature for making lines of text even at the margins.

<→>, moves the cursor one space to the right (The left arrow key should not be confused with the <Backspace> key.)

3. In order to use the cursor-control keys, the <Num Lock> key must be off. If the number 8, 6, 2, or 4 appears on the screen when a cursor-control key is pressed, press the <Num Lock> key once. Delete the number using the <Backspace> key. Press the cursor-control key again. Instead of a number appearing on the screen, the cursor should move in the direction indicated by the arrow.

4. To select a format using the cursor-control keys, move the highlighting to the format you want to select and press the <Return> key.

YOUR TURN Select the format called MEMOFORM.FRM for your file JOB.MEM.

Recording a Document's History

WordStar 2000 can record the history of any document. It can keep track of the number of keystrokes used to create and edit a document. It can store useful information about each document such as the title of the document, the author of the document, the name of the person who typed the document, and where copies of the document were sent.

This information is typed in on the History Screen. Every time a new document is created, the History Screen appears after the format for the document has been selected. When the History Screen appears, either type in information about the document, or bypass the History Screen by using the command ^Q.

Table 8-2
Standard WordStar Formats

			SETTINGS				
FORMATS	Top Margin (lines)	Bottom Margin (lines)	Right Margin (inches from left margin)	Lines per Page	Line Spacing	Text (Justified or Ragged)	Page Numbers
Justify	6	6	6.5	66	single	justified	none
Memoform	6	6	6.5	66	single	justified	none
Manuscript	1	2	6.9	33	double	ragged	centered at bottom of page
Normal	6	6	6.5	66	single	justified	centered at bottom of page
Ragged	6	6	6.5	66	single	ragged	centered at bottom of page
Convert	3	6	6.5	66	single	justified	centered at bottom of page

Table 8-2 Continued

```
                    Justify
     Are you nervous about using a computer?  Perhaps you haven't
had much experience with electronic equipment.  "What will I do
if something goes wrong?" you think.  Maybe you turn on the power
switch...and nothing happens.  Maybe the printer won't print.  Or
you put a disk in the disk drive and the disk drive just keeps on
whirring and whirring and whirring...  Before you panic, here are
some simple things to check.
     If the computer does not start, be sure the power cord is
firmly plugged into an outlet that you know is working.  Be sure
the other end of the cord is firmly plugged into the equipment.
It may look plugged in, but may be loose enough to stop the flow
of electricity.
     Are the brightness and contrast switches on the monitor ad-
justed properly?  Maybe nothing shows up on the screen because
the brightness switch is turned to "dark."
     When you put in a disk, the disk drive may not start or the
disk keeps spinning.  Take out the disk and reinsert it.  If that
doesn't work, the disk may be warped or bent.  Try another disk.
Of course, be sure all cables are correctly plugged in.
     Printer won't print?  Be sure the cables are correctly in-
serted and the proper switches are turned on.  Be sure there's
enough paper and that it is correctly feeding into the printer.
     If these simple remedies fail, it's time to seek the help of
you instructor or a computer repairman.
```

```
                    Manuscript

Are you nervous about using a computer?  Perhaps you haven't had

much experience with electronic equipment.  "What will I do if

something goes wrong?" you think.  Maybe you turn on the power

switch...and nothing happens.  Maybe you put a disk in the disk drive

and the disk drive just keeps on whirring and whirring and

whirring...  Before you panic, here are some simple things to check.

     If the computer does not start, be sure the power cord is firmly

plugged into an outlet that you know is working.  Be sure the other

end of the cord is firmly plugged into the equipment.  It may look

plugged in, but may be loose enough to stop the flow of electricity.

     Are the brightness and contrast switches on the monitor adjusted

properly?  Maybe nothing shows up on the screen because the

brightness switch is turned to "dark."

     When you put in a disk, the disk drive may not start or the disk

keeps spinning.  Take out the disk and reinsert it.  If that doesn't

work, the disk may be warped or bent.  Try another disk.  Of course,

be sure all cables are correctly plugged in.
```

```
                                   MEMORANDUM
TO:        All Students
FROM:      Your Instructor
DATE:      October 18, 1987
SUBJECT:   Troubleshooting a Computer

     Are you nervous about using a computer?  Perhaps you haven't
had much experience with electronic equipment.  "What will I do
if something goes wrong?" you think.  Maybe you turn on the power
switch...and nothing happens.  Maybe the printer won't print.  Or
you put a disk in the disk drive and the disk drive just keeps on
whirring and whirring and whirring...  Before you panic, here are
some simple things to check.
     If the computer does not start, be sure the power cord is
firmly plugged into an outlet that you know is working.  Be sure
the other end of the cord is firmly plugged into the equipment.
It may look plugged in, but may be loose enough to stop the flow
of electricity.
     Are the brightness and contrast switches on the monitor
adjusted properly?  Maybe nothing shows up on the screen because
the brightness switch is turned to "dark."
     When you put in a disk, the disk drive may not start or the
disk keeps spinning.  Take out the disk and reinsert it.  If that
doesn't work, the disk may be warped or bent.  Try another disk.
Of course, be sure all cables are correctly plugged in.
     Printer won't print?  Be sure the cables are correctly
inserted and the proper switches are turned on.  Be sure there's
paper and that it is correctly feeding into the printer.
     If these simple remedies fail, it's time to seek my help.
```

```
                    Normal
     Are you nervous about using a computer?  Perhaps you haven't
had much experience with electronic equipment.  "What will I do
if something goes wrong?" you think.  Maybe you turn on the power
switch ...and nothing happens.  Maybe the printer won't print.
Or you put a disk in the disk drive and the disk drive just keeps
on whirring and whirring and whirring...  Before you panic,
here are some simple things to check.
     If the computer does not start, be sure the power cord is
firmly plugged into an outlet that you know is working.  Be sure
the other end of the cord is firmly plugged into the equipment.
It may look plugged in, but may be loose enough to stop the flow
of electricity.
     Are the brightness and contrast switches on the monitor ad-
justed properly?  Maybe nothing shows up on the screen because
the brightness switch is turned to "dark."
     When you put in a disk, the disk drive may not start or the
disk keeps spinning.  Take out the disk and reinsert it.  If that
doesn't work, the disk may be warped or bent.  Try another disk.
Of course, be sure all cables are correctly plugged in.
     Printed won't print?  Be sure the cables are correctly in-
serted and the proper switches are turned on.  Be sure there's
paper and that it is correctly feeding into the printer.
     If these simple remedies fail, it's time to seek the help of
your instructor or a computer repairman.
```

YOUR TURN

When the History Screen appears after selecting the format MEMOFORM.FRM, bypass it using the appropriate command.

Entering Text

When entering text, usually you need to use both uppercase and lowercase letters. If all the letters are capitals when you begin typing, press the <Caps Lock> key once. You should then be able to type both uppercase and lowercase letters.

CHAPTER 8: INTRODUCTION TO WORD PROCESSING AND WORDSTAR 2000   223

Table 8-2 Continued

Ragged	Convert

Are you nervous about using a computer? Perhaps you haven't had much experience with electronic equipment. "What will I do if something goes wrong?" you think. Maybe you turn on the power switch...and nothing happens. Maybe the printer won't print. Or you put a disk in the disk drive and the disk drive just keeps on whirring and whirring and whirring... Before you panic, here are some simple things to check.
 	
    If the computer does not start, be sure the power cord is firmly plugged into an outlet that you know is working. Be sure the other end of the cord is firmly plugged into the equipment. It may look plugged in, but may be loose enough to stop the flow of electricity.
 	
    Are the brightness and contrast switches on the monitor adjusted properly? Maybe nothing shows up on the screen because the brightness switch is turned to "dark."
 	
    When you put in a disk, the disk drive may not start or the disk keeps spinning. Take out the disk and reinsert it. If that doesn't work, the disk may be warped or bent. Try another disk. Of course, be sure all cables are correctly plugged in.
 	
    Printer won't print? Be sure the cables are correctly inserted and the proper switches are turned on. Be sure there's paper and that it is correctly feeding into the printer.
 	
    If these simple remedies fail, it's time to seek the help of your instructor or a computer repairman.
	Are you nervous about using a computer? Perhaps you haven't had much experience with electronic equipment. "What will I do if something goes wrong?" you think. Maybe you turn on the power switch...and nothing happens. Maybe the printer won't print. Or you put a disk in the disk drive and the disk drive just keeps on whirring and whirring and whirring... Before you panic, here are some simple things to check.
	
	    If the computer does not start, be sure the power cord is firmly plugged into an outlet that you know is working. Be sure the other end of the cord is firmly plugged into the equipment. It may look plugged in, but may be loose enough to stop the flow of electricity.
	
	    Are the brightness and contrast switches on the monitor adjusted properly? Maybe nothing shows up on the screen because the brightness switch is turned to "dark."
	
	    When you put in a disk, the disk drive may not start or the disk keeps spinning. Take out the disk and reinsert it. If that doesn't work, the disk may be warped or bent. Try another disk. Of course, be sure all cables are correctly plugged in.
	
	    Printer won't print? Be sure the cables are correctly inserted and the proper switches are turned on. Be sure there's paper and that it is correctly feeding into the printer.
	
	    If these simple remedies fail, it's time to seek the help of your instructor or a computer repairman.

WORD WRAP
The feature by which a word is automatically moved to the beginning of the next line if it goes past the right margin.

The <Return> key need not be pressed when the end of a line is reached, because WordStar 2000 uses the **word wrap** feature. Word wrap automatically moves a word to the beginning of the next line if it goes past the right margin. The text is automatically wrapped around to the line below and is hyphenated if necessary. If you want to start a new paragraph or create blank lines in your text, the <Return> key needs to be pressed.

In order to begin entering text, the Editing Menu must be on the computer screen. The Editing Menu appears after you leave the History Screen, when you are creating a new document, or after you select a preexisting document to edit.

WS Tip: Do not worry if you make a mistake and either quit too soon or somehow get caught in a problem you do not know how to remedy. You can always just start over. Once a document has been named, it will be in the Directory. If something unforeseen happens and you want to start over, press either ^**Q** or <Esc> until the Opening Menu is on the screen. Press **E.** When the directory of all the files appears, select the one on which you were working and continue your work.

YOUR TURN

The Editing Menu with the MEMORANDUM format should be on the screen. Type the following memo exactly as it appears here. Any errors you find are intentional. Follow closely the directions given in parentheses, and do not worry if you make mistakes; they can be corrected later. The cursor is under the *M* in MEMORANDUM. Press the down arrow key < ↓ > twice so that the cursor is to the right of TO: in column 11.

PART TWO: APPLICATIONS SOFTWARE

- Type: `Ms. Kim Landon`
- (Press the <↓> key once so the cursor is to the right of FROM:)
- Type: `Dr. Nancy Dillon`
- (Press the <↓> key once so the cursor is to the right of DATE:)
- Type: `December 12, 1987`
- (Press the <↓> key once so the cursor is to the right of SUBJECT:)
- Type: `Job Opening`
- Press the <↓> key three times so the cursor is below the line that appears on the screen.
- Type the following message:

`As your advisor, I want to help you in any way possible with your job hunt. Since graduation is only six short months away, I'm sure finding a job is a top priority for you right now. I just recieved some information from the placement service office that I would like to pass along to you. I think this information will help you in your job-search efforts.`

(Press <Return> twice to create a space between paragraphs.)

`The placement service is sponsoring a cerees of semenars designed to help upcoming graduates locate potential employers, write cover letters and resumes, and improve interviewing skills. There is no cost for attending this semenar, but if you plan to attend, you must register with the placement office no later than Monday, Feburary 17. These semenars will be divided up according to majors. The semenar for Accounting majors is scheduled for Saturday, Feburary 21.`

(Press <Return> twice to create a space between paragraphs.)

`I hope you plan to attend this semenar. I think it will be well worth your time.`

Saving a Document

To save a document, press ^Q for the Quit command in the Editing Menu. The Quit Editing Menu appears next.

There are four commands in the main part of the Quit Editing Menu. Table 8-3 describes each command and explains the circumstances under which that command would be chosen. If you have to stop working on any of the following Your Turn exercises, remember to save your work before turning off the computer.

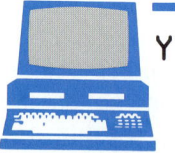

YOUR TURN Save your file JOB.MEM. Use the command from the Quit Editing Menu which returns the Opening Menu to the screen after the document is saved.

CHAPTER 8: INTRODUCTION TO WORD PROCESSING AND WORDSTAR 2000

Command	Description	Uses
S for **S**ave changes	Document is saved; Opening Menu appears on the screen.	Use the **S** command to save your file before working on a different document, or if you wish to leave WordStar.
C for **C**ontinue after saving	Document is saved; document remains on the screen; the Editing Menu reappears.	Use the **C** command to continue working on the current document after saving it.
A for **A**bandon changes	The message THIS DOCUMENT HAS BEEN CHANGED. ABANDON CHANGES? (Y/N)N appears on the screen. Pressing **N** or <Return> returns the current document without saving anything. Pressing **Y** returns the Opening Menu. If the document has never been saved before, pressing **Y** erases the document. If the document has been saved before, the document is saved as it was before the current edit session. Changes made since the document was last opened are not saved.	Use the **A** command if changes made to the document are not to be saved. Press **N** or <Return> if the current document is to remain on the screen. Press **Y** if work on the document is completed. If it is a new document that has never been saved before, pressing **Y** erases the document.
P for **P**rint after saving	Document is saved; a series of questions appears, regarding the printing of the document.	Use the **P** command to print the document immediately after saving it.

Table 8-3
Commands From the Quit Editing Menu

WS Tip: Remember to save your work on the work disk in drive B. The Program Disk in drive A does not have enough space on it to save new documents.

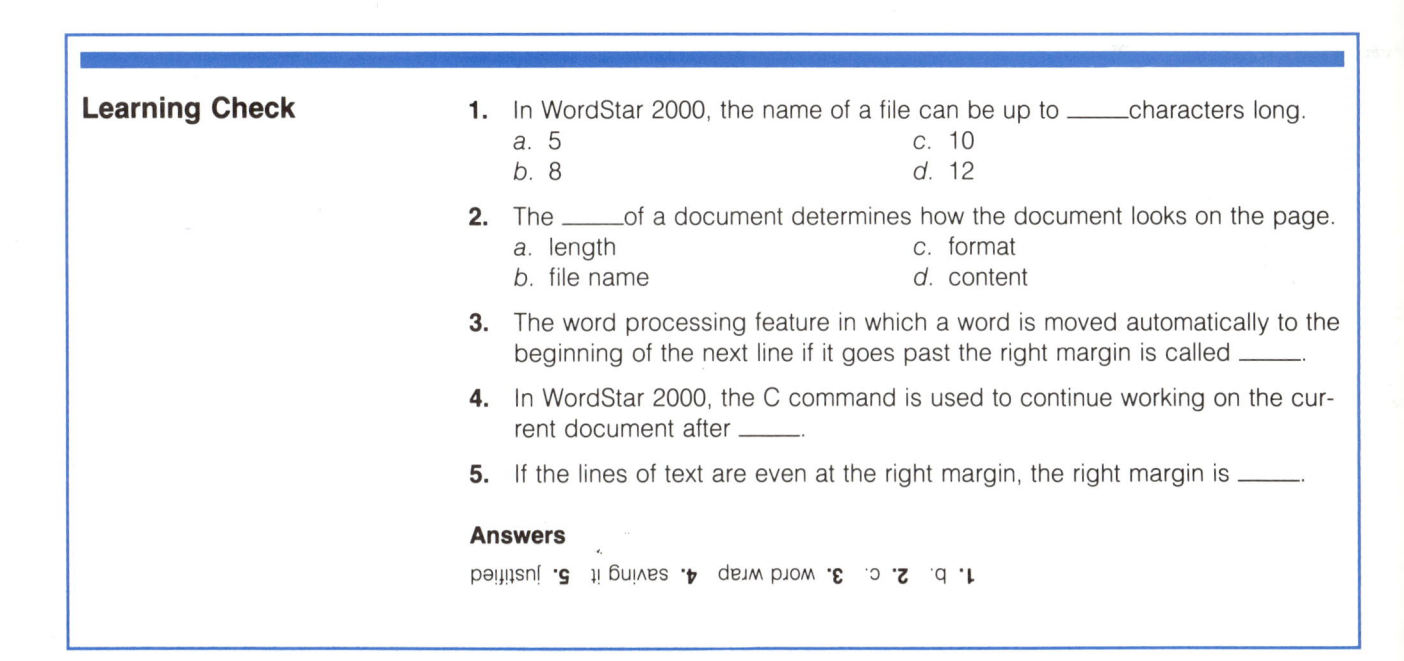

Learning Check

1. In WordStar 2000, the name of a file can be up to ____ characters long.
   a. 5
   b. 8
   c. 10
   d. 12

2. The ____ of a document determines how the document looks on the page.
   a. length
   b. file name
   c. format
   d. content

3. The word processing feature in which a word is moved automatically to the beginning of the next line if it goes past the right margin is called ____.

4. In WordStar 2000, the C command is used to continue working on the current document after ____.

5. If the lines of text are even at the right margin, the right margin is ____.

Answers

1. b.   2. c.   3. word wrap   4. saving it   5. justified

Editing a Document

TEXT EDITING
The function of a word processor which enables the user to enter and edit text.

INSERTION
A word processing feature in which a character, word, sentence, or larger block of text can be added to the existing text.

DELETION
A word processing feature in which a character, word, sentence, or larger block of text can be removed from the existing text.

STATUS LINE
A message line above or below the text area on a display screen which gives format and system information.

Figure 8-3
Components of the Editing Menu

Now that a document has been saved on disk, it can be edited. The **text editing** function of a word processor enables the user to enter and edit text. The most fundamental aspect of this function is the word processor's ability to accept and store the text that is typed in at the keyboard. Without this ability, all the other functions and procedures would be useless.

Text editing also includes the ability of the word processor to **insert** and **delete** characters, words, lines, paragraphs, and larger blocks of text. The insert and delete modes are two of the most often-used text editing features of any word processor. The text editing features of most word processors, including WordStar, also allow blocks of text to be moved and copied. These features facilitate the rearranging and retyping of documents.

The more familiar WordStar's Editing Menu becomes, the easier the editing process will be. Figure 8-3 shows the various components of the Editing Menu. The **status line** at the top of the screen displays the name of the document and where the cursor is located. The number following Pg is the screen page number. The number following Ln is the number of the horizontal line where the cursor is located. The number following Col is the column number, or the number of spaces from the left margin, where the cursor is located. The number in parentheses, following the column number, is the number of inches the cursor is from the left margin.

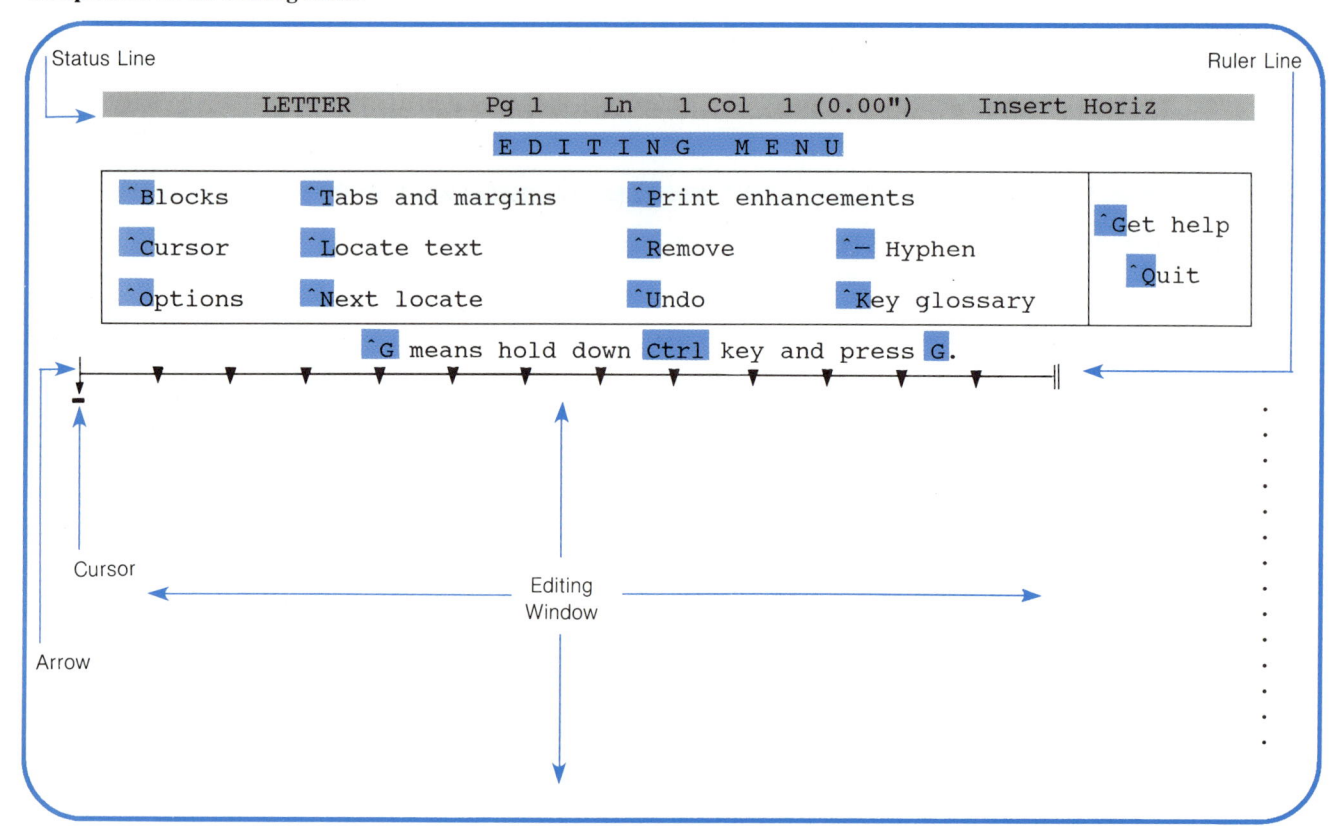

```
Status Line                                                          Ruler Line

           LETTER         Pg 1    Ln  1 Col  1 (0.00")    Insert Horiz
                              E D I T I N G   M E N U

    ^Blocks        ^Tabs and margins    ^Print enhancements        ^Get help
    ^Cursor        ^Locate text         ^Remove        ^- Hyphen
    ^Options       ^Next locate         ^Undo          ^Key glossary    ^Quit

              ^G means hold down Ctrl key and press G.

Cursor
                              Editing
Arrow                         Window
```

The exercises in this section demonstrate the commands used to edit a document. You will practice using these commands on the JOB.MEM document you created.

Copying a Document

It is a good idea to make a copy of a document before it is edited. If a copy is made, the original document can be retrieved even after changes have been made to it.

To copy a file, press **C** for **C**opy at the Opening Menu. The question FILE TO COPY FROM? appears on the screen. Type **b:** and press the <Return> key. A list of files on the data disk in drive B appears on the screen.

There are three ways to select the file to copy from. To select the first file in the list, simply press <Return>. To select a file other than the first one in the list, the name of the file can be entered at the blinking cursor next to the prompt FILE TO COPY FROM. Press <Return> after typing the name. The third way to select a file is to use the cursor control keys to move the highlighting to the name of the document being copied and press the <Return> key.

The message FILE TO COPY TO? appears on the screen next. Give the file a new name so that it can be distinguished from the original. For example type newname and press the <Return> key. The Opening Menu returns to the screen.

> *Hard Disk Differences:* Omit typing **b:**. As soon as you press **C,** the list of files that are saved appears under the question FILE TO COPY TO? Move the cursor control keys to select the document you want to copy, and press the <Return> key.

YOUR TURN Copy your file JOB.MEM. Name the copy NEWJOB.MEM.

Moving the Cursor

There are three ways to move the cursor: (1) by using the cursor command from the editing menu; (2) by using the <PgUp>, <PgDn>, <Home>, and <End> keys; or (3) by using the four arrow keys: <↑>, <↓>, <←>, <→>.

To use the cursor command from the Editing Menu, press ^**C.** The first screen of the Cursor Menu appears. Table 8-4 describes the commands most commonly used from the Cursor Menu.

After practicing using these commands, try using a shortcut method that bypasses the Cursor Menu: give the commands all at once. For example, to move the cursor to the beginning of the document, press ^**CB** all at the same time.

> *WS Tip:* Remember that the **T** command from the Cursor Menu can be used with characters as well as with letters. Using the **T** command with a period moves the cursor to the end of a sentence. Using the **T** command with the <Return> key moves the cursor to the end of a paragraph.

Table 8-4
Commands from the Cursor Menu

Command		Description
B	for **B**eginning of document	Moves the cursor to the beginning of the document.
L	For **L**eft side of line	Moves the cursor to the first position in the current line.
T	for **T**o a character	Moves the cursor to the next occurrence of the character you type in response to the question CHARACTER TO GO TO?
E	for **E**nd of document	Moves the cursor to the end of the document.
R	for **R**ight of document	Moves the cursor to the position just after the end of the current line.

A second way to move the cursor is with the <Home>, <End>, <PgUp>, and <PgDn> keys located on the numeric keypad. Pressing <Home> places the cursor at the top left corner of the screen. Depending on the computer system used, pressing <End> places the cursor at the beginning of the next-to-last line or last line of text on the screen. Pressing <PgUp> moves the cursor up one screen. Pressing <PgDn> moves the cursor down one screen.

Besides moving the cursor, the <PgUp> and <PgDn> keys also cause the screen to **scroll.** If a document is too long to fit on the screen, it cannot be viewed all at once. Scrolling is the process of moving a line or lines of text onto or off the screen. When the <PgUp> and <PgDn> keys are used to move the cursor up or down past the lines on a full screen, the new lines move onto the screen, and the lines at the opposite edge of the screen move off.

SCROLLING
Moving a line or lines of text onto or off the screen.

A third way to move the cursor is with the four cursor-control arrow keys, <↑>, <↓>, <←>, and <→>, as previously explained. These keys are located at the right of the keyboard, and the direction of the arrow on each key illustrates its function.

YOUR TURN

Use the command from the Opening Menu which enables you to edit the NEWJOB.MEM document.

If the NEWJOB.MEM document is already highlighted, simply press the <Return> key. If it is not highlighted, move the highlighting with the arrow keys until it is highlighted, and press the <Return> key.

Practice all three ways to move the cursor: with the **C** command, the <Home>, <End>, <PgUp>, <PgDn> keys, and the cursor-control keys. Watch the line numbers and the column numbers in the status line as the cursor moves. Watch the arrow in the ruler line as the cursor moves.

Removing Text

There are four ways to remove text using WordStar 2000: with commands from the Remove Menu or with the <Backspace> key, the <Ins> key, or the <Del>

key. The appropriate method depends upon the text to be removed and the user's typing style.

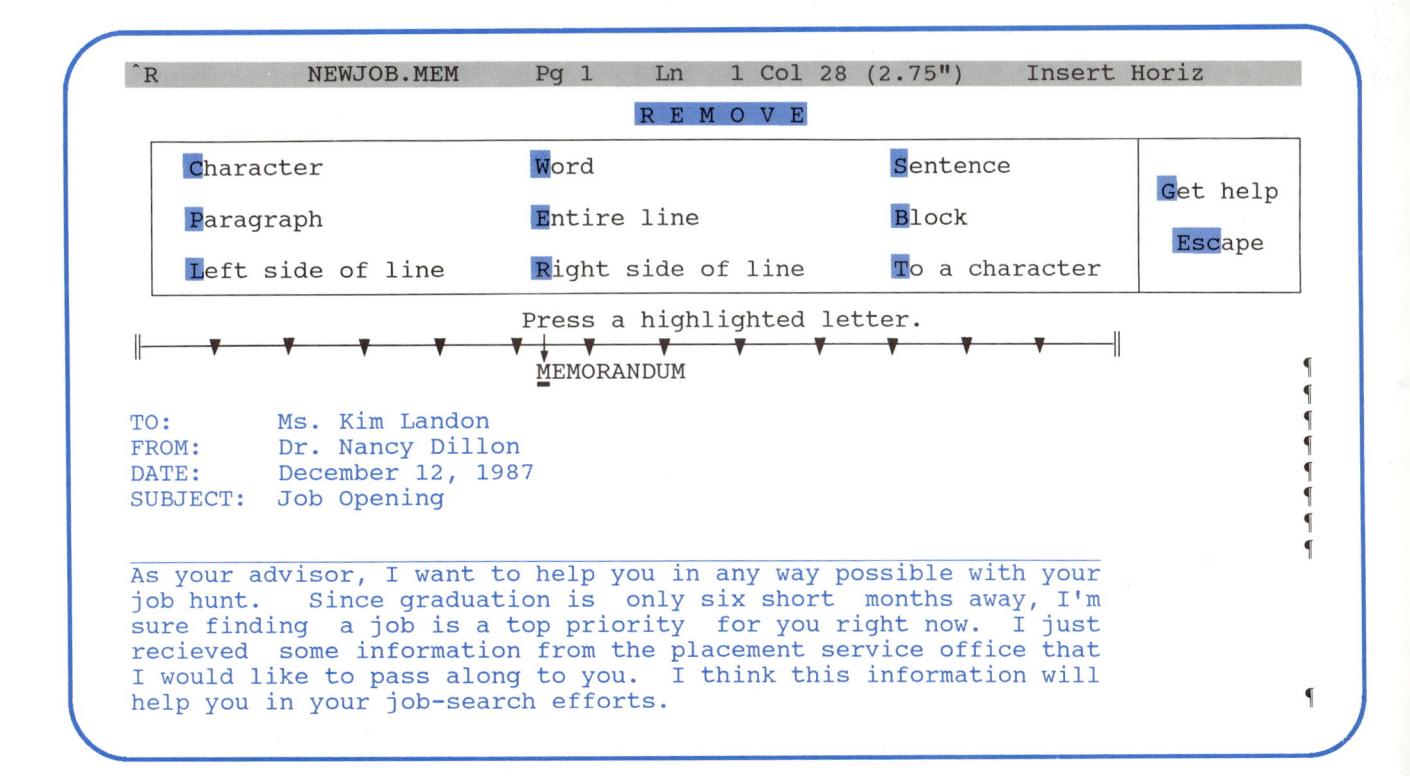

Commands from the Remove Menu remove anything from a character to an entire paragraph (see Figure 8-4). Before a command from the Remove Menu is used, the text to be deleted must be indicated by the cursor. For example, if a specific word is to be deleted, the cursor must be placed somewhere within that word. Table 8-5 describes commands available from the Remove Menu.

A second way to delete text is with the <Backspace> key located next to the <Num Lock> key at the top of the keyboard. Pressing the <Backspace> key once deletes the character to the left of the cursor. If the <Backspace> key is held down, it deletes characters until released.

A third way to delete characters is with the <Ins> key located at the bottom of the keyboard to the right of the <Caps Lock> key. At the right of the status line is the word Insert. Pressing the <Ins> key changes Insert to Over. Pressing the <Ins> key again changes it back to Insert. If the word Over is in the status line, then the **Overtype** mode is on. In this mode, text is changed by typing over it. For example, to change the phrase *green sports car* to *magenta roadster,* place the cursor under the *g* in *green,* make sure Overtype is on, and type `magenta roadster`. The words *green sports car* are deleted automatically.

Overtype does exactly what it says: it types over the existing characters. If the text inserted has fewer characters than that deleted, the leftover characters still need to be deleted, using the <Del> or <Backspace> key. If the insertion is longer than the deletion, it overwrites the following text, so that characters are deleted that should not be. Although Overtype is a useful function, it should be turned off most of the time to prevent information from being lost accidentally.

OVERTYPE
To type directly over an existing character, replacing it with a new character.

Figure 8-4
Remove Menu

```
^R            NEWJOB.MEM      Pg 1    Ln   1 Col 28 (2.75")    Insert Horiz
                             R E M O V E

   Character            Word                 Sentence
                                                              Get help
   Paragraph            Entire line          Block
                                                              Escape
   Left side of line    Right side of line   To a character

                        Press a highlighted letter.
                             MEMORANDUM

   TO:       Ms. Kim Landon
   FROM:     Dr. Nancy Dillon
   DATE:     December 12, 1987
   SUBJECT:  Job Opening

   As your advisor, I want to help you in any way possible with your
   job hunt.  Since graduation is  only six short  months away, I'm
   sure finding  a job is a top priority  for you right now.  I just
   recieved  some information from the placement service office that
   I would like to pass along to you.  I think this information will
   help you in your job-search efforts.
```

Table 8-5
Commands from the Remove Menu

Command	Description
C for Character	Deletes the character over the cursor.
P for Paragraph	Deletes the entire paragraph that contains the cursor.
L for Left side of line	Deletes from the character position where the cursor is located to the left end of that line.
W for Word	Deletes the entire word that contains the cursor.
E for Entire line	Deletes the entire line that contains the cursor.
R for Right side of line	Deletes from the character position where the cursor is located to the right end of that line.
S for Sentence	Deletes the entire sentence that contains the cursor.
B for Block	Deletes a currently selected block of text.
T for To a character	Deletes from the cursor's current location to a character you select.

A fourth way to delete characters is with the <Del> key, which is located in the bottom right corner of the keyboard. Pressing the <Del> key deletes the character above the cursor.

If text is deleted by accident, the **Undo** command restores that text. For example, suppose that you intend to remove a sentence but you press ^**RP** by mistake. An entire paragraph is deleted. To restore that text, simply press ^**U** and the deleted paragraph reappears. **Undo** has some limitations: it can restore only the most recently removed text, and it cannot restore a single character.

> *WS Tips:* Make sure the cursor is located exactly where you want it before pressing ^**R**. For example, if you want to delete a sentence and press ^**RS** without checking to make sure the cursor is located within the sentence you want to delete, you may delete a different sentence. If this happens, restore what you accidentally deleted using ^**U**.
>
> If you remove text using ^**RT** (**T**o a specified character), make sure that character actually exists. If it does not exist the rest of the text to the end of the paragraph will be removed. If this happens, restore the deleted text using ^**U**.
>
> Make sure Overtype is off, except when you need to use it. Otherwise you may type over important text.

YOUR TURN

- Start with the NEWJOB.MEM file on the screen.
- Move the cursor to Line 6. Remove the words *Job Opening* by using the command that deletes everything from the cursor to the right side of the line. Type `Placement Service Seminar` in place of the deleted text.

- Move the cursor to Line 10. Remove the word *graduation* by using the command that deletes an entire word. Type commencement in its place.
- Move the cursor to under the *p* in *placement* in Line 12. Delete the *p* using the command that removes one character. Type a capital P in its place. Change the *s* in *service* and the *o* in *office* to capital letters, using the same method.
- Move the cursor to the sentence in Line 13 that starts: "I think this information . . ." Delete the entire sentence.
- Move the cursor to Line 15 and place it under the *p* in *placement*. Delete the *p* using the <Del> key. Type a capital P in its place. Change the lowercase *s* in *service* to a capital S, using the same method.
- Delete this entire sentence: "These semenars will be divided up according to majors." Replace it with the following sentence: Each semenar will focus on a different major.
- Change the lowercase *p* and *o* in *placement office* in Line 19 to capital letters by turning on Overtype.
- Move the cursor to *I* at the beginning of the sentence "I think it will be well worth your time." Delete the words *I think it* by using the command that enables you to delete to a specified character. Remove text from the cursor to the letter *w*. Type It followed by a space in front of *will*.

Moving Blocks of Text

BLOCK MOVEMENT
A feature that enables the user to define a block of text and then perform a specific operation on the entire block. Common block operations include block move, block copy, block save, and block delete.

Manipulating a document a character at a time is extremely slow when working with large blocks of text. To help speed operations, WordStar 2000 includes a **block movement** feature. This feature defines a block of text and then performs a specific operation on that block, such as copying it, deleting it, or moving it. A block of text can range in length from one character to several pages.

First, the beginning and end of the block of text must be marked. To define a block of text, press ^B, for **B**lock, from the Editing Menu. The Blocks Menu appears (see Figure 8-5). Table 8-6 explains the function of each command in the Blocks Menu. Some of the commands in this menu are advanced commands that are not covered in this chapter, but they are defined in Table 8-6 for your future reference.

To mark the beginning of the block, place the cursor where the block of text is to begin and use the ^**BB** command. A beginning block marker is displayed as <B>. Move the cursor to the end of the block of text and use the ^**BE** command. Both block markers are now in place, but invisible. If the Display mode is on, the block of text is highlighted. Either marker can be set first, but the <B> marker must precede the <E> marker in the text. There can only be one <B> and one <E> at any time.

The <B> and <E> markers cannot be removed. They remain in effect until a new pair of markers is established. The only way to remove markers is by saving a file using ^**QS** or ^**QP,** or by abandoning a document using ^**QA.** Markers remain in place if the ^**QC** command is used.

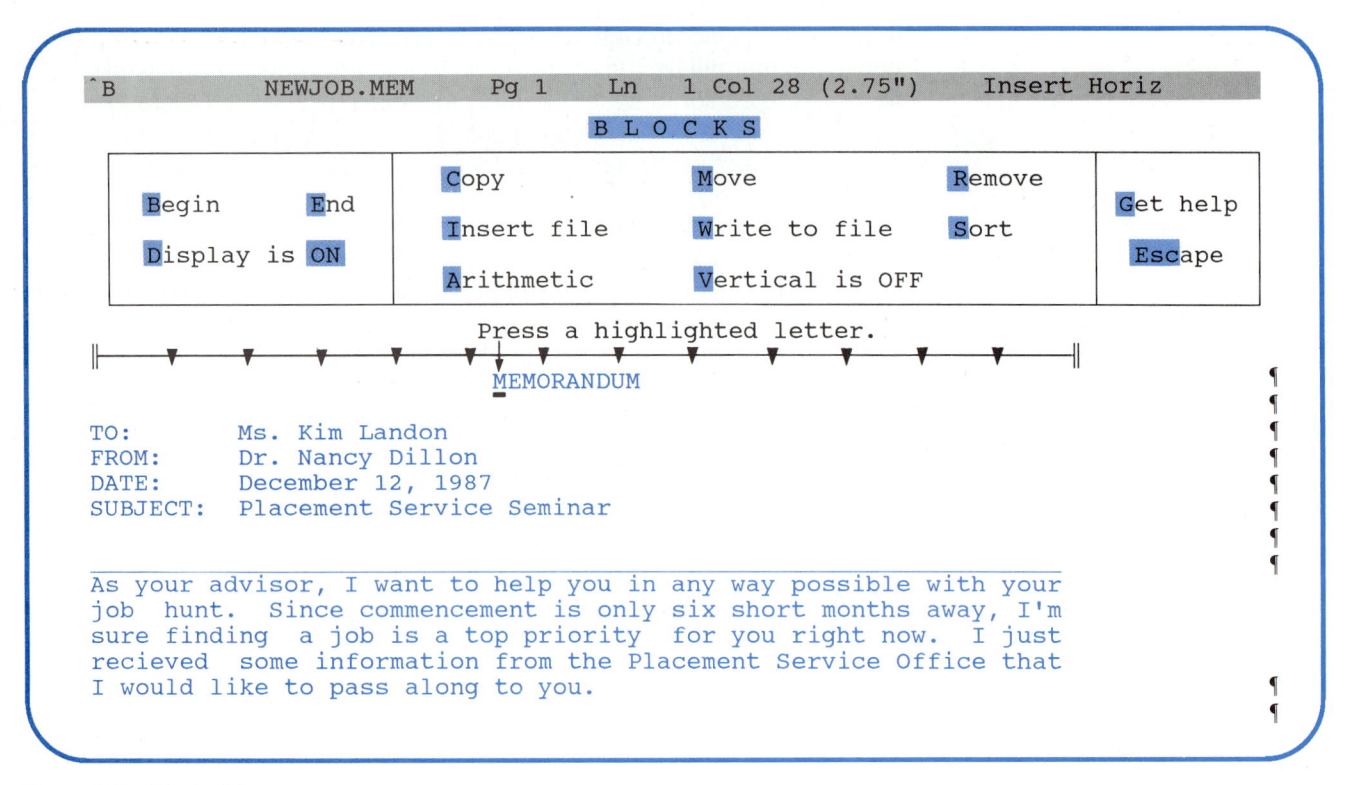

```
^B          NEWJOB.MEM      Pg 1    Ln   1 Col 28 (2.75")      Insert Horiz
                                  B L O C K S
┌─────────────────────┬──────────────────────────────────────────────┬──────────────┐
│                     │ Copy            Move             Remove      │              │
│  Begin      End     │                                              │  Get help    │
│                     │ Insert file     Write to file    Sort        │              │
│  Display is ON      │                                              │  Escape      │
│                     │ Arithmetic      Vertical is OFF              │              │
└─────────────────────┴──────────────────────────────────────────────┴──────────────┘
                            Press a highlighted letter.

                              MEMORANDUM

TO:         Ms. Kim Landon
FROM:       Dr. Nancy Dillon
DATE:       December 12, 1987
SUBJECT:    Placement Service Seminar

As your advisor, I want to help you in any way possible with your
job  hunt.  Since commencement is only six short months away, I'm
sure finding  a job is a top priority  for you right now.  I just
recieved  some information from the Placement Service Office that
I would like to pass along to you.
```

Figure 8-5 Blocks Menu

YOUR TURN

- Start with the NEWJOB.MEM file on the screen.
- Using the Block commands, select the following sentence as a block of text "As your advisor, I want to help you in any way possible with your job hunt."
- Move the cursor to the word *I* in the sentence that begins "I just recieved some information. . . ." Use the Block command that moves the block of text you just selected to this new location.
- Select the entire first paragraph as a block of text. Move the cursor to a new line at the end of the memo. Use the Block command that copies the paragraph to this new location. You decide you do not like this paragraph in its new location. Use the Block command that removes this block of text from the end of the memo. The paragraph should remain as the opening paragraph to the memo.
- Select the sentence in the second paragraph that begins: "There is no cost for attending this semenar. . . ." Move it so that it is the last sentence in the second paragraph.

Correcting Spelling Mistakes

WordStar 2000 comes with a very useful function called CorrectStar. CorrectStar checks the spelling in a document, and if it finds a misspelled word, it suggests

Table 8-6
Commands From the Blocks Menu

Command	Description
B for **B**egin	Marks the beginning of a block of text. The block begins at the cursor's location.
E for **E**	Marks the end of a block of text. The block ends at the cursor's location.
D for **D**isplay	After the beginning and the end of a block of text are marked, the block of text can be highlighted so that it is easily identifiable. If the Display mode is on, the text is highlighted. If the Display mode is off, the text is not highlighted, even though it is still selected as a block of text. Pressing **D** once turns the display off. Pressing **D** again turns the Display back on.
C for **C**opy	Inserts a copy of the block at the cursor's location. The block of text is not be deleted from its original location.
M for **M**ove	Moves the block to the cursor's location. The block of text is deleted from its original location.
R for **R**emove	Removes the block of text.
I for **I**nsert file	Inserts a copy of a file into a document at the cursor's location.
A for **A**rithmetic	Performs simple arithmetic on a block of numbers.
W for **W**rite to file	Copies a block of text to another file.
V for **V**ertical	Allows a vertical column (rather than a series of horizontal lines) to be selected as a block of text. Pressing **V** once turns Vertical on. VERT appears on the status line. When Vertical is on, columns of text can be selected as a block. Pressing **V** again turns Vertical off. HORIZ (rather than VERT) appears in the status line.
S for **S**ort	Sorts lines or columns alphabetically or numerically in either ascending or descending order.

the correct spelling. CorrectStar can analyze a word phonetically (by sound). If a word is close to the correct spelling, CorrectStar can suggest the right spelling.

To use CorrectStar, you need the WordStar 2000 Dictionary disk. Press ^**O** for **O**ptions from the Editing Menu. The Options Menu appears. Next press **S** for **S**pelling correction, and the Spelling Correction Menu appears. Table 8-7 explains each of the commands in the Spelling Correction Menu.

After pressing ^**OS** and either **W** for **W**ord, **P** for **P**aragraph, or **R** for **R**est of document, the message REPLACE THE PROGRAM DISK WITH THE DICTIONARY DISK appears. Remove the program disk from drive A and replace it with the dictionary disk. Press <Esc>. CorrectStar then asks PERSONAL DICTIONARY TO USE? Press <Return>. CorrectStar begins looking for misspelled words. When it finds a suspect word, CorrectStar searches for a replacement to suggest. Once it suggests a replacement, you must select one of seven options. These options from the CorrectStar Menu are listed in Table 8-8.

> *Hard Disk Differences:* If the dictionary is already installed on the hard disk, after you press ^**OS** and either **W, P,** or **R,** CorrectStar immediately begins searching for misspelled words.

Table 8-7
Commands From the Spelling Correction Menu

Command	Description
W for Word	Checks the spelling of the individual word at the cursor's location.
P for Paragraph	Checks the spelling of all the words in the paragraph where the cursor is located.
R for Rest of document	Checks all the spelling from the cursor's location to the end of the document. If the cursor is placed at the beginning of the document, this command checks the spelling of the entire document.
S for Select dictionary	Creating a personal dictionary is possible with WordStar 2000. For example, if a research paper uses special terminology, those terms can be entered in a personal dictionary and then checked throughout the paper. This command creates a new dictionary or uses a dictionary already created.

When CorrectStar finds no more spelling errors, the message REPLACE THE DICTIONARY DISK WITH THE WS2000 PROGRAM DISK appears. Remove the Dictionary disk from drive A and replace it with the program disk. Press <Esc>. The Editing Menu returns to the screen.

Hard Disk Differences: When CorrectStar has completed the search for misspelled words, the Editing Menu automatically returns to the screen.

Table 8-8
Commands from the CorrectStar Menu

Command	Description
A for Add to dictionary	Adds a suspect word to a personal dictionary. The word is not changed, and CorrectStar looks for the next misspelled word. The next time this word is encountered, CorrectStar does not consider it to be misspelled.
I for Ignore	Ignores the suggested replacement. The suspect word is not changed, and CorrectStar looks for the next misspelled word. The next time this word is encountered, CorrectStar again considers it to be misspelled and suggests a replacement word.
T for Type correction	Enables the user to type in his or her own replacement word.
C for Correct all occurrences	Replaces all occurrences of the suspect word with the suggested replacement.
N for Next suggestion	Provides another suggestion for a replacement word.
P for Previous suggestion	Returns to the previous suggestion for a replacement word.
<Return>	Pressing the <Return> key replaces the suspect word with the suggested replacement at the current location only. The suspect word is not be corrected anywhere else in the document.

CorrectStar can be selected from either the Editing Menu or the Opening Menu. At the Opening Menu, select **S** for Spelling correction and the question CHECK SPELLING OF WHICH DOCUMENT? appears on the screen. After you select a document, the question PERSONAL DICTIONARY TO USE? appears on the screen. After you have selected a dictionary, the process for correcting spelling errors is the same as when you enter CorrectStar through the Editing Menu. If CorrectStar is entered through the Opening Menu, however, the spelling of the entire document is automatically checked. If CorrectStar is entered through the Editing Menu, the spelling of either the entire document or just part of it can be checked.

YOUR TURN

- Start with the NEWJOB.MEM file on the screen.
- Move the cursor to Line 1 of the document. Use the command that checks the spelling of the entire document. If CorrectStar finds spelling errors other than the ones mentioned in this exercise, correct them as you go along.
- When CorrectStar finds the words *Kim, Landon,* and *Dillon,* add them to the dictionary.
- When CorrectStar finds *recieved,* use the command that corrects it as suggested for this one time only.
- When CorrectStar finds *cerees,* its first suggestion is not the correct word. Use the command that allows CorrectStar to offer another suggestion. Continue to use the command until *series* is the suggested replacement. Then correct the word for this one time only.
- When CorrectStar finds *semenars,* use the command that corrects all occurrences of the word in the rest of the document.
- When CorrectStar finds *semenar,* use the command that corrects all occurrences of the word in the rest of the document.
- When CorrectStar finds *Feburary,* correct it for the entire document.
- When CorrectStar can find no more errors, replace the Dictionary Disk with the Program Disk. Press <Esc>.
- Read over the entire memo carefully. You can get back to the beginning by using the <PgUp> or <↑> key. Be sure to check the spacing between words and sentences. You may need to create a space or delete a space. The space bar creates spaces, and the <Del> or <Backspace> key or the Remove commands delete them.
- When you are satisfied with the memo, use the ^**QC** command to save the document.

Printing

There are two ways to print with WordStar 2000. The **P** (**P**rint) command at the Opening Menu prints any document in the files. The ^**QP** (**Q**uit and **P**rint) command saves the document currently being edited and then prints that document.

After the ^QP command, the Choose a Name screen appears, followed by the question PRINTER TO USE? At this point, a printer needs to be selected. If the computer is connected to only one printer, simply press the <Return> key. If it is connected to more than one printer, move the highlighting using the cursor-control keys to the name of the printer to be used, or type the name of the printer. Press the <Return> key.

If you use the ^P command at the Opening Menu instead, the question DOCUMENT TO PRINT? appears. Select the document by typing its name or moving the highlighting. Then the question PRINTER TO USE? appears, and you proceed as described in the last paragraph.

The Decisions screen appears next (see Figure 8-6). Six questions need to be answered about how the document is to be printed. There is already an answer by each of the questions. To see all of the questions and answers, press ^V. To accept the answer on the screen, press <Return>. Using the <Return> key answers the questions one at a time. To accept all of the answers, press ^Q.

When all the questions have been answered, the message PREPARE THE PRINTER AND PRESS RETURN appears. Make sure the printer is turned on and online, and that there is enough paper. Press the <Return> key to print the document.

YOUR TURN

Use the ^QP command to print the NEWJOB.MEM document. When the DECISIONS screen appears, accept all the answers by pressing ^Q.

Learning Check

1. The _____ provides information regarding the document name, cursor location, and typing and text modes.

2. How many ways are there to move the cursor within a file or document?
   a. 1   c. 3
   b. 2   d. 4

3. The Undo command can restore any previously deleted text. (True or False?)

4. Text block markers can be removed only by _____ or _____ a document.

5. CorrectStar not only can search for misspelled words, but also can suggest correct spellings. (True or False?)

6. CorrectStar can be accessed through the _____ or _____ Menu.

7. After editing, the ^QP command instructs the computer to _____ and _____ your document.

Answers

1. status line 2. c 3. False 4. saving, abandoning 5. True 6. Editing, Opening 7. save, print

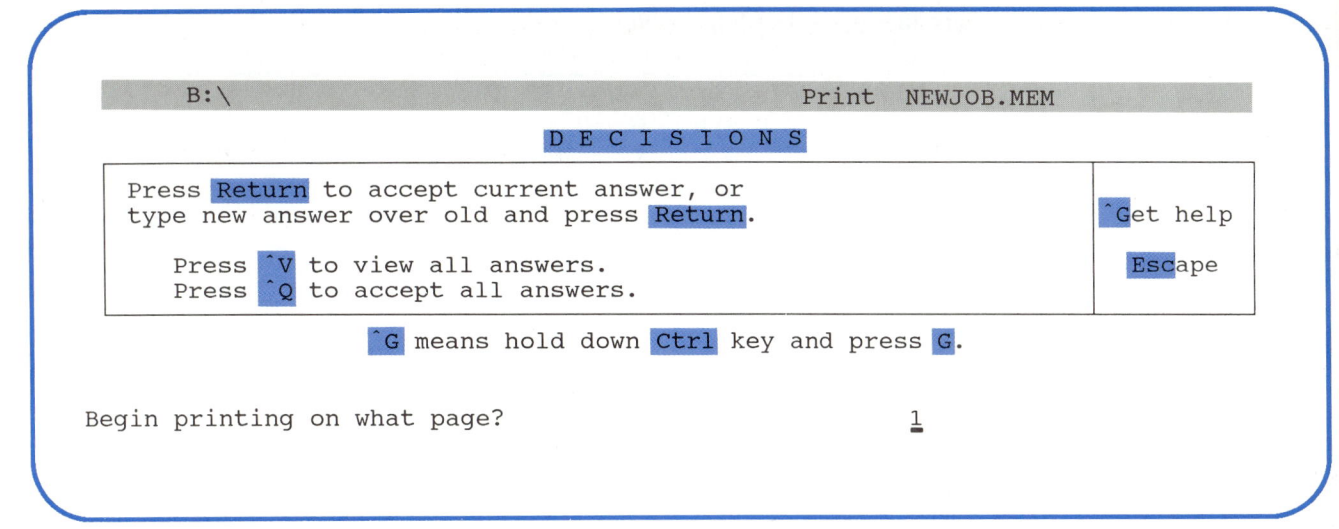

```
            B:\                                    Print  NEWJOB.MEM
                            D E C I S I O N S
   ┌─────────────────────────────────────────────────────┬──────────────┐
   │ Press Return to accept current answer, or           │              │
   │ type new answer over old and press Return.          │  ^Get help   │
   │                                                     │              │
   │    Press ^V to view all answers.                    │   Escape     │
   │    Press ^Q to accept all answers.                  │              │
   └─────────────────────────────────────────────────────┴──────────────┘
                   ^G means hold down Ctrl key and press G.

    Begin printing on what page?                              1
                                                              ─
```

Figure 8-6 Printing Decisions Screen

Summary of Frequently Used WordStar 2000 Menus

1. Opening Menus

1-a. The following menu appears after you type WS2:

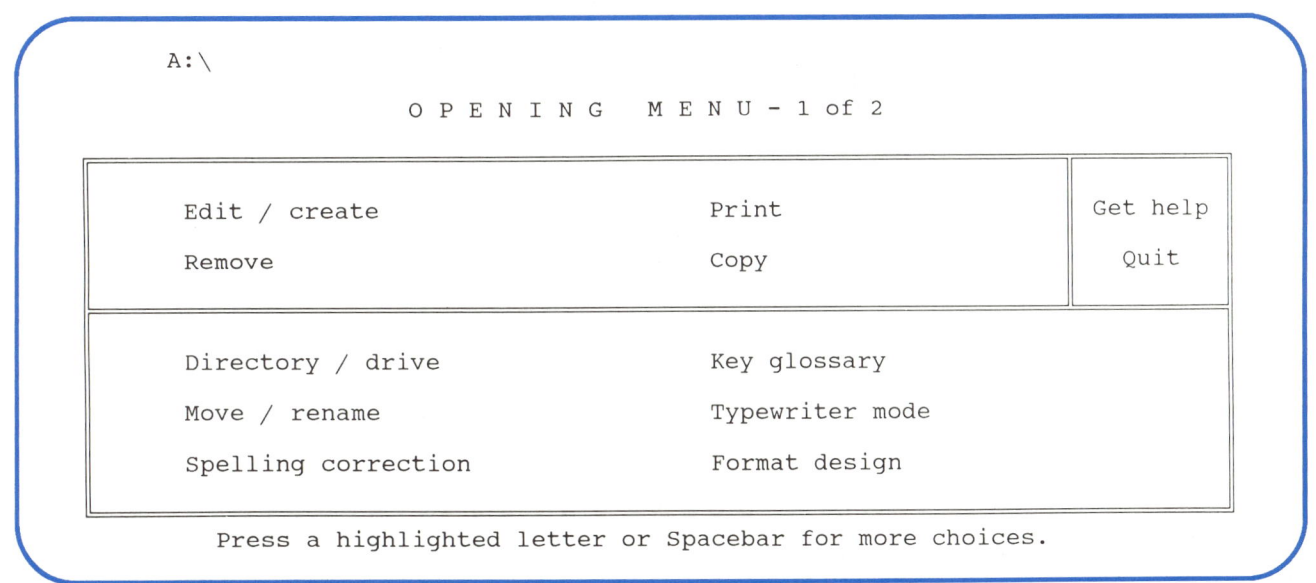

```
       A:\
                      O P E N I N G    M E N U - 1 of 2

       ┌──────────────────────────────────────────────────┬──────────────┐
       │   Edit / create              Print               │  Get help    │
       │                                                  │              │
       │   Remove                     Copy                │   Quit       │
       ├──────────────────────────────────────────────────┴──────────────┤
       │                                                                 │
       │   Directory / drive          Key glossary                       │
       │                                                                 │
       │   Move / rename              Typewriter mode                    │
       │                                                                 │
       │   Spelling correction        Format design                      │
       └─────────────────────────────────────────────────────────────────┘
             Press a highlighted letter or Spacebar for more choices.
```

1-b. The following menu appears after you select Edit/Create:

```
    B:\
                      C H O O S E   A   N A M E
   ┌──────────────────────────────────────────────────┬──────────┐
   │ Type or highlight name.  Press Return.           │          │
   │                                                  │ ^Get help│
   │    Move highlighting with cursor keys.           │          │
   │    Erase errors with Backspace.                  │ Escape   │
   │    Transfer highlighted letters to answer line with ^T.     │
   └──────────────────────────────────────────────────┴──────────┘
              ^G means hold down Ctrl key and press G.


 Document to edit or create?_




   JUSTIFY.FRM       MEMOFORM.FRM      MSCRIPT.FRM      NORMAL.FRM
   RAGGED.FRM        UNFORM.FRM        WS2.KEY
```

1-c. After you have created a new file, the history screen appears, filled with information regarding the new file:

```
              NEW                                          Insert
                         H I S T O R Y
   ┌──────────────────────────────────────┬───────────────────────┬──────────┐
   │ On the lines below, enter or update any │ Created:  02/04/87 │          │
   │ information you want to keep on file:   │ Modified: 02/04/87 │ ^Get help│
   │                                         │ — Keystrokes —     │          │
   │   Press Return to move to the next line.│ Total: 0           │ Escape   │
   │   Press ^Q to leave screen or save data.│ Last edit: 0       │          │
   └──────────────────────────────────────┴───────────────────────┴──────────┘
              ^G means hold down Ctrl key and press G.

      Title:_
     Author:
   Operator:

   Distribution:              Key Words:
      1.                         1.
      2.                         2.
      3.                         3.
      4.                         4.
      5.                         5.
   Comments:
```

2. Editing Menus

2-a. The Editing menu always appears in the upper part of the editing window:

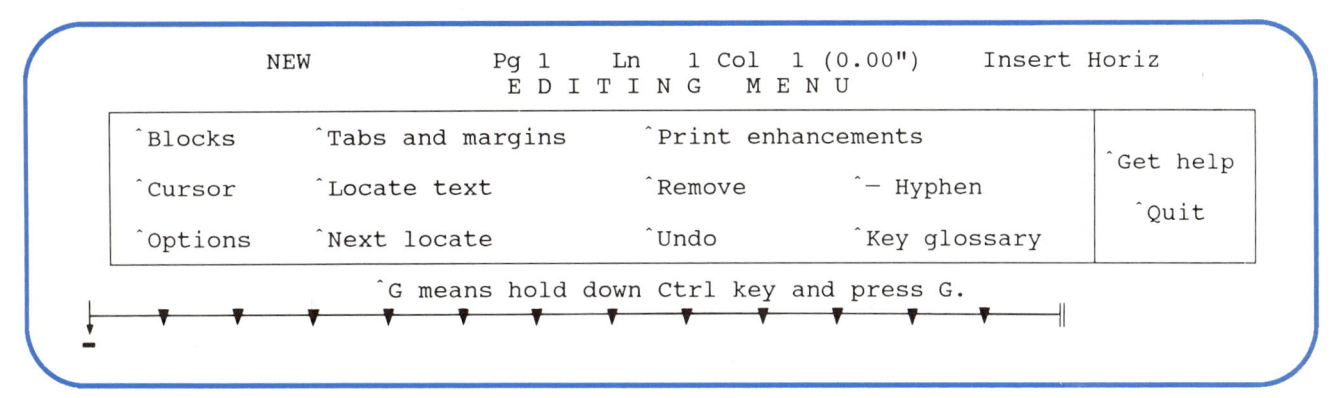

```
            NEW              Pg 1    Ln   1 Col   1 (0.00")    Insert Horiz
                                  E D I T I N G    M E N U
    ┌─────────────────────────────────────────────────────────┬──────────────┐
    │  ^Blocks       ^Tabs and margins    ^Print enhancements │   ^Get help  │
    │  ^Cursor       ^Locate text         ^Remove    ^— Hyphen│              │
    │  ^Options      ^Next locate         ^Undo      ^Key glossary│ ^Quit    │
    └─────────────────────────────────────────────────────────┴──────────────┘
              ^G means hold down Ctrl key and press G.
```

2-b. Some of the Editing Submenus appear as follows:

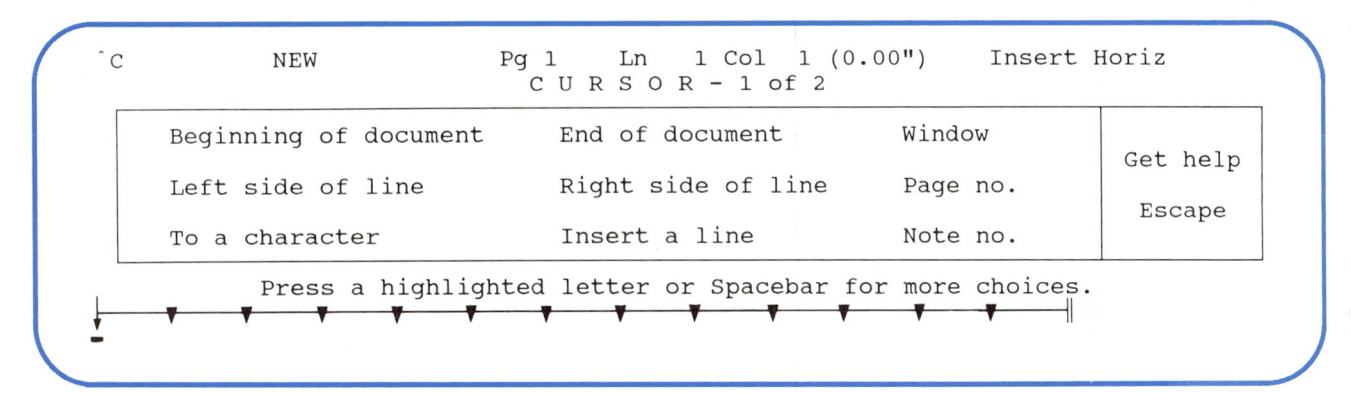

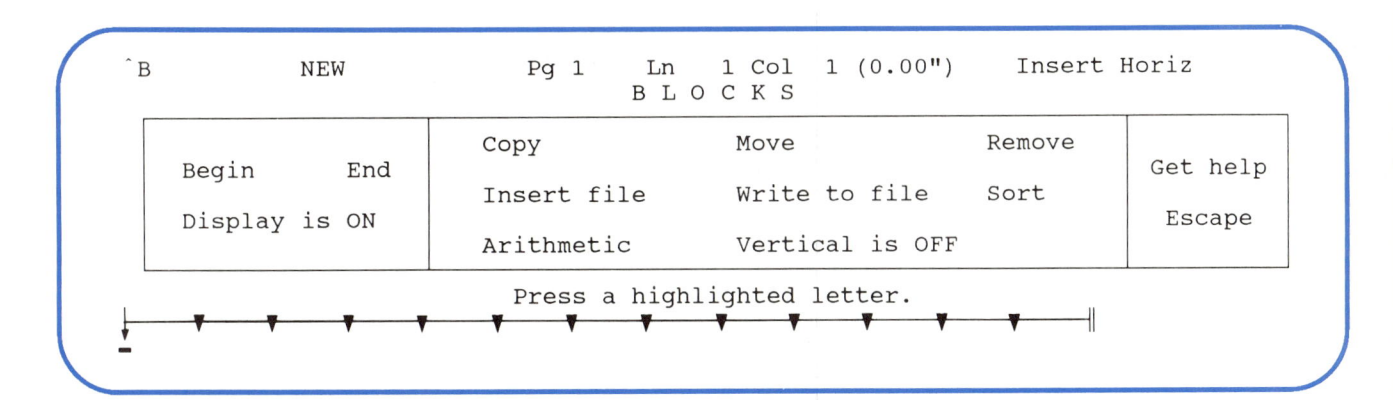

```
   ^C        NEW              Pg 1    Ln   1 Col   1 (0.00")    Insert Horiz
                                  C U R S O R - 1 of 2
    ┌─────────────────────────────────────────────────────────┬──────────────┐
    │  Beginning of document   End of document      Window    │   Get help   │
    │  Left side of line       Right side of line   Page no.  │              │
    │  To a character          Insert a line        Note no.  │   Escape     │
    └─────────────────────────────────────────────────────────┴──────────────┘
         Press a highlighted letter or Spacebar for more choices.
```

```
   ^B        NEW              Pg 1    Ln   1 Col   1 (0.00")    Insert Horiz
                                      B L O C K S
    ┌─────────────────────────────────────────────────────────┬──────────────┐
    │                        Copy           Move        Remove│   Get help   │
    │  Begin      End        Insert file    Write to file  Sort│             │
    │  Display is ON         Arithmetic     Vertical is OFF   │   Escape     │
    └─────────────────────────────────────────────────────────┴──────────────┘
                        Press a highlighted letter.
```

PART TWO: APPLICATIONS SOFTWARE

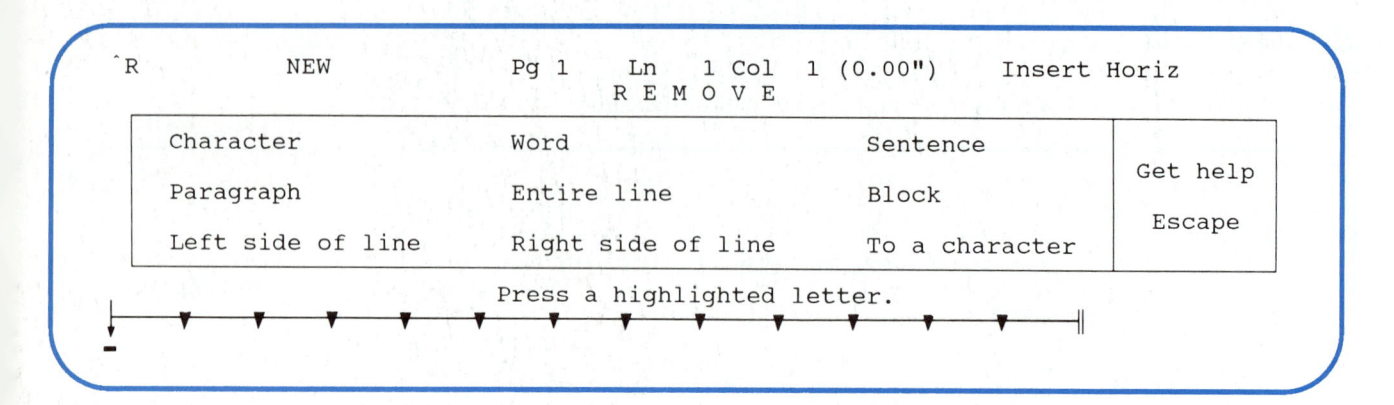

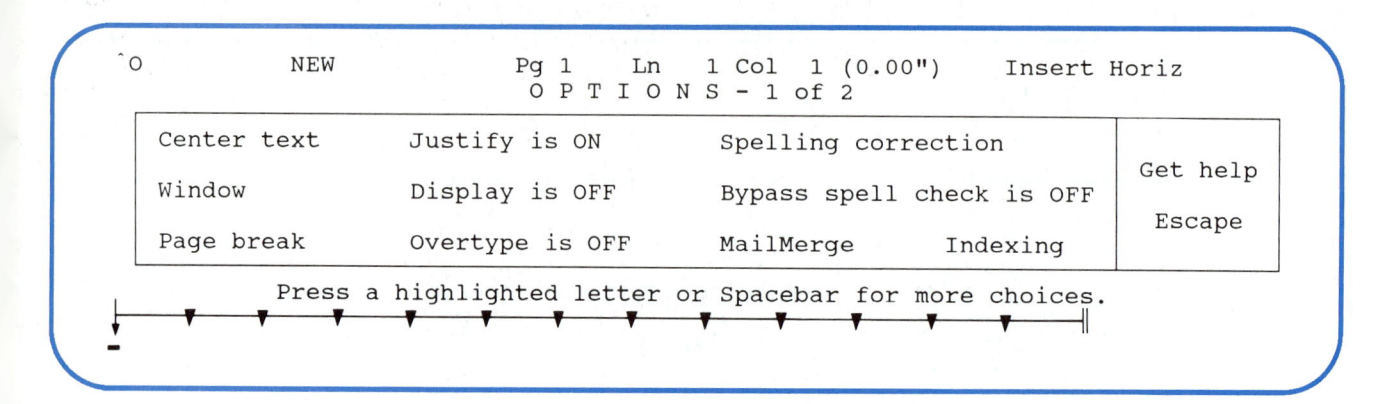

```
^R            NEW           Pg 1    Ln   1 Col  1 (0.00")    Insert Horiz
                              R E M O V E
    ┌─────────────────────────────────────────────────────────┬──────────┐
    │ Character          Word                  Sentence       │          │
    │                                                         │ Get help │
    │ Paragraph          Entire line           Block          │          │
    │                                                         │ Escape   │
    │ Left side of line  Right side of line    To a character │          │
    └─────────────────────────────────────────────────────────┴──────────┘
                    Press a highlighted letter.
```

```
^O            NEW           Pg 1    Ln   1 Col  1 (0.00")    Insert Horiz
                           O P T I O N S - 1 of 2
    ┌─────────────────────────────────────────────────────────┬──────────┐
    │ Center text       Justify is ON       Spelling correction│          │
    │                                                          │ Get help │
    │ Window            Display is OFF      Bypass spell check is OFF     │
    │                                                          │ Escape   │
    │ Page break        Overtype is OFF     MailMerge    Indexing│        │
    └─────────────────────────────────────────────────────────┴──────────┘
         Press a highlighted letter or Spacebar for more choices.
```

3. Quit Editing Menu

3-a. This menu appears after typing ^Q:

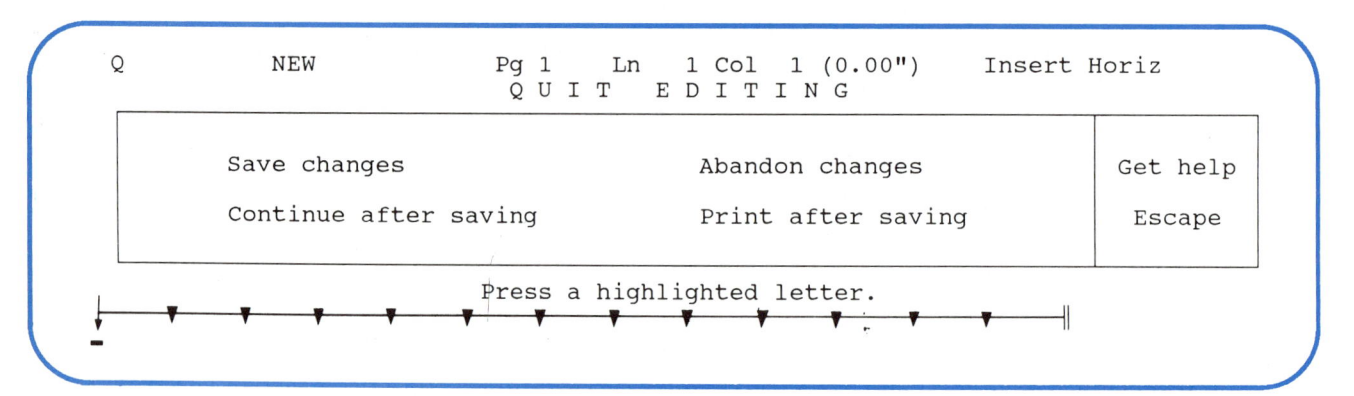

```
Q             NEW           Pg 1    Ln   1 Col  1 (0.00")    Insert Horiz
                              Q U I T   E D I T I N G
    ┌─────────────────────────────────────────────────────────┬──────────┐
    │   Save changes                 Abandon changes          │ Get help │
    │                                                         │          │
    │   Continue after saving        Print after saving       │ Escape   │
    └─────────────────────────────────────────────────────────┴──────────┘
                    Press a highlighted letter.
```

CHAPTER 8: INTRODUCTION TO WORD PROCESSING AND WORDSTAR 2000   241

3-b. The Printing Menus appear as follows:

```
     B:\
                    C H O O S E   A   N A M E
  ┌─────────────────────────────────────────────────────┬──────────┐
  │ Type or highlight name.  Press Return.              │          │
  │                                                     │ ^Get help│
  │    Move highlighting with cursor keys.              │          │
  │    Erase errors with Backspace.                     │ Escape   │
  │    Transfer highlighted letters to answer line with ^T.│       │
  └─────────────────────────────────────────────────────┴──────────┘
              ^G means hold down Ctrl key and press G.


Printer to use? _



PRINTER

PRINTER
```

```
     B:\                                     Print  NEW
                      D E C I S I O N S
  ┌─────────────────────────────────────────────────────┬──────────┐
  │ Press Return to accept current answer, or           │          │
  │ type new answer over old and press Return.          │ ^Get help│
  │                                                     │          │
  │    Press ^V to view all answers.                    │ Escape   │
  │    Press ^Q to accept all answers.                  │          │
  └─────────────────────────────────────────────────────┴──────────┘
              ^G means hold down Ctrl key and press G.


Begin printing on what page?                             1
Stop printing after what page? (L for LAST)              L
Print how many copies?                                   1
Pause between pages for paper change? (Y/N)              N
Obey page formatting commands? (Y/N)                     Y
Print and continue working? (Y/N)                        N
Send document to Printer or to Disk file? (P/D)          P
Prepare the printer and press Return.                    _
```

Summary Points

- Word processing is the act of composing and manipulating text with the aid of a computer.
- A word processor is a program (software) or set of programs which enables you to write, edit, format, and print data.
- A word processing system includes both the hardware and software that enable you to operate a word processor. There are two general types of word-processing systems: (1) dedicated systems, which can handle only word processing, and (2) multipurpose systems, which are equipped to handle various processing tasks including word processing.
- Word processors can be used in many different places, such as businesses, schools, and homes. Uses for word processors include writing business letters, school reports, and letters.
- The two primary functions of a word processor are text editing (which involves entering and manipulating text) and print formatting (which involves communicating to the printer how to format the printed copy).
- Common writing and editing features of a word processor include cursor positioning, word wrap, scrolling, insertion, replacement, deletion, spelling correction, block movement, searching, undo, and save.

WordStar 2000 Exercises

1. Starting up WordStar 2000
   a. Assuming the computer is shut off, describe all the steps you must take to start WordStar 2000. Start WordStar 2000. What is the name of the first WordStar 2000 menu? What are the six commands listed on the upper part of the menu?
   b. The characters A:\ in the upper left corner of the screen indicate that disk drive A: is the current drive. Change the drive to B. Describe the steps taken to change the drive to B. (Omit this question if your computer has a hard disk.)

2. Creating a New Document
   a. Choose the appropriate command to create a new document. What is the name of this command? What is the name of the screen that appears after you select the command to create a new document? Type a name and press the <Return> key. What happens? How is a format selected?
   b. What is the name of the screen that appears after you press the <Return> key? What is its purpose? How do you quit this screen?
   c. After you quit this screen, the Editing Menu appears. What information does the first line on the screen provide? How do you use the editing commands that appear on the upper part of the screen?

3. Entering a Document

Type the following paragraph:

```
A soap opera deal with the plights and problems
brought about in the lives of its permanent princi-
pal characters by the advent and interference of one
group of individuals after another. Thus, a soap op-
era ia an endlesss sequence of narratives whose only
cohesive element is the eternal presence of bedev-
iled and beleaguered principal characters. A nara-
tive, or story sequence, may run from eight weeks to
several months. The ending of one plot is always
hooked up with the beginning of the next, but the
connection is unimportant and soon forgotten. Almost
all the villains in the small town daytime serials
are emigres from the cities--gangsters, white-collar
criminals, designing women, unnatural mothers, cold
wives, and selfish, ruthless, and just plain cursed
rich men. They always come up against a shrewdness
that ouwits them or destroys them, or a kindness
that wins them over to the god way of life.

                            E. B. WHITE, ''Soapland''
```

4. Using the Editing Commands
   a. Correct the following typing mistakes:
- Add an *s* to *deal* in the first sentence.
- In the second sentence, change *ia* to *is* and remove the extra *s* from *endless*.
- In the third sentence, correct the misspelled word *narative*.
- Using the ˆ**C**ursor command, move the cursor to the end of the text; change the word *god* to *good* in the last sentence.

   b. Delete the following sentence using the ˆ**B**locks command: ''A narrative, or story sequence, may run from eight weeks to several months.'' (Note: Make sure you delete the two spaces following this text.)

   c. Move the cursor back to the first line of the paragraph and copy the first sentence at the end of the text, using the ˆ**B**locks command.

5. Saving and Retrieving a Document
   a. Save the work you have completed, and quit WordStar 2000. What steps are taken to do this? Explain the four options displayed on the Quit/Editing window.

   b. You decide to restore the sentence previously removed. Retrieve the file containing the document. Describe the steps taken to accomplish this. Retype the sentence at the appropriate place, and save the document again.

6. Review

List the various menus used for creating, editing, saving, and retrieving a document.

WordStar 2000 Problems

To complete the following problems, use the ORDER file included on the Student File Disk. To start WordStar 2000, boot the system with the DOS disk. At the A> prompt, insert the program disk in drive A and type **ws2**. Insert the Student File Disk in drive B.

> *Hard Disk Differences:* You need to copy the ORDER file included on your diskette onto the hard disk. When you turn on your computer, at the C> prompt, type **a:** and press <Return> to switch to drive A. Insert your diskette with the ORDER file on it into drive A, type **copy order c:\ws2000,** and press <Return>. Switch back to drive C by typing **c:** and pressing the <Return> key. Type **ws2** and press <Return>.

1. To be able to read the ORDER file in drive B, change the directory by using the appropriate command. (If you have a hard disk, omit this step.)

2. Copy the ORDER file to the ESSAI file by using the copy command. Describe the steps taken to copy the file.

3. Use the ESSAI file to answer the remaining questions. Retrieve the ESSAI file.

4. The document is an order to a publishing firm. Assume that you are Helen Turoff, the documentalist. You want to use the same format in the ORDER file to order another magazine. Because you made a copy of the ORDER file, you can make changes to it and still have the original format saved. Change the date of the order to the current date.

5. Using the ^**B**lock and ^**R**emove commands, delete the supplier address and replace it with the following new address:

   Midwest Publishing
   112 Lassalle Street
   Chicago, IL 60610

6. Change the word *monthly* to *weekly*.

7. Add the text *starting next month* to the beginning of the first sentence. Change the *P* in *Please* from uppercase to lowercase.

8. Add the following name to the list of persons receiving the subscription:

   Mr. Mark Steiner
   M.I.S. Department

9. Using the ^Remove Sentence command, delete the following sentence: I am accepting your special offer--$15 for the first subscription, $8 for each additional copy.

10. Save and print your work.

CHAPTER 9

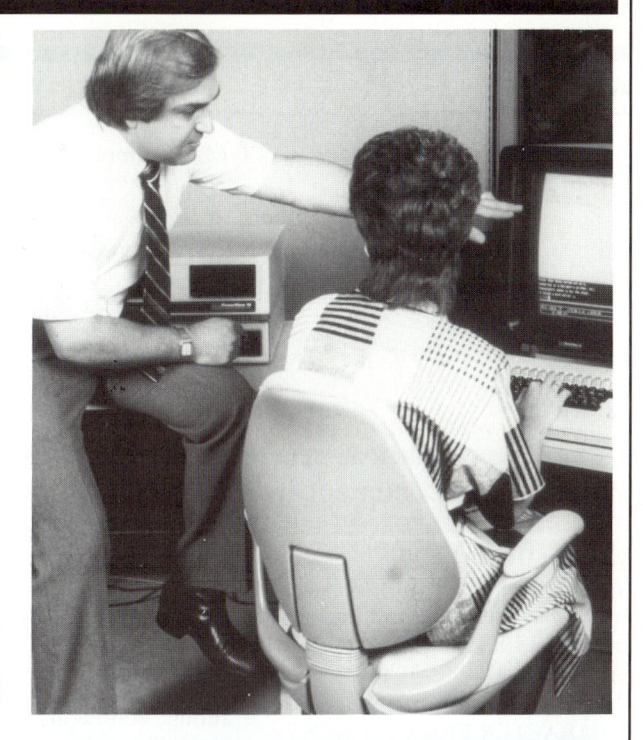

Advanced WordStar 2000

Outline

Introduction
Formatting a Document
  Setting Tabs and Margins
  The Options Menu
  Viewing Command Tags
  Print Enhancements

Learning Check
More Advanced Features
  Headers and Footers
  Footnotes
  Locate and Replace
  Changing a Format Design

Learning Check
Summary Points
WordStar 2000 Exercises
WordStar 2000 Problems

Introduction

Many simple documents, such as memos, letters, and outlines, can be created with the WordStar 2000 commands learned in the previous chapter. Other types of documents, however, such as resumes or term papers, require the use of WordStar 2000's more advanced features. These features can make the creation of a complicated document a relatively easy task. This chapter explains how to use print formatting features to enhance the appearance of a document, and how to add headers, footers, and footnotes to a document.

Formatting a Document

PRINT FORMATTING
The function of a word processor which communicates with the printer to tell it how to print the text on paper.

CHARACTER ENHANCEMENT
Underlining, boldfacing, subscripting, and superscripting.

The **print formatting** function of a word processor involves a variety of features that communicate with the printer to tell it how to print the text on paper. Some of the more common print formatting features include setting margins and tab stops; selecting single- or double-spaced text; reformatting paragraphs after editing; marking page breaks; and performing **character enhancements,** such as underlining, boldfacing, superscripting, and subscripting. Figure 9-1 illustrates a typical page format.

As mentioned in the previous chapter, WordStar 2000 provides six standard formats. When one of these formats is chosen, the overall shape of the document is defined, but parts of it can still be changed. The exercises in this chapter guide you through the process of formatting a document so that it looks exactly as you want it to look.

Setting Tabs and Margins

The Ruler Line, the line separating the menus from the window, shows the tabs and margins as they are set in the format being used (see Figure 9-2). The two parallel lines at the left edge of the ruler indicate the left margin. The ▼ symbol indicates a normal tab. The arrow (↓) in the Ruler Line indicates the cursor's column position in the text; it covers any other symbol at that position in the Ruler Line. The # symbol (if present) indicates a decimal tab, and the two parallel lines at the right edge of the Ruler Line indicate the right margin.

The <Tab> key is the <⇆> key located above the <Ctrl> key. Pressing the <Tab> key moves the cursor one tab stop to the right. All the standard formats have the same tab setting: a tab stop every five spaces, starting in column 6. These tab settings can be changed easily. To change the tab settings, press ^T, for Tabs and Margins, from the Editing Menu. The Tabs and Margins Menu appears on the screen. Table 9-1 explains the function of each of the commands in the Tabs and Margins Menu.

Format commands relating to indenting margins (^TI, ^TB, ^TP, ^TH, etc.) take effect on the current line if the cursor is at the current left margin when the command is issued. For example, if ^TP is typed first when text for a new document

**Figure 9-1
A Typical Page Format**

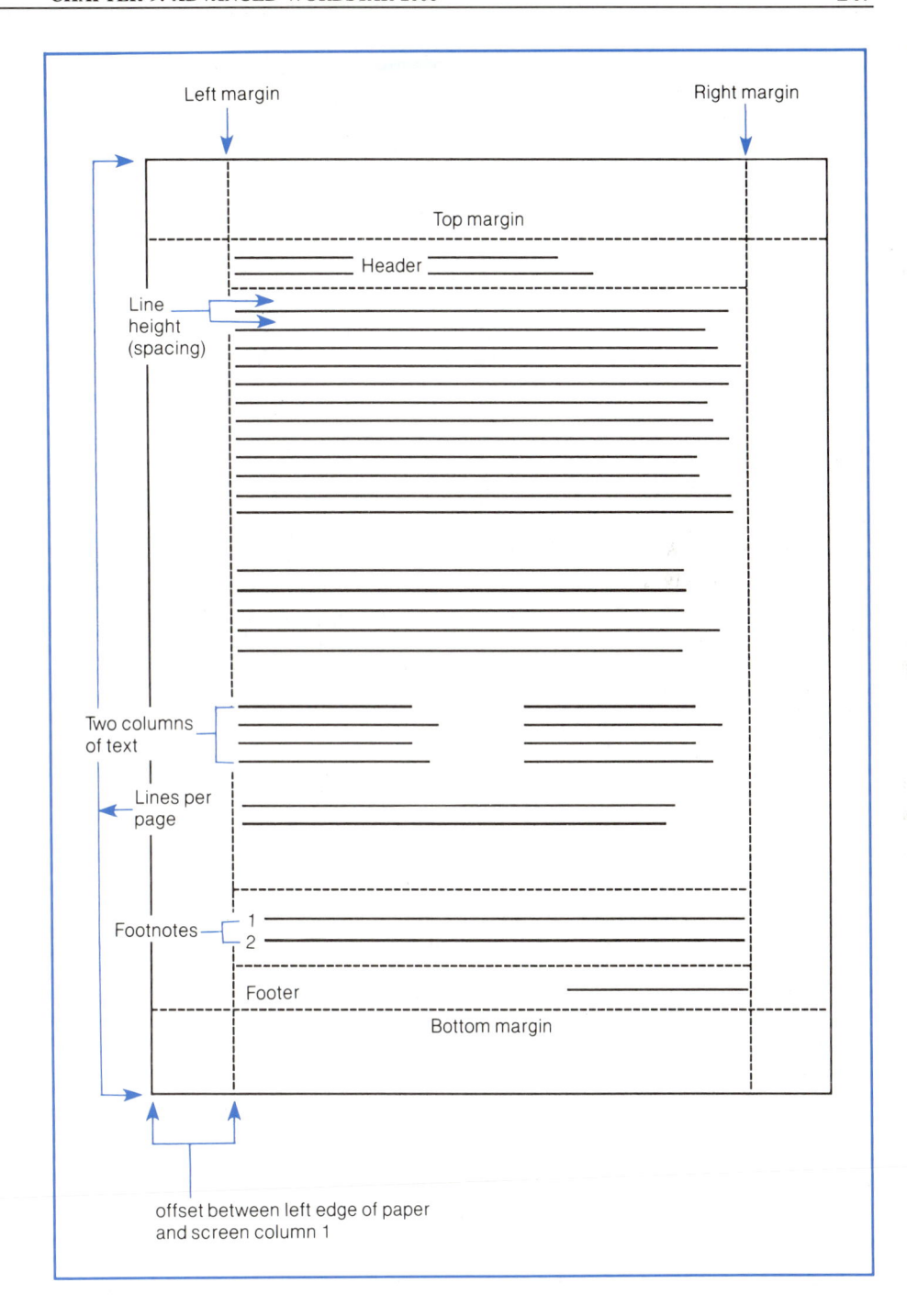

is being entered, the first line of the text will be indented, because the cursor is always at the current left margin at the start of a new document. If the cursor is not at the current left margin, the indentation begins at the next line. For example, if there is a long quotation in the middle of a document, the left margin of the quotation needs to be indented. Press ^TI at the end of the line immediately

248   PART TWO: APPLICATIONS SOFTWARE

[Diagram showing a ruler line with labels: The Left Margin, The Right Margin, Decimal Tab Settings, Cursor's current location, Tab Settings]

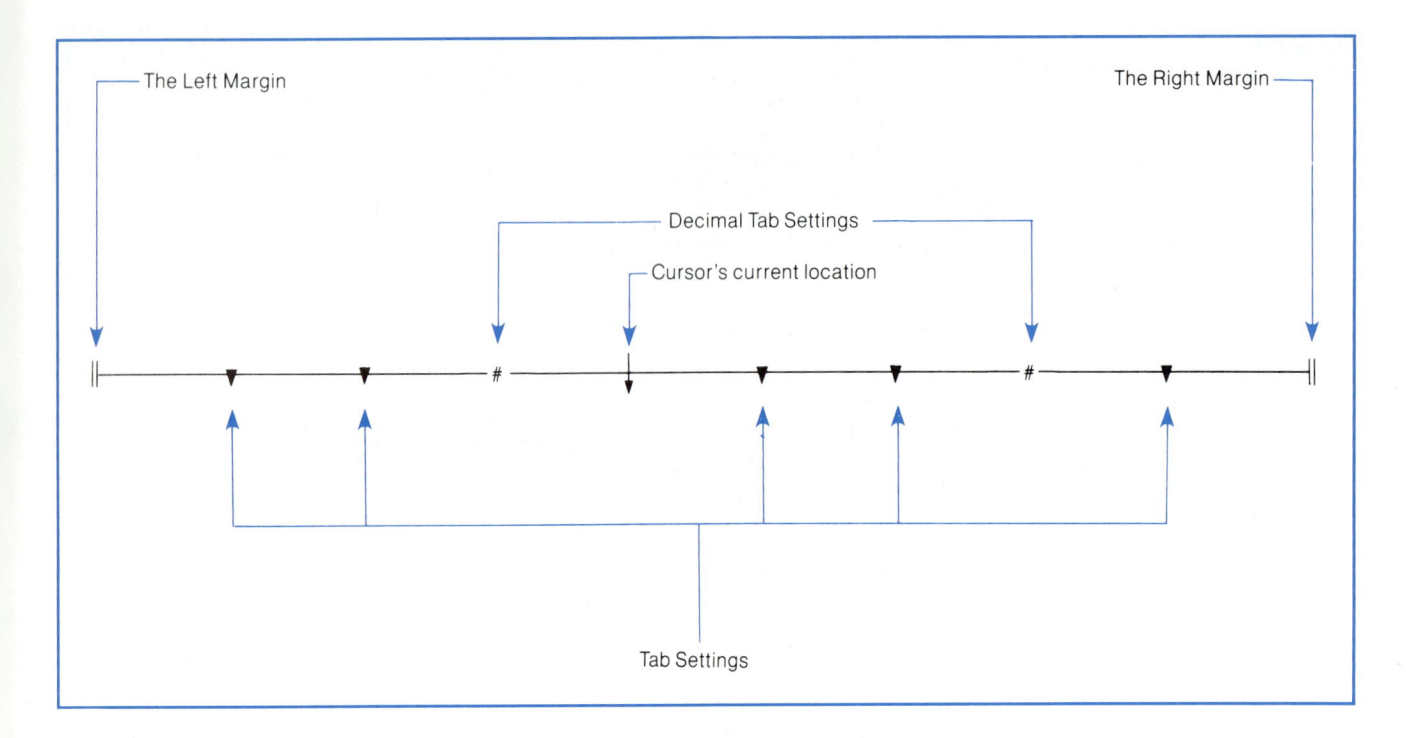

Figure 9-2
The Ruler Line

preceding the first line of the quotation. If the command is issued when the cursor is already on the first line of the quotation, the first line may not indent at all. In this case, the indentation begins at the second line of the quotation.

> *WS Tip:* If you want to indent more than one tab stop, repeat the ^TI command.

The Options Menu

Many commands relating to the format of a document are found in the Options Menu. To view the Options Menu, press ^O for Options from the Editing Menu. The Options Menu has two screens. After viewing the first one, press the space bar to view the second one. Table 9-2 describes the commands from the Options Menu. You will not use all these commands in this chapter, but they are listed in Table 9-2 for your future reference.

Viewing Command Tags

A command tag is an editing command that is stored with the text. Command tags do not appear on the screen unless the user turns the Display mode on. Being able to view command tags is an important part of formatting a document. If you do

Table 9-1
Commands from the Tabs and Margins Menu

Command		Description
S	for Set	Sets a tab at the cursor's current location, or a specified number of inches from the left margin.
C	for Clear	Clears the tab at the cursor's current location, or the tab located a specified number of inches from the left margin.
D	for Decimal tab	Sets a decimal tab at the cursor's current location, or a specified number of inches from the left margin. A decimal tab is used when you are typing a column of numbers that contain decimal points. Using the decimal tab lines up a column of numbers along their decimal points.
L	for Left margin	Sets the left margin at the cursor's current location, or a specified number of inches from the current left margin.
R	for Right margin	Sets the right margin at the cursor's current location, or a specified number of inches from the current right margin.
M	for Margins on page	Brings the user to the Margins on Page Menu. From this menu, the user can change the format setting for the top margin, the bottom margin, the page length, the even page offset, and the odd page offset.
I	for In left	Indents the left margin one tab stop from the current margin.
O	for Out left	Moves the indented left margin one tab stop to the left. Moves the indentation out.
B	for Both sides in	Indents both the left and right margins one tab stop from the current margins.
P	for Paragraph	Indents the first line of each paragraph.
H	for Hanging	Indents all but the first line of each paragraph one tab stop from the current margin.

not like the way a paragraph is formatted, for example, or if you have made a mistake in formatting a document, you can delete the original editing commands when the command tags are visible on the screen.

When the Display mode is on, command tags appear on the screen embedded between brackets. Figure 9-3 a and b shows the same computer screen twice: first with the Display mode on, so that the command tags are visible, and then with the Display mode off. Notice the [TU], [TI], and [TH] in Figure 9-3a. These are the command tags that affect the format of this document.

To turn the display on, press ^O for Options; then press D for Display. When ^O is first pressed, the phrase in the Options Menu reads DISPLAY IS OFF. After you press D, the phrase reads DISPLAY IS ON. Pressing ^OD a second time turns the Display mode off again. This command, ^OD, acts as a toggle switch. That is to say, when the command is executed, it switches the program to whichever mode it is not currently using: Display mode on or Display mode off. Whether the Display mode is on or off is reflected in the Options Menu.

Command tags can be deleted when the Display mode is on. They are deleted by the same methods used to delete other characters. Perhaps the easiest way to delete a command tag is to place the cursor under the command tag and press the <Del> key. Another method is to place the cursor under the command tag and use the command ^RW for Remove Word. Once the command tag has been deleted

Table 9-2
Commands from the Options Menu

Command	Description
C for **C**enter Text	Centers the text on the current line.
W for **W**indow	Opens another window below the current text or window.
P for **P**age Break	Starts a new page at the cursor's location.
J for **J**ustify (ON or OFF)	If the Justify mode is on, text at the right margin aligns evenly. If the Justify mode is off, text at the right margin is ragged, or uneven.
D for **D**isplay (ON or OFF)	If the Display mode is on, command tags embedded between brackets are visible on the screen. If the Display mode is off, command tags are not visible on the screen.
O for **O**vertype (ON or OFF)	If the Overtype mode is on, whatever is typed replaces the text on the screen. The status line displays the word *Over*. If the Overtype mode is off, whatever is typed pushes the text to the right. The status line displays the word *Insert*.
S for **S**pelling correction	Corrects spelling errors in a document.
B for **B**ypass spell check (ON or OFF)	Instructs CorrectStar to bypass a designated portion of a document during the spelling correction.
M for **M**ailMerge	Creates a master document that contains MailMerge commands and variable data for the purpose of printing personalized form letters.
I for **I**ndexing	Defines index and table of contents entries.
H for **H**eader	Defines text to be used as a header (a line to be printed at the top of specified pages).
F for **F**ooter	Defines text to be used as a footer (a line to be printed at the bottom of specified pages).
N for **N**ote	Enters a footnote and footnote reference in a document.
K for **K**eep lines together	Prevents a specified number of lines from being split by a page break.
A for **A**ssign	Assigns or resets the current printed page number.
U for **U**nprinted comment	Inserts a comment in the document which shows on the screen, embedded between brackets, but does not appear when the document is printed.
R for **R**epeat	Repeats commands or text. Pressing any key stops the command.
L for **U**nder**l**ine between words (ON or OFF)	If the Underline mode is on, underlining appears between words. If the Underline mode is off, only words and not the spaces between them are underlined.
- Auto hyphenation (ON or OFF)	If the Auto hyphenation mode is on, words that do not fit on a line are hyphenated. If the Auto hyphenation mode is off, words that do not fit on a line are moved onto the next line.
V Column Break	Starts a new column in a document with several columns.

and the format of the document changes accordingly, a new command tag can be inserted or the document can be left as is. Command tags are inserted in the same way a character is inserted: place the cursor at the point where the command is to be effective, and press the command.

CHAPTER 9: ADVANCED WORDSTAR 2000   251

Figure 9-3 Command Tags
a. This screen has the display on so the command tags can be seen.

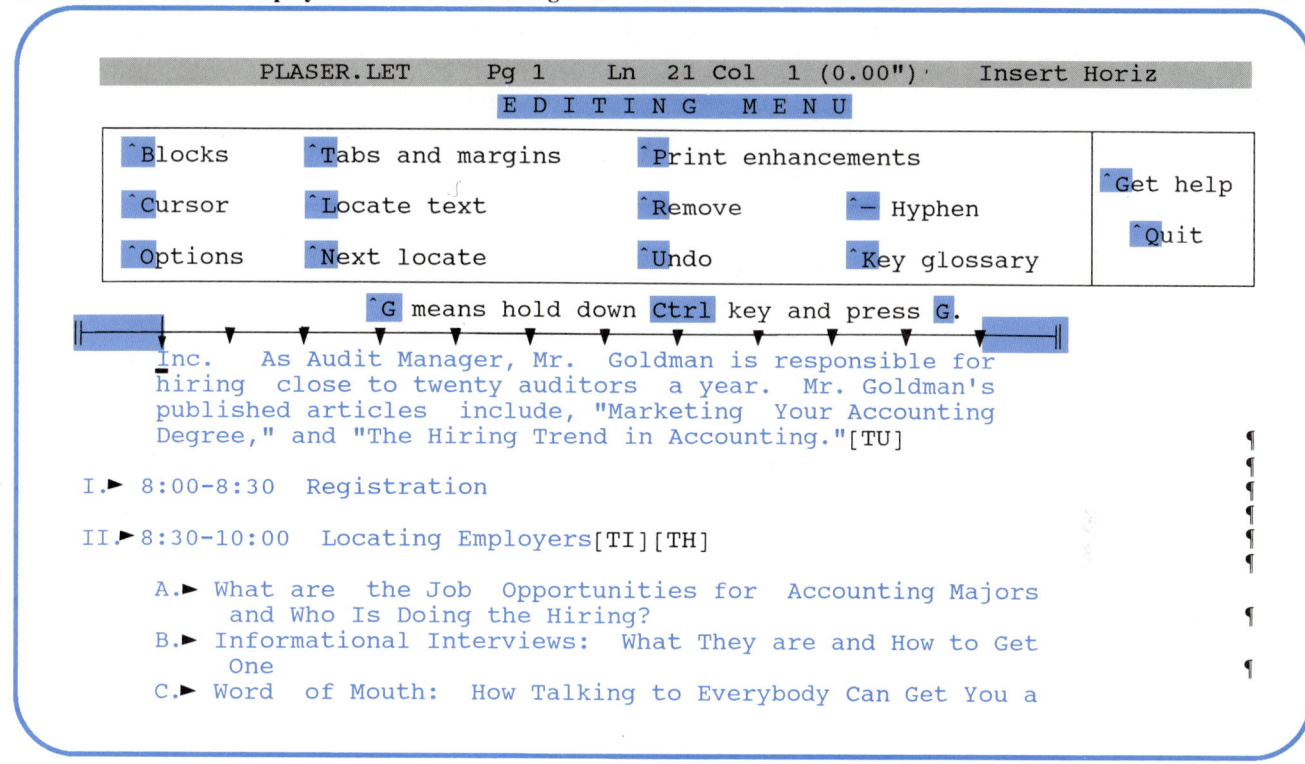

```
              PLASER.LET      Pg 1    Ln  21 Col  1 (0.00")·     Insert Horiz
                               E D I T I N G    M E N U

   ^Blocks        ^Tabs and margins     ^Print enhancements
                                                                      ^Get help
   ^Cursor        ^Locate text          ^Remove         ^- Hyphen
                                                                      ^Quit
   ^Options       ^Next locate          ^Undo           ^Key glossary

                       ^G means hold down Ctrl key and press G.

      Inc.   As Audit Manager, Mr.  Goldman is responsible for
      hiring  close to twenty auditors  a year.  Mr. Goldman's
      published  articles  include, "Marketing  Your Accounting
      Degree," and "The Hiring Trend in Accounting."[TU]

   I.► 8:00-8:30   Registration

  II.►8:30-10:00   Locating Employers[TI][TH]

         A.► What are  the Job  Opportunities for  Accounting Majors
             and Who Is Doing the Hiring?
         B.► Informational Interviews:  What They are and How to Get
             One
         C.► Word  of Mouth:  How Talking to Everybody Can Get You a
```

b. This is the same computer screen, only the display is off so the command tags are no longer visible.

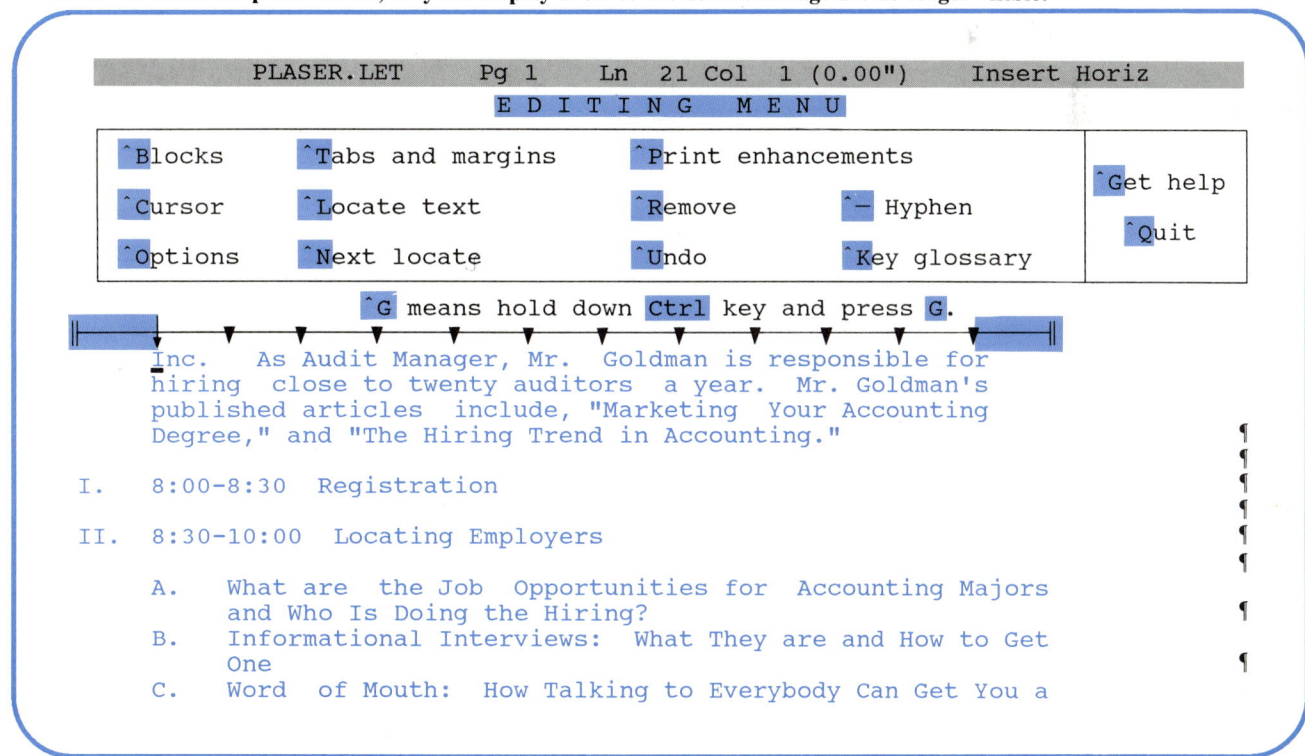

```
              PLASER.LET      Pg 1    Ln  21 Col  1 (0.00")      Insert Horiz
                               E D I T I N G    M E N U

   ^Blocks        ^Tabs and margins     ^Print enhancements
                                                                      ^Get help
   ^Cursor        ^Locate text          ^Remove         ^- Hyphen
                                                                      ^Quit
   ^Options       ^Next locate          ^Undo           ^Key glossary

                       ^G means hold down Ctrl key and press G.

      Inc.   As Audit Manager, Mr.  Goldman is responsible for
      hiring  close to twenty auditors  a year.  Mr. Goldman's
      published  articles  include, "Marketing  Your Accounting
      Degree," and "The Hiring Trend in Accounting."

   I.   8:00-8:30   Registration

  II.   8:30-10:00   Locating Employers

         A.   What are  the Job  Opportunities for  Accounting Majors
              and Who Is Doing the Hiring?
         B.   Informational Interviews:  What They are and How to Get
              One
         C.   Word  of Mouth:  How Talking to Everybody Can Get You a
```

YOUR TURN   For this hands-on exercise you are going to create a new document. Figure 9-4 depicts the final document. Start with the Opening Menu of WordStar 2000 on the screen. Make sure the disk drive being accessed is drive B.

Use the command for creating a new document.

When asked the name of the document to edit or create, type PLASER.LET (for Placement Service Letter). When asked what format to use, select NORMAL.FRM.

Bypass the History screen by using the ^**Q** command.

The first part of the document has two indented paragraphs. To select the format for indented paragraphs, use the ^**TP** command. Remember, once this command is selected, the paragraphs will automatically indent. When you start a new paragraph, do not press the <Tab> key, or the paragraph will be indented to the second rather than the first tab stop. Type the following two paragraphs. After you type the last word, do not press the <Return> key.

    The Placement Service Office is pleased you are attending one of our job placement seminars. This is the third year we have sponsored these seminars and they have proven to be quite successful.

    The seminar for Accounting majors is Saturday, February 22 from 8:00 a.m. to 5:00 p.m. The following introduces you to the people leading the seminar and outlines the day's schedule.

Because the next part of the document does not use indented paragraphs, that particular command needs to be removed. Use the ^**TU** command to undo the tab setting.

The next part of the document indents the paragraphs on both sides. Use the ^**TB** command to indent both sides of the next two paragraphs.

Press the <Return> key twice, and type the following two paragraphs. After you type the last word, do not press the <Return> key.

Dr. Kate Clifford, Head of Placement Service. Dr. Clifford has been the head of the Placement Service Office at Ohio State for over fifteen years. Before coming to Ohio State, she worked for the executive recruiting firm, Cyphers and Porter, Inc.

Mr. Keith Goldman, Audit Manager, Thales Electronic, Inc. As Audit Manager, Mr. Goldman is responsible for hiring close to twenty auditors a year. Mr. Goldman's published articles include, ''Marketing Your Accounting Degree,'' and ''The Hiring Trend in Accounting.''

The remainder of the document is an outline. Because the format will change again, the previous format needs to be removed. Use the ^**TU** command to undo the tab setting.

Figure 9-4 Letter from the Placement Service Office Using Various Formatting Commands

       The Placement Service Office is pleased you are attending one of our job placement seminars. This is the third year we have sponsored these seminars and they have proven to be quite successful.
       The seminar for Accounting majors is Saturday, February 22 from 8:00 a.m. to 5:00 p.m. The following introduces you to the people leading the seminar and outlines the day's schedule.

    Dr. Kate Clifford, Head of Placement Service. Dr. Clifford has been the head of the Placement Service Office at Ohio State for over fifteen years. Before coming to Ohio State, she worked for the executive recruiting firm, Cyphers and Porter, Inc.

    Mr. Keith Goldman, Audit Manager, Thales Electronic, Inc. As Audit Manager, Mr. Goldman is responsible for hiring close to twenty auditors a year. Mr. Goldman's published articles include, "Marketing Your Accounting Degree," and "The Hiring Trend in Accounting."

I.   8:00-8:30 Registration

II. 8:30-10:00 Locating Employers

    A. What are the Job Opportunities for Accounting Majors and Who is Doing the Hiring?
    B. Informational Interviews: What They are and How to Get One
    C. Word of Mouth: How talking to Everybody Can Get You a Job

III. 10:00-12:00 Cover Letters and Resumes

    A. The Content of a Resume: What Should and Should Not Be Included
    B. The Form of a Resume: What a Resume Should and Should Not Look Like
    C. How to Write a Cover Letter

IV. 12:00-1:00 Break for Lunch

V.   1:00-2:00 Interviewing Skills

    A. First Impressions: How to Make a Positive Impression in the First Five Minutes of an Interview
    B. Being Prepared For Any Interview Question
    C. Knowing What Questions You Should Ask

VI. 2:00-5:00 Utilizing the Placement Service Office

    A. Using the Career Library
    B. Interviews Through the Placement Office

Press the <Return> key twice. Begin the outline by typing I. (press the <Tab> key once) 8:00-8:30 Registration (press the <Return> key twice). Type II. (press the <Tab> key once) 8:30-10:00 Locating Employers (do not press the <Return> key).

You are now ready to start formatting the outline. This part of the outline is indented, so use the ^TI command to indent the text.

Once the ^TI command is issued, the left margin is set one tab stop to the right. All the second-level points in the outline (A., B., C., etc.) will begin at this new left margin. If a second-level heading is longer than one line, however, you do not want the second line to start at the left margin. Rather, you want the second line to start one tab stop in from what is now the left margin. To ensure that second-level headings that continue onto a second line are indented one tab stop, use the ^TH command for a hanging indent.

Once the ^TH command has been issued, press the <Return> key twice. Type A. (press the <Tab> key once) What Are the Job Opportunities for Accounting Majors and Who Is Doing the Hiring? (press the <Return> key once). Type B. (press the <Tab> key once) Informational Interviews: What They Are and How to Get One (press the <Return> key once). Type C. (press the <Tab> key once) Word of Mouth: How Talking to Everybody Can Get You a Job (do not press the <Return> key).

In order to type the third point in the outline, you need to undo your current format. Use the ^TU command to undo the tab settings. Press the <Return> key twice and type III. (press the <Tab> key once) 10:00-12:00 Cover Letters and Resumes (do not press the <Return> key).

Again, you want to move the left margin in one tab stop and issue the hanging indentation command, so the headings that continue onto a second line will be indented one tab stop from the current left margin. Issue the ^TI and ^TH commands.

Press the <Return> key twice. Type the following. Remember to press the <Tab> key once after typing A., once after typing B., and once after typing C.

    A. The Content of a Resume: What Should and Should Not Be Included
    B. The Form of a Resume: What a Resume Should and Should Not Look Like
    C. How to Write a Cover Letter

Use the command to undo the current tab settings. Press the <Return> key twice and type:

    IV. 12:00-1:00 Break for Lunch (press the <Return> key twice)
    V. 1:00-2:00 Interviewing Skills

Set the format to move the left margin one tab stop to the right and to set up hanging indents. Press the <Return> key twice. Type:

    A. First Impressions: How to Make a Positive Impression in the First Five Minutes of an Interview

>   B. Being Prepared For Any Interview Question
>   C. Knowing What Questions You Should Ask

Undo the current tab stops. Press the <Return> key twice. Type:

>   VI. 2:00—5:00 Utilizing the Placement Service Office

Set the format to move the left margin one tab stop to the right and to set up hanging indents. Press the <Return> key twice. Type:

>   A. Using the Career Library
>   B. Interviews Through the Placement Office

Look over the document carefully. The format should match Figure 9-4. If it does not match, use the command that displays the command tags, and make sure they correspond to the command tags you were instructed to use in this exercise. If you have an incorrect or misplaced command tag, delete the incorrect command and insert the correct one. Check the spacing of the document. Remember that the <Del> key, the <Backspace> key, and the Remove commands delete spaces as well as text. If spaces need to be inserted, make sure the Overtype mode is off and the word INSERT appears in the status line. Use CorrectStar to correct spelling errors. When you are satisfied that the document matches Figure 9-4, print the document.

Now you are going to print the document as two pages instead of one. Use the command that edits the document PLASER.LET. Move the cursor to line 20, which is the space between the description of the people leading the seminar and the outline. Use the command from the Options Menu which puts in a page break. If you insert the page break in the wrong location, use the command that displays the command tags, place the cursor under the command tag [PAGE], and press the <Del> key. Print the Placement Service letter as a two-page document.

Print Enhancements

A **character enhancement**, or print enhancement, is any special printing effect. Print enhancements such as underlining, boldface, and italics can be used to improve the appearance of the document. Whether or not you can use all the print enhancements included in WordStar 2000 depends on the printer you are using. Not all printers can print italics, for example. Your instructor can tell you which print enhancements your printer is capable of producing.

Pressing ^P from the Editing Menu accesses the Print Enhancements Menu (Figure 9-5). There are so many commands in the Print Enhancement Menu that it takes two screens to hold them all. To see the second screen, press the space bar. Table 9-3 describes commands from the Print Enhancement Menu.

Print enhancements can be specified as a document is being typed for the first time, or they can be inserted into text that has already been typed. Print enhancements also can be combined. The title of a chapter, for example, can be both boldfaced and underlined.

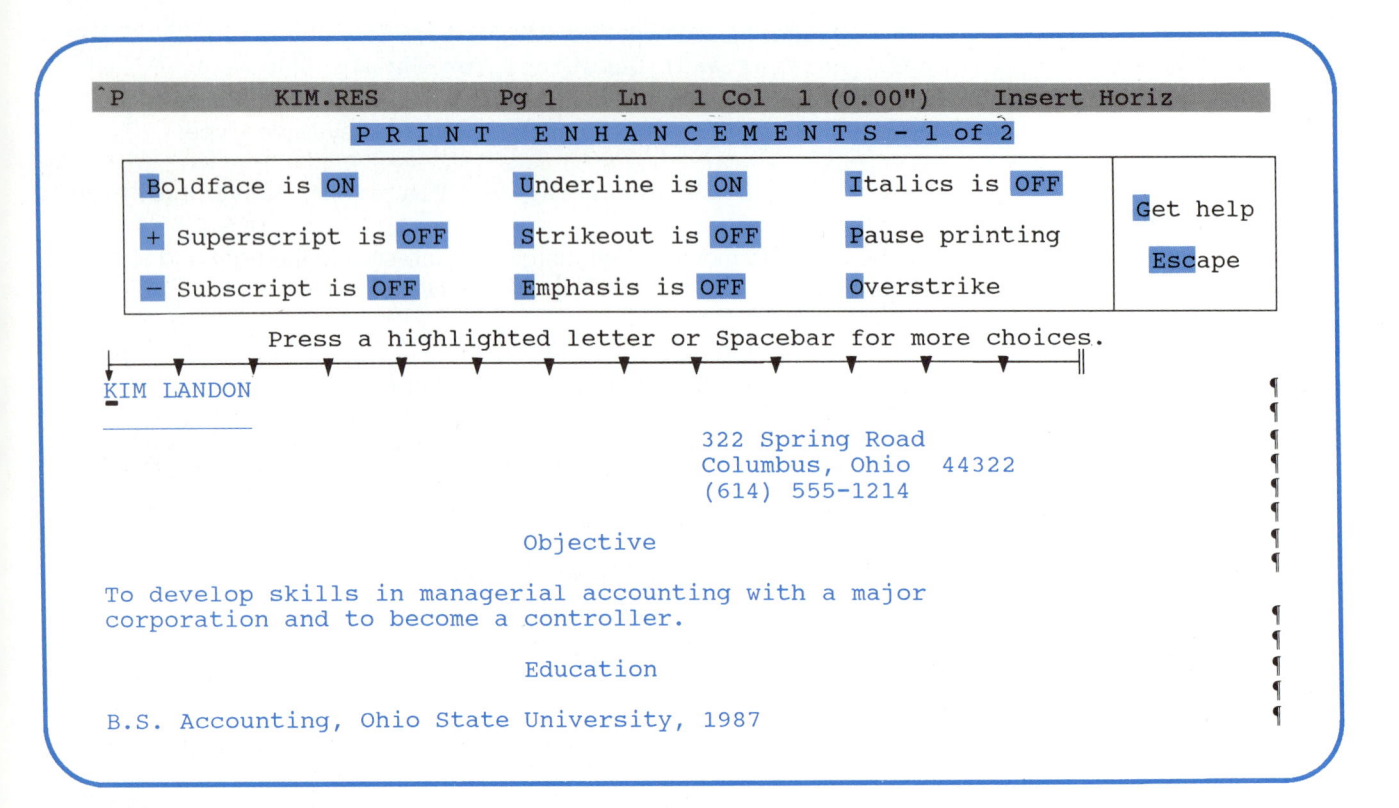

```
^P            KIM.RES        Pg 1    Ln   1 Col   1 (0.00")      Insert Horiz
                    P R I N T   E N H A N C E M E N T S - 1 of 2
  ┌─────────────────────────────────────────────────────────────┐  ┌──────────┐
  │ Boldface is ON       Underline is ON       Italics is OFF   │  │ Get help │
  │+ Superscript is OFF  Strikeout is OFF      Pause printing   │  │          │
  │- Subscript is OFF    Emphasis is OFF       Overstrike       │  │ Escape   │
  └─────────────────────────────────────────────────────────────┘  └──────────┘
           Press a highlighted letter or Spacebar for more choices.
```

KIM LANDON

                              322 Spring Road
                              Columbus, Ohio 44322
                              (614) 555-1214

                    Objective

To develop skills in managerial accounting with a major
corporation and to become a controller.

                    Education

B.S. Accounting, Ohio State University, 1987

Figure 9-5
The Print Enhancements Menu

To delete a print enhancement, the command tags must be displayed using the ^OD command. The command tags for print enhancements are embedded between brackets. The easiest way to remove them is to move the cursor to the command tag for the print enhancement to be deleted and press the <Del> key. If the print enhancement has two command tags, both must be deleted. For example, text that is to be underlined has the command tag [U] before the first word and after the last word. To delete underlining, delete both the beginning [U] and the ending [U].

YOUR TURN

For this exercise, a resume is created utilizing many of the print enhancements. Figure 9-6 depicts the completed resume. Start with the Opening Menu of WordStar 2000 on your screen.

- Issue the command for creating a new document.
- When asked the name of the document to edit or create, type KIM.RES (for Kim's resume).
- When asked what format to use, select JUSTIFY.FRM.
- Issue the command that bypasses the History screen.

Before you start typing the resume, some formatting commands need to be issued. First, the right margin is not justified. Issue the ^OJ command to turn

**Table 9-3
Commands from the Print
Enhancements Menu**

Command	Description
B for Boldface	Marks the beginning and end of text to be printed in **boldface** (extra dark).
+ for Superscript	Marks the beginning and end of text to be printed as a superscript (slightly above the current line).
- for Subscript	Marks the beginning and end of text to be printed as a subscript (slightly below the current line).
U for Underline	Marks the beginning and end of text to be underlined when printed.
S for Strikeout	Marks the beginning and end of text to be crossed out with hyphens when printed.
E for Emphasis	Marks the beginning and end of text to be emphasized when printed. The exact effect depends on the printer being used. Emphasized text may look like double strike.
I for Italics	Marks the beginning and end of text to be italicized when printed.
P for Pause	Marks a place where the printer is to pause during the printing of a document so that a manual task can be completed, such as changing a print wheel on a daisy wheel printer.
O for Overstrike	Creates special characters by printing two characters in the same space (prints a character over the previous one).
W for Word grouping	Marks words to be kept together on the same line when printed.
X for Extras	Marks text to be printed with a special printer feature. How this command works depends on the special feature capabilities of the printer being used. The choices of extra features vary from being able to select a foreign language character set to being able to select draft or letter quality printing.
N for No new line	Marks two lines of text to be printed on the same line (prints a line of text on top of the previous one).
1 for Single, 2 for Double, or 3 for Triple Columns	Allows two or three newspaper-type columns to be formatted into the document.
F for Font	Marks the beginning and end of text to be printed in a particular lettering style. After pressing ^PF a list of possible fonts appears. Move the highlighting to the desired font and press <Return>.
H for Height	Marks the beginning and end of text to be printed with a line height (changes the spacing between lines). After pressing ^PH the prompt LINE HEIGHT (SPACING) appears. Move the highlighting to the Lines Per Inch you want and press <Return>. 3.00 LPI is double space. 6.00 LPI is single space.
C for Color	Marks the beginning and end of text to be printed in a particular color. The effect of this command depends on the printer being used and the ribbon in it.
T for Tray	Directs the printer to change the type of paper. How this command works depends on the printer being used.

Figure 9-6 Resume Using Several Print Enhancements

```
KIM LANDON
                                      322 Spring Road
                                      Columbus, Ohio  44322
                                      (614) 555-1214

                          Objective

To develop skills in managerial accounting with a major
corporation and to become a controller.

                          Education

B.S. Accounting, Ohio State University, 1985
Minor: Economics with emphasis in corporate finance.
Significant courses include:

Accounting                     Business
Financial Accounting           Topics in Corporate Management
Cost Accounting                Industrial Economics
Advanced Accounting            Management Information Systems
Advanced Federal Tax Law       Business Communications

                          Experience

Summers    Intern, Price Waterhouse, Columbus, Ohio, 1986
           Worked on various audit assignments, including stock
           inventory at Mills International.

           Intern, Johnson & Johnson, Cincinnati, 1985
           Worked in the budget department on data collecting for
           the preparation of the next-fiscal-year budget.

College    Assistant, University Financial Aid Office, 1986
           Reviewed applications for financial aid; verified their
           conformity with tax returns and other supportive
           documents.

           Orientation Leader, University Admissions Office, 1985
           Met with prospective students and their parents;
           conducted tours of campus; wrote reports for each
           orientation meeting.

                      Computer Experience

Proficient in running Lotus 1-2-3 and WordStar 2000 on an IBM PC.

                          Activities

Alpha Beta Psi, 1984-1986
Student Senator, Served on budget committee, 1985-1986

                          References

Credentials and references available upon request.
```

the Justify mode off. Next, for this resume, words are not hyphenated. Press ^O to access the Option Menu. The Auto hyphenation command is found on the second screen of the Options Menu. Press the space bar to access the second screen .Press - (hyphen sign) to turn off Auto hyphenation.

Now you are ready to start typing the resume. The name *Kim Landon* is in all capital letters and boldface. Press ^PB to issue the command to boldface the name. Type **KIM LANDON** in capital letters. Press ^PB again to turn off the boldface. Press <Return>.

Notice that the address appears on the right side of the resume. In order to achieve this, temporarily reset the left margin. Press ^TL. In response to the question SET LEFT MARGIN WHERE?, type 4.0 and press the <Return> key. Typing 4.0 sets the left margin 4 inches from the left offset. The Ruler Line now reflects the new left margin. Type:

> 322 Spring Road (press the <Return> key once)
> Columbus, Ohio 44322 (press the <Return> key once)
> (614) 555-1214 (press the <Return> key twice)

Move the left margin back to where it was as follows: Press ^TL to change the left margin. When asked where to set the left margin, type **0,** and press the <Return> key.

All the titles for the major divisions in the resume are boldfaced and centered. Press ^PB to issue the boldface command and ^OC to issue the center command. Type **Objective**. Press ^PB to turn off the boldface command. The ^OC command affects only one line at a time, so there is no need to turn this command off. Press the <Return> key twice. Type:

> To develop skills in managerial accounting with a major corporation and to become a controller. (Press the <Return> key twice.)

Issue the command to boldface and center the next title. Type **Education**. Turn off the boldface command. Press the <Return> key twice and type:

> B.S. Accounting, Ohio State University, 1985 (press the <Return> key once)
> Minor: Economics with emphasis in corporate finance. (press the <Return> key once)
> Significant courses include: (press the <Return> key twice)

The next part of the resume is formatted in two columns. To set up the column format, first press ^P to access the Print Enhancement Menu. The commands for setting columns are found on the second screen of the Print Enhancement Menu. Press the space bar to access the second screen. Now press **2** to set up double columns.

Columns are entered one at a time. The titles to these columns are underlined, so before typing the first column, issue the underline command.

Type `Accounting`. Turn the underline command off. Press the <Return> key once. Type:

    `Financial Accounting` (press the <Return> key once)
    `Cost Accounting` (press the <Return> key once)
    `Advanced Accounting` (press the <Return> key once)
    `Advanced Federal Tax Law` (press the <Return> key once)

Now you are going to enter the second column. Columns do not appear side-by-side on the screen. After the first column is typed, the column break command needs to be issued to let the computer know you are beginning to type the second column. To issue the column break command, press ^**O**. The column break command is found on the second screen of the Options Menu. Press the space bar. Press **V** to issue the column break command. A double line appears across the screen, and the cursor automatically moves to the position where the second column starts.

Issue the underline command. Type `Business`. Turn off the underline command. Press the <Return> key once. Type:

    `Topics in Corporate Management` (press the <Return> key once)
    `Industrial Economics` (press the <Return> key once)
    `Management Information Systems` (press the <Return> key once)
    `Business Communications` (press the <Return> key twice)

You are now finished typing columns. The way to signal the computer that you no longer want the text lined up in columns is to issue a command telling it to format everything in one column. Press ^**P1** to tell the computer to start formatting everything in one column. The cursor automatically moves to the left side of the screen.

The next item to be typed is another division head. Issue the command to center and boldface the title. Type **Experience**. Turn off the boldface command. Press the <Return> key twice.

In the next section of the resume there are some indented paragraphs. These paragraphs are indented two tab stops. First type **Summers**. Next press ^**TI** twice to format the paragraphs so that they will begin at the second tab stop. Because this command does not take effect until the next line, press the tab key once so that the first line in the paragraph will line up with the lines to follow. Type:

    `Intern, Price Waterhouse, Columbus, Ohio, 1986` (press the <Return> key once)
    `Worked on various audit assignments, including stock inventory at Mills International.` (press the <Return> key twice)
    `Intern, Johnson & Johnson, Cincinnati, 1985` (press the <Return> key once)

> Worked in the budget department on data collecting for the preparation of the next-fiscal-year budget.

Press ^**TU** to undo the command to indent the paragraphs two tab stops. Press the <Return> key twice. Type **College**. Press ^**TI** twice. Press the <Tab> key once. Type:

> Assistant, University Financial Aid Office, 1986

(press the <Return> key once)

> Reviewed applications for financial aid; verified their conformity with tax returns and other supportive documents.

(press the <Return> key twice)

> Orientation Leader, University Admissions Office, 1985

(press the <Return> key once)

> Met with prospective students and their parents; conducted tours of campus; wrote reports for each orientation meeting.

Press ^**TU** to undo the command to indent the paragraphs two tab stops. Press the <Return> key twice.

Issue the command to boldface and center the next title. Type **Computer Experience**. Turn off the boldface command. Press the <Return> key twice. Type:

> Proficient in running Lotus 1-2-3 and WordStar 2000 on an IBM PC.

Press the <Return> key twice. Center and boldface the next title. Type **Activities**. Turn off the boldface command. Press the <Return> key twice. Type:

> Alpha Beta Psi, 1984-1986 (press the <Return> key once)
> Student Senator, Served on budget committee, 1985-1986

(press the <Return> key twice)

Center and boldface the final title. Type **References**. Unbold the text. Press the <Return> key twice and type:

> Credentials and references available upon request.

Look over the resume carefully. The format should match Figure 9-6. If it does not match, use the command that displays command tags, and make sure they correspond to the command tags you were instructed to use in this exercise. If you have an incorrect or misplaced command tag, delete the incorrect tag and insert the correct one. Check the spacing of the document. Use CorrectStar to correct spelling errors. When you are satisfied that the document matches Figure 9-6, print the resume.

Learning Check

1. When the Editing Menu is on the screen, the _____ separates the menu from the text window and indicates tabs and margins settings.
2. To indent margins on the current line of text, the cursor must be located _____.
   a. at the left margin of that line
   b. anywhere in the affected line
   c. in the middle of the affected line
   d. at the right margin
3. Command tags are visible at all times while editing or formatting a document. (True or False?)
4. Print enhancements can be specified as you type or inserted at a later time. (True or False?)
5. Print enhancements can be combined in the same text. (True or False?)

Answers

1. ruler line 2. a. 3. False 4. True 5. True

More Advanced Features

WordStar 2000 includes sophisticated features that are not mandatory for all documents. If mastered, however, they can be convenient time-savers. These features, which are covered in the remainder of this chapter, can help you create professional-looking documents with little effort.

Headers and Footers

HEADER
A piece of text that is stored separately from the main text and printed at the top of each page.

FOOTER
A piece of text that is stored separately from the main text and printed at the bottom of each page.

A **header** is a piece of text which is printed at the top of a page, such as a title that appears on each page of text (see Figure 9-7). A **footer** is a piece of text which is printed at the bottom of a page, such as a page number. Headers and footers are stored separately from the text and are printed automatically at the appropriate place on every page in the document. Headers and footers can take up as many lines as needed. They can be printed on odd pages only, even pages only, or on both odd and even pages.

When headers and footers are created on WordStar 2000, the Display mode must be on so that the header and footer command tags can be viewed. Press ^**OD** if the Display mode currently is off.

The header and footer commands are found in the second screen of the Option Menu. Before using the command to create a header or footer, make sure the cursor is at the top of the first page on which the header or footer is to appear. A header or footer command can be placed anywhere in the document. It does not have to appear at the top of the page. If a header or footer command is not placed at the top of the page, however, the header or footer does not begin printing until the following page.

> Job Placement Seminar
> February 21
> 2
>
> This is not the impression most people looking for jobs have of
>
> those who have the power to hire or not hire them.
>
> > Bolles explains why interviewers may be so uncomfortable
>
> with the process:
>
> > The odds are very great that the executive who does the
> > interviewing was hired because of what they could con-
> > tribute to the company, and not because they were such a
> > great interviewer. In fact, their gifts in this arena
> > may be rather miserable.[2]
>
> David Roman agrees with Bolles. Roman states:
>
> > As interviewers, ... managers ...a may be out of their
> > element. They're in the business of running a
> > department, not of interviewing job applicants.[3]
>
> Since the person running the interview is probably just as uncom-
>
> fortable as you are, there are several things you as a prospec-
>
> tive employee can do to take advantage of the situation and turn
>
> the interview into a pleasant and rewarding experience.
>
> ────────────────────
> 1. Bolles, Richard. _What Color is Your Parachute?_, Berkeley: 10
> Speed Press, 1983, p. 181.
>
> 2. Ibid.
>
> 3. Roman, David. "Why MIS/DP Job Interviews Go Wrong," in _Computer Decisions_, November 19, 1985, p. 66.

Figure 9-7
Headers and Footnotes

To place a header in a document, press ^OH. The Header Placement Menu appears next, asking whether the header is to be placed on both odd and even pages, odd pages only, or even pages only. Press **B** for **B**oth odd and even, **O** for **O**dd pages only, or **E** for **E**ven pages only.

Once the header has been placed, WordStar 2000 returns to the Edit Menu and automatically turns on the Display mode if it is not already on. The following command tags appear in the document:

[HEADER]

[HEADER]

The cursor is on the blank line between the two command tags. Type the header in this line. If the header is more than one line long, simply press the <Return> key at the end of each line.

When the document is printed, one blank line is placed automatically between the header and the body of the document. If you want to have more space between the header and the document's text, press the <Return> key after the header has been typed. A blank line will appear on the screen between the last line of the header and the second command tag.

To remove a header, delete all the text between the command tags: place the cursor anywhere on the header text, and use the ^**RE** command, for **R**emove **E**ntire line. Remember that blank lines and spaces count as text. If you use the ^**RE** command and the command tags are still on the screen, place the cursor on the blank line between the two command tags and issue the ^**RE** command again.

To place a footer in a document, press ^**OF** for **O**ption **F**ooter and follow the directions for placing a header. WordStar 2000 inserts one blank line between the last line of text on the page and the first line of the footer. If you want more space, insert blank lines between the first footer command tag and the first line of text in the footer.

Page numbers can be embedded within a header or a footer. To insert a page number in either a header or a footer, type **&%page&** between the header or footer command tags in the column and line where you want the number to appear.

Footnotes

One of the most tedious tasks involved in writing any term paper is typing the footnotes. WordStar 2000 simplifies this task tremendously.

To create a footnote, place the cursor on the space following the sentence or paragraph being referenced by a footnote. The footnote command is found on the second screen of the Options Menu. Press ^**ON** for **O**ption **N**ote. Once the command is issued, the Display mode is turned on automatically. The following footnote command tags appear:

[FOOTNOTE 1]

[FOOTNOTE 1]

WordStar 2000 automatically numbers the footnotes. The next time the ^**ON** command is issued, the command tag will read [FOOTNOTE 2], and so on. The cursor is on the blank line between the two command tags. Type the footnote on this line. A footnote can take up as many lines as necessary. When the footnote has been typed, move the cursor past the second command tag and continue typing the text of the document.

When the Display mode is turned off, the footnote information typed between the footnote command tags disappears, and the appropriate footnote number appears superscripted at the end of the quotation. If a footnote is deleted, inserted, or moved, WordStar 2000 automatically changes the numbers accordingly. To remove a footnote, delete all the text between the command tags.

When a document containing footnotes is printed, the footnotes automatically appear at the bottom of the page, separated from the text by a line (refer to Figure 9-7).

Locate and Replace

SEARCH AND FIND
A routine that searches for a specific string of characters and places the cursor at that location.

SEARCH AND REPLACE
A routine that searches for a specified character string and replaces it with a specified replacement string.

GLOBAL SEARCH AND REPLACE
A search and replace operation that is carried out throughout the entire document, without user intervention.

If you have ever written a large document and discovered that a key term has been misspelled throughout, you know how difficult and time-consuming it is to correct the mistake. Most word processors, like WordStar 2000, have alleviated this problem by incorporating various search routines. The most basic is the **search and find** routine. You tell the program the specific character string to search for, and it finds and positions the cursor at the first occurrence of the string. Usually you have the option of continuing the search to find each successive occurrence of the specified string.

Another type of search routine is the **search and replace** routine, in which the word processor searches for each occurrence of a specified string and replaces it with a specified replacement string. Usually there are two options for this search routine. In the first option, the cursor moves to the first occurrence of the string to be replaced, and the user is asked if that particular occurrence of the string should be replaced. The user responds accordingly at each occurrence of the string. The second option is what is known as **global search and replace:** The word processor searches for all occurrences of a specified string and replaces them with the specified replacement string, without user intervention.

WordStar 2000 incorporates all three of these search routines. All are part of the locate command, which is found in the Editing Menu. To locate a word or phrase, press ^L for Locate. The question TEXT TO LOCATE? appears on the screen. When identifying text for WordStar 2000 to locate, be very specific. If you tell WordStar 2000 to locate every occurrence of the word *their*, but occasionally you misspelled it as *there*, the misspelled words will not be found. WordStar 2000 can locate a maximum number of 39 characters per string.

Enter the text to be located (up to 39 characters) and press the <Return> key. Next, the question LOCATE ONLY/REPLACE? (L/R) appears. If you want to find the word only, press L. If you want to find the word and then replace it with another word, press R.

After you press L or R, an Options Menu appears. You can select all, some, or none of these options. Table 9-4 lists the options for the locate and replace commands. (Some of them appear in the menu only if you select the Replace option.) If you do not want to select any options, simply press the <Return> key in response to the question OPTIONS? If you want to select an option, type the letter or letters of the option or options you want to select and press <Return>. WordStar 2000 begins the search for the text at the cursor's current locations. If the entire document is to be searched, make sure the cursor is in page 1, line 1, column1 before issuing the locate text command.

Table 9-4
Options for the Locate and Replace Commands

Option		Description
B	for **B**ackwards search	Searches backwards through the text, from the cursor to the beginning of the text.
C	for **C**ase match	Locates the exact UPPERCASE/lowercase match only. For example, if you search for *She,* WordStar 2000 will not find *she.*
D	for **D**on't ask approval	Replaces text without first asking for the user's approval.
n	(any number) for nth occurrence	Locates the nth occurrence of the text. For example, if the number 3 is entered, the third occurrence is located. If no number is specified, the first occurrence is located.
n	(any number) for n of times to search and replace	Replaces the next n occurrences of the text. For example, if the number 9 is entered, the next nine occurrences are replaced. If no number is specified, all occurrences are replaced.
S	for **S**how onscreen	Shows each replacement briefly on the screen. Can be used only with the **D** option.
U	for **U**se case from replacement	Inserts the new text exactly as it is typed, rather than following the uppercase/lowercase format of the word being replaced. For example if *green* is typed in to replace the word *Red* in the text, *green,* not *Green,* is the replacement.
W	for **W**hole words only	Matches only whole words. For example, *the* matches only *the* and not *there, thesis,* and so on.

If a particular option is not selected, the opposite condition applies. For example, if **C** for **C**ase match is not selected, words are located whether or not the case matches the specified text.

Any text can be located, including command tags such as [U]. When searching for a command tag, the Display mode must be on. The Display mode also must be on if your document contains footnotes that are to be included when using the locate and replace commands.

Once a particular word or phrase has been located, you may want to find the next occurrence of that word or phrase. The command ^**N** (**N**ext locate) from the Editing Menu enables you to move to the next occurrence of the word or phrase. When no more occurrences of the word or phrase can be found, the message CAN'T FIND TEXT appears. To cancel the locate and replace operations while they are in progress, press the <Esc> key.

YOUR TURN

In this hands-on exercise, you are going to create the first two pages of a paper that includes footnotes. Start with the Opening Menu of WordStar 2000 on your screen.

Issue the command for creating a new document. When asked the name of the document to edit or create, type `INTER.PAP` for interview paper. When asked what format to use, select JUSTIFY.FRM. Issue the command that bypasses the History screen.

CHAPTER 9: ADVANCED WORDSTAR 2000

Before typing the paper, you need to issue some formatting commands. First, this paper has a header that includes page numbers. Use the ^**OH** command to insert a header. When the Header Placement screen appears, select **B** for **B**oth odd and even pages. Type the following header between the two [HEADER] command tags:

```
Job Placement Seminar (Press the <Return> key once)
February 21 (Press the <Return> key once)
&%page&
```

(Remember that **&%page&** places the page number in the header.)

Move the cursor outside the second header command tag. Press the <Return> key once. Before typing the title of the paper, issue the commands that will center and underline the title. Type:

```
Interviews: Wretched or Rewarding?
```

Turn off the underline command. Press the <Return> key twice.

For this paper, the right margin does not need to be justified, so issue the command that turns off the justification.

This paper uses both double and single spacing. The body of the paper is double-spaced and the quotations are single-spaced. Since the JUSTIFY format is single-space, switch to double space to start typing the paper. Press ^**P.** The command for adjusting the spacing is on the second screen of the Print Enhancements Menu. Next to the word HEIGHT it says 6.00 LPI. This stands for six lines per inch, meaning that the document is single-spaced. Press **H.** The question LINE HEIGHT (SPACING)? appears on the screen. Depending on the printer being used, various line heights are listed. Three lines per inch is double spacing, so select 3.00 LPI.

Now you are ready to start typing the paper. Type the following:

```
    For many people, interviews have a peculiar Dr.
Jekyll and Mr. Hyde quality to them. While these
people are job hunting, they anxiously await the phone
call or letter issuing the coveted invitation for an
interview. After all their hard work of scouting out
the job market, finding openings in their field,
writing resumes and cover letters, an interview seems
like a well-deserved reward. But, once attained, the
golden interview turns into a nerve-shattering
monster. Sleepless nights are spent worrying over such
questions as, what will I wear, what will I say, what
if they ask a question I can't answer? All of a
sudden, the job hunter feels like the hunted as
visions of the mighty interviewer, whose sole purpose
is to expose all the inadequacies of the interviewee,
become inescapable.
    Interviews do not have to turn into such horrible
monsters. Exposing some of the myths about interviews
```

> helps to alleviate the fear we all attach to the
> interviewing process.
>   Often, the interviewee has a totally inaccurate
> image of the interviewer. Many prospective employees
> assume the interviewer is highly skilled in conducting
> interviews. This is not necessarily the case as
> Richard Boles points out in the following quotation:

You are now ready to type the first quotation. Some of the formatting needs to be changed. The cursor should still be in the space following the colon after the word *quotation*. Issue the ^**TU** command to undo the tab setting. Both sides of the quotation are to be indented, so issue the ^**TB** command. Press the <Return> key once. The quotation is single-spaced, so press ^**PH** and change the line height to 6.00 LPI. Type the following quotation:

> . . . the interviewer may be as uncomfortable with
> this process as you are, and as ill-equipped to know
> how to find out what he or she wants to know, as the
> newest college graduate just coming into the job-
> market.

The cursor should be in the space after the period following the word *market*. Press ^**TU** to undo the tab setting for the quotation. Now you need to insert the first footnote. Press ^**ON,** for **O**ption foot**n**ote. Type the following between the two [FOOTNOTE 1] command tags (do not forget to underline the book title):

> Boles, Richard. What Color is Your Parachute?
> Berkeley: 10 Speed Press, 1983, p. 181.

Move the cursor outside the second footnote command tag. Press the <Return> key twice. Change the spacing back to double, and type the following:

> This is not the impression most people looking for
> jobs have of those who have the power to hire or not
> hire them.
>   Boles explains why interviewers may be so
> uncomfortable with the process:

The cursor should remain at the space after the colon following the word *process*. Issue the command to indent both sides of the quotation. Press the <Return> key once. Issue the command to change the spacing to single. Type the following:

> The odds are very great that the executive who does
> the interviewing was hired because of what they could
> contribute to the company, and not because they were
> such a great interviewer. In fact, their gifts in this
> arena may be rather miserable.

The cursor should remain at the space after the period following the word *miserable.* Undo the tab setting. Issue the footnote command. Type `Ibid.` between the [FOOTNOTE 2] command tags. Move the cursor outside the second command tag. Press the <Return> key twice. Change the spacing to double, and type the following:

```
David Roman agrees with Boles. Roman states:
```

Issue the command to indent both sides of the quotation. Press the <Return> key once. Change the spacing to single. Type:

```
As interviewers, . . . managers . . . may be out of
their element. They're in the business of running a
. . . department, not of interviewing job applicants.
```

Undo the tab setting. Issue the command to insert the third footnote. Type the following between the [FOOTNOTE 3] command tags (do not forget to underline the magazine title):

```
Roman, David. ''Why MIS/DP Job Interviews Go Wrong,''
in Computer Decisions, November 19 1985, p. 66.
```

Move the cursor outside the second command tag. Press the <Return> key twice. Change the spacing to double, and type the following:

```
Since the person running the interview is probably
just as uncomfortable as you are, there are several
things you as an interviewee can do to take advantage
of the situation and turn the interview into a
pleasant and rewarding experience.
```

You just discovered that you misspelled a name throughout the text. The spelling of the author's name is *Bolles,* not *Boles.* Move the cursor to page 1, line 1, column 1. Make sure the Display mode is on, because this name needs to be corrected in footnotes as well. Press ^**L** for the **L**ocate command. When asked what text to locate, type **Boles.** When asked LOCATE ONLY/REPLACE? (L/R), TYPE **R** for replace. When asked for the replacement text, type **Bolles.** When the Options Menu appears, select **U** for **U**se case from replacement. Because this is a proper name, you want to make sure it is capitalized.

When WordStar 2000 finds the first occurrence of the name Boles, the question REPLACE? (Y/N) appears in the upper right corner of the screen. Type **Y.** The program will continue to find all the occurrences of this name, and you should replace them all. Then the Editing Menu returns to the screen.

Next, you decide that there is no such word as *interviewee.* Return the cursor to page 1, line 1, column 1. You want to locate all occurrences of *interviewee,* but the same word should not be used in all cases as a replacement, so you cannot use the replace option. Activate the Locate text command. Type **interviewee** as the text to locate. Next, type **L** for Locate only. There are no options you want to select, so press the <Return> key when the question OPTIONS? appears.

When WordStar 2000 finds the first occurrence of *interviewee,* the cursor appears under the first character of the word, and the Editing Menu returns to the screen. Use the command that will remove the word *interviewee.* Type the word `applicant` to take its place. Since "interviewee" occurs throughout the paper, press ^N for Next locate to find the next occurrence of the term. Again, remove the term *interviewee.* Type `person being interviewed` in its place. Activate the next locate command. Remove the next occurrence of *interviewee.* Type `prospective employee` to take its place. The sentence now reads, ". . . as an prospective employee . . ." Change the *an* to *a.*

Look over the document carefully. Use CorrectStar to check your spelling. Correct any errors, and then print the paper.

Changing a Format Design

Selecting one of the six standard formats in WordStar 2000 is a fast and easy way to start a document. Just by selecting one format, you can automatically set margins, tabs, and page numbers.

But what if none of the standard formats suits your needs for a particular document? With WordStar 2000, one or more settings of a particular format design can be changed, or an entirely new format can be designed. Referring to Figure 9-1 may help when you are considering changing a format design.

In order to change the settings of a standard format, or to design an entirely new format, press **F** for **F**ormat at the Opening Menu. The question FORMAT OR FORMATTED DOCUMENT NAME? appears on the screen. How this question is answered depends on whether you want to change settings in a standard format, change settings in a document that already exists, or create an entirely new format. The following list explains how to perform these functions.

■ To change one or more settings in an existing format, move the highlighting to the name of the standard format to be changed and press <Return>.

■ To change the format of an existing document, type **b:** and the name of the document. For example, to change the format of the document INTER.PAP, type **b:INTER.PAP** and press <Return>. (If you have switched to drive B, using the D command from the Opening Menu, then you may omit the b:.)

■ To create a new format, type the name of the format followed by the file extension **.FRM.** For example, to create a format called REPORT, type **REPORT.FRM** and press <Return>.

> *Hard Disk Differences:* Omit typing **b:.** Simply type the name of the document, for example, **INTER.PAP**.

The question PRINTER TO USE? appears on the screen next. Select a printer and press <Return>. The next question, FONT TO USE?, determines the font—the type size and style—of the document. Select a font and press <Return>. The next question, LINE HEIGHT (SPACING)?, determines how many lines will be printed per inch. For example, 6.00 LPI stands for six lines per inch. If this option is selected, the document will be single-spaced. 3.00 LPI stands for three lines per inch, or double spacing. Select the spacing for your document and press <Return>.

After these initial questions have been answered, the Decisions Menu appears. There are seventeen questions regarding format design options. Table 9-5 lists these questions with their **default settings,** and explains the function each option performs. If you do not want to change the default setting, press the <Return> key to go on to the next question. If you want to change the setting, type the change and press the <Return> key.

DEFAULT SETTING
The setting that a program automatically assumes when no other setting is designated by the user.

Learning Check

1. Header and footer commands must be placed at the top of each affected page. (True or False?)

2. Headers, footers, and footnotes are removed by deleting the comment tags. (True or False?)

3. WordStar 2000 can search for and/or replace text up to ____ characters long.
   a. 15   *c.* 39
   b. 24   *d.* 50

4. In order to locate a command tag, the Display mode must be on. (True or False?)

5. When using the locate and replace command, all occurrences of the search text are replaced automatically without the user's approval. (True or False?)

Answers

1. False 2. False 3. c. 4. True 5. False

Table 9-5
Questions Regarding Format Design from the Decisions Menu

Format Questions	Default Answers
HOW MANY LINES IN THE TOP MARGIN?	6

This determines the width of the top margin. There are 66 lines on a standard 8½ × 11 inch piece of paper. If the line height is set to 6.00, six lines in the top margin equal 1 inch. If the document is single-spaced, three lines in the top margin equal ½ inch, nine lines equal 1½ inches, and so on. If the line height is set to 3.00 for double spacing, answering 3 to this question produces a 1-inch top margin, 1.5 produces a ½-inch margin, and 4.5 produces a 1½-inch margin. The top margin can be adjusted from 0 to 500 lines.

HOW MANY LINES IN THE BOTTOM MARGIN?	6

This determines the width of the bottom margin. The bottom margin is set the same way as the top margin.

SET RIGHT MARGIN WHERE? (IN INCHES)	6.5

This determines the width of the right margin. The number typed as an answer to this question is the distance between the left margin and the right margin. If the left margin is set at 1 inch and the right margin is set at 6.5 inches (the default answer), the width of the right margin is 1 inch (1 + 6.5 + 1 = 8.5, the width of the paper). An easy way to determine where to set the right margin is to add the width of the left margin to the width of the right margin, and subtract the sum from 8.5. For example, if the left margin is set at 2 inches and the width of the right margin is to be 1.5 inches, add 1.5 to 2 and subtract the sum from 8.5. The result, 5, should be the answer to this question.

SET TAB AT EVERY N INCHES—TYPE A NUMBER FOR N:	0.5

This sets tabs at established intervals. For example, the default setting of 0.5 sets a tab every ½ inch. Changing the answer to 1.0 sets tabs every inch, 2.0 sets tabs every 2 inches, 2.5 sets them every 2½ inches, and so on.

NUMBER OF LINES PER PAGE?	66

The length of the paper being used and the spacing of the document determine the answer to this question. If the paper is 11 inches long and the document is set at 6.00 LPI, single-spaced, then there are 66 lines per page. If the paper is 12 inches long and the document is set at 6.00 LPI, there are 72 lines per page. If the paper is 14 inches long and the document is set at 6.00 LPI, there are 84 lines per page.

EVEN-NUMBERED PAGE OFFSET? (IN INCHES)	1.0

This determines the width of the left margin on even-numbered pages. Type the number of inches this width is to be.

ODD-NUMBERED PAGE OFFSET? (IN INCHES)	1.0

This determines the width of the left margin on odd-numbered pages. Type the number of inches this width is to be.

TEXT JUSTIFIED OR RAGGED-RIGHT? (J/R)	J

This determines whether the text at the right margin is aligned evenly or unaligned. Typing **J** aligns the text. Typing **R** leaves the text unaligned or ragged.

AUTOMATIC HYPHENATION ON? (Y/N)	Y

Y, for yes, automatically hyphenates words at the end of the line. **N,** for no, moves the entire word to the next line rather than hyphenating it.

Continued

Table 9-5 Continued

Format Questions	Default Answers
USE FORM FEEDS WHEN PRINTING? (Y/N)	Y

This determines whether or not WordStar 2000 sends form-feed signals to the printer. If your printer accepts form-fe 1 signals, type **Y.** If your printer does not accept form feed signals, type **N** and WordStar 2000 issues a number of line feeds to advance from one page to the next.

UNDERLINE BETWEEN WORDS? (Y/N)	Y

This determines whether or not the spaces between words being underlined will be underlined as well. If the answer is **Y,** the spaces will be underlined. If the answer is **N,** the spaces will not be underlined.

DISPLAY PAGE BREAKS? (Y/N)	Y

This determines whether or not the lines indicating page breaks appear on the screen. **Y** displays page break lines; **N** does not display them.

PAGE NUMBERS: CENTERED, LEFT, RIGHT, ALTERNATING OR NONE? (C/L/R/A/N)	C

This determines whether or not page numbers appear on the printed pages of the document, and if so, where the page numbers are located. Typing **C** locates page numbers in the center of the line; **L** locates them at the left margin; **R** locates them at the right margin; **A** locates them at the left margin on the left-hand pages and at the right margin on right-hand pages. Page numbers are not printed if the answer is **N.**

PRINT FOOTNOTES AT THE END OF THE DOCUMENT? (Y/N)	N

This determines whether footnotes appear at the bottom of the page where they occur, or at the end of the document. **N** prints footnotes at the bottom of the page that contains their reference. **Y** prints footnotes together at the end of the document.

NUMBER OF COLUMNS?	1

This determines the number of columns of text on a page. The answer can be from 1 to 3.

SPACES BETWEEN DOUBLE COLUMNS? (IN INCHES)	0.3

This determines the number of inches between two columns of text. Answers can be from .1 to 9.9.

SPACES BETWEEN TRIPLE COLUMNS? (IN INCHES)	0.2

This determines the number of inches between three columns of text. Answers can be from .1 to 9.9.

Summary Points

■ Word Processors, such as WordStar 2000, include print-formatting features that determine how the text is printed on paper.

- Common print-formatting features include setting tab and margin stops, single- or double-spacing the text, reformatting paragraphs after editing, marking page breaks, and performing character enhancements.
- Common character enhancements include underlining, boldfacing, superscripting, and subscripting.
- Headers and footers are pieces of text that are stored separately from the main text in a word processing program. A header is printed at the top of a page, and a footer is printed at the bottom of a page.
- Searching routines—search and find, search and replace, and global search and replace—locate a specific string of characters and, if desired, replace it with a specified replacement string.

WordStar 2000 Exercises

The following exercises require you to create a document of your own. Assume you have a term paper due next week and you want to use WordStar to type it. You have the DOS disk, the WordStar 2000 program disk, the dictionary disk, and your own data disk to save your work. You are therefore ready to start. Boot the system with the DOS disk and start WordStar 2000. Make sure that your data disk is in drive B.

> *Hard Disk Differences:* With WordStar 2000 already saved on the hard disk, you simply need to start WordStar 2000.

1. Change the directory so you can save your work on your own disk later.

> *Hard Disk Differences:* Omit step 1.

2. At the Opening Menu, select the Edit/create command and create a new file. Give it the name you want and select the manuscript format. Note that this format is double spaced. Fill in the history screen. Why is the history screen useful?

3. Prepare the front page by typing the title of the paper in the middle of the page and typing your name, your professor's name, the name of the class, and the date in the lower part of the page. Underline the paper's title. Center all the text on this page. How do you underline text? Which command do you use to center text?

4. Move the cursor to the last blank line of the text and use the appropriate key to start a new page.

5. Type the title of the paper again and underline it.

6. Type at least two pages of text.

7. Assume you want to enter a footnote and a footnote reference at the end of your last paragraph. Use the ^ON command and type the footnote appropriately.

8. Now that you have finished typing the text, you want to check the spelling of the entire document. Move the cursor to the beginning of the document, using the ^C command. Use the ^OS command to check the spelling of the text. Remember that you will need the dictionary disk at this time. Describe all the steps you followed to check the spelling of your document.

9. Save and print your work.

WordStar 2000 Problems

To complete the following problems, use the JOB file included on the Student File Disk. To start WordStar 2000, boot the system with the DOS disk. At the A> prompt, insert the program disk in drive A and type **ws2**. Insert the Student File Disk in drive B.

> *Hard Disk Differences:* You need to copy the JOB file included on the Student File Disk onto the hard disk. When you turn on your computer, at the C> prompt, type **a:** and press <Return> to switch to drive A. Insert your Student File Disk with the JOB file on it into drive A, and type **copy job c:\ws2000** and press <Return>. Switch back to drive C by typing **c:** and pressing the <return> key. Type **ws2** and press <Return>.

1. To be able to read the JOB file in drive B, change the directory by using the appropriate command.

> *Hard Disk Differences:* Omit Step 1.

2. Copy the JOB file to the REQUEST file by using the copy command. Describe the steps taken to copy the file.

3. Use the REQUEST file to answer the remaining questions. Retrieve the REQUEST file.

4. Read the REQUEST file. REQUEST is a solicited application letter used to answer an advertisement for an accounting job. Assume that you have just graduated from your college with a major in marketing rather than accounting. You are looking for a job in the marketing field. Delete the sender address using the Blocks and Remove commands from the Editing Menu. Replace it with your own address.

5. Change the date to the current date.

6. Delete the company address, and replace it with the address of a company that you know.

7. Delete the phrase "Daily Mirror on April 9" from the first sentence of the letter. Insert the following to take its place: `in the Tribune No 350.` (Make sure that the word Tribune is underlined.)

8. Using the Locate and replace command, replace all occurrences of the word *accounting* with the word *marketing*.

9. In the second paragraph, delete *Ohio State University* using the Remove Word command. Type the name of your college.

10. Delete the following sentence:

As an intern at Price Waterhouse, I worked on the audit of Mills International.

11. Insert the following in place of the sentence just deleted:

> `As a project assignment, I conducted a market survey on fast food business in Northwest Ohio. This survey was used for the implementation of a new fast food chain in the area.`

12. Move the cursor to the name of the applicant. Replace the name Kim Landon with your own name.

13. Print the letter.

14. Now that you have seen a hard copy of the letter you would like to make some changes to the format design. Make the following changes:
  a. Change the top margin from 1 inch to 1½ inches.
  b. Set the right and left margins so that they are both 1½ inches wide.
  c. Have the right margin be ragged rather than justified.
  d. Change the format so that there are no page numbers on your letter.

15. Print the letter again.

CHAPTER 10

Introduction to Word Processing and WordPerfect

Three snaking side-by-side columns on screen?

WORDPERFECT 4.1 - NETWORK VERS

Along with Satellite Software's new version of WordPerfect 4.1, they will release WordPerfect 4.1 Network version.

The network version of the popular word processing program contains all the features the regular version of WordPerfect has and supports over 100 printers, just as does the regular version. Some of these features are a thesaurus, a new

and on AST-PC Net, Novell Network, and IBM Network.

SSI has added a new feature to the network version - it now has file locking capabilities. The first retrieved file will automatically be locked so someone at another terminal will not be able to edit the same file. If the person who initially retrieved the locked file saves this file as another name, the

Doc 1

Outline

Introduction
Definitions
Uses of Word Processors
Learning Check
Guide to WordPerfect
Getting Started with WordPerfect
Getting Help with WordPerfect
Learning Check

Creating a New Document
   Entering Text
   Saving a Document
   Retrieving a Document
Learning Check
Editing a Document
   Moving the Cursor
   Removing Text

Moving Blocks of Text
Correcting Spelling Mistakes
Printing
Learning Check
Summary Points
WordPerfect Exercises
WordPerfect Problems

Introduction

Human beings are constantly in search of more efficient and effective methods to accomplish their tasks. The written word has been no exception. The evolution of the writing instrument has progressed from rocks and twigs to what many thought to be the ultimate writing instrument—the typewriter. But the evolution did not stop there; the computer revolution has brought the word processor.

To gain a little perspective, think of the difference between writing with a pen and pad and writing with a typewriter; this comparison approximates the difference between using a typewriter and using a word processor. In terms of speed, power and capabilities, the word processor is to the pen and pad as the Ferrari is to the Model T.

One of the biggest advantages of word processing is that the words typed are not immediately committed to paper, but rather are displayed on a video screen where they can easily be manipulated electronically. Word processors have made it simple to insert or delete text and to move text from one place to another without having to retype or spend hours cutting and pasting. Gone are the days of overflowing wastepaper baskets and messy correction paper or fluid. A word processor enables the writer to be completely satisfied with what has been written before one word is printed on paper.

This chapter introduces word processing—what it is and what its uses are. In addition, it provides instructions on how to get started using WordPerfect, one of the most popular word processing packages on the market today.

Definitions

WORD PROCESSOR
A program or set of programs designed to enable the user to enter, manipulate, format, print, store, and retrieve text.

WORD PROCESSING
The act of composing and manipulating text electronically.

WORD PROCESSING SYSTEM
The hardware and software used for word processing.

DEDICATED SYSTEM
A computer equipped to handle only one function, such as word processing.

A **word processor** is a program (software) or set of programs which enables a computer user to write, edit, format, and print text. As characters are typed on a keyboard, they appear on the computer screen. Mistakes can be corrected easily because the text has not yet been put on paper. Words, sentences, and even entire paragraphs can be moved by special commands. Nothing is printed on paper until the user is satisfied with the results.

Word processing refers to the act of composing and editing text. The words are composed and rearranged in the writer's mind; the word processor and the hardware provide a convenient way to display, store, edit and recall the work that has been done.

A **word processing system** includes the hardware and software used for the purpose of word processing. There are two general types of word processing systems: (1) **dedicated systems,** which are basically microcomputers equipped to handle only word processing; and (2) multipurpose microcomputers, which are equipped to handle a wide variety of processing tasks, including word processing.

In the early days of word processing, the serious user's only choice was a dedicated system. With the development of faster and more sophisticated microcomputers, however, came the development of microcomputer-compatible word processors such as WordPerfect. Today most, if not all, multipurpose microcomputers on the market have at least one word processor available for them.

Although a word processor is actually a program or programs, many people refer to the combination of both software and hardware as a word processor. Table 10-1 provides a quick reference to other terms often used in connection with word processors.

Uses of Word Processors

Word processors are used in homes, businesses, schools, and many other places. At home they can be used to write school reports, letters or the minutes from a meeting. Most word processors for home use are easier to use and have fewer features than those designed for business use.

In offices, word processors take over much of the paperwork involved in running a business. They produce reports, letters, brochures, legal papers, and other important documents. A word processor can print a letter many times, with different names and addresses inserted to make the letter more personal.

Word processors have revolutionized the publishing industry. Books, newspapers, and magazines can be produced faster and with fewer mistakes. Sometimes these documents are not printed on paper until they are ready to be distributed. Writers enter text at computer terminals, and editors review the work at their terminals. Then designers lay out the pages electronically, choosing the type style, size, and column width. Finally, the document is printed for the first and only time.

Schools also are increasing their use of word processors. Students can write essays or reports on the computers in their classrooms. Teachers can format tests and worksheets on a computer much faster than on a typewriter. Of course, school secretaries can use word processors to prepare reports and letters.

No matter how word processors are used, they enable the writer to think more about organizing ideas rather than the mechanics of writing. A word processor makes it easy for a person to revise a document before it is printed.

Guide to WordPerfect

The remainder of this chapter focuses on how to use WordPerfect. WordPerfect, a state-of-the-art word processing program from WordPerfect Corporation, is extremely powerful yet easy to use. Memos, letters, reports, and term papers can be created with WordPerfect.

Some of the directions for using WordPerfect vary depending on whether the computer has two floppy disk drives or a hard disk drive. The directions in this chapter are written for computers with two floppy disk drives. Differences for computers with a hard disk drive are written in difference boxes. The instructions

**Table 10-1
Frequently Encountered Word Processing Terms**

Term	Definition
Automatic pagination	A feature that enables a word processor to number the pages of the printed copy automatically.
Block	A group of characters, such as a sentence or paragraph.
Block movement	A feature that allows the user to define a block of text and then perform a specific operation on the entire block. Common block operations include block move, block copy, block save, and block delete.
Boldface	Heavy type, for example, **this is boldface.**
Character	A letter, number, or symbol.
Character enhancement	Underlining, boldfacing, subscripting, and superscripting.
Control character	A coded character that does not print but is part of the command sequence in a word processor.
Cursor	The marker on the display screen indicating where the next character can be displayed.
Default setting	A value used by the word processor when it is not instructed to use any other.
Deletion	A feature by which a character, word, sentence, or larger block of text can be removed from the existing text.
Document-oriented word processor	A word processor that operates on a text file as one long document.
Editing	The act of changing or amending text.
Format	The layout of a page; for example, the number of lines, margin settings, and so on.
Global	An instruction that will be carried out throughout an entire document, for example, global search and replace.
Header	A piece of text that is stored separately from the text and printed at the top of each page.
Incremental spacing	A method by which the printer inserts spaces between words and letters to produce justified margins; also called *microspacing*.
Insertion	A feature in which a character, word, sentence, or larger block of text is added to the existing text.
Justification	A feature for making lines of text even at the margins.
Line editor	The type of editor that allows the user to edit only one line at a time.
Memory-only word processor	A word processor that cannot exchange text between internal memory and disk during the editing process.
Menu	A list of commands or prompts on the display screen.

Table continued on next page

Table 10-1 Continued

Term	Definition
Page-oriented word processor	A word processor that operates on a text file as a series of pages.
Print formatting	The function of a word processor which communicates with the printer to tell it how to print the text on paper.
Print preview	A feature that enables the user to view a general representation on the screen of how the document will look when printed.
Screen editor	The type of editor that enables the user to edit an entire screen at a time.
Screen formatting	A function of a word processor which controls how the text will appear on the screen.
Scrolling	Moving a line of text onto or off the screen.
Search and find	A routine that searches for, and places the cursor at, a specified string of characters.
Search and replace	A routine that searches for a specified character string and replaces it with the specified replacement string.
Status line	A message line above or below the text area on a display screen which gives format and system information.
Subscript	A character that prints below the usual text baseline.
Superscript	A character that prints above the usual text baseline.
Text buffer	An area set aside in memory to hold text temporarily.
Text editing	The function of a word processor that enables the user to enter and edit text.
Text file	A file that contains text, as opposed to a program.
Virtual representation	An approach to screen formatting which enables the user to see on the screen exactly how the printed output will look.
Word wrap	The feature in which a word is moved automatically to the beginning of the next line if it goes past the right margin.

Learning Check

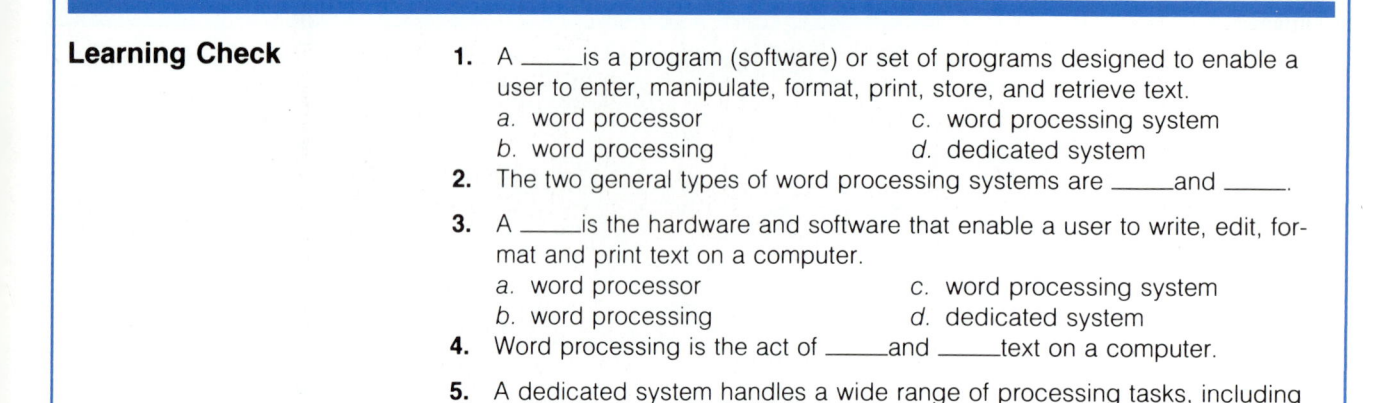

1. A _____ is a program (software) or set of programs designed to enable a user to enter, manipulate, format, print, store, and retrieve text.
   a. word processor
   b. word processing
   c. word processing system
   d. dedicated system
2. The two general types of word processing systems are _____ and _____.
3. A _____ is the hardware and software that enable a user to write, edit, format and print text on a computer.
   a. word processor
   b. word processing
   c. word processing system
   d. dedicated system
4. Word processing is the act of _____ and _____ text on a computer.
5. A dedicated system handles a wide range of processing tasks, including word processing. (True or False?)

Answers

1. a. 2. dedicated systems; multipurpose microcomputers. 3. c. 4. composing; editing. 5. False

---

in the difference boxes assume WordPerfect has been stored on the hard disk in a subdirectory named ''wp.''

Each of the following sections introduces one or more features of WordPerfect. At the end of each section there is a hands-on activity called YOUR TURN. Do not try the hands-on activities until after you have carefully read the section preceding them.

From now on, the key marked ↵ is referred to as the <Return> key (sometimes it is also called the <Enter> key). Throughout this chapter, when instructed to press the <Return> key, press the key marked ↵.

WordPerfect uses the ten function keys on the left side of the keyboard to activate most of its features. Usually a template is provided with the software to place around these ten keys (see Figure 10-1). The template lists, beside each key, the four functions that key activates. If you are not provided with a template refer to Figure 10-1.

Each key has four functions, which are activated by pressing the key alone or at the same time the <Alt>, <Shift>, or <Ctrl> key is pressed. The template's functions are color coded to indicate whether the key is pressed alone or with one of the other keys:

Black	Press the indicated function key only
Blue	Hold down the <Alt> key and press the indicated function key
Green	Hold down the <Shift> key and press the indicated function key
Red	Hold down the <Ctrl> key and press the indicated function key

Figure 10-1
The WordPerfect Template

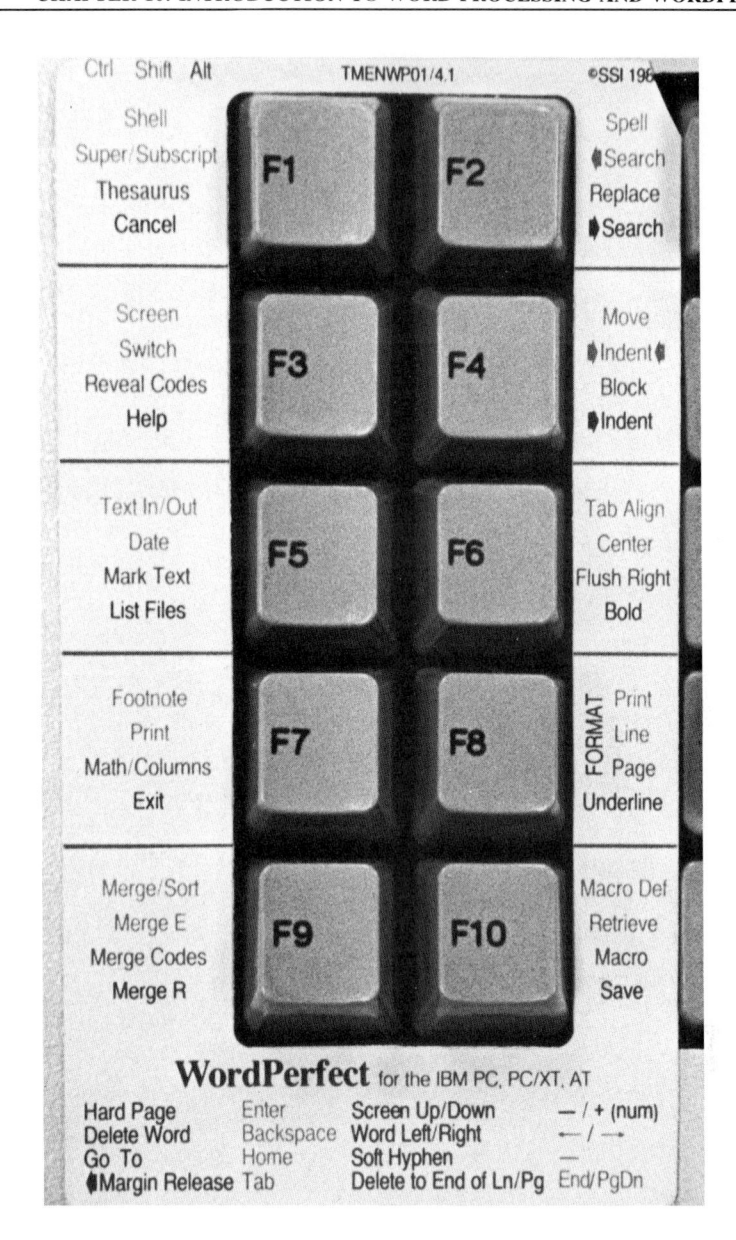

A few other keys are important in using WordPerfect. The <Num Lock> key is used to control the ten-key number pad on the right side of the keyboard. If the <Num Lock> key is pressed once, the pad is used for writing numbers to the screen. If not pressed, or pressed twice, it allows the keypad to be used for controlling the cursor. The <←> key, hereafter referred to as the <Backspace> key, allows mistakes to be erased by backing the cursor over them. The Cancel function, which is activated by pressing the <F1> key, allows a feature to be cancelled after it has been called up. It can also restore text that has been accidentally deleted.

The following symbols and typefaces appear throughout the chapter. This is what they mean:

Type **b:**	The information in boldface indicates a command that should be typed to the screen.
Press the <Return> key	The angle brackets (<>) are used to signify a specific key on the keyboard. Press the key whose name is enclosed by the angle brackets.
WP Tip:	This phrase introduces important information needed to run WordPerfect successfully.
EXIT WP? (Y/N)	All capital letters indicate phrases that appear on the computer screen. They also indicate the names of WordPerfect functions or commands.
Type `Job Opening`	Typewriter font indicates text that is to be entered into a document.

Getting Started with WordPerfect

BOOT
To load an operating system into a computer's main memory.

To **boot** the computer and start WordPerfect, you need a DOS disk, a WordPerfect Program disk, and a formatted disk that will serve as your data disk. All the documents or files you create will be saved on your data disk.

If a two-disk drive system is used, the data disk is always inserted in drive B. Unless instructed otherwise, the computer automatically saves files on whatever disk is in drive A. Because your data disk is always in drive B, you need to instruct the computer to store the documents you create on the data disk in drive B.

Follow these steps to boot the computer, start WordPerfect, and set the computer to store documents on the disk in drive B:

1. Insert the DOS disk into drive A. Close the disk drive door. Turn on the computer.
2. When asked to type the date enter the current date (for example, 9-28-1987) and press <Return>. When asked to enter the correct time, either enter the time using military form (14:26:24) and press <Return>, or simply press the <Return> key to bypass the time set feature.
3. When the system prompt A> appears on the screen, remove the DOS disk from drive A. Insert the WordPerfect Program disk into drive A and close the disk drive door.
4. Insert your data disk into drive B. Close the disk drive door.
5. Type **b:** and press <Return>. This command causes your work to be saved on drive B, where your data disk is. The program disk does not have enough room on it to save other files. If you forget this step, you may get an error message when you try to save files, and you may lose your work.
6. When the B> system prompt appears on the screen, type **a:wp** and press the <Return> key.

CHAPTER 10: INTRODUCTION TO WORD PROCESSING AND WORDPERFECT 285

> *Hard Disk Differences:* Turn on your computer. When you see the system prompt C>, type **cd\wp** (''wp'' is the name of the subdirectory where WordPerfect is located) and press the <Return> key. When the system prompt appears again, type **wp** and press the <Return> key.

STATUS LINE
A message line above or below the text area on a display screen that gives format and system information.

After typing **a:wp** and pressing <Return>, information about WordPerfect appears for a moment on the screen. Then, if a printer has been selected, the screen goes blank, except for the blinking cursor in the upper left corner and the **status line** in the lower right corner (see Figure 10-2). If a printer has not been selected, the information stays on the screen and you are prompted to press any key to continue. If the prompt ARE OTHER COPIES OF WORKPERFECT RUNNING appears, type **N**.

YOUR TURN Turn on and boot your computer, and start WordPerfect. Your screen should match Figure 10-2.

Figure 10-2 The WordPerfect Status Line and Editing Window

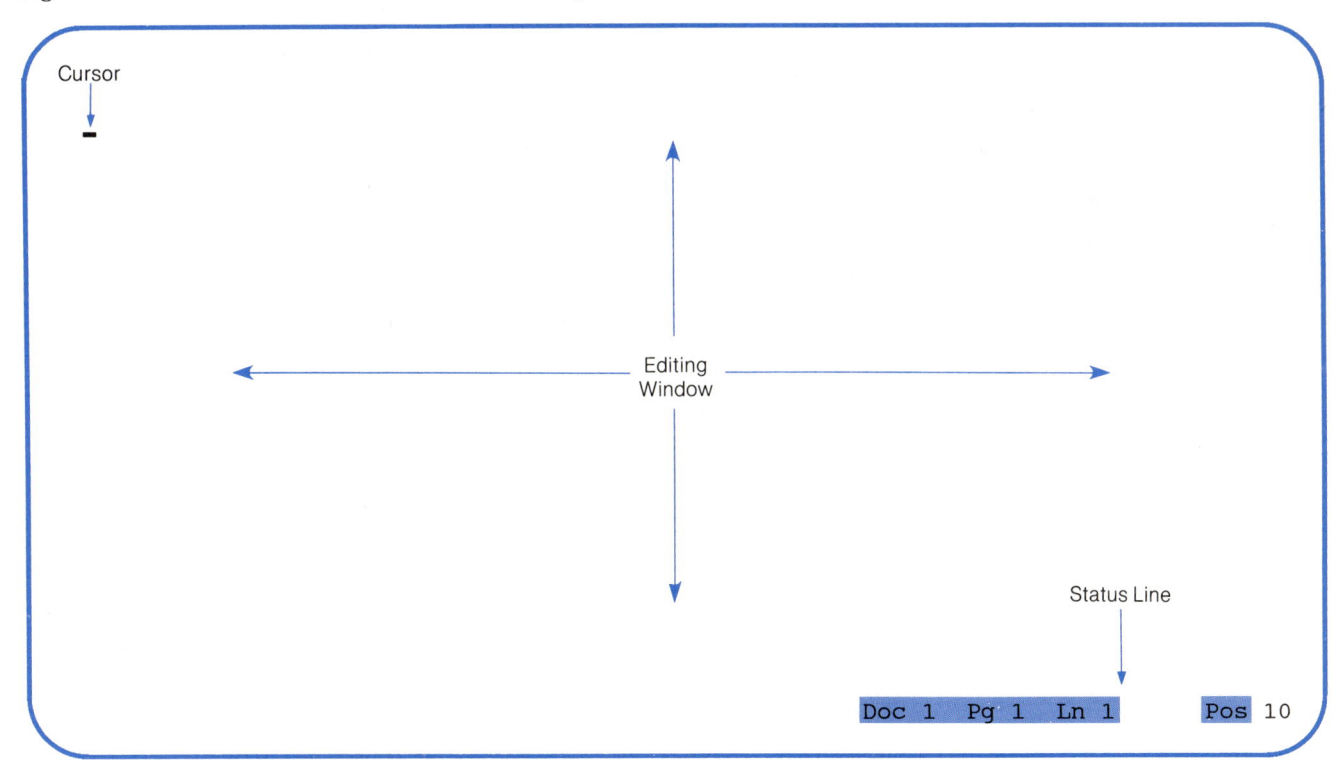

PART TWO: APPLICATIONS SOFTWARE

Getting Help with WordPerfect

To get help with any of WordPerfect's functions, you must have a WordPerfect Learning disk. Press <F3> (the <F3> key is marked Help in black on the template). The prompt INSERT LEARNING DISKETTE AND PRESS DRIVE LETTER appears at the bottom of the screen. Remove your data disk from drive B and insert the Learning disk into drive B. Type **B.**

To get more information about a specific function, press the function key that activates that particular function. Information about that function appears on the screen. Pressing a different function key brings up information on that function key. When you are ready to return to the document, press the <Space Bar>. The WordPerfect Learning disk then has to be replaced with your data disk.

YOUR TURN

In this exercise you are going to practice getting help with WordPerfect. To complete this exercise, you need a copy of the WordPerfect Learning disk. A blinking cursor should be in the upper left corner of your screen and the WordPerfect status line should be in the lower right corner.

   Press <F3> for HELP

When the prompt INSERT LEARNING DISKETTE AND PRESS DRIVE LETTER appears, remove your data disk from drive B and place the WordPerfect Learning disk into drive B. Close the disk drive door.

   Type **B**

Now you can get help with any of WordPerfect's functions.

   Press <F10> for SAVE

A Help screen appears with information about saving a document. Read the screen.

   Press <Shift> <F7> for PRINT

A Help screen appears with information about printing a document. Read the screen.

   Press <F7> for EXIT

A Help screen appears with information about exiting a document. Read the screen. Notice the last line on the Help screen. It says to exit WordPerfect without saving the document, you press EXIT (which is the <F7> key) and then type **n** and **y**. You are now going to exit WordPerfect using this method.

> Press the <Space Bar> to exit from the Help screens
> Press <F7> for EXIT

The prompt SAVE DOCUMENT appears at the bottom of the screen.

> Type **n**

The prompt EXIT WP appears on the screen.

> Type **y**

The A> or B> system prompt appears at the bottom of the screen. You know you have exited WordPerfect when the system prompt appears. When the red light on both disk drives goes off, it is safe to remove the disks from the disk drives. Never remove a disk when the red light on the drive is on. Removing a disk while the red light on the disk drive is on can cause damage to both the computer and the software. Turn off the computer and monitor.

Hard Disk Differences: When the C> system prompt appears, turn off the computer and monitor.

Learning Check

1. WordPerfect uses _____ to activate most of its features.
   - a. letter keys
   - b. menus
   - c. function keys
   - d. the ten-key number pad
2. Each function key has _____ function(s).
   - a. one
   - b. two
   - c. three
   - d. four
3. In order to find out how to set up footnotes with WordPerfect, press _____.
   - a. <F1> and then <F3>
   - b. <H> and then <F7>
   - c. <F3> and then <F>
   - d. <F3> and then <Ctrl><F7>
4. If the function that you want to use is printed on the function key template in red, what key do you press with the listed function key? _____
   - a. <Ctrl>
   - b. <Shift>
   - c. <Alt>
   - d. Press the function key alone
5. What key do you press in order to restore deleted text? _____
   - a. <F3>
   - b. <Delete>
   - c. <F2>
   - d. <F1>

Answers

1. c 2. d 3. d 4. a 5. d

Creating a New Document

The files created with WordPerfect are similar to files in a file cabinet—each file is a unit of storage. Files can be used to store memos, letters, and term papers. For example, when a memo or letter is completed, that file is saved on a disk. Once saved, that file can be reentered in order to revise, edit, or print its contents.

Entering Text

Each time WordPerfect is started, a blank screen appears with a blinking cursor in the upper left corner. The status line is in the lower right corner (refer to Figure 10-2). The status line displays the number of the document and the cursor's location. The number following Pg is the document's page number where the cursor is currently located. The number following Ln is the number of the horizontal line where the cursor is located. The number following Pos is the position number, or the number of spaces from the left margin, where the cursor is located.

The remainder of the screen is often referred to as the **editing window.** The editing window displays the words as they are typed. All editing of a document takes place in the editing window, which can contain twenty-four lines of text. When you type a document that is longer than twenty-four lines, the lines at the beginning of the document **scroll** off the top of the screen to make room for any additional lines.

When entering text, you need to use both upper and lowercase letters. If the letters are all capitals when you begin typing, press the <Caps Lock> key. Letters should appear in both upper and lowercase. Pressing the <Caps Lock> key again produces all capital letters.

The <Return> key does not need to be pressed when the end of a line is reached. WordPerfect has a feature called **word wrap,** which automatically moves a word to the beginning of the next line if it crosses the right margin. The <Return> key is used to begin new paragraphs and to add blank lines to the text.

Features such as margins, tabs, and spacing are set automatically according to **default** settings. These settings can be changed easily, but for now you should just use the default settings.

EDITING WINDOW
The area on a computer screen that contains the typed words in a document; also, the area in which changes can be made in a document.

SCROLLING
Moving a line or lines of text onto or off the screen.

WORD WRAP
The feature by which a word is automatically moved to the beginning of the next line if it goes past the right margin.

DEFAULT SETTING
The setting that a program automatically assumes when no other setting is designated by the user.

YOUR TURN

In this exercise, you are going to start WordPerfect on the computer and enter a letter.

Insert the DOS disk into drive A. Close the disk drive door. Turn on the computer and monitor. The date prompt appears on the screen. Enter the current date. The time prompt appears on the screen. Press <Return>.

The system prompt A> appears on the screen. Remove the DOS disk from drive A. Insert the WordPerfect Program disk into drive A and close the disk drive door. Insert your data disk into drive B. Close the disk drive door.

Type **b:**
Press <Return>

CHAPTER 10: INTRODUCTION TO WORD PROCESSING AND WORDPERFECT   289

The B> system prompt appears on the screen.

>Type **a:wp**
>Press the <Return> key

Information about WordPerfect appears for a moment on the screen. If a printer has been selected, the editing window appears. If a printer has not been selected, the information stays on the screen and you are prompted to press any key to continue. If this message appears, press any key. If the prompt ARE OTHER COPIES OF WORDPERFECT RUNNING appears, type **N**. The editing window should be on the screen and the blinking cursor should be in the upper left corner.

You are now going to enter a letter that should be typed exactly as it appears here. Any errors you find are intentional. Do not worry about any errors you make; they can be corrected easily later. Do not press <Return> unless instructed to do so. Let word wrap move the cursor to the next line. Follow the directions closely.

Before typing the letter, you are going to activate the FLUSH RIGHT and DATE functions. Remember that functions are activated through the combined use of the ten function keys and the <Ctrl> <Shift> and <Alt> keys. Use the color-coded function key template to find the proper combination. In this case, FLUSH RIGHT appears in blue beside the <F6> key and DATE appears in green beside the <F5> key.

>Press the <Alt> and <F6> keys for FLUSH RIGHT

The cursor jumps to the right side of the screen.

>Press the <Shift> and <F5> keys for DATE

At the bottom of the screen, a line with three numbered choices for the Date function appears.

>Type **1**

The date is inserted automatically, flush with the right margin. (Note: If you bypassed setting the date when starting up DOS, the date will read January 1, 1980).

>Press <Return> four times
>Type Kim Landon
>Press <Return>
>Type 4332 University Road
>Press <Return>
>Type Toledo, Ohio 43403
>Press <Return> twice
>Type Dear Ms. Landon,
>Press <Return> twice

Now type the body of the letter as follows:

> As your advisor, I want to help you in any way
> possible with your job hunt. Since graduation is only
> six short months away, I'm sure finding a job is a top
> priority for you right now. I just recieved some
> information form the placement service office that I
> would like to pass along to you. I think this
> information will help you in your job-search efforts.

Press <Return> twice

> The placement service is sponsoring a searees of
> semenars designed to help upcoming graduates locate
> potential employers, write cover letters and resumes,
> and imporve interviewing skills. There is no cost for
> attending this semenar, but if you plan to attend, you
> must register with the placement office no later than
> Monday, February 17. These semenars will be divided up
> according to majors. The semenar for Accounting majors
> is scheduled for Saturday, February 21. I have
> enclosed a tenative schedule of events.

Press <Return> twice

> I hope you plan to attend this semenar. I think it
> will be well worth your time.

Press <Return> twice

> Sincerly,

Press <Return> four times

> Professor Hubert Melville

Press <Return> twice

> See enclosure

When you have finished, your screen should look like Figure 10-3. Leave the letter on the screen. You are going to save it in the next hands-on exercise.

Saving a Document

To save a document, activate the EXIT function by pressing the function key marked <F7>. When the prompt SAVE DOCUMENT?(Y/N) Y appears in the lower left corner of the screen, press the <Return> key to save the document. You do not have to type **Y** because the program's default setting is **Y.** If you do

> recieved some information form the placement service office that
> I would like to pass along to you. I think this information will
> help you in your job-search efforts.
>
> The placement service is sponsoring a searees of semenars
> designed to help upcoming graduates locate potential employers,
> write cover letters and resumes, and imporve interviewing skills.
> There is no cost for attending this semenar, but if you plan to
> attend, you must register with the placement office no later than
> Monday, February 17. These semenars will be divided up according
> to majors. The semenar for Accounting majors is scheduled for
> Saturday, February 21. I have enclosed a tenative schedule of
> events.
>
> I hope you plan to attend this semenar. I think it will be well
> worth your time.
>
> Sincerly,
>
>
> Professor Hubert Melville
>
> See enclosure_
>
>   Doc 1 Pg 1 Ln 37   Pos 23

Figure 10-3 Entering Text

not wish to save the document before leaving it, type **N,** which will replace the **Y.**

The prompt DOCUMENT TO BE SAVED appears next. Enter a name for the document. It is helpful to give your files names that will remind you of their contents.

> *WP TIP:* When naming a file, remember the following rules:
>
> 1. The name can be from 1 to 8 characters long, with no spaces.
> 2. The characters in a filename can be the letters of the alphabet, the numbers 0 through 9, or the special characters $#@!()-{}__.
> 3. An optional extension can be used following the filename. The extension can have from 1 to 3 characters with no spaces, and is separated from the filename by a period (.).
> 4. Try to give the file a name that reminds you of what it contains.

After naming a file the prompt EXIT WP? (Y/N) N appears. If you want to continue using WordPerfect, press <Return> to accept the default setting of N for No. If you want to exit the program, type **Y.** When the system prompt appears and the red lights on the disk drives are off, you can take the disks out of the disk drives and turn off the computer and monitor.

YOUR TURN

In this exercise, you are going to save the letter just entered. The letter should appear on the screen.

    Press <F7> for EXIT

The prompt SAVE DOCUMENT appears at the bottom of the screen.

    Press <Return> to accept the default setting **Y** for Yes

The prompt DOCUMENT TO BE SAVED appears at the bottom of the screen. You are going to name the document JOBSEM.1 for job seminar.

    Type `JOBSEM.1`
    Press <Return>

The prompt EXIT WP appears.

    Type **Y**

The system prompt appears in the lower left corner of the screen.

Retrieving a Document

To edit a document that already exists, activate the RETRIEVE command by pressing the <Shift> and <F10> keys. The prompt DOCUMENT TO BE RETRIEVED appears. Type the name of the document that is to be edited, and press <Return>. If there is a file that corresponds to the name entered, the document appears on the screen, ready to be edited.

If you do not remember the name of the document you want to retrieve, activate the LIST FILES command by pressing <F5>. The prompt DIR B:/*.* appears in the lower left corner of the screen and the instruction USE = TO CHANGE DEFAULT DIRECTORY appears in the lower right corner. Press <Return> to get the listing of files in Directory B which contains your data disk. Highlight the name of the file to be retrieved by typing the name of the file. Press <Return>.

A list of options appears at the bottom of the screen. Next to the RETRIEVE option is the number one. To retrieve the highlighted file, type **1.** The desired document appears on the screen.

> *Hard Disk Differences:* The prompt DIR C:/*.* appears in the lower right corner of the screen. Pressing <Return> provides you with a list of the WordPerfect files in Directory C.

YOUR TURN

In this exercise, you are going to retrieve the JOBSEM.1 file. Start WordPerfect. A blank editing window should be on the screen.

> Press <Shift> <F10> for RETRIEVE
> Type jobsem.1
> Press <Return>

The letter appears on the screen. Now you are going to retrieve the letter again using the directory. First you have to exit from the file.

> Press <F7> for EXIT

The SAVE DOCUMENT prompt appears. You do not have to save the letter again since it has already been saved once and you have not yet made any changes to it.

> Type **N**
> Press <Return>

A blank editing window appears.

> Press <F5> for LIST FILES
> Press <Return>

The directory for disk B appears on the screen. The JOBSEM.1 file is listed.

> Type jobsem.1

The highlighting is on the JOBSEM.1 file in the directory. The filename appears in the lower left corner as you type it.

> Press <Return>

A list of options appears at the bottom of the screen.

> Type **1** for RETRIEVE

The letter appears in the editing window. Leave the letter on the screen. Exit WordPerfect.

Learning Check

1. Each time WordPerfect is started up, _____ appears
   a. a menu
   b. a blank screen
   c. a blank screen with a blinking cursor in the upper left corner
   d. a list of formatting options
2. What key do you press to save a file?
3. How long can a WordPerfect filename be?
4. What is the feature called which automatically moves words that run over the right margin to the next line?
5. Which function keys activate the LIST FILES and RETRIEVE functions?

Answers

1. c. 2. The EXIT function key, <F7> 3. Eight characters, with three additional characters following a period if desired 4. word wrap 5. <F5>; <F10> and the <Shift> keys together

Editing a Document

TEXT EDITING
The function of a word processor which enables the user to enter and edit text.

INSERTION
A word processing feature in which a character, word, sentence, or larger block of text can be added to the existing text.

DELETION
A word processing feature in which a character, word, sentence, or larger block of text can be removed from the existing text.

Now that a document has been saved on a disk, it can be edited. The **text editing** function of a word processor enables the user to enter and edit text. The most fundamental aspect of this function is the word processor's ability to accept and store the text that is typed in at the keyboard. Without this ability, all the other functions and procedures would be useless.

Text editing also includes the ability of the word process to **insert** and **delete** characters, words, lines, paragraphs, and larger blocks of text. The insert and delete modes are two of the most often used text editing features of any word processor. The text editing features of most word processors, including WordPerfect, also allow blocks of text to be moved and copied. These features make it easier to rearrange and retype documents.

The exercises in this section demonstrate the commands used to edit a document. You will practice using these commands on the JOBSEM.1 document you created.

Moving the Cursor

Before starting to work on a file, you need to be able to control the position of the cursor. The cursor is controlled by the arrow keys in the numeric keypad on the right side of the keyboard. The down arrow $<\downarrow>$ moves the cursor one line down. The up arrow $<\uparrow>$ moves the cursor one line up. The left arrow $<\leftarrow>$, which should not be confused with the <Backspace> key, moves the cursor one position to the left. The right arrow $<\rightarrow>$ key moves the cursor one position to

Table 10-2
Commands for Moving the Cursor

Keys	Description
<←>	Moves the cursor one character to the left
<→>	Moves the cursor one character to the right
<Ctrl><→>	Moves the cursor one word to the right
<Ctrl><←>	Moves the cursor one word to the left
<Home><→>	Moves the cursor to the right edge of the screen
<Home><←>	Moves the cursor to the left edge of the screen
<Home><Home><→>	Moves the cursor to the far right of the line
<Home><Home><←>	Moves the cursor to the far left of the line
<↑>	Moves the cursor up one line
<↓>	Moves the cursor down one line
<Home><↑>	Moves the cursor to the top of the screen
<Home><↓>	Moves the cursor to the bottom of the screen
<Ctrl><Home><↑>	Moves the cursor to the top of the current page
<Ctrl><Home><↓>	Moves the cursor to the end of the current page
<Pg Up>	Moves the cursor to the top of the previous page
<Pg Dn>	Moves the cursor to the top of the next page
<Home><Home><↑>	Moves the cursor to the beginning of the document
<Home><Home><↓>	Moves the cursor to the end of the document
<Ctrl><Home>#	Moves the cursor to the page number entered
<Esc>#<↑>	Moves the cursor up the number of lines entered
<Esc>#<↓>	Moves the cursor down the number of lines entered

the right. Remember, the keypad can be used to move the cursor only when the <Num Lock> key is off. If the numbers 2, 4, 6, 8 appear on the screen when you are trying to move the cursor, then the <Num Lock> key is on. Press it once to turn it off, and use the <Backspace> key to delete the numbers.

The cursor can also be moved a specified number of lines by using the <Esc> key. Press <Esc> and the prompt N = 8 appears in the lower left corner of the screen. Enter the number of lines you want the cursor to move and press either the <↓> or <↑> key. The cursor moves down the number of lines specified if the <↓> key was pressed and up the specified number of lines if the <↑> key was pressed.

The cursor can also be moved word by word or page by page through the document. Table 10-2 summarizes the cursor commands.

YOUR TURN

In this exercise, you are going to practice moving the cursor. Start WordPerfect. A blank editing window should be on the screen. Retrieve the JOBSEM.1 file. Look at the status line. The cursor should be on Page 1, Line 1, Position 10.

Press <↓> 10 times

The cursor should be under the A in the first word of the first sentence. Look at the status line. It now reads Line 11 rather than Line 1.

Press <Home><Home><→>

The cursor is now on Line 11, Position 75, at the very end of the first line of the letter.

Press <Home><↓>

The cursor will move to the bottom of the screen.

Press <Home><Home><↓>

The word Repositioning flashes briefly on the screen as the cursor repositions itself at the end of the document.

Press <Esc>

The prompt N = 8 appears in the lower left corner of the screen.

Type **10**
Press <↑>

The cursor moves up ten lines. Continue to practice all the ways to move the cursor. Watch the Line and Position numbers in the status line as you move the cursor.

Removing Text

There are several ways to remove text from a WordPerfect document. The most efficient method depends upon the text to be removed and the user's typing style.

Pressing the <Backspace> key moves the cursor one space to the left, removing the character from that position. If you hold the <Backspace> key down, it continues to remove characters until it is released.

Pressing the <Del> key removes the character above the cursor. The <Del> key can also be used in conjunction with the BLOCK command (<Alt><F4>). Position the cursor at the beginning of the block of text that is to be deleted. Press <Alt><F4> to activate the block command. The words BLOCK ON begin flashing in the lower left corner of the screen. Use the arrow keys to highlight the block of text to be deleted. Press <Del>. The prompt DELETE BLOCK? (Y/N) N appears in the lower left corner of the screen. To delete the block of text that

OVERTYPE
To type directly over an existing character, replacing it with a new character.

is highlighted, press **Y.** To cancel the Block command, press <Return> and then press <F1> for CANCEL. The highlighting disappears from the text.

The <Ins> key can be used for removing and replacing text. If the <Ins> key is pressed once, the word TYPEOVER appears in the lower left corner of the screen and the **overtype** mode is on. When WordPerfect is in overtype mode, text can be changed by typing over the characters above the cursor. For example, if the cursor is under the *d* in "The *d*og ran up the street" and TYPEOVER appears on the screen, typing *cat* produces the sentence "The cat ran up the street." Typing *elephant,* however, results in the sentence "The elephantup the street." For one word to replace another, the two must have the same number of letters. Usually it is not efficient to work with the overtype feature on, because important information could easily be written over. Pressing the <Ins> key again puts WordPerfect back into Insert mode.

Text can also be deleted by pressing either <Ctrl><End> or <Ctrl><PgDn>. Pressing <Ctrl> <End> deletes text from the cursor's position to the end of the line. Pressing <Ctrl><PgDn> deletes text from the cursor's position to the end of the page.

If text is deleted by accident, pressing <F1> for the CANCEL command enables you to undo the deletion. This function has limitations, however. It can restore only the most recently removed text.

YOUR TURN

In this exercise you are going to practice the various ways to delete text. The JOBSEM.1 document should be on the screen. If necessary, move the cursor to position it in Page 1, Line 1, Position 10.

Because the JOBSEM.1 document is a modified block form letter, the date needs to be moved back to the left margin.

> Press the <→> key to position the cursor under the first letter in the date.
> Press the <Backspace> key once

The prompt DELETE [ALN/FLSR]? (Y/N) N appears in the lower left corner of the screen. The prompt is asking if you want to delete the Flush Right function.

> Press **Y**

The date moves over the left margin. Move the cursor to Line 14 Position 37, under the *o* in *form*.

> Press <Del> twice to delete *or*

Make sure TYPEOVER does not appear in the lower left corner of the screen.

> Type `ro`

The word should now be *from*. Keep the cursor in Line 14 and move it until it is under the *p* in *placement*. You are going to change the lowercase *p, s,* and *o* in *placement service office* to uppercase letters.

    Press <Ins>

TYPEOVER appears in the lower left corner of the screen.

    Type P

Move the cursor until it is under the *s* in *service*.

    Type S

Move the cursor until it is under the *o* in *office*.

    Type O
    Press <Ins> to turn the Typeover mode off

The word TYPEOVER should no longer be on the screen. Move the cursor to the beginning of the sentence in Line 15 that starts: "I think this information . . ." You are going to delete the entire sentence using the BLOCK command. The cursor should be under the *I*.

    Press <Alt><F4> for BLOCK

The words BLOCK ON start flashing in the lower left corner of the screen.

    Press <↓> once

The entire sentence is now highlighted.

    Press <Del>

The prompt DELETE BLOCK appears.

    Type **Y**

The entire sentence is deleted. Move the cursor to Line 17. Using the <Ins> key, change the lowercase *p* and *s* in *placement service* to uppercase letters.

    Move the cursor to Line 22. Using the BLOCK command and the <Del> key, delete this entire sentence: "These semenars will be divided up according to majors." Replace it with the following sentence: `Each semenar will focus on a different major.`

    Change the lowercase *p* and *o* in *placement office* in Line 21 to capital letters using the <Ins> key. Do not forget to turn the overtype mode off when the corrections have been made.

Move the cursor to the *i* in the word *it* in the following sentence which starts on Line 27: "I think *it* will be well worth your time." Use the <Backspace> key to change this sentence to: "It will be well worth your time."

 Press the <Backspace> key eight times

Move the cursor to the *l* in the word *Sincerly* in Line 30.

 Type e

You are now going to save the corrections you just made.

 Press <F10> for SAVE

The prompt DOCUMENT TO BE SAVED: B\WP\JOBSEM.1 appears at the bottom of the screen.

 Press <Return>

The prompt REPLACE B\WP\JOBSEM.1? (Y/N) N appears at the bottom of the screen. This prompt is asking if you want to replace the original JOBSEM.1 file with the file you just created by making corrections. There is no need to save the first letter so you are going to replace the file.

 Type **Y**

The new JOBSEM.1 file with corrections should stay on the screen. You are going to continue to make more changes in the next hands-on exercise.

Moving Blocks of Text

BLOCK MOVEMENT
A feature that enables the user to define a block of text and then perform a specific operation on the entire block. Common block operations include block move, block copy, block save, and block delete.

Manipulating a document a character at a time is extremely slow when working with large blocks of text. To help speed operations, WordPerfect includes a **block movement** feature. This feature defines a block of text—either a sentence, paragraph, or page—and then either copies it or moves it elsewhere in the document.

 To be able to move a block of text, it first must be highlighted. Position the cursor under the first letter of the text to be moved. Activate the MOVE function by pressing <Ctrl><F4>. A menu appears at the bottom of the screen that offers three move options: 1 SENTENCE; 2 PARAGRAPH; 3 PAGE. Select the appropriate number. Depending on the number selected, either a sentence, paragraph or page is highlighted.

 Next, the prompt 1 CUT; 2 COPY appears at the bottom of the screen. If the text is to be moved to another part of the document, type **1** for CUT. Move the cursor to the position where the cut text should be inserted. Activate the MOVE function again by pressing <Ctrl><F4>. When the menu reappears, press **5** for TEXT to place the text at its new position.

The MOVE function can also be used to copy a block of text that is to be repeated a number of times throughout a document. Move the cursor to the beginning of the block of text to be copied. Activate the MOVE function (<Ctrl><F4>). Select either **1, 2,** or **3,** depending on whether a sentence, paragraph or page needs to be copied. When the 1 CUT; 2 COPY prompt appears, type **2** for COPY. The text is copied into memory, but also is left in its original position. The block of text can be reproduced as many times as needed. Simply place the cursor at the position where the copied text is to appear and activate the MOVE function (<Ctrl><F4>). Select **5** to place the copied text at the cursor's position. To reproduce the text again, move the cursor to the next location where the copied text is to appear, activate the MOVE function and press **5** for text. This process can be repeated as many time as necessary to place copied text. The text stays in memory until a new block of text is copied.

YOUR TURN

Use the JOBSEM.1 document, which should be on your screen, to practice using the BLOCK function.

Move the cursor to the *A* in the sentence "As your advisor, I want to help you in any way possible with your job hunt."

 Press <Ctrl><F4> for MOVE

The menu appears at the bottom of the screen.

 Type **1** for SENTENCE

The entire first sentence is highlighted and the prompt 1 CUT; 2 COPY appears at the bottom of the screen (see Figure 10-4). You are going to cut this sentence and move it to a new location.

 Type **1**

The sentence is cut from the letter. Move the cursor to the word *I* in the sentence that begins "I just recieved some information . . .,"

 Press <Ctrl><F4> for MOVE
 Type **5** for TEXT

The sentence that was cut is now inserted as the second sentence of the letter.

Move the cursor to the first letter of the sentence in the second paragraph that begins: "There is no cost for attending this semenar . . ." You are going to move this sentence so that it is the last sentence of the paragraph.

```
          February 6, 1987


     Kim Landon
     4332 University Road
     Toledo, Ohio  43402

     Dear Ms. Landon,

     As your advisor, I want to help you in any way possible with your
     job hunt.  Since graduation is only six short months away, I'm
     sure finding a job is a top priority for you right now.  I just
     recieved some information from the Placement Service Office that
     I would like to pass along to you.

     The Placement Service is sponsoring a searees of semenars
     designed to help upcoming graduates locate potential employers,
     write cover letters and resumes, and imporve interviewing skills.
     There is no cost for attending this semenar, but if you plan to
     attend, you must register with the Placement Office no later than
     Monday, February 17.  Each semenar will focus on a different
     major.  The semenar for Accounting majors is scheduled for
     Saturday, February 21.  I have enclosed a tenative schedule of
  1 Cut; 2 Copy: 0
```

Figure 10-4
Moving a Block of Text

Press <Ctrl><F4> for MOVE
Type **1** for SENTENCE
Type **1** for CUT

Move the cursor to the space immediately following the period at the end of the last sentence in the paragraph. Press the <Space Bar> once so that there are two spaces after the period.

Press <Ctrl><F4> for MOVE
Type **5** for TEXT

The sentence that was cut now appears as the last sentence of the paragraph. Save the corrections you have made. Again, you can replace the old JOBSEM.1 with the newly revised file JOBSEM.1.

Correcting Spelling Mistakes

WordPerfect comes with a very useful function called the Speller. The speller checks the spelling in a document and if it finds a misspelled word, it suggests the correct spelling. The Speller can analyze a word phonetically (by sound). If a word is close to the correct spelling, the Speller can suggest the right spelling.

To use the Speller, you need a WordPerfect Speller disk. First, retrieve the document that is to be checked. Remove the data disk that is in drive B and replace it with the Speller disk. Activate the SPELL function by pressing <Ctrl><F2>. Depending on which version of WordPerfect you are using, a message may appear at this point indicating that the program cannot locate the Speller in drive A. If this happens, type **B:** and press <Return> to tell WordPerfect to look for the Speller in drive B. The Check menu appears at the bottom of the screen.

> *Hard Disk Differences:* Retrieve the document to be checked. Start the Speller by pressing <Ctrl><F2>. If the Speller has been saved on the hard disk, the Check menu appears immediately, eliminating the need to specify a drive letter.

The Speller can check a document a word at a time, page at a time, or it can check the spelling of the entire document. To check the spelling of one word or page, the cursor must be placed anywhere within the word or page before activating the SPELL function. When the Check menu appears, type **1** for WORD to check a single word, or type **2** for Page to check the entire page. To check the spelling of an entire document, type **3** for document.

The message PLEASE WAIT appears at the bottom of the screen while the Speller program checks the spelling. If the Speller comes across a word that is not in its dictionary, that word is highlighted in the document and the message NOT FOUND! SELECT WORD OR MENU OPTION appears at the bottom of the screen along with a replacement list. The replacement list includes words that are similar to the misspelled word and its purpose is to help you find the correct spelling of the highlighted word. If the highlighted word can be replaced by one of the words in the replacement list, simply press the letter corresponding to the correct word. The Speller replaces the highlighted word with the word selected from the replacement list, and continues checking the spelling.

The Not Found Menu contains six options. If a highlighted word in this particular instance is acceptable, type **1** for SKIP ONCE. The Speller will continue to check the spelling. If that word is found again, it will be highlighted again. If the highlighted word is acceptable in all cases of its use, type **2** for SKIP and the Speller will continue to check the spelling. If that word is found again, the Speller will skip over it. If the word should be added to a supplementary dictionary because it is used often and you want the Speller to recognize it, type **3** for ADD WORD.

If the highlighted word needs to be corrected but cannot be corrected by using one of the words from the replacement list, type **4** for EDIT. The cursor moves to the first letter of the misspelled word. Make the necessary correction and press <Return>.

If you need to look up a word you do not know how to spell, type **5** for LOOK UP. The prompt WORD OR WORD PATTERN appears. Enter the word, spelled as closely as possible using "wild-card" characters for those letters you are not sure about. Type **?** if you are unsure of a single letter and ***** if unsure of more than one letter. For example, say you do not know how to spell *boutonniere* but know it begins with a *bo*, and has a *t* in it somewhere and ends with an *e*. At the WORD OR WORD PATTERN prompt enter **bo*t*e** and press <Return>. A list of words appears on the screen, one of which is *boutonniere*.

The last option on the Not Found menu is **6** for PHONETIC. This option checks the dictionary for words that sound like the highlighted word.

When the Speller can find no more misspelled words, the message WORD COUNT: nnn PRESS ANY KEY TO CONTINUE appears on the screen. The word count provides the total number of words in the document. Press any key. Remove the Speller disk from drive B. Insert your data disk in drive B. Save the revised document.

> *WP TIP:* WordPerfect's Speller makes corrections on the screen only so they must be saved. However, do not save them until the WordPerfect Speller disk in drive B has been replaced by your data disk. Otherwise the document will be saved on the wrong disk.

YOUR TURN

You are going to practice using WordPerfect's Speller function using the JOBSEM.1 file. In order to complete this exercise, you need a copy of the WordPerfect Speller disk. The JOBSEM.1 document should be on your screen and the cursor should be on Page 1, Line 1, Position 10. Remove your data disk from drive B and replace it with the Speller disk.

Press <Ctrl><F2> for SPELL

Depending on which version of WordPerfect you are using, a message may appear at this point indicating that the program cannot locate the Speller in drive A. If this happens, type **B:** and press <Return> to tell WordPerfect to look for the Speller in drive B. The Check menu appears at the bottom of the screen (see Figure 10-5). Check the spelling of the entire document. If the Speller finds errors other than the ones mentioned in this exercise, correct them as you go along.

Type **3** for DOCUMENT

The Speller finds the word *Kim* and highlights it. The Not Found menu appears at the bottom of the screen. A list of replacement words also appears (see Figure 10-6). The word *Kim*, however, does not need to be changed in this letter.

Type **2** for SKIP

The speller finds *Landon*.

PART TWO: APPLICATIONS SOFTWARE

```
February 6, 1987


Kim Landon
4332 University Road
Toledo, Ohio  43402

Dear Ms. Landon,

Since graduation is only six short months away, I'm sure finding
a job is a top priority for you right now.  As your advisor, I
want to help you in any way possible with your job hunt.  I just
recieved some information from the Placement Service Office that
I would like to pass along to you.

The Placement Service is sponsoring a searees of semenars
designed to help upcoming graduates locate potential employers,
write cover letters and resumes, and imporve interviewing skills.
Each semenar will focus on a different major.  The semenar for
Accounting majors is scheduled for Saturday, February 21.  I have
enclosed a tenative schedule of events.  There is no cost for
attending this semenar, but if you plan to attend, you must
register with the Placement Office no later than Monday, February
```
Check: **1** Word; **2** Page; **3** Document; **4** Change Dictionary; **5** Look Up; **6** Count

Figure 10-5
WordPerfect's Check Menu

Type **2** for SKIP

The speller finds the first occurrence of *recieved*. The correct spelling is offered in the replacement list next to A.

Type **A**

The Speller immediately replaces the misspelled word with the correct word from the replacement list and moves on. The next word it finds is *searees*.

Type **M**

The next word found is *semenars*.

Type **A**

The next word found is *imporve*.

Type **A**

The next word found is *semenar*

Type **A**

CHAPTER 10: INTRODUCTION TO WORD PROCESSING AND WORDPERFECT 305

```
                February 6, 1987


          Kim Landon
          4332 University Road
          Toledo, Ohio  43402

          Dear Ms. Landon,

          Since graduation is only six short months away, I'm sure finding
==============================================================================
     A. kid                  B. kin                   C. kip
     D. kit                  E. km                    F. cam
     G. came                 H. chem                  I. chime
     J. chum                 K. chyme                 L. com
     M. comb                 N. come                  O. coomb
     P. cum                  Q. cyme                  R. quam
     S. quem


  Not Found!   Select Word or Menu Option (0=Continue): 0
   1 Skip Once;  2 Skip;  3 Add Word;  4 Edit;  5 Look Up;  6 Phonetic
```

Figure 10-6
WordPerfect's Not Found Menu

The next word found is *tenative*

    Type **A**

The next word found is *Hubert.*

    Type **2** for SKIP

The message WORD COUNT 165 PRESS ANY KEY TO CONTINUE appears at the bottom of the screen. Press any key. Remove the Speller disk from drive B. Insert your data disk in drive B.

    Press <F10> for SAVE

The message DOCUMENT TO BE SAVED: B:\WP\JOBSEM.1 appears.

    Press <Return>

The message REPLACE B:\WP\JOBSEM.1 appears.

    Type **Y**

All the corrections are now saved.

Printing

There are several ways to print with WordPerfect. One way is to retrieve the document to be printed. Make sure that the computer is hooked up to the printer, the printer has plenty of paper and is online. With the document on the computer screen, press <Shift><F7> for PRINT. A menu appears at the bottom of the screen. Press **1** to print the entire text or press **2** to just print a page of the text. The document is printed.

A document also can be printed without retrieving it. With a blank editing window on the screen, press <Shift><F7> for PRINT. When the menu appears, press **4** for PRINTER CONTROL. The Printer Control menu appears (see Figure 10-7). Press **P** for PRINT A DOCUMENT. Type the name of the document. Both the disk drive and filename have to be included. For example, to print the JOB-SEM.1 document using this method, you would type **B:JOBSEM.1** and press <Return>.

> *Hard Disk Differences:* You do not have to designate the disk drive when typing the name of the document; simply type the filename and press <Return>.

Figure 10-7 WordPerfect's Printer Control Menu

```
Printer Control                         C - Cancel Print Job(s)
                                        D - Display All Print Jobs
1 - Select Print Options                G - "Go" (Resume Printing)
2 - Display Printers and Fonts          P - Print a Document
3 - Select Printers                     R - Rush Print Job
                                        S - Stop Printing
Selection: 0


Current Job

Job Number: n/a                         Page Number:  n/a
Job Status: n/a                         Current Copy: n/a
Message:    The print queue is empty

Job List

Job   Document              Destination         Forms and Print Options




Additional jobs not shown: 0
```

CHAPTER 10: INTRODUCTION TO WORD PROCESSING AND WORDPERFECT 307

The prompt STARTING PAGE appears. If desired, only certain pages from a document can be printed. For example, pages 4 through 6 from a ten-page document could be printed. Enter the page number of the first page to be printed. If the entire document is to be printed, enter **1**. Press <Return>.

Next the prompt ENDING PAGE appears. If the entire document is to be printed, press <Return>. If only a portion of the document is to be printed, enter the page number of the last page that is to be printed and press <Return>.

When you are finished using the Printer Control menu, press <F1> for CANCEL. A blank text editing window appears on the screen.

YOUR TURN You are going to print the JOBSEM.1 document. If necessary, retrieve the document so that it appears on the screen.

Press <Shift><F7>

A menu appears at the bottom of the screen (see Figure 10-8).

Type **1** for FULL TEXT to print the entire document.

The message PLEASE WAIT flashes briefly in the lower left corner of the

Figure 10-8 Printing a Document

```
February 6, 1987


Kim Landon
4332 University Road
Toledo, Ohio  43402

Dear Ms. Landon,

Since graduation is only six short months away, I'm sure finding
a job is a top priority for you right now.  As your advisor, I
want to help you in any way possible with your job hunt.  I just
received some information from the Placement Service Office that
I would like to pass along to you.

The Placement Service is sponsoring a series of seminars designed
to help upcoming graduates locate potential employers, write
cover letters and resumes, and improve interviewing skills.  Each
seminar will focus on a different major.  The seminar for
Accounting majors is scheduled for Saturday, February 21.  I have
enclosed a tentative schedule of events.  There is no cost for
attending this seminar, but if you plan to attend, you must
register with the Placement Office no later than Monday, February
```
1 Full Text; **2** Page; **3** Change Options; **4** Printer Control; **5** Type-thru: **0**

```
February 6, 1987


Kim Landon
4332 University Road
Toledo, Ohio  43402

Dear Ms. Landon,

Since graduation is only six short months away, I'm sure finding
a job is a top priority for you right now.  As your advisor, I
want to help you in any way possible with your job hunt.  I just
received some information from the Placement Service Office that
I would like to pass along to you.

The Placement Service is sponsoring a series of seminars designed
to help upcoming graduates locate potential employers, write
cover letters and resumes, and improve interviewing skills.  Each
seminar will focus on a different major.  The seminar for
Accounting majors is scheduled for Saturday, February 21.  I have
enclosed a tentative schedule of events.  There is no cost for
attending this seminar, but if you plan to attend, you must
register with the Placement Office no later than Monday, February
17.

I hope you plan to attend this seminar.  It will be well worth
your time.

Sincerely,


Professor Hubert Melville

See enclosure
```

Figure 10-9
The JOBSEM.1 Document

screen and the document is printed. When your document is printed, it should look like Figure 10-9.

Summary Points

■ Word processing is the act of composing and manipulating text with the aid of a computer.

■ A word processor is a program (software) or set of programs which enables users to write, edit, format, and print data.

CHAPTER 10: INTRODUCTION TO WORD PROCESSING AND WORDPERFECT

Learning Check

1. The _____ function of a word processor enables the user to enter and edit text.
2. What function needs to be activated to move blocks of text in a document?
3. If the <Ins> key is pressed once, _____ appears in the lower left corner of the screen.
4. If text is deleted by accident, the _____ function allows the text to be recovered.
5. The WordPerfect Speller can not only search for misspelled words, but also can suggest correct spellings. (True or False?)

Answers

1. text editing 2. MOVE; <Ctrl><F4> 3. TYPEOVER 4. CANCEL; <F1> 5. True

---

■ A word processing system includes both the hardware and software that enable users to operate a word processor. There are two general types of word-processing systems: (1) dedicated systems, which can handle only word processing, and (2) multipurpose systems, which are equipped to handle various processing tasks including word processing.

■ Word processors can be used in many different places, such as businesses, schools, and homes. Uses for word processors include writing business letters, school reports, and letters.

■ The two primary functions of a word processor are text editing (which involves entering and manipulating text) and print formatting (which involves communicating to the printer how to format the printed copy).

■ Common writing and editing features of word processors include cursor positioning, word wrap, scrolling, insertion, replacement, deletion, spelling correction, block movement, searching, undo and save.

WordPerfect Exercises

1. Starting up WordPerfect
   a. Assume that the computer is shut off and describe all the necessary steps to start WordPerfect. Start WordPerfect. How are most of WordPerfect's functions activated? What is the significance of the color coding on the function key template?
   b. How do you activate the HELP function to find out about a feature of WordPerfect? Activate the HELP function to find out about the PAGE FORMAT, REPLACE, and SPELL functions (along with any others you have questions about).

2. Creating a New Document
   a. What actions do you have to take to begin working on a new document in WordPerfect? Take steps necessary to begin entering text into a document.
   b. How do you tell where you are in a document? Locate the status line on your screen.

3. Entering a Document
   a. Type the following paragraph:

   A soap opera deal with the plights and problems brought about in the lives of its permanent principal characters by the advent and interference of one group of individuals after another. Thus, a soap opera ia an endlesss sequence of narratives whose only cohesive element is the eternal presence of bedeviled and beleaguered principal characterrs. A narative, or story sequence, may run from eight weeks to several months. The end of one plot is always hooked up with the beginning of the next, but the connection is unimportant and soon forgotten. Almost all the villains in the small town daytime serials are emigres from the cities—gangsters, white-collar criminals, designing women, unnatural mothers, cold wives, and selfish, ruthless, and just plain cursed rich men. They always come up against a shrewdness that ouwits them or destroys them, or a kindness that wins them over to the god way of life.

   E. B. WHITE, ''Soapland''

4. Using the Editing Commands
   a. Correct the following typing mistakes:
   • Add an *s* to *deal* in the first sentence.
   • In the second sentence, change *ia* to *is* and remove the extra *s* from *endless*.
   • In the third sentence, correct the misspelled word *narative*.
   • Using the <Pg Dn> key, move the cursor to the end of the text; change the word *god* to *good* in the last sentence.
   • Correct any other errors that you may find.
   b. Delete the following sentence using the BLOCK function and the <Del> key. Make sure you also delete the two spaces following this sentence: "A narrative, or story sequence, may run from eight weeks to several months."
   c. Move the cursor back to the beginning of the paragraph. Copy the first sentence. Reproduce this sentence at the end of the text, using the MOVE function.
   d. Use the Speller to check the spelling of the paragraph. Make any necessary corrections.

5. Saving and Retrieving a Document
a. Save the work you have completed and quit WordPerfect. What steps are taken to do this? Save the document and exit WordPerfect.
b. You decide to restore the sentence previously removed so you need to reboot WordPerfect and retrieve the file containing the document. Describe the steps required to do this. Retype the sentence at the appropriate place and save the document again.

6. Review
List all of the WordPerfect functions that you used in this chapter.

WordPerfect Problems

To complete the following problems, use the SUBSCRIP file included on the Student File Disk. To start WordPerfect, boot the system with the DOS disk. At the A> prompt, insert the WordPerfect program disk in drive A and type **B:**. When the B> prompt appears on the screen, type **a:wp** and press <Return>. Insert the Student File Disk in drive B.

> *Hard Disk Differences:* You need to copy the SUBSCRIP file included on the Student File Disk onto the hard disk. When you turn on your computer, at the C> prompt, type **a:** and press <Return> to switch to drive A. Insert your Student File Disk with the SUBSCRIP file on it into drive A and type **copy subscrip c:\wp** and press <Return>. Switch back to drive C by typing **c:** and pressing the <Return> key. Type **wp** and press <Return>.

1. Make a copy of the SUBSCRIP file by using the LIST FILES command and selecting the appropriate choice from the menu beneath the directory. Name the copy SUBSCRIP.2. Describe the steps necessary to copy the file.

2. Use the SUBSCRIP.2 file to answer the remaining questions. Retrieve the SUBSCRIP.2 file.

3. The document is an order to a publishing firm. Assume that you are Helen Turoff, the documentalist. You want to use the same format in the SUBSCRIP.2 file to order another magazine. Because you made a copy of the SUBSCRIP file, you can make changes to it using the SUBSCRIP.2 file and save the original format. Change the date of the order to the current date.

4. Using the BLOCK function and the <Del> key, delete the supplier address and replace it with the following new address:

Midwest Publishing
112 Lassalle Street
Chicago, IL 60610

5. Change the name of the magazine to **News Weekly.**

6. Add the following to the beginning of the first sentence: *Starting next month,*. Change the *P* in *Please* from uppercase to lowercase.

7. Add the following name to the list of persons receiving the subscription:

Mr. Mark Steiner
M.I.S. Department

8. Using the Block function and the <Del> key, delete the following sentence: "I am accepting your special offer—$15 for the first subscription, $8 for each additional copy."

9. Use the Speller to check the spelling in your letter. Make any necessary corrections.

10. Save and print your work.

CHAPTER 11

Advanced WordPerfect

Outline

Introduction
Formatting a Document
  Print Format
  Line Format
  Indenting Paragraphs

Learning Check
  Character Enhancements
  Viewing Command Codes
More Advanced Features
  Page Format
  Footnotes and Endnotes

Search
Learning Check
Summary Points
WordPerfect Exercises
WordPerfect Problems

Introduction

Many simple documents such as memos, letters, and short papers can be created with the WordPerfect functions learned in the previous chapter. Resumes, term papers, and other types of documents, however, require the use of WordPerfect's more advanced features. These features can make the creation of a complicated document a relatively easy task. This chapter explains how to use formatting features to enhance the appearance of a document, and how to add footnotes or endnotes to a document.

Formatting A Document

FORMATTING
The function of a word processor which communicates with the printer to tell it how to print the text on paper.

CHARACTER ENHANCEMENTS
A special printing effect such as underlining or boldfacing.

The **formatting** function of a word processor involves a variety of features that communicate with the printer to tell it how to print the text on paper. Some of the more common formatting features include setting margins and tab stops; selecting single- or double-spaced text; and performing **character enhancements,** such as underlining and boldfacing. Figure 11-1 illustrates a typical page format.

As mentioned in Chapter 10, WordPerfect's default settings provide a standard page format; the user does not have to enter any information. These default settings can be changed, however. Most of WordPerfect's formatting functions fall into one of three categories: print format, line format, and page format. Each of these categories is controlled by the function key <F8>. Notice that the word FORMAT is printed vertically on the WordPerfect template next to the <F8> function key. The exercises in this chapter will guide you through the process of formatting a document so that it can be custom-designed.

Print Format

JUSTIFICATION
A feature for making lines of text even at the margins.

The PRINT FORMAT function is activated by pressing <Ctrl> <F8>. Do not confuse this with the PRINT function (<Shift> <F7>). The PRINT function actually prints the document. The PRINT FORMAT function enables the user to select print enhancements, such as right **justification,** that determine how the document will look when it is printed. When the PRINT FORMAT function is activated, the Print Format Menu appears (see Figure 11-2). When an option from the Print Format Menu is selected, a code is placed in the document at the cursor's position. The printing is affected from the cursor's position forward. This means that several different print formats can be selected for the same document.

There are nine options on the Print Format menu. Table 11-1 explains the purpose of each option.

At the bottom of the Page Format Menu is the prompt SELECTION. To select a prompt option, enter its selection number. The cursor moves to that option. Type the appropriate number and press <Return>. When all the selections have been made, press the EXIT function (<F7>) to return to the document.

Figure 11-1
A Typical Page Format

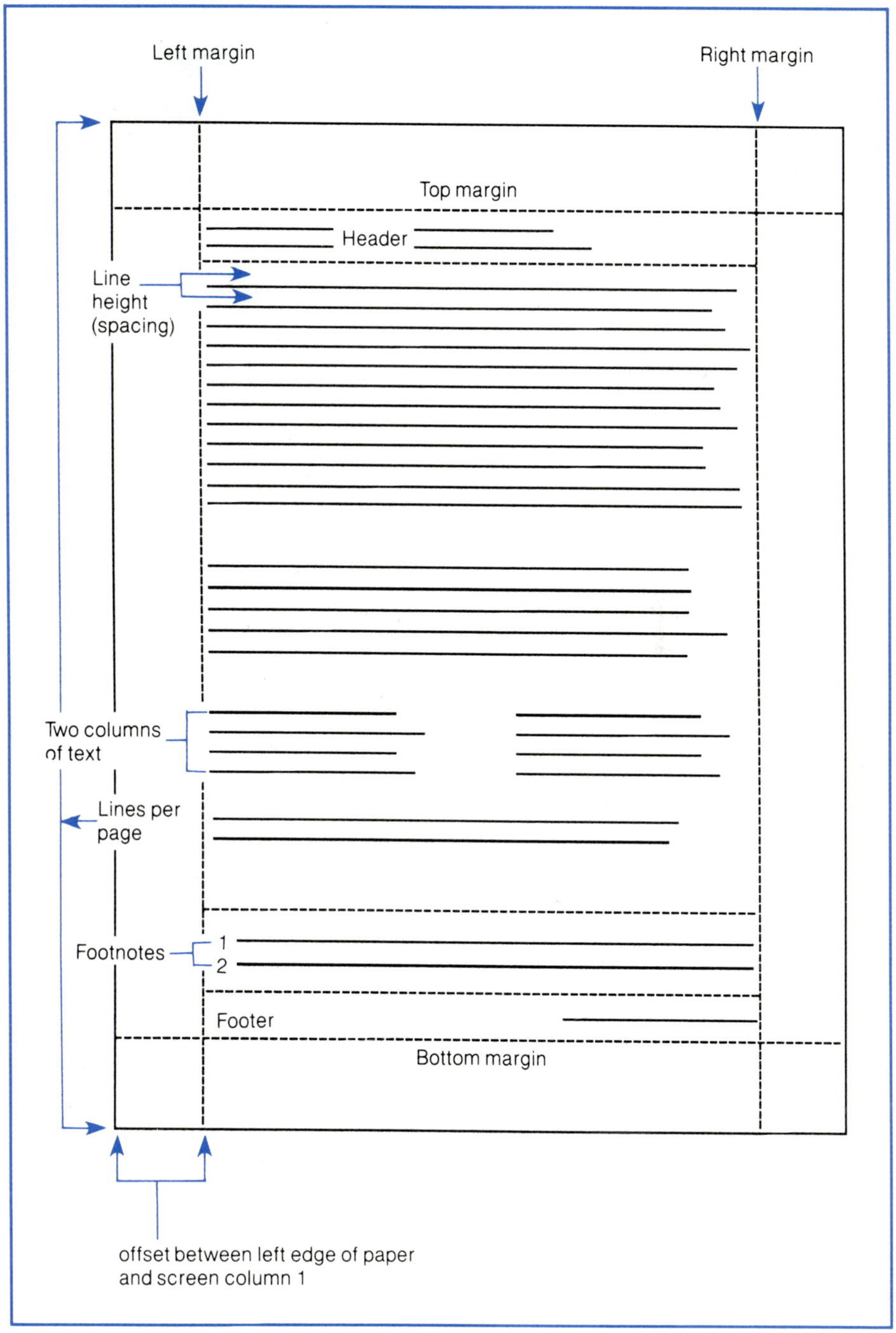
Left margin
Right margin
Top margin
Header
Line height (spacing)
Two columns of text
Lines per page
Footnotes
1
2
Footer
Bottom margin
offset between left edge of paper and screen column 1

Line Format

The LINE FORMAT function, which enables the user to set margins, tabs, spacing, and hyphenation, is activated by pressing <Shift> <F8>. The Line Format menu

Figure 11-2
The Print Format Menu

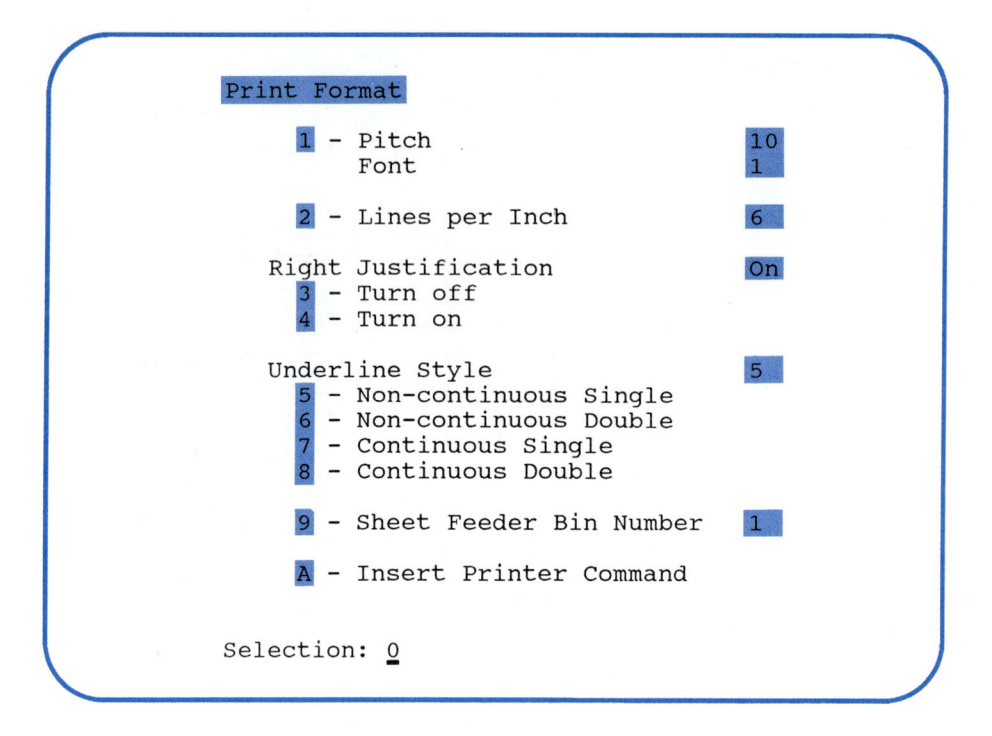

```
Print Format

    1 - Pitch                              10
        Font                                1

    2 - Lines per Inch                      6

        Right Justification                On
    3 - Turn off
    4 - Turn on

        Underline Style                     5
    5 - Non-continuous Single
    6 - Non-continuous Double
    7 - Continuous Single
    8 - Continuous Double

    9 - Sheet Feeder Bin Number             1

    A - Insert Printer Command


        Selection: 0
```

(see Figure 11-3) has six options. Table 11-2 explains the purpose of each option.

To set the right and left margins, press **3** for margins when the Line Format Menu appears. The prompt [MARGIN SET] 10 74 TO LEFT = appears in the lower left corner of the screen. A standard size piece of paper is 8-½ inches wide. If the document is to be printed at 10 characters per inch, there will be 85 columns across the page, assuming that the first column is 0. If the document is to be printed at 12 characters per inch, there will be 101 columns across the page. The margin setting designates the column number of the left and right margin. For example, if a document is printed at 10 characters per inch, setting the margins at 10 and 74 would provide 1-inch margins. If the pitch is set at 12 characters per inch, setting the margins at 18 and 83 would provide 1-½ inch margins.

To set the left margin, enter the column number of the left margin at the prompt and press <Return>. The prompt RIGHT = appears. Enter the column number of the right margin and press <Return>. The editing window returns to the screen.

To select tab stops, press **1** when the Line Format Menu appears. Two lines representing the width of the document appear. Along the lines are *T*'s which indicate the current tab settings.

Figure 11-3
The Line Format Menu

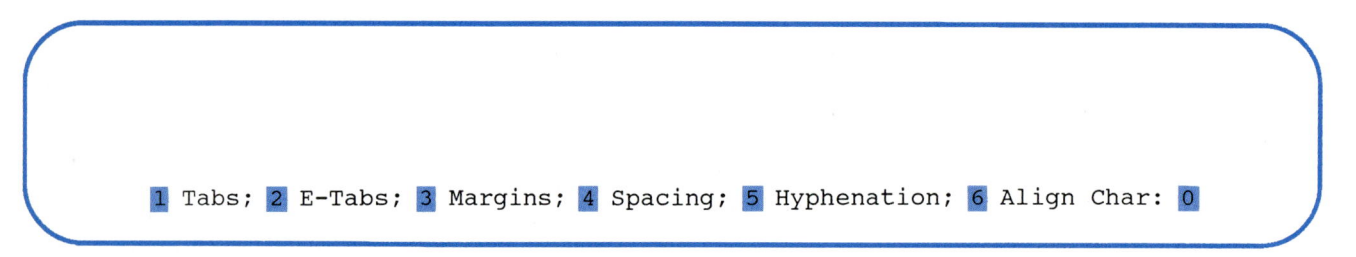

```
1 Tabs;  2 E-Tabs;  3 Margins;  4 Spacing;  5 Hyphenation;  6 Align Char: 0
```

**Table 11-1
Options from the Print Format
Menu**

Selection Number	Option	Description
1	Pitch	The Pitch sets how many characters there are per inch. Ten characters per inch, which is the default setting, and 12 characters per inch are the pitches most commonly used.
1	Font	The Font sets the print style. To use this option, you must know which fonts your printer is capable of printing.
2	Lines per Inch	Lines per Inch sets the number of vertical lines printed in an inch. WordPerfect prints either six or eight lines per inch. The default setting is six.
Right Justification:		
3	Off	The Right Justification option can either be turned on or off. If it is set to ON the right margin is justified which means that the lines of text are even at the right margin. If it is set to OFF the lines at the right margin are ragged or uneven. The default setting is ON.
4	On	
Underline Style:		
5	Non-continuous-Single	Non-continuous underlining, which does not underline the spaces between words; one-line underlining.
6	Non-continuous-Double	Non-continuous underlining, which does not underline the spaces between words; two-line underlining.
7	Continuous-Single	Continuous underlining does underline between spaces; one-line underlining.
8	Continuous-Double	Continuous underlining; underlines between spaces; two-line underlining.
		The default setting is for non-continuous, single underlining.
9	Sheet Feeder Bin Number	Applies only to printers with sheet feeders. Selects the bin from which the paper will come when the document is printed.

There are several ways to set or delete tabs. First, the column number can be entered by typing the number of the column where the tab is to be set and pressing <Return>. Another method is to place the cursor on the line at the bottom of the screen where the tab is to be set and type **t.** Finally, multiple tab stops can be set by typing the column number where the first tab is to be set, followed by a comma and the interval at which the tabs are to occur. For example, if tabs are to be set every 15 spaces starting at the left margin, **0,15** would be entered.

To delete all set tabs, position the cursor on or before the first tab setting. Activate the DELETE TO EOL (end of line) function by pressing <Ctrl> <End>. All the tabs from the cursor forward are deleted. To delete individual tabs, move the cursor to the *T* representing the tab stop to be deleted and press <Del>.

When you have finished setting the tabs, press <F7> for EXIT to exit the Tab menu. To return to the text without saving any of the tabs that were set, press

Table 11-2
Options from the Line Format Menu

Selection Number	Option	Description
1	Tabs	Enables the user to set tab stops. The default setting is one tab stop every five spaces.
2	E-Tabs (extended tabs)	Enables the user to set tab stops between the positions 160 and 250.
3	Margins	Enables the user to set the left and right margins. The default setting is right margin = 10; left margin = 74.
4	Spacing	Enables the user to set the line spacing. A setting of 1.5 = one-and-a-half lines of spacing; 1 = single spacing, 2 = double spacing, 3 = triple spacing; and so on. The default setting is 1 for single spacing.
5	Hyphenation	Enables the user to set the hyphenation feature either on or off. If the feature is off, none of the words are hyphenated. If the feature is on, the user can select where words should be hyphenated. The default setting is off.
6	Alignment	Enables the user to select the symbol around which characters are aligned when the TAB ALIGN function is used. The default setting is a decimal point.

<F1> for CANCEL. Tabs can be set as many times as necessary in a document. Only the text entered after tabs have been set will be affected.

To select the line spacing, press **4** when the Line Format Menu appears. The prompt [SPACING SET] 1 appears in the lower left corner of the screen. Enter the desired spacing and press <Return>. The editing window returns to the screen.

Indenting Paragraphs

In addition to using tab stops, WordPerfect has two INDENT functions that enable the user to easily indent an entire paragraph from either the left margin only or both the left and right margins. The INDENT function that indents a paragraph from both the right and left margin is activated by pressing <Shift> <F4>. The tab stops also are used for indent stops, so the cursor moves to the next tab stop when the INDENT function is activated. Every line is then indented an equal distance from the left and right margins. Pressing the <Return> key cancels the INDENT function and the lines that follow return to the normal margin.

To indent a paragraph from the left margin only, press <F4>. The paragraph indents one tab stop each time <F4> for INDENT is pressed. Pressing <Return> cancels the function and the lines that follow return to the normal margin.

A hanging paragraph, in which the first line begins at the left margin while the remaining lines are indented, can also be created using the INDENT function. To create a hanging indent, press <F4> for INDENT. Then press <Shift> <Tab> to move the first line of the paragraph one tab stop to the left. Type the paragraph. The first line of the paragraph starts at the left margin while the remaining text is indented. To end a hanging paragraph, press the <Return> key.

CHAPTER 11: ADVANCED WORDPERFECT

Learning Check

1. For the most part, WordPerfect formatting changes are controlled by ____.
2. To change margins, activate the ____ function.
3. How do you turn off the right justification?
4. What is a hanging paragraph indention?
5. Examples of character enhancements are ____ and ____.

Answers

1. <F8> 2. LINE FORMAT 3. Activate the PRINT FORMAT function and press 3 when the menu appears. 4. It indents every line of a paragraph except the first one. 5. underlining; boldfacing

YOUR TURN

For this exercise, you are going to practice using the PRINT FORMAT, LINE FORMAT, and INDENT functions by creating an outline. Figure 11-4 depicts the final document. Start WordPerfect on the computer. There should be a blank editing window on the screen.

First, turn the right justification off.

Press <Ctrl> <F8> for PRINT FORMAT
Type **3** for RIGHT JUSTIFICATION OFF

The word OFF now appears next to RIGHT JUSTIFICATION on the Print Format Menu. You are now going to exit the Print Format Menu.

Press <F7> for EXIT

Next, change the margin settings.

Press <Shift> <F8> for LINE FORMAT

The Line Format menu appears.

Type **3** for MARGINS

The prompt [MARGIN SET] 10 74 TO LEFT = appears. Set the margins at 5 and 79.

Type **5**
Press <Return>
Type **79**
Press <Return>

> The Placement Service Office is pleased you are attending one of our job
> placement seminars. This is the third year we have sponsored these
> seminars and they have proven to be quite successful. The seminar for
> Accounting majors is Saturday, February 22 from 8:00 a.m. to 5:00 p.m. The
> following introduces you to the people leading the seminar and outlines the
> day's schedule.
>
>   Dr. Kate Clifford, Head of Placement Service. Dr. Clifford has
> been the head of the Placement Service Office at Ohio State for
> over fifteen years. Before coming to Ohio State, she worked
> for the executive recruiting firm, Cyphers and Porter, Inc.
>
>   Mr. Keith Goldman, Audit Manager, Thales Electronic, Inc. As
> Audit Manager, Mr. Goldman is responsible for hiring close to
> twenty auditors a year. Mr. Goldman's published articles
> include, "Marketing Your Accounting Degree," and "The Hiring
> Trend in Accounting."
>
> I.   8:00-8:30   Registration
>
> II.   8:30-10:00 Locating Employers
>
>   A. What Are the Job Opportunities for Accounting Majors and Who is Doing the Hiring?
>   B. Informational Interviews: What They Are and How to Get One
>   C. Word of Mouth: How Talking to Everyone Can Get You a Job
>
> III. 10:00-12:00 Cover Letters and Resumes
>
>   A. The Content of a Resume: What Should and Should Not Be Included
>   B. The Form of a Resume: What a Resume Should and Should Not Look Like
>   C. How to Write a Cover Letter
>
> IV. 12:00-1:00 Break for Lunch
>
> V.   1:00-2:00   Interviewing Skills
>
>   A. First Impressions: How to Make a Positive Impression in the First Five Minutes of an Interview
>   B. Being Prepared for Any Interview Question
>   C. Knowing What Questions You Should Ask
>
> VI. Utilizing the Placement Service Office
>
>   A. Using the Career Library
>   B. Interviews Through the Placement Office

Figure 11-4
Using Formatting Functions to Create an Outline

The editing window appears. Now you are going to reset the tab stops.

    Press <Shift> <F8> for LINE FORMAT
    Type **1** for TABS

The Tab Menu appears (see Figure 11-5).

    Press <Ctrl> <End> to delete all the tab stops

CHAPTER 11: ADVANCED WORDPERFECT

```
Delete EOL (clear tabs); Enter number (set tab); Del (clear tab)
Press EXIT when done.
         10        20        30        40        50        60        70
0123456789012345678901234567890123456789012345678901234567890123456789
T....T....T....T....T....T....T....T....T....T....T....T....T....T....T...
80        90       100       110       120       130       140       150
012345678901234567890123456789012345678901234567890123456789012345678
T....T....T....T....T....T....T....T....T....T....T....T....T....T....T...
```

Figure 11-5
The Tab Menu

The left margin is set in column 5. You want the first tab stop to be six spaces in from the left margin and the second tab stop to be four spaces from the first tab stop.

>Type **11**
>Press <Return>
>Type **15**
>Press <Return>

A **T** appears on the line at column 11 and column 15.

>Press <F7> for EXIT

The editing window appears. You are ready to start entering the outline. Type the following:

>The Placement Service Office is pleased you are attending one of our job placement seminars. This is the third year we have sponsored these seminars and they have proven to be quite successful. The seminar for Accounting majors is Saturday, February 22 from 8:00 a.m. to 5:00 p.m. The following introduces you to the people leading the seminar and outlines the day's schedule.

>Press <Return> twice.

The following two paragraphs are to be indented from both the left and right margins.

>Press <Shift> <F4> for INDENT

Type the following:

>Dr. Kate Clifford, Head of Placement Service. Dr. Clifford has been the head of the Placement Service

> Office at Ohio State for over fifteen years. Before coming to Ohio State, she worked for the executive recruiting firm, Cyphers and Porter, Inc.

Press <Return> twice.

Pressing <Return> cancels the INDENT function, so you need to reactivate the INDENT function before entering the second paragraph.

Press <Shift> <F4> for INDENT

Type the following:

> Mr. Keith Goldman, Audit Manager, Thales Electronic, Inc. As Audit Manager, Mr. Goldman is responsible for hiring close to twenty auditors a year. Mr. Goldman's published articles include, ''Marketing Your Accounting Degree,'' and ''The Hiring Trend in Accounting.''

Press <Return> twice.

You are now going to enter the outline.

Type I.
Press the <Tab> key
Type 8:00-8:30 Registration
Press <Return> twice
Type II.
Press the <Tab> key
Type 8:30-10:00 Locating Employers
Press <Return> twice

Now you want to use the INDENT function that indents lines from the left margin only.

Press <F4> for INDENT
Type A.
Press <F4> for INDENT

Type the following:

> What Are the Job Opportunities for Accounting Majors and Who is Doing the Hiring?

Notice that when the line wraps around, it lines up under the indentation.

Press <Return>
Press <F4> for INDENT

Type B.
Press <F4> for INDENT

Type the following:

Informational Interviews: What They Are and How to Get One

Press <Return>
Press <F4> for INDENT
Type C.
Press <F4> for INDENT

Type the following:

Word of Mouth: How Talking to Everybody Can Get You a Job

Press <Return> twice.

You should now be familiar with how the INDENT function works. Type the rest of the outline as follows:

    III. 10:00-12:00 Cover Letters and Resumes

          A. The Content of a Resume: What Should and Should Not Be Included
          B. The Form of a Resume: What a Resume Should and Should Not Look Like
          C. How to Write a Cover Letter

    IV.   12:00-1:00 Break for Lunch

    V.   1:00-2:00 Interviewing Skills

          A. First Impressions: How to Make a Positive Impression in the First Five Minutes of an Interview
          B. Being Prepared for Any Interview Question
          C. Knowing What Questions You Should Ask

    VI.   2:00-5:00 Utilizing the Placement Service Office

          A. Using the Career Library
          B. Interviews Through the Placement Office

Use the Speller to check for spelling errors. Save the document. Name it PLASER.LET for Placement Service letter. Use the PRINT function (<Shift>

<F7>) to print the document. Your printed document should look like Figure 11-4. Exit from the document.

Character Enhancements

A character enhancement is any special printing effect. Character enhancements such as underlining and boldfacing are quite useful when creating reports, resumes and other documents. Whether you can use all the print enhancements included in WordPerfect depends on your printer. Your instructor can tell you which print enhancements your printer is capable of producing.

To activate the BOLD function, press <F6>. Any text entered after activating the BOLD function appears in boldface when printed. To end the BOLD function, press <F6> again.

To bold text that has already been entered, use the BLOCK function to define the text to be bolded. While the words BLOCK ON are still flashing in the lower left corner of the screen, activate the BOLD function by pressing <F6>. The text that was marked with the BLOCK function will be in boldface when printed. Activating the BOLD function turns the BLOCK function off. The words BLOCK ON stop flashing in the lower left corner of the screen.

To activate the UNDERLINE function, press <F8>. Any text entered after activating the UNDERLINE function is underlined when printed. To end the UNDERLINE function, press <F8> again.

To underline text that has already been entered, use the BLOCK function to define the text to be underlined. While the words BLOCK ON are still flashing in the lower left corner of the screen, activate the UNDERLINE function by pressing <F8>. The text that was marked with the BLOCK function will be underlined when printed. Activating the UNDERLINE function turns the BLOCK function off. The words BLOCK ON stop flashing in the lower left corner of the screen.

Text can be centered by pressing <Shift> <F6> for the CENTER function. Any text entered after pressing <Shift> <F6> is automatically centered. Pressing <Return> cancels the CENTER function and the text that follows returns to the margin settings.

Viewing Command Codes

WordPerfect is a what-you-see-is-what-you-get word processor. That is, what you see on the screen resembles as closely as possible how the text will look when printed on a piece of paper. However, when most of WordPerfect's functions are activated, command codes are inserted into the text. Because codes are not printed, they do not appear on the screen unless the user wants to view them. Revealing the command codes enables a user to easily delete commands.

Pressing <Alt> <F3> activates the REVEAL CODES function. When the REVEAL CODES function is activated, the screen is divided in two by the Tab Ruler. The same text is displayed above and below the Tab Ruler, but the text below the Tab Ruler also displays all the codes. Seven lines of text can be displayed

CHAPTER 11: ADVANCED WORDPERFECT   325

in both windows: the line where the cursor is currently positioned and three lines above and below it. The cursor on the bottom window is displayed as a blinking caret ([^]). The cursor can be moved using the arrow keys. Either the <Backspace> key or the <Del> key can be used to delete command codes. Pressing any other key cancels the REVEAL CODES function and the editing window returns to normal.

YOUR TURN

For this exercise, you are going to create a resume. Figure 11-6 illustrates the final, corrected document. Start with a blank editing window on your screen.

Before you start typing the resume, some formatting changes need to be made. First, the right margin is not justified.

> Press <Ctrl> <F8> for PRINT FORMAT

The Print Format Menu appears.

> Type **3** for RIGHT JUSTIFICATION; TURN OFF

The word OFF now appears next to the words RIGHT JUSTIFICATION.

> Press <F7> for EXIT

The blank editing window returns to the screen. Next you need to set the tab stops.

> Press <Shift> <F8> for LINE FORMAT
> Press **1** for TABS
> Press <Ctrl> <End> to clear all the current tabs
> Type **20**
> Press <Return>
> Type **45**
> Press <Return>

You now have tabs set at position 20 and position 45.

> Press <F7> for EXIT

Now you are ready to start typing the resume. The name Kim Landon is in all capital letters and boldface.

> Press <F6> for BOLD
> Type **KIM LANDON**
> Press <F6> for BOLD
> Press <Return>
> Press the <Tab> key twice

Figure 11-6 Resume Using Several Print Enhancements

<u>KIM LANDON</u>
                                    322 Spring Road
                                    Columbus, Ohio 44322
                                    (612) 555-1214

                        Objective

To develop skills in managerial accounting with a major
corporation and to become a controller.

                        Education

B.S. Accounting, Ohio State University, 1987
Minor: Economics with emphasis in corporate finance.
Significant courses include:

<u>Accounting</u>   <u>Business</u>
Financial Accounting   Topics in Corporate Management
Cost Accounting   Industrial Economics
Advanced Accounting   Management Information Systems
Advanced Federal Tax Law   Business Communications

                        Experience

Summers   Intern, Pricewaterhouse, Columbus, Ohio, 1986
           Worked on various audit assignments, including stock
           inventory at Mills International.

College   Assistant, University Financial Aid Office, 1986
           Reviewed applications for financial aid; verified their
           conformity with tax returns and other supportive
           documents.

           Orientation Leader, University Admissions Office, 1985
           Met with prospective students and their parents;
           conducted tours of campus; wrote reports for each
           orientation meeting.

                    Computer Experience

Proficient in running Lotus 1-2-3 and WordPerfect on an IBM PC.

                        Activities

Alpha Beta Psi, 1984-1986
Student Senator, Served on budget committee, 1985-1986

                        References

Credentials and references available upon request.

Type 322 Spring Road
Press <Return>
Press the <Tab> key twice
Type Columbus, Ohio 44322
Press <Return>
Press the <Tab> key twice
Type (612) 555-1214
Press <Return> twice

All the titles for the major divisions in the resume are boldfaced and centered.

Press <Shift> <F6> for CENTER
Press <F6> for BOLD
Type **Objective**
Press <F6> for BOLD
Press <Return> twice
Type the following:

To develop skills in managerial accounting with a major corporation and to become a controller.

Press <Return> twice
Press <Shift> <F6> for CENTER
Press <F6> for BOLD
Type **Education**
Press <F6> for BOLD
Press <Return> twice
Type the following:

B.S. Accounting, Ohio State University, 1987

Press <Return>

Minor: Economics with emphasis in corporate finance.

Press <Return>

Significant courses include:

Press <Return> twice

The next subtitles are to be underlined.

Press <F8> for UNDERLINE
Type Accounting
Press the <Tab> key
Type Business
Press <F8> for UNDERLINE

Press <Return>
Type Financial Accounting
Press the <Tab> key
Type Topics in Corporate Management
Press <Return>
Type Cost Accounting
Press the <Tab> key
Type Industrial Economics
Press <Return>
Type Advanced Accounting
Press the <Tab> key
Type Management Information Systems
Press <Return>
Type Advanced Federal Tax Law
Press the <Tab> key
Type Business Communications
Press <Return> twice
Press <Shift> <F6> for CENTER
Press <F6> for Bold
Type **Experience**
Press <F6> for BOLD
Press <Return> twice

The next two subheadings also are going to be underlined.

Press <F8> for UNDERLINE
Type Summers
Press <F8> for UNDERLINE

Indent the next paragraph.

Press <F4> for INDENT
Type Intern, Price Waterhouse, Columbus, Ohio, 1986
Press <Return>
Press <F4> for INDENT
Type the following:

Worked on various audit assignments, including stock inventory at Mills International.

Press <Return> twice
Press <F8> for UNDERLINE
Type College
Press <F8> for UNDERLINE
Press <F4> for INDENT
Type Assistant, University Financial Aid Office, 1986
Press <Return>
Press <F4> for INDENT

Type the following:

> Reviewed applications for financial aid; verified their conformity with tax returns and other supportive documents.

> Press <Return> twice
> Press <F4> for INDENT
> Type Orientation Leader, University Admissions Office, 1985
> Press <Return>
> Press <F4> for INDENT

> Type the following:

> Met with prospective students and their parents; conducted tours of campus; wrote reports for each orientation meeting.

> Press <Return> twice

Now type the remainder of resume using the CENTER and BOLD functions as necessary.

Computer Experience

Proficient in running Lotus 1-2-3 and WordPerfect on an IBM PC.

Activities

Alpha Beta Psi, 1984-1986
Student Senator, Served on budget committee, 1985-1986.

References

Credentials and references available upon request.

Next, save the document.

> Press <F10> for SAVE
> Type Kim.Res (For Kim's resume)
> Press <Return>

You have decided you want to underline the name at the top. To do this, mark the name as a block of text and activate the underline function. Move the cursor under the *K* in *Kim* (Page 1, Line 1, Position 10).

> Press <Alt> <F4> for BLOCK
> Press <→> 10 times so that the entire name is highlighted
> Press <F8> for UNDERLINE

330   PART TWO: APPLICATIONS SOFTWARE

```
                          Experience

      Summers    Intern, Pricewaterhouse, Columbus, Ohio, 1986
                 Worked on various assignments, including stock
                 inventory at Mills International.

                                        Doc 1   Pg 1   Ln 25      Pos 10
   [               ▲                             ▲                      ]
[HRt]
[C][B]Experience[b][c][HRt]
[HRt]
[^][U]Summers[u][->Indent]Intern, Pricewaterhouse, Columbus, Ohio, 1986[HRt]
[->Indent]Worked on various assignments, including stock[SRt]
inventory at Mills International.[HRt]
[HRt]
```

Figure 11-7
Revealing Command Codes

The name will now be underlined when printed. Now you have decided to delete the underlining from the subtitles *Summers* and *College*. Move the cursor so that it is under the *S* in *Summers*.

    Press <Alt> <F3> for REVEAL CODES

The screen is divided in two (see Figure 11-7). Below the Tab Ruler line is the text with all the command codes revealed. Notice the word *Summers* has a [U] symbol in front of it and a [u] symbol after it. These are the command codes for underlining. To delete the underlining, delete the command code. The blinking cursor ([^]) is next to the [U] symbol.

    Press <Del>

Notice both the [U] and the [u] are deleted. Now you need to delete the underlining from *College*.

    Press the <↓> key four times

The [^] cursor is next to the [U] in front of *College*.

    Press <Del>

Both the [U] in front of *College* and the [u] after *College* are deleted.

    Press <Return>

The editing window returns to normal. Look over the resume carefully. The formatting should match Figure 11-6. Use the SPELL function to check for spelling errors. When you are satisfied with the resume, print it.
    Before exiting from this document, however, make sure you save it again because changes were made to the resume after it was saved the first time.

More Advanced Features

WordPerfect includes sophisticated features that are not mandatory for all documents. If mastered, however, they can be convenient time-savers. These features, which are covered in the remainder of this chapter, can help you create professional-looking documents with little effort.

Page Format

The PAGE FORMAT function is activated by pressing <Alt> <F8>. After activating the PAGE FORMAT function, the Page Format Menu appears (see Figure 11-8). This menu has 10 options.

Options on the Page Format Menu that help users create professional-looking documents include **headers** or **footers.** A header is a piece of text that is printed at the top of a page, such as a title that appears on each page (see Figure 11-9). A footer is a piece of text that is printed at the bottom of a page, such as a page number. Headers and footers can take up as many lines as needed. They can be printed on odd-numbered pages only, even-numbered pages only, or on both odd and even pages.

The Page Format Menu also offers the option of eliminating "widows" and "orphans" from documents. In publishing, a widow is a single line that has been separated from a paragraph and appears by itself at the top of a page. An orphan

HEADER
A piece of text that is stored separately from the main text and printed at the bottom of each page.

FOOTER
A piece of text that is stored separately from the main text and printed at the bottom of each page.

Figure 11-8
The Page Format Menu

```
Page Format

    1 - Page Number Position

    2 - New Page Number

    3 - Center Page Top to Bottom

    4 - Page Length

    5 - Top Margin

    6 - Headers or Footers

    7 - Page Number Column Positions

    8 - Suppress for Current page only

    9 - Conditional End of Page

    A - Widow/Orphan

Selection: 0
```

Figure 11-9 Headers and Footnotes

Job Placement Seminar
February 21

2

find out what he or she wants to know, as the newest college graduate just coming into the job market.[1]

This in not the impression most people looking for jobs have of those who have the power to hire or not hire them.

Bolles explains why interviewers may be so uncomfortable with the process:

The odds are very great that the executive who does the interviewing was hired because of what they could contribute to the company, and not because they were such a great interviewer. In fact, their gifts in this arena may be rather miserable.[2]

David Roman agrees with Bolles. Roman states:

As interviewers, ... managers may be out of their element. They're in the business of running a ... department, not of interviewing job applicants.[3]

Since the person running the interview is probably just as uncomfortable as you are, there are several things you as a person being interviewed can do to take advantage of the situation and turn the interview into a pleasant and rewarding experience.

---

[1] Bolles, Richard. *What Color Is Your Parachute?*, Berkeley: 10 Speed Press, 1983, p. 181.

[2] Ibid.

[3] Roman, David. "Why MIS/DP Job Interviews Go Wrong," in *Computer Decisions*, November 19, 1985, p. 66.

is a single line separated from a paragraph that appears at the bottom of a page. All the options in the Page Format Menu are explained in Table 11-3.

Footnotes and Endnotes

One of the most tedious tasks involved in writing documents such as term papers is typing the footnotes. WordPerfect simplifies this task tremendously.

With WordPerfect, both footnotes and endnotes can be included in the same document. Footnotes and endnotes provide information about the cited work. The only difference is footnotes appear at the bottom of the page and endnotes are compiled at the end of the document. Footnotes and endnotes created with WordPerfect are automatically numbered. All the user has to do is type the text of the note.

To create a footnote or endnote, the cursor must be placed at the space where the note number is to appear. Activate the FOOTNOTE function by pressing <Ctrl> <F7>. The Footnote Menu appears. Type **1** for CREATE to create a footnote; type **3** for CREATE ENDNOTE to create an endnote. A special editing screen appears. The number of the note is in the upper left corner of the screen. Enter the note and press <F7> for EXIT. The document returns to the editing window.

To edit a note that has already been entered, activate the FOOTNOTE function (<Ctrl> <F7>). When the footnote Menu appears, type **2** for EDIT to edit a footnote or type **6** for EDIT ENDNOTE to edit an endnote. Next, the number of the footnote or endnote has to be entered. The note is retrieved and changes can then be made to it. Once the changes are made, press <F7> for EXIT. The document returns to the screen.

To delete a footnote or endnote, move the cursor to the note number in the document. Press <Backspace> or <Del> to delete the note number. The prompt DELETE [NOTE]? (Y/N) appears. Type **Y** and the note is deleted.

Search

SEARCH AND FIND
A routine that searches for a specified string of characters, and places the cursor at that location.

If you have ever written a lengthy document and discovered that a key term has been used incorrectly throughout the text you know how difficult and time-consuming it is to correct the mistake. This problem has been eliminated by incorporating a **search and find** routine in WordPerfect and most other word processors. The user tells the program the specific character string to search for, and it finds and positions the cursor at the first occurrence of the string.

WordPerfect can search for text in a forward or reverse direction. The SEARCH function activated by pressing <F2> searches for the specified text forward from the cursor's position. The SEARCH function activated by pressing the <Shift> <F2> keys searches for the specified text backward from the cursor's position. Once the SEARCH function is activated, the SRCH prompt appears at the bottom of the screen with an arrow that indicates the direction of the search. Enter the character string to be searched for and press either <F2> or <Shift> <F2> again. The cursor stops after the first match is found.

Table 11-3
Options from the Page Format Menu

Selection Number	Option	Description
1	Page Number Position	Enables the user to select where on the page the page number is placed. The default setting is for no page numbers to appear.
2	New Page Number	Enables the user to renumber pages; the user can choose either Roman- or Arabic-style numbers
3	Center Page Top to Bottom	Centers a page from top to bottom when it is printed.
4	Page Length	Enables the user to change the page length and the number of lines that are to be printed on the page.
5	Top Margin	Enables the user to set the top margin. The top margin is set in half lines. The default setting is 12, which provides a one-inch margin.
6	Headers or Footers	Enables the same text to be printed at the top or bottom of each page.
7	Page Number Column Positions	Enables the user to define the column positions for the Page Number Position option. The default settings are: 10 for page numbers appearing on the left side of the page; 42 for page numbers appearing on the center of the page; 74 for page numbers appearing on the left side of the page.
8	Suppress for Current Page Only	Enables the user to turn off any combination of page formats for the current page only.
9	Conditional End of Page	Enables the user to keep a block of text together at all times.
A	Widow/Orphan	Enables the user to keep at least two lines of a paragraph together at the top or the bottom of a page.

YOUR TURN In this exercise, you are going to type a paper that includes footnotes. A blank editing window should be on the screen.

Before you start typing the paper, some formatting changes have to be made. First, you want each page of the paper to have a header.

Press <Alt> <F8> for PAGE FORMAT

The Page Format Menu appears.

    Type **6** for HEADERS OR FOOTERS

The Header/Footer Specification screen appears (see Figure 11-10).

    Type **1** for HEADER A

The cursor moves to the OCCURRENCE column. You want the header to occur on every page.

    Type **1** for EVERY PAGE

A special screen appears in which the header is entered. Type the following header:

    Job Placement Seminar (Press <Return>)
    February 21
    Press <F7> for EXIT

The Page Format Menu returns to the screen. Now you want to place the page number position. You want the page numbers to appear at the top right corner of every page.

    Type **1** for PAGE NUMBER POSITION
    Type **3** for TOP RIGHT OF EVERY PAGE

The Page Format Menu returns to the screen. Finally, you want to eliminate any widows or orphans.

    Press **A** for WIDOWS/ORPHANS
    Type **Y** in response to the Widow/Orphan Protect prompt
    Press <F7> for EXIT

The blank editing window reappears. The right margin in this paper is not to be justified.

    Press <Ctrl> <F8> for PRINT FORMAT
    Type **3** for RIGHT JUSTIFICATION; TURN OFF
    Press <F7> for EXIT

This term paper uses both double- and single-spacing. The body of the paper is double-spaced and the quotations are single-spaced. As you type the paper, you will switch back and forth between double- and single-spacing. Because the default setting is single-spacing, you need to switch to double-spacing to begin typing the body of the paper.

Figure 11-10
The Header/Footer Specification Screen

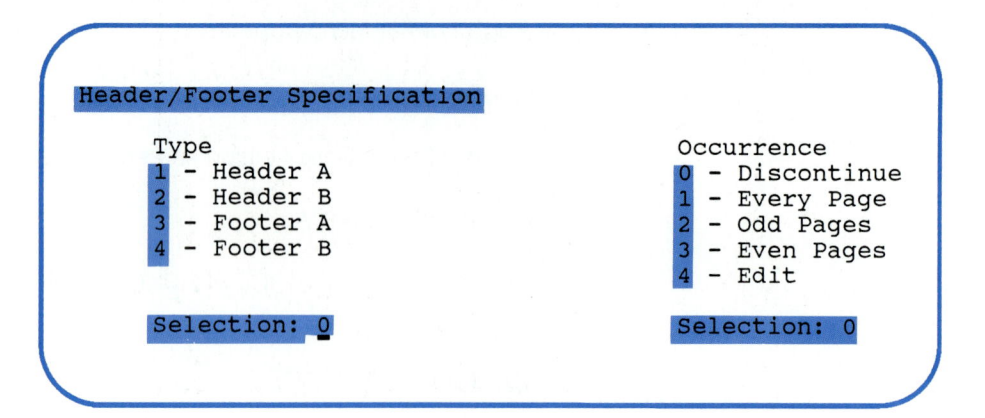

```
Header/Footer Specification

    Type                           Occurrence
    1 - Header A                   0 - Discontinue
    2 - Header B                   1 - Every Page
    3 - Footer A                   2 - Odd Pages
    4 - Footer B                   3 - Even Pages
                                   4 - Edit

    Selection: 0                   Selection: 0
```

Press <Shift> <F8> for LINE FORMAT
Type **4** for SPACING
Type **2**
Press <Return>

The editing window returns to the screen. Now you are ready to begin typing the paper. First, type the title.

Press <Shift> <F6> for CENTER
Press <F8> for UNDERLINE
Type `Interviews: Wretched or Rewarding?`
Press <F8> for UNDERLINE
Press <Return>
Type the following:

   For many people, interviews have a peculiar Dr. Jekyll and Mr. Hyde quality to them. While these people are job hunting, they anxiously await the phone call or letter issuing the coveted invitation for an interview. After all their hard work of scouting out the job market, finding openings in their field, writing resumes and cover letters, an interview seems like a well-deserved reward. But, once attained, the golden interview turns into a nerve-shattering monster. Sleepless nights are spent worrying over such questions as, what will I wear, what will I say, what if they ask a question I can't answer? All of a sudden, the job hunter feels like the hunted as visions of the mighty interviewer, whose sole purpose is to expose all the inadequacies of the interviewee, become inescapable.
   Interviews do not have to turn into such horrible monsters. Exposing some of the myths about interviews helps to alleviate the fear we all attach to the interviewing process.

> Often, the interviewee has a totally inaccurate image
> of the interviewer. Many prospective employees assume
> the interviewer is highly skilled in conducting
> interviews. This is not necessarily the case as
> Richard Boles points out in the following quotation:

Now you are ready to type the first quotation. The cursor should still be in the space following the colon. Press the <Return> key once to create space between the text and the quotation. The quotation should be single spaced, so you need to activate the LINE FORMAT function.

Press <Shift> <F8> for LINE FORMAT
Type **4** for SPACING
Type **1**
Press <Return>

The quotation needs to be indented five spaces from each margin.

Press <Shift> <F4> for INDENT

Type the quotation as follows:

> . . . the interviewer may be as uncomfortable with
> this process as you are, and as ill-equipped to know
> how to find out what he or she wants to know, as the
> newest college graduate just coming into the job
> market.

Now you need to insert the first footnote.

Press <Ctrl> <F7> for FOOTNOTE

The Note Menu appears at the bottom of the screen.

Type **1** for CREATE

The special screen for entering the footnote text appears. Notice the *1* for footnote 1 has already been inserted. Type the footnote as follows, underlining the title of the book.

> Boles, Richard, What Color Is Your Parachute?,
> Berkeley: 10 Speed Press, 1983, p. 181.

After entering the footnote text, activate the EXIT function. The *1* for footnote 1 is automatically placed in the text (see Figure 11-11). The series of dashes that go across the screen indicates a page break. Notice that there is one line from the quotation by itself at the top of the second page. This is a widow. Change the spacing back to double space. Press <Return> to create space between the quotation and the next line of text in the

```
         inadequacies of the interviewee, become inescapable.

             Interviews do not have to turn into such horrible monsters.
         Exposing some of the myths about interviews helps to alleviate
         the fear we all attach to the interviewing process.
             Often, the interviewee has a totally inaccurate image of the
         interviewer.  Many prospective employees assume the interviewer
         is highly skilled in conducting interviews.  This is not
         necessarily the case as Richard Boles points out in the following
         quotation:
             . . . the interviewer may be as uncomfortable with this
             process as you are, and as ill-equipped to know how to
             find out what he or she wants to know, as the newest
         ------------------------------------------------------------------------
             college graduate just coming into the job market.1_
                                               Doc 1  Pg 2  Ln 1    Pos 65
```

Figure 11-11
Adding Footnotes to a Document

document. After pressing <Return> notice that WordPerfect automatically moves a second line from the quotation onto the second page to eliminate the widow.

Type the following:

```
This is not the impression most people looking for
jobs have of those who have the power to hire or not
hire them.
   Boles explains why interviewers may be so
uncomfortable with the process:
```

Press <Return> to create a space before the next quotation. Change the spacing to single and activate the INDENT function that indents the paragraph from both margins. Enter the quotation as follows:

```
The odds are very great that the executive who does
the interviewing was hired because of what they could
contribute to the company, and not because they were
such a great interviewer. In fact, their gifts in this
arena may be rather miserable.
```

Activate the FOOTNOTE function and type the following footnote.

```
Ibid.
```

Activate the EXIT function to return to the document. Return to double spacing. Press <Return> to create space between the quotation and the next line of text. Type the following:

> David Roman agrees with Bolles. Roman states:

Press <Return>. Change the spacing to single, and activate the INDENT function to indent the quotation from both margins. Type the following:

> As interviewers, . . . managers . . . may be out of their element. They're in the business of running a . . . department, not of interviewing job applicants.

Activate the FOOTNOTE function and type the following footnote:

> Roman, David, ''Why MIS/DP Job Interviews Go Wrong,'' in Computer Decisions, November 19, 1985, p. 66.

Exit back to the document. Change the spacing to double. Press <Return> to create space between the quotation and the next line of text. Finish typing the text:

> Since the person running the interview is probably just as uncomfortable as you are, there are several things you as an interviewee can do to take advantage of the situation and turn the interview into a pleasant and rewarding experience.

You now discover that you misspelled a name throughout the text. The author's name is Bolles, not Boles. Move the cursor to the beginning of the document (Page 1, Line, 1, Position 10). Use the REPLACE function to locate and correct all occurrences of Boles.

> Press <Alt> <F2> for REPLACE

The prompt WITH CONFIRM? (Y/N) N appears. The prompt is asking if you want to confirm every correction.

> Type **Y**

The prompt -> SRCH appears in the lower-left corner of the screen.

> Type Boles
> Press <Alt> <F2> for REPLACE

The prompt REPLACE WITH appears in the lower-left corner of the screen.

> Type Bolles
> Press <Alt> <F2> for REPLACE

The cursor stops on the first occurrence of Boles. The prompt CONFIRM? (Y/N) N appears in the lower left corner of the screen.

    Type **Y**

The cursor stops on the second occurrence of Boles and the confirm prompt appears at the bottom of the screen.

    Type **Y**

The cursor stops on the third occurrence of Boles and the confirm prompt appears at the bottom of the screen.

    Type **Y**

The corrections have now been made in the text; but footnote 1 still contains a misspelling of the author's name, so you need to edit a footnote.

    Press <Ctrl> <F7> for FOOTNOTE
    Type **2** for EDIT

The prompt FTN #? 3 appears in the lower left corner of the screen.

    Type **1**
    Press <Return>

The first footnote appears on the screen. Change the spelling of Boles to Bolles. Exit from the note screen after the correction has been made.
    Now you decide that there is no such word as *interviewee*. Return the cursor to the beginning of the document (Page 1, Line 1, Position 10).

    Press <F2> for SEARCH

The prompt -> SRCH appears on the screen, with Boles entered as the search string because that was the last text searched for.

    Type `interviewee`
    Press <F2> for SEARCH

The cursor stops at the first occurrence of interviewee. Use the <Backspace> key to delete interviewee. Enter `applicant` to take its place. Press <F2> for SEARCH again. The prompt appears with interviewee entered as the search string, and you must press <F2> for SEARCH one more time. The cursor stops at the next occurrence of interviewee. Use the <Backspace> key to delete interviewee and enter `person being interviewed` to take its place. Activate the SEARCH function again. When the program finds the third occurrence of interviewee, replace it with `prospective employee`. Notice that you will also have to change the preceding `an` to `a`.
    After making this final change, the last sentence of the document may

have to be reformatted if it runs past the right margin. Use the <→> key to move the cursor to the end of the sentence, past the period. Press <Return>. The end of the sentence should wrap around to the next line.

Return the cursor to the beginning of the document one more time. Use the SPELL function to check the spelling in the entire document. Correct any errors. Save the document as INTER.PAP (for interview paper). Print the entire document. Exit WordPerfect.

Learning Check

1. What are the functions required for bolding existing text?
2. What function enables the user to delete command codes from an existing document?
3. What function is activated to create a footnote?
4. What function is activated to create a header?
5. In a word processor program, the _____ routine can locate a specified character string.

Answers

1. BLOCK (<Alt> <F4>); BOLD (<F6>) 2. REVEAL CODES (<Alt> <F3>) 3. FOOTNOTE (<Ctrl> <F7>) 4. PAGE FORMAT (<Alt> <F7>) 5. Search and Find

Summary Points

- Word processors, such as WordPerfect, include formatting features that determine how the text is printed on paper.
- Common formatting features include setting tab and margin stops, single- or double-spacing the text, and performing character enhancements.
- Common character enhancements include underlining and boldfacing.
- Headers and footers are pieces of text that are printed on every page in a document. A header is printed at the top of a page, and a footer is printed at the bottom of a page.
- Search and find routines locate a specific string of characters.

WordPerfect Exercises

1. Changing a Document's Formatting
   a. What are the steps required to change the formatting for a WordPerfect

document? Start up WordPerfect to begin a new document.

b. Describe the process for setting margins. Set the margins for your document at 15 and 70.

c. How do you change the spacing in a document? Change to double-spacing for this exercise.

d. Center and underline the title of the document which is <u>Monitoring Chemical Spills</u>.

e. Ignore spelling errors, which will be corrected later in the exercise, and type the following:

```
Since a recent chemical spill at the Union Carbide
plant in Bhopal, India resulted in the daeths of
more than 2,000 people, cehmical companies have
become much more interested in computerized
tracking and warning systems designed to protect
communities around their plants. The old method for
predicting the path and level of toxicity of a
chemical cloud (still in use at most chemical
palnts) involves the use of lengthy charts and
tables and relies on human calculations.
  Safer Emergency Systems, Inc., has designed
computerized emergency systems for 25 chemical
plants. The system combines a computer, a 19-inch
color graphics screen, and a printer with sensors
placed at key locations in the plant to detect
leaks early and sound alarms in the central
computer. A tower placed on the rooftop of a nearby
open field has sensors that help plot the
temperature and directrion of a chemical cloud.
```

2. Changing Command Codes in an Existing Document

a. How can you view the commands made in a document? Describe the procedure used for changing those commands. Use the REVEAL CODES function. Change the spacing to single in the preceding document by deleting the double-space command in the command screen.

b. Delete the Underline command for the title.

3. Spell Checking

a. What actions are required to use the WordPerfect Speller? Describe the features of the Speller.

b. Use the WordPerfect Speller to check the spelling in the document.

4. Footnotes

a. What is the procedure for inserting footnotes in a WordPerfect document? Insert the following footnote after the first paragraph:

```
Johnson, Dale. Safety With the Computer, Chicago:
University Press, 1985, p. 74.
```

b. Return to the document. Now use the FOOTNOTE function again to edit the footnote. Change 1985 to 1986.

5. Review all of the functions that you have used in this chapter.

WordPerfect Problems

To complete the following problems, use the APPLY file included on the Student File Disk. To start WordPerfect, boot the system with the DOS disk. At the A> prompt, insert the WordPerfect system disk in drive A and the Student File Disk in drive B. Type **b:** and press <Return>. Type **a:wp** and press <Return>.

> *Hard Disk Differences:* You need to copy the APPLY file included on the Student File Disk onto the hard disk. When you turn on your computer, at the C> prompt, type **a:** and press <Return> to switch to drive A. Insert your Student File Disk with the APPLY file on it into drive A, and type **copy apply c:\wp** and press <Return>. Switch back to drive C by typing **c:** and pressing the <Return> key. Type **wp** and press <Return>.

> *Hard Disk Differences:* Omit Step 1.

1. Copy the APPLY file to the APPLY2 file by retrieving APPLY and saving it with the new name, APPLY2. Describe the steps taken to copy the file.

2. Use the APPLY2 file to answer the remaining questions. Retrieve the APPLY2 file if necessary.

3. Read the APPLY2 file. APPLY2 is a solicited application letter used to answer an advertisement for an accounting job. Assume that you have just graduated from your college with a major in marketing rather than accounting. You are looking for a job in the marketing field. Delete the sender address using the BLOCK function and the <Del> key. Replace it with your own address.

4. Change the date to the current date.

5. Delete the company address, and replace it with the address of a company that you know.

6. Delete the phrase "Daily Mirror on April 9" from the first sentence of the

letter. Insert the following to take its place: `in the Tribune No. 350`. (Make sure that the word <u>Tribune</u> is underlined.)

7. Using the SEARCH and REPLACE functions, replace all occurrences of the word *accounting* with the word *marketing*.

8. In the second paragraph, delete *Ohio State University*. Type the name of your college.

9. Delete the following sentence:

As an intern at Price Waterhouse, I worked on the audit of Mills International.

10. Insert the following in place of the sentence just deleted:

```
As a project assignment, I conducted a market sur-
vey on fast food business in Northwest Ohio. This
survey was used for the implementation of a new
fast food chain in the area.
```

11. Move the cursor to the name of the applicant. Replace the name Kim Landon with your own name.

12. Print the letter.

13. Now that you have seen a hard copy of the letter you would like to make some changes to the format design. Make the following changes:
    a. Change the top margin from 1 inch to 1½ inches.
    b. Set the right and left margins so that they are both 1½ inches wide.
    c. Have the right margin be ragged rather than justified.

14. Print the letter again.

CHAPTER 12

Introduction to Spreadsheets and Lotus 1-2-3

Outline

Introduction
Definitions
Uses of Spreadsheets
Learning Check
Guide to Lotus 1-2-3
   Identifying Parts of the Worksheet
Learning Check
   Getting Started with Lotus 1-2-3
   Moving Around the Worksheet
   Menus and Menu Options
   Saving and Retrieving Files
   Saving an Amended File
   Getting Help with Lotus 1-2-3
   Quitting a File and Quitting the Access System
Creating a Worksheet
   Entering Labels
   Entering Values
   Ranges
   Entering Formulas
   Formatting Cells
   Erasing a Cell
Learning Check
Changing the Appearance of a Worksheet
   Aligning Labels
   Adjusting Column Widths
   Inserting and Deleting Rows and Columns
Printing a Worksheet
Learning Check
Summary Points
Lotus 1-2-3 Exercises
Lotus 1-2-3 Problems

Introduction

SPREADSHEET
A ledger or table used in a business environment for financial calculations and for the recording of transactions.

SPREADSHEET PROGRAM
A set of computer instructions which generates and operates an electronic spreadsheet.

A manual **spreadsheet** is used to record business transactions and to perform calculations. A **spreadsheet program** uses a computer's memory capability to solve mathematically oriented problems. With a spreadsheet program, columns of numbers can be set up to keep track of money or objects.

Typically, a pencil, a piece of paper, and a calculator are the tools used to solve mathematical problems. A spreadsheet program makes the process much faster and easier. This capability is useful with complicated formulas or lengthy, tedious calculations. Imagine that, after finishing your tax returns, you realized you did not include income you received from a temporary job. Every calculation following that part of the form would be incorrect. With a spreadsheet program, you would simply insert the forgotten number and direct the program to recalculate all the totals. With the ability to calculate, store, print, merge, and sort numeric information, a spreadsheet is an extremely useful tool.

This chapter looks at some of the features that make spreadsheet programs so popular. It also provides instructions on how to get started using Lotus 1-2-3.

Definitions

Ledger sheets are used primarily by accountants and business managers for financial calculations and the recording of transactions. A spreadsheet actually is a ledger sheet like the one shown in Figure 12-1. To keep numbers in line, ledger sheets have columns in which the numbers are written.

Figure 12-1 Ledger Sheet

	HOME BUDGET		
	Expenses:		
	Rent	235 00	
	Food	100 00	
	Gas	97 00	
	Electric	75 00	
	Phone	25 00	
	Car	100 00	
	TOTAL EXPENSES	632 00	

ELECTRONIC SPREADSHEET
A large computerized grid divided into rows and columns, which uses computer storage and computational capabilities for financial analysis.

WORKSHEET
The grid of rows and columns created using a spreadsheet software package. The worksheet falls within the row and column borders.

VALUE
A single piece of numeric data used in the calculations of a spreadsheet.

CELL
A storage location within a spreadsheet.

An **electronic spreadsheet** keeps numbers in line with a grid consisting of columns and rows which appear on the display screen. The spreadsheet is used to manipulate numeric data that is stored in the computer's memory. Some software packages, like Lotus 1-2-3, refer to an electronic spreadsheet as a **worksheet.** For the remainder of this chapter, the word *worksheet* refers to the grid of rows and columns used by Lotus 1-2-3 to store and manipulate numeric data. Table 12-1 provides a quick reference to other terms frequently encountered when using an electronic spreadsheet.

In a spreadsheet numbers, or **values,** are entered into **cells** formed by the columns and rows. Each cell relates to a certain storage location in the computer's memory. **Labels** also can be entered to tell the user what the numbers mean (see Figure 12-2).

Formulas, as well as values, can be entered into cells. A formula is a mathematical expression that can contain constant numbers and numbers from other cells. If one number in a cell is changed, the program automatically recalculates any formula that uses the changed number. This is probably one of the most significant advantages of an electronic spreadsheet over a traditional spreadsheet.

Uses of Spreadsheets

Because electronic spreadsheets instantaneously recalculate formulas, they can be used to answer ''what if'' questions such as the following:

- What if I spend $50 more at the grocery store each month?
- What if the interest earned by my savings account goes up ½ percent?
- What if I take a job working on commission rather than on salary?

Manually calculating the answers to these questions could take a person several hours while a computer and spreadsheet program enable the user to see the answers almost immediately on the display screen.

Table 12-1
Terms Associated with Electronic Spreadsheets

Term	Definition
Cell	A storage location within a spreadsheet used to store a single piece of information relevant to the spreadsheet.
Coordinates	The column letter and row number that define the location of a specific cell.
Formula	A mathematical expression used in a spreadsheet.
Label	Information used for describing some aspect of a spreadsheet. A label can be made up of alphabetic or numeric information, but no arithmetic can be performed on a label.
Value	A single piece of numeric information used in the calculations of a spreadsheet.
Window	The portion of a worksheet which can be seen on the computer display screen.

348 PART TWO: APPLICATIONS SOFTWARE

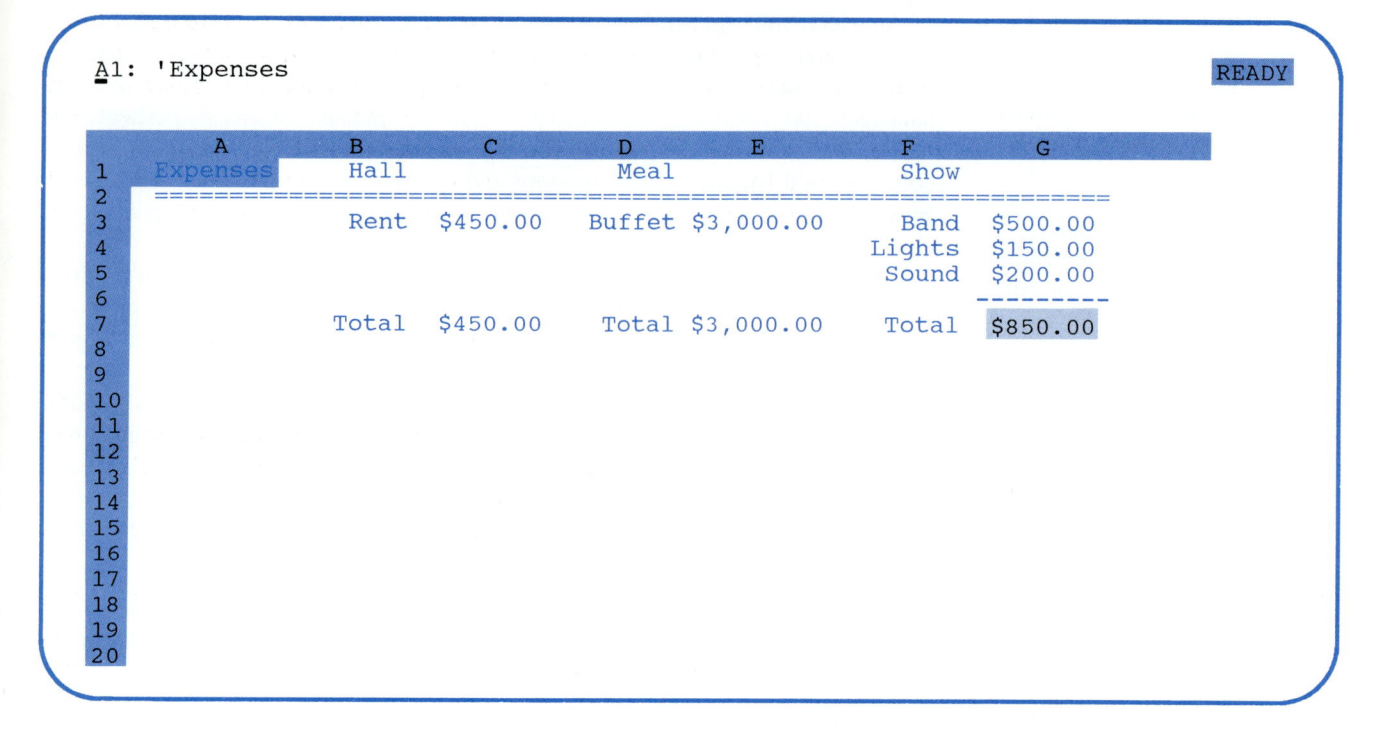

```
A1: 'Expenses                                                      READY

         A          B          C          D          E          F          G
  1    Expenses    Hall                  Meal                  Show
  2    ================================================================
  3                Rent      $450.00    Buffet   $3,000.00     Band     $500.00
  4                                                            Lights   $150.00
  5                                                            Sound    $200.00
  6                                                                     --------
  7                Total     $450.00    Total    $3,000.00     Total    $850.00
  8
  9
 10
 11
 12
 13
 14
 15
 16
 17
 18
 19
 20
```

Figure 12-2
Values and Labels.
Columns A, B, D, and F contain labels. Columns C, E, and G contain values.

In business, decision makers also use spreadsheets to help answer "what if" questions. For example, an executive might use a spreadsheet to calculate the effect on a company's profit margin if a new tax law is passed (what if the tax law is changed?). Business people also use spreadsheets to keep track of data, such as sales figures, expenses, payroll, and prices. Any calculation that can be performed by hand can be performed with a spreadsheet.

Home computer owners can use spreadsheets to keep track of household expenses. Spreadsheets can calculate the percentages of each paycheck going to rent,

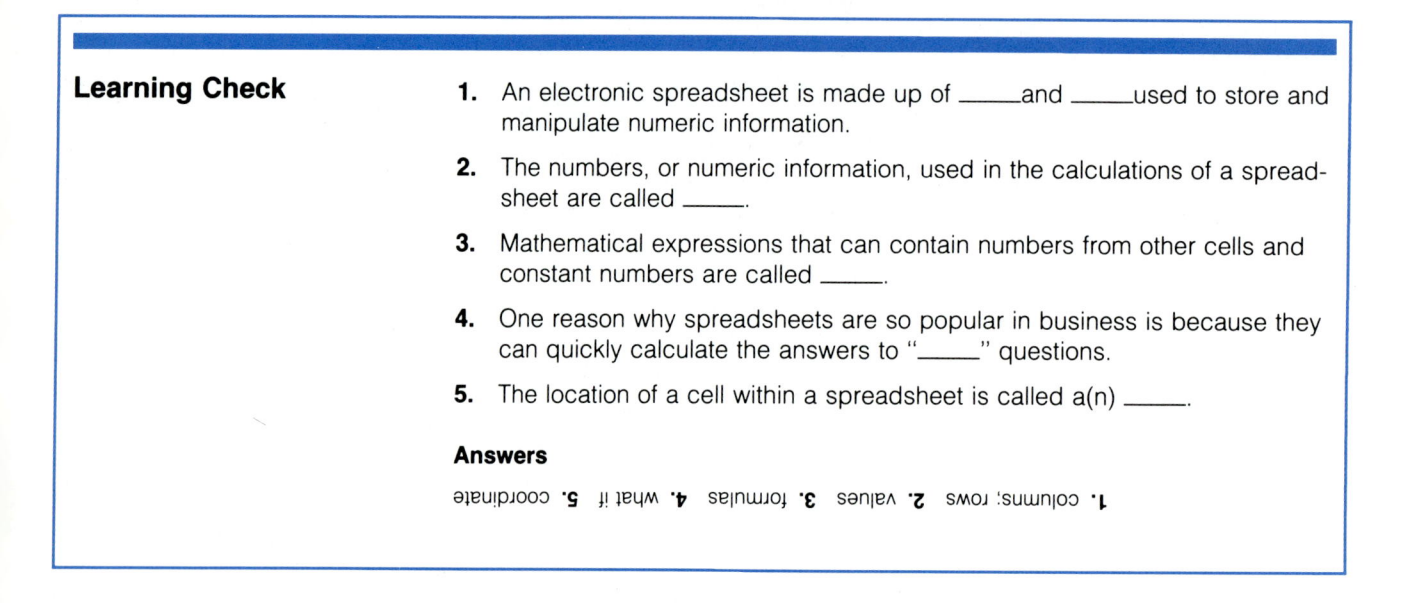

Learning Check

1. An electronic spreadsheet is made up of _____ and _____ used to store and manipulate numeric information.

2. The numbers, or numeric information, used in the calculations of a spreadsheet are called _____.

3. Mathematical expressions that can contain numbers from other cells and constant numbers are called _____.

4. One reason why spreadsheets are so popular in business is because they can quickly calculate the answers to "_____" questions.

5. The location of a cell within a spreadsheet is called a(n) _____.

Answers

1. columns; rows 2. values 3. formulas 4. what if 5. coordinate

CHAPTER 12: INTRODUCTION TO SPREADSHEETS AND LOTUS 1-2-3

utilities, and food so that the user can see which expenses increase and decrease each month. Spreadsheets can be used in other ways; for example, they can help determine how much money should be saved each month for a vacation or a new car.

Engineers and scientists use spreadsheets to help answer "what if" questions, too. The recalculating feature of spreadsheets helps cut down on the trial and error involved in research. Scientists use complex spreadsheets to calculate the outcomes of experiments conducted under varying conditions.

Guide To Lotus 1-2-3

The remainder of this chapter introduces Lotus 1-2-3, a software package that combines a spreadsheet with file management and graphics functions. This chapter focuses on 1-2-3's spreadsheet.

Identifying Parts of the Worksheet

When a new 1-2-3 worksheet is loaded into the computer, a screen like the one shown in Figure 12-3 appears. Numbers listed down the left side of the grid represent the rows. The letters listed across the top of the grid represent the columns.

COORDINATE
The location of a cell within a spreadsheet.

CELL POINTER
The highlight that indicates the active cell in a spreadsheet.

ACTIVE CELL
The cell on a spreadsheet currently available for use; the active cell is indicated by the cell pointer.

CONTROL PANEL
The portion of the spreadsheet which provides status and help information. The control panel is composed of a status line, an entry line, and a prompt line.

Each cell in the spreadsheet has a cell address or **coordinate.** The coordinate of a cell consists of a letter for its column and a number for its row. For example, the coordinate or cell address C4 represents the cell where column C and row 4 intersect. The **cell pointer** is a highlighted bar that indicates which cell or cells are active or can accept information. The cell indicated by the cell pointer is called the **active cell.** In Figure 12-3, the cell pointer is in cell A1, so A1 is the active cell.

The top three lines of the screen constitute the **control panel.** The first line of the control panel is the status line, which provides information such as the cell address, the cell contents, and whether the cell contains a label, value, or formula.

The second line of the control panel, the entry line, is a work line that displays data as it is typed in at the keyboard. The entry line is called a work line because the data appearing there can be edited and changed before the <Return> key is pressed. Once the <Return> key is pressed, however, the data moves from the entry line to the status line and enters the worksheet. The entry line may also contain a menu of Lotus 1-2-3 options.

The third line of the control panel, the prompt line, contains either a submenu or an explanation of a specific command.

The mode indicator, in the upper right corner of the worksheet, displays 1-2-3's current mode of operation. Lotus 1-2-3 is always in the READY mode when first started. This is the mode that enables you to move the cell pointer around the worksheet. Typing any other valid character or command activates one of the other modes. Table 12-2 describes some of 1-2-3's mode indicators.

In the bottom left corner of the worksheet is the error message area, and at the bottom right corner are the indicators. If a mistake is made, error messages provide a brief description of what has gone wrong. There are four indicators: CALC, NUM, CAPS, and SCROLL. If the <Num Lock> key is on, NUM is displayed;

350   PART TWO: APPLICATIONS SOFTWARE

[Diagram of a blank Lotus 1-2-3 worksheet with labels: Cell Address, Status Line, Entry Line, Promt Line, Column Border, Mode Indicator, Control Panel, Cell Pointer, Row Border, Window, Error Message Area, Indicators (CALC, NUM, CAPS, SCROLL), READY, A1:]

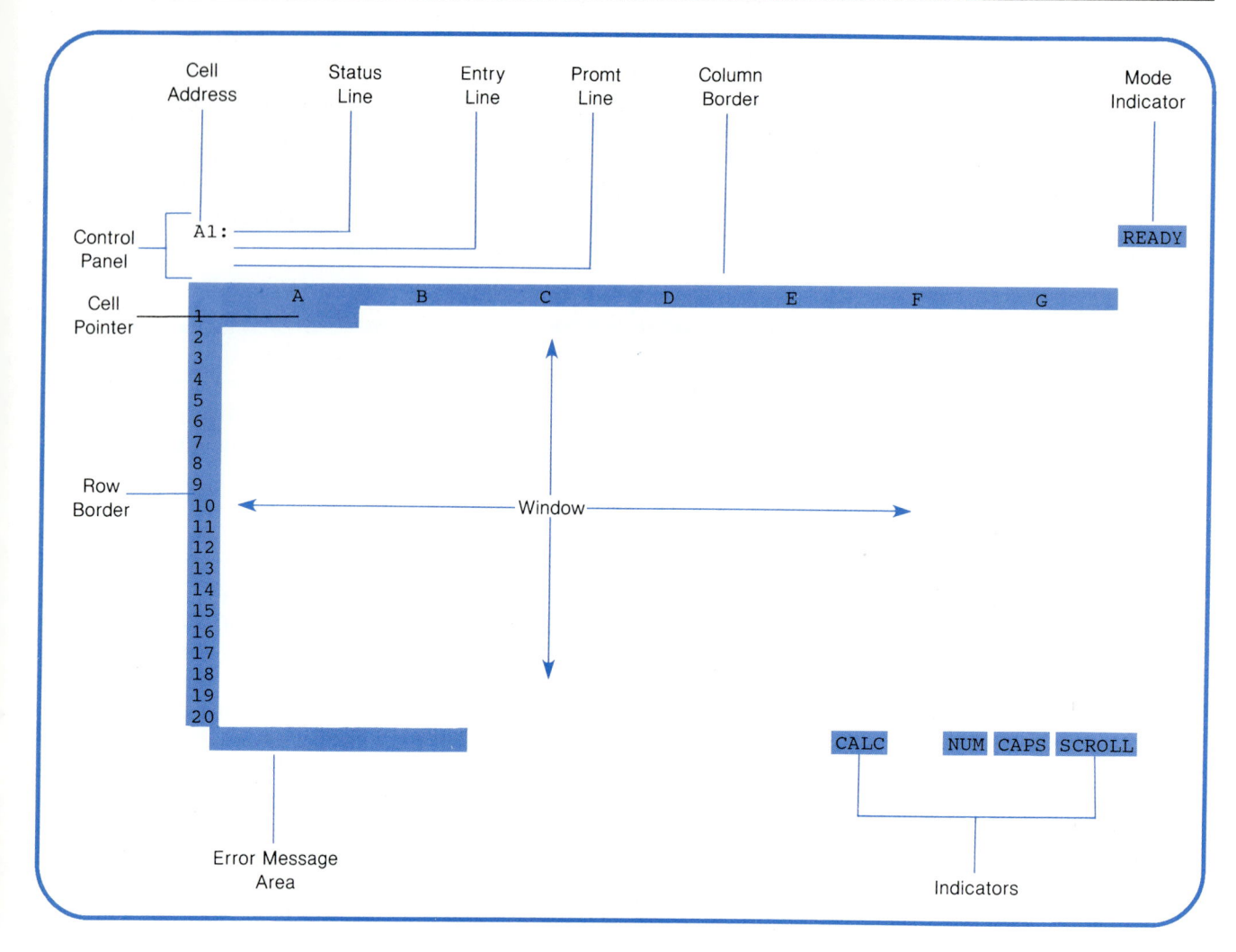

Figure 12-3
A Blank Lotus 1-2-3 Worksheet

if the <Caps Lock> key is on, CAPS is displayed; if the <Scroll Lock> key is on, SCROLL is displayed. The CALC indicator is displayed when changes requiring recalculation have been made to a worksheet.

Table 12-2
Lotus 1-2-3 Mode Indicators

Indicator	Description
EDIT	An entry is being edited.
ERROR	An error was made; 1-2-3 is waiting for the <Return> or <Esc> key to be pressed in response to the error.
HELP	1-2-3's Help facility is being used.
LABEL	A label is being entered.
MENU	A menu is displayed and a menu option is being selected.
POINT	1-2-3 is pointing to a cell or a range of cells.
READY	1-2-3 is waiting for a command or cell entry.
VALUE	A number or formula is being entered.
WAIT	1-2-3 is calculating; commands cannot be processed.

Learning Check

1. The top three lines of a Lotus 1-2-3 worksheet are called the _____.
2. The _____ is the first line of the control panel and includes information such as the cell address and cell contents.
3. The entry line can contain either data as it is typed in at the keyboard or a _____.
4. The _____ is the third line of the control panel and contains either a submenu or an explanation of a Lotus 1-2-3 command.
5. The mode indicator displays 1-2-3's current _____.

Answers

1. control panel 2. status line 3. menu 4. prompt line 5. mode of operation

Getting Started With Lotus 1-2-3

Some of the procedures for using Lotus 1-2-3 depend on whether you are using a system with two floppy disk drives or one with a hard disk drive. The directions in this chapter are for a system with two floppy disk drives. Differences for systems with a hard disk drive are written in difference boxes.

Each of the following sections introduces one or more features of Lotus 1-2-3. At the end of each section, there is a hands-on activity marked YOUR TURN. Be sure to read the preceding section carefully before trying the hands-on activity.

The key on the IBM PC keyboard marked ↵ is the <Return> key, also called the <Enter> key. Whenever you are instructed to press the <Return> key, press the key marked ↵.

Throughout this chapter, the following symbols and typefaces appear. This is what they mean:

Select Worksheet	Italicized text indicates that a specific option from a menu should be selected.
Type **C12**	The characters in boldface are Lotus 1-2-3 commands that should be typed to the screen.
Press the <Return> key	The angle brackets (<>) are used to signify a specific key on the keyboard. Press the key whose name is enclosed by the angle brackets.
1-2-3 Tip:	This phrase introduces important information needed to run Lotus 1-2-3 successfully.
ENTER RANGE OF LABELS	All capital letters indicate phrases that appear on the computer screen.
Type MONTHLY BUDGET	Typewriter font indicates text that is to be entered into the worksheet.

To start Lotus 1-2-3, you need a DOS disk, a 1-2-3 system disk, and a formatted disk that is your data disk. Follow these steps whenever you need to start Lotus 1-2-3:

1. Insert the DOS disk in drive A. Turn on the computer.
2. When asked to type the date, either bypass the prompt by pressing <Return> or enter today's date using the same format that appears next to "Current Date" on the screen. When asked to type the time, either bypass the prompt by pressing <Return> or enter the current time using the same format that appears next to "Current Time" on the screen.
3. When the system prompt (A>) appears, remove the DOS disk from drive A. Insert the 1-2-3 system disk in drive A.
4. Insert the data disk, the disk onto which the Lotus files you create are stored, into drive B.
5. Type either **Lotus** or **123** and press <Return>.

If you type **Lotus,** the Lotus Access System appears. The menu pointer is on 1-2-3. You can either press the <Return> key or type **1** to select 1-2-3. You can bypass the Access System by typing **123**. This takes you directly to the spreadsheet.

If the Lotus Access System is activated, notice there are six options included in the menu at the top of the screen. The first option, 1-2-3, activates Lotus and places a blank worksheet on the screen. PrintGraph enters the Lotus graphics printing program so that a graph which has been created can be printed. Translate allows a user to read files from certain other programs. Install begins the procedure to install Lotus. View provides an introduction to many of 1-2-3's most commonly used features and procedures. Finally, Exit exits the Lotus program to the system prompt.

> *Hard Disk Differences:* Depending upon the installation procedure used, you may or may not be able to start 1-2-3 directly from the hard disk. Ask your instructor if 1-2-3 can be started directly from the hard disk. If it can't, each time you start 1-2-3 you must insert the 1-2-3 system disk in drive A even though 1-2-3 is on the hard disk. When the C> prompt appears, type **CD** and the name of the directory where 1-2-3 is located. Press <Return>. At the C> prompt, type either **Lotus** or **123.**

YOUR TURN Start Lotus 1-2-3. A blank worksheet should be on the screen.

Moving Around the Worksheet

WINDOW
The portion of an electronic spreadsheet which can be seen on the computer display screen.

The Lotus 1-2-3 worksheet contains 256 columns, which are labeled A–IV, and 8,192 rows, which are numbered 1–8192. The part of the worksheet that appears on the screen at one time is the **window.** For example, in Figure 12-3, cells A1 through G20 appear in the window.

There are several ways to move around the 1-2-3 worksheet and to see parts of the worksheet outside the window. The first is by using the pointer-movement keys (also called cursor control keys) located on the numeric keypad at the right of the keyboard. Table 12-3 lists the pointer-movement keys, and describes where the cell pointer moves when each key is pressed. (The <Ctrl> key is located at the left side of the keyboard.)

> *1-2-3 Tip:* Because the 1-2-3 worksheet is so large, it is possible to lose track of your position on it. If this happens, simply press <Home>—returning the cell pointer to cell A1—to reorient yourself on the worksheet.

The other way to move the cell pointer around the worksheet is by using the GOTO key. The GOTO key is the <F5> key, one of the ten function keys at the left of the keyboard. Pressing <F5> moves the cell pointer to any cell on the worksheet. For example, if the cell pointer is in cell A1 and you want to go to cell R30, simply press <F5>, type R30, and press <Return>. The cell pointer immediately moves to cell R30. The GOTO key quickly moves the cell pointer large distances in the spreadsheet.

Table 12-3
Pointer-Movement Keys

Key	Description
7 Home	Pressing the <Home> key returns the cell pointer to cell A1.
9 PgUp	Pressing the <Page Up> key moves the cell pointer up 20 cells.
3 PgDn	Pressing the <Page Down> key moves the cell pointer down 20 cells.
8 ↑	Pressing <↑>, the up arrow key, moves the cell pointer one cell up.
6 →	Pressing <→>, the right arrow key, moves the cell pointer one cell to the right.
2 ↓	Pressing <↓>, the down arrow key, moves the cell pointer one cell down.
4 ←	Pressing <←>, the left arrow key (not to be confused with the <Backspace> key), moves the cursor one space to the left.
Ctrl 4 ←	Pressing these keys together moves the cursor eight columns to the left.
Ctrl 6 →	Pressing these keys together moves the cursor eight columns to the right.

YOUR TURN

Start with a blank 1-2-3 worksheet on the screen. Practice moving the cell pointer by doing the following:

- Press the <↓> key three times. The cell address in the status line should say A4.
- Press the <→> key ten times. The cell address should be K4.
- Press <Pg Dn>. Watch the row border. The cell pointer remains in the same place and the row numbers change. The cell address should be K24.
- Press <Ctrl> <→>. The cell address should be L24.
- Press <Home>. The cell pointer should be back to A1.
- Press <F5>, the GOTO key. Type **L24** and press <Return>. The cell pointer immediately moves to cell L24. Check the cell address to make sure that is the location of the cell pointer.
- Press <Pg Up>. The cell address should be L4.
- Press <Home>.
- Press <F5>. Type **Z1998** and press <Return>.
- Press <Home>.

Continue practicing moving the cell pointer with the pointer movement keys and with <F5>, the GOTO key. When you have finished practicing, press <Home> to return to A1.

Menus and Menu Options

For the main menu to be activated, Lotus must be in the READY mode. Typing the slash </> key activates the MENU mode, and the Main menu appears in the entry line of the control panel (see Figure 12-4). The Main menu lists ten options. When the Main menu is first selected, the menu pointer is on the Worksheet option. The menu pointer is the highlight that indicates which option is currently selected.

There are two ways to select an option. The first is by highlighting the option with the menu pointer. To highlight an option, move the menu pointer to the option using the <←> and <→> keys. When the option is highlighted, press <Return>. The second way to select an option is by pressing the first letter of the option name. Selecting an option using this second method is faster, as it eliminates having to move the menu pointer and press the <Return> key.

In addition to the Main menu, Lotus 1-2-3 has several submenus. That is, when you select one option on the Main menu, a submenu with additional options moves to the entry line. For example, if you select the Worksheet option from the Main menu, a submenu with nine additional options moves from the prompt line to the entry line.

If a menu is activated by mistake, or if you begin to use an option and decide you do not want that option, pressing the <Esc> key lets you back out of any selection one menu at a time until you return to the READY mode. Each time <Esc> is pressed, the current menu is replaced with the one previous to it.

Figure 12-4 The Lotus 1-2-3 Main Menu

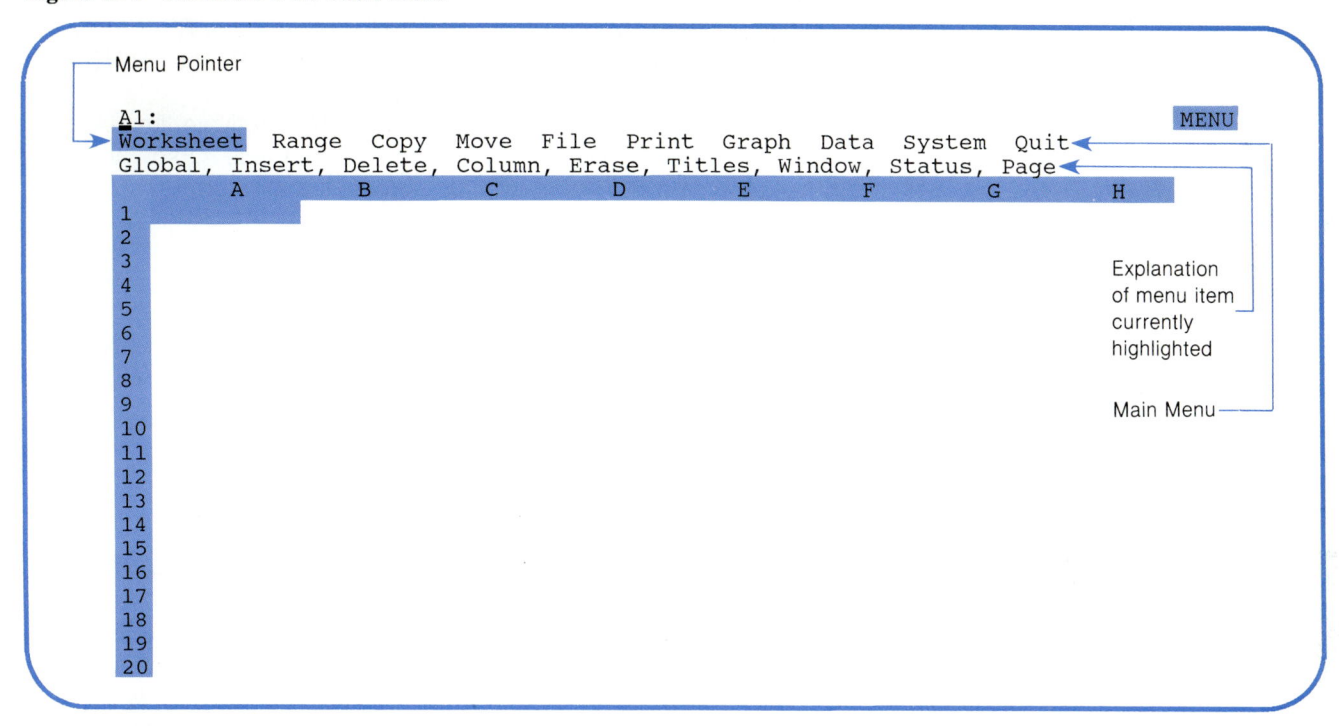

```
Menu Pointer
  ↓
A1:                                                                    MENU
Worksheet  Range  Copy  Move  File  Print  Graph  Data  System  Quit
Global,  Insert,  Delete,  Column,  Erase,  Titles,  Window,  Status,  Page
           A        B        C        D        E        F        G        H
 1
 2
 3                                                              Explanation
 4                                                              of menu item
 5                                                              currently
 6                                                              highlighted
 7
 8
 9                                                              Main Menu
10
11
12
13
14
15
16
17
18
19
20
```

YOUR TURN

Start with a blank 1-2-3 worksheet on the screen.

- Press the slash key (/). The Lotus 1-2-3 Main menu appears. Note that the mode indicator says MENU, the current cell address is A1, and the cell pointer is on WORKSHEET, the first word of the menu. Read the prompt line. This is a submenu for the WORKSHEET command.
- Press the <→> key. The cell pointer is on RANGE, and a submenu for the RANGE option is in the prompt line.
- Press the <→> key again. Now the cell pointer is on COPY. A description of the COPY option appears in the prompt line.
- Move through the Main menu one command at a time using the <→> key. When the cell pointer is on QUIT, press the <→> key. The cell pointer moves back to the first command, WORKSHEET.
- With the cell pointer on the WORKSHEET command, press the <Return> key. The WORKSHEET submenu now appears on the entry line. The cell pointer is on GLOBAL, the first option in the submenu. The prompt line describes the GLOBAL command.
- Press the <→> key. The cell pointer moves to the second command. Move through the entire menu using the <→> key. When the PAGE command is highlighted, use the <←> key to move backward through the menu until the cell pointer is on GLOBAL.
- Press the <Esc> key. Pressing the <Esc> key moves Lotus 1-2-3 back one command level. The Main menu is now back in the entry line.

- Press the <Esc> key again. The entry and prompt lines are empty, and the mode indicator has changed from the MENU mode to the READY mode.
- Press the slash key (/). The Main menu appears. Type **P**. The PRINTER command is immediately activated. Press <Esc>.
- Type **R** to activate the RANGE command. Type **N** to activate the NAME command. Type **D** to activate the DELETE command. Press <Esc> three times to move backwards through all the submenus and return to the main menu.
- Practice moving through the main menu and the submenus, both by using the <→> and <←> keys and pressing <Return> and by using the first letter of the command name.
- When you have finished practicing, return the worksheet to the READY mode by using the <Esc> key.

Saving and Retrieving Files

Worksheets are permanently saved in files on your data disk. Once saved, a file can be retrieved at any time to be used and changed as necessary.

Lotus saves files to a **directory** located on a disk. When instructed to save a file, Lotus checks the location of the current directory. The current directory can be on the disk in drive A or the disk in drive B. The **default setting** is the disk in drive A, but your data disk is in drive B, so you want the current directory to be in drive B.

To find where the current directory is located, type the slash character (\) to view the Main menu. Type **F** for File and then **D** for Directory. The entry line reads ENTER CURRENT DIRECTORY: followed by either A:\ or B:\. If it says B:, the location of the current directory does not need to be changed. It is already in drive B, where your data disk is. If it says A:, the current directory has to be changed to drive B.

DIRECTORY
A special kind of file that organizes the other files stored on a disk.

DEFAULT SETTING
The setting that a software package automatically uses when no other setting is designated by the user.

Hard Disk Differences: To find where the current directory is located, follow the same procedure used for a system with two floppy disk drives. If, after you type **F** for File and **D** for Directory, the entry line reads ENTER CURRENT DIRECTORY: C:\ SUBDIRECTORY NAME, the current directory does not need to be changed, assuming your hard disk drive is designated as drive C. Press the <Esc> key three times to return to the READY mode.

If the current directory is not located in your hard disk drive, type the letter that designates your hard disk drive, followed by a colon, a backslash, and the part of the subdirectory where 1-2-3 is to store your data. For example, if your hard disk drive is C and 1-2-3 is to store data in a subdirectory called 123, type **C:\123** and press <Return>. If you do not have any subdirectories, just type **C:** and press <Return>. To save the directory designation, type **U** for Update when the previous menu returns, and type **Q** for Quit.

CHAPTER 12: INTRODUCTION TO SPREADSHEETS AND LOTUS 1-2-3 357

To change the drive, activate the Main menu. Type **W** for Worksheet, **G** for Global, **D** for Default, and **D** again for Directory. Now the entry line reads DIRECTORY AT STARTUP: A:\. Press <Esc> to erase the current directory designation. Type **B:** and press <Return> to change the current directory designation to drive B. The previous submenu returns. Type **U** for Update to save the change from drive A to drive B. After a few seconds, the same submenu returns. Type **Q** for Quit to return to the READY mode.

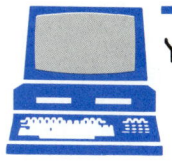

YOUR TURN

Start with a blank 1-2-3 worksheet on the screen.

Find out where the current directory is located by doing the following:

    Type /
    Select File
    Select Directory

If the entry line reads ENTER CURRENT DIRECTORY: B:\, press <Return>. If the entry line reads ENTER CURRENT DIRECTORY: A:\, change the location of the current directory to drive B by doing the following:

    Return to the Main menu by pressing <Esc> twice
    Select Worksheet
    Select Global
    Select Default
    Select Directory

The entry line reads DIRECTORY AT STARTUP: A:\

    Press <Esc>
    Type **B:**
    Press <Return>
    Select Update

When the worksheet displays the Main menu, return to the READY mode:

    Select Quit

Once the current directory designation is drive B, a worksheet can be saved. To save a worksheet in a file, type a slash (/) to view the Main menu. Next, select the File command and the Save command.

You are then prompted to specify a filename. A filename can be up to eight characters long, and it can be a combination of letters and numbers. Try to give the file a name that indicates the information contained on that worksheet. Type the name of the file and press <Return>. The mode indicator switches to WAIT for a few seconds and then changes to READY. When 1-2-3 returns to the READY mode, the worksheet has been saved.

When 1-2-3 saves the worksheet, an extension is automatically added to the name given the worksheet. The extension is separated from the filename by a period. The extension given to the filenames depends on whether the original Lotus 1-2-3 or Lotus 1-2-3 Release 2 is being used. The first release of 1-2-3 adds the extension WKS to the filename, whereas Release 2 adds the extension WK1. This extension may be displayed briefly when the prompt appears.

To retrieve an existing file, type the slash (/) when the worksheet is in the READY mode. Type **F** for File and **R** for Retrieve. 1-2-3 then prompts you to enter the name of the file to be retrieved. The files stored on the disk are listed on the prompt line. To select a file to retrieve, highlight its name using the $<\leftarrow>$ and $<\rightarrow>$ keys if necessary, and press <Return>.

The entry line can display up to five filenames. If there is more than one file on the disk, the filenames are listed alphabetically from left to right. If there are more than five files saved on the disk, press the $<\downarrow>$ key to see the next five files. Once the line containing the name of the file to be retrieved is reached, use the $<\leftarrow>$ and $<\rightarrow>$ keys to highlight it and press <Return>. Pressing <Home> returns the menu pointer to the first filename in the list.

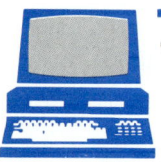

YOUR TURN

Start with a blank 1-2-3 worksheet on the screen.

Lotus 1-2-3 should be in the READY mode, with the cell pointer at A1.

Type Lotus 1-2-3
Press <Return>

Something is now entered into the worksheet. To save this worksheet, do the following:

Type /
Select File
Select Save
Type Practice
Press <Return>

Retrieve the file just saved by doing the following:

Type /
Select Retrieve
Select PRACTICE.WK1 (Your extension might read WKS)

The worksheet with "Lotus 1-2-3" typed into cell A1 should appear on the screen.

Saving An Amended File

Once a worksheet has been created, it can be retrieved and changes can be made to it. Data can be added or deleted, values and labels can be changed, and so on.

CHAPTER 12: INTRODUCTION TO SPREADSHEETS AND LOTUS 1-2-3

When a previously saved file has been retrieved and amended, there are two methods by which to save it.

The first method is to save the amended file as a new file, in which case the original file remains in 1-2-3's memory and can be retrieved again if necessary. The second method is to replace the original file with the amended file, so that only the amended file is saved and the original file is erased from memory.

To save an amended file, first select the File option from the Main menu. Next, select Save. The prompt ENTER SAVE FILE NAME appears. The response to this prompt determines whether the amended file replaces the original file or is saved as a new file.

To save the amended file as a new file, type in a different filename and press <Return>. To replace the original file, press <Return>, indicating that the filename of the original file is to be used as the filename of the amended file. After pressing <Return>, you can either cancel the Save command, keeping the original file intact, or, by selecting Replace, you can erase the original file and replace it with the amended file.

YOUR TURN

Start with the PRACTICE worksheet on the screen. "Lotus 1-2-3" is in A1.

Go to A2
Type `Practice File`
Press <Return>

The PRACTICE file has now been amended, because new data has been entered into A2. To save the amended file, do the following:

Type /
Select File
Select Save

The prompt ENTER SAVE FILE NAME appears. To save the amended file as a separate file from the original PRACTICE file, type a new filename. To replace the original PRACTICE file with the amended PRACTICE file, which now has data in A2, do the following instead:

Press <Return>
Select Replace

The mode indicator returns to READY, and the new PRACTICE worksheet remains on the screen.

Getting Help With Lotus 1-2-3

Lotus 1-2-3 includes a Help facility that provides information about how to use the program. If an error is made, ERROR appears in the mode indicator. No harm is caused to the data or to the program if ERROR appears in the mode indicator,

PART TWO: APPLICATIONS SOFTWARE

but you cannot continue working until the error is corrected. If you do not know how to correct the error, use 1-2-3's Help facility.

To call up the Help facility, press <F1>, the Help key. As soon as <F1> is pressed, the worksheet disappears and a detailed explanation of the current activity on the worksheet appears. After you have read the information provided by the Help facility, press <Esc>. The worksheet returns to the screen.

YOUR TURN

Start with the PRACTICE file on the screen.

Press <F5>

1-2-3 prompts you to enter the address to go to:

Type **G8200**
Press <Return>

ERROR appears in the mode indicator.

Press <F1>

The Help facility appears. Read the information on the screen. The last line of the screen, INVALID CELL OR RANGE ADDRESS, identifies your error: you specified a row that does not exist, row 8200. The final row on the worksheet is 8192.

At the bottom of the screen, there are four commands to choose from. They are:

RETURNING TO READY MODE
/RANGE NAME CREATE
FIXING TYPING MISTAKES
HELP INDEX

Currently, RETURNING TO READY MODE is highlighted. Move the highlighting to HELP INDEX, using the <→> and <↓> keys. Press <Return>.

The Help Index appears on the screen. The Help Index lists and accesses all the Help screens available on 1-2-3. The highlighting is now on USING THE HELP FACILITY. Press <Return> and read the information that appears on the screen.

Move the highlighting to HELP INDEX and press <Return>. Select other Help screens and read about them. After becoming familiar with using Help screens, press <Esc> to return to the worksheet

ERROR is still in the mode indicator. Press <Esc> again to erase the invalid cell address.

> ***1-2-3 Tip:*** When using 1-2-3 you are bound to make a mistake at some point. First try using the Help facility, which provides useful information on whatever function or command is being performed when the <F1> key is pressed. If you still don't know what to do, press the <Esc> key to terminate your last command. Repeatedly pressing the <Esc> key takes you back to the READY mode. Once back to the READY mode, you can start all over.

Quitting a File and Quitting the Access System

When you no longer want to work on a particular worksheet, you need to leave 1-2-3. Be sure to save the file before leaving 1-2-3. Once the file is saved, type a slash (/) to view the Main menu. Next type **Q** for Quit. The words NO and YES appear on the entry line of the control panel, and NO is highlighted. Pressing the <Return> key at this point cancels the Quit command and returns the worksheet to the READY mode.

If you do not wish to cancel the Quit command, move the menu pointer to YES. The prompt line of the control panel prompts you to save the worksheet first. Press the <Return> key.

If 1-2-3 was started directly, by typing **123** at the system prompt, a message appears, prompting you to insert the COMMAND.COM disk in drive A and press any key. Follow these instructions and the operating system prompt appears. If 1-2-3 was started through the Access System, by typing **LOTUS**, the Access System screen appears. If the Access System menu appears, move the menu pointer to EXIT and press <Return>. A message appears, prompting you to insert COMMAND.COM in drive A.

Lotus suggests that the file COMMAND.COM be copied from your DOS disk to the System disk. If the COMMAND.COM file is not present on the System disk you are using, a message appears prompting you to insert COMMAND.COM in drive A. This message will appear whenever you exit Lotus if your System disk does not contain the COMMAND.COM file. If this message does appear, insert the operating system disk in drive A and press <Return>. The operating system prompt A> appears. When the operating system prompt appears, remove the disks and turn off the computer and monitor.

> ***Hard Disk Differences:*** If 1-2-3 was started directly, by typing **123** at the C> prompt, then the operating system prompt appears immediately. If 1-2-3 was started through the Access System, by typing **LOTUS,** the Access System screen appears. If the Access System menu appears, move the menu pointer to EXIT and press <Return>. The operating system prompt appears.

If you don't want to exit the system but you do want to leave one worksheet to start working on a new one, move the cell pointer to 1-2-3 when the Access

System menu appears. Press <Return>. If the Access System menu was bypassed by typing **123** and you want to start a new worksheet rather than exit the system, type **123** again when the system prompt appears and press <Return>.

YOUR TURN

Start with the PRACTICE file on the screen and the worksheet in the READY mode.

Type /
Select Quit
Select Yes

If the Access System menu appears, move the menu pointer to EXIT and press <Return>.

Creating A Worksheet

In previous sections, you learned how to move around the worksheet and how to use menus and submenus. You used two commands, Save and Retrieve, and you entered data into the worksheet (when you typed "Lotus 1-2-3" into cell A1). This section introduces more commands and basic worksheet moves by having you create a monthly budget.

Learning Check

1. The _____ is the part of the worksheet that appears on the screen at one time.

2. The GOTO key is _____.
   a. F1   c. F5
   b. F3   d. F7

3. The Help key is _____.
   a. F1   c. F5
   b. F3   d. F7

4. Typing the slash (/) key always calls up the _____ when Lotus is in the READY mode.

5. A filename can be up to _____ characters long.
   a. four   c. ten
   b. six   d. eight

Answers

1. window 2. c. 3. a. 4. Main menu 5. d.

Entering Labels

As explained at the beginning of the chapter, one of three categories of data can be entered in a cell: a label, a value, or a formula. Labels usually are letters or words, used as titles or captions to help identify the items in a column or a row.

Labels can be entered only when the worksheet is in the READY mode. If an attempt is made to enter a label while in any other mode, 1-2-3 beeps and nothing happens. Before you enter a label, check to make sure the worksheet is in the READY mode.

Entering a label in a cell involves three steps:

1. First, the cell pointer has to be moved to the cell where the label is to be entered. Either the GOTO key <F5> or the pointer-movement keys can be used to move the cell pointer.
2. Next, the label is typed. As soon as you start typing the label, the mode indicator changes to LABEL and the label appears in the entry line.
3. The final step is to store the label in the cell. There are two ways to store the label. The first is by pressing the <Return> key. The second is by pressing the Up <↑>, Down <↓>, Left <←>, or Right <→> pointer-movement keys. As soon as one of these keys is pressed, the label is stored in the cell.

Three things happen once the label is stored: The label moves to the status line, it appears in the appropriate cell on the worksheet and the mode indicator returns to READY.

Using the pointer-movement keys, rather than the <Return> key, to store a label can be a timesaver because the pointer-movement keys perform two functions with one keystroke. If <Return> is pressed to store the label, the label is stored, but the cell pointer remains in the same cell. Before you can make the next entry, the cell pointer has to be moved to a new cell. If the <↑>, <↓>, <←>, or <→> key is used to store a label, the cell pointer also moves automatically one cell in the direction the arrow is pointing. For example, if labels must be entered in cells A1, A2, A3, and A4, time is saved by pressing <↓> after each label is typed, because the cell pointer moves to the next cell where the label is to be entered.

A typing error can be corrected before the <Return> key or one of the cell pointer keys is pressed by using the <Backspace> key, which is located to the left of the <Num Lock> key. The <Backspace> key should not be confused with the Left pointer-movement key, which also has a left arrow on it (←). Each time <Backspace> is pressed, one character is erased. After erasing the mistake, retype and store the label.

There are two ways to edit data already stored in a cell. One way is to go to the cell where the label is located, retype the entire label, and store it. The new label replaces the old one. Once a label has been replaced, it is erased from memory and cannot be retrieved. The second way is to use the Edit key, <F2>, which allows the information in the entry line to be edited. To use the Edit key, go to the cell to be edited, press <F2>, and make the correction.

The default setting for the width of a cell in Lotus 1-2-3 is nine characters. That is, unless otherwise specified, a cell can hold only nine characters. When entering labels, however, Lotus 1-2-3 uses an automatic spill-over feature: If a label longer than nine characters is entered, it spills over automatically into the next cell.

364 PART TWO: APPLICATIONS SOFTWARE

YOUR TURN

Start with a blank 1-2-3 worksheet on the screen. Make sure the worksheet is in the READY mode and the current cell address is A1.

    Type MONTHLY BUDGET
    Press <Return>

Notice that the title MONTHLY BUDGET spills over into cell B1 because it is longer than nine characters. Also, notice that the cell pointer remains in cell A1.

    Go to cell A3. Use either the GOTO key <F5> or the pointer movement key < ↓ >. When you are instructed to go to a specific cell, always check the cell address to make sure the cell pointer is in the correct cell.

    In cell A3, type Income
    Press < ↓ >

Notice that the cell pointer automatically moves one cell down, to cell A4.

    Press the space bar twice and type Take-Home Pay
    Press < ↓ > three times. The cell address now should read A7
    Type Expenses
    Press <Return>

By now you should be familiar with the three steps involved in entering a label: going to a specific cell location, typing the label, and pressing either the <Return> key or the Up < ↑ >, Down < ↓ >, Left <←>, or Right <→> key. For the remainder of the chapter, when you are instructed "Enter A Label in A1", for example, this means go to cell A1, type "A Label," and press either <Return>, < ↓ >, < ↑ >, <←>, or <→>.

    Enter Rent in A9
    Enter Phone in A10
    Enter Food in A11
    Enter Personal in A12
    Enter Clothing in A13
    Enter Transportation in A14
    Enter Student Loan in A15
    Enter Car Loan in A16
    Enter Insurance in A17
    Enter Savings in A18
    Enter TOTAL in A20
    Enter Budgeted in C7
    Enter Actual in D7
    Enter Difference in E7
    Enter Per of Income in G7

Now practice using <F2>, the Edit key:

    Go to G7
    Press <F2>

CHAPTER 12: INTRODUCTION TO SPREADSHEETS AND LOTUS 1-2-3

The mode indicator reads EDIT and the label moves from the status line to the entry line.

> Press <←> ten times, or until the cursor is one space to the right of the *r* in *Per*
> Press the <Backspace> key three times to erase *Per*
> Type %
> Press <Return>

When all the labels are entered, the screen should look like Figure 12-5. Save the worksheet under the filename BUDGET1.

Entering Values

Values are either numbers or formulas. Like all spreadsheet programs, Lotus 1-2-3 processes labels and values differently. A value, unlike a label, can be used in an arithmetic calculation. A label can spill over into several cells, but a value must be confined to one cell. Because 1-2-3 distinguishes labels from values, care must be taken in making entries.

The first character of an entry distinguishes it as either a label or a value. Because most labels are words, 1-2-3 assumes that an entry is a label if its first character is a letter. If the first character is a number, 1-2-3 assumes the entry is a value. For the most part, the following rules apply:

■ The entry is interpreted as a value if the first character is one of the following: 0123456789 + − (.@#$.

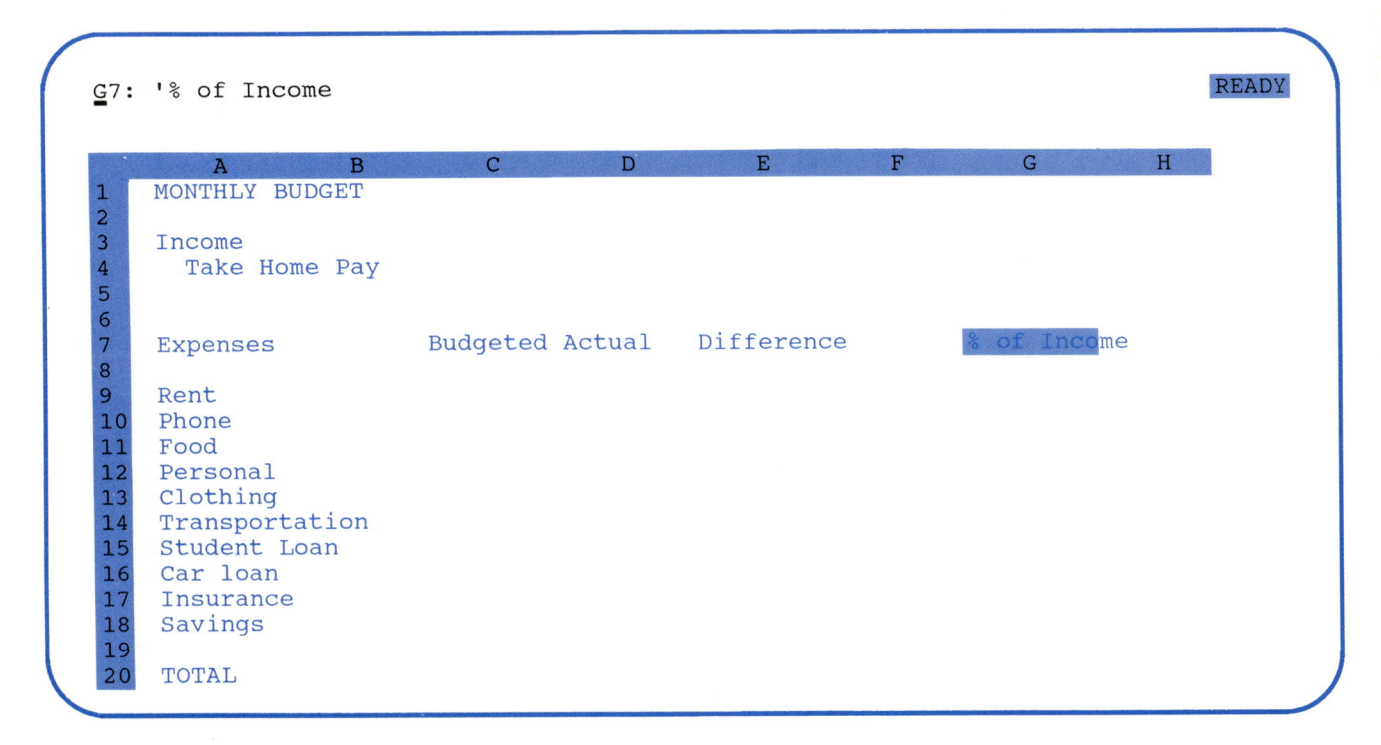

Figure 12-5
Entering Labels in the BUDGET1 Worksheet

```
G7: '% of Income                                                    READY

         A         B         C         D         E         F         G         H
  1  MONTHLY BUDGET
  2
  3  Income
  4     Take Home Pay
  5
  6
  7  Expenses            Budgeted  Actual    Difference          % of Income
  8
  9  Rent
 10  Phone
 11  Food
 12  Personal
 13  Clothing
 14  Transportation
 15  Student Loan
 16  Car loan
 17  Insurance
 18  Savings
 19
 20  TOTAL
```

366   PART TWO: APPLICATIONS SOFTWARE

■ If the first character is any character other than those listed above, the entry is interpreted as a label.

Values are entered into a cell in the same way as labels. The worksheet must be in the READY mode. The cell pointer is moved to the appropriate cell, the number is typed into the cell, and the number is stored in the cell by pressing <Return>, <↑>, <↓>, <←>, or <→>.

Values also are edited the same way as labels. A value can be edited with the <Backspace> key before it has been stored in the cell. After a value has been stored, it can be changed either by typing a new entry or by using the <F2> key.

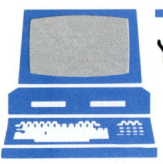

YOUR TURN

Start with the BUDGET1 file on your screen. For this hands-on exercise, you are going to enter numbers into cells on the worksheet.

    Enter 1100 in C4

Notice that the mode indicator changes to VALUE as soon as a number is typed.

    Enter 240 in C9
    Enter 20 in C10
    Enter 200 in C11
    Enter 100 in C12
    Enter 70 in C13
    Enter 120 in C14
    Enter 40 in C15
    Enter 150 in C16
    Enter 50 in C17
    Enter 110 in C18
    Enter 240 in D9
    Enter 35 in D10
    Enter 178 in D11
    Enter 95 in D12
    Enter 114 in D13
    Enter 108 in D14
    Enter 40 in D15
    Enter 150 in D16
    Enter 50 in D17
    Enter 90 in D18

When all the values have been entered, your worksheet should look like Figure 12-6.

RANGE
A rectangular block of one or more cells in the worksheet, which is treated as one unit.

Ranges

A **range** is a rectangular block of one or more cells in the worksheet which 1-2-3 treats as one unit. A range can be composed of a single cell, one row, one

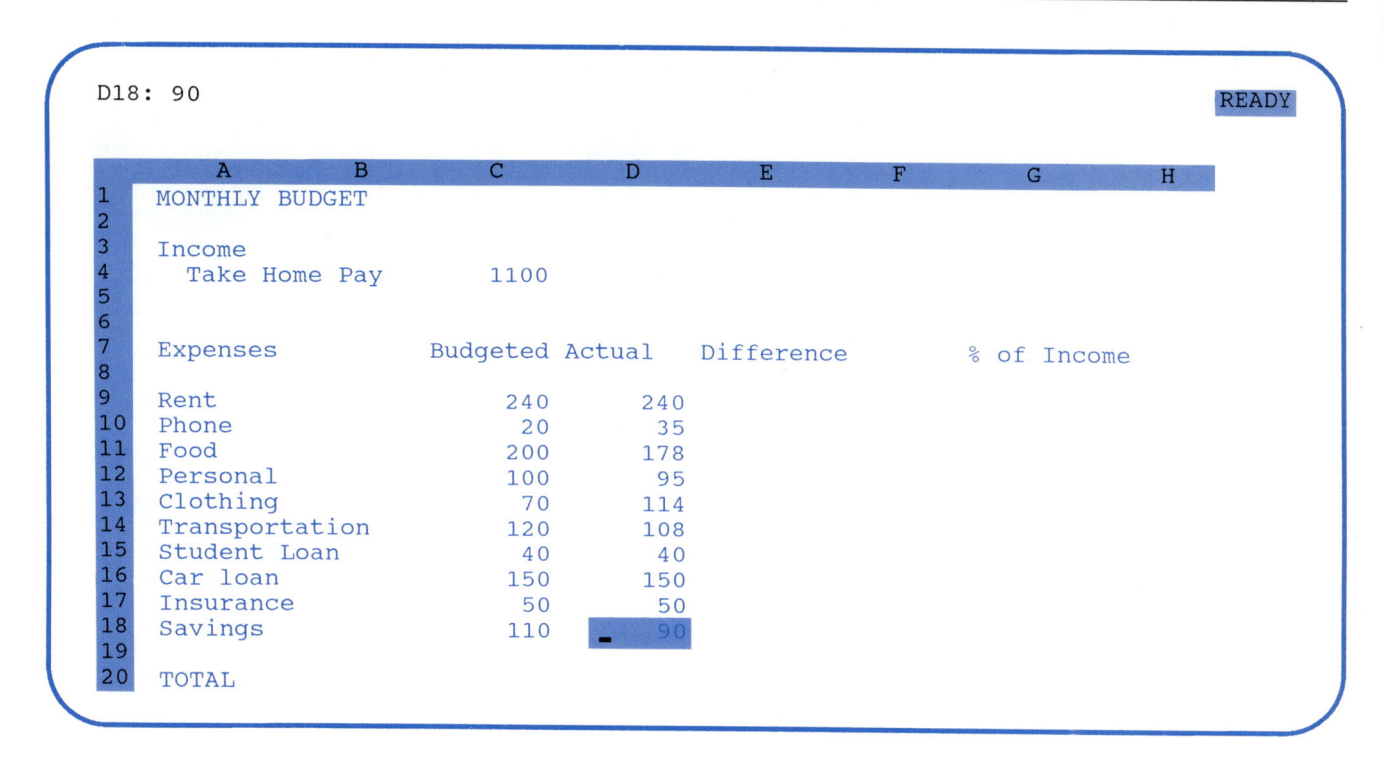

CHAPTER 12: INTRODUCTION TO SPREADSHEETS AND LOTUS 1-2-3   367

```
D18: 90                                                              READY

        A         B         C         D         E         F         G         H
 1  MONTHLY BUDGET
 2
 3  Income
 4     Take Home Pay     1100
 5
 6
 7  Expenses           Budgeted  Actual    Difference          % of Income
 8
 9  Rent                 240       240
10  Phone                 20        35
11  Food                 200       178
12  Personal             100        95
13  Clothing              70       114
14  Transportation       120       108
15  Student Loan          40        40
16  Car loan             150       150
17  Insurance             50        50
18  Savings              110        90
19
20  TOTAL
```

Figure 12-6
Entering Values in the BUDGET1 Worksheet

column, or a block of rows and columns that form a rectangle (see Figure 12-7). Ranges are among the valuable assets of electronic spreadsheets. Instead of performing a particular function on one cell at a time, the user can define a range of cells and have a function performed on the entire range. For example, ranges can be used to copy, move, or erase entire sections of a worksheet.

YOUR TURN   Start with the BUDGET1 worksheet on the screen.

Go to cell A5
Type \ = (the backslash key followed by the equal sign)
Press <Return>

Notice that, even though the equal sign was typed only once, the double lines fill the entire cell. That is because the backslash was typed before the equal sign. In Lotus 1-2-3, the backslash functions as a repeating label prefix. Whatever is typed after the backslash repeats itself until it fills the entire cell.

Type /
Select Copy

The message ENTER RANGE TO COPY FROM: A5..A5 appears in the entry line, and the mode indicator says POINT. A5 is the current location of the

**Figure 12-7
Ranges**

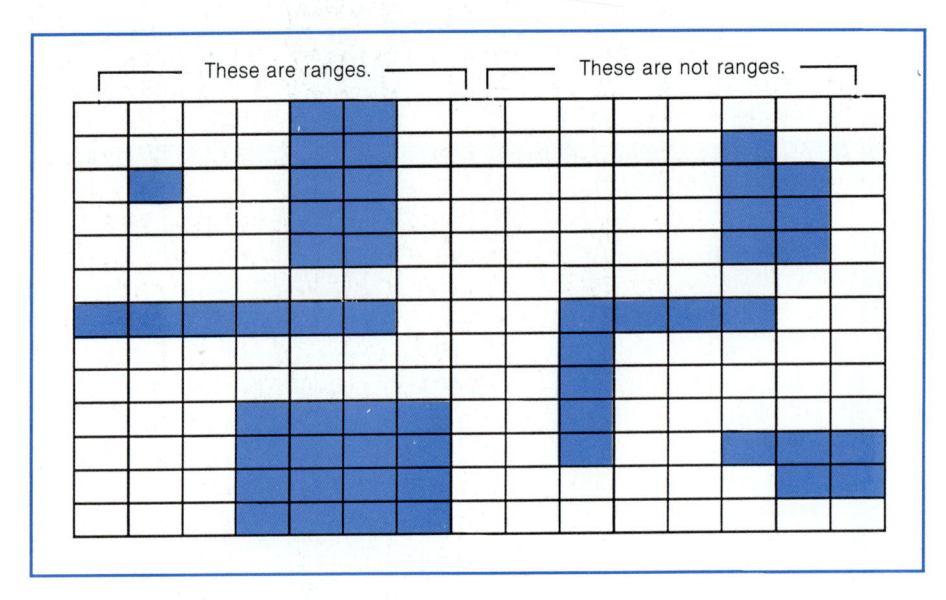

cell pointer, and it is also a one-cell range. You are now going to copy this one-cell range. Because A5 is the only cell to be copied, press the <Return> key. The entry line now reads ENTER RANGE TO COPY TO: A5. You now need to indicate the range of cells where you want the double lines copied to. There are two ways to indicate a range. The first way is to type the cell addresses that comprise the range, separated by a period:

Type **B5.H5**
Press <Return>

The second way to indicate a range is to extend the highlighting to include all the cell addresses that constitute the range:

Go to A8.
Type \-
Press <Return>
Type /
Select Copy

The prompt ENTER RANGE TO COPY FROM: A8..A8 appears in the entry line. Again, this one-cell range is what you want to copy, so press <Return>. The prompt ENTER RANGE TO COPY TO: A8 now appears in the entry line. This time you are going to indicate the range by expanding the highlighting. The range must first be "anchored" before the highlighting can be expanded. Typing a period after the cell address where the highlighting is to begin anchors the highlighting—that is, it indicates the address of the first cell in the range.

Type **.** (period) to anchor the first cell of the range in cell A8

Notice that the entry line of the control panel now reads ENTER RANGE TO COPY TO: A8..A8. Once the period was pressed, 1-2-3 automatically added

..A8. You can tell if a range is anchored by looking at this notation by the prompt. If there is only one cell address, such as A8, the range is not anchored. If there is a notation of a range, such as A8..A8, the range is anchored.

Press <→> seven times

Notice that the highlighting now extends through the range of cells A8-H8, and that the notation by the prompt in the entry line now reads A8..H8.

Press <Return>

Pressing <Return> confirms the range indicated by the highlighting. The single line is copied into that range of cells.

1-2-3 Tip: If the range is anchored in the wrong cell, press <Esc> to release the range, move the cell pointer to the correct cell, and type a period (.) to reanchor the range.

Entering Formulas

Formulas are mathematical expressions. When writing formulas with 1-2-3, you can use addition, subtraction, multiplication, division, and exponentiation, as well as advanced financial and statistical analysis. Formulas can contain references to particular cells (using their cell addresses) and can indicate mathematical operations to be performed on the values within those cells.

Formulas are entered on a worksheet in the same way that labels and numbers are entered—by typing them into cells. A formula typically is created by entering either a value or a cell address, then a mathematical operator, and then another value or cell address, and so on. The mathematical operators most frequently used in formulas are:

+ add
− subtract
* multiply
/ divide

Formulas often contain cell addresses. For example, a formula might be A5+A6+A7. Because formulas are values, and Lotus assumes an entry beginning with a letter is a label, formulas often begin with a plus sign (+) to indicate what follows is a formula, not a label. If the previous example were entered into a worksheet, it would be entered as +A5+A6+A7.

There are two ways to enter formulas into cells: (1) by typing the formula, and (2) by pointing to the cells included in the formula. The following exercise uses both methods.

PART TWO: APPLICATIONS SOFTWARE

YOUR TURN

Start with the BUDGET1 worksheet on your screen. For this hands-on exercise, you are going to enter formulas into cells on the worksheet. First, you are going to enter formulas by typing them.

>Go to C20
>Type **240+20+200+100+70+120+40+150+50+110**

Notice that the mode indicator changes to VALUE and that the formula you typed appears in the entry line.

>Press <Return>

The mode indicator changes to READY, the formula moves to the status line, and the sum (1100) appears in cell C20. The next formula is entered using cell addresses rather than numbers:

>Go to D20
>Type **+D9+D10+D11+D12+D13+D14+D15+D16+D17+D18**

Remember that the plus sign (+) must be the first character typed, to indicate to Lotus that this is a value, not a label.

>Press <Return>

Again, the sum appears in the cell where the formula was entered, even though you used cell addresses rather than numbers in the formula.
    When a formula is long, like this one, typing in all the numbers or cell addresses is time-consuming and making a typing error is easy. A more efficient way to enter formulas is by pointing to the cells included in the formula. Reenter the two formulas just entered using this method:

>Go to C20
>Type **+**
>Using the <↑> key, move to C18

Notice that the mode indicator says POINT and that +C18 is in the entry line. You had to use the <↑> key rather than the <F5> key to move to C18 because the GOTO key, <F5>, does not function while you are pointing to cells in a formula.

>Type **+**

The cell pointer moves back to C20.

>Using the <↑> key, move to C17
>Type **+**

Again, the cell pointer moves back to C20.

    Move to C16
    Type +
    Move to C15
    Type +
    Move to C14
    Type +
    Move to C13
    Type +
    Move to C12
    Type +
    Move to C11
    Type +
    Move to C10
    Type +
    Move to C9
    Press <Return>

The formula, using cell addresses, is in the status line. The sum is in cell C20. Using the same pointing method, reenter the formula for cell D20.

The column titled Difference shows the difference between what was budgeted for the month and what was actually spent. Enter formulas in cells E9 through E18 to show this difference:

    Go to E9
    Type +
    Move to C9
    Type −
    Move to D9
    Press <Return>

The formula appears in the status line, the mode indicator says READY, and the difference appears in cell E9.

    Go to E10
    Type +
    Move to C10
    Type −
    Move to D10
    Press <Return>

Because $15.00 more than what was budgeted was actually spent, the number appears as a negative.

    Go to E11
    Type +
    Move to C11

Type –
Move to D11
Press <Return>

Continue to enter formulas into cells E12 through E18 which calculate the difference between what was budgeted and what was actually spent. Save the amended worksheet.

Formatting Cells

Values in a Lotus 1-2-3 worksheet can be formatted. That is, they can be made to appear with dollar signs, with commas, or rounded off to a certain number of decimal places. Either one cell or a range of cells can be formatted.

To format a cell, first select the Range option from the Main menu. Then select Format. The options for the Format command appear in the entry line. Table 12-4 lists these options and the functions they perform.

If Fixed, Scientific, Currency, Comma (,), or Percent is selected as a format, 1-2-3 prompts you to enter the number of decimal places you would like displayed. Up to 15 decimal places can be displayed. No matter how many decimal places are actually displayed, however, 1-2-3 remembers the number to maximum precision. That is, formatting a value only changes the way it is displayed; the value itself does not change. For example, suppose the value in cell B12 is 13.9812. If cell B12 is formatted using the Fixed option to be rounded to two decimal places, the number 13.98 appears in cell B12 on the worksheet. If B12 is used in a formula, however, 1-2-3 uses 13.9812 in its calculations; it does not use 13.98.

YOUR TURN

Start with the BUDGET1 worksheet on the screen.

Go to C9
Type /
Select Range
Select Format
Select Currency

Lotus 1-2-3 prompts you to enter the number of decimal places. The default setting is 2. Select the default setting by pressing <Return>. The entry line reads ENTER RANGE TO FORMAT: C9..C9.

Press the <↓> key nine times, or until the range reaches C18
Press <→> twice

The range from C9 to E18 is now selected, as indicated in the entry line.

Press <Return>

Table 12-4
Format Command Options

Option	Description
Fixed	Values are rounded to a fixed number of places. Example: 8.67
Scientific	Exponential notation. Example: 2.56E+05
Currency	Dollars and cents. Example: $30.45
,	Commas are added to long numbers. Example: 32,450. Negative numbers are placed in parentheses. Example: (5,469)
General	No fixed number of decimal places is set. Example: 8.671
Percent	Value is multiplied by 100 and a % sign added. Example: 58%
Date	Date format. Example: DD-MMM-YY (28-Sep-53)
Text	Displays formula in the cell.
Hidden	Hides the cell entries.
Reset	Returns cell or cells to the global default format, which, if not changed, is General.

All the values in cells C9 to E18 now appear in the currency format. Notice that the negative numbers now appear within parentheses rather than having a minus sign in front of them. The status line reads C9: (C2) 240. The C2 within parentheses indicates how the cell has been formatted. It stands for Currency rounded to 2 decimal places.

The column titled % of Income is used for figuring out what percentage of the monthly take-home pay was actually spent on each of the budgeted expenses. The formula used to figure this percentage is the amount spent divided by the monthly take-home pay. For example, the formula to be entered into G9 is 240/1100 or D9/C4. Enter the appropriate formulas into cells G9 through G18. Remember, if you use cell addresses in your formulas, you must use the + prefix.

Next, format cells G9–G18 using the Percent format option:

Go to G9
Type /
Select Range
Select Format
Select Percent

The entry line reads ENTER NUMBER OF DECIMAL PLACES (0..15): 2.

Type **0**
Press <Return>
Press <↓> nine times, or until the cell range G9 through G18 is selected
Press <Return>

The percentages appear in column G. In the first line of the control panel, (P0) stands for the Percentage format carried out to 0 decimal places. Save the amended BUDGET1 worksheet.

374 PART TWO: APPLICATIONS SOFTWARE

Erasing A Cell

Erasing a cell or a range of cells on a 1-2-3 worksheet is easy. First select Range from the Main menu; then select Erase. The prompt ENTER RANGE TO ERASE appears. Using the <→>, <←>, <↑> and <↓> keys, select the range to be erased and press <Return>.

If a value that has been used in a formula is erased, the formula using that value automatically recalculates without the value.

YOUR TURN

Start with the BUDGET1 worksheet on your screen.

Go to A12
Type /
Select Range
Select Erase

The prompt ENTER RANGE TO ERASE: A12..A12 appears in the entry line. Only one cell, A12, is to be erased, so press <Return>.

Enter `Spending $` in A12

Save the amended worksheet as BUDGET1.

Learning Check

1. The Edit key is _____.
   a. F1   c. F5
   b. F2   d. F10

2. If the first character of an entry is a number, Lotus assumes the entry is a _____.

3. A _____ is a rectangular block of cells in a worksheet which Lotus treats as one unit.

4. If the first entry in a formula is a cell address, the formula must be preceded with a _____.

5. When a cell is formatted, both the way the value is displayed and the value itself are changed. (True or False?)

Answers

1. b. 2. value 3. range 4. plus sign (+) 5. False

Changing the Appearance of a Worksheet

Having a worksheet that is easy to read is important. Lotus 1-2-3 includes such options as being able to align labels, adjust column widths, and insert and delete rows and columns, in order to help create a neat and easily understandable worksheet. These options are discussed in the following sections.

Aligning Labels

A label prefix determines the alignment of a label—that is, whether it aligns on the left side of the cell, is centered within the cell, or is aligned on the right side of the cell. A label prefix is the first character typed when entering a label. Table 12-5 lists the label prefixes and explains their functions.

Lotus 1-2-3's default prefix is the apostrophe. That is, if no prefix is indicated, Lotus aligns the labels on the left side of the cell.

Label prefixes also enable a heading that begins with a number to be used as a label. For example, if you wanted to use 1986, 1987, and 1988 as labels, Lotus would read them as values unless you used a label prefix. Just as the plus sign is typed in as the first character of a formula beginning with a cell address, so a label prefix must be the first character of a label beginning with a number. In this example, you would type the following into the cells: ^1986, ^1987, ^1988. (The label prefix character does not appear in the cell as part of the label.)

There are two methods for setting up label prefixes. The first is to type in the prefix as part of the title. The second, which is explained in the following exercise, is to align a range of labels.

YOUR TURN Start with the BUDGET1 worksheet on your screen.

Go to A7
Type /
Select Range
Select Label

LEFT, RIGHT, and CENTER appear in the entry. Currently the labels are aligned at the left side of the cell. Move the menu pointer to RIGHT and press <Return>.

**Table 12-5
Label Prefixes**

Label Prefix	Purpose
' (apostrophe)	To align labels on the left side of the cell
^ (caret)	To center labels within the cell
" (double quotation mark)	To align labels on the right side of the cell
\ (backslash)	To repeat a single character or a set of characters for the length of the cell

ENTER RANGE OF LABELS: A7..A7 appears on the entry line.

Press <→> seven times, or until the range of cells from A7 through H7 is selected
Press <Return>

Move the cell pointer through row 7. Notice that each label is preceded by the label prefix ".

Go to A7
Type /
Select Range
Select Label
Select Center
Enter the range of labels A7 through H7
Press <Return>

Move the cell pointer through row 7. Now the ^ label prefix is in front of each label. Save the amended worksheet BUDGET1.

Adjusting Column Widths

The default column width in Lotus 1-2-3 is nine characters. The column width can be adjusted, however, from 1 to 240 characters. The width of individual columns can be set, or the width of all the columns in the worksheet can be set.

YOUR TURN   Start with the BUDGET1 worksheet on your screen.

Go to C4

In the previous hands-on exercise, when cells were changed to the currency format, cells C4, C20, and D20 were not formatted. Now you are going to format these cells.

Type /
Select Range
Select Format
Select Currency
Press <Return> to accept the default setting at two decimal places
Press <Return> again to accept a range of one cell, C4

Notice that asterisks now fill C4. Changing the format to currency added enough characters to 1100 that it is now too long to fit in the column at its present width. Look at the control panel. Even though asterisks appear on the worksheet, Lotus still has the value 1100 stored in cell C4.

Keep the cell pointer at C4. You are going to change the width of the column so that the actual value, rather than asterisks, appears on the worksheet in cell C4.

Type /
Select Worksheet
Select Column
Select Set-Width

ENTER COLUMN WIDTH (1..240): 9 now appears in the entry line, because 9 is the current width of the column.

Press <→> once

Notice that the 9 in the entry line changed to a 10. The current column width is now 10. $1,100.00 now appears on the worksheet in C4. A column width of 10 is enough space for this value.

Press <Return>

The control panel now reads C4: (C2) [W10] 1100. This indicates that cell C4 is formatted as currency carried out to two decimal places, the width of C4 is 10, and the value in C4 is 1100.

Go to C20
Format C20 as currency carried out to two decimal places

Because the width of the column is 10, the value appears in C20. When you are changing the width of a column, the cell pointer can be on any cell in the column. Move the cell pointer to any cell in column D and change the width of column D to 10. Then format D20 as currency carried out to two decimal places.
   Column F is too wide. Move the cell pointer to column F and change the width to 3. When the prompt ENTER COLUMN WIDTH (1..240) appears in the entry line, type **3** and press <Return>.
   Save the amended worksheet BUDGET1.

Inserting and Deleting Rows and Columns

Sometimes the appearance of a worksheet can be enhanced by adding a row or column. Perhaps a row or column has to be added to accommodate additional data, or data that is no longer relevant has to be deleted from a worksheet. Adding or deleting rows and columns on a Lotus worksheet is a simple task that involves pointing to the location where the row or column is to be added or deleted.
   To add a row or column, first position the cell pointer. The cell pointer must be positioned to the right of where a column is to appear and under where a row is to appear. Select the Worksheet option from the Main menu. Next select Insert. The option of selecting either Column or Row appears next. After you select Row

or Column, the prompt ENTER COLUMN (ROW) INSERT RANGE appears in the entry line. If only one column or row is to be inserted, simply press <Return>. If more than one column or row is to be inserted, the range of the insertion can be indicated either by using the pointer movement keys or by typing in the range. Once the <Return> key is pressed, the row or column is added, and the worksheet returns to the READY mode.

Deleting a row or column is similar to adding a row or column. Select Worksheet from the Main menu, and select Delete. Next you choose to delete either a row or a column, and indicate the range of columns or rows to be deleted. Pressing the <Return> key deletes the designated rows or columns and the worksheet returns to the READY mode.

Be very careful when deleting rows and columns. Once a row or column is deleted, it is erased from memory and cannot be retrieved. Accidentally deleting a row when you intended to delete a column could be disastrous.

YOUR TURN

Start with the BUDGET1 worksheet on the screen. You are going to delete row 6 from the worksheet.

> Go to A6
> Type /
> *Select Worksheet*
> *Select Delete*
> *Select Row*
> Press <Return>, because you want to delete row 6 only.

Now you are going to add a row between Take-Home Pay and the double lines:

> Go to A5
> Type /
> *Select Worksheet*
> *Select Insert*
> *Select Row*
> Press <Return>, because you want to add one row only.

Your worksheet should look like Figure 12-8 when completed.
Save the amended BUDGET1 file.

Printing A Worksheet

There are times when it is useful to have a hard copy of a worksheet. Printing a Lotus worksheet is described in this section.

Before printing a worksheet, make sure to save the file so that the hard copy will include the latest changes or additions. Select the Print option from the Main

```
A5:                                                                    READY


      A         B           C           D           E         F    G       H
 1  MONTHLY BUDGET
 2
 3  Income
 4    Take Home Pay   $1,100.00
 5
 6  ============================================================
 7  Expenses              Budgeted    Actual    Difference   % of Income
 8  ------------------------------------------------------------
 9  Rent                  $240.00    $240.00      $0.00        22%
10  Phone                  $20.00     $35.00    ($15.00)        3%
11  Food                  $200.00    $178.00     $22.00        16%
12  Spending $            $100.00     $95.00      $5.00         9%
13  Clothing               $70.00    $114.00    ($44.00)       10%
14  Transportation       $120.00    $108.00     $12.00        10%
15  Student Loan           $40.00     $40.00      $0.00         4%
16  Car loan              $150.00    $150.00      $0.00        14%
17  Insurance              $50.00     $50.00      $0.00         5%
18  Savings               $110.00     $90.00     $20.00         8%
19
20  TOTAL              $1,100.00  $1,100.00
```

Figure 12-8
Changing the Appearance of the BUDGET1 Worksheet

menu. The options PRINTER and FILE appear next. A Lotus worksheet can be sent directly to a printer, or it can be stored in a print file for later processing. Select Printer. Eight Printer options appear in the entry line. These options offer choices regarding the appearance and format of the printout. Table 12-6 lists the Printer options and describes their functions.

The only printer option that must be selected is Range. After you select range, the prompt ENTER PRINT RANGE appears in the entry line. To specify the range to be printed, move the cell pointer to the first cell to be printed. The address of that cell appears after the prompt in the entry line. Type a period (.) to anchor the range, and then move the cell pointer to the last cell to be printed. Press <Return>. The Printer options return to the entry line.

Table 12-6
Printer Options

Option	Description
Range	Specifies the range of the worksheet to be printed. The range must be specified even if all the data on the worksheet is being printed.
Line	Advances the paper one line.
Page	Advances the paper one page.
Options	Allows a number of choices to be made regarding the appearance of the worksheet. These choices include specifying a header or footer to be printed on each page, setting margins, specifying border columns and rows, and specifying the number of lines per page.
Clear	Resets some or all of the print settings.
Align	Resets the alignment of the paper to the top of the page.
Go	Starts the printing process.
Quit	Returns 1-2-3 to the READY mode.

PART TWO: APPLICATIONS SOFTWARE

Make sure the printer is connected to your computer and is online. Select Go from the Printer options, and the worksheet is printed. The Printer options remain in the entry line after the worksheet has been printed. When you no longer want to print, select Quit and the worksheet returns to the READY mode.

YOUR TURN

You are going to print the entire BUDGET1 worksheet.

Type /
Select Print
Select Printer
Select Range

Move the cell pointer to A1. Remember, <F5> cannot be used to go to a specific cell when the mode indicator says POINT.

Type a period (.) to anchor the range
Press <→> 7 times to select the columns A through H
Press <↓> 19 times to select the rows 1 through 20

The entire worksheet should now be highlighted.

Press <Return>

Learning Check

1. The label prefix _____ aligns labels on the right side of the cell.
   a. ' (apostrophe)   c. ^ (caret)
   b. " (double quotation mark)   d. \ (backslash)

2. The label prefix _____ repeats a single character or set of characters for the length of the cell.
   a. ' (apostrophe)   c. ^ (caret)
   b. " (double quotation mark)   d. \ (backslash)

3. A heading beginning with a number can only be used as a label if a label prefix precedes it. (True or False?)

4. The default column width in Lotus is _____ characters.
   a. 6   c. 8
   b. 9   d. 10

5. When a row has been deleted accidentally on a Lotus worksheet, it can be retrieved. (True or False?)

Answers

1. b. 2. d. 3. True 4. b. 5. False

The worksheet is no longer highlighted, and the Printer options return to the entry line. Make sure your printer is connected to the computer and online.

Select Go

The BUDGET1 worksheet is printed. It should look like Figure 12-9.

Select Quit

Summary Points

- A spreadsheet program simulates the operations of a calculator and stores the results in the computer's memory.
- An electronic spreadsheet is displayed as a table of columns and rows.
- The three categories of items which can be entered into an electronic spreadsheet are labels, values, and formulas.
- Labels are used to identify the contents of a spreadsheet. A value is a single piece of numeric information used in the calculations of a spreadsheet.
- A formula is a mathematical expression that is assigned to a cell in the spreadsheet.
- The two major areas of a worksheet are the control panel and the window. The control panel displays important information about the worksheet. The window is the portion of the worksheet which is currently displayed.

Figure 12-9
The BUDGET1 Worksheet

```
MONTHLY BUDGET

Income
   Take Home Pay    $1,100.00

================================================================
Expenses            Budgeted    Actual    Difference    % of Income
----------------------------------------------------------------
Rent                $240.00    $240.00      $0.00          22%
Phone                $20.00     $35.00    ($15.00)          3%
Food                $200.00    $178.00     $22.00          16%
Spending $          $100.00     $95.00      $5.00           9%
Clothing             $70.00    $114.00    ($44.00)         10%
Transportation      $120.00    $108.00     $12.00          10%
Student Loan         $40.00     $40.00      $0.00           4%
Car loan            $150.00    $150.00      $0.00          14%
Insurance            $50.00     $50.00      $0.00           5%
Savings             $110.00     $90.00     $20.00           8%

TOTAL             $1,100.00  $1,100.00
```

Lotus 1-2-3 Exercises

To complete the following exercises you need a DOS disk, a Lotus system disk, and a formatted disk that will be your data disk.

1. Starting Lotus 1-2-3
   a. Start the computer with a DOS disk. At the A> prompt, insert the Lotus system disk in drive A and type **Lotus.** What are the six menu options offered on the screen? What are their meanings? How do you select an option?
   b. *Select 123* and press <Return>. What appears on the screen?

2. Moving through the worksheet and entering data.

Now that a worksheet is displayed, you are going to practice moving through the worksheet. First, insert your data disk in drive B.
   a. The cell pointer is positioned on cell A1. Enter the words **last name** into that cell. Describe the steps you use to do this. Which key do you press to go to B1?
   b. In B1, type **first name** and press <↓>. Where is the cell pointer positioned after this action? Which key do you press to go to A2?
   c. Use the GOTO key to go to cell L130. Enter the number **145.6**.
   d. Use the <Home> key to return to cell A1.

3. Building a new worksheet

Now you are going to enter a new worksheet. First, type a slash (/) to activate the Main menu. Then *select Worksheet* and *Erase* to clear the screen and start a new worksheet. This step deletes the information you previously entered. Assume that you want to prepare the following report on the total quantity of items ordered by customers during the past week. In the report X stands for a figure to be computed.

Summary of Products Ordered During Week 30

PRODUCT NAME	CODE	MON	TUE	WED	THR	FRI	TOT
Skirts	1	80	90	50	70	110	X
Shorts	2	120	130	110	140	150	X
Blouses	3	30	30	20	60	70	X
Shirts	4	180	170	150	180	180	X
Socks	5	110	105	120	140	150	X
Jeans	6	165	170	140	150	170	X
Total		X	X	X	X	X	X

   a. Make sure the cell pointer is positioned at cell A1 and start typing the title of the report: **Summary of Products Ordered During Week 30**. In which cell(s) is the text displayed? What do you call this?

b. Start typing the labels. Move the cell pointer to cell A3. Type PRODUCT NAME and press <→>. Where is the cell pointer positioned now? Type the next label, CODE, and press <→> again. Type all the labels in row 3.

c. Move the cell pointer back to cell A3. What happens to the cell entry? *Select Worksheet* and *Column-Width* to set the width of Column A to 15 characters. Describe all the steps taken to change the column width.

d. Move the cell pointer to cell A5. You are now ready to enter the data for each line.

    1. Type the first product name and press <→> to move the pointer to the right. Use the label prefix ^ to center the name.

    2. Type the code and press <→> again to move the cell pointer to the right.

    3. Type the quantities ordered during the week for product 1 in the appropriate cells.

    4. Repeat steps 1 through 3 for the remaining products.

e. You are now ready to compute the totals and complete the report.

    1. Start with the totals per day. For this purpose, move the cell pointer to cell C12. Total orders for the first day are equal to +C5+C6+C7+C8+C9+C10. Enter this formula, using the pointing method.

    2. Enter the appropriate formulas in cells D12, E12, F12, and G12, using the pointing method.

    3. Move the cell pointer to H5. This cell should contain the total for skirts ordered during week 30, that is, the sum of cells B5 through G5. Enter the appropriate formula in cell H5.

    4. Enter the appropriate formulas in cells H6, H7, H8, H9, H10, and H12. What is the grand total of products ordered during the week?

f. To improve the appearance of the report, you want to draw a horizontal line between the last line of data and the totals. Move the cell pointer to cell C11. Type \ — . What appears in that cell? Copy this cell entry to the remaining cells through H11.

4. The report is now ready. Save the worksheet under the name SALES30.
5. Print the report.
6. When you have finished, return to DOS by the appropriate steps.

Lotus 1-2-3 Problems

You are an administrative assistant in the sales department. The manager asks you to prepare a variance report, in order to analyze each division's activity and the performance of the sales force during the past year. To complete the problem, you need to use the Lotus 1-2-3 system disk and the SALES file included on your Student File Disk.

1. Following the appropriate steps, start Lotus and insert the Student File Disk with the permanent files into drive B.

2. Retrieve the file SALES and save it under the name NEW. From now on, use the file NEW. The original data will always be in the file SALES if you need to start over, or if you want to work through the questions again.

3. Retrieve the file NEW. You now have access to the data provided to you by the manager. Move the cell pointer through the worksheet to familiarize yourself with the information. Notice that this worksheet contains the forecast and actual sales for the previous calendar year.

4. You want to compute all the totals per division and per quarter, and the grand total for the year. First compute the annual forecasted sales for each division:
    a. Go to cell F7. Using the pointing method, enter the formula that finds the total of the Northwest division's yearly forecasted sales.
    b. Using the pointing method, enter the formulas in cells F8, F9, and F10 which find the total yearly forecasted sales for the East Coast, Midwest, and Central divisions respectively.

Next, compute the total forecasted sales per quarter and for the total year:

    c. Go to B12. Using the pointing method, enter the formula that finds the total of all the divisions' forecasted sales in the first quarter.
    d. Using the pointing method, enter the formulas in cells, C12, D12, and E12 which find the totals for all the divisions' forecasted sales in the second, third, and fourth quarters respectively.
    e. Go to F12. Compute the total forecasted sales for all the divisions for the entire year.

Repeat steps a through e for realized sales, starting at cell F15.

5. Now you want to compute the variances per quarter and per division. Variances are deviations of the actual results from what was expected. For one quarter, the variance is equal to realized sales minus forecasted sales. For example, the formula to compute the variance for the Northwest division in the first quarter is B15 − B7.
    a. Go to B23. Enter the formula that computes the variance for the Northwest division in the first quarter.
    b. In cells C23, D23, and E23, enter the formulas that compute the variances for the Northwest division in the second, third and fourth quarters respectively.
    c. Follow the same procedure to find the variances for the East Coast, Midwest, and Central divisions.
    d. In cells B28, C28, D28, and E28, compute the total variances per quarter.
    e. In cells F23, F24, F25, and F26 compute the total variances per division.
    f. In cell F28, compute the total variance for the entire company for the entire year.

6. Now that you have finished building the worksheet, you would like to improve its appearance.
    a. Insert a row below the subtitles (Forecasted sales, Realized sales, and Variance report).

    b. Insert a column before the "Total Y1" column.
    c. Increase the first column width to 15 in order to be able to read "East Coast" completely.
    d. Type Thousands $ under the main title.
    e. Above each total line, draw a horizontal line using the repeating label prefix (\ −). Start at column B.
    f. Below each total line, draw a double line using the repeating label prefix (\ =).

7. Save and print the report.
8. Look over the report. What are your first conclusions concerning the activity of the firm? Which division has performed best? Do you think that there is a problem with the forecasts?

CHAPTER 13

Advanced Lotus 1-2-3

Outline

Introduction
   Copy and Move
The Difference Between Global
   and Range Commands
Functions
Copying Formulas
Freezing Titles
Order of Precedence
Spreadsheet Analysis

Learning Check
Graphics
   Bar Graphs and Pie Charts
   Creating a Bar Graph and a Pie
     Chart
   Printing a Graph
Learning Check
Summary of Frequently Used
   Lotus 1-2-3 Menus and

Submenus
Summary of Lotus 1-2-3
   Commands
Summary Points
Lotus 1-2-3 Exercises
Lotus 1-2-3 Problems

Introduction

In the previous chapter, the fundamentals for creating a basic worksheet were covered. Lotus 1-2-3 also has many advanced features that simplify the task of creating more complex worksheets. These features, such as copy and move and @functions, are covered in this chapter. In addition, this chapter describes how to create graphs using Lotus 1-2-3.

Another important concept covered in this chapter is **spreadsheet analysis.** Spreadsheet analysis (or what-if analysis) is the mental process of evaluating information contained within an electronic spreadsheet. Often it involves comparing various results generated by the spreadsheet. A **model,** in terms of a spreadsheet, is a numeric representation of a real-world situation. For example, a home budget is a numeric representation of the expenses involved in maintaining a household and therefore can be considered a model. The hands-on exercises in this chapter provide an introduction to spreadsheet analysis.

SPREADSHEET ANALYSIS
A mental process of evaluating information contained in an electronic spreadsheet; also called what-if analysis.

MODEL
A numeric representation of a real-world situation.

Copy and Move

Some of the data entered into complex worksheets is repetitive. For example, the same labels or the same formulas may be repeated. Lotus 1-2-3 has a copy and move feature that enables the user to copy any cell or cells in the worksheet and move them to any other part of the worksheet, instead of having to type the same data two or more times.

The Copy command is one of the options from 1-2-3's Main menu. After the user selects Copy, the prompt ENTER RANGE TO COPY FROM appears in the entry line. The range to be copied is then selected, either by using the pointer-movement keys or by typing the range of cells. After this range has been selected, the prompt ENTER RANGE TO COPY TO appears in the entry line. Move the pointer to the first cell of the range where the data is to be copied, and press <Return>. All the data moves automatically to the new range. You need not specify a range equal in size to the range that was copied.

YOUR TURN

Because you are now familiar with Lotus commands, the hands-on exercises in this chapter use an abbreviated method to indicate what commands are to be selected. For example, the following instructions indicate that you should type a slash to activate the Main menu, select Worksheet from the Main menu options, and select Erase from the worksheet options:

/ WORKSHEET ERASE

Start with a blank worksheet on the screen. Enter the following labels in the cells indicated:

CHAPTER 13: ADVANCED LOTUS 1-2-3

Cell	Label	
A1	INCOME	
A3	Rent	
A5	Apt. #1	
A6	Apt. #2	
A7	Apt. #3	
A9	EXPENSES	
A11	Repairs	
B3	^1983	(Remember to use the ^ label prefix, because these dates are labels, not values).
C3	^1984	
D3	^1985	
E3	^1986	
F3	^1987	
G3	^1988	

Now you are going to copy cells B3 through G3 and move the copy to cells B11 through G11. You also will copy cells A5 through A7 and move the copy to cells A13 through A15.

    Go to B3
    / COPY

When the ENTER RANGE TO COPY FROM prompt appears, move the cell pointer using the <→> key to G3. Press <Return>. When the prompt ENTER RANGE TO COPY TO appears, move the cell pointer to B11 using the <↓> key. Press <Return>. The labels are copied automatically to cells B11 through G11.

    Go to A5
    / COPY
    Select the range A5 through A7
    Go to A13
    Press <Return>

The labels are copied automatically to cells A13 through A15. Save this worksheet as EXAMPLE on your data disk.

1-2-3 Tip: Before copying a range, make sure there is no data in the range where the data will be written. If there is data in that range, the Copy command will write over it, and that data will be irretrievably lost.

**Table 13-1
Global Options**

Option	Description
Format	Sets a global format. For example, the entire worksheet could be formatted as currency.
Label-Prefix	Sets a global label alignment prefix. For example, all the labels in the worksheet could be centered.
Column-width	Sets a global column width. For example, every column in the worksheet could be 12 characters wide.
Recalculation	Determines when, in what order, and how many times formulas in the worksheet are recalculated.
Protection	Prevents changes from being made to cells.
Default	Enables the user to select his or her own default settings for the type of printer being used and its connection; the directory 1-2-3 automatically uses when searching for files; international display formats; the method of using the Help facility; and the type of clock display on the screen.
Zero	Determines whether values of zero are displayed on the screen.

The Difference Between Global and Range Commands

Many Lotus 1-2-3 commands can be applied either to a specific range of cells or to the entire worksheet. For example, if every value in a particular worksheet is currency, the entire worksheet can be formatted one time and all the values in that worksheet will appear as currency.

To use the Global command, first select Worksheet from the Main menu. Next, select Global and a menu of all the Global options appears. Table 13-1 lists these options and describes their functions.

YOUR TURN

Start with the EXAMPLE file on the screen and enter the following values in the cells indicated:

Cells	Values	Cells	Values
B5	2280	B13	250
B6	4080	B14	190
B7	3880	B15	312
C5	2460	C13	235
C6	4260	C14	285
C7	4060	C15	345
D5	2700	D13	310
D6	4500	D14	308
D7	4300	D15	296
E5	3000	E13	433
E6	4800	E14	507
E7	4600	E15	472

```
E15: 472                                                              READY


          A            B            C            D            E            F
 1   INCOME
 2
 3   Rent         1983         1984         1985         1986         1987
 4
 5   Apt #1       $2,280.00    $2,460.00    $2,700.00    $3,000.00
 6   Apt #2       $4,080.00    $4,260.00    $4,500.00    $4,800.00
 7   Apt #3       $3,880.00    $4,060.00    $4,300.00    $4,600.00
 8
 9   EXPENSES
10
11   Repairs      1983         1984         1985         1986         1987
12
13   Apt #1       $250.00      $235.00      $310.00      $433.00
14   Apt #2       $190.00      $285.00      $308.00      $507.00
15   Apt #3       $312.00      $345.00      $296.00      $472.00
16
17
18
19
20
```

Figure 13-1
The EXAMPLE File With a Global Currency Format and Global Column-Width Setting

All the values in this particular worksheet are currency, so you are going to format the entire worksheet as currency:

/ WORKSHEET GLOBAL FORMAT CURRENCY

When the prompt ENTER NUMBER OF DECIMAL PLACES appears, press <Return> to accept the default setting of 2.

Asterisks appear in many of the cells because the columns are not wide enough to display some of the values. You are going to change the column width of the entire worksheet:

/ WORKSHEET GLOBAL COLUMN-WIDTH

When the prompt ENTER GLOBAL COLUMN WIDTH appears, type **12** and press <Return>. The worksheet is now globally formatted for currency and for a column width of 12. A value entered in any cell on the worksheet appears on the screen as currency, and every column on the worksheet has a width of 12 characters. When completed, your worksheet should look like Figure 13-1.

Save the amended EXAMPLE file.

Functions

In the previous chapter, you learned how to enter formulas either by typing them or by using the pointing method. Using 1-2-3's @functions is a quicker and more

Table 13-2
@Functions

Function	Description
@AVG	Calculates the average of a list of values
@MAX	Determines the maximum value in a list
@MIN	Determines the minimum value in a list
@SUM	Determines the sum of a list of values
@RAND	Determines a random number between 0 and 1
@ROUND	Rounds a value to a specified number of places
@SQRT	Determines the positive square root of a value

FUNCTION
A built-in formula or process included in a spreadsheet program. When a function is used in a formula, a calculation is automatically performed. For example, a sum function automatically adds a range of numbers.

accurate way to enter certain formulas. **Functions** reduce the number of keystrokes needed to enter a formula as well as reduce the likelihood of an error occurring. The @functions are built-in formulas that perform specialized calculations.

In Lotus, these functions are called ''at functions'' because each one begins with the ''at'' character (@). An @function is comprised of three parts: the at symbol (@), the name of the function, and an argument or arguments enclosed by parentheses. The argument, which indicates what data the function applies to, can be a single value or a range of cells.

Lotus includes both simple @functions, such as one that adds a range of cells, and more complex @functions, such as those that calculate loans, annuities, and cash flows over a period of time. Lotus includes eight categories of functions:

Mathematical functions
Logical functions
Special functions
String functions
Date and Time functions
Financial functions
Statistical functions
Database Statistical functions

Table 13-2 lists some of the more commonly used @functions.

YOUR TURN

Start with the EXAMPLE file on the screen. You are going to use an @function to find the total income from rent in 1983 and the total expenses spent on repairs in 1983.

First, some changes need to be made to the worksheet. You have to add two rows for the totals.

Go to A9
/ WORKSHEET INSERT ROW

When the prompt ENTER ROW INSERT RANGE appears, enter the range A9 to A8. Press <Return>.

```
B19: @SUM(B15..B17)                                                    READY

        A           B            C            D            E          F
  1  INCOME
  2
  3  Rent          1983         1984         1985         1986       1987
  4
  5  Apt #1     $2,280.00    $2,460.00    $2,700.00    $3,000.00
  6  Apt #2     $4,080.00    $4,260.00    $4,500.00    $4,800.00
  7  Apt #3     $3,880.00    $4,060.00    $4,300.00    $4,600.00
  8
  9  Total     $10,240.00
 10
 11  EXPENSES
 12
 13  Repairs       1983         1984         1985         1986       1987
 14
 15  Apt #1       $250.00      $235.00      $310.00      $433.00
 16  Apt #2       $190.00      $285.00      $308.00      $507.00
 17  Apt #3       $312.00      $345.00      $296.00      $472.00
 18
 19  Total        $752.00
 20
```

Figure 13-2
Using @Functions

Enter **Total** in cell A9
Enter **Total** in cell A19
Go to B9
Enter **@SUM(B5.B7)**
Press <Return>

The total of cells B5, B6, and B7 immediately appears in cell B9.

Go to B19
Enter **@SUM(B15.B17)**
Press <Return>

Your worksheet should look like Figure 13-2. Notice that the formula using the @SUM function is in the status line.
Save the amended EXAMPLE file.

Copying Formulas

Previously you learned how to use the Copy command by copying and moving labels in the EXAMPLE file. The Copy command also can be used to copy formulas, but it works differently in this case, as explained in this section.

When a cell containing a formula is copied, Lotus does not copy the value displayed in the cell on the worksheet. Rather, Lotus copies the formula displayed in the status line. When the formula is copied, Lotus automatically inserts the appropriate argument or arguments. For example, suppose a worksheet contains a list of values in columns B, C, and D, and a sum for each column needs to be calculated. First, the @SUM function is used to calculate the total for column B. Then, that formula is copied into columns C and D to calculate the totals for those columns. Lotus automatically inserts the appropriate range of cells in the arguments for each formula.

YOUR TURN

Start with the EXAMPLE file on the screen. You are going to copy the formula in B9 into C9, D9, and E9. You also will copy the formula in B19 into C19, D19, and E19.

Go to B9
/ COPY

When the prompt ENTER RANGE TO COPY FROM appears, press <Return> to copy just the formula in B9. When the prompt ENTER RANGE TO COPY TO appears, move the cell pointer to C9. Type a period (.) to anchor the range and move the cell pointer to E9. Press <Return>.

The totals for columns C, D, and E immediately appear. Go to C9 and look at the formula in the status line. It should say @SUM(C5..C7). Lotus automatically changed the argument from (B5..B7) to (C5..C7) when the formula was copied into cell C9.

Go to B19
/ COPY
Press <Return>
Move the cell pointer to C19
Type .
Move the cell pointer to E19
Press <Return>

The totals appear in cells C19, D19, and E19. Your worksheet should look like Figure 13-3.

Save the amended EXAMPLE file.

Freezing Titles

Up to this point, all the worksheets you have used fit within the window. More complex and larger worksheets, however, may not fit within the window. As the user moves around a large worksheet, columns and rows of information scroll off the computer screen. Usually this is not a problem, unless titles identifying the rows and columns also scroll off the screen. A screen full of numbers with no identifying labels can be confusing. Lotus solves that problem by including a feature that "freezes" titles. If a row or column of titles is frozen, those titles do not scroll off the computer screen as the user moves around a large worksheet.

```
B19: @SUM(B15..B17)                                                          READY

         A           B           C           D            E          F
 1  INCOME
 2
 3  Rent         1983        1984        1985         1986       1987
 4
 5  Apt #1     $2,280.00   $2,460.00   $2,700.00    $3,000.00
 6  Apt #2     $4,080.00   $4,260.00   $4,500.00    $4,800.00
 7  Apt #3     $3,880.00   $4,060.00   $4,300.00    $4,600.00
 8
 9  Total     $10,240.00  $10,780.00  $11,500.00   $12,400.00
10
11  EXPENSES
12
13  Repairs      1983        1984        1985         1986       1987
14
15  Apt #1       $250.00     $235.00     $310.00      $433.00
16  Apt #2       $190.00     $285.00     $308.00      $507.00
17  Apt #3       $312.00     $345.00     $296.00      $472.00
18
19  Total        $752.00     $865.00     $914.00    $1,412.00
20
```

Figure 13-3
Copying @Functions

To freeze titles, the user must position the cell pointer one row below the rows to be frozen and one column to the right of the columns to be frozen. After positioning the cell pointer, select the Worksheet option from the Main menu; then select Titles. There are four Titles options from which to select. Table 13-3 lists these options and describes their functions.

The cell pointer keys cannot be used to move into a row or column that has been frozen. To go to a cell within a row or column that is frozen, use the GOTO key, <F5>.

A second copy of the title rows or columns is displayed on the screen. There are two ways to remove this second copy. If the Clear option is selected from the Titles menu, all the existing titles are unfrozen and the second copy is removed. Another way to remove the second copy is to press the <PgDn> key and then the <PgUp> key for rows, or the <Tab> key and then the <Backtab> key for columns. (The <Backtab> key is the <Shift> key used in combination with the <Tab> key.)

Table 13-3
Titles Options

Option	Description
Both	Both the rows above the cell pointer and columns to the left of the cell pointer will not scroll off the screen.
Horizontal	The rows above the cell pointer will not scroll off the screen.
Vertical	The columns on the screen to the left of the cell pointer will not scroll off the screen.
Clear	All the existing titles are unfrozen.

YOUR TURN Start with the EXAMPLE file on your screen. You are going to freeze column A.

>Go to B1
>/ WORKSHEET TITLES VERTICAL

Column A is now frozen and will not scroll off the screen. Suppose you want to start projecting some costs for 1988. To do that, you need to move to column G:

>Go to G1

If you use the GOTO key, <F5>, your screen should look like Figure 13-4. Notice that column A remains on the screen. Without those titles, the worksheet would not make much sense.

>Go to A1

Notice that there are now two column A's. That is because Lotus copied the frozen column. Remove the second column by pressing <Tab> and then <Backtab>. Clear the frozen column.

Figure 13-4
Freezing Titles

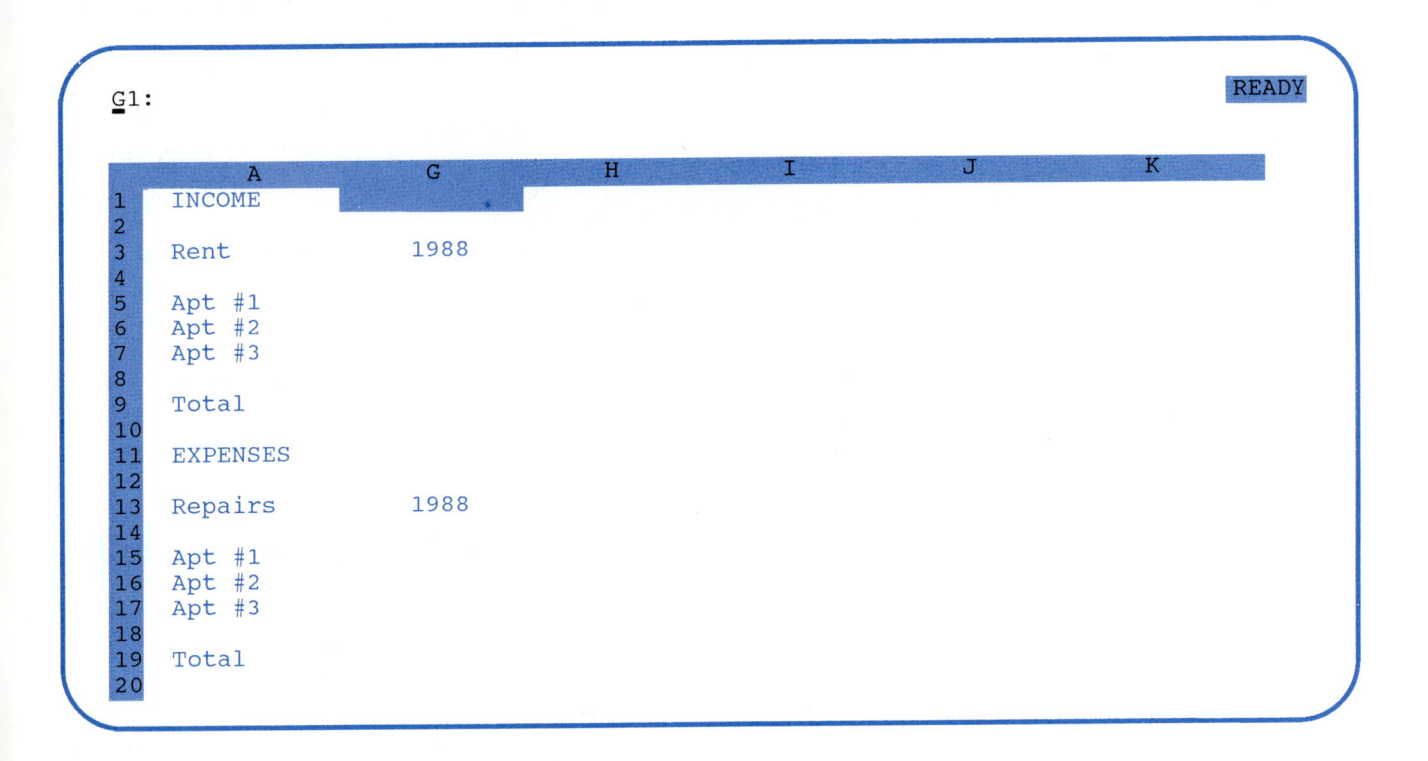

```
G1:                                                           READY

             A           G           H           I           J           K
 1   INCOME
 2
 3   Rent          1988
 4
 5   Apt #1
 6   Apt #2
 7   Apt #3
 8
 9   Total
10
11   EXPENSES
12
13   Repairs       1988
14
15   Apt #1
16   Apt #2
17   Apt #3
18
19   Total
20
```

**Table 13-4
Order of Precedence**

Order	Operator	Operation
First	^	Exponentiation
Second	*/	Multiplication, Division
Third	+−	Addition, Subtraction

Order of Precedence

**PRECEDENCE
In a spreadsheet program, the order in which calculations are executed in a formula containing several operators.**

When more complex formulas are used on a worksheet, Lotus performs calculations in a specific order of **precedence.** The order of precedence, or the order of operations, is the order in which calculations are performed in a formula that contains several operators. Table 13-4 shows operators that can be used in formulas, together with the order in which the operations are performed. If a formula contains operations that have the same precedence, they are performed sequentially from left to right.

There is a way to override the order of precedence listed in Table 13-4: Operations contained within parentheses are calculated before operations outside the parentheses. The operations within the parentheses are performed according to the order of precedence. For example, the formula (C12*B12)+C12 would be calculated in the following order:

1. The contents of cell C12 are multiplied times the contents of cell B12.
2. The result of the calculation in step 1 is added to the contents of cell C12.

YOUR TURN

For this hands-on exercise, you will design a model to help the owner of an apartment building project the income each unit in the building will generate per month. Start with a blank worksheet on the screen.

First, you will globally change the column width and enter all the labels:

/ WORKSHEET GLOBAL COLUMN-WIDTH

When prompted to ENTER GLOBAL COLUMN WIDTH, enter **10.** Now enter the following labels in the cells indicated:

Cells	Label
A1	^803 NORTH WOOSTER, BOWLING GREEN, OHIO

(Remember, any number used as a label must be preceded by the ^ symbol).

B3	Yearly	D5	^1988
D3	Projected	E5	^1989
E3	Projected	F5	^1990

(continued)

Cells	Label		
F3	Projected	A7	Apt #1
B4	Increase	A8	Apt #2
D4	Income	A9	Apt #3
E4	Income	A10	Apt #4
F4	Income	A11	Apt #5
A5	Unit	A12	Apt #6
B5	Rate	A13	Apt #7
C5	^1987	A15	Average
		A17	Total

Next, format cells B7 through B13 to percentages, carried out one decimal place:

Go to B7
/ RANGE FORMAT PERCENT

When the prompt ENTER NUMBER OF DECIMAL PLACES appears, enter **1**. Format the range B7 through B13.

The rest of the worksheet values should be formatted as currency, carried out to 0 decimal places:

Go to C7
/ RANGE FORMAT CURRENCY

When the prompt ENTER THE NUMBER OF DECIMAL PLACES appears, enter **0**. Format the range C7 through F17.

Enter the following values in the appropriate cells.

Cells	Values
B7	.065
B8	.08
B9	.065
B10	.05
B11	.08
B12	.05
B13	.10
C7	250
C8	530
C9	275
C10	350
C11	540
C12	325
C13	750

To find the average rent for the apartments in this building, use the @AVG function:

CHAPTER 13: ADVANCED LOTUS 1-2-3

Go to C15
Enter **@AVG(C7.C13)**

Copy this formula into cells D15 through F15:

Go to C15
/ COPY

Press <Return> when the prompt ENTER RANGE TO COPY FROM appears. When the prompt ENTER RANGE TO COPY TO appears, select the range D15 through F15. Notice that the letters ERR, for error, appear in cells D15, E15, and F15. This is because the formulas entered into those cells include the contents of cells that are currently empty. For now, ignore the ERR message.

To find the Total rent per month for each year, use the @SUM function:

Go to C17
Enter **@SUM(C7.C13)**

Copy this formula into cells D17 through F17:

Go to C17
/ COPY

Press <Return> when the prompt ENTER RANGE TO COPY FROM appears. When the prompt ENTER RANGE TO COPY TO appears, select the range D17 through F17. Notice that $0 appears in cells D17 through F17. That is because the cells in columns D, E, and F currently are empty.

Now you need to enter a formula that finds the new monthly rent, given the yearly increase percentage rate for each apartment.

Go to D7
Enter **(C7*B7)+C7**

Because of the order of precedence, the operation within the parentheses is calculated first. This operation (C7*B7) finds the rent increase each month, given the yearly increase rate. That amount then is added to the current rent, which is the value in C7. The result is the rental cost for the apartment in 1988. This formula can now be copied into cells D8 through D13:

Go to D7
/ COPY
Press <Return> to copy from D7
Select the range D8 through D13 to copy to

Notice that, once formulas were entered into column D, ERR in cell D15 was replaced by a value. Now formulas need to be entered into cells E7 and F7.

```
F7: (C0) (E7*B7)+E7                                                    READY

           A         B         C         D         E         F        G
 1    803 NORTH WOOSTER, BOWLING GREEN, OHIO
 2
 3              Yearly               Projected  Projected  Projected
 4              Increase             Income     Income     Income
 5    Unit      Rate       1987      1988       1989       1990
 6
 7    Apt #1    6.5%       $250      $266       $284       $302
 8    Apt #2    8.0%       $530      $572       $618       $668
 9    Apt #3    6.5%       $275      $293       $312       $332
10    Apt #4    5.0%       $350      $368       $386       $405
11    Apt #5    8.0%       $540      $583       $630       $680
12    Apt #6    5.0%       $325      $341       $358       $376
13    Apt #7    10.0%      $750      $825       $908       $998
14
15    Average              $431      $464       $499       $537
16
17    Total                $3,020    $3,248     $3,495     $3,762
18
19
20
```

Figure 13-5
The RENT Worksheet

Go to E7
Enter **(D7*B7)+D7**
Go to F7
Enter **(E7*B7)+E7**
Copy the formula in cell E7 into cells E8 through E13
Copy the formula in cell F7 into cells F8 through F13

When completed, your worksheet should look like Figure 13-5. Save this worksheet under the file name RENT.

Spreadsheet Analysis

Once a worksheet has been created, it is easy to experiment with various options. After changes are made, Lotus automatically recalculates the worksheet to reflect those changes. Numerous alternatives to a single plan can be projected and evaluated, so the spreadsheet is an invaluable tool in decision-making.

YOUR TURN Start with the RENT file on the screen. You are going to experiment with what-if analysis by making changes to the Yearly Increase Rate and to the rent for each unit.
   The owner of this apartment building is thinking of hiring a building manager in 1988. The owner cannot afford to pay a building manager's

salary, however, unless the total income per month from the apartments is $3,800. The owner wants to know if raising the Yearly Increase Rate for each unit by 1 percent would generate enough income to hire a building manager in 1988.

Change the values in cells B7 through B13 to reflect a 1 percent increase in the Yearly Increase Rate. Could the owner afford to hire a building manager in 1988? What year could the owner afford to hire a building manager?

The other option for increasing income is to raise the rent. Increase each apartment's rent in column C by $30.00. In what year can the owner afford to hire a building manager?

Continue to experiment with what-if analysis. When you have finished, do not save the amended file. You want to save the file as it was before you began experimenting with what-if analysis. The following commands enable you to save the RENT file in its original form:

/ QUIT YES

If you quit without using the / FILE SAVE command, the file remains as it was originally entered.

Learning Check

1. In _____, different results generated by the spreadsheet often are compared.
2. A(n) _____ is a numeric representation of a real-world situation.
3. Lotus commands that apply to the entire worksheet are called _____ commands.
4. A built-in formula already stored in a spreadsheet program is called a(n) _____.
5. The order in which calculations are performed in a formula with several operators is called the _____.

Answers

1. spreadsheet analysis 2. model 3. global 4. function 5. order of precedence

Graphics

ANALYTICAL GRAPHS
Charts and graphics used for financial analysis and other types of numerical comparison.

The purpose of business graphics is to develop charts and **analytical graphs** for financial analysis. Numeric data can be transformed into multicolored charts and graphs for analyzing markets, forecasting sales, comparing stock trends, and planning business and home finances. Frequently used in presentations and reports, business graphics often can present information more effectively than a column of numbers. Two of the more commonly used types of graphs are bar graphs and pie charts.

Bar Graphs and Pie Charts

A bar graph can be used to make a quantitative comparison of several subjects' performances. Numeric values are represented as vertical bars, each of which depicts the value of a single cell in the worksheet. The X axis, a horizontal line, has labels identifying what each bar represents. The Y axis, a vertical line, has scaled numeric divisions corresponding to the worksheet values being represented.

Two types of bar graphs often are used as analytical graphs. A simple bar graph depicts the changes in one set of values, whereas a multiple bar graph depicts the relationships among changes in several sets of values. For example, a simple bar graph might chart how many blue jeans a clothing store sold in 1984, 1985, and 1986 (see Figure 13-6). A multiple bar graph might compare the numbers of blue jeans sold to the numbers of corduroy slacks and chino pants sold in 1984, 1985, and 1986. Each year would have three bars above it: one bar for blue jeans, one for corduroy slacks, and one for chino pants (see Figure 13-7).

In Figure 13-6, the vertical line or Y axis contains the numeric data ranges from 0 to 45. Notice the word *Thousands* in parentheses to the left of the graph. This means each of the numeric values along the vertical line should be multiplied

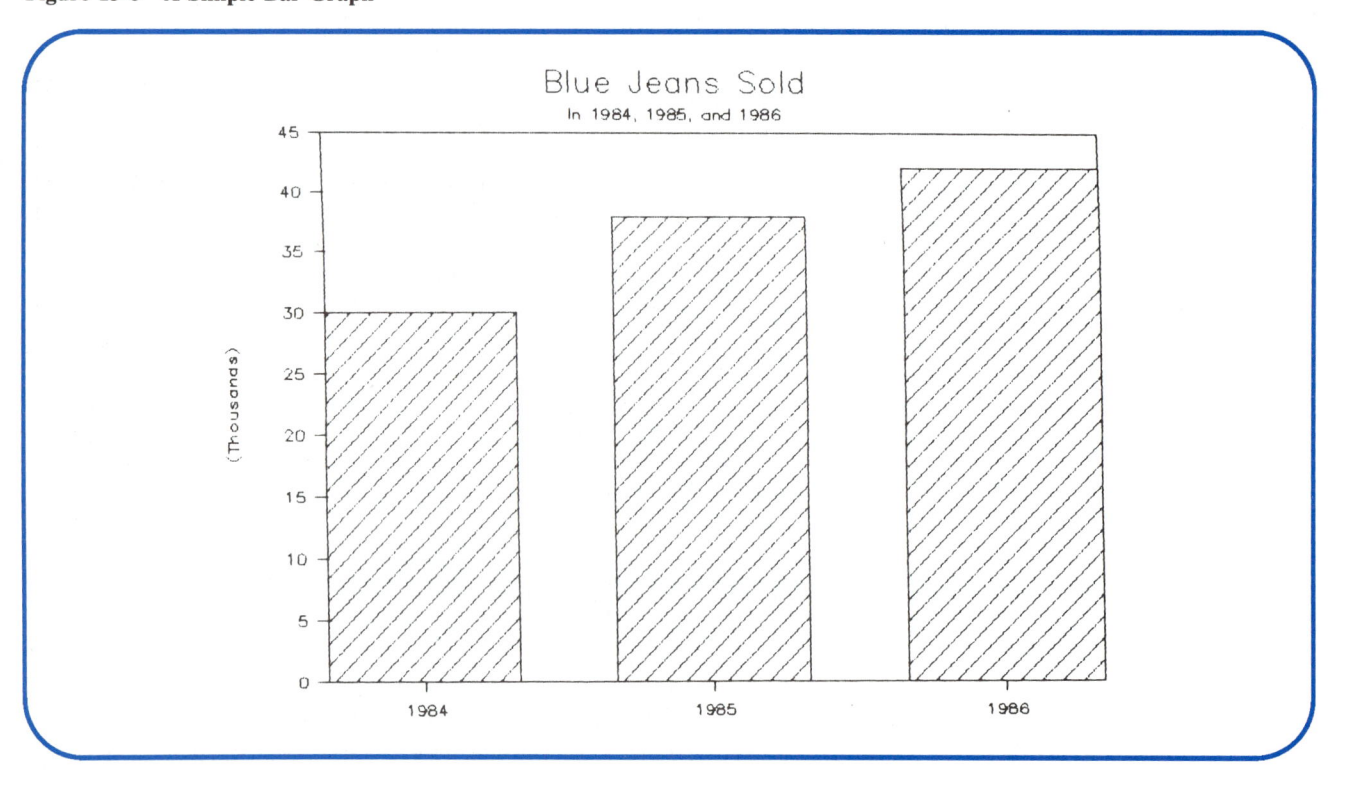

Figure 13-6   A Simple Bar Graph

CHAPTER 13: ADVANCED LOTUS 1-2-3

After you have selected Type from the Graph menu, the options LINE, BAR, XY, STACKED-BAR, and PIE appear in the entry line. Select the type of graph to be drawn.

Once the type of graph has been selected, the Graph menu reappears in the entry line. The next step in creating a graph is to specify which data ranges are to be used for this graph, and what labels are to be used to describe that data. The options used to accomplish this step are the range commands (X, A, B, C, D, E, F) from the Graph menu.

The X option is used to select the range of labels. On a bar graph, each label on the X axis corresponds to a bar or multiple bars. On a pie chart, each label corresponds to one slice of the pie. The A–F options are used to specify ranges of data. Up to six ranges can be specified for a bar graph, but only one range can be specified for a pie chart. After the data ranges and labels have been specified, the graph can be viewed using the View option from the Graph menu.

YOUR TURN

You are going to create a simple bar graph and a multiple bar graph using the RENT file. Start with the RENT file on the screen. The first bar graph you will create compares the rent paid for all the apartments in 1987.

/ GRAPH TYPE BAR

The Graph menu reappears in the entry line. You need to identify the labels to be used for the bar graph. Because the graph will compare the rents for the apartments, the apartment numbers are the appropriate labels.

Select X from the Graph menu

The prompt ENTER X AXIS RANGE appears.

Go to A7
Type a period (.) to anchor the range
Using the <↓> key, move to A13
Press <Return>

Now you need to specify the range of data to be used in the graph. You want to compare the rent for each unit in 1987, so the data to be used is in cells C7 through C13. The Graph menu should be in the entry line.

Select A from the Graph menu.

The prompt ENTER FIRST DATA RANGE appears.

Go to C7
Type a period (.) to anchor the range
Using the <↓> key, move to C13
Press <Return>

You can now view the graph. Select View from the Graph menu. What happens after you select View depends on the hardware being used and on how the system is configured. The system must be equipped with both a graphics monitor and a graphics card. If it is not, when View is selected, the computer beeps and nothing happens. Even though the graph is not displayed, it does exist in the computer's memory and can be printed at a later date.

If the computer you are using has a graphics card and either a monochrome or color screen, the bar graph is displayed after selecting View. What you see on the screen is only a rough version of what the printed graph would look like. When you have finished viewing the graph, press <Esc>.

Now you are going to create a multiple bar graph that includes three more data ranges. Say you wanted to compare the rent paid on each unit in 1987 with the projected rent to be paid on each unit in 1988, 1989, and 1990. Option B from the Graph menu can hold the data from the data range D7 through D13, option C can hold the data from E7 through E13, and option D can hold the data from the range F7 through F13.

Select B from the Graph menu
Enter the data range D7 through D13
Select C from the Graph menu
Enter the data range E7 through E13
Select D from the Graph menu
Enter the data range F7 through F13
Select View from the Graph menu

Now there are four bars for each apartment unit. The four bars represent the monthly rents for that unit in 1987, 1988, 1989, and 1990 respectively. When you are finished viewing the graph, press <Esc>.

The graph would become more meaningful if it had a title. A two-line title can be printed at the top of the graph. Each line can contain up to 39 characters. You are now going to provide a title for the graph.

Select Options from the Graph menu
Select Titles from the Options menu
Select First from the Titles menu

When the prompt ENTER GRAPH TITLE, TOP LINE appears, type RENT INCREASE ON EACH UNIT and press <Return>.

Select Titles again
Select Second

When the prompt ENTER GRAPH TITLE SECOND LINE appears, type FOR 1987, 1988, 1989, AND 1990 and press <Return>.

Now you want to save the bar graph. Press <Esc> once to return to the Graph menu. Select Save. When the prompt ENTER GRAPH FILE NAME appears, type RENTBAR and press <Return>. When Lotus saves the

CHAPTER 13: ADVANCED LOTUS 1-2-3

graph, the extension PIC is added automatically to whatever name the graph is given. Select Quit to return the worksheet to the READY mode.

YOUR TURN

In this hands-on exercise, you will use the RENT file to create a pie chart to compare apartment unit rents in 1987. Start with the RENT file on the screen.

/ GRAPH TYPE PIE

The Graph menu returns to the entry line. Select option X. Because each piece of the pie is to represent one apartment, you want to leave the X range setting intact. It should already be set at the range A7 through A13. Press <Return>.

Select A

The range C7 through C13 should still be selected. Because the pie chart is to compare rents in 1987, you want to leave the A range setting intact. Press <Return>.

Unlike a bar graph, a pie chart is limited to comparisons based on one criterion. Therefore, the only settings to be made from the Graph menu are X, to set the X-range, and A to set the first (and only) data range.

None of the other data used in the bar graph is to be used in the pie chart, so you need to reset options B, C, and D. Select Reset from the Graph menu. Select B and press <Return>. Select C and press <Return>. Select D and press <Return>. Select Quit.

Next, you need to provide a title for the pie chart. Select the following:

OPTIONS TITLES FIRST

The prompt ENTER GRAPH TITLE, TOP LINE appears. The title from the bar graph may be entered after the prompt. If it is, use the <Backspace> key to erase it. Enter `MONTHLY INCOME 803 NORTH WOOSTER`. Press <Return>. Select the following:

TITLES SECOND

The prompt ENTER GRAPH TITLE, SECOND LINE appears. If the second line from the bar graph appears after the prompt, erase it using the <Backspace> key. Enter `FOR THE YEAR 1987`. Press <Return>. Select Quit.

Look at the pie chart by selecting View. The pie chart illustrates what percentage the rent on each unit contributes to the total monthly income for the building. When you are finished viewing the pie chart, press <Esc>. Now you need to save the pie chart. Select Save. When the prompt ENTER GRAPH FILE NAME appears, enter `RENTPIE`. Select Quit to return the worksheet to the Ready mode.

Printing a Graph

Before trying to print a graph, you need to perform three steps. First, make sure the printer being used is capable of printing graphics. Next, check to make sure the 1-2-3 Install program for the printer has been run. Finally, make sure the printer is properly hooked up to the computer, is turned on, and has plenty of paper.

The PrintGraph program is started from the Access menu, so you need to exit 1-2-3. Before exiting, make sure the final version of the worksheet and the graph file or files have been saved. If you accessed 1-2-3 by typing Lotus at the system prompt, the Access menu appears after exiting. If you started by typing 123, the operating system prompt appears (or a message telling you to insert the COMMAND.COM disk). At the system prompt, type **Lotus** in order to have the Access menu on the screen.

You will need the 1-2-3 PrintGraph Program disk to be able to print graphs. Remove the 1-2-3 System Disk from drive A and insert the PrintGraph Program Disk. Leave your data disk in drive B.

> *Hard Disk Differences:* If the PrintGraph Program Disk files have been installed on the hard disk, you do not need to switch disks. To print a graph, you must be in the subdirectory in which all the 1-2-3 disks are copied, and the Access menu must be on the screen.

Figure 13-9
The PrintGraph Screen

Select PrintGraph from the Access menu. The PrintGraph screen appears (see Figure 13-9). The PrintGraph screen offers several options to enhance the printed

```
Copyright 1985 Lotus Development Corp.   All Rights Reserved.   Release 2    MENU
Select graphs for printing
Image-Select  Settings  Go  Align  Page  Exit

    GRAPH       IMAGE OPTIONS                        HARDWARE SETUP
    IMAGES      Size              Range Colors       Graphs Directory:
    SELECTED    Top       .395    X Black              C:\123
                Left      .750    A Black            Fonts Directory:
                Width    6.500    B Black              C:\123
                Height   4.691    C Black            Interface:
                Rotate    .000    D Black              Parallel 1
                                  E Black            Printer Type:
                Font              F Black              Epson FX,RX/Hi
                1  BLOCK1                            Paper Size
                2  BLOCK1                              Width      8.500
                                                      Length    11.000

                                                    ACTION OPTIONS
                                                      Pause: No    Eject: No
```

Table 13-6
The PrintGraph Options

Option	Description
Image-Select	Selects the graph file to be printed.
Settings	Enables the user to define the hardware setup for the particular printer being used, along with setting type styles and colors (if the printer is capable of printing colors).
Go	Prints the graph
Align	Tells 1-2-3 where the top edge of the paper starts.
Page	Advances the paper in the printer to insert blank pages between graphs.
Exit	Exits the PrintGraph program.

version of the graph. At the top of the screen, under the copyright information, is the PrintGraph menu. This menu has six options, which are defined in Table 13-6.

YOUR TURN

You are going to print the bar graph and pie chart created from the rent worksheet. Start with the Access menu on the screen. If the Rent worksheet is currently on the screen, exit 1-2-3. When the system prompt appears on the screen, type **Lotus.**

Remove the 1-2-3 System Disk from drive A and insert the PrintGraph Program disk. Your data disk remains in drive B. Select PrintGraph from the Access menu. The PrintGraph screen appears.

Select Settings. The Settings menu appears. You need to specify the hardware setup, so select Hardware from the Settings menu. Next, the Hardware menu appears. Included in the Hardware menu is the Graphs-Directory option. The purpose of this option is to let the PrintGraph program know where the graph files are stored. As you can see in the first entry under the title HARDWARE SETUP on the PrintGraph screen, the setting for the Graphs Directory is now drive A. Since your graph files are all stored on the data disk in drive B, this setting has to be changed.

Select Graphs-Directory. Press <Esc> to clear the current directory. Type **B:** and press <Return>.

> *Hard Disk Differences:* Type **C:\123** and press <Return>.

The Hardware menu appears on the screen, and the Graphs Directory listing under the title HARDWARE SETUP should now say B:\.

Next you have to specify the printer you are using. To do this, select Printer from the Hardware menu. The Printer screen appears, listing the printer or printers that were defined when the 1-2-3 Install program for the printer was run. In addition to a list of printers, you are given a choice of densities. The higher the density, the longer it takes the printer to print the graph, but the high-density graphs are darker and easier to read. Select the appropriate printer and density.

Learning Check

1. Business graphics used for financial analysis are called _____.

2. A _____ bar graph illustrates the changes in one set of values and a _____ bar graph illustrates the relationships among changes in several sets of values.

3. A pie chart makes comparisons based on only one criterion. (True or False?)

4. Each bar in a bar graph depicts an entire range of cells from a worksheet. (True or False?)

5. In a bar graph, the labels identifying what the bars represent appears along the _____ and the scaled numeric divisions appear along the _____.

Answers

1. analytic graphs 2. simple; multiple 3. True 4. False 5. X axis; Y axis

---

Hard Disk Differences: If you are using a computer with a hard disk, you have to make one more change on the PrintGraph screen. Look at the Fonts Directory listing under HARDWARE SETUP. It may be set to drive A. If it is, you must change it to drive C. To do this, select Fonts-Directory from the Hardware menu. Press <Esc> to erase the setting. Type **C:\123**. Press <Return>.

Once hardware settings have been specified, you are ready to save them. Select Quit to leave the Hardware menu. Select Save to save the hardware settings.

Now that the settings are saved, you can select the specific graph you want to print. Select the Image-Select command from the PrintGraph menu. A list of all the graph files is displayed. You can move through the list using the <↑> and <↓> keys. Highlight the RENTBAR graph and press <Return>. The PrintGraph screen returns, and the name RENTBAR appears under the heading GRAPH IMAGES SELECTED.

Make sure the printer is turned on and the paper is aligned at the top of the page. Once the paper is aligned, select Align from the PrintGraph menu. Now select Go. After a few seconds, 1-2-3 will print the graph. Your bar graph should look like Figure 13-10.

Now print the pie chart. Select the Image-Select command from the PrintGraph menu. Notice the # symbol next to RENTBAR. This symbol indicates that this graph is selected for printing. Move the highlighting to RENTBAR and press the space bar. The # symbol disappears, and

Figure 13-10
Bar Graph Generated From the RENT Worksheet

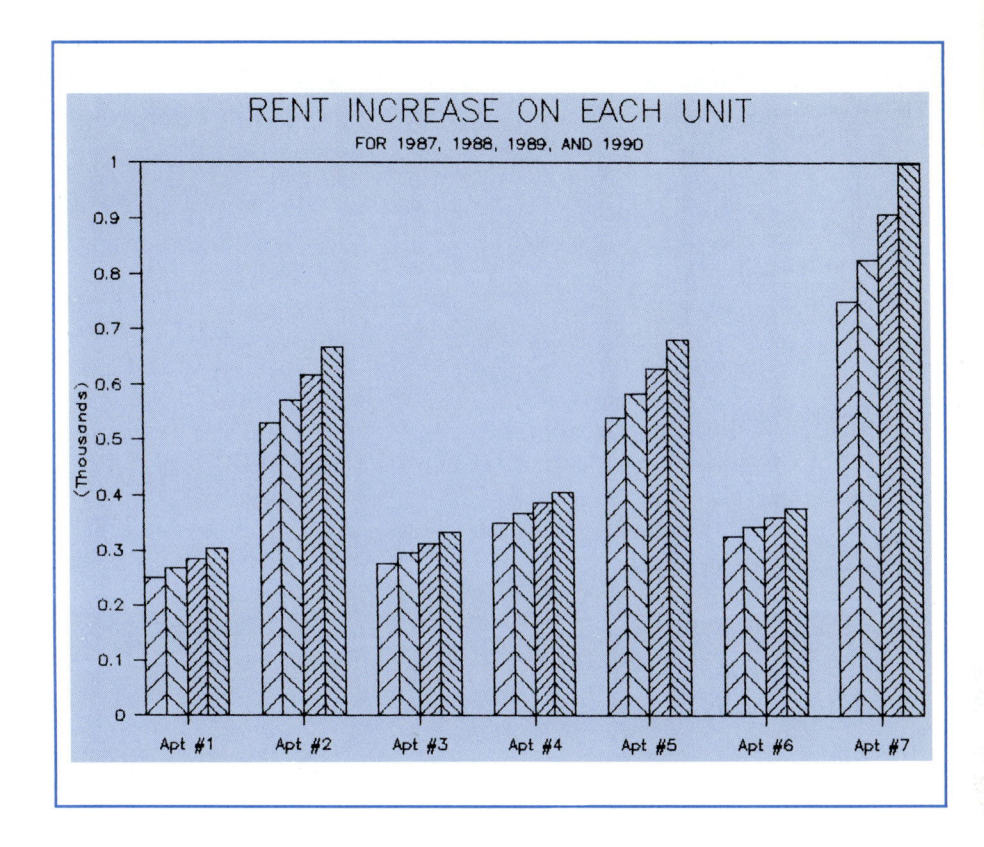

RENTBAR is no longer selected. Move the highlighting to the RENTPIE graph and press <Return>. Check to make sure RENTPIE appears under the title GRAPH IMAGES SELECTED on the PrintGraph screen. Align the paper in the printer. Select Align. Select Go. Your pie chart should look like Figure 13-11 when printed.

To exit the PrintGraph program, select Exit from the PrintGraph menu. Then select Yes when the prompt END PRINTGRAPH SESSION? appears. The Access menu appears on the screen.

Summary Points

■ Spreadsheet analysis is the mental process of evaluating information contained within a spreadsheet. It often involves comparing various results generated by a spreadsheet.

■ A model is a numeric representation of a real-world situation.

■ Functions, built-in formulas included in a spreadsheet program, save time by reducing the number of keystrokes needed to enter a formula as well as reduce the likelihood of error.

■ Formulas involving several operators are calculated according to the order of precedence. Parentheses can be used to override the order of precedence.

Figure 13-11
Pie Chart Generated from the RENT Worksheet

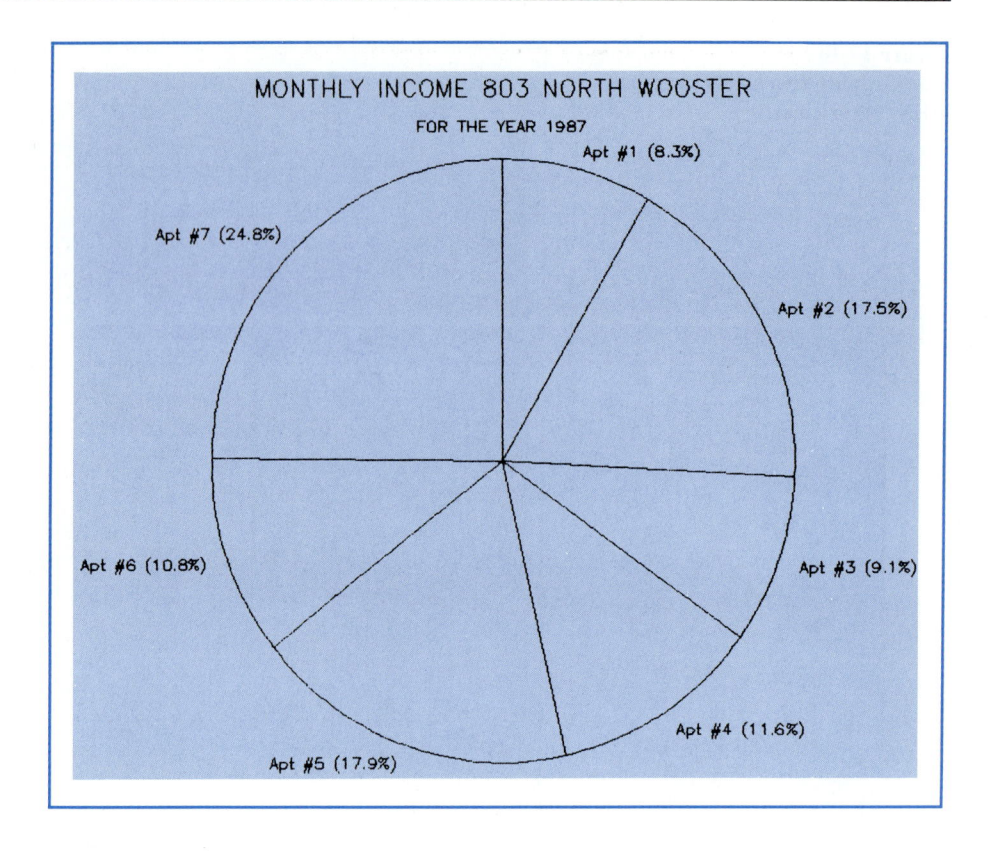

[Pie chart: MONTHLY INCOME 803 NORTH WOOSTER FOR THE YEAR 1987 — Apt #1 (8.3%), Apt #2 (17.5%), Apt #3 (9.1%), Apt #4 (11.6%), Apt #5 (17.9%), Apt #6 (10.8%), Apt #7 (24.8%)]

- Analytical graphs are used in business for financial analysis.
- Bar graphs can be used to provide a quantitative comparison of several subjects' performances. Pie charts depict an entire subject divided into parts, showing the relationships between the parts and the whole.

Lotus 1-2-3 Exercises

In this exercise, you are going to design a model to help you to follow your performance and determine your final grade in the courses you are taking. Assume that you are a business major taking the following courses during the Fall semester:

Course	Credit Hours
ACCT 221	3
MIS 200	3
POLS 360	3
ECON 310	3
STATS 210	3

1. At the DOS A> prompt, insert the Lotus System disk in drive A and your data disk in drive B. Start Lotus and load a new worksheet.

CHAPTER 13: ADVANCED LOTUS 1-2-3

Summary of Frequently Used Lotus 1-2-3 Menus And Submenus

Main Command Menu	Submenus
WORKSHEET	GLOBAL, INSERT, DELETE, COLUMN, ERASE, TITLES, WINDOW, STATUS, PAGE
RANGE	FORMAT, LABEL, ERASE, NAME, JUSTIFY, PROTECT, UNPROTECT, INPUT, VALUE, TRANSPOSE
COPY	
MOVE	
FILE	RETRIEVE, SAVE, COMBINE, XTRACT, ERASE, LIST, IMPORT, DIRECTORY
PRINT	PRINTER → RANGE, LINE, PAGE, OPTIONS, CLEAR, ALIGN, GO, QUIT FILE
GRAPH	TYPE, X, A, B, C, D, E, F, RESET, VIEW, SAVE, OPTIONS, NAME, QUIT
DATA	FILL, TABLE, SORT, QUERY, DISTRIBUTION, MATRIX, REGRESSION, PARSE
SYSTEM	
QUIT	

Summary of Lotus 1-2-3 Commands

\multicolumn{3}{c}{**A. MAIN COMMAND MENU**}
Command	*Keys*	*Description*
Worksheet	/W	Set of commands that affect the entire worksheet. Format, Erase the entire worksheet. Insert and Delete rows and columns. Set titles, windows, page break characters.
Range	/R	Set of commands that affect particular cells. Format, Label, Erase, Name, Justify, Protect, Unprotect a range of cells.
Copy	/C	Copy cell entries to other locations in the worksheet.
Move	/M	Move cell entries to other locations in the worksheet.
File	/F	Retrieve, Save, Combine, Import files. Set the current directory drive.
Print	/P	Output a range to a printer or a print file.
Graph	/G	Create graphs.
Data	/D	Create, Modify, Sort a database. Search for records.
System	/S	Invoke the DOS command interpreter.
Quit	/Q	End 1-2-3 session and return to Lotus Access System or DOS.

\multicolumn{3}{c}{**B. WORKSHEET COMMAND MENU**}
Command	*Keys*	*Description*
Global	/WG	Select entire worksheet settings.
Insert	/WI	Insert a blank column to the left of the specified range or a row above the specified range.
Delete	/WD	Delete specified rows or columns.
Column	/WC	Set individual column widths.
Titles	/WT	Set titles horizontal, vertical, or both. Clear titles.
Erase	/WE	Erase the entire worksheet. Worksheet should be saved before using this command.
Window	/WW	Set split screen and synchronized scrolling.
Status	/WS	Display worksheet settings.
Page	/WP	Insert a page break above the cell pointer.

continued

Summary of Lotus 1-2-3 Commands (cont.)

C. RANGE COMMAND MENU

Command	Keys	Description
Format	/RF	Format a cell or range of cells.
Label	/RL	Align a label or range of labels.
Erase	/RE	Erase a cell or range of cells.
Name	/RN	Create, delete, or modify range names.
Justify	/RJ	Adjust width of a column of labels.
Protect	/RP	Disallow changes to a range if protection is enabled.
Unprotect	/RU	Allow changes to a range.
Input	/RI	Enter data into the unprotected cells in a range.
Value	/RV	Copy range, converting formulas to values.
Transpose	/RT	Copy range, switching columns and rows.

D. FILE COMMAND MENU

Command	Keys	Description
Retrieve	/FR	Erase the current worksheet and display the selected worksheet.
Save	/FS	Store the entire worksheet in a worksheet file.
Combine	/FC	Incorporate all or part of a worksheet file into the worksheet.
Xtract	/FX	Store a cell range in a worksheet file.
Erase	/FE	Erase a worksheet, print, or graph file.
List	/FL	Display names of 1-2-3 files in the current directory.
Import	/FI	Read text or numbers from a print file into the worksheet.
Directory	/FD	Display and or set the current directory.

E. PRINT COMMAND MENU TO PRINTER

Command	Keys	Description
Range	/PPR	Specify a range to print.
Line	/PPL	Advance one line.
Page	/PPP	Advance one page.
Options	/PPO	Header, Footer, Margins, Borders, Setup, Page-length, Others.
Clear	/PPC	Reset some or all print settings.
Align	/PPA	Reset to top of page.
Go	/PPG	Print the specified range.
Quit	/PPQ	Return to Ready mode.

continued

Summary of Lotus 1-2-3 Commands (cont.)

F. GRAPH COMMAND MENU		
Command	Keys	Description
Type	/GT	Set graph type.
X	/GX	Set X range.
A	/GA	Set first data range.
B	/GB	Set second data range.
C	/GC	Set third data range.
D	/GD	Set fourth data range.
E	/GE	Set fifth data range.
F	/GF	Set sixth data range.
Reset	/GR	Cancel graph settings.
View	/GV	View the current graph.
Save	/GS	Save the current graph in a file for later printing.
Options	/GO	Legend, Format, Titles, Grid, Scale, Color, B & W, Data, Labels.
Name	/GN	Use, Create, Delete, or Reset named graphs.
Quit	/GQ	Return to Ready mode.

G. DATA COMMAND MENU		
Command	Keys	Description
Fill	/DF	Fill a range with numbers.
Table	/DT	Create a table of values.
Sort	/DS	Sort data records.
Query	/DQ	Find all data records satisfying the given criteria.
Distribution	/DD	Calculate frequency distribution of a range.
Matrix	/DM	Perform matrix operations.
Regression	/DR	Calculate linear regression.
Parse	/DP	Parse a column of labels into a range.

2. Move the cell pointer to cell A1 and enter `Fall Semester`. Move the cell pointer to cell A3 and enter `Course`. In the next cell to the right, enter `Cr. Hrs.` Then move the cell pointer to cell D3 and enter `Assignments`.

3. Starting at cell C5 and leaving a blank column after each assignment number, enter your assignment list in row 5 as follows:

`1    2    3    4    5    TOT.    TOT.POS.    PERC.`

What is the cell address of TOT.POS.?

4. Enter your course list and the credit hours allocated to each course. Start entering the information for the first course, ACCT 221, in cells A7 and B7. Repeat this for the other courses, but make sure you leave a blank row after each course.

5. Now assume that your grades for the semester are as follows:

COURSE	1	2	3	4	5	TOT.	TOT.POS.
ACCT 221	180	80	95	178			600
MIS 200	180	190	170	190	188		1000
POLS 360	45	47	80				200
ECON 310	75	180	140	184			650
STATS 210	150	180	170				600

Enter the data in the appropriate cells.

6. Compute your total for each course in column M, using the @SUM function. Then move to the PERC. column and compute your percentage for each course, which is equal to +Tot./Tot.Pos. Format cells Q7 through Q15 to percent, with two decimal places.

7. What is your standing in Accounting 221? In Economics 310?

8. In order to improve the appearance of the spreadsheet, you would like to change your column widths.
    a. Reduce the size of columns C, E, G, I, and K to 4 characters.
    b. Reduce the blank columns between the data columns to 2 characters.

9. You realize that, in MIS 200, your professor gave a last assignment that does not show in your records. The assignment was worth 50 points and you received a grade of 47. Insert a column before the TOT. column to include this new assignment. Type the assignment number (6) and your grade in the appropriate cells. Change the total possible points for the course, and correct the formula in order to include this new grade in your total. What is your standing in MIS 200 now?

10. Save your work using the /FILE SAVE command. Name your file GRADE.

11. Print your work using the /PRINT RANGE command.

Lotus 1-2-3 Problems

To complete the following problems, use the INCOME file included on the Student File Disk. If you are not yet in Lotus, use the necessary steps to start the worksheet program. Insert the Student File Disk in drive B.

> **Hard Disk Difference:** To be able to access the INCOME file, you should copy the Student File Disk onto the hard disk.

1. Select the /FILE RETRIEVE command. When asked the name of the file to retrieve, type **INCOME.** You should see the worksheet with the title INCOME STATEMENT on the screen. Select the /FILE SAVE command. When asked the name of the file to save, type **INCOME1.** When you do this, the file INCOME is copied to INCOME1. From now on, you are going to use the file INCOME1 and keep the file INCOME intact, in case you want to start over again or you make a mistake. Use the /FILE RETRIEVE command again to retrieve the file INCOME1.

2. The file INCOME1 contains the summary of income statements for the L L&T CO. for the past seven years. You will have to update it and make a comparative analysis of the data.

    a. Use the arrow keys to move around the worksheet and discover the structure of the model. Look closely at column D. This column contains simple entries in cells D6, D7, D10, D13, and D16; and formulas for totals and subtotals in cells D9, D12, D15, and D18. This structure is the same for all years.

    b. Go to cell D3 and enter the following: (Thousand dollars)

    c. Now assume that you have just received the following data for 1986:

NET SALES	1 650.41
COST OF GOODS SOLD	1 251.30
GENERAL EXPENSES	214.68
INTEREST EXPENSE	15.65
STATE TAXES	73.26
COMMON SHARES	27 500
DIVIDENDS PAID	29 900

You are going to update the worksheet in column B.

- Go to cell B4 and type 1986 with the label prefix that centers the label.
- Enter the numbers in the appropriate columns.
- Copy the formulas from cells D9, D12, D15, and D18 to the equivalent cells in column B. As you can see, the totals are updated as you enter the formulas.

3. Now you would like to compute the differences between years for the following items: NET SALES, COST OF GOODS SOLD, GROSS PROFIT, GEN.ADM.EXPENSES, and NET INCOME.

a. First, freeze column A so that you will always be able to see those titles. To do this, move the cell pointer to column B. Select the /WORKSHEET TITLES VERTICAL command. Now column A will remain on the screen as you move one screen to the right.

b. Now start with the differences between 1986 and 1985.
- Move the cell pointer to cell E4 and type **D86/85.**
- Move the cell pointer to cell E6 to calculate the first difference in NET SALES. The formula should be: (+B6-D6)/D6. Type the formula into that cell.
- Copy it to the cells corresponding to the other items for which a difference is requested.

c. Change the format of the cells in that range to the percent format.
- Move the cursor to cell E6.
- Select the /RANGE FORMAT PERCENT command.
- When asked for the decimal places, type **2.**
- When asked for the range, use the pointing method to define the following range: E6..E18. You should see all the differences displayed on the worksheet in the PERCENT format.

d. Now compute the differences for the remaining years.
- Enter the column titles as above (for example, **D85/84** in cell G4 for the differences between 1985 and 1984).
- Because the formulas already have been computed once, simply use the COPY command to copy them to the appropriate cells for the remaining columns.
- Change the format of the cells to PERCENT, as in 3c, to display the differences using the PERCENT format.
- Move the cell pointer to cell A20. Enter \ = (using the repeating label prefix) and copy this cell entry to the range B20..R20, to draw a horizontal line.

4. Compute the income per share and the dividends per share for each year. Start with 1986.

INCOME PER SHARE = NET INCOME/COMMON SHARES
DIVIDEND PER SHARE = DIVIDENDS PAID/COMMON SHARES

a. Define the formulas with their cell addresses and enter them in the appropriate cells (B23 and B27).
b. Copy the formulas to the remaining columns.
c. You would like to show a $ sign before INCOME/SHARE, DIVIDENDS PAID, and DIVIDEND/SHARE. Use the RANGE FORMAT CURRENCY command to change the cells to this format. When asked the number of decimal places, type **2** and press <Return>. When asked for a range, use the pointing method to define the range B23 through P27.

5. Use the FILE SAVE command to save the changes you have made to this file. When asked CANCEL REPLACE, select REPLACE.

6. Use the WORKSHEET TITLES CLEAR command to clear the title you have previously set. Use the PRINT RANGE command to print your model. Use the pointing method to cover the range that you want to print.

7. Now assume that you want to draw a bar graph showing the evolution of NET SALES over the past seven years. To draw this graph, you need the years for the horizontal axis and the net sales for the vertical axis. The data should be in a continuous set of cells. First you have to copy them.

    a. Copy the net sales for the seven years to cells S6 to S13. For example, the cell B6 entry (net sales for 1986) should be copied to cell S6, and cell D6 should be copied to cell S7.

    b. Move the cell pointer to cell R6 and type 1986. Type 1985 in cell R7. Repeat this until you have typed the appropriate year for each net sales amount.

    c. Select the GRAPH command from the Main menu. The Graph menu should appear in the control panel.

    d. Select the TYPE command from this menu, and then the Bar option from the submenu. Notice that, after the graph type is selected, the main Graph menu reappears in the control panel.

    e. Select X from the Graph menu. When asked for the range, enter **R6..R13** and press <Return>.

    f. Select A from the Graph menu. When asked for the range, use the pointing method to define the range S6..S13 and press <Return>.

    g. Select the View command from the Graph menu to see the Bar graph on the screen. Press <Esc> after you have viewed the graph.

    h. To give a title to the graph, select the OPTIONS TITLES FIRST command. Enter the following title: Evolution of sales from 1979 to 1986. Select Quit to return to the Graph menu.

    i. Select the NAME GENERATE command to name and save the graph with the worksheet. Name the graph SALES. This step saves all the settings of the graph. If you want to use it again, you use the NAME USE command from the Graph menu.

    j. Select the SAVE command from the Graph menu. This time, you will save the graph in a different file for printing with the PrintGraph program. When the prompt appears asking for the graph file name, enter **Sales.**

    k. Press <Esc> to return to the Ready mode.

    l. Use the /FILE RETRIEVE command to save all the changes that have been made to the worksheet.

8. Print the bar graph SALES.

CHAPTER 14

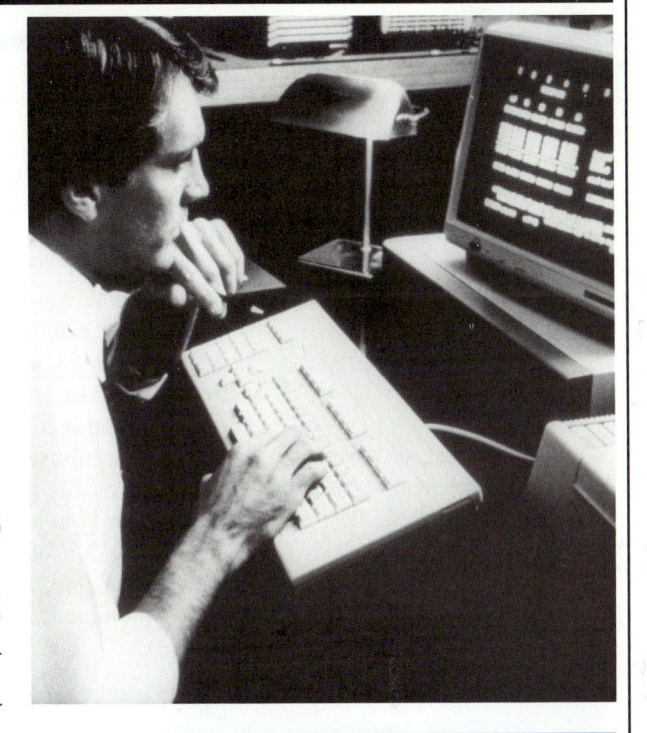

Introduction to Data Managers and dBase III

Outline

Introduction
   Definitions
Uses of Data Managers
Learning Check
Guide to dBase III
   Getting Started with dBase III
   Creating a Database File
   Entering Records

Using dBase III Commands
   QUIT
   USE
   HELP
   DISPLAY
   DISPLAY FOR
   DISPLAY STRUCTURE
   MODIFY STRUCTURE
Learning Check
   LIST
   APPEND
   BROWSE
   PACK
   EDIT
   DELETE and RECALL
   GOTO
   GO TOP and GO BOTTOM

dBase III Summary Commands
   COUNT
   SUM
   AVERAGE
Learning Check
Printing a dBase III File
Summary Points
dBase III Exercises
dBase III Problems

Introduction

Schools, hospitals, restaurants, and all types of businesses store data. The ability to retrieve, sort, and analyze data quickly and efficiently can make the difference between a company's success and failure. The types of data collected include employee records, bills, supply lists, budgets, and insurance information. Before microcomputers became standard business equipment, the most common way to organize data was to store the records in folders in file cabinets. File cabinets use a lot of space, however, and sometimes several departments may keep the same data. This duplication of data is a waste of time, effort, and space, and can lead to confusion or errors if one copy is changed.

Data managers are software packages that computertize record-keeping tasks. The term **database management system (DBMS)** also is often used when referring to the systematic organization and handling of a large collection of data stored in a computer system. In this book, we will refer to the computerization of record-keeping tasks as data management and the programs that make this task possible as data managers. This chapter explains what a data manager is and how it works. It also introduces dBase III, a sophisticated and powerful data management tool.

DATA MANAGER
A data management software package that consolidates data files into an integrated whole, allowing access to more than one data file at a time.

Definitions

A data manager software package is used to organize files. Data managers use secondary storage devices, such as floppy disks, to store the type of data that is kept in folders and envelopes in a manual filing system.

Understanding how data is stored in a filing cabinet is easy. Folders with related data are kept in the drawers of the cabinet. Each folder has a label that identifies the contents. All the folders in each drawer may be related to a certain topic. To find one data item, the appropriate drawer has to be selected, and then the specific folder containing the needed information has to be found.

With a data manager, data is recorded electronically on floppy disks, hard disks, or magnetic tapes. Instead of people looking through drawers and folders for a certain item, the computer searches the disk or tape for it.

Each data item, such as a student name, an insurance-policy number, or the amount of a bill, is called a **field.** A group of related fields forms a **record.** Your school may keep a record about each student. A student record contains fields such as the student's name, home address, parents' names, class standing, courses taken, and grade-point average.

A **file** is a group of related records. For example, all the student records in a school could make up one file. The school might have other files for teacher records, financial records, and school-board records. Figure 14-1 illustrates how a database software package might be organized for a business.

Data managers are useful because they perform many tasks faster and more easily than a manual filing system. Most data managers can perform the following:

- Add or delete data within a file
- Search a file for certain data
- Update or change data in a file

FIELD
A subdivision of a record that holds a meaningful item of data, such as an employee number.

RECORD
A collection of related data fields that constitute a single unit, such as an employee record.

FILE
A group of related data records, such as employee records.

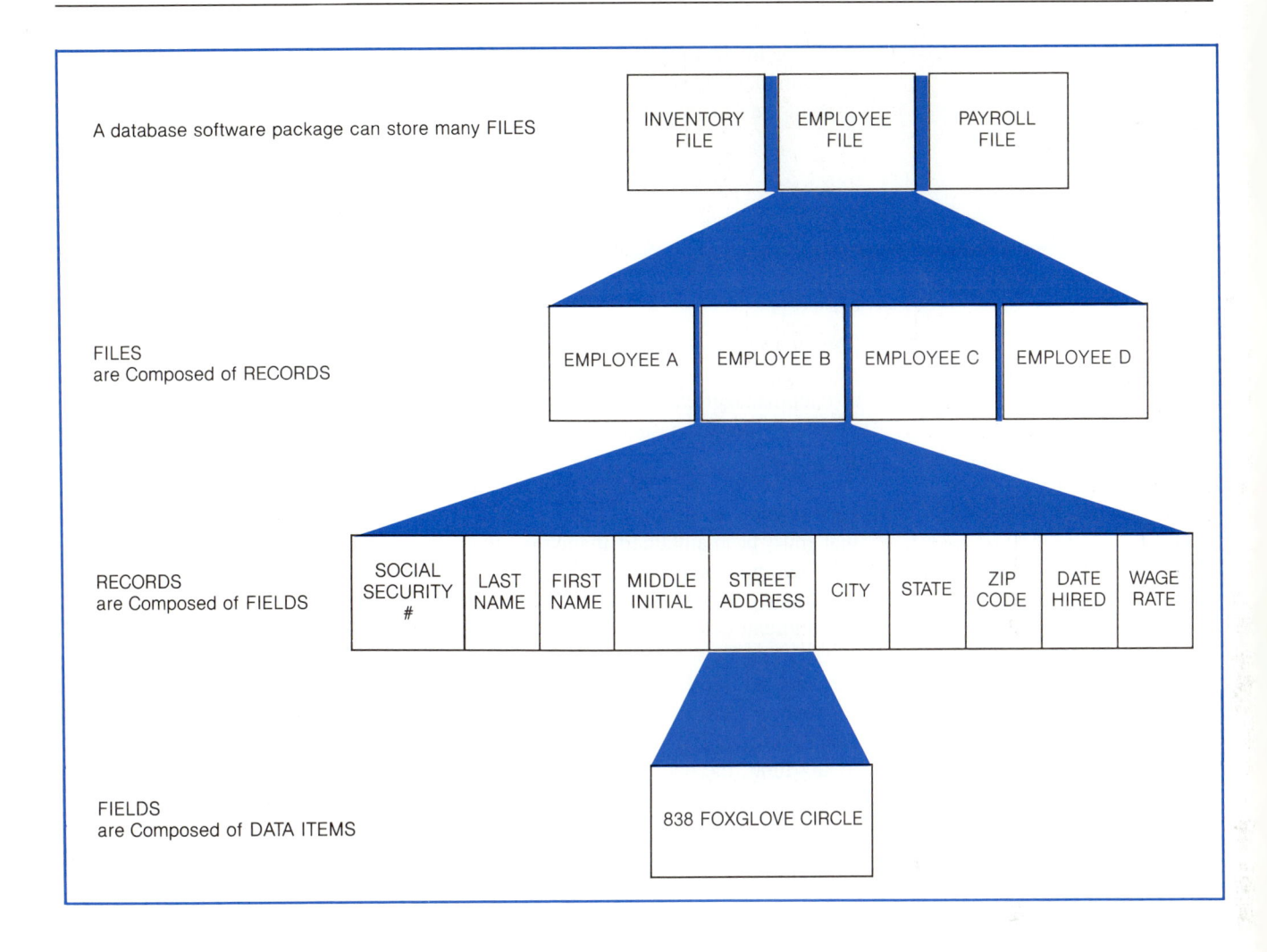

CHAPTER 14: INTRODUCTION TO DATA MANAGERS AND dBASE III

Figure 14-1
The Organization of a Sample Database File

A database software package can store many FILES: INVENTORY FILE, EMPLOYEE FILE, PAYROLL FILE

FILES are Composed of RECORDS: EMPLOYEE A, EMPLOYEE B, EMPLOYEE C, EMPLOYEE D

RECORDS are Composed of FIELDS: SOCIAL SECURITY #, LAST NAME, FIRST NAME, MIDDLE INITIAL, STREET ADDRESS, CITY, STATE, ZIP CODE, DATE HIRED, WAGE RATE

FIELDS are Composed of DATA ITEMS: 838 FOXGLOVE CIRCLE

DATA REDUNDANCY
The repetition of the same data in several different files.

DATABASE
A grouping of independent files into one integrated whole that can be accessed through one central point; a database is designed to meet the information needs of a wide variety of users within an organization.

- Sort data into some order
- Print all or part of the data in a file

Because different files may contain the same information, **data redundancy** can occur and cause problems for a business. Data redundancy is the repetition of data in different files. Because of the difficulty of keeping one piece of information—such as an employee address—current in several files, large companies have developed database packages. A **database** consolidates various independent files into one integrated unit while allowing users access to the information they need. Each data item is stored once, so it is easy to maintain. Users can search for, update, add, or delete data on all the records at one time.

Database packages store data so it can be accessed in many ways. A university database might be accessed by the admissions office, the registrar's office, the financial aid office, and the deans' offices. A college dean might request the names of students who will graduate with academic honors, whereas the financial aid director might need a listing of all students participating in a work-study program.

Since microcomputers were introduced, data managers have become popular with smaller businesses and with home users. The following section discusses the uses of data managers.

Uses of Data Managers

Data managers are popular software packages for home use. They can be used to create and organize a computerized address book, holiday card list, or recipe file. A data manager can be used for just about any type of record keeping. Collectors of coins, stamps, baseball cards, or other items can keep up-to-date files on their collections.

By computerizing these recording and filing tasks in the home, the user can keep records in a compact form. Instead of having numerous notebooks and folders that must be maintained manually, the user enters new data into the computer. Files can be stored on several floppy disks or cassette tapes. Other home uses of data managers include keeping personal records, creating mailing lists, keeping appointment calendars, and indexing books in a personal library.

Data managers also are much faster than manual record keeping. For example, they can be used in homes and businesses to prepare reports for filing taxes. They can keep a record of financial transactions throughout the year, and place a field labeled TAX DEDUCTIBLE in the data record to indicate tax-related transactions. At tax time, the data manager can pick out these transactions and print a report. Thus data managers free the users to concentrate on tasks that can be done only by humans, such as talking to customers or planning new displays.

Data managers can replace the traditional filing system of papers, folders, and filing cabinets. A data manager can maintain employee records, control inventory, and list suppliers and customers. A small sporting goods retail store, for example, can computerize its inventory to improve sales. By recording daily sales, managers can see when the stock levels are low and reorder as necessary.

Some data managers perform mathematical tasks. They can total the values of the same field in all records, find the average of the values in the same field, or find records with the lowest or highest value in a given field. A data manager with mathematical capabilities can determine dollar sales of an item for a certain period. The mathematical features of a data manager also can be used for inventory control, so that employees need not count the items in the store. The data manager can display, subtotal, and total inventory for tax reporting at the end of the year.

Some data managers are designed for use in special situations, such as mass mailing. Creating mailing lists is one popular application. A data manager can store data about people, such as names, addresses, interests, hobbies, and purchases. (People's interests and hobbies can be determined from studying the products they order or magazines they receive.) For example, the data manager can sort and print a list of people who order a sewing or craft item or who receive craft catalogs. Data managers can be used with word processors to produce mailing labels and personalized form letters for individuals or organizations found on mailing lists.

Learning Check

1. A _____ is a meaningful item of data, such as an employee address.
   a. database
   b. record
   c. field
   d. file
2. A _____ is a collection of related data fields that constitute a single unit, such as all the relevant data about one employee.
   a. database
   b. record
   c. field
   d. file
3. A grouping of independent data files into an integrated whole is a _____.
   a. database
   b. record
   c. field
   d. file
4. A _____ is a group of related data records.
   a. database
   b. record
   c. field
   d. file
5. By storing each data item only once, eliminating duplication of information in many different files, a database reduces problems caused by _____.

Answers

1. c 2. b 3. a 4. d 5. data redundancy

Guide to dBase III

The remainder of this chapter focuses on how to use dBase III, developed by Ashton-Tate. dBase III is a data management program that enables you to perform many functions of database management easily.

Some of the directions for using dBase III vary depending on whether the computer has two floppy disk drives or a hard disk drive. The directions in this chapter are written for computers with two floppy disk drives. Differences for computers with a hard disk drive are written in difference boxes.

Over the years, Ashton-Tate has developed several different versions of this popular data management program. The one you are using may be called either dBase II, dBase III or dBase III Plus. Also, there are at least two different releases of dBase III and dBase III Plus (1.0 and 1.1). You can find out which one you are using by reading the opening screen or the diskette label, or by asking your instructor.

This book will focus on the major features that dBase II, dBase III and dBase III Plus have in common. Once you have mastered these basic functions, you should be able to use any version of the program without difficulty. Some of the screens may look slightly different from the ones shown in this book, but the menus and prompts will tell you what to do. If you have dBase III Plus and you want to learn more about its advanced features, you should consult the user manual.

The name "dBase III" or "dBase," as used in this book, refers to all versions of the program unless stated otherwise. Specific versions of the program are named only where it is necessary to clarify differences in the way they are used.

Each of the following sections introduces one or more features of dBase III. At the end of each section there is a hands-on activity marked with this symbol: YOUR TURN. Do not try the hands-on activity until you have carefully read the section preceding it.

The key on the IBM PC keyboard marked ↵ is the <Return> key, also called the <Enter> key. Throughout this chapter, when you are instructed to press the <Return> key, press the key marked ↵.

The following symbols and typefaces appear throughout the chapter:

Press ^A *or:* Press <Ctrl> A	The ^ symbol represents the <Ctrl> key, which is always used in conjunction with another key. In this example, the <Ctrl> key is held down while the letter A key is pressed. Both keys are released together.
Type Number	Typewriter font indicates text that should be entered into a file.
Press the <Return> key	The angle brackets are used to signify a specific key on the keyboard. Press the key whose name is enclosed by the angle brackets.
dBase Tip:	This phrase introduces important information needed to run dBase successfully.
CREATE	All capital letters and boldface indicates a dBase III command name.
DISPLAY ALL (field name #1)	Information contained within parentheses indicates a generic name for a variable that the user must supply. In this example, the user would type something such as DISPLAY ALL Last_Name.

Getting Started with dBase III

BOOT
To load an operating system into a computer's main memory.

To **boot** the computer and start dBase III, you need a DOS disk, a dBase III System Disk (*or* dBase III Plus System Disks #1 and #2), and a formatted data disk. All the files you create are saved on your data disk. Follow these steps to boot the computer and start dBase III:

1. Insert the DOS disk into drive A. Close the disk drive door. Turn on the computer.
2. When asked to type in a date, either bypass the prompt by pressing <Return> or enter today's date using the same format that appears next to CURRENT DATE on the screen. When asked to type the time, either bypass the prompt by pressing <Return> or enter the current time using the same format that appears next to CURRENT TIME on the screen.

CHAPTER 14: INTRODUCTION TO DATA MANAGERS AND dBASE III

3. When the system prompt (A>) appears on the screen, remove the DOS disk from drive A. Insert the dBase III System Disk (*or* the dBase III Plus System Disk #1) into drive A and close the disk drive door.
4. Insert your data disk into drive B. Close the disk drive door.
5. Type **dbase** and press the <Return> key. The screen that comes up depends on the version of the program you are using:

- If you have dBase II or dBase III, you get the copyright notice and a dot prompt, as discussed in the next section.

- If you have dBase III Plus, follow the instructions on the screen. Remove System Disk #1 and insert System Disk #2 when you are instructed to do so. A menu of options appears. Press the <Esc> key to get the dot prompt.

Hard Disk Differences: The dBase III System Disk can be copied to hard disk by entering the following command:

COPY A:*.* C:
Press the <Return> key

Once the system disk has been copied to hard disk, dBase III can be run from the hard disk, but the system disk still has to be in drive A when you first start up the program. The system disk can be removed from drive A once the program is up and running.

If you have dBase III Plus, just copying the files to the hard disk may not work. Some releases of dBase III Plus have copy protection on System Disk #1, so you may need to follow the instructions in your user manual to install the program on your hard disk.

YOUR TURN   Turn on and boot your computer. Start dBase III.

Creating a Database File

After you type **dBase** at the A> system prompt, a copyright notice appears on the screen. At the bottom of the screen is a single period, called the dot prompt, followed by a blinking cursor. (If you have dBase III Plus, you need to press <Esc> in order to get the dot prompt, as explained in the previous section.)

Whenever the dot prompt appears on the screen, dBase is ready to accept a new command, and it is said to be in the Command mode. dBase III commands are easy to use because they are all English words.

The **default** drive the dBase III automatically accesses when first started is drive A. Your data disk—the disk onto which you want to save all the files you

DEFAULT SETTING
The setting that a software package automatically uses when the user does not designate another setting.

create using dBase III—is in drive B, so the default drive has to be changed. The dBase command that changes the default drive is **SET DEFAULT to b.** The SET DEFAULT command tells dBase which disk drive to access when reading from or writing to disk files. The default drive needs to be set to B only once during a work session.

When you are typing commands in dBase, it does not matter if you use uppercase letters, lowercase letters, or a combination of both. For example, the SET DEFAULT command can be entered as SET DEFAULT, Set Default, set default, or sEt deFault. This is true only of commands entered at the dot prompt. When data items are entered into fields, dBase stores the data items exactly as they are typed.

YOUR TURN

The dot prompt should be at the bottom of the screen.

Type **SET DEFAULT to b**
Press <Return>

After you press <Return>, another dot prompt with a blinking cursor next to it appears at the bottom of the screen.

The first step in creating a database file is to give the file a name. Filenames can be up to eight characters long. They can be made up of any combination of letters and numbers, but they must begin with a letter. Try to name a file according to what the file contains. That way, the filename is easier to remember.

The dBase command for creating a file is CREATE. To create a file, prompt type **CREATE** and the filename at the dot prompt, and then press <Return>.

YOUR TURN

The command prompt should be at the bottom of the screen. You are going to create a file to keep track of all the books in a personal library.

Type **CREATE Library**
Press <Return>

The dBase III field definition form appears on the screen (see Figure 14-2).

Different versions of the program may have the field definition form arranged somewhat differently, but its content and purpose are basically the same for all versions.

The purpose of the field definition form is to enable the user to specify all the fields needed for the particular file being created. A field can contain information such as first name, last name, street address, phone number, or order number—any item or type of data that the file is to keep track of. In the upper left corner of the field definition form is a line that indicates the disk drive currently being

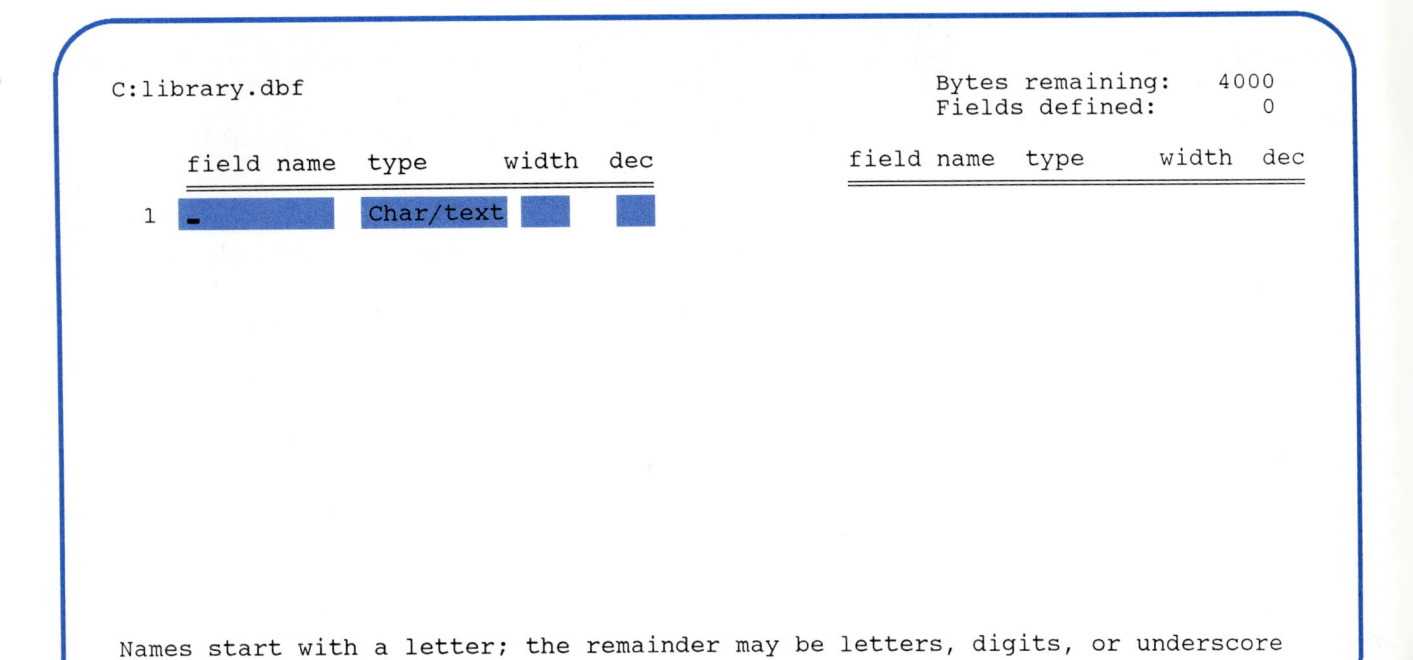

```
C:library.dbf                                    Bytes remaining:    4000
                                                 Fields defined:        0

        field name   type      width  dec         field name   type      width  dec
        ──────────────────────────────────         ──────────────────────────────────
    1   ▮            Char/text  ▮      ▮









    Names start with a letter; the remainder may be letters, digits, or underscore
```

Figure 14-2
The Field Definition Form

accessed and the name of the current file. dBase automatically adds the extension .DBF to the filename. In the upper right corner of the screen are two lines: one that shows the amount of available memory, and another that shows the number of fields that have been defined. At the very bottom of the screen is a prompt that helps to explain the entry that is to be made.

dBase III asks for four categories of information on each field. The first category is the field name, which can be up to ten characters long. The characters can be letters, numbers, or underscores, but the first character has to be a letter. A field name cannot include any spaces. Underscores often are used to separate words in a field name.

> ***dBase Differences:*** In dBase II, underscores cannot be used in field names.

The second category is field type. Five types of data fields can be defined, according to the kind of information being stored in the field. Table 14-1 lists the five field types and explains how they are used.

The default field type is character/text, so pressing the <Return> key selects character/text as the field type.

Table 14-1
Types of Data Fields

	Field Type	Description
C	Character/text fields	Character/text fields store any character that can be enterd from the keyboard: letters, numbers, and symbols. The maximum field width for a character/text field is 254.
N	Numeric fields	There are two types of numeric fields: integer and decimal. An integer numeric field does not have any decimal places. The number of salaried employees is an example of an integer numeric field. The field width of a numeric field is the number of digits the field can hold, with a decimal point counting as one digit.
D	Date fields*	Date fields store dates. The field width of a date field is always 8 (mm/dd/yy).
L	Logical Fields	Logical fields are used to test for true/false conditions. The field width of a logical field is always one.
M	Memo fields*	The purpose of a memo field is to store a large block of textual information.

*In dBase II, Date and Memo Fields are not available. Dates and large blocks of textual information have to be handled as one of the other three field types.

The width of the data field is the maximum number of characters allowed in that field. Table 14-1 defines the possible field width for each field.

Dec stands for decimal. A number entered in this category represents the number of decimal places if the field type is a decimal numeric field.

YOUR TURN

Start with the field definition form on your screen. The file name LIBRARY should be in the upper left corner of the screen (or at the bottom of the screen, if you are using dBase III Plus).

The purpose of this file is to keep track of books in a personal library. For each book, you want to keep a record of the following information:

1. Number — Allocated sequentially to each new book
2. Title — Title of the book
3. Author — Author's last name and first name
4. Date of purchase — Month and year when the book was bought
5. Cost — Amount paid for the book
6. Usage — School usage or personal usage

You are going to start defining these six fields in the field definition form. The blinking cursor should be under the heading Field Name.

Type **Number**
Press <Return>

CHAPTER 14: INTRODUCTION TO DATA MANAGERS AND dBASE III

The cursor moves to the Field Type column. You want this field to be Character/Text, so press the <Return> key to accept the Character/Text default setting. The cursor moves to the field width column.

The field width for the NUMBER field is 3, because you doubt that you will own over 999 books in your personal library:

Type **3**
Press <Return>

Since the field type was not decimal numeric, the cursor automatically skips the decimal column and jumps down so that you can enter the information on the second field. Enter the information on the remaining fields as follows. If you notice a typing mistake before you have pressed <Return>, use the <Backspace> key to delete the necessary characters and retype the entry. If you notice a typing mistake in a field that has already been entered, use the <↑>, <←>, <↓>, and <→> keys to move the cursor to the entry where the mistake occurred. Then use the <Del> key to delete characters and the <Ins> key to insert characters to help you correct the error.

Type **Title**
Press <Return>
Press <Return> again
Type **25**
Press <Return>
Type **Last_Name**
Press <Return>
Press <Return> again
Type **15**
Press <Return>
Type **First_Name**

At this point, the computer beeps and the cursor automatically moves to the Type column. This happens because the field name FIRST_NAME is 10 characters long, the maximum length a field name can be. dBase does not accept more than 10 characters for a field name, so it automatically moves the cursor to the next column. The beep alerts you to the fact the cursor has moved to the next column, so you do not have to press the <Return> key to advance to that column. Again, accept the default setting for Type and enter the field width:

Press <Return>
Type **15**
Press <Return>
Type **Pur_Month**
Press <Return>
Press <Return> again
Type **2**
Press <Return>
Type **Pur_Year**

(Continued)

Press <Return>
Press <Return> again
Type **2**
Press <Return>
Type **Cost**
Press <Return>

The COST field is not a character/text field. It is a decimal numeric field with two decimal places. Notice the prompt line at the bottom of the screen: HIT SPACE FOR OPTIONS (or PRESS SPACE TO CHANGE THE FIELD TYPE, or a similar message). Press the space bar once. The word NUMERIC now appears in the field type column for the COST field.

Press <Return>
Type **8**
Press <Return>

This time the cursor moves to the decimal column, because the field type is numeric. Two decimal places are required.

Type **2**
Press <Return>
Type **Usage**
Press <Return>

You want the USAGE field to be a logical field. This time, instead of pressing the space bar to select the field type, type **L** (for Logical). dbase III immediately selects logical for the field type and 1 for the field width, and moves the cursor to the next line. (You could also select Logical by pressing the space bar several times.)

All the fields for this data file are now defined. Your screen should look like Figure 14-3. Look over all your entries to make sure there are no mistakes. If there are mistakes use the <↑>, <←>, <↓>, <→>, <Del>, and <Ins> keys to help you correct them.

There are two ways to end the field definition process. One way is to press the <Return> key. The second way is to press <Ctrl> <End>. The second method is used in dBase III Plus.

Press <Return>

The message HIT RETURN TO CONFIRM—ANY OTHER KEY TO RESUME (or a similar message) appears at the bottom of the screen. If you want to enter more data fields or to edit those fields already entered, press any key. To end the field definition process, press <Return> one more time.

Press <Return>

After a few seconds the field definition form disappears and the message

```
C:library.dbf                                    Bytes remaining:    3929
                                                 Fields defined:        8

     field name    type       width  dec        field name  type      width  dec
     ==========    ====       =====  ===        ==========  ====      =====  ===
  1  NUMBER        Char/text      3
  2  TITLE         Char/text     25
  3  LAST_NAME     Char/text     15
  4  FIRST_NAME    Char/text     15
  5  PUR_MONTH     Char/text      2
  6  PUR_YEAR      Char/text      2
  7  COST          Numeric        8    2
  8  USAGE         Logical        1
  9                Char/text




Names start with a letter; the remainder may be letters, digits, or underscore
```

Figure 14-3
Defining the Fields for the LIBRARY File

INPUT DATA RECORDS NOW? (Y/N) appears on the screen. The data structure has now been saved.

Entering Records

Once all the fields in a record have been defined, data can be entered into as many records as needed. Typing **Y,** for yes, at the INPUT DATA RECORDS NOW prompt displays the data entry form (see Figure 14-4). Notice that the first line says Record No. 1. dBase automatically keeps track of how many records are entered.

> *dBase Differences:* In dBase III Plus, the data entry form does not display the record number. Also, a menu appears at the top of the data entry form, defining the functions of the various cursor movement keys. This menu is discussed further in the section on the BROWSE command.

Figure 14-4 is the data entry form for the LIBRARY file that was started in the previous hands-on exercise. Below the record number is a list of all the fields defined in the field definition form. The highlighting indicates the width of each

Figure 14-4
A Data Entry Form

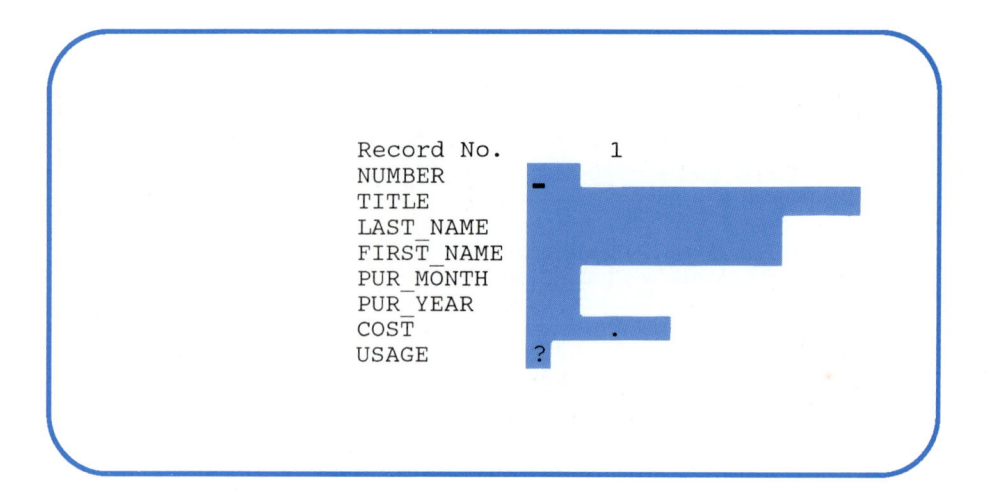

```
                    Record No.         1
                    NUMBER      ▬
                    TITLE
                    LAST_NAME
                    FIRST_NAME
                    PUR_MONTH
                    PUR_YEAR
                    COST              .
                    USAGE       ?
```

field. For example, the TITLE field has a width of 25, the longest field in the record. By looking at the highlighting on the data entry form, you can see that the TITLE field has the greatest width. Also notice that dBase has automatically placed a decimal point in the COST field, and that the USAGE field, which was defined as a logical field, has a question mark next to it.

YOUR TURN

The INPUT DATA RECORDS NOW prompt should be on your screen. Type **Y** for yes.

The data entry form appears. You are now ready to create records for the LIBRARY file by entering data into all of the fields. If you notice a typing error before you press the <Return> key, use the <Backspace> key to correct the error. If you notice an error after pressing the <Return> key, you can use the arrow keys to take you back to the place where the error occurred. The cursor is now in the highlighted area next to the field name Number.

Type 1
Press <Return>
Type A Short Course in PL/C
Press <Return>
Type Clark
Press <Return>
Type Ann
Press <Return>
Type 07

The computer beeps and the cursor automatically moves to the next field without your having to press <Return>. It does this because the field width is 2 and you typed two characters. The beep alerts you to the fact that the cursor is already in the next field. This also happens with the next two entries.

PART TWO: APPLICATIONS SOFTWARE

mand is for creating a database file. The following section introduces the more frequently used dBase commands.

When you are using dBase commands, you must follow a specific **syntax**. Like English or any other language, dBase has a set of rules which governs its structure.

If you make a mistake typing a command, dBase returns the prompt VARIABLE NOT FOUND or SYNTAX ERROR. Both prompts are followed by the question DO YOU WANT SOME HELP? (Y/N). Typing **Y** brings up a help screen that explains the correct syntax for whatever command is being entered. If either of these messages appears as you go through the hands-on exercises, first check to make sure there is not a typing or spelling error in the command. If you believe the command is typed correctly, you can obtain additional help by typing **Y** and reading the help screen.

hat must be followed
rogram instructions;
ructure of the

QUIT

The procedure for exiting from dBase is simple: At the dot prompt, type **QUIT** and press <Return>. The system prompt appears on the screen.

YOUR TURN

Record 16, with nothing in it, should be at the top of your screen. The dot prompt should be at the bottom of the screen.

    Type **QUIT**
    Press <Return>

The system prompt appears on the screen.

USE

The USE command retrieves a previously saved dBase file. To retrieve a file, type **USE** and the name of the file to be retrieved at the dot prompt. dBase then opens that file for use.

If you are unsure of the name of the file to be retrieved, you can use the DIR command, which displays the name of all the files along with the total number of records in each file, the amount of memory used by the files, and the date when each file was last updated. To use the DIR command, type **DIR** at the dot prompt and press <Return>.

YOUR TURN

Start the dBase program. The dot prompt should be on the screen.

    Type **DIR**
    Press <Return>

CHAPTER 14: INTRODUCTION TO DATA MANAGERS 436

Type 86
Type 25.00

The next field is logical, meaning that the entr
no. You will insert Y if the book is for use at s

Type N

After you enter the last field, dBase automatic
record. The record number appears in the fir
track of your entries. (dBase III Plus may not
You are now going to add fourteen more rec
point, do not worry about any typing mistake
the chapter you will learn how to return to the
Enter the following information:

Number	Title	Last_Name	First_Name	Pur_Mor
2	Accounting Today	Asman	Mark	01
3	Advanced Structured COBOL	Welburn	Tyler	10
4	Business Policies	Christensen	Roland	01
5	COBOL For The 80's	Spence	John	11
6	Computers are Fun	Rice	Jean	02
7	Consumer Behavior	Williams	Terrel	01
8	Economics	McConnel	Campbell	12
9	International Marketing	Kramer	Roland	09
10	Introduction to Basic	Mandell	Steven	01
11	Using 1-2-3	Leblond	Geoffrey	04
12	Discovering PC DOS	Worcester	Clark	07
13	Harbrace College Handbook	Hodges	John	10
14	Facts From Figures	Moroney	M	11
15	Financial Accounting	Eskew	Robert	09

Once all the records are entered, record n
Press <Return>. The 15 records are save
the bottom of the screen, indicating that d
command.

SYNTAX
The structure
when writing
in dBase, the
commands.

Using dBase III Commands

All commands in dBase are simple Englis
usually describes the purpose of the comm

CHAPTER 14: INTRODUCTION TO DATA MANAGERS AND dBASE III

A list of the files appears. You want to use the LIBRARY file.

>Type **USE LIBRARY**
>Press <Return>

Another dot prompt appears at the bottom of the screen.

HELP

The HELP command provides information about dBase III commands and their operational rules. These help messages can provide useful information if you are having trouble with any part of dBase III. You can exit from the help message at any time by pressing <Esc>.

YOUR TURN

The LIBRARY file should be active and there should be a dot prompt at the bottom of the screen.

>Type **HELP**
>Press <Return>

The dBase III Main menu appears. There are six options to choose from on the Main menu. The first selection, GETTING STARTED, is highlighted. Press <Return>. Read the information on the screen and press <Return> again. Read the information on the next screen. Press <Ctrl> <Home>. The Main menu returns to the screen.

> *dBase Differences:* In dBase III Plus, if you type **HELP** at the dot prompt, you get the Help Main menu. It has the same six options as the dBase III Main menu. The first option, GETTING STARTED, is highlighted. You may press <Return> and read the information on the first help screen. To scroll to the next help screen, press <PgDn> rather than <Return>. The instructions on the screen tell you which keys to press. dBase II does not include a HELP command.

Move the highlighting to option 2 by pressing the <↓> key. Press <Return>. A list of ten items is displayed. More information about any of those items can be displayed by moving the highlighting to the item, using the arrow keys, and pressing <Return>. Select one or two items from the

"What Is A . . ." list and read about them. When you have finished, press <PgUp> twice to take you back to the Main menu.

Become familiar with the information provided by the HELP command. Select some other options from the Main menu to read about. When you have finished familiarizing yourself with the HELP command, press <Esc>. The dot prompt appears at the top of the screen.

DISPLAY

The DISPLAY command shows all or part of the records in an active file. To show all the records in a file, the DISPLAY ALL command is used. To use this command, type **DISPLAY ALL** at the dot prompt.

> *dBase Differences:* In dBase II, the DISPLAY command is activated by pressing the <F2> key.

YOUR TURN

The dot prompt should be on the screen and the LIBRARY file should be active.

Type **DISPLAY ALL**
Press <Return>

Your screen should look like Figure 14-5. It may seem a bit confusing. Monitors are limited to a screen width of 80 columns. The records in the LIBRARY file have more than 80 characters, so dBase wraps the remaining characters around to the next line. The first line in the list of records shows the record number, the number of the book, the title of the book, the last and first name of the book's author, and the purchase month. The second line still pertains to book 1. On this line is the Purchase Year field, the Cost field, and the Usage field for book 1. The last three fields of each record have to wrap around to the next line.

Look at the entries on the screen for the Usage field. The data you entered into the Usage field was either a Y for yes or a N for no. dBase translated that input into T for true and F for false. An F appears in the fields where you entered a N, and a T appears in the fields where you entered a Y.

At the bottom of the screen is the prompt PRESS ANY KEY TO CONTINUE. All the records do not fit on one screen. To see the rest of the

```
. display all
Record#    NUMBER  TITLE                        LAST_NAME    FIRST_NAME    PUR_MO
NTH PUR_YEAR       COST USAGE
      1    1       A Short Course in PL/C       Clark        Ann            07
 86                25.00 .F.
      2    2       Accounting Today             Asman        Mark           01
 87                50.50 .T.
      3    3       Advanced Structured COBOL    Welburn      Tyler          10
 85                35.00 .F.
      4    4       Business Policies            Christensen  Roland         01
 84                45.00 .T.
      5    5       COBOL For The 80's           Spence       John           11
 85                28.00 .F.
      6    6       Computers are Fun            Rice         Jean           02
 83                34.00 .F.
      7    7       Consumer Behavior            Williams     Terrel         01
 84                40.00 .F.
      8    8       Economics                    McConnel     Campbell       12
 83                65.00 .F.
      9    9       International Marketing      Kramer       Roland         09
 84                52.00 .T.
     10   10       Introduction to Basic        Mandell      Steven         01
 83                54.00 .F.
Press any key to continue..._
```

Figure 14-5
The DISPLAY ALL Command

records, press any key. The remaining records appear at the bottom of the screen.

Reading the records that wrap around to a second line can be confusing. To prevent this situation, you can display only some of the fields rather than all the fields. To use the DISPLAY ALL command to display specific fields, type **DISPLAY ALL (field name #1), (field name #2) . . .**

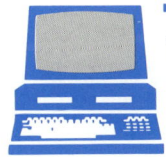

YOUR TURN

The dot prompt should be on the screen and the LIBRARY file should be active. You are going to display only fields 2, 3, 4, and 7 of the LIBRARY file.

Type **DISPLAY ALL Title, Last_Name, First_Name, Cost**
Press <Return>

Fields 2, 3, 4, and 7 for each record appear on the screen. The records are now easier to read, because each record fits on one line.

Table 14-2
Relational Operators

Relational Operator	Relation
=	Equal to
<	Less than
>	Greater than
<=	Less than or equal to
>=	Greater than or equal to
<> or #	Not equal to

DISPLAY FOR

The DISPLAY command can be used to display only those records that meet certain conditions. Those conditions are specified in the DISPLAY FOR command by using relational operators. Table 14-2 defines the acceptable relational operators.

To use the DISPLAY FOR command, type **DISPLAY FOR** (search key) (relationship) (search object).

Using the LIBRARY file as an example, suppose you want to know which books cost over $40.00. The command that provides this information is DISPLAY FOR COST>40.00. The field title COST is the search key, because the COST field is the field to be searched. The > relational symbol is used because you wish to list only those books costing *more than* $40.00, which is the search object.

A search key can be either character/text or numeric. If it is character/text, the search object has to be a character/text string, and it must be enclosed in quotation marks. If the search key is numeric, then the search object also must be a number or a value. In this example, the COST field is numeric, so the search object also is a number.

Numbers can be used as search objects if the search key is character/text. Enclosing the search object in quotation marks tells dBase that the number should be read as text rather than as a value.

In addition to relational operators, dBase uses logical operators, which generate a result from comparing two expressions. Table 14-3 lists and explains the logical operators.

Logical operators allow more than one condition to be set up for displaying records.

Table 14-3
Logical Operators

Logical Operator	Comparison
.AND.	Both expressions must be true.
.OR.	Either one expression or the other must be true (or both).
.NOT.	The condition opposite to the expression must be true.

CHAPTER 14: INTRODUCTION TO DATA MANAGERS AND dBASE III   441

YOUR TURN

The LIBRARY file should be active and a dot prompt should be on the screen.

Type **DISPLAY FOR Cost>40.00**
Press <Return>

A list of the five books costing more than $40.00 appears on the screen.
Now you want to display all the books purchased for 1984. The purchase year field is the search key and is also character/text. Whenever the search key and search object are character/text, the search object has to be enclosed in quotation marks.

Type **DISPLAY FOR Pur_Year>"84"**
Press <Return>

The eight books that were purchased after 1984 are displayed. Now you want to know how many books you have by the author Steven Mandell. To do this, you are going to use the = relational operator. When you use this relation, the condition is met only if the search key and search object are an identical match. If you type "mandell" instead of "Mandell" as the search object, dBase cannot find the record.

Type **DISPLAY FOR Last_Name="Mandell"**
Press <Return>

The one book by Mandell is displayed on the screen. Now suppose you want to combine the first two commands to display the titles of all the books purchased after 1984 which cost more than $40.00. The logical operator .AND. has to be used.

Type **DISPLAY Title FOR Cost>40.00 .AND. Pur_Year>"84"**
Press <Return>

dBase displays the title of the book that was purchased after 1984 and that cost more than $40.00.
If you want to display the titles of all the books that are not for school use, for example, use the .NOT. command.

Type **DISPLAY Title FOR .NOT. Usage**
Press <Return>

All the books that were purchased for personal rather than school use are displayed.

DISPLAY STRUCTURE

In addition to displaying records in a file, dBase can display the data structure of the file—that is, the structure of the file as it was defined on the field definition form. To display the structure of the currently active file, type **DISPLAY STRUCTURE** at the dot prompt.

YOUR TURN

The dot prompt should be on the screen and the LIBRARY file should be active.

Type **DISPLAY STRUCTURE**
Press <Return>

In addition to listing the name, type, and width of each field, the DISPLAY STRUCTURE command lists the number of data records in the file and the date of the last update if the current date was entered when starting DOS.

MODIFY STRUCTURE

The MODIFY STRUCTURE command is used to change the structure of the active database file. Existing database fields can be changed or new database fields can be added using the MODIFY STRUCTURE command.

To use this command, type **MODIFY STRUCTURE** at the dot prompt. The structure is displayed in the same form as it was entered on the field definition form. The structure can then be edited using the < ↑ >, < ↓ >, <←>, and <→> keys to position the cursor at the beginning of the field to be changed. The <PgUp> and <PgDn> keys can be used to display more fields, if the fields take up more than one screen.

To insert a new field, place the cursor at the location where the field is to be inserted and press <Ctrl> **N**. A blank field is then displayed. Field definitions are entered the same way as they are when first creating a database file.

To delete a field, place the cursor at the beginning of the field to be deleted and press <Ctrl> **U**. When all the changes or additions have been made to the data fields, press <Ctrl> <End> to save the changes that were made and to end the structure modification.

YOUR TURN

The LIBRARY file should be active and the dot prompt should be on the screen. You are going to add a new field to the file using the MODIFY STRUCTURE command. Some of the books have more than one author, but only one author's name is stored in each database record. The field you are going to add is a logical field named Code. If a book has more than one author, you will enter Y for Yes. If it has only one author, enter N for No.

Type **MODIFY STRUCTURE**
Press <Return>

The field definition form appears with the eight fields that were entered. Press the < ↓ > key eight times. When the highlighting moves past field eight, spaces appear for entering field 9. The blinking cursor is in the Field Name column.

Type **Code**
Press <Return>
Type **L** (for logical field)

The new field is now entered. Press <Ctrl> <End>.
  The prompt HIT RETURN TO CONFIRM—ANY OTHER KEY TO RESUME (or a similar prompt) appears on the screen. Once you press <Return> the database file reflects the changes that were made and the original file becomes irretrievable. When modifying a structure, you should make sure the changes are exactly what you want before pressing <Ctrl> <End> and <Return>.

Press <Return>

After you press the <Return> key, the MODIFY STRUCTURE command appends the database file to match the new structure. Because a new field was just added to the structure, blank spaces are written in the new field in all the existing data records. A message stating how many records were added briefly flashes on the screen, indicating that blank space for the new field has been added to all the records. The dot prompt then returns to the screen. The DISPLAY STRUCTURE command can be used as a check to make sure the new field has been added.

Type **DISPLAY STRUCTURE**
Press <Return>

The new field, Code, should be listed as field 9. The next step is to add data into the new field. That process is covered in a hands-on exercise later in the chapter.

LIST

Another way to display data records is with the LIST command. The LIST command is similar to the DISPLAY command. The only difference between them is how they display files that are too large to fit on one screen. The DISPLAY

Learning Check

1. In dBase, the filename for the database file can be up to eight characters long and must begin with a letter. (True or False?)
2. _____ fields are used to test for true/false conditions.
   a. Character/text   c. Logical
   b. Numeric   d. Date
3. _____ fields store any character that can be entered from the keyboard.
   a. Character/text   c. Logical
   b. Numeric   d. Date
4. The specific structure that must be followed when writing a dBase command is called the _____.
5. Whenever a dot prompt appears on the screen, dBase is said to be in the _____ mode.

Answers

1. True 2. c 3. a 4. syntax 5. Command

---

command pauses when the screen is full. To see more records, the user presses a key and more records appear on the screen. The LIST command does not pause, but instead displays the records continuously.

If all the records in a file can be displayed on the screen, LIST and DISPLAY work identically. If there are too many records in a file to fit on the screen, however, using the DISPLAY command is more convenient.

The LIST command has the same formats as the DISPLAY command:

LIST STRUCTURE	Displays the structure of the data fields as defined on the field definition form.
LIST ALL	Displays all the records in a database file.
LIST (Field name #1, Field name #2, . . .)	Includes only those fields specified when displaying records in a file.
LIST FOR (search key)(relationship)(search object)	Displays only those records that meet certain conditions.

YOUR TURN

The LIBRARY file should be active and the dot prompt should be on the screen.

Type **LIST ALL**
Press <Return>

CHAPTER 14: INTRODUCTION TO DATA MANAGERS AND dBASE III

The LIST command displays all the records in the LIBRARY file without pausing. The first four records scroll off the top of the screen.

APPEND

Records can be added to the end of a database file by using the APPEND command. To add a record, type **APPEND** at the dot prompt. An entry form for the new record appears. As many records as needed can be added to the file.

YOUR TURN

The LIBRARY file should be active and the dot prompt should be on the screen.

Type **APPEND**
Press <Return>

An entry form for record 16 appears on the screen. The entry form that appears is always for the new record following the last record in the database. In this case there are 15 records in the LIBRARY file, so an entry form for record 16 appears. Notice that the new field Code is included.
Enter the following five records:

Number	Title	Last_Name	First_Name	Pur_Month	Pur_Year	Cost	Usage	Code
16	Getting Things Done	Bliss	Edwin	02	85	23.60	N	N
17	Intermediate Algebra	Mangan	Frances	09	84	22.30	Y	N
18	Management	Glueck	William	07	86	28.45	N	N
19	Learning to Program in C	Plum	Thomas	07	86	48.90	N	N
20	Information Systems	Burch	John	01	86	52.60	Y	Y

When the entry form for record 21 appears, press <Return> to save the added records and to end the APPEND command.

BROWSE

Another command that displays the records in a file is the BROWSE command. The BROWSE command is different from the DISPLAY and LIST commands in that records can be modified with the BROWSE command. The data in the records can be edited, additional records can be added, and existing records can be deleted.

If a data record contains more than 80 characters, the entire record will not fit across the screen. The BROWSE command displays only the first 80 characters. Just as with the DISPLAY and LIST commands, specific fields can be displayed by indicating the field names, using a BROWSE FIELD command. For example, to display fields 2 and 3 of the LIBRARY file using the BROWSE command, type **BROWSE FIELDS Last_Name, First_Name.**

When you are using the BROWSE command, dBase's commands and control functions are helpful for moving the cursor around the screen. The SET MENUS ON command displays a cursor movement key menu that is useful to have on the screen as you move through the records. (If you do not want to display this menu, use the command SET MENUS OFF.) The $<\uparrow>$ and $<\downarrow>$ keys are used to move through the records one record at a time. The $<\leftarrow>$ and $<\rightarrow>$ keys are used to move through each record one character at a time. The <Return> key moves the cursor to the next field.

A new data record can be added to the file by using the $<\downarrow>$ key beyond the last data record. The prompt ADD NEW RECORDS? (Y/N) appears on the screen. Typing **Y** places a row of blank spaces after the last record. A new data record can be entered in these blank spaces. As many records as needed can be added at the end of the file.

Either a field or an entire record can be deleted using the BROWSE command. To delete a field, position the cursor within the field to be deleted and press <Ctrl> **Y**. To delete a record, place the cursor within the record to be deleted and press <Ctrl> **U**.

YOUR TURN

The LIBRARY file should be active and the dot prompt should be on the screen. You are going to use the BROWSE command to display fields 2, 3, 4, and 7. First you are going to display the menu.

Type **SET MENU On**
Press <Return>

The dot prompt appears again.

Type **BROWSE FIELDS Title, Last_Name, First_Name, Cost**
Press <Return>

Your screen should look like Figure 14-6. Only one record, record number 20, is listed. This is because record 20 is the active record. The last record accessed in the database file is always the active or current record. Notice on the menu that the $<\uparrow>$ key moves the file up one record.

Press $<\uparrow>$

Record 19 now appears on the screen.

Press the $<\uparrow>$ key until record number 1 is the first record listed.

Look over the menu at the top of the screen. Practice using the cursor movement commands listed in the menu.

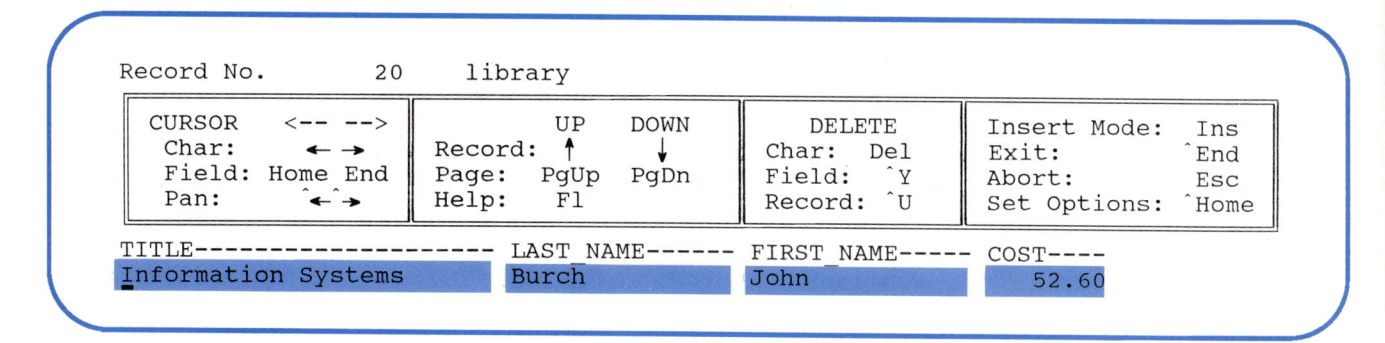

```
Record No.      20     library
┌─────────────────────┬───────────────────┬─────────────────┬──────────────────────┐
│ CURSOR   <-- -->    │         UP  DOWN  │ DELETE          │ Insert Mode:   Ins   │
│  Char:    ← →       │ Record:  ↑   ↓    │  Char:   Del    │ Exit:          ^End  │
│  Field: Home End    │ Page:   PgUp PgDn │  Field:  ^Y     │ Abort:         Esc   │
│  Pan:    ^←^→       │ Help:    F1       │  Record: ^U     │ Set Options:   ^Home │
└─────────────────────┴───────────────────┴─────────────────┴──────────────────────┘
TITLE-------------------- LAST NAME------ FIRST NAME----- COST----
Information Systems       Burch           John              52.60
```

Figure 14-6
The BROWSE Command

Go through each record a field at a time using the <Return> key. If you find any typing mistakes, use the <←> and <→> keys to move the cursor to the mistake to correct it. The <Del> key deletes characters and the <Ins> key inserts characters.

When you get to the last record on the screen, press <PgDn>. The remaining records in the LIBRARY file appear. Read through these records for typing mistakes and correct your mistakes as needed.

You have decided to sell your book titled *Intermediate Algebra*, which is record 17. Move the highlighting to record 17. Press <Ctrl> **U.** Notice the top line of the screen now has the word *DEL* or Del. This record is now marked for deletion, but it still remains in the file. Press <Ctrl> **U** again. The word *DEL* disappears from the top of the screen. The record is no longer marked for deletion. <Ctrl> **U** acts as a toggle function. If it is pressed once, the delete function is on, and if it is pressed again, the function is off.

Press <Ctrl> **U**

Record 17 is now marked for deletion. To exit from the BROWSE command and save any changes made to the records press <Ctrl> <End>. To exit BROWSE without saving any changes, press <Esc> instead.

Press <Ctrl> <End>

The changes you made are saved, and the dot prompt returns to the screen. The command SET MENU Off turns the menu off.

Type **SET MENU Off**
Press <Return>

PACK

Simply marking records for deletion does not actually remove them from the file. To remove the record, use the PACK command. The PACK command removes the record or records previously marked for deletion and repacks the remaining records.

> *dBase Tip:* Always use the PACK command with care. Make sure the records that are marked for deletion are the ones you really do not want removed. Once you use the PACK command, those records are removed permanently.

YOUR TURN

The LIBRARY file should be active and the dot prompt on the screen. In the previous hands-on exercise, record 17 was marked for deletion. Now you are going to remove it permanently from the file with the PACK command.

Type **PACK**
Press <Return>

The message 19 RECORDS COPIED appears on the screen. dBase has repacked the LIBRARY file by deleting record 17 and renumbering the remaining records. Use the DISPLAY command to look at record 17.

Type **DISPLAY Record 17**
Press <Return>

Record 17, which is now for the book *Management,* is displayed on the screen. Display all the book titles to see if *Intermediate Algebra* is listed.

Type **DISPLAY All Title**
Press <Return>

All the titles are displayed and *Intermediate Algebra* has been deleted.

EDIT

The contents of a data record can be modified using the EDIT command as well as the BROWSE command. To edit a specific record, type EDIT RECORD (record number). For example, to edit record 3 of the LIBRARY file, the command to be typed is **EDIT RECORD 3**.

Once the record is displayed, move the cursor through the record using the arrow keys. The current record remains on the screen as long as the cursor remains within that record. If the cursor is positioned in field 1 and the <↑> key is pressed, the previous record appears on the screen. If the cursor is positioned in the last field in the record and the <↓> key is pressed, the next record appears on the screen. Regardless of where the cursor is positioned in the record, the <PgUp> key displays the previous data record and the <PgDn> key displays the next data record.

CHAPTER 14: INTRODUCTION TO DATA MANAGERS AND dBASE III

There are two ways to exit the EDIT command. To exit without saving any changes that were made, press <Esc>. To exit and save all the changes that were made, press <Ctrl> <End>.

YOUR TURN

The LIBRARY file should be active and the dot prompt should be on the screen.

Type **EDIT Record 1**
Press <Return>

Record 1 appears on the screen. Read through the record for mistakes. In the previous hands-on exercise, when you used the BROWSE command to check for typing errors, you did not check fields 1, 5, 6, 8, or 9. Check these fields for errors now. Notice that there is a question mark next to the field name Code. The field Code was added with the MODIFY STRUCTURE command, but data was not entered into the new field. You are now going to enter data into this field.

Using the <↓> key, move the cursor to the Code field.

Type N

Record 2 now appears on the screen. Move the cursor to the Code field.

Type Y

Continue to add data to the Code field as follows:

Record No.	Data
3	N
4	Y
5	N
6	Y
7	N
8	N
9	N
10	N
11	Y
12	N
13	N
14	N
15	Y

When you reach record 16, data is already in the Code field. Records 16 through 20 were inserted after the Code field was added, so they do not need to have data added into this field.

The <Ctrl> Y command for deleting a field and the <Ctrl> U command for deleting a record work the same way as they did in the BROWSE command. Using the <PgUp> or <PgDn> key as needed, move the cursor to record 10.

Press <Ctrl> **U**

The word *DEL* appears at the top of the screen. Record 10 is marked for deletion.

Press <Ctrl> <End>

The dot prompt appears at the bottom of the screen. All the changes you made have been saved.

Type **PACK**
Press <Return>

This command removes record 10 from the file and repacks the remaining records. There are now 18 records in the LIBRARY file.

DELETE and RECALL

As previously discussed, the process of deleting a data record involves two steps: the record has to be marked for deletion, and the file has to be repacked with the PACK command. Records can be deleted not only with the BROWSE command and the EDIT command, but also with the DELETE command.

The DELETE command can be used to delete a specific record, to delete all the records in a file, or to delete only those records that meet certain conditions. The following are the DELETE command formats:

DELETE RECORD (record number)	Marks the specified data record for deletion.
DELETE ALL	Marks every data record in the file for deletion.
DELETE FOR (search key)(relationship)(search object)	Marks for deletion only those records that meet specified conditions.

After records have been marked for deletion using the DELETE command, the file has to be repacked using the PACK command.

If a record has been marked for deletion but the PACK command has not yet been issued, the deletion marks can be erased using the RECALL command. The following are the formats for the RECALL command:

RECALL RECORD (record number) — Erases the deletion mark from the data record specified.

RECALL ALL — Erases the deletion marks from all the data records marked for deletion.

RECALL FOR (search key)(relationship)(search object) — Erases the deletion marks only from those records that meet specified conditions.

Once a data record has been removed with the PACK command, it can never be retrieved.

YOUR TURN

The library file should be active and the dot prompt should be on the screen.

Suppose your library is getting too large and you have decided to sell or give away all the books purchased prior to 1985. Now you want to delete them from the file.

Type DELETE FOR Pur_Year<"85"
Press <Return>

The message 6 RECORDS DELETED appears on the screen. Look at the data file to see which records were deleted.

Type DISPLAY ALL Title, Pur_Year
Press <Return>

This command displays a list of all the book titles and the year each book was purchased. Notice that the book titles in records 4, 6, 7, 8, 9, and 12 have asterisks next to them. This means that these records are marked for deletion. Also notice that the purchase year of each of these books was before 1985.

Now suppose you have decided that you cannot part with so many books, no matter how large your library is, and you do not want to delete these books from the file. Use the RECALL command to erase the deletion marks.

Type RECALL FOR Pur_Year<"85"
Press <Return>

The message 6 RECORDS RECALLED appears on the screen. Check to make sure the deletion marks have been erased.

Type DISPLAY ALL Title, Pur_Year
Press <Return>

The asterisks are erased from the file.

GOTO

A specific data record can be displayed by using the GOTO command. The format for the GOTO command is GOTO (data record number).

YOUR TURN

The library file should be active and the dot prompt should be on the screen. You are going to use the GOTO command to go to record 15.

    Type **GOTO 15**
    Press <Return>
    Type **DISPLAY Title, Last_name, First_name**
    Press <Return>

Record 15 is displayed.

GO TOP and GO BOTTOM

The first or last data record in a file can be selected by using the GO TOP or GO BOTTOM commands. To go to the first record in a file, type **GO TOP**. Record 1 then becomes the active record. To go to the last record, type **GO BOTTOM**. The last record in the file becomes the active record.

YOUR TURN

The library file should be active and the dot prompt should be on the screen.

    Type **GO TOP**
    Press <Return>
    Type **DISPLAY Title, Last_name, First_name**
    Press <Return>

Record 1 is displayed.

    Type **GO BOTTOM**
    Press <Return>
    Type **DISPLAY Title, Last_name, First_name**
    Press <Return>

Record 18, the last record in the file, is displayed.

dBase III Summary Commands

So far this chapter has introduced dBase commands that enable a user to create, edit, and display a data file. Once a file has been created, it can provide a wide variety of valuable information through the use of dBase's summary commands. In fact, the summarizing of data is one of dBase's most significant functions. The summary commands COUNT, TOTAL, and AVERAGE summarize data to provide useful information.

COUNT

The COUNT command can be used in several ways to tally the records in a file. An unconditional COUNT command counts all the data records in a file. To use the unconditional COUNT command, type **COUNT**. A message such as 28 RECORDS appears on the screen, indicating the total number of records currently stored in the file.

A conditional COUNT command counts only those records that meet a specified condition. The format for the conditional COUNT command is COUNT FOR (search key) (relationship) (search object). A message appears on the screen, indicating how many records meet the condition specified.

More than one condition can be specified in the COUNT command by using the logical operators AND, OR, and NOT. These logical operators perform the same functions when used with the COUNT command as they do when used with the DISPLAY command.

YOUR TURN

The LIBRARY file should be active and the dot prompt should be on the screen.

Type **COUNT**
Press <Return>

The message 18 RECORDS appears on the screen, because the LIBRARY file currently has 18 data records stored in it.
Now you want to find out how many books you purchased in 1986.

Type **COUNT FOR Pur_Year="86"**
Press <Return>

The message 7 RECORDS appears on the screen. Now you want to know how many books you purchased in 1986 which cost $25.00 or more.

Type **COUNT FOR Pur_Year="86" .AND. Cost>=25.00**
Press <Return>

The message 5 RECORDS appears on the screen.

SUM

The contents of numeric fields can be added using the SUM command. The unconditional SUM command calculates the sum of all the values in the specified data field. To use the unconditional SUM command, type **SUM (name of field)**. This command adds together all the data records in the file.

The SUM command also can include relational and logical operators. The format for a conditional SUM command is SUM (name of data field) FOR (search key) (relationship) (search object). More conditions can be added to the SUM command by using the logical operators AND, OR, and NOT.

YOUR TURN

The LIBRARY file should be active and the dot command should be on the screen. You are going to find out the total cost of your library by using the SUM command.

Type **SUM Cost**
Press <Return>

A message appears, telling you that 18 records have been added together and that the total cost for all the books is $639.60. Now you are going to find out how much money you spent on buying books in 1986.

Type **SUM Cost FOR Pur_Year="86"**
Press <Return>

Now you want to find out how much money you spent in 1986 for books other than those for school use.

Type **SUM Cost FOR .NOT. Usage .AND. Pur_Year="86"**
Press <Return>

Notice that the qualifier .NOT. Usage does not include a relational operator or the search object. This is because the field Usage is a logical field. A logical field never needs a search object, because the field contains one of only two options: T for true or F for false. When you entered data into the Usage field, you entered Y for yes (which equates to T for True) if the book was used at school. The qualifier .NOT. Usage tells the computer to include only those fields where Usage does not contain the value true. If you wanted to find the cost of the books used in school, you would use the logical operator .AND. When used in conjunction with a logical field, the logical operator .AND. tells the computer to include only those fields that contain the value true.

Type **SUM Cost FOR Pur_Year="86" .AND. Usage**
Press <Return>

AVERAGE

The AVERAGE command calculates an average value for the contents of a numeric field. The unconditional AVERAGE command, AVERAGE (name of numeric field), computes the average using the specified field from all the records. The conditional AVERAGE command computes the average using the numeric fields that meet the specified conditions. The format for a conditional AVERAGE command is AVERAGE (name of numeric field) FOR (search key) (relationship) (search object). The AVERAGE command also can include logical operators.

> *dBase Differences:* In dBase II, the AVERAGE command is not available.

YOUR TURN

The LIBRARY file should be active and the dot prompt should be on the screen.

You are going to find the average cost of all your books.

Type AVERAGE Cost
Press <Return>

A prompt appears, indicating that 18 records have been averaged and that the average price you paid for a book was $35.53.

Now you would like to know the average price of a book you use at school.

Type AVERAGE Cost FOR Usage
Press <Return>

A prompt appears, indicating that 6 records have been averaged and that the average price you paid for books used at school is $42.61.

Printing a dBase III File

A hard copy of a data file often is useful. There are a number of different ways to print a dBase file. If the hard copy should appear the same as the file displayed on the screen, the command TO PRINT along with the LIST and DISPLAY commands can be used.

Before trying to print a dBase file, make sure the printer is connected to the printer, is online and has plenty of paper. Use either one of the following commands and press the <Return> key to print a hard copy of designated fields within a file:

Learning Check

1. Once a dBase record has been marked for deletion, it is removed from the file. (True or False?)

2. Which of the following commands does not display the records in a dBase file?
   - a. BROWSE
   - b. DISPLAY
   - c. APPEND
   - d. LIST

3. Once a data record has been removed with the PACK command, it can be retrieved with the RECALL command. (True or False?)

4. When using the BROWSE and EDIT command, press _____ to exit the command and save any changes that were made.

5. Which of the following is not a dBase summary command?
   - a. COUNT
   - b. NOT
   - c. TOTAL
   - d. AVERAGE

Answers

1. False 2. c 3. False 4. <Ctrl> <End> 5. b

    LIST (names of fields to be printed) TO PRINT
    DISPLAY (names of fields to be printed) TO PRINT

To print the entire contents of a file, use either the command LIST TO PRINT or the command DISPLAY TO PRINT.

---

dBase Differences: In dbase II, the following commands have to be entered from the dot prompt in order to print a copy of the data file:
    SET PRINT ON
    LIST
    SET PRINT OFF

YOUR TURN

The LIBRARY file should be active and the dot prompt should be on the screen.

    Type **LIST Title, First_Name, Last_Name, Cost TO PRINT**
    Press <Return>

Your hard copy of the LIBRARY file should look like Figure 14-7.

Figure 14-7 Selected Fields from the LIBRARY File

```
Record#  Title                         First_Name   Last_Name      Cost
      1  A Short Course in PL/C        Ann          Clark         25.00
      2  Accounting Today              Mark         Asman         50.50
      3  Advanced Structured COBOL     Tyler        Welburn       35.00
      4  Business Policies             Roland       Christensen   45.00
      5  COBOL For The 80's            John         Spence        28.00
      6  Computers are Fun             Jean         Rice          34.00
      7  Consumer Behavior             Terrel       Williams      40.00
      8  Economics                     Campbell     McConnel      65.00
      9  International Marketing       Roland       Kramer        52.00
     10  Using 1-2-3                   Geoffrey     Leblond       21.50
     11  Discovering PC DOS            Clark        Worcester     18.50
     12  Harbrace College Handbook     John         Hodges        16.75
     13  Facts From Figures            M            Moroney       16.00
     14  Financial Accounting          Robert       Eskew         38.80
     15  Getting Things Done           Edwin        Bliss         23.60
     16  Management                    William      Glueck        28.45
     17  Learning to Program in C      Thomas       Plum          48.90
     18  Information Systems           John         Burch         52.60
```

Summary Points

- A data manager (data management package) can be used for the same purposes as a manual filing system: to record and file information.
- Data managers can be used in the home for such tasks as creating a computerized holiday card list or recipe index file, helping balance a checkbook, and keeping a personal appointment calendar.
- In business, data managers have many uses, such as keeping employee and inventory control records and lists of customers and suppliers.
- Data managers enable businesses to maintain records quickly and efficiently.
- Some specialized uses of data managers include preparing mass mailings and creating form letters, in conjunction with word processors.

dBase III Exercises

To complete the following exercises, you will need a DOS disk, the dBase III system disk, and your data disk.

1. Start dBase. Describe the steps required. At the dot prompt, use the command to set the default directory to drive B.
2. Assume you have been hired by Kenneth Fretwell, D.D.S. to establish a database management system for his office using dBase III. Using the CREATE command, create a file named PATIENTS.

3. Your PATIENTS file has eight fields. For each field, enter the following information into the field description form.

Field Name	Type	Width	Dec
First_Name	Character/Text	10	
Last_Name	Character/Text	10	
Address	Character/Text	15	
City	Character/Text	10	
St	Character/Text	2	
Zip	Character/Text	5	
Age	Character/Text	2	
Balance	Numeric	6	2

4. Enter the following data into the PATIENTS file:

First_Name	Last_Name	Address	City	St	ZIP	Age	Balance
David	Busch	552 Wallace	Columbus	OH	78654	27	58.60
Patricia	Busch	552 Wallace	Columbus	OH	78654	28	0
Tom	Allen	67 Curtis	Columbus	OH	78653	78	8.90
Eileen	Spires	890 Pine	Columbus	OH	78651	56	120.00
Dave	Jenkins	10 W. Wooster	Columbus	OH	89123	13	93.50
Pamela	Weaver	16 Clough	Columbus	OH	78654	10	0
Bradley	Busch	552 Wallace	Columbus	OH	78654	7	25.00
William	Bentley	77 Palmer	Dayton	OH	89213	45	0

After the eighth record has been added, press the <Return> key to end the process of adding data records.

5. Using the EDIT command, go over all the records to check for any mistakes. Make any corrections necessary and save the changes.

6. Add the following records to the PATIENTS file:

First_Name	Last_Name	Address	City	St	ZIP	Age	Balance
Wilma	Lukes	909 Clough	Columbus	OH	78653	89	280.090
Douglas	Swartz	9 Main	Dayton	OH	89213	32	46.90
Linda	Plazer	12 Vine	Columbus	OH	78651	25	176.00
Ann	Bressler	25 Baldwin	Columbus	OH	78653	25	0

7. Tom Allen and William Bentley changed dentists. Delete their records from the file.

8. The Busch family moved. Their new address is 41 Normandie in Columbus. Update their records, assuming their ZIP code will be the same.

9. Dr. Fretwell is going to start a No Cavities Club for children under the age of 16. List all of Dr. Fretwell's patients who might be eligible for this club.

10. What is the total balance due from all of the patients? Who are the patients who owe over $35.00? Who are the patients with a zero balance?

11. Print a hard copy of the PATIENTS file.

dBase III Problems

To complete the following exercise, you need a DOS disk, the dBase III system disk, and the Student File Disk.

1. Start dBase and insert the data disk in drive B. Set the default drive to B.
2. You are going to use a database that has already been created. Assume that you are working in the payroll department of your company. The company uses two major files to store employee information: A permanent file called PAYROLL to keep permanent information (such as name, address, job name, and hourly salary), and a temporary file that is created each month based on the specific data for the month. Retrieve the file PAYROLL. Before you start using this file, you need to make a copy of it. That way, if you make a mistake, you will always have the original file. Type **COPY TO PAYROLL1** at the dot prompt.
3. Open the file PAYROLL1. What are the two ways of displaying the file's structure? Use one of them to display the file's structure. How many fields are there in the file? How many numeric fields? What is the width of the field Jobname? The field Status defines the personnel status (F for full-time and P for part-time). What is its type? How many data records are there in the file?
4. Now you want to see the records of the employees. First display the first five records. What is the command to display these records? What is the name of the employee corresponding to record number 5? What is his job title? Use the command to display all records. What is the name of the last employee?
5. Now you would like to list only the last name, first name, and job title of all employees. Describe the steps you have to follow to list this information.
6. Now list the same information for all full-time employees. How many full-time employees are there in the company?
7. List the last name, first name, employee number, and job title for all employees who are part-time and writers.
8. What is the average hourly wage of all the employees? Who are the employees earning more than $9.00 an hour?
9. Now the manager gives you all the information about the employees who worked during March. He asks you to create a file for this data. The file should contain the following information:

Field Name	Field Type	Width	Dec	Description
EMPLNUM	N	3		Employee number
MONTH	N	2		Month of work
ENDPER	C	6		Ending period
NORMHRS	N	5	2	Total hours of work

Exit from the PAYROLL1 file. Start dBase again so you can create the new file. What is the first instruction to start creating a new file? Use this command to start the new file. Name it MONTH3.

10. Enter the structure of the new file, using the information in exercise 9. How do you end the session? What does dBase ask you at this moment? Answer **N** and

use the DISPLAY STRUCTURE command to review the file structure.

11. You realize that the following field is missing:

Field Name	Field Type	Width	Dec	Description
EXTRAHRS	N	6	2	Extra hours

Use the MODIFY STRUCTURE command to add this new field. Change the Normhrs field width to 6. Now that you are satisfied with your structure, use the appropriate command to save your modifications.

12. What is the command to add records to a file? Using this command, start entering the following data into the file:

EMPLNUM	MONTH	ENDPERIOD	NORMHRS	EXTRAHRS
1	3	033187	160.00	30.00
2	3	033187	160.00	40.00
3	3	033187	160.00	0.00
4	3	033187	140.00	0.00
6	3	033187	160.00	0.00
7	3	033187	160.00	20.00
8	3	033187	160.00	20.00
9	3	033187	160.00	0.00
10	3	033187	160.00	0.00
11	3	033187	100.00	0.00
13	3	033187	160.00	0.00
15	3	033187	80.00	0.00
16	3	033187	90.00	0.00

Save the data. Exit from dBase.

CHAPTER 15

Advanced dBase III

Outline

Introduction
  SORT TO
  Conditional Sorts
  INDEX ON
  Indexing on Multiple Fields
  FIND
Learning Check
Creating a Report with dBase III

CREATE REPORT
  Filling in the Report Headings
    Screen
  Defining Report Columns
  MODIFY REPORT
  Printing a Report
Using Multiple Database Files
  SELECT

Learning Check
  Joining Two Files
Summary of dBase III Commands
Summary Points
dBase III Exercises
dBase III Problems

Introduction

The previous chapter presented all the commands needed to create a database file with dBase III. Once a file has been created, it can be manipulated in many useful ways. The purpose of this chapter is to introduce the more advanced dBase commands that enable a user to arrange the data stored in a database file so that it can be used efficiently. Other advanced topics covered in this chapter include creating a report with a dBase file and joining two dBase files.

SORT TO

As discussed in the previous chapter, a database file is made up of records that a user enters into the data entry form. As each record is entered, dBase automatically assigns a chronological record number to it. The data records are stored in the file in the order in which they were entered, but this may not be the order that provides the most useful information. For example, records in a payroll file are not entered in alphabetical order. They are added when employees are hired and deleted when employees leave the company. To be useful, however, a database program must be able to arrange a payroll file in alphabetical order. In dBase, the SORT TO command enables the user to rearrange data records.

Data records can be arranged in either ascending or descending order. Sorting physically rearranges the records in the active database file, so in order to maintain the original database file, dBase copies the sorted database file to a working file. The command to sort the records in a file is:

SORT TO (filename) ON (field)

The filename is the new filename under which the sorted records are saved. The field is the data field used to sort the file. This field must be a character, numeric, or date field; it cannot be a logical or memo field. Unless otherwise specified, dBase assumes the sort will be in ascending order (for example, A to Z for a character field). If the sort is to be in descending order, /D must be added to the end of the field name.

> *dBase Differences:* In dBase II, the command to sort the records in a file is:
> SORT ON (field) TO (filename)

YOUR TURN

You are going to sort a database file using the SORT TO command. First, you must create the file to be sorted. You are going to create a file called STUDENT that contains the name, classification, grade point average, birthdate, social security number, account balance, and address for students at a college. Numbers are used to designate the student's classification: 4 = senior, 3 = junior, 2 = sophomore, and 1 = freshman.

Start dBase. Set the default directory drive to B. Using the CREATE command, create a database file named STUDENT. Enter the following information in the field definition form:

Field	Field name	Type	Width	Dec
1	Name	Char/text	20	
2	Year	Char/text	1	
3	GPA	Numeric	4	2
4	Birthdate	Date	8	
5	SS_Number	Char/text	11	
6	Account	Numeric	8	2
7	Address	Char/text	15	
8	City	Char/text	10	
9	State	Char/text	2	
10	Zip_Code	Char/text	5	

You may wonder why some of the field types are character even though the data entered into them is actually numeric. There are two reasons for this. First, a general rule to follow is that a field should always be character unless it is to be used for calculations. Zip codes and social security numbers are not used in calculations, so their field type is character. The second reason is that character fields are easier to index, as explained later in this chapter.

Once the field information has been entered, input the following into the data records:

#	NAME	YR	GPA	BDATE	SS_NUMBER	ACCOUNT	ADDRESS	CITY	ST	Z CODE
1	Faulks, Tim	4	3.20	03/01/65	343-61-1101	286.59	78 Main St.	Miami	FL	32109
2	Bulas, Irene	3	3.00	07/19/66	289-89-4672	1203.87	908 W. Summit	Cygnet	OH	43409
3	Klein, Tom	4	2.55	10/20/65	278-45-7891	96.95	12 Yong St.	Hampton	NC	27710
4	Wilcox, Bill	1	2.00	06/08/68	524-68-4099	0.00	6 Williams Rd.	Fremont	OH	43098
5	Ornelas, Tina	2	3.12	03/05/67	468-71-9002	2005.32	123 First St.	Canton	OH	43012
6	Lord, Pamela	4	3.78	03/03/65	208-46-4096	576.94	98 Pike St.	Oregon	OH	42876
7	Busch, Brad	3	3.70	04/04/61	782-28-1598	803.52	32 Bradner	Columbus	OH	43219
8	Weaver, Chris	2	2.15	10/10/67	411-69-4774	68.07	909 Clough	Portage	OH	43213
9	Engel, Chuck	4	2.34	03/10/60	778-61-8723	12.18	1432 Indian Rd.	Hamler	OH	43406
10	Wilks, Cleo	1	3.81	11/02/68	428-18-9972	1096.20	76 Gorrel	Lima	OH	43420
11	Bressler, Ann	1	2.08	07/16/63	789-22-6615	0.00	45 S. Luke St.	Palma	OH	43316
12	Hocks, Arthur	3	2.89	03/12/66	558-79-5151	446.29	90 Kellog Rd.	Portage	OH	43213
13	DeSalvo, Liz	4	2.22	06/14/65	879-43-6291	0.00	9 W. Second St.	Columbus	OH	43207
14	Friedman, Mark	1	3.98	09/02/68	271-64-4049	33.68	3426 Little St.	Palma	OH	43316
15	Crope, Trish	2	3.21	03/11/65	491-11-9984	175.50	67 Baldwin	Cygnet	OH	43409

Once all the records have been entered, use the SORT TO command to sort all the records alphabetically by name.

Type **SORT TO Alphaname ON Name**
Press <Return>

ALPHANAME is the new name for the file that now stores the records listed in alphabetical order by name. Name is the field that determines the sort. After pressing <Return>, the message 100% SORTED 15 RECORDS SORTED appears on the screen.

In order to see the new sorted file, you have to type the USE command to change the active file to ALPHANAME. Currently, STUDENT is the active file.

Type **USE Alphaname**
Press <Return>

To check and see if the records have been sorted alphabetically by name, use the DISPLAY command.

Type **DISPLAY ALL Name**
Press <Return>

The names should be listed in alphabetical order. Now you are going to sort all the records by GPA in descending order. The sorted file will be called DESGPA. (Remember that dBase does not distinguish uppercase and lowercase letters in commands.)

Type **SORT TO Desgpa ON Gpa/d**
Press <Return>
Type **USE Desgpa**
Press <Return>
Type **DISPLAY ALL Name, Gpa**

The records are now sorted from the highest GPA to the lowest GPA.

Conditional Sorts

A condition can be added to the dBase SORT command so that only those records that satisfy the condition are included in the sort. The format for a SORT command with a condition is:

SORT TO (new filename) ON (field name) FOR (search key) (relationship) (search object)

dBase tests each record for the condition and includes the record in the sort only if the condition is met.

YOUR TURN

You are going to use the STUDENT file to perform a conditional sort. You would like to know which students have a GPA of 3.5 or above, and you would like the list to be in descending order. The STUDENT file should be active and the dot prompt should be on the screen.

Type **USE Student**
Type **SORT TO Deanslist ON Gpa/d FOR Gpa>=3.5**
Press <Return>

Use the DISPLAY command to see who made the dean's list.

Type **USE Deanslist**
Press <Return>
Type **DISPLAY ALL Name, Year, Gpa**
Press <Return>

Four records are displayed, each one showing the student's name, year, and GPA. The GPA values range from 3.98 to 3.70.

INDEX ON

The INDEX ON command might appear to be similar to the SORT ON command. Both commands can arrange records in ascending order, alphabetically, chronologically or numerically, and place the newly sorted file into a separate target file. There are, however, some significant differences between the two commands.

Indexed files, unlike sorted files, automatically update changes made to the database. For example, if a record is added or deleted, or if the information stored in a record is edited, the changes are made automatically in all open INDEX files. Thus, as the database gets larger or as it is modified, the records do not have to be reordered constantly.

With the INDEX command, as with the SORT command, the field being indexed must be a numeric, character, or date field. The INDEX command, however, can arrange only numeric fields in descending order. If database records need to be arranged in descending order based upon a character or date field, the SORT command must be used instead.

The format for the INDEX command is as follows:

INDEX ON (field name) TO (new filename)

The field name is the name of the field to be indexed, and the new filename is the name of the file that will hold the indexed records.

Once a file is indexed, it must be made the active file before it can be viewed. The command to establish an indexed file as active is:

SET INDEX TO (index filename)

The SET INDEX command actually performs two functions. First, the command establishes a file as active. Second, the command opens all specified indexed files. More than one indexed file can be listed in the SET INDEX command. The format for listing more than one file is:

SET INDEX TO (index filename #1), (index filename #2), (index filename #3)

466 PART TWO: APPLICATIONS SOFTWARE

Up to seven indexed files can be open at one time. As was mentioned earlier, an indexed file must be open in order for changes made to the database file to be reflected automatically in the indexed file. The SET INDEX TO command opens the files so that they can receive all additions, deletions, or editing changes made to database file.

The first index file in the list is the active file. The LIST or DISPLAY command displays the contents of the first index file listed.

YOUR TURN

You are going to use the INDEX command to create three index files. The STUDENT file should be active and the dot prompt should be on the screen.

The three fields you are going to index are SS_Number, Zip_Code, and Year. The students' social security numbers are used as their student identification numbers. The index on the SS_Number field will list the students according to these identification numbers. The index on the Zip_Code field will list the students according to zip code. This list could then be used for a mass mailing. The index on the Year field is going to list the students according to their class standing—whether the student is a senior, junior, sophomore, or freshman.

Type **USE Student**
Type **INDEX ON SS_Number TO ID_Number**
Press <Return>
Type **INDEX ON ZIP_Code TO Mailing**
Press <Return>
Type **INDEX ON Year TO Class**
Press <Return>

Now you are going to open all the indexed files.

Type **SET INDEX TO ID_Number, Mailing, Class**
Press <Return>

Now you want to view one of the indexed files.

Type **DISPLAY ALL Name, Year, SS_Number**
Press <Return>

Your screen should look like Figure 15-1. There are two things to notice about this list. First, the ID_Number index is displayed. You can tell it is the ID_Number index because the records are listed in ascending order according to social security number. Of the three indexes created, the ID_Number index is displayed because it was the first index listed in the SET INDEX TO command.

Next, look at the record numbers. Recall that the SORT command renumbered the records consecutively in ascending order. When a file is indexed, however, records maintain their original record numbers. The record numbers in Figure 15-1 are 6, 14, 3, 2, 1, 8, and so on.

Figure 15-1
INDEX ON Command

```
. set index to id_number, mailing, class
. display all name, year, ss_number
Record#  name                  year  ss_number
      6  Lord, Pamela             4  208-46-4096
     14  Friedman, Mark           1  271-64-4049
      3  Klein, Tom               4  278-45-7891
      2  Bulas, Irene             3  289-89-4672
      1  Faulks, Tim              4  343-61-1101
      8  Weaver, Chris            2  411-69-4774
     10  Wilks, Cleo              1  428-18-9972
      5  Ornelas, Tina            2  468-71-9002
     15  Crope, Trish             2  491-11-9984
      4  Wilcox, Bill             1  524-68-4099
     12  Hocks, Arthur            3  558-79-5151
      9  Engel, Chuck             4  778-61-8723
      7  Busch, Brad              3  782-28-1598
     11  Bressler, Ann            1  789-22-6615
     13  DeSalvo, Liz             4  879-43-6291
.
```

Now you are going to add a record to the file. All the indexes are open because you used the SET INDEX TO command. Therefore, the added record will be incorporated into the indexes automatically.

Type **Append**
Press <Return>

A data entry form for record 16 appears. Use the following information to fill in the form:

NAME:	Diaz, Kate
YEAR:	3
GPA:	3.6
BIRTHDATE:	09/27/59
SS_NUMBER:	009-56-0983
ACCOUNT:	8.38
ADDRESS:	75 Hilltop Dr.
CITY:	Leominster
STATE:	MA
ZIP_CODE:	03402

Press <Return> after the data is entered to return to the dot prompt. Now check to make sure the indexes were updated.

Type **DISPLAY ALL Name, Year, SS_Number**
Press <Return>

Record 16, for Kate Diaz, is the first record listed. The ID_Number index is still the active index, so the records are listed in ascending order according to social security number. Now check to make sure record 16 also is in the mailing index. To do this, you have to change the active index using the SET INDEX TO command.

Type **SET INDEX TO Mailing**
Press <Return>
Type **DISPLAY ALL Name, Address, City, State, Zip_Code**
Press <Return>

Again, record 16 is the first record listed, but this time it is first because it is the record with the lowest zip code number. Notice that the records are now listed in ascending order according to zip code. They are listed this way because the active index is now the Mailing index.

Indexing on Multiple Fields

There are times when indexing on more than one field is useful. To index on more than one field, join the fields with plus signs:

INDEX ON (field #1)+(field #2)+ . . . TO (new filename)

This command can be used only on fields of the same type. It cannot be used to index on a field that is character/text and on a field that is numeric. All the fields must be either character/text or numeric.

The order in which the fields are listed in this command is significant. dBase first arranges all the records by the first field listed, then by the second field listed, and so on. When using this command, make sure the fields are listed in the order that produces the desired results.

YOUR TURN

You are going to use the INDEX command on multiple fields to list the students alphabetically by class. The dot prompt should be on the screen.

Type **SET INDEX TO Class**
Press <Return>
Type **DISPLAY ALL Name, Year**
Press <Return>

Look at how the names are listed. They are grouped according to class standing, but the names are in no particular order. This index would be more useful if the students were listed alphabetically within each class. Indexing on multiple fields enables you to do this. You are now going to index both the year field and the name field.

Type **INDEX ON Year+Name TO Class**
Press <Return>

Because an index named CLASS was created previously, the message CLASS.NDX ALREADY EXISTS, OVERWRITE IT? (Y/N) appears. Type **Y** for yes. The message 16 RECORDS INDEXED appears. Take another look at the CLASS index.

Figure 15-2
Indexing on Multiple Fields

```
. index on year+name to class
class.ndx already exists, overwrite it? (Y/N) Yes
     16 records indexed
. display all Name, Year
Record#  Name                     Year
    11   Bressler, Ann             1
    14   Friedman, Mark            1
     4   Wilcox, Bill              1
    10   Wilks, Cleo               1
    15   Crope, Trish              2
     5   Ornelas, Tina             2
     8   Weaver, Chris             2
     2   Bulas, Irene              3
     7   Busch, Brad               3
    16   Diaz, Kate                3
    12   Hocks, Arthur             3
    13   DeSalvo, Liz              4
     9   Engel, Chuck              4
     1   Faulks, Tim               4
     3   Klein, Tom                4
     6   Lord, Pamela              4
.
```

Type **DISPLAY ALL Name, Year**
Press <Return>

Your screen should look like Figure 15-2. The records still are grouped by class—all the freshmen together, all the sophomores together, etc.—but now the names also are listed alphabetically within each class.

FIND

When database files become large, finding one particular record can be tedious. dBase eliminates that problem with the FIND command, which searches an indexed file for a particular alphanumeric string. The format for the FIND command is as follows:

FIND (alphanumeric string)

dBase searches the indexed file for the first record containing the string specified. When a record with the string is found, dBase places a record pointer on it. That record can then be displayed. The FIND command works only on indexed files.

YOUR TURN

You are going to create an index with all the students listed alphabetically. Then you are going to use that index to search for specific students. The dot prompt should be on the screen and the STUDENT file should be active.

Type **USE Student**
Press <Return>
Type **INDEX ON Name TO Alphaname**
Press <Return>

If the message ALPHANAME.NDX ALREADY EXISTS, OVERWRITE IT? (Y/N) appears, type **Y**.

Type **SET INDEX TO Alphaname**
Press <Return>

Now you are going to use the FIND command with the ALPHANAME index.

Type **FIND Desalvo**
Press <Return>

The message NO FIND appears. There is a student with the last name DeSalvo in the database file, but dBase did not find this record because it distinguishes capital and lowercase letters. For dBase to find the record, the name must be typed exactly as it appears in the record.

Type **FIND DeSalvo**
Press <Return>
Type **DISPLAY name, gpa, address, city, state, zip_code**
Press <Return>

Learning Check

1. The _____ command rearranges records in either ascending or descending order, and renumbers the records according to their new order.
   a. FIND
   b. INDEX ON
   c. SET INDEX TO
   d. SORT TO
2. All types of dBase III fields—character, numeric, date, logical, and memo—can be sorted using the SORT TO command. (True or False?)
3. With the INDEX ON command, only _____ fields can be arranged in descending order.
   a. character
   b. numeric
   c. date
   d. logical
4. The _____ command establishes an indexed file as active and opens all specified indexed files.
   a. FIND
   b. INDEX ON
   c. SET INDEX TO
   d. SORT TO
5. Indexing on more than one field requires that the fields be of the same type. (True or False?)

Answers

1. d 2. False 3. b 4. c 5. True

This time, dBase finds DeSalvo's record.

> Type **FIND Weaver**
> Press <Return>
> Type **DISPLAY name, year, gpa, ss_number**
> Press <Return>

Chris Weaver's record is displayed.

Creating a Report with dBase III

Having data stored in a database file certainly can provide some useful information. Until that information can take the form of a report on paper, however, its usefulness is limited. The following section explains the basic commands needed to create a report with dBase files.

CREATE REPORT

A dBase report is created with the CREATE REPORT command. The format for this command is as follows:

   CREATE REPORT (name of report)

The CREATE REPORT command is a menu-based command. That is, it guides the user through the creation of the report by displaying a series of screens and prompts.

> *dBase Differences:* In dBase II, the format of the command to create a report is:
>   REPORT FORM (name of report)
> If the report does not already exist, it is created based on answers the user gives to several questions.

YOUR TURN

Start dBase III if necessary. The next several hands-on exercises take you through the creation of a report using the STUDENT file. The dot prompt should be on the screen.

> Type **USE Student**
> Press <Return>
> Type **CREATE REPORT Student**
> Press <Return>

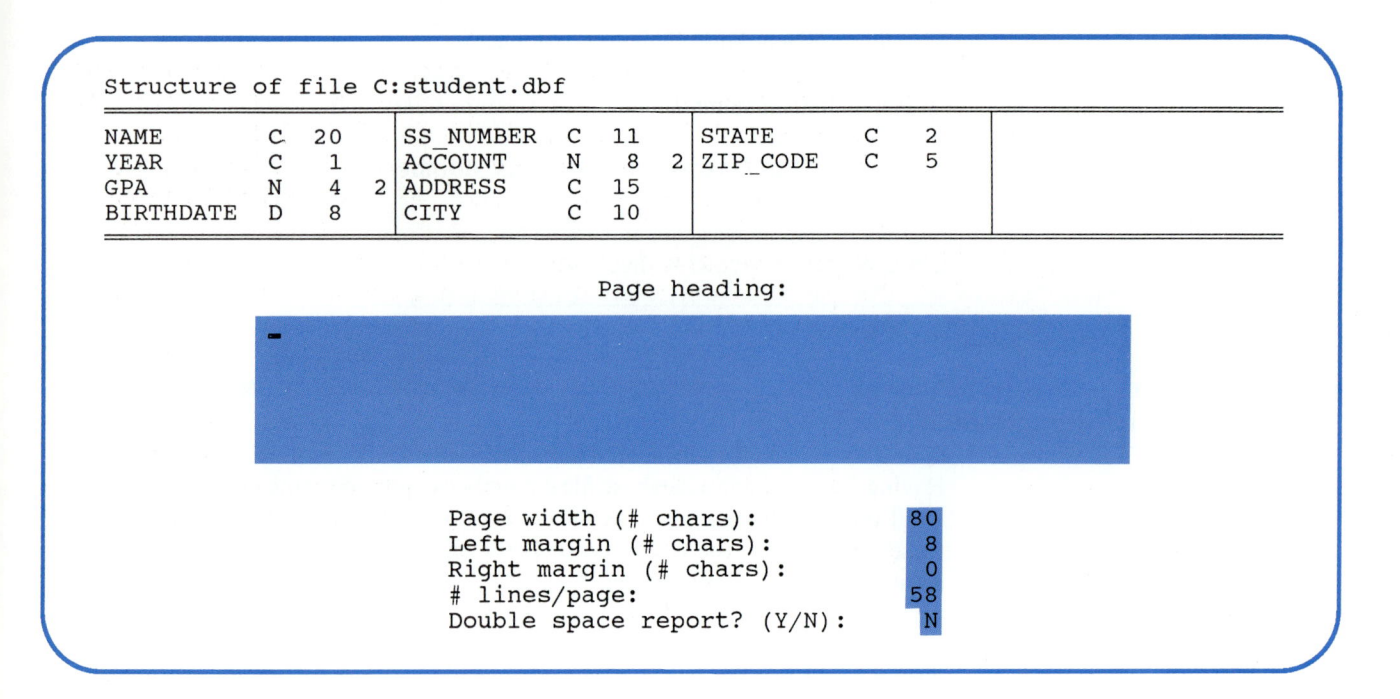

```
Structure of file C:student.dbf
═══════════════════════════════════════════════════════════════════════
NAME        C  20    SS_NUMBER  C  11      STATE      C  2
YEAR        C   1    ACCOUNT    N   8   2  ZIP_CODE   C  5
GPA         N   4  2 ADDRESS    C  15
BIRTHDATE   D   8    CITY       C  10
═══════════════════════════════════════════════════════════════════════

                         Page heading:
          ┌─────────────────────────────────────────────┐
          │ _                                           │
          │                                             │
          │                                             │
          │                                             │
          └─────────────────────────────────────────────┘

                    Page width (# chars):        80
                    Left margin (# chars):        8
                    Right margin (# chars):       0
                    # lines/page:                58
                    Double space report? (Y/N):   N
```

Figure 15-3
Report Headings Screen

The name of the database file and the report are the same: STUDENT. This does not cause a problem because dBase automatically adds the extension .FRM to the report. The two files, STUDENT.DBF and STUDENT.FRM, are stored as two separate files. Using the same name for the database file and the report can help to clarify the contents of the files.

The report headings screen is displayed (see Figure 15-3). Note: In dBase III Plus, the report headings screen is arranged differently and lists several additional format options. You should consult the user manual for details.

Filling in the Report Headings Screen

The dBase III report headings screen is made up of three parts. At the top of the screen is a description of the file's structure. The top line indicates the name of the file. Under that, each field in the file, along with its type and width, is listed.

In the center of the screen are the words PAGE HEADING and a large highlighted area that consists of four lines. Each line is 60 characters long. The cursor appears at the beginning of the first line. Whatever is entered into this space will print at the top of each report page.

The third area, at the bottom of the screen, lists the default settings for the format of the report. The width of the report, the number of positions in the right and left margins, the number of lines per page, and the line spacing (single or double) can be changed by changing the default settings.

> ***dBase Differences:*** In dBase III Plus, the report headings screen does not include the description of the file structure. The top line of the screen lists five headings: OPTIONS, GROUPS, COLUMNS, LOCATE, and EXIT. While the report headings screen is displayed, OPTIONS is highlighted. The format options are listed at the top of the screen, and a cursor menu appears at the bottom. The first option in the list is PAGE TITLE. When you select this option (by pressing <Return> when the option is highlighted), a box appears at the right. You type the text that you want to appear at the top of the page, and then press <Ctrl> <End> to accept it. Then you proceed with the other format options in the list, such as the page width and margins, as described for dBase III.
>
> Pressing <PgDn> in dBase III Plus won't get you to the subtotals screen. Instead, when you are finished with the format settings, use the right arrow key (at the right-hand side of the keyboard) to highlight GROUPS. The groups screen is displayed. It is equivalent in function to the dBase III subtotals screen but is arranged somewhat differently.
>
> To access the report columns screen in dBase III Plus, use the right arrow key again to highlight COLUMNS.

YOUR TURN

The STUDENT file should be active and the report headings screen should be on the screen.

>   Type **STATE COLLEGE**
>   Press <Return>
>   Type **STUDENT NAME AND ADDRESS**
>   Press <Return> three times

The cursor is now in front of the 80, which is the default setting for page width. All the default settings can be accepted by pressing the <PgDn> key.

>   Press <PgDn>

The subtotals screen appears (see Figure 15-4). This screen allows subtotals to be established for a report. Subtotals can be used only on a sorted or indexed file. Subtotals are not needed for the purposes of this report. Pressing the <PgDn> key advances you to the next menu.

>   Press <PgDn>

The report columns screen appears (see Figure 15-5).

```
Structure of file C:student.dbf
```

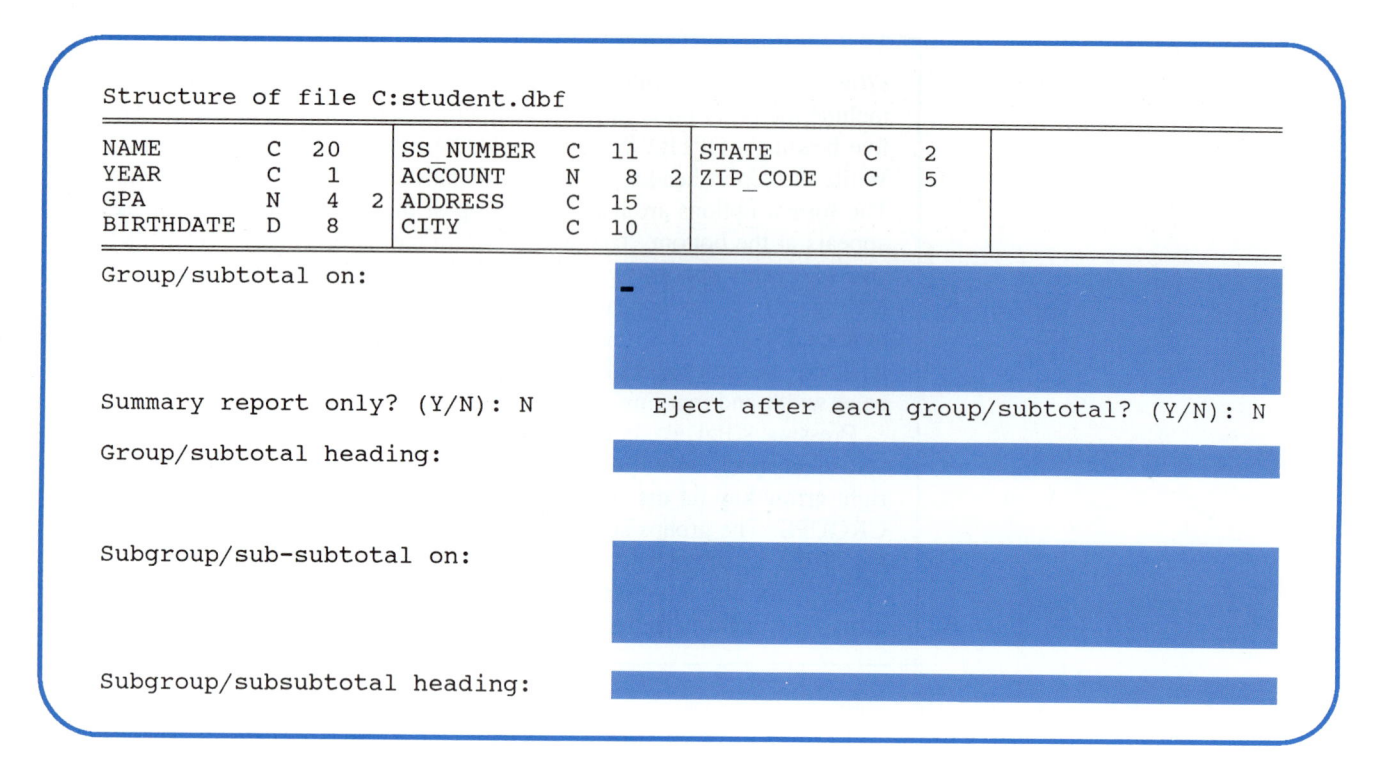

NAME	C	20		SS_NUMBER	C	11		STATE	C	2
YEAR	C	1		ACCOUNT	N	8	2	ZIP_CODE	C	5
GPA	N	4	2	ADDRESS	C	15				
BIRTHDATE	D	8		CITY	C	10				

Group/subtotal on:

Summary report only? (Y/N): N   Eject after each group/subtotal? (Y/N): N

Group/subtotal heading:

Subgroup/sub-subtotal on:

Subgroup/subsubtotal heading:

Figure 15-4
Subtotals Screen

Defining Report Columns

The report columns screen is used to define columns to be printed by the report. Each screen defines the information to be printed in a column. You can define as many columns as will fit across the width of the page.

At the top of the report columns screen is the information on the structure of the file (refer to Figure 15-5). Under that are the words FIELD 1 and COLUMNS LEFT = 72. The words FIELD 1 indicate that this particular screen is defining the first field to be printed in the report. This field will appear in the first column when the report is printed.

Look at the line underneath the words FIELD 1. This line helps the user to keep track of the format of the printed report. The line begins with eight > symbols, which signify the number of spaces taken up by the left margin. Refer to the default settings on Figure 15-3 and note that the left margin is eight characters wide. COLUMNS LEFT = 72 indicates that there are 72 spaces left across the width of the page. If the page width is 80 (refer to the default settings), and 8 spaces are taken up by the left margin, then there are 72 spaces left.

The highlighted area next to the words FIELD CONTENTS is for specifying the field to appear in column 1. If the field specified is numeric, the user can respecify the number of decimal positions and can indicate whether or not a total of the field is to be printed.

The highlighted area next to the words FIELD HEADER is for defining a header to describe the contents of this column. The header can be up to four lines long and 60 characters wide. The field headers are printed at the top of each page above the corresponding columns.

After FIELD 1 has been entered, a report columns screen for FIELD 2 appears.

CHAPTER 15: ADVANCED dBASE III   475

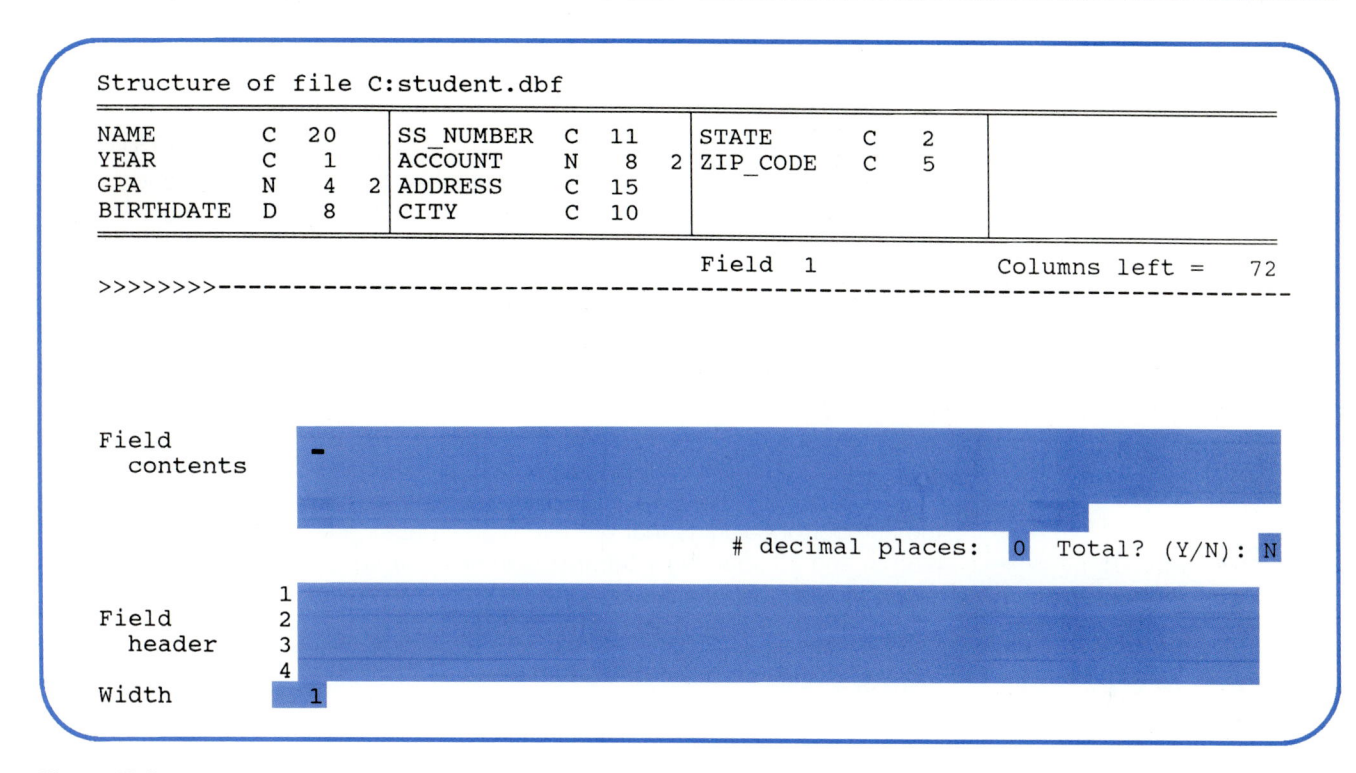

```
Structure of file C:student.dbf
NAME        C   20    SS_NUMBER   C   11      STATE      C   2
YEAR        C    1    ACCOUNT     N    8   2  ZIP_CODE   C   5
GPA         N    4  2 ADDRESS     C   15
BIRTHDATE   D    8    CITY        C   10

                                              Field  1         Columns left =   72
>>>>>>>>-------------------------------------------------------------------------



  Field
 contents     ▬


                                      # decimal places:  0   Total? (Y/N):  N

               1
  Field        2
 header        3
               4
  Width       1
```

Figure 15-5
Report Columns Screen for Field 1

Information on the field to appear in column 2 is entered into this screen. Save the report by pressing <PgDn> after the last field of the last report column has been defined.

> *dBase Differences:* In dBase III Plus, the report columns screen looks different from the one described for dBase III, but it performs the same functions. It does not display the file structure. Instead of FIELD CONTENTS, it says CONTENTS. You move the highlighting to this option, press <Return>, and specify the field that you want to appear in column 1. The next option, HEADING, is the same thing as FIELD HEADER. After you select this option, a box appears in which you can type the heading. Accept the heading by pressing <Ctrl> <End> and continue working through the list of options. When you are finished with column 1, press <PgDn> to display a new screen for column 2. You can also back up to a previous column by pressing <PgUp>. The status line at the bottom of the screen includes the number of the current column.

YOUR TURN

The report columns screen for Field 1 should be on the screen. The cursor should be in the highlighted area next to the words FIELD CONTENTS. This report is going to contain the name, address, city, state, and balance for each of the students in the file.

Type **Name**
Press <Return>

Because the NAME field is not a numeric field, the cursor automatically bypasses the questions regarding the number of decimal places and whether or not the field should be totaled. The cursor is now at the beginning of the first line in the highlighted area next to the words FIELD HEADER. Notice the words WIDTH 20 at the bottom of this box. This is the width of the NAME field.

Type **NAME**
Press <PgDn>

Your screen should look like Figure 15-6. Notice the X's above the FIELD CONTENTS box. These X's represent the width of the first column. Also note the number of columns that are left. Eight spaces are taken up by the left margin and 20 spaces by the first column. One space is inserted automatically between the first and second column.

The cursor is in the FIELD CONTENTS box.

Type **address**
Press <Return>
Type **ADDRESS**
Press <PgDn>

The screen for Field 3 appears.

Type **city**
Press <Return>
Type **CITY**
Press <PgDn>

The screen for Field 4 appears.

Type **state**
Press <Return>
Type **ST**
Press <PgDn>

The screen for Field 5 appears.

Type **account**
Press <Return>

ACCOUNT is a numeric field, so the cursor moves to the space next to the words # OF DECIMAL PLACES. Because the field originally was defined to be carried out to two decimal places, the number 2 already appears next to the words # OF DECIMAL PLACES. You want to retain the two decimal places.

CHAPTER 15: ADVANCED dBASE III 477

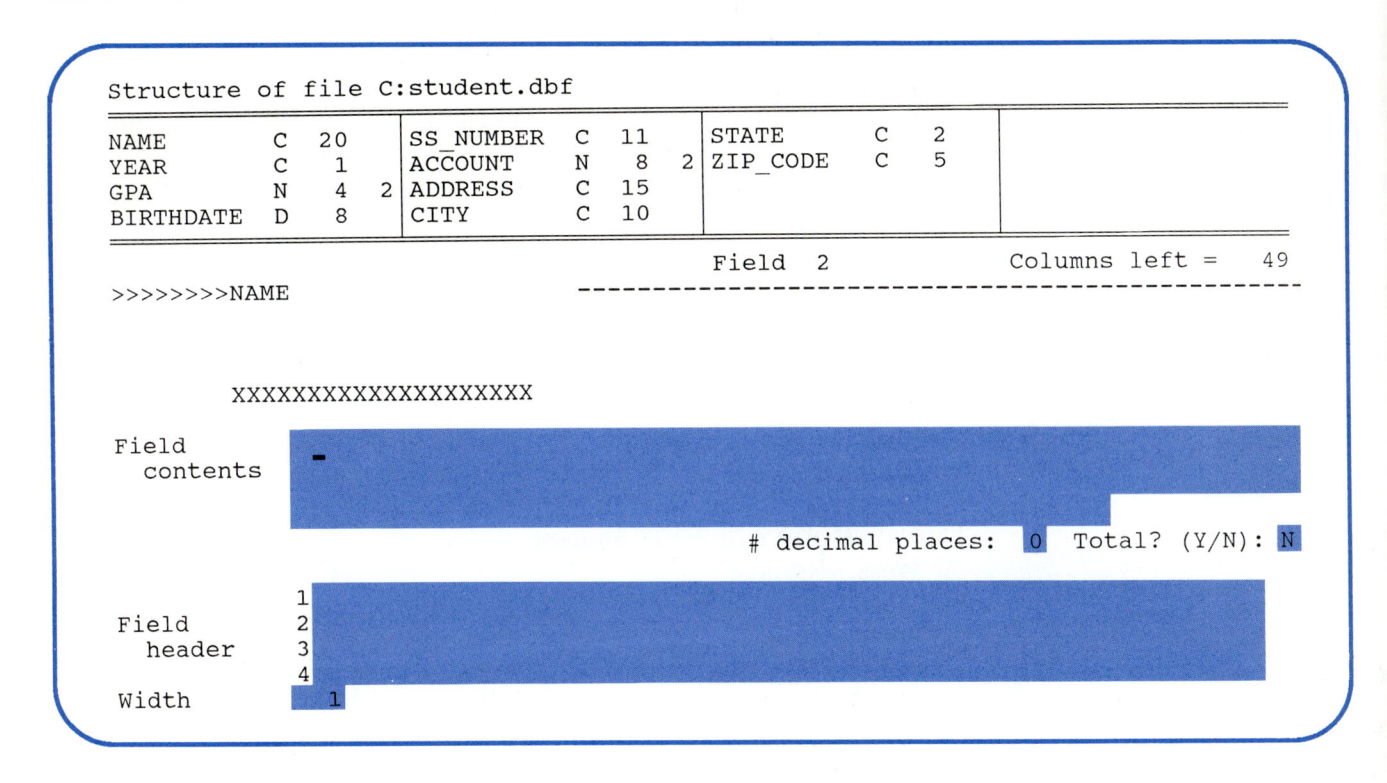

```
Structure of file C:student.dbf
NAME        C   20    SS_NUMBER   C   11      STATE      C   2
YEAR        C    1    ACCOUNT     N    8    2 ZIP_CODE   C   5
GPA         N    4  2 ADDRESS     C   15
BIRTHDATE   D    8    CITY        C   10
                                          Field  2           Columns left =    49
>>>>>>>>NAME                       ---------------------------------------------


               XXXXXXXXXXXXXXXXXXXX
    Field
  contents       -


                                            # decimal places:  0   Total? (Y/N):  N

               1
    Field      2
   header      3
               4
    Width        1
```

Figure 15-6
Report Columns Screen for Field 2

    Press <Return>

The number 2 stays in the highlighted box and the cursor moves to the space next to the words TOTAL? (Y/N). You want a total of this column.

    Type **Y**

The cursor moves to the FIELD HEADER box.

    Type **ACCOUNT**
    Press <Return>
    Type **BALANCE**
    Press <PgDn> twice

The report is now saved.

MODIFY REPORT

Once the report form has been designated and saved, it can be recalled for editing or modification if necessary. The format for the command to modify a report form is:

    MODIFY REPORT (name of report form file)

When this command is used, the report file is retrieved and displayed in the same screen sequence as it was when created.

The contents of the report form can be edited using the following keystrokes:

<Ctrl> U	Deletes the current field shown.
<Ctrl> N	Inserts a new field.
<Ctrl> <End>	Leaves the report form design process and saves all changes.

YOUR TURN

You are going to modify the STUDENT report form. The dot prompt should be on the screen.

    Type **MODIFY REPORT Student**
    Press <Return>

The report columns screen appears. The name of the report needs to be changed. The cursor is now in the first line of the page heading. Press the <↓> key once to move the cursor to the second line in the page heading. Delete the words NAME AND ADDRESS and insert **ACCOUNT BALANCE.** When you are finished, the Page heading box should have STATE COLLEGE in line 1 and STUDENT ACCOUNT BALANCE in line 2.

    Press <PgDn> twice

Look at the report headings screen for Field 1. Make sure there are no typing errors. if there are, correct them.

    Press <PgDn>

Look at the report headings screen for Field 2. Again, make sure there are no typing errors. Continue to press <PgDn> to check for mistakes until you get to the report headings screen for Field 5, which is for the account balance. You are going to add a new Field 5.

    Press <Ctrl> **N**

The screen still says Field 5, but the Field contents box and the Field header box are empty. You can now add a new field. You are going to include the zip code in the report. The cursor should be in the Field contents box.

    Type **zip_code**
    Press <Return>
    Type **ZIP**
    Press <Return>
    Type **CODE**
    Press <PgDn>

CHAPTER 15: ADVANCED dBASE III

The report headings screen for Field 6 is on the screen. The account balance is now Field 6. Check this screen over for typing errors. If you want to go back to a previous screen, press <PgUp>. Once you are sure everything in the report is correct, press <Ctrl> <End> to save the modifications you made to the report.

Printing a Report

Once a report is entered into a database file, a hard copy of the report can be printed. The command to print a report is as follows:

REPORT FORM (file name of report) TO PRINT

YOUR TURN

You are going to print a copy of the report STUDENT. Make sure your printer is hooked up to the computer and online. The STUDENT file should be active and the dot prompt should be on the screen.

Type **REPORT FORM Student TO PRINT**
Press <Return>

Your printed report should look like Figure 15-7.

Figure 15-7
Student Account Balance Report

```
Page No.     1
02/19/87
                       STATE COLLEGE
                    STUDENT ACCOUNT BALANCE

NAME                ADDRESS             CITY         ST    ZIP      ACCOUNT
                                                          CODE      BALANCE
Faulks, Tim         78 Main St.         Miami        FL    32109     286.59
Bulas, Irene        908 W. Summit       Cygnet       OH    43409    1203.87
Klein, Tom          12 Yong St.         Hampton      NC    27710      96.95
Wilcox, Bill        6 Williams Rd.      Fremont      OH    43098       0.00
Ornelas, Tina       123 First St.       Canton       OH    43012    2005.32
Lord, Pamela        98 Pike St.         Oregon       OH    42876     576.94
Busch, Brad         32 Bradner          Columbus     OH    43219     803.52
Weaver, Chris       909 Clough          Portage      OH    43213      68.07
Engel, Chuck        1432 Indian Rd.     Hamler       OH    43406      12.18
Wilks, Cleo         76 Gorrel           Lima         OH    43420    1096.20
Bressler, Ann       45 S. Luke St       Palma        OH    43316       0.00
Hocks, Arthur       90 Kellog Rd        Portage      OH    43213     446.29
DeSalvo, Liz        9 W. Second St.     Columbus     OH    43207       0.00
Friedman, Mark      3426 Little St.     Palma        OH    43316      33.68
Crope, Trish        67 Baldwin          Cygnet       OH    43409     175.50
Diaz, Kate          75 Hilltop Dr.      Leominster   MA    03402       8.38
*** Total ***
                                                                    6813.49
```

Using Multiple Database Files

Up to this point, the hands-on exercises in this chapter have used only one database file at a time. With dBase III, however, several database files can be open at one time. The following section explains how to open more than one database file, and how to join information from two different files to form a third file.

SELECT

In order for you to open more than one database file at a time, the files have to be stored in an active area using the SELECT command. In dBase III, up to ten different files can be stored in active work areas. The format for the SELECT command is as follows:

SELECT (work area)

The work area can be signified either by a number (1 through 10) or by a letter (A through J). Only one database file can be assigned to each work area. Once a database file has been assigned to a work area, that file cannot be activated with the USE command; the SELECT command must be used to activate the file. For example, the following commands would place a file named LIBRARY into an active work area:

SELECT 1
USE Library

After the LIBRARY file has been assigned to work area 1, the command to activate the LIBRARY file is SELECT 1. If the USE Library command were given, the error message ALIAS NAME ALREADY IN USE would appear. An alias name is an alternative name of a database. SELECT 1 becomes an alias for the LIBRARY file. The only way to open a file that has been assigned to a work area is by using its alias. In the example of the LIBRARY file, the user would type SELECT 1.

Another way to avoid the ALIAS NAME ALREADY IN USE message is to close all the open files. Closing an open file returns the field to its original name rather than its alias. To close all the files assigned to work areas, use the command CLOSE DATABASE.

Even though up to ten different work areas can be used, only one database file is active at a time. The last file used with the SELECT command is the active file and remains in the foreground. The other work areas are in the background. In order to move a file from the background to the foreground, use the SELECT command.

> *dBase Differences:* In dBase II only two data files can be open in different work areas. These work areas are called Primary and Secondary.

CHAPTER 15: ADVANCED dBASE III

YOUR TURN

You are going to create a new file called BOOKS, which lists the names of students who have books overdue at the library. Create a new file called BOOKS using the following structure:

Field	Field name	Type	Width	Dec
1	NAME	Char/text	20	
2	DATE	Date	8	
3	DAYS	Numeric	3	0
4	BOOK	Char/text	20	

Once the structure has been defined, enter the following data into the records:

Record #	Name	Date	Days	Book
1	Bulas, Irene	10/02/87	2	Learning dBase III
2	Busch, Brad	10/02/87	1	Trigonometry
3	Engel, Chuck	10/09/87	17	Data Management
4	Bressler, Ann	10/12/87	5	Geometry Made Easy
5	Hocks, Arthur	10/12/87	4	Science Fiction
6	Crope, Trish	10/12/87	3	Design and Analysis
7	Wilks, Cleo	10/12/87	1	Apple II
8	Ornelas, Tina	10/12/87	10	Modern Science
9	DeSalvo, Liz	10/20/87	5	Home Computers
10	Lord, Pamela	10/20/87	2	Calculus
11	Friedman, Mark	10/20/87	15	Basic Programming
12	Faulks, Tim	10/20/87	3	Computer Games

Now you are going to create a report using the BOOKS file.

> Type **USE Books**
> Press <Return>
> Type **CREATE REPORT BOOKS**
> Press <Return>

Input the page heading.

> Type **STATE COLLEGE LIBRARY**
> Press <Return>
> Type **BOOKS OVERDUE REPORT**
> Press <PgDn> twice to bypass the subtotals screen

Input the report columns information for Field 1. The cursor should be in the FIELD CONTENTS box.

> Type **Name**
> Press <Return>
> Type **STUDENT'S NAME**
> Press <Return>

482 PART TWO: APPLICATIONS SOFTWARE

In line 2, type 14 hyphens. These hyphens will act as an underline for the column headings. Your screen should look like Figure 15-8.

>   Press <PgDn>

Input the report columns information for Field 2. The cursor should be in the FIELD CONTENTS box.

>   Type **Book**
>   Press <Return>
>   Type **TITLE**
>   Press <Return>
>   Type 5 hyphens
>   Press <PgDn>

Input the following for Field 3.

>   Type **Days**
>   Press <Return>

The DAYS field is numeric, so the cursor moves to the zero next to the decimal places prompt.

>   Press <Return> twice (because you do not want a total of this column in the report)
>   Type **DAYS OVERDUE**

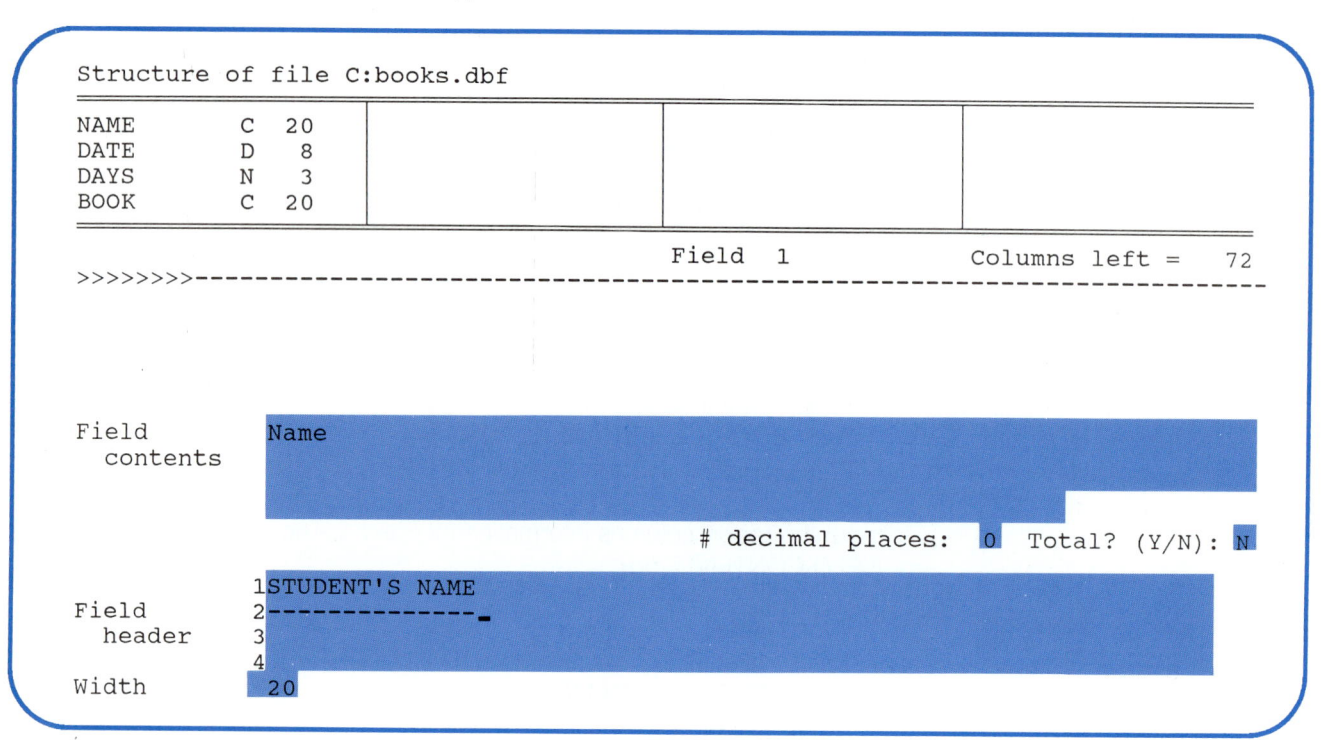

Figure 15-8
Field 1 of the Books Overdue Report

```
Structure of file C:books.dbf
NAME       C   20
DATE       D    8
DAYS       N    3
BOOK       C   20
                                        Field 1           Columns left =  72
>>>>>>>>----------------------------------------------------------------

Field
 contents   Name


                                    # decimal places: 0  Total? (Y/N): N

            1STUDENT'S NAME
Field       2--------------
 header     3
            4
Width        20
```

CHAPTER 15: ADVANCED dBASE III

Press <Return>
Type 12 hyphens
Press <PgDn>

Input the following for Field 4. The cursor is in the FIELD CONTENTS box. You are going to enter a formula to calculate how much each student owes in fines. The library charges 25 cents a day for each overdue book.

Type **days * .25**
Press <Return>
Press <Return> to accept 2 as the number of decimal places
Type **Y** for a total of this column to be printed in the report
Type **AMOUNT DUE**
Press <Return>
Type 10 hyphens
Press <PgDn> twice to save the report

Use the MODIFY REPORT command to check for errors. When you are satisfied with the entries, print the report.

Type **REPORT FORM Books TO PRINT**
Press <Return>

Your report should look Figure 15-9.
The next hands-on exercise joins the BOOKS file with the STUDENT file. In preparation for this exercise, place the STUDENT file and the BOOKS file in work areas A and B respectively.

**Figure 15-9
Books Overdue Report**

```
Page No.      1
02/19/87
                          STATE COLLEGE LIBRARY
                          BOOKS OVERDUE REPORT

STUDENT'S NAME         TITLE                DAYS OVERDUE  AMOUNT DUE
---------------        -----                ------------  ----------


Bulas, Irene           Learning dBase III          2         0.50
Busch, Brad            Trigonometry                1         0.25
Engel, Chuck           Data Management            17         4.25
Bressler, Ann          Geometry Made Easy          5         1.25
Hocks, Arthur          Science Fiction             4         1.00
Crope, Trish           Design and Analysis         3         0.75
Wilks, Cleo            Apple II                    1         0.25
Ornelas, Tina          Modern Science             10         2.50
DeSalvo, Liz           Home Computers              5         1.25
Lord, Pamela           Calculus                    2         0.50
Friedman, Mark         Basic Programming          15         3.75
Faulks, Tim            Computer Games              3         0.75
*** Total ***
                                                            17.00
```

Type **SELECT A**
Press <Return>
Type **USE STUDENT**
Press <Return>
Type **SELECT B**
Press <Return>
Type **USE BOOKS**
Press <Return>

Now both the STUDENT file and the BOOKS file are open.

Learning Check

1. When you are creating a report, the default settings for the format of the report are found on the _____.
   a. Main menu
   b. report headings screen
   c. report columns screen
   d. subtotals screen
2. When you are creating a report, the columns to be printed in the report are defined on the _____.
   a. Main menu
   b. report headings screen
   c. report columns screen
   d. subtotals screen
3. When you are modifying a report that has already been created, the _____ command deletes the current field shown.
   a. <Ctrl> **U**
   b. <Ctrl> **N**
   c. <Ctrl> <End>
   d. <Ctrl> <Home>
4. In dBase III, up to _____ different files can be stored in active work areas.
   a. five
   b. six
   c. eight
   d. ten
5. The last file used with the SELECT command is the active file. (True or False?)

Answers

1. b 2. c 3. a 4. d 5. True

Joining Two Files

To join fields from two different files to create a third file, the two files first must be placed in active work areas. Once the two files are in active work areas, they are open.

As the previous section explained, even though these two files may be open, only one of them can be active at a time. The last file named with the SELECT command is the active or primary file. The other file is open, but it is a secondary file because it is not currently active.

The format for joining two files is as follows:

JOIN WITH (secondary filename) TO (new filename) FOR (condition) FIELDS (list of field names)

At first glance this command may seem complicated, but breaking it down into parts helps to clarify it. The primary filename does not appear in the command because it is the active file. Therefore, the first part of the command tells dBase to join whatever file is active with the secondary file.

The second part of the command, TO (new filename), designates the name of the third file that is going to be created as a result of merging the primary and secondary files.

The third part of the command, FOR (condition), states the condition under which the two files should be merged. dBase uses the primary file and evaluates all the records in the secondary file based upon this condition. Whenever the condition is true, the record is placed in the new third file.

The last part of the command, FIELDS, lists all the fields to be included in the new file. Fields from either the primary or secondary file can be listed. If a field from the secondary file is listed, however, a special syntax must be used because the file is not active. This syntax is

(filename) -> (field name)

The arrow is created by typing a hyphen followed by the "greater than" symbol >. For example, suppose the name of the secondary file is LIBRARY, and the AUTHOR field from the LIBRARY file is to be included in the new file being created. The FIELDS portion of the command would appear as follows:

Library -> Author

After the new file has been created, it can be activated with the USE command.

> *dBase Differences:* In dBase II, there are minor differences in executing the JOIN command.

YOUR TURN

You are going to create a new file, OVERDUE, by merging the BOOKS file with the STUDENT file. Both the BOOKS file and the STUDENT file should be open from the previous hands-on exercise. The BOOKS file is the active file because it was the last file chosen with the SELECT command. STUDENT is the secondary file.

Type **JOIN WITH Student TO Overdue FOR Name = Student -> Name FIELDS Name, Student -> SS_Number, Date, Days, Book**

486   PART TWO: APPLICATIONS SOFTWARE

Before pressing <Return>, examine the command. It instructs dBase to join the BOOKS file with the STUDENT file to create a new file named OVERDUE. The two files are to be merged if the field NAME from the BOOK file matches (is equal to) the field NAME from the student file. (Notice that, every time the command refers to a field from the secondary file, the expression STUDENT -> appears before the field name.) The fields to be included in the OVERDUE file are: NAME (from the primary file), SS_NUMBER (from the secondary file), DATE (primary file), DAYS (primary file), and BOOK (primary file).

    Press <Return>
    Type **USE Overdue**
    Press <Return>
    Type **DISPLAY ALL**
    Press <Return>

Your screen should look like Figure 15-10.

Now you are going to modify the report BOOKS. You want to add a new Field 2 that will contain the student's social security number.

    Type **MODIFY REPORT Books**
    Press <PgDn> until you reach the report columns screen for Field 2
    Press <Ctrl> **N** to insert a new field
    Type **SS_Number**
    Press <Return>
    Type **ID #**
    Press <Return>

Figure 15-10
OVERDUE File

```
. select a
. use student
. select b
. use books
. join with student to overdue for name = student -> name fields name, student -
> ss_number, date, days, book
     12 records joined
. use overdue
. display all
Record#  NAME                 SS_NUMBER     DATE      DAYS BOOK
      1  Bulas, Irene         289-89-4672  10/02/87      2 Learning dBase III
      2  Busch, Brad          782-28-1598  10/02/87      1 Trigonometry
      3  Engel, Chuck         778-61-8723  10/09/87     17 Data Management
      4  Bressler, Ann        789-22-6615  10/12/87      5 Geometry Made Easy
      5  Hocks, Arthur        558-79-5151  10/12/87      4 Science Fiction
      6  Crope, Trish         491-11-9984  10/12/87      3 Design and Analysis
      7  Wilks, Cleo          428-18-9972  10/12/87      1 Apple II
      8  Ornelas, Tina        468-71-9002  10/12/87     10 Modern Science
      9  DeSalvo, Liz         879-43-6291  10/20/87      5 Home Computers
     10  Lord, Pamela         208-46-4096  10/20/87      2 Calculus
     11  Friedman, Mark       271-64-4049  10/20/87     15 Basic Programming
     12  Faulks, Tim          343-61-1101  10/20/87      3 Computer Games
```

CHAPTER 15: ADVANCED dBASE III

```
Page No.     1
02/19/87
                        STATE COLLEGE LIBRARY
                         BOOKS OVERDUE REPORT

STUDENT'S NAME          ID #         TITLE                AMOUNT DUE
--------------          ----         -----                ----------


Bulas, Irene            289-89-4672  Learning dBase III         0.50
Busch, Brad             782-28-1598  Trigonometry               0.25
Engel, Chuck            778-61-8723  Data Management            4.25
Bressler, Ann           789-22-6615  Geometry Made Easy         1.25
Hocks, Arthur           558-79-5151  Science Fiction            1.00
Crope, Trish            491-11-9984  Design and Analysis        0.75
Wilks, Cleo             428-18-9972  Apple II                   0.25
Ornelas, Tina           468-71-9002  Modern Science             2.50
DeSalvo, Liz            879-43-6291  Home Computers             1.25
Lord, Pamela            208-46-4096  Calculus                   0.50
Friedman, Mark          271-64-4049  Basic Programming          3.75
Faulks, Tim             343-61-1101  Computer Games             0.75
*** Total ***
                                                               17.00
```

Figure 15-11
Modified Books Overdue Report

Type four hyphens
Press <PgDn> until you reach Field 4, the column for DAYS OVERDUE
Press <Ctrl> **U** to delete this field
Press <Ctrl> <End> to save the changes

Now print the modified report.

Type **Report Form Books TO PRINT**

Your report should look like Figure 15-11.

Summary of dBase III Commands

Creating Files

Command	Description
CREATE	Creates a new database file.
COPY TO	Copies the file in use to a new file.
JOIN WITH (secondary filename) TO (new filename) FOR (condition) FIELDS (list of field names)	Combines specified fields from two database files to form a new database file.

Using a Database File

Command	Description
SET DEFAULT TO	Specifies the active drive or directory for database files.
DIR	Displays the file directory.
USE (filename)	Indicates which file is to be used.
HELP	Activates the help screens.
SET MENUS ON (OFF)	Displays (deletes) a cursor-movement menu.
SELECT	Places a database file into a designated work area so that several files can be open at once.
QUIT	Closes all open files and exits to DOS.

Modifying Files

Command	Description
MODIFY STRUCTURE	Allows changes to be made to the structure of the active database file.
MODIFY REPORT	Allows changes to be made to a report form.

Manipulating Files

Command	Description
SORT TO (filename) ON (field)	Rearranges data records in ascending or descending order according to the field(s) specified.
INDEX ON (field name) TO (new filename)	Creates a key file in which all records are ordered according to the field specified.
COUNT	Counts the number of records in the active database file.
COUNT FOR (search key) (relationship) (search object)	Counts the records that meet a specified condition.
SUM (field name)	Calculates the sum of all the values in the specified numeric field.
SUM (name of field) FOR (search key) (search object)	Calculates the sum of values in a numeric field which meet a specified condition.

Command	Description
AVERAGE (name of field)	Calculates the average value for the contents of a numeric field.
AVERAGE (name of field) FOR (relationship) (search object)	Calculates an average value using numeric fields that meet specified conditions.
CLOSE DATABASES	Closes all open database files.

Displaying Data

Command	Description
DISPLAY	Displays the contents of the first record in the file.
DISPLAY ALL	Displays the contents of all the records in the file.
DISPLAY ALL (field name), (field name)	Displays specified fields from all the records in the file.
DISPLAY FOR (search key) (relationship) (search object)	Displays only those records that meet specified conditions.
DISPLAY STRUCTURE	Displays the data structure of the active file.
LIST ALL	Displays the contents of all the records in the file continuously, without pausing.
LIST (field name), (field name)	Lists specified fields from all the records in the file continuously, without pausing.
LIST (field name), (field name) FOR (search key) (relationship) (search object)	Lists continuously (without pausing) only those records that meet specified conditions.

Editing Records

Command	Description
EDIT RECORD (record number)	Displays a record for editing.
APPEND	Allows records to be added to the end of a database file.
BROWSE	Displays an entire database file for editing.
BROWSE FIELDS (field name) (field name)	Displays specified database fields from an entire file for editing.

Deleting Records

Command	Description
DELETE RECORD (record number)	Marks the specified record for deletion.
DELETE ALL	Marks every data record in the file for deletion.
DELETE FOR (search key) (relationship) (search object)	Marks for deletion only those records that meet specified conditions.
PACK	Permanently removes all deleted records from the file.
RECALL RECORD (record number)	Erases the deletion mark from the data record specified.
RECALL ALL	Erases the deletion marks from all the data records marked for deletion.
RECALL FOR (search key) (relationship) (search object)	Erases the deletion marks only from those records that meet specified conditions.

Creating Reports

Command	Description
CREATE REPORT	Menu-based command that guides the user through the creation of a report form file.

Printing

Command	Description
LIST TO PRINT	Prints the entire contents of a file.
LIST (field name), (field name) TO PRINT	Prints designated fields in a database file.
REPORT FORM (filename) TO PRINT	Prints a hard copy of a report.

Selecting Specific Records

Command	Description
GOTO (record number)	Selects the designated record.
GO TOP	Select the first record in a database file.

GO BOTTOM   Selects the last record in a database file.

FIND (alphanumeric string)   Searches for and selects the first data record in an indexed file which contains a specified string.

Summary Points

- There are two ways to rearrange the order of records within a dBase file: the SORT command and the INDEX command.
- The FIND command searches indexed files for relevant data.
- The CREATE REPORT command is a menu-based command that guides the user through the creation of a report by displaying a series of screens.
- The SELECT command allows more than one database file to be open at a time. Once two files are opened, the JOIN command can be used to join specified fields from both files to form a third file.

dBase III Exercises

In this exercise you are going to prepare the rosters for classes at a state university. The database is organized as follows:

- A master file called ENROLL contains general student information such as personal data, program, and major.
- A movement file records registration information for each semester.

1. If you are not in dBase, use the procedures to start it. Make sure your work disk is in drive B. Set the default drive to B.

2. Use the CREATE command to start a new file and name it ENROLL. You are going to create the master file that contains information about the students. The file should have the following structure:

Field Name	**Type**	**Width**
NUMBER	Char/text	2
LAST_NAME	Char/text	10
FIRST_NAME	Char/text	10
ADDRESS	Char/text	16
CITY	Char/text	15
STATE	Char/text	2
MAJOR	Char/text	10
PROGRAM	Char/text	3

Enter the structure information. At the end of the last field, press <Return> to end the CREATE process.

3. At the prompt INPUT DATA RECORDS NOW? (Y/N), type **Y** and enter the following information:

Number	Last_Name	First_Name	Address	City	State	Major	Program
1	Mansfield	Carolyn	190 Main Street	Bowling Green	OH	Education	BA
2	Magpoc	William	1200 Victory Blvd.	Toledo	OH	Business	BA
3	Rath	Alexis	221 Maple Ave.	Perrysburg	OH	Business	BA
4	Byrtum	Laura	849 Napoleon Rd.	Bowling Green	OH	Health	BA
5	Burkett	Lynn	12 Central	Toledo	OH	Music	MA
6	Catayee	Monique	110 Main Street	Maumee	OH	Theater	MA
7	Marin	Bernard	12 King Rd.	Huron	OH	Accounting	BA
8	Byler	Diane	Anderson Hall	Bowling Green	OH	Business	BA
9	Heil	Pascal	302 West Hall	Bowling Green	OH	Education	BA
10	Jaccoud	Lynn	120 S. Main St.	Sandusky	OH	Finance	BA
11	Wegman	Nelly	430 Clough	Dearborn	MI	Accounting	BA
12	Pinkston	Mark	65 High St.	Detroit	MI	Statistics	MA
13	Burroughs	Beverly	26 S. Summit	Huron	OH	Journalism	BA
14	King	Stephen	201 E. Wooster	Bloomdale	OH	History	MA
15	Paulin	Jack	102 High	Sylvania	OH	Math	MA
16	Proctor	Christopher	34 Eighth St.	Lancaster	OH	Chemistry	MA
17	Priess	Ronald	120 Prout Hall	Bowling Green	OH	Marketing	BA
18	Atkins	Lee	12560 Euclid Ave.	Cleveland	OH	Education	BA
19	Asik	Jennifer	22 Mercer	Cleveland	OH	History	MA
20	Dowell	Gail	112 Ridge	Toledo	OH	Business	MA
21	Wacker	Annick	320 East Merry	Sandusky	OH	Economics	BA
22	Garret	Lynda	39 Vine Street	Detroit	MI	Music	MA
23	McGovern	Alice	12000 Sand Ridge	Bowling Green	OH	Theater	PhD
24	McLaughlin	Francoise	210 Main Street	Tiffin	OH	Education	BA
25	Augustin	Liliane	333 Jeffers Rd.	Dearborn	MI	Finance	BA

Once all the records are entered, press <Ctrl> <End> to end the process.

4. Use the BROWSE command to review the data and make sure that everything is correct. Make any necessary corrections.

5. Now you are going to create a second file for registration for the fall semester. The file should have the following structure:

Field name	Type	Width	Description
NUMBER	Character	3	Student number allocated at registration
CLASS	Character	8	Class name

| SEMESTER | Character | 2 | 01 for Fall semester, 02 for Spring semester, 03 for first Summer term, and 04 for second Summer term |
| YEAR | Character | 2 | Year of registration |

Use the CREATE command to start the new file and name it MOVE. Enter the structure information. At the end of the last field, press <Return> to end the process.

6. At the prompt INPUT DATA RECORDS NOW? (Y/N), type **Y**. Enter the following information:

Number	Class	Semester	Year
1	EDCI421	01	87
1	HIST430	01	87
1	EDCI441	01	87
1	ECON301	01	87
2	BUS300	01	87
2	LEGS301	01	87
2	FIN400	01	87
2	ECON301	01	87
3	BUS300	01	87
3	LEGS301	01	87
3	HIST430	01	87
4	PRG200	01	87
4	PRG205	01	87
4	ENG200	01	87
7	ACCT322	01	87
7	ACCT441	01	87
7	FIN400	01	87
7	LEGS301	01	87
10	FIN400	01	87
10	ACCT322	01	87
10	ECON301	01	87
12	STATS511	01	87
12	STAT520	01	87
12	MATH540	01	87
12	CS500	01	87
13	JOURN301	01	87
13	FREN300	01	87
13	ITAL201	01	87
14	HIST430	01	87
14	ECON301	01	87
14	HIST540	01	87
15	MATH540	01	87
15	CS500	01	87
15	MATH660	01	87
15	MATH610	01	87
16	CHEM500	01	87
16	STAT501	01	87
16	MATH540	01	87

16	CHEM529	01	87
17	BUS300	01	87
17	ECON301	01	87
17	LEGS301	01	87
19	HIST430	01	87
19	HIST410	01	87
19	LEGS301	01	87
24	EDCI421	01	87
24	EDCI441	01	87
24	HIST430	01	87
25	FIN400	01	87
25	ACCT322	01	87
25	ECON301	01	87

Once all the information is entered, press <Return> to end the process.

7. Use the BROWSE command to review the data and make sure that everything is correct. Make any necessary corrections.

8. Now you want to index the file on the CLASS field. What is the command to index a file? Use it to index the MOVE file. Name the indexed file COURSE.

9. Use the DISPLAY command to see all the records now. Is there any difference in the order of the records? What is it?

10. Use the LIST command to see the student number for all students who registered for ECON301. (Remember, when searching for a character field the search object has to be enclosed in quotation marks and must be entered exactly as it appears in the database record.) How many students are there in this class? Repeat listing the NUMBER field for the following classes: LEGS301, HIST430, and ACCT322.

11. Now you want to produce a complete roster that includes the last name, first name, program, and major for each student in all the classes. You need the following information from the ENROLL and MOVE files:

ENROLL	**MOVE**
Number	Number
Last_Name	Class
First_Name	
Major	
Program	

As you notice, the common field is NUMBER. Therefore, you have to join the two files based on this field. How do you join two files?

12. Use this procedure to join the file MOVE with the file ENROLL on the NUMBER field to the new file ROSTER. Remember that the file ROSTER should contain all the fields listed above from the ENROLL file and the MOVE file.

13. Open the file ROSTER and use the DISPLAY STRUCTURE command to make sure that all these fields have been created.

14. List Last_Name, First_Name, Major, Program, and Class for the class EDCI421. How many students are there in that class? What are their last names, first names, and majors?

15. Repeat question 14 for the classes MATH540, LEGS301, and ECON301.

16. Print a hard copy of the rosters listed in questions 14 and 15.

dBase III Problems

To complete the following problems, you need the DOS disk, the dBase III system disk and the Student File Disk.

1. The Museum of Sciences and Industry, located in Toledo, Ohio, has two types of associates who participate in different programs:

■ *Exhibition Program*. Under this program, the public can get a membership that provides the following rights:

Free parking
Free access to all permanent and temporary exhibitions
Free publications (newsletter and quarterly magazine)
Discount at the gift shop

■ *Science Clubs*. Under this program, a member has access to a series of activities and can use the Museum facilities allocated to each club. Currently there are three science clubs:

Club A: for specific events and lectures by major scientists
Club B: for in-house workshops
Club C: for field trips

In addition, the members of each club have the right to free parking and a discount at the gift shop. They also receive a bi-monthly publication issued by the club.

An associate can be a member of one program or of both programs.

The director of public relations, who is in charge of these programs, would like to reorganize the data structure using dBase III. She would like to be able to retrieve information easily, in order to prepare for the mailing of the magazines. She also would like to be able to follow the expiration dates for membership in each program and to assure the renewal of membership cards. She wants to control the activity of each program (total number of new members per month, year, etc.).

1. A permanent file called MASTER, with general information on all associates, already exists. It has the following structure:

Field name	Width	Type	Description
NUMBER	3	Char/text	Associate number
LASTNAME	15	Char/text	Last name of associate
FIRSTNAME	15	Char/text	First name of associate
DATEBIRTH	6	Char/text	Date of birth of associate
ADDRESS	20	Char/text	Street address
CITY	15	Char/text	City
STATE	2	Char/text	State
TYPE	1	Char/text	1 for exhibition membership, 2 for club membership, and 3 for both

Start the computer with the DOS disk. At the A> prompt, start dBase III and insert the Student File Disk in drive B. At the dot prompt, open the file MASTER. Remember to set the default drive to B. Copy the MASTER file to MASTER1 using the COPY TO command. From now on, you are going to use the file MASTER1.

2. Open the MASTER1 file and display its structure. How many data records are there in the file? Use the BROWSE command to review all the records. How do you go to the last record? What is the name, address, city, and type of the associate in the last record? How do you end the BROWSE command?

3. Assume that the director asks you to provide her with a master list of all associates. Use the LIST TO PRINT command to print the following information: NUMBER, LASTNAME, FIRSTNAME, ADDRESS, CITY, STATE, TYPE.

4. Use the DISPLAY command to show LASTNAME and FIRSTNAME for associates who are in both programs (TYPE=3). How many associates are in both programs?

5. Now the director would like you to create a file for each category of associate. The structure of each file should be as follows:

Filename: MEMBER

Field name	Width	Type	Description
NUMBER	3	Char/text	Associate Number
DATEORIG	4	Char/text	Month and year of first membership
DATEEXP	4	Char/text	Month and year when current membership expires
DATEPAY	4	Char/text	Month and year when last payment was received
RENEWNOTIC	1	Logical	Y if membership renewal notice for next year has been sent, otherwise N
AMOUNT0	4	Numeric	Amount paid in current year

AMOUNT1	4	Numeric	Amount paid in previous year
AMOUNT2	4	Numeric	Amount paid in second previous year
CATEGORY	1	Char/text	Category of membership—1 for children, 2 for students, 3 for adults, 4 for senior citizens

Filename: SCIENCE

Field Name	Width	Type	Description
NUMBER	3	Char/text	Associate number
DATEORG	4	Char/text	Month and year of first membership
DATEEXP	4	Char/text	Month and year when current membership expires
DATEPAY	4	Char/text	Month and year when payment for current year was received
RENEWNOTIC	1	Logical	Y if membership renewal notice for next year has been sent, otherwise N
AMOUNT0	4	Numeric	Amount paid in current year
AMOUNT1	4	Numeric	Amount paid in previous year
AMOUNT2	4	Numeric	Amount paid in second previous year
CLUBCATEG	1	Char/text	Club category—A for club A, B for club B, C for club C

Using all this information, create the two other files. For each file, use the CREATE command and enter the structure. Remember that the filenames are MEMBER and SCIENCE.

6. Use the DISPLAY STRUCTURE command to review each structure. Make sure that it corresponds exactly to the information given to you. If necessary, use the MODIFY STRUCTURE command to make any corrections.

7. Now use the APPEND command to enter the data for each file:

MEMBER file

Number	Dateorig	Dateexp	Datepay	No	Amnt0	Amnt1	Amnt2	Category
1	0185	1287	1286	N	0	32	27	2
2	0587	0488	0587	N	35	0	0	4
5	0385	0288	0287	N	25	23	19	1
6	0686	0587	0686	Y	0	45	0	3
7	0285	0187	0286	Y	0	23	19	1
8	0680	0587	0686	N	0	23	0	1
10	0287	0188	0287	N	35	0	0	4
11	0885	0787	0886	N	0	32	27	2
12	0986	0887	0986	N	0	32	0	4
15	0387	0288	0387	N	50	0	0	3
16	0685	0587	0686	N	0	45	38	3
17	0685	0587	0686	N	0	45	38	3
19	0486	0388	0487	N	35	32	0	4
22	0487	0388	0487	N	35	0	0	2
24	1285	1187	1286	N	0	45	38	3
25	1085	0986	1085	Y	0	0	27	2

498 PART TWO: APPLICATIONS SOFTWARE

SCIENCE File

Number	Dateorig	Dateexp	Datepay	Not	Amnt0	Amnt1	Amnt2	Category
3	0185	1287	0187	N	150	130	110	C
4	0387	0288	0387	N	150	0	0	C
6	1284	1187	1286	N	0	80	70	B
9	0686	0587	0686	N	0	30	0	A
12	0986	0887	0986	N	0	30	0	A
13	0686	0587	0686	Y	0	80	0	B
14	0485	0388	0487	N	150	130	110	C
16	0985	0987	0986	N	0	130	110	C
17	0486	0388	0487	N	50	45	0	A
18	0685	0587	0686	N	0	30	25	A
20	0986	0887	0986	N	0	130	0	C
21	0184	1287	0187	N	100	80	70	B
23	0685	0587	0686	Y	0	80	70	A
25	1086	0987	1086	N	0	30	0	A

8. Now that all files are complete, you are going to use the data to issue various reports. Open the MEMBER file. List NUMBER and DATEORIG for all student members. How many members are students? List NUMBER and DATEORIG for new members in March 1987 (members who have DATEORIG = 0387).

9. Assume you want to prepare a notice letter for all members whose expiration date is equal to May 1987 (0587). For this purpose, you need the following data from the MEMBER and the MASTER1 files:

Member	**Master1**
NUMBER	NUMBER
DATEEXP	LASTNAME
RENEWNOT	ADDRESS
	CITY
	STATE

The common field for the two files is NUMBER.

How do you join two files? Use this procedure to join MASTER1 with MEMBER on NUMBER to RENEW. The file RENEW should contain all the fields previously mentioned. (Remember that the MEMBER file is already open.)

10. Open the file RENEW. To prepare the mailing list, use the command LIST TO PRINT for the fields NUMBER, LASTNAME, ADDRESS, CITY, STATE, and DATEEXP.

11. Now you want to prepare a mailing list for the active members of club B in order to send them a newsletter. You need the following information from the MASTER1 file and the SCIENCE file:

Science	**Master1**
NUMBER	NUMBER
DATEEXP	LASTNAME
CLUBCATEG	ADDRESS
	CITY
	STATE

Join the file SCIENCE with the file MASTER1 to the form the file CLUBB. Again, the common field is NUMBER. Use SELECT 3 and SELECT 4 to open the MASTER1 and SCIENCE files respectively. The file CLUBB should contain all the fields previously mentioned.

12. Open the file CLUBB. Print NUMBER, LASTNAME, ADDRESS, CITY, STATE, DATEEXP, and CLUBCATEG for members in club B for whom DATEEXP is equal to 0587.

13. Use the command to close the database files and to return to the DOS system.

APPENDIX
Installation Procedures

Following are basic instructions for installing WordStar 2000, WordPerfect, Lotus 1-2-3, and dBase III. For more complete instructions on installing any of these programs, consult the user's manual.

Installing WordStar 2000

To install WordStar 2000 you will need the following:

- A copy of the DOS disk
- A copy of the WordStar 2000 Installation Disk
- A copy of the WordStar 2000 Program Disk
- Blank formatted disks.

Refer to pp. 45–46 for instructions on formatting a disk.
Refer to p. 47 for instructions on copying a disk.

Installing WordStar 2000 on a Two Floppy Disk Computer

1. Make a copy of each original WordStar 2000 disk. Store the original disks in a safe place. Always use the copies when running WordStar 2000.
2. Insert the DOS disk in drive A. Turn on the computer and monitor. Press <Return> in response to the date and time prompts. The system prompt (A>) appears on the screen.
3. Put the copy of the Installation Disk in drive B. Close the disk drive door.

A-1

4. Type **b:** and press <Return>.
5. Type **ws2ins** and press <Return>.
6. Follow the instructions on the screen.

Installing WordStar 2000 on a Hard Disk Computer

1. Make sure the computer is turned on and booted. The system prompt (C>) should be on the screen.
2. Put the Installation Disk in drive A. Close the disk drive door.
3. Type **a:ws2copy**. Press <Return>. Follow the instructions on the screen.

Installing WordPerfect

To install WordPerfect you will need the following:

- A copy of the DOS disk
- A copy of the WordPerfect Program Disk
- A copy of the WordPerfect Speller, Thesaurus, and Printer disks
- Blank formatted disks.

Refer to pp. 45–46 for instructions on formatting a disk.
Refer to p. 47 for instructions on copying a disk.

Installing WordPerfect on a Two Floppy Disk Computer

1. Make a copy of each original WordPerfect disk. Store the original disks in a safe place. Always use the copies when running WordPerfect.
2. Insert the DOS disk in drive A. Turn on the computer and monitor. Press <Return> in response to the time and date prompts. The system prompt (A>) appears on the screen.
3. Remove the DOS disk from drive A. Put the copy of the WordPerfect Program Disk in drive A. Close the disk drive door. Put a copy of the Printer Disk into drive B. Close the disk drive door.
4. Type **b:** and press <Return>.
5. Type **a:wp** and press <Return>.
6. Press <Shift> <F7> for PRINT. Press 4 for PRINTER CONTROL. The Printer Control Menu appears.
7. Type 3 for SELECT PRINTERS. Press <Pg Dn> to display an alphabetical list of defined printers. If your printer is not listed on the first screen, press <Pg Up> or <Pg Dn> until you find it. Type the number of your printer.
8. Answer the questions that follow regarding the specifications of your printer.

Installing WordPerfect on a Hard Disk Computer

1. Make sure the computer is turned on and booted. The system prompt (C>) should be on the screen.
2. To make a subdirectory for the WordPerfect system files, type **md\wp**.
3. To change the WP directory type **cd\wp**.
4. Place the WordPerfect Program Disk in drive A. Close the disk drive door. Type **copy a:*.*** and press <Return> to copy the WordPerfect files to the C:/WP directory.
5. Repeat step 4 to copy the remaining WordPerfect disks to the C:/WP directory.
6. Place the Printer disk into drive A. Start WordPerfect by typing **wp**. Follow steps 6 through 8 in the installation instructions for a two floppy disk drive system to install a printer.

Installing Lotus 1-2-3

To install Lotus 1-2-3 you will need the following:

- A copy of the DOS disk
- The six 1-2-3 disks
- Blank formatted disks.

Refer to pp. 45–46 for instructions on formatting a disk.
Refer to p. 47 for instructions on copying a disk.

Installing Lotus 1-2-3 on a Two Floppy Disk Computer

1. Make a copy of each original Lotus 1-2-3 disk. Store the original disks in a safe place. Always use the copies of all the Lotus disks, except the 1-2-3 System Disk, when running Lotus 1-2-3.
2. Insert the DOS disk in drive A. Turn on the computer and monitor. Press <Return> in response to the time and date prompts. The system prompt (A>) appears on the screen.
3. Place the copy of the Utility Disk in drive A. Close the disk drive door.
4. Type **install**. After a few seconds, the Install Main menu appears on the screen. Follow the instructions on the screen.

Installing Lotus 1-2-3 on a Hard Disk Computer

1. Make sure the computer is turned on and booted. The system prompt (C>) should be on the screen.

2. To make a subdirectory for the Lotus 1-2-3 files, type **md\123**.
3. To change to the 123 directory, type **cd\123**.
4. Place the 1-2-3 System Disk disk in drive A. Close the disk drive door. Type **copy a:*.*** and press <Return> to copy the 1-2-3 System Disk to the C:/123 directory.
5. Repeat step 4 to copy the remaining Lotus 1-2-3 disks to the C:/123 directory.
6. Type **install**. Press <Return>.
7. Read the introductory screen and press <Return>. Follow the instructions on the screen.

Installing dBase III

To install dBase III you will need the following:

- A copy of the DOS disk
- The dBase III System Disk
- A blank formatted disk.

Refer to pp. 45–46 for instructions on formatting a disk.
Refer to p. 47 for instructions on copying a disk.

Installing dBase III on a Two Floppy Disk Computer

1. Make a copy of the dBase III System Disk. The dBase III System Disk is copy-protected. This does not prevent the disk from being copied, but copies of the System Disk are useless unless the original System Disk is in one of the floppy drives.
2. Insert the DOS disk in drive A. Turn on the computer and monitor. Press <Return> in response to the time and date prompts. The system prompt (A>) appears on the screen.
3. Insert the dBase III System Disk in drive A. Type **dBase**. Press <Return>.

Installing dBase III on a Hard Disk Computer

1. Make sure the compter is turned on and booted. The system prompt (C>) should be on the screen.
2. To make a subdirectory for the dBase III files, type **md\dBase**.
3. To change to the dBase directory, type **cd\dBase**.
4. Place the dBase III System Disk disk in drive A. Close the disk drive door. Type **copy a:*.*c:** and press <Return> to copy the dBase III System Disk to the C:/dBase directory.
5. dBase III can only be run from the hard disk provided the original System Disk is in a floppy disk drive during execution of the program.

PART THREE

BASIC Supplement

SECTION I

Introduction to BASIC

Outline

Introduction
Background on BASIC
The Programming Process
   Defining the Problem
   Designing a Solution
   Writing the Program
   Submitting the Program to the
     Computer

Learning Check
Getting Started
DOS Commands
BASIC Commands
   NEW
   RUN
   SAVE
   LOAD
   LIST
   FILES and KILL

Learning Check
Summary Points
Review Questions

Introduction

Part III of this book shows you how to write programs using Microsoft BASIC on the IBM PC. Each chapter introduces new topics in a readable, easily understood, step-by-step format. In time, you will become proficient in writing BASIC programs, but remember that learning to write computer programs is like building a house: unless there is a solid foundation, the entire house will collapse. For the time being, you should not skip around the book. Once you have a firm foundation, you can move to more advanced techniques.

This section discusses the process programmers follow to develop well-designed programs. It also explains several commands that enable you to manipulate BASIC programs—for example, to save them on a diskette or to execute them.

Background on BASIC

BASIC, an acronym for *B*eginner's *A*ll-*P*urpose *S*ymbolic *I*nstruction *C*ode, was developed in the mid-1960s at Dartmouth College by Professors John Kemeny and Thomas Kurtz. It is a high-level language that uses English-like words and statements, such as LET, READ, and PRINT. It is easy to learn and is considered a general-purpose programming language, because it is useful for a wide variety of programming tasks.

BASIC, like English and other languages used for communication, includes rules for spelling, grammar, and punctuation. In BASIC, however, these rules are very precise and allow no exceptions. They enable the programmer to tell the computer what to do in such a way that the computer is able to carry out the instructions.

The Programming Process

A computer program is a step-by-step series of instructions which a computer can use to solve a problem. Because the computer can perform only the instructions submitted to it the program must be written precisely. In order to know what instructions are required to solve a problem efficiently, the programmer follows four steps, commonly referred to as the programming process:

1. Define the problem.
2. Design a solution.
3. Write the program.
4. Submit the program to the computer and debug and test the program.

To show how these steps are used in the programming process, we will describe a sample data processing problem: calculating a distance in miles, given the distance in kilometers.

SECTION I: INTRODUCTION TO BASIC

Defining the Problem

INPUT
The data needed to solve a problem.

PROCESSING
The producing of output or information from the input or data.

OUTPUT
Information that is the result of processing.

The first step is to define the problem. To do so, we analyze it by using the basic steps involved in all data processing: **input, processing,** and **output.** Input is data used to solve the problem, output is the information that results when the problem is solved, and processing includes the steps needed to convert the input to output.

Often it is easier to determine what processing is needed by working backward: first determine what output is required, and then determine what input is needed to obtain the output. The gap between the available input and the required output is the processing needed in the program.

Determining the output for this sample is quite simple: we need to know the distance in miles. The input available is the distance in kilometers. The processing step requires a conversion factor that translates the distance in kilometers to the distance in miles. One kilometer equals 0.621 miles; hence, to calculate the distance in miles, we multiply the distance in kilometers by 0.621.

Designing a Solution

ALGORITHM
The sequence of instructions needed to solve a problem, arranged in a specific, logical order.

TOP-DOWN DESIGN
A method of solving a problem which proceeds from the general to the specific.

The second step, designing a solution, requires developing an **algorithm,** a sequence of instructions or statements arranged in a specific, logical order to solve the problem. Using **top-down design** to accomplish this step produces the most logical and efficient algorithm. When using top-down design, the programmer looks first at the most general task to be performed, then breaks this task into smaller, more specific subtasks. Top-down design makes the programmer's job easier by reducing a large task into smaller, more manageable portions that can be dealt with one at a time.

Applying this approach to the distance conversion problem, we see that the most general task is to calculate the distance in miles given the distance in kilometers. We can divide this task into at least three subtasks:

1. Input the number of kilometers to be converted.
2. Convert the distance from kilometers to miles.
3. Display the distance in miles.

Next, we examine each of these subtasks to see if any of them can be divided into smaller tasks. Because each of these three subtasks is very simple, we will not subdivide them further.

STRUCTURE CHART
A diagram that visually illustrates how a problem solution has been developed using stepwise refinement.

FLOWCHART
A graphic representation of the solution to a programming problem.

The design step of the programming process always should be accompanied by good documentation. Documentation can consist of either written or graphic descriptions of the solution. A **structure chart** graphically depicts the step-by-step breakdown, or refinement, of a problem. Figure I–1 shows a structure chart for the distance conversion problem. Because this problem is so simple, there are only two levels to this chart: Level 0 contains the general statement of the problem, and Level 1 contains the three basic steps. More complex programming problems usually contain many levels of refinement.

Once the various tasks making up the problem have been determined, we must decide what program steps are needed to perform those tasks. One way of visualizing these steps and their logical order is by using a **flowchart.** A flowchart

**Figure I–1
Structure Chart for Distance Conversion Problem**

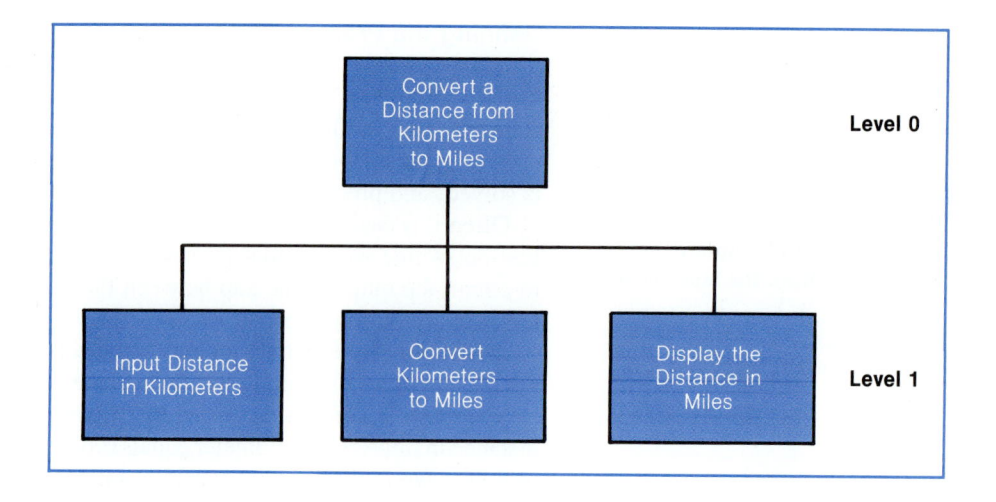

shows the actual flow of the logic of a program, whereas a structure chart simply contains statements of the levels of subproblems used to reach a solution. Flowcharts are composed of symbols that stand for various types of program operations. Figure I–2 shows some of the symbols and the steps they represent.

Figure I–3 shows a flowchart depicting the steps of the programming example. Notice how the symbols are shown in logical top-down order and connected by arrows. The first symbol shows the start of the program. The second symbol shows an input step: the distance in kilometers is entered. The third symbol shows the processing done by the program; that is, the conversion of the distance in kilometers to the distance in miles. Next, the result is displayed on the monitor. Finally, another terminal symbol signifies the end of the program. The flowchart makes it easy to see the input, processing, and output steps of the program.

Writing the Program

If the solution has been designed carefully, the next step—coding (writing) the program in a programming language—should be relatively easy. All that is required is to translate the flowchart into program statements. Figure I–4 shows the sample program written in BASIC. As you can see, many BASIC words, such as INPUT and PRINT, are easy to interpret.

Compare the coded BASIC statements in Figure I–4 to the flowchart in Figure I–3. The correspondence between the two is obvious. The remaining sections of this supplement will explain the exact meaning and use of the program statements shown in the sample program.

Submitting the Program to the Computer

The fourth step of the programming process involves sitting down at the keyboard and typing the program, line for line, into the computer. After this is done, the program can be executed. In order to execute a program, the programmer enters

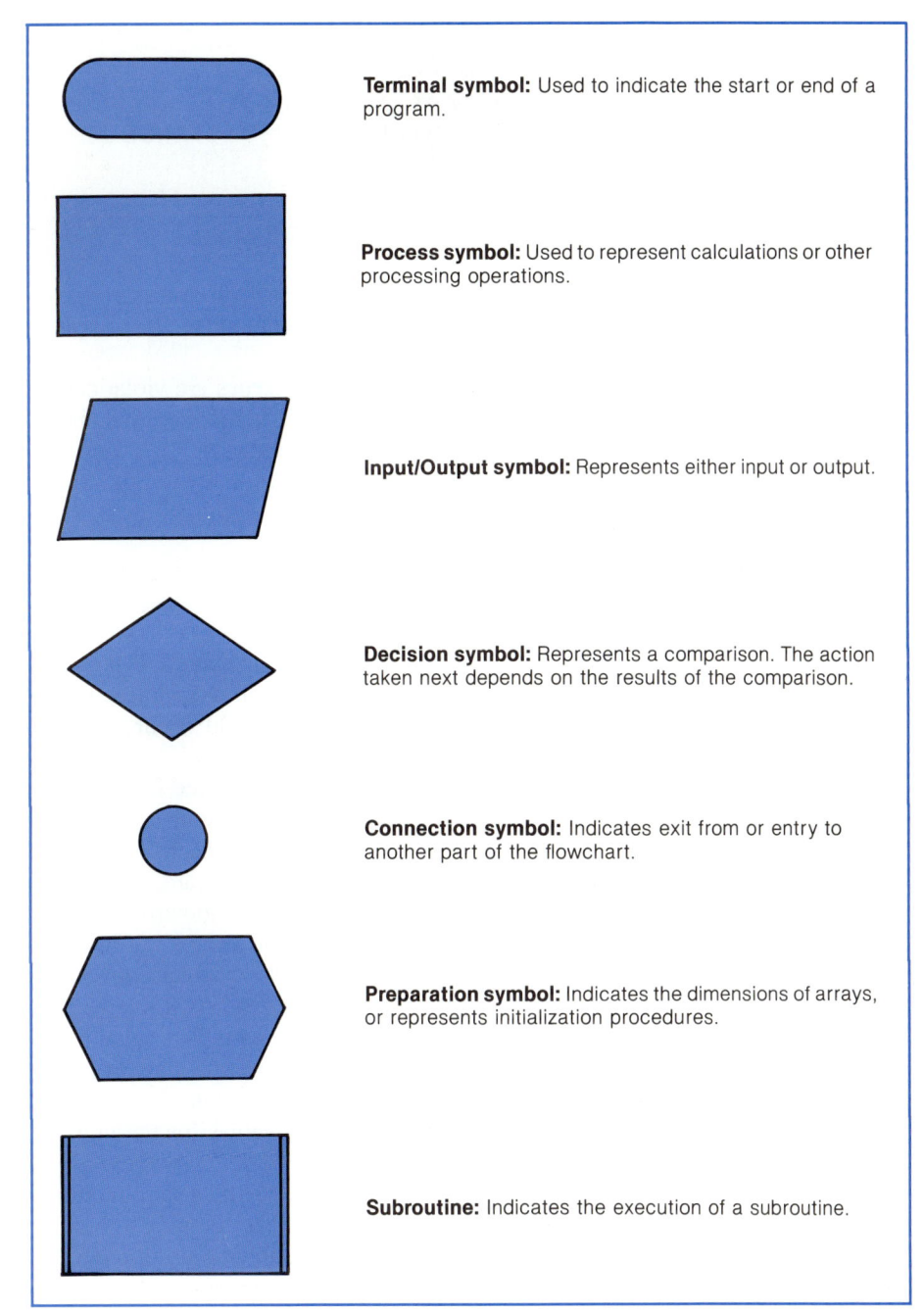

SECTION I: INTRODUCTION TO BASIC

**Figure I–2
Flowcharting Symbols**

Terminal symbol: Used to indicate the start or end of a program.

Process symbol: Used to represent calculations or other processing operations.

Input/Output symbol: Represents either input or output.

Decision symbol: Represents a comparison. The action taken next depends on the results of the comparison.

Connection symbol: Indicates exit from or entry to another part of the flowchart.

Preparation symbol: Indicates the dimensions of arrays, or represents initialization procedures.

Subroutine: Indicates the execution of a subroutine.

**Figure I–3
Flowchart for Distance Conversion Problem**

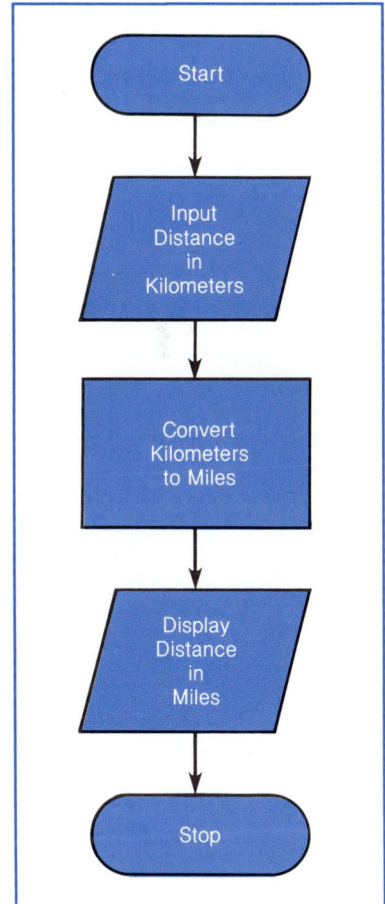

Start → Input Distance in Kilometers → Convert Kilometers to Miles → Display Distance in Miles → Stop

**DEBUG
To locate and correct program errors.**

the RUN command and presses the Return key. This process will be discussed in more detail later in this chapter.

Few programs of significant length are error-free when first written. **Debugging** is the process of finding and correcting errors. Debugging should begin before the program is entered to the computer. Once the program code has been written, the

Figure I–4
Distance Conversion Program

```
10 INPUT "ENTER KILOMETERS";KILOMETERS
20 LET DISTANCE = KILOMETERS * .6210001
30 PRINT "THE DISTANCE IN MILES IS ";DISTANCE
99 END
```

programmer should carefully check the typing and logic of each program statement. Errors detected in this way are far easier to correct than those found by the computer once the program has been submitted.

There are three basic types of program errors. **Syntax errors** are violations of the grammar rules of a language. Programming languages, like natural languages such as English, are governed by rules that determine how the language must be written. A frequent source of syntax errors is typing mistakes. For example, if the following BASIC statement were entered to the computer, a syntax error would occur because of the misspelling of PRINT:

```
10 PRING "THE DISTANCE IN MILES IS ";D
```

SYNTAX ERROR
A violation of the grammatical rules of a language.

RUN-TIME ERROR
An error that causes program execution to stop prematurely.

LOGIC ERROR
A flaw in an algorithm which results in the program's output being incorrect.

A **run-time error** occurs when the computer is unable to execute the program instructions as given. If the sample program instructed the computer to input two numbers but the user entered only one, a run-time error would occur, causing program execution to stop prematurely.

The worst type of error is a **logic error.** A program may be free from syntax errors and execute with no problems, yet produce incorrect output because the logic does not properly solve the problem. For instance, if an incorrect formula for converting kilometers to miles were used in the sample program, the output would be incorrect even though no error messages appeared. Logic errors can be detected only by carefully examining the program output and comparing it to the expected results. Figure I–5 shows the execution results of the distance conversion program. Check the answer by hand to see if it is correct.

Testing a program involves running it with a variety of data to determine if the results are always correct. A program may produce correct results when it is run with one set of data, but incorrect results when run with different data. The distance conversion program could be tested by using a variety of values for the number of kilometers to be converted.

This sample program is relatively simple, but it shows each of the steps required to complete a program. Although other problems may be more complex, the steps involved are the same. Successful programming can come about only through the diligent application of the four steps in the programming process.

Getting Started

The IBM Personal Computer runs an enhanced version of Microsoft BASIC. There are two versions of BASIC on the IBM Personal Computer: Disk and Advanced.

Figure I–5
Output of Distance Conversion Program

```
RUN
ENTER KILOMETERS? 500
THE DISTANCE IN MILES IS  310.5001
```

Disk BASIC (referred to simply as BASIC) has the ability to input data from diskette and to output data to diskette, and an internal clock that keeps track of the date and time. Advanced BASIC, known as BASICA, has these same capabilities but also offers advanced graphic and sound support. The commands and statements for BASIC and BASICA are the same, except for some graphics and sound features that are offered only in BASICA. Because the last chapter of this

---

Learning Check

1. The steps in an algorithm can be listed in any order. True or false?
2. Top-down design always proceeds from the _____ to the _____.
3. A(n) _____ _____ is a diagram that depicts the levels of refinement of a problem solution.
4. A(n) _____ is used to represent the logic of a programming problem solution visually.
5. _____ is the process of writing a problem solution in a programming language.

Answers

1. false 2. general, specific 3. structure chart 4. flowchart 5. coding

section deals with graphics and sound, we will use BASICA in that chapter; until then, however, we will use BASIC.

To start BASIC on an IBM PC with standard configuration (two external drives, no hard disk), you need to start DOS (disk operating system). To do so, place the DOS diskette into Drive A, the left drive. Then turn on the computer. The power switch is located at the right rear of the machine. Remember to turn on the monitor and to turn up the brightness dial, too. Once the DOS has been booted, or loaded, the computer asks for the date and time. If you do not wish to enter the date and/or time, merely press the ⏎ (Return) key after each of the prompts, which appear as follows:

```
Current date is Tue  1-01-1980
Enter new date:
Current time is  0:00:08.95
Enter new time:
```

After you have responded to the time prompt and pressed ⏎ , the computer responds with a display similar to the following:

```
The IBM Personal Computer DOS
Version 2.10 (C)Copyright IBM Corp 1981,1982,1983
A>
```

The A> is the DOS prompt. Type BASIC and press ⏎ to load the disk BASIC interpreter. The screen will look similar to this:

```
The IBM Personal Computer Basic
Version D2.10 Copyright IBM Corp. 1981, 1982, 1983
61327 Bytes free
Ok
```

Notice the word "Ok" on the screen. It is the BASIC prompt, which tells you the computer is ready to accept BASIC commands and statements.

DOS Commands

Chapter 3 introduced DOS commands, which we will review in this section. These commands are executed at the DOS level (that is, at the A> symbol).

The FORMAT command enables you to prepare a disk so that files can be stored on it. The command

   FORMAT *drive:*

allows you to specify the drive the disk to be formatted is in. For example,

SECTION I: INTRODUCTION TO BASIC

    FORMAT B:

would format the disk currently in Drive B.

    The DISKCOPY command enables you to make backup copies of disks, as a precaution in case a disk is damaged. The command

    DISKCOPY A: B

copies the contents of the disk currently in Drive A to the disk in Drive B. If your system only has one drive, use the following command:

    DISKCOPY A:

You will then be instructed to remove the disk being copied and to place the target disk into the drive. Both commands, FORMAT and DISKCOPY, can be used without qualifiers. If you do use only the FORMAT or DISKCOPY command, a prompt will appear on the screen telling you what to do next.

    The DIR (short for directory) command displays the names of all files stored on the disk.

    To remove a file from a disk, use either the ERASE or the DEL command:

    ERASE *filename*

or

    DEL *filename*

A file can easily be copied by using the COPY command:

    COPY *sourcedrive: filename targetdrive:*

To change the name of a file, use RENAME:

    RENAME *drive: oldfilename newfilename*

BASIC Commands

Whereas DOS commands are entered at DOS level (A>), BASIC commands are entered while you are in BASIC mode, which is indicated by the Ok prompt. To get into the BASIC mode, simply type BASIC, as we showed you before:

    A>BASIC

IMMEDIATE MODE
The BASIC mode in which commands are executed as soon as the RETURN key is pressed: it is used without line numbers.

and press [↵]. You must be in the BASIC mode to enter BASIC commands and programs. BASIC commands are **immediate-mode** instructions; that is, they are executed as soon as the carriage control key ([↵]) is pressed. They differ from BASIC language statements, which usually are not executed until the program is run. The most commonly used BASIC commands are discussed in this section.

NEW

The NEW command tells the computer that the programmer is ready to enter a new program. It does so by instructing the computer to erase any programs in main memory, thereby making room for the new program. The syntax is as follows:

NEW

If you want to store the program currently in main memory for future use, you must save it on a diskette (see SAVE) before entering the NEW command. Otherwise, the NEW command will erase the old program from main memory to make room for the new program, and you will not be able to recover it.

RUN

EXECUTE
To carry out the instructions in a program.

To see if a program works, use the RUN command. This command will cause the computer to **execute** the program currently in main memory. That is, the computer will carry out the instructions in the program.

There are three forms of the RUN command. The first form simply executes the program currently in memory from start to finish (unless an error is encountered). In the following example the last line is the output from the one line program that is executed when the computer receives the RUN command.

RUN ⏎

For example:

```
10 PRINT "THIS IS A TEST"
RUN

THIS IS A TEST
```

The second form also executes the program currently in main memory, but it begins at the line number that you indicate. (A line number accompanies every program statement, as discussed in the next chapter.) The syntax is as follows:

RUN line number ⏎

For example:

```
10 PRINT "THIS IS"
20 PRINT "A TEST"
30 PRINT "ON RUN"
40 PRINT "COMMANDS"
```

RUN 30

ON RUN COMMANDS

The third form gets a program from the diskette, puts it into main memory, and runs it. This form erases any program currently in main memory. The syntax is as follows:

RUN "filename" ⏎

(The "filename" is the name given to the program when it is saved on diskette, as discussed later in this chapter.)
For example:

RUN "PAYROLL"

This command gets the program PAYROLL from the diskette, places it into main memory, and executes it.

Notice that quotation marks have been placed around the filename. The set of quotation marks on the right side of the filename is optional. Thus the file PAYROLL could also be executed by this statement:

RUN "PAYROLL

SAVE

Once a program has been entered into main memory, you can save it on a diskette by using the SAVE command. This command copies the program from main memory, which is temporary, to a diskette for long-term storage. Once the program is copied to a diskette, the programmer can perform other tasks that access the computer's main memory without worrying about erasing or changing the program. The syntax is

SAVE "filename"

For example:

SAVE "PAYROLL"

This command saves the program in main memory under the filename PAYROLL. As with the RUN command, the set of quotation marks on the right side of the filename is optional. Thus the filename PAYROLL could also be saved by this statement:

SAVE "PAYROLL

The filename is the name given to the program to be saved on the diskette. It must contain eight or fewer characters. If a file already on the diskette has the same name as the filename just used, the old file will be written over and lost.

LOAD

A program that has been saved is stored on a diskette. When it is needed, it can be retrieved from the diskette and placed into the computer's main memory. This procedure is called loading a program, and it is carried out by the BASIC command LOAD. When the program you request is retrieved from the diskette and placed into main memory, any program currently in main memory is erased.

There are two basic forms of the LOAD command. The first form simply loads the specified program from the diskette into main memory. The syntax is as follows:

LOAD "filename" ⏎

For example:

```
LOAD "PAYROLL"
```

The second form of the command loads the specified program from the diskette to the computer's main memory and then runs it. The syntax is as shown here:

LOAD "filename",R ⏎

For example:

```
LOAD "PAYROLL",R
```

This command loads the program PAYROLL and executes it.

LIST

It is often necessary to view part or all of a program that is being worked on. The LIST command displays the program that is currently in main memory, either on the screen or on the printer. There are two basic forms of the LIST command, one to list the entire program and the other to list only part of the program.

To view the entire program in main memory, use the following syntax:

LIST ⏎

This command lists on the screen the program that is in main memory.

When the LIST command is used to display a program on the monitor screen, the program **scrolls;** that is, the display image moves vertically in such a way that the next line of the program appears at the bottom of the text already on the screen. If your program contains more lines than the number of lines your screen is capable of displaying, part of it will disappear off the top of the screen. For example, if your program contains 40 lines but your screen only has a 24-line capacity, the first 16 lines will move vertically off the top of the screen. Scrolling occurs so quickly that the program disappears from the screen before you can read it. There is a way to control the display, however, thus enabling you to see a portion of the program and then continue displaying the remaining portion of the program.

SCROLL
To move vertically off the top of the monitor screen.

SECTION I: INTRODUCTION TO BASIC   B-15

Table I-1
LIST Command

Command	Explanation
LIST	List the entire program on the screen.
LIST,"LPT1:"	List the entire program on the printer.
LIST 10	List line 10 on the screen.
LIST 10-20	List lines 10 through 20 on the screen.
LIST 10-20,"LPT1:"	List lines 10 through 20 on the printer.
LIST 100 -	List the program from line 100 to the end of the program.
LIST -200	List the program from beginning through line 200.

This is known as controlling the scroll, and it is done by holding down the <Ctrl> key and pressing the <NumLock> key *at the same time*. To continue scrolling, simply press any key other than [↑], <Break>, or <Ins>. To stop the LIST command once it has been started, press the <Ctrl> and <Break> keys at the same time.

To view a portion of the program, use the following syntax:

LIST line1 - line2

The lines from line1 through line2 are displayed. This form of the LIST command has several options. If only line1 is given, with the hyphen following it, that line and all higher-numbered lines are listed. If only line2 is given, with the hyphen preceding it, all lines from the beginning of the program through line2 are listed. If only line1 is given and no hyphen follows it, only that line is printed. (See Table I-1 for the forms of the LIST command.)

All of the LIST commands discussed here can be used to print all or part of the program to a printer, if the "LPT1:" extension is added to the end of the LIST command before the [↵] key is typed. For example:

LIST,"LPT1:" [↵]

"LPT1:" stands for line printer. This extension, preceded by a comma, tells the computer to print to the printer.

FILES and KILL

The FILES command lists all of the files stored on a disk. It works in the same way as the DOS DIR command, except that the DIR command is used at DOS level (the A> symbol), whereas FILES is used in BASIC mode.

The KILL command is used to delete a file that is saved on disk. Again, it is used in BASIC mode, whereas DEL is used to remove files at DOS level. The format of the KILL command is as shown here:

KILL "filename"

Learning Check

1. When is the NEW command used?
2. What is the syntax of the instruction to execute a program that has been saved on a diskette?
3. The LOAD command erases anything currently in the computer's main memory. True or false?
4. What is the command to list a program through Line 990 on the printer?

Answers

1. When the programmer is ready to enter a new program. 2. RUN "filename" 3. true 4. LIST -990,"LPT1:"

Summary Points

- BASIC (*B*eginner's *A*ll-Purpose *S*ymbolic *I*nstruction *C*ode) was developed in the mid-1960s by Professors John G. Kemeny and Thomas E. Kurtz at Dartmouth College.
- The four steps in the programming process are (1) Define the problem, (2) Design a solution, (3) Write the program, and (4) Submit the program to the computer, and debug and test it.
- Programs are best designed by the top-down approach, in which a large task is divided into smaller and smaller subtasks, moving from the general to the specific.
- Program design can be documented by structure charts to show the results of the top-down design process, and by flowcharts to display the order and type of program steps to be performed.
- BASIC has rules of grammar (syntax) to which programmers must adhere.
- The BASIC NEW command clears any programs in the computer's main memory, in preparation for a new program.
- The RUN command causes the computer to execute a program.
- The SAVE command transfers a program from main memory to diskette.
- The LOAD command places a saved program into main memory.
- The LIST command is used to display on the screen or printer all or part of a program that is in main memory.
- The FILES command lists files on disk.
- The KILL command deletes a stated file.

Review Questions

1. What are the steps in the programming process?
2. What is an algorithm, and what is its importance to programmers?
3. What information is needed to define a problem?
4. Design a solution to the problem of making a pizza, using the top-down approach. Draw a structure chart to document your design.
5. List the three types of program errors.
6. Why are logic errors in a program difficult to detect?
7. Name the seven BASIC commands presented in this chapter.
8. Give examples of the three different ways the LIST command can be used.
9. What does the SAVE command do?
10. When is the NEW command used? What does it do?

SECTION II

Getting Started with BASIC

Outline

Introduction
Data Types
Constants
   Numeric Constants
   Character String Constants
Variables
   Numeric Variables
   Character String Variables

Reserved Words
Line Numbers
Learning Check
Elementary BASIC Statements
   The REM Statement
   The Assignment Statement
   The PRINT Statement
   The END Statement
Learning Check

Comprehensive Programming
   Problem
   Problem Definition
   Solution Design
   The Program
Summary Points
Review Questions
Debugging Exercises
Additional Programming Problems

Introduction

In this section, you will learn how to write simple BASIC programs, including those that perform mathematical operations. Four BASIC statements are covered: REM, assignment, PRINT, and END. These statements will build a strong foundation for future programming, so it is important that you understand clearly how to use them.

Data Types

Two general types of data values are used within a program: numeric and string. BASIC enables the programmer to use these data types in two different ways, as constants or as variables. The following discussion clarifies the uses of these data types and the differences between them.

Constants

CONSTANT
A value that cannot change during program execution.

Constants are values that do not change during the execution of a program. There are two types of constants: numeric and character string.

Numeric Constants

A numeric constant is a number that is included in a BASIC statement (other than line numbers, which are discussed later). Numeric constants can be represented as real or as integer numbers.

A real constant is a number with a decimal part. The following are valid real constants:

```
   6.0      6.782
    .95     0.58
 -7.302   -0.09
```

Very small or very large numbers can be represented in scientific notation (also called exponential notation), which has the following form: $\pm x.xxxxE\pm n$. The symbol $\pm$ represents the sign of the number, positive or negative. The E in the number represents the number 10, and the signed number following the E is the power to which 10 is raised. The symbol x.xxxx is called the mantissa, and it represents a number that may be carried to a maximum of eight decimal places. Table II-1 gives some examples of numbers in exponential notation.

An integer constant is a number with no decimal portion. The following numbers are examples of integer constants:

Table II-1
Examples of Exponential Notation

Decimal	Power Equivalent	Scientific Notation
53860	5.386×10^4	5.386E+04
0.00531	5.31×10^{-3}	5.31E−03
−658310	-6.5831×10^5	−6.5831E+05

```
29      123765
453     -25
204     -101
```

The following rules must be observed when using numbers in BASIC.

1. No commas can be embedded within numbers, because the computer interprets the digits before and after a comma as belonging to two separate numbers. For example, the computer would interpret 3,751 as the number 3 *and* the number 751. The valid form of the number is 3751.

2. If a number is negative, it must be preceded by a minus sign, as in the example −21.

3. If no sign is included, the number is assumed to be positive: 56 is the same as +56.

4. Fractions must be written in decimal form. For example, 2.75 is the correct representation for 2¾.

Character String Constants

A character string constant is a collection of symbols called alphanumeric characters. These can include any combination of letters, numbers, and special characters. The character string is enclosed in double quotation marks. The following are examples of character string constants:

"April 25, 1986"
"Friday night we went out for dinner."
"My name is Sam!"

Variables

VARIABLE
A storage location whose contents can change during program execution.

Values that can change during the execution of a program are **variables.** Variable names can be of any length, but the IBM PC recognizes only the first 40 characters of a name. The name must begin with a letter, followed by letters, numbers and a decimal point, with no embedded blanks. There are two types of variables, numeric and string, as explained in the following paragraphs.

Table II-2
Valid Numeric and String Variable Names

Numeric	String
SUM (Real)	HEADING$
D6E7% (Integer)	DAY$
M1% (Integer)	M1$
AMT (Real)	NME$

Numeric Variables

A numeric variable is used to store a number that is either supplied to the computer by the programmer or internally calculated during program execution. As with numeric constants, there are both integer and real numeric variables. Integer variable names have a percent sign (%) as the last character. Some examples of integer variable names are EMP%, PAY%, and X%. Real variable names do not have to end with a special character GROSSPAY, RTE, and PRCNT are all real variables. It is possible to assign an integer value to a real variable, however, because the computer can convert the integer to a real number without changing its value. For example, the integer 17 can be assigned to the real variable name NMBR because it can be changed to the real number 17.0.

Character String Variables

A character string variable is used to store a character string, such as a name, an address, or a social security number. A string variable name must be terminated with a dollar sign($). Table II-2 shows valid numeric and character string variable names.

Reserved Words

RESERVED WORD
A word that has a specific meaning to the BASIC system and therefore cannot be used as a variable name.

Certain words have specific meanings in the BASIC language. These are called **reserved words,** and they cannot be used as variable names. Table II-3 lists all the reserved words in PC BASIC.

Line Numbers

INDIRECT MODE
The mode in which BASIC statements are not executed until the RUN command is given. The statements must have line numbers.

As mentioned earlier, BASIC commands usually are executed in immediate or direct mode. BASIC statements, or instructions, can be executed in either direct mode or **indirect mode.** In indirect mode, the statements are executed until the RUN command is given. **Line numbers** tell the computer that the statements

Table II-3
Reserved Words in BASIC

ABS	EOF	LPRINT	RIGHT$
AND	EQV	LSET	RND
ASC	ERASE	MERGE	RSET
ATN	ERL	MID$	RUN
AUTO	ERR	MKD$	SAVE
BEEP	ERROR	MKI$	SCREEN
BLOAD	EXP	MKS$	SGN
BSAVE	FIELD	MOD	SIN
CALL	FILES	MOTOR	SOUND
CDBL	FIX	NAME	SPACE$
CHAIN	FN*xxxxx*	NEW	SPC(
CHR$	FOR	NEXT	SQR
CINT	FRE	NOT	STEP
CIRCLE	GET	OCT$	STICK
CLEAR	GOSUB	OFF	STOP
CLOSE	GOTO	ON	STR$
CLS	HEX$	OPEN	STRIG
COLOR	IF	OPTION	STRING$
COM	IMP	OR	SWAP
COMMON	INKEY$	OUT	SYSTEM
CONT	INP	PAINT	TAB(
COS	INPUT	PEEK	TAN
CSNG	INPUT#	PEN	THEN
CSRLIN	INPUT$	PLAY	TIME$
CVD	INSTR	POINT	TO
CVI	INT	POKE	TROFF
CVS	KEY	POS	TRON
DATA	KILL	PRESET	USING
DATE$	LEFT$	PRINT	USR
DEF	LEN	PRINT#	VAL
DEFDBL	LET	PSET	VARPTR
DEFINT	LINE	PUT	VARPTR$
DEFSNG	LIST	RANDOMIZE	WAIT
DEFSTR	LLIST	READ	WEND
DELETE	LOAD	REM	WHILE
DIM	LOC	RENUM	WIDTH
DRAW	LOCATE	RESET	WRITE
EDIT	LOF	RESTORE	WRITE#
ELSE	LOG	RESUME	XOR
END	LPOS	RETURN	

LINE NUMBER
A number preceding a BASIC statement which is used to reference the statement and determine its order of execution.

following them are to be executed in indirect mode. Therefore, the computer does not execute numbered statements until it is instructed to do so.

Line numbers determine the sequence of execution of BASIC statements. They also are used as reference points for branching and editing (which are discussed later). Figure II-1 gives an example of a program using line numbers.

Line numbers must be integers between 0 and 65529. No commas or embedded spaces can be included in a line number. Line numbers do not have to be in increments of 1. In fact, it is best to use increments of 10 or 20, in order to allow for insertion of lines at a later time if necessary. Here is a simple example:

```
60 LET NUMBER = 10
70 PRINT NUMBER,NUMBER1
```

If you determine later that a line has been omitted, you can enter it out of sequence as shown here:

```
60 LET NUMBER = 10
70 PRINT NUMBER,NUMBER1
65 LET NUMBER1 = 11
```

When this program segment is listed, the lines are rearranged in their numeric order.

If you find that you have made an error on a line, simply retype the line number and the correct BASIC statement. This procedure corrects the error because, if two lines are entered with the same line number, the computer saves and executes only the most recently typed one. To demonstrate this fact, assume that line 160 should print SUM, but the following was typed instead:

```
160 PRINT SUN
```

Figure II-1
Program Showing Use of Line Numbers

```
10 REM * * * THIS PROGRAM ADDS TWO NUMBERS * * *
20 LET A = 9
30 LET D1 = 4
40 LET P3 = A + D1
50 PRINT "THE ANSWER IS ";P3
99 END
```

```
RUN
THE ANSWER IS  13
```

SECTION II: GETTING STARTED WITH BASIC   B-25

To correct this, simply retype line 160 as follows:

```
160 PRINT SUM
```

The computer discards the current line 160 and replaces it with the newest version of line 160.

Learning Check

1. Real numbers are numbers that do not include a decimal portion. True or false?

2. Which of the following are valid real variable names?
   a. CX   b. AA$ c. TOM%

3. How would you write the following in exponential notation?
   a. 73.92   b. 0.00010   c. 93240

4. Name the two ways numeric and character strings can be used in BASIC.

5. What are the two main purposes of line numbers?

Answers

1. false 2. a 3a. 7.392E-1 3b. 1.0E-4 3c. 9.3240E+4 4. Constants and variables 5. Line numbers tell the computer the order in which to execute program statements. They also tell the computer that the following statements are to be executed in indirect mode.

Elementary BASIC Statements

BASIC statements are composed of programming command words (special words recognized by the BASIC system) and elements of the language: constants, numeric and string variables, and operators. A BASIC program is a sequence of statements which tells the computer how to solve a problem. Figure II-2 is an example. This program calculates the gross pay of an employee whose wage rate is $4.50 an hour and who has worked 40 hours. We will now turn our attention to four elementary BASIC statements: REM, LET, PRINT, and END.

The REM Statement

DOCUMENTATION
Comments that explain a program to people; documentation is ignored by the computer.

REM, short for REMark, is a statement that provides information for the programmer or anyone else reading the program. It is ignored by the computer; in other words, it is a nonexecutable statement. This information is referred to as **documentation,** and its function is to explain the purpose of the program, what the variable names represent, or any special instructions for the benefit of human

**Figure II-2
Gross Pay Program**

```
10 REM * * * THIS PROGRAM COMPUTES AN * * *
20 REM * * * EMPLOYEE'S GROSS PAY.     * * *
30 REM
40 LET RTE = 4.5
50 LET HOURS = 40
60 LET PAY = RTE * HOURS
70 PRINT "GROSS PAY = $ ";PAY
99 END
```

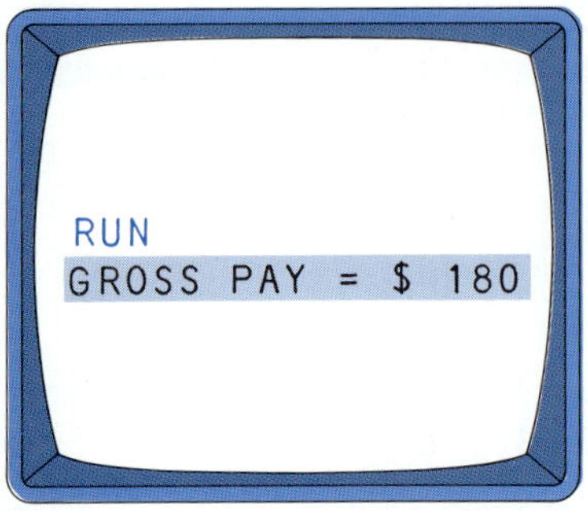

```
RUN
GROSS PAY = $ 180
```

readers. Because REM statements do not affect program execution, they can be placed anywhere in the program. The only restriction is that the statement must begin with the reserved word REM.

The format for the REM statement is as follows:

line# REM comment

The comment can be any statement that the programmer regards as appropriate documentation. Figure II-3 is a sample program that uses the REM statement. Lines 10 and 20 describe the purpose of the program. Lines 30 through 70 explain the major variables that are used in the program. These lines are helpful to a reader who is not the original programmer. Notice that line 80 contains no comment after the REM statement. This statement makes the program listing easier to read by separating the opening remarks from the executable statements listed later in the program.

Notice the asterisks that surround the descriptive comments. Although this device is simply a matter of personal taste, many programmers use asterisks to separate comments from the rest of the program. This technique allows the REM statement to be identified easily when the programmer is looking through long program listings.

The Assignment Statement

**ASSIGNMENT STATEMENT
A statement that causes a value to be stored in a variable.**

The LET Statement is an **assignment statement**—that is, a statement that stores a value in the memory location allotted to the specified variable. In a flowchart, an assignment statement is illustrated by a processing symbol (▢). The general format of the LET statement is as follows:

line# LET variable = expression

```
10   REM * * * THE PURPOSE OF THIS PROGRAM IS     * * *
20   REM * * * TO COMPUTE AN AVERAGE TEST SCORE   * * *
30   REM * * * MAJOR VARIABLES:                   * * *
40   REM * * *    FTEST    FIRST TEST SCORE       * * *
50   REM * * *    STEST    SECOND TEST SCORE      * * *
60   REM * * *    TTEST    THIRD TEST SCORE       * * *
70   REM * * *    AV       AVERAGE                * * *
80   REM
90   LET FTEST = 89
100  LET STEST = 85
110  LET TTEST = 78
120  LET AV = (FTEST + STEST + TTEST) / 3
130  PRINT "AVERAGE ",AV
999  END
```

```
RUN
AVERAGE         84
```

Figure II-3
Program Showing Use of the REM Statement

The variable can be a numeric or string variable. If it is a numeric variable, the expression can be a numeric constant, an arithmetic formula, or another numeric variable. If the variable is a string variable, the expression can be either a string constant or another string variable.

The LET statement can be used to assign values to numeric or string variables directly, or to assign the results of a calculation to a numeric variable. In either case, the expression on the right side of the equal sign is assigned to the variable on the left side. This operation causes the value of the expression to be placed in the memory location identified by the variable name on the left side of the LET statement.

In Figure II-3, lines 90 through 110 assign three numeric constants to three numeric variables. Line 120 assigns the result of an arithmetic calculation to the numeric variable AV, which represents the average of the three scores. Table II-4 shows some valid and invalid examples of the LET statements.

The use of the reserved word LET is optional. Therefore, the following two lines are equivalent:

```
10 LET X = A + B
10      X = A + B
```

For simplicity's sake, we will discontinue using the LET in programs after this chapter.

Table II-4
Valid and Invalid LET Statements

```
INVALID                 VALID
LET 8 + B = X           LET X = 8 + B
LET T$ = A              LET T$ = A$
LET B$ = DON            LET B$ = "DON"
LET X = "PAUL"          LET X = 34
LET L + M = K           LET K = L + M
```

Arithmetic Expressions. In BASIC, arithmetic expressions are composed of constants, numeric variables, and arithmetic operators. Table II-5 shows the arithmetic operators that can be used.

Some examples of valid arithmetic expressions in assignment statements are shown here:

```
10 LET VOLUME = LNGTH * WDTH * HGHT
20 LET AREA = (BASE * HGHT) / 2
30 LET SUM = A + 7
```

HIERARCHY OF OPERATIONS
The order in which arithmetic operations are performed. In BASIC the order is: (1) anything in parentheses, (2) exponentiation, (3) multiplication and division, and (4) addition and subtraction.

Hierarchy of Operations. When more than one operation is to be performed within an arithmetic expression, the computer follows a **hierarchy,** or priority, **of operations.** If parentheses are present in an expression, as they are in line 20 of the preceding example, the operation within the parentheses is performed first. If parentheses are nested—that is, if one set of parentheses is inside another—the operation in the innermost set of parentheses is performed first. Thus, in the following expression, the first operation to be performed is to add 2 to the value in Y:

$$30 * (8 - 5 / (2 + Y) * 6)$$

In the absence of parentheses, operations are performed according to the rules of priority shown in Table II-6. Operations with high priority are performed before operations with lower priority (subject to parentheses). If more than one operation is to be performed at the same level, as in the following expression, the computer evaluates them from left to right:

Table II-5
BASIC Arithmetic Symbols

BASIC Arithmetic Operation Symbol	Operation	Arithmetic Example	BASIC Expression
+	Addition	A + B	A + B
−	Subtraction	A − B	A − B
*	Multiplication	A × B	A * B
/	Division	A ÷ B	A / B
^	Exponentiation	A^B	A ^ B

**Table II-6
Rules of Priority**

Priority	Operation	Symbol
First	Exponentiation	^
Second	Multiplication or division	*, /
Third	Addition or subtraction	+, −

```
5 * 4 / 2
```

In this example, the 5 would be multiplied by 4, and then the result, 20, would be divided by 2. The answer is 10.

The following are more examples of these hierarchical rules:

Statement	Computer Evaluation
1. Y = 2 * 5 + 1	First: 2 * 5 = 10 Second: 10 + 1 = 11 Result: Y = 11
2. Y = 2 * (5 + 1)	First: 5 + 1 = 6 Second: 2 * 6 = 12 Result: Y = 12
3. Y = (3 + (6 + 2) /4) + 10 ^ 2	First: 6 + 2 = 8 Second: 8 / 4 = 2 Third: 3 + 2 = 5 Fourth: 10 ^ 2 = 100 Fifth: 5 + 100 = 105 Result: Y = 105

Two operators cannot be placed next to each other. For example, the expression P/−X is invalid, because parentheses should be used to separate the operators. Thus, P/(−X) is valid.

The PRINT Statement

The PRINT statement is used to print or display the results of computer processing. It also permits formatting, or arranging, of output. The PRINT statement can take several forms, depending on the output required. In a flowchart, a PRINT statement is illustrated by the input/output symbol (▱). The general format of the PRINT statement is as shown here:

$$\text{line\# PRINT} \begin{cases} \text{variables} \\ \text{literals} \\ \text{arithmetic expressions} \\ \text{any combination of the above} \end{cases}$$

If more than one item is included in the PRINT statement, the items are separated by commas. These commas also are used to format or arrange the output; this topic is discussed in detail in the next chapter. For now, it is sufficient to know that the commas automatically space the items across the output line.

Printing the Values of Variables. We can tell the computer to print values assigned to storage locations by using the reserved word PRINT with the variables listed after it:

```
100 PRINT AMOUNT,DAY,YEAR
```

Printing has no effect on the contents of the storage location. The PRINT statement only gets the value of a variable and prints it to the monitor screen.

LITERAL
An expression in a PRINT statement which contains any combination of letters, numbers, and/or special characters.

Printing Literals. A **literal** is an expression consisting of alphabetic, numeric, or special characters, or a combination of any of these. It is essentially the same as a constant, but the term *literal* is applied to constants used in PRINT statements. There are two types: character string literals and numeric literals.

A character string literal is a group of letters, numbers, or special characters enclosed in quotation marks. Whatever is inside the quotation marks is printed. For example,

```
10 PRINT "EXAMPLES$%#"
```

would appear on the screen as

```
EXAMPLES$%#
```

Note that the quotation marks are not printed.

Literals can be used to print headings in output. To print column headings, for example, put each heading in quotation marks and separate them with commas:

```
50 PRINT "ITEM","PRICE","QUANTITY"
```

When line 50 is executed, the following output appears:

```
ITEM     PRICE    QUANTITY
```

Numeric literals are numbers placed within the PRINT statement which are printed in the output. They do not have to be enclosed in quotation marks. For example, the statement

```
40 PRINT 100
```

prints the following:

```
100
```

Printing the Values of Expressions. The computer can print not only the values of literals and variables, but also the values of arithmetic expressions. Consider the following program segment:

```
50 LET X = 15.0
60 LET Y = 26.0
70 PRINT (X + Y) / 2,X / Y
```

The computer evaluates each expression in line 70, according to the hierarchy of operations, and then prints the result:

```
20.5     .5769231
```

If the expression has an extremely large or small positive or negative value, the computer may print it in exponential notation.

Printing Blank Lines. A blank line in output makes the output more readable, and can be achieved by using a PRINT statement alone:

```
100 PRINT
```

To skip more than one line, simply include more than one such statement:

```
110 PRINT
120 PRINT
```

The END Statement

The END statement instructs the computer to stop program execution. In a flowchart, it is indicated by the termination symbol (⌐). The general format of the END statement is as follows:

line# END

To make the END statement readily identifiable, many programmers give it a line number of all 9's, such as 999. All programs in this supplement follow this practice.

Comprehensive Programming Problem

Problem Definition

Smith's Warehouse needs a program to calculate its monthly ending inventory and the value of that inventory. Smith's has provided you with the following inventory data:

Learning Check

1. When a variable is printed, the contents of that variable's storage location are changed. True or false?
2. The _____ statement causes the computer to stop program execution.
3. What is documentation? What is the BASIC statement used for internal documentation?
4. List the hierarchy of operations in BASIC.
5. A(n) _____ is an expression consisting of any combination of letters, numbers, or special characters.

Answers

1. false 2. END 3. Documentation consists of REM statements placed in a program to explain the program or give instructions to humans. 4. Parentheses; exponentiation; multiplication and division; addition and subtraction. 5. literal

---

Beginning inventory = 430 units
Receipts = 86 units
Orders issued = 112 units
Cost per unit = $11.50

The program should produce a report that displays the beginning inventory, receipts, orders issued, ending inventory, and the value of the ending inventory.

The input and output for the program are easily seen. The input is simply the data given, and the output consists of three of the input values, plus two calculated values: the ending inventory and its value. Because the output is in the form of a report, an appropriate heading also should be displayed. The processing requires a formula to calculate the ending inventory:

Ending inventory = Beginning inventory + Receipts − Orders issued

From the result, we can calculate the value of the ending inventory using the following formula:

Value of ending inventory = Ending inventory × Cost per unit

With the input, processing, and output defined, we must now design a solution.

Solution Design

We now consider the general problem of producing the specified report, and see if it can be divided into subproblems. Keeping in mind the flow of data processing, we can determine at least three smaller tasks to be performed:

SECTION II: GETTING STARTED WITH BASIC   B-33

1. Access the given data.
2. Perform the calculations.
3. Display the report.

The second step involves two formulas, so this step can be further divided as follows:

2.A. Calculate the ending inventory.
2.B. Calculate the ending inventory value.

The report should contain a heading plus the requested values, so the third step can be divided as follows:

3.A. Display a heading.
3.B. Display the requested values.

All of the tasks listed are pictured in the structure chart in Figure II-4.

Next we need to consider what program steps will accomplish these tasks. A flowchart of a possible solution is shown in Figure II-5. In order to use the given data, we assign the input values to variables. Next, the two calculations are performed. A heading is then printed, followed by the needed values.

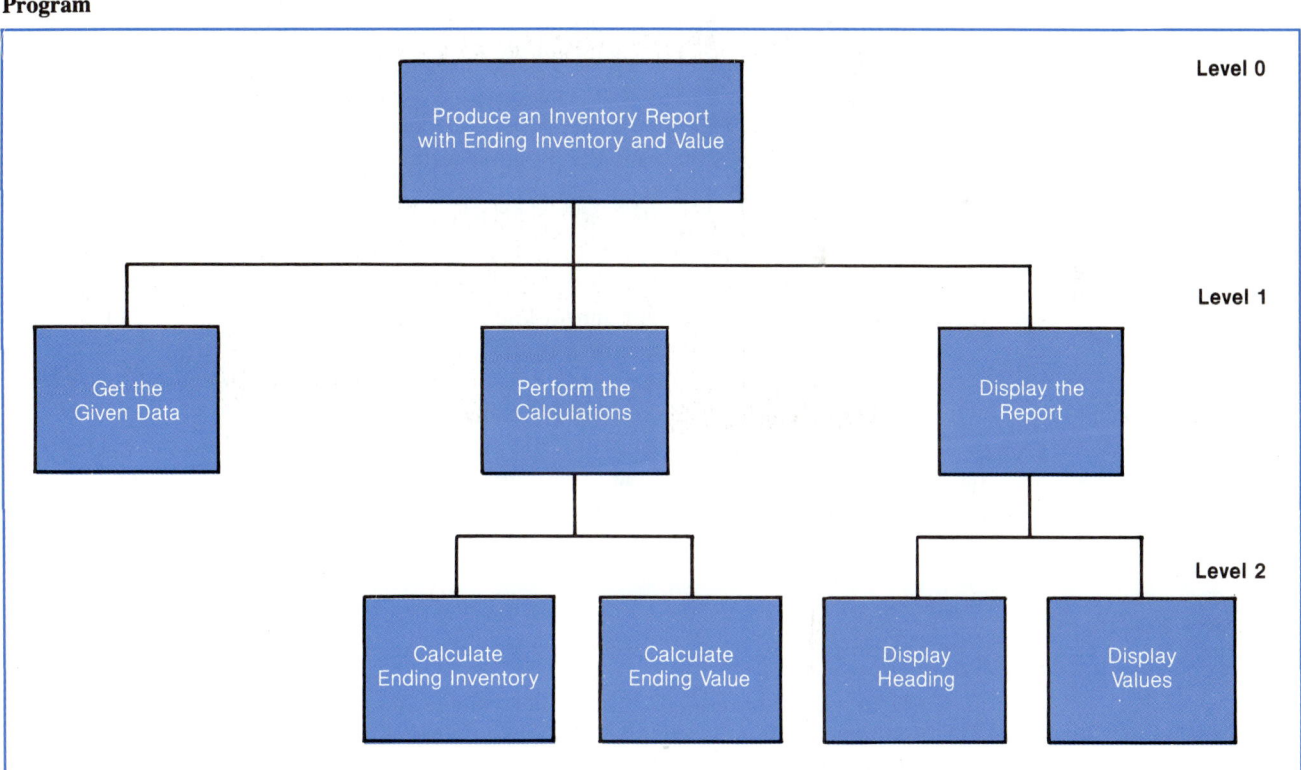

Figure II-4
Structure Chart for Inventory Program

```
                    ┌─────────────────────────────┐                    Level 0
                    │  Produce an Inventory Report│
                    │ with Ending Inventory and Value│
                    └──────────────┬──────────────┘
         ┌─────────────────────────┼─────────────────────────┐          Level 1
  ┌──────┴──────┐          ┌───────┴───────┐          ┌──────┴──────┐
  │   Get the   │          │  Perform the  │          │ Display the │
  │ Given Data  │          │  Calculations │          │   Report    │
  └─────────────┘          └───────┬───────┘          └──────┬──────┘
                          ┌────────┴────────┐        ┌───────┴────────┐ Level 2
                   ┌──────┴──────┐   ┌──────┴──────┐ ┌──────┴──────┐ ┌──────┴──────┐
                   │  Calculate  │   │  Calculate  │ │   Display   │ │   Display   │
                   │Ending Inventory│ │Ending Value │ │   Heading   │ │   Values    │
                   └─────────────┘   └─────────────┘ └─────────────┘ └─────────────┘
```

**Figure II-5
Flowchart for Inventory Program**

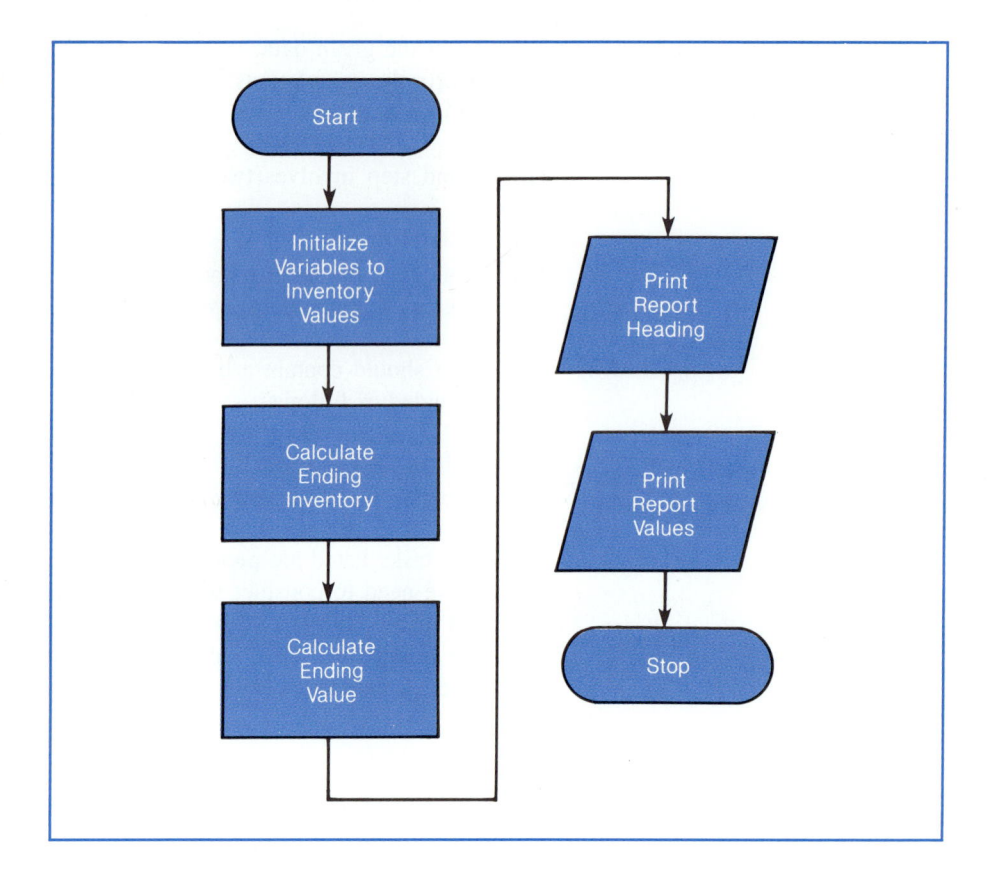

The Program

Figure II-6 shows the listing and output of this program. The REM statements in lines 10 through 110 document the purpose of the program and the contents of the variables. Lines 130, 190, and 230 give descriptions of the statements that follow them. Lines 140 through 170 assign the inventory values to variables. Line 200 calculates the ending inventory and assigns it to EINV. The result is then multiplied by the cost per unit in line 210. This operation yields the value of the ending inventory and assigns it to the variable VLUE.

Lines 240 and 250 improve the readability of the output by causing two blank lines to be printed before the next statement, line 260, prints the heading of the report. Each of the remaining PRINT statements prints a label for a field of output, followed by the field value. The program concludes with the END statement.

Summary Points

- Constants are values that do not change during program execution. A valid numeric constant is any integer or real number. Character strings are alphanumeric data enclosed in quotation marks.

```
10  REM * * * THIS PROGRAM COMPUTES THE MONTHLY ENDING INVENTORY * * *
20  REM * * * AND VALUE FOR SMITH'S WAREHOUSE, AND PRINTS AN IN-   * * *
30  REM * * * VENTORY REPORT.                                      * * *
40  REM
50  REM * * * MAJOR VARIABLES:                                     * * *
60  REM * * *     BINV      BEGINNING INVENTORY                    * * *
70  REM * * *     EINV      ENDING INVENTORY                       * * *
80  REM * * *     ISSUED    NUMBER OF UNITS ISSUED                 * * *
90  REM * * *     RECPT     NUMBER OF UNITS RECEIVED               * * *
100 REM * * *     CST       COST PER UNIT                          * * *
110 REM * * *     VLUE      ENDING INVENTORY VALUE                 * * *
120 REM
130 REM * * * ASSIGN THE INPUT VALUES TO THE VARIABLES.  * * *
140 LET BINV = 430
150 LET RECPT = 86
160 LET ISSUED = 112
170 LET CST = 11.5
180 REM
190 REM * * * CALCULATE THE ENDING INVENTORY AND VALUE.  * * *
200 LET EINV = BINV + RECPT - ISSUED
210 LET VLUE = EINV * CST
220 REM
230 REM * * * PRINT THE INVENTORY REPORT.  * * *
240 PRINT
250 PRINT
260 PRINT "INVENTORY STATUS"
270 PRINT
280 PRINT "BEGIN INV.",BINV
290 PRINT "RECEIPTS",RECPT
300 PRINT "ISSUED",ISSUED
310 PRINT "ENDING INV.",EINV
320 PRINT "VALUE   $",VLUE
999 END
```

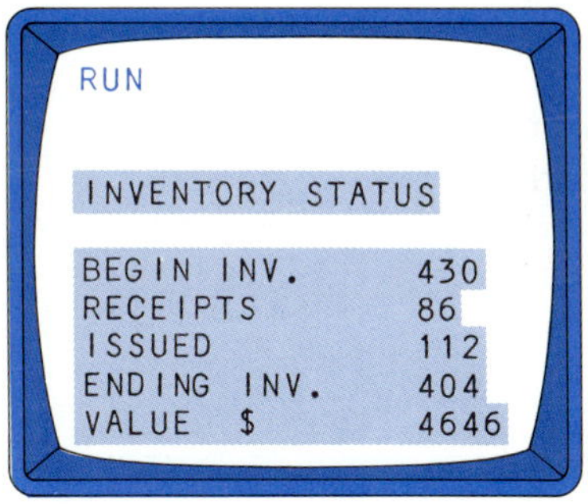

```
RUN

INVENTORY STATUS

BEGIN INV.      430
RECEIPTS         86
ISSUED          112
ENDING INV.     404
VALUE    $     4646
```

**Figure II-6
Inventory Program**

■ Variables are storage locations containing values that can change during program execution. Variable names are programmer-supplied names that identify specific variables. Numeric variables represent numbers. String variables contain character strings; their names are distinguished from those of numeric variables by the $ symbol used as the last character.

■ Line numbers serve to specify the order of execution of the program statements, and also to label statements so that they can be referenced.

■ Using line numbers in large increments, such as 10, permits easy insertion of new statements.

- A BASIC statement is composed of reserved words, constants, variables, and operators.
- REM statements document the program; they are not executed by the computer.
- The purpose of the LET statement is to assign values to variables. The computer evaluates the expression on the right side of the equal sign and stores its value in the variable on the left side of the equal sign.
- Arithmetic expressions are evaluated according to a hierarchy of operations: (1) operations in parentheses, (2) exponentiation, (3) multiplication or division, and (4) addition or subtraction. Multiple operations at the same level are evaluated from left to right.
- The PRINT statement prints or displays the results of processing. It can be used to print the values of variables, literals, arithmetic expressions, or a combination of these.
- The END statement causes program execution to stop and is the last statement executed.

Review Questions

1. What are the two main purposes of line numbers?
2. What is a constant? Name two types of constants.
3. What are numbers called which do not have a decimal portion?
4. What is alphanumeric data?
5. What is the name of a storage location that contains a value that can change during program execution?
6. What are the two types of variables?
7. What is the purpose of the REM statement?
8. What purpose does the LET statement perform?
9. What is the hierarchy of operations?
10. Define a literal, and give three examples.

Debugging Exercises

Examine the following programs and correct any programming errors.

1.
```
10 REM THIS PROGRAM PRINTS
20 A NAME AND AGE OF A PERSON.
30 REM
40 LET A = 21
50 LET N$ = STACY
60 PRINT N$,A
99 END
```

2.  ```
    10 REM *** THIS PROGRAM CALCULATES    ***
    20 REM *** THE AVERAGE OF TWO NUMBERS. ***
    30 LET A + 1 = 10
    40 LET B = 15
    50 LET X = A + B / 2
    60 PRINT X
    99 END
    ```

Additional Programming Problems

1. You want to know how much it would cost you to fly your plane to Hollywood for the Oscars. Hollywood is 2,040 nautical miles from your home. Your plane gets 14 miles per gallon, and you can get gas for $10.50 per gallon. Your output should have the following format:

DISTANCE   TOTAL COST
XXX $XXX.XX

2. A cassette tape with a list price of $8.98 is on sale for 15 percent off. Write a program that will calculate and output the sale price of the tape.

3. You own an apartment building with eight identical apartments, each having two rooms that need carpeting. One room has a length of twelve feet and a width of nine feet, and the other has a length of ten feet and a width of eight feet. The carpeting costs $9.50 a square yard. Write a program that will calculate the amount of carpeting needed to carpet the entire building, as well as the total cost of the carpeting. The output should include both figures. The area of a room is equal to the length multiplied by the width. Be sure to document your program.

4. Write a program that will print the date, time, and telephone number of the following telephone log entries:

8/9/90	8:09 am	(419) 353-7789
9/1/90	3:51 pm	(614) 366-6443
1/7/91	6:42 am	(313) 557-5864

The output should have the following format:

DATE   TIME   TELEPHONE #
X/X/X   X:XXxx   (XXX)XXX-XXXX

5. Write a program that converts 72 degrees Fahrenheit to its centigrade equivalent and prints the result, appropriately labeled. Use the formula $C = 5/9(F - 32)$, where C equals the degrees centigrade and F equals the degrees Fahrenheit.
    ```

SECTION III

Input and Output

Outline

Introduction
The INPUT Statement
   Printing Prompts for the User
The READ and DATA Statements
   The RESTORE Statement
Comparison of the Two Data
   Entry Methods
Learning Check

Clearing the Screen
Printing Results
   Print Zones and Commas
   Using Semicolons
   The TAB Function
   SPC
   LOCATE
   The PRINT USING Statement
Learning Check

Comprehensive Programming
   Problem
   Problem Definition
   Solution Design
   The Program
Summary Points
Review Questions
Debugging Exercises
Additional Programming Problems

Introduction

The first part of this section explains two methods of entering data to a program: the INPUT statement and the READ and DATA statements. The INPUT statement enables the user to enter data while the program is running. When the READ and DATA statements are used, the data is entered as part of the program itself.

The remainder of the section discusses ways of printing program output so that it is attractive and easy to read. It also explains how to print output in table form.

The INPUT Statement

In many programming situations, the data changes each time the program is executed. For example, think of a program that calculates the gas mileage for your car. Each time you run this program, you need to enter new values for the number of miles traveled and the amount of gas used. If such a program used assignment statements to assign these values to variables, the statements would have to be rewritten every time you wanted to calculate your gas mileage. A more practical approach to this programming problem is to use the INPUT statement.

The INPUT statement enables the user to enter data at the keyboard while the program is executing. The format of the INPUT statement is as follows:

line# INPUT variable1[,variable2,...]

Brackets ([]) indicate that the item enclosed is optional. In this statement, for example, it is not necessary to specify more than one variable.

The following are all valid INPUT statements:

```
110 INPUT STUDENT$,GPA,YR
120 INPUT ADDRESS$
130 INPUT PAY,TAX,NETPAY
```

The following are examples of invalid INPUT statements:

```
180 INPUT CITY$ ST$              (No comma separating variables)
INPUT BEANS,CARROTS,CELERY       (No line number)
240 TABLES,INPUT CHAIRS          (Reserved word INPUT in wrong place)
```

Note that one or more variables can be listed in a single INPUT statement. If there are two or more variables, their names must be separated by commas. The programmer places INPUT statements in a program at the point where user-entered data is needed, as determined by the logic of the program.

When a program is running and an INPUT statement is encountered, the program temporarily stops executing and a question mark appears on the monitor screen. The user then must enter the required data and press the Return key. After each value is stored in its corresponding variable, program execution continues at the next statement.

Figure III-1 shows a program that uses INPUT statements to enter the data needed to calculate the gas mileage. When this program is run, the computer encounters the INPUT statement in line 30, prints a question mark, and waits for the user to enter the distance traveled. Once the user has entered this value and pressed the Return key, the computer continues executing the program.

This process is repeated when the INPUT statement in line 40 is encountered. After the user has entered the amount of gas used and pressed the Return key, the program continues execution, calculates the mileage, and prints the results.

In Figure III-1 the INPUT statements request that a numeric value be entered by the user. If the user enters a character string instead, an error message is printed and program execution stops prematurely. If an INPUT statement requests a character string, the input need not be surrounded by quotation marks.

If an INPUT statement contains more than one variable, only one question mark appears on the screen when the program is run. In this case, the user needs to enter the correct number of data items and must separate them with commas. For example:

```
10 INPUT CITY$,ST$,ZIP
```

When this statement is executed, only one question mark appears on the monitor screen, but three data items must be entered by the user:

```
? CEDAR RAPIDS, IOWA, 12500
```

Figure III-1
Gas Mileage Program Using INPUT Statements

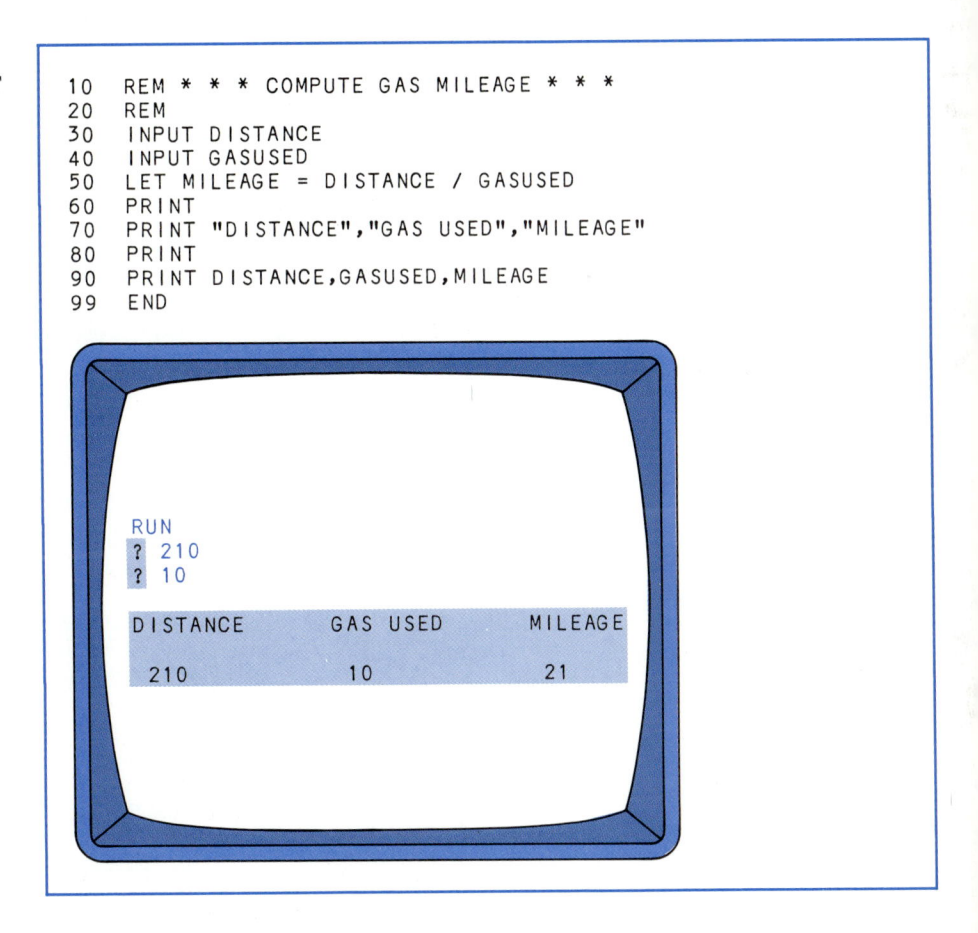

```
10  REM * * * COMPUTE GAS MILEAGE * * *
20  REM
30  INPUT DISTANCE
40  INPUT GASUSED
50  LET MILEAGE = DISTANCE / GASUSED
60  PRINT
70  PRINT "DISTANCE","GAS USED","MILEAGE"
80  PRINT
90  PRINT DISTANCE,GASUSED,MILEAGE
99  END
```

```
RUN
? 210
? 10

DISTANCE        GAS USED        MILEAGE
  210              10              21
```

The user must enter the exact number of data items needed by the INPUT statement and must include the commas. If fewer data items are entered, an error message is printed.

Printing Prompts for the User

In the previous example, when the INPUT statement was executed, only a question mark (?) appeared on the monitor screen when it was time for the user to enter data. The user was not told what type of data or how many data items to enter. Therefore, the programmer should also have included a **prompt** to tell the user what to enter.

A prompt can consist of a PRINT statement placed before the INPUT statement in the program, or it can be contained within the INPUT statement itself. Figure III-2 shows the program in Figure III-1 with prompts using PRINT statements preceding the INPUT statements.

Line 30 of the program prints the prompt:

```
30 PRINT "ENTER THE DISTANCE TRAVELED"
```

PROMPT
A message telling the user to enter data. Usually a prompt also specifies the type of data to be entered.

Figure III-2
Gas Mileage Program with Prompts

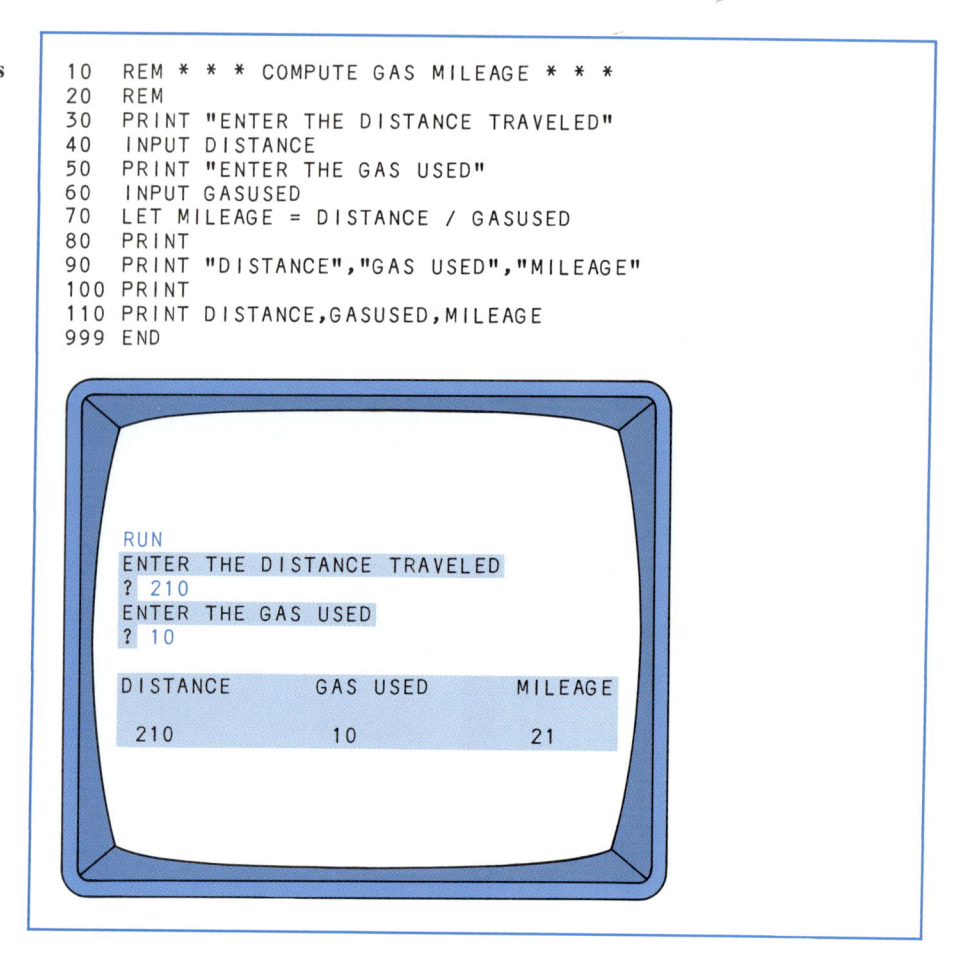

```
10  REM * * * COMPUTE GAS MILEAGE * * *
20  REM
30  PRINT "ENTER THE DISTANCE TRAVELED"
40  INPUT DISTANCE
50  PRINT "ENTER THE GAS USED"
60  INPUT GASUSED
70  LET MILEAGE = DISTANCE / GASUSED
80  PRINT
90  PRINT "DISTANCE","GAS USED","MILEAGE"
100 PRINT
110 PRINT DISTANCE,GASUSED,MILEAGE
999 END
```

```
RUN
ENTER THE DISTANCE TRAVELED
? 210
ENTER THE GAS USED
? 10

DISTANCE        GAS USED        MILEAGE

 210              10              21
```

SECTION III: INPUT AND OUTPUT

Line 40 is the INPUT statement:

```
40  INPUT DISTANCE
```

After line 40 is executed, the computer stops and waits for the user to enter the distance traveled. Then execution continues until the second INPUT statement is encountered. Again, the program waits for the user to enter the requested data and then continues execution.

The prompt can be included within the INPUT statement, using the following syntax:

line# INPUT prompt;variable1[,variable2,...]

Therefore, lines 30 and 40 of the program in Figure III-2 could be replaced with the following single statement:

```
30  INPUT "ENTER THE DISTANCE TRAVELED";DISTANCE
```

When the program is run with this modification, the question mark and the prompt appear on the same line as shown in Figure III-3. Using this format simplifies the writing of the program and makes the logic easy to follow.

Figure III-3
Gas Mileage Program with the INPUT Statement and Prompts

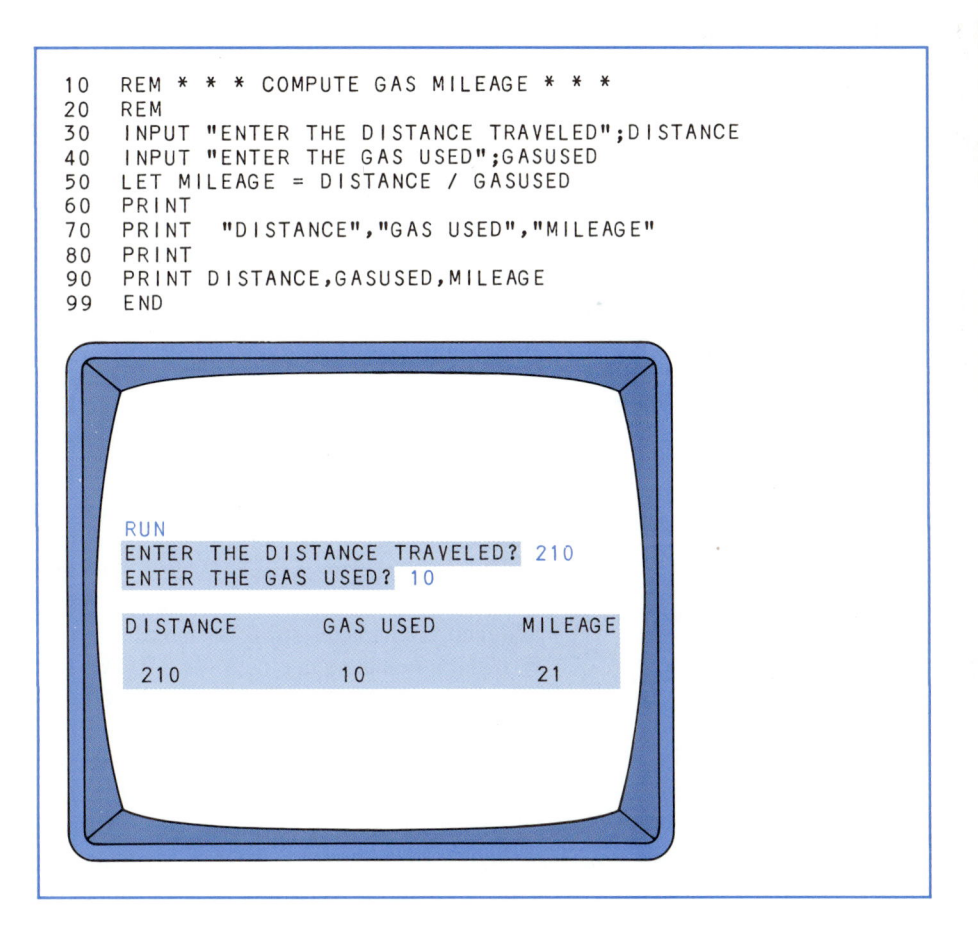

```
10  REM * * * COMPUTE GAS MILEAGE * * *
20  REM
30  INPUT "ENTER THE DISTANCE TRAVELED";DISTANCE
40  INPUT "ENTER THE GAS USED";GASUSED
50  LET MILEAGE = DISTANCE / GASUSED
60  PRINT
70  PRINT  "DISTANCE","GAS USED","MILEAGE"
80  PRINT
90  PRINT DISTANCE,GASUSED,MILEAGE
99  END
```

```
RUN
ENTER THE DISTANCE TRAVELED? 210
ENTER THE GAS USED? 10

DISTANCE        GAS USED        MILEAGE

 210              10              21
```

INQUIRY-AND-RESPONSE MODE (INTERACTIVE MODE)
A mode of operation in which the program asks a question and the user enters a response.

The method of data entry discussed in this section, in which the user enters a response to a prompt printed on the monitor screen, is called **inquiry-and-response, interactive mode,** or **conversational mode.**

The READ and DATA Statements

A second method of entering data to a BASIC program is to use the READ and DATA statements. The READ and DATA statements differ from the INPUT statement in that data values are not entered by the user during program execution, but instead are assigned by the programmer within the program itself.

The general formats for the READ and DATA statements are as follows:

line# READ variable1[,variable2,...]
line# DATA value1[,value2,...]

The values in the DATA statement are assigned to the corresponding variables in the READ statement. The following is a list of rules explaining the use of the READ and DATA statements.

■ A program can contain any number of READ and DATA statements.
■ The placement of READ statements is determined by the program logic. The programmer places these statements at the point where data needs to be read.
■ DATA statements are nonexecutable, and therefore can be placed anywhere in the program.
■ The computer collects the values from all the DATA statements in a program and places them in a single list, referred to as the **data list.** The values in this list are arranged in order, from the lowest to the highest line number and from left to right within a single DATA statement.
■ When two or more data values are placed in a single DATA statement, the values are separated by commas. Character strings require quotation marks only if they contain leading or trailing blanks, commas, or semicolons.
■ When the program encounters a READ statement, it goes to the data list and assigns the next value in that list to the corresponding variable in the READ statement. If the variable is numeric, the data value also must be numeric. If it is a character string variable, however, the computer allows a numeric value to be assigned to it. No computation can be performed with numbers that have been assigned to character string variables.
■ If there is inadequate data for a READ statement (that is, if there are no more data values in the data list), an OUT OF DATA error message appears and the program stops execution.
■ If there are more data values than variables, these extra data values remain unread. This condition does not result in an error message.

Figure III-4 shows a program segment that contains READ and DATA statements. When the computer executes this segment, it first encounters the READ

DATA LIST
A single list containing the values in all of the data statements in a program. The values appear in the list in the order in which they occur in the program.

**Figure III-4
READ/DATA Segment**

```
00100 READ NME$,S1,S2,S3
00110 READ NME$
00120 READ S1,S2
00130 READ S3
00140 DATA JACOBS,48
00150 DATA 60,53,GUINARD
00160 DATA 62,58
00170 DATA 54
```

statement in line 100. The statement instructs it to read four data values from the data list, and to assign these values to the variables NMNE$, S1, S2, and S3 respectively. After this task is completed, program execution continues at line 110, where the next value in the data list, GUINARD, is assigned to the variable NME$. This new value of NME$ replaces JACOBS, the previous value.

Note that the computer "remembers" where it is in the data list. Whenever it encounters another READ statement, it assigns the next value in the list to that variable. Study Figure III-4 to make certain you understand how the READ and DATA statements are used in reading data values.

Figure III-5 shows the sample gas mileage program rewritten using READ and DATA statements. Line 30 tells the computer to take the first value in the data list and put it in the storage location named DISTANCE. The statement also says to take the next value in the data list and assign it to the variable GASUSED. The program then goes on to calculate and print the gas mileage. To run this program again with different data, we would need to change line 100, the DATA line.

The RESTORE Statement

Usually, when READ and DATA statements are used, each data value is read only once. If it is necessary to use the same data value more than once, the RESTORE statement can be used. Consider the following program segment:

```
110 READ A,B
120 TT = A + A * B
130 RESTORE
140 READ C,D,E
150 SUM = C + D + E
160 DATA 44,790,1,,15,138
```

When line 110 of this program segment is executed, the value 44 is assigned to variable A and the value 790 is assigned to variable B. Normally, the next data value available to be read would be 1, but the RESTORE statement in line 130 returns the computer to the beginning of the data list. When line 140 is encountered, the value 44 will be read to variable C, 790 to variable D, and 1 to variable E.

Figure III-5
Gas Mileage Program Using READ and DATA Statements

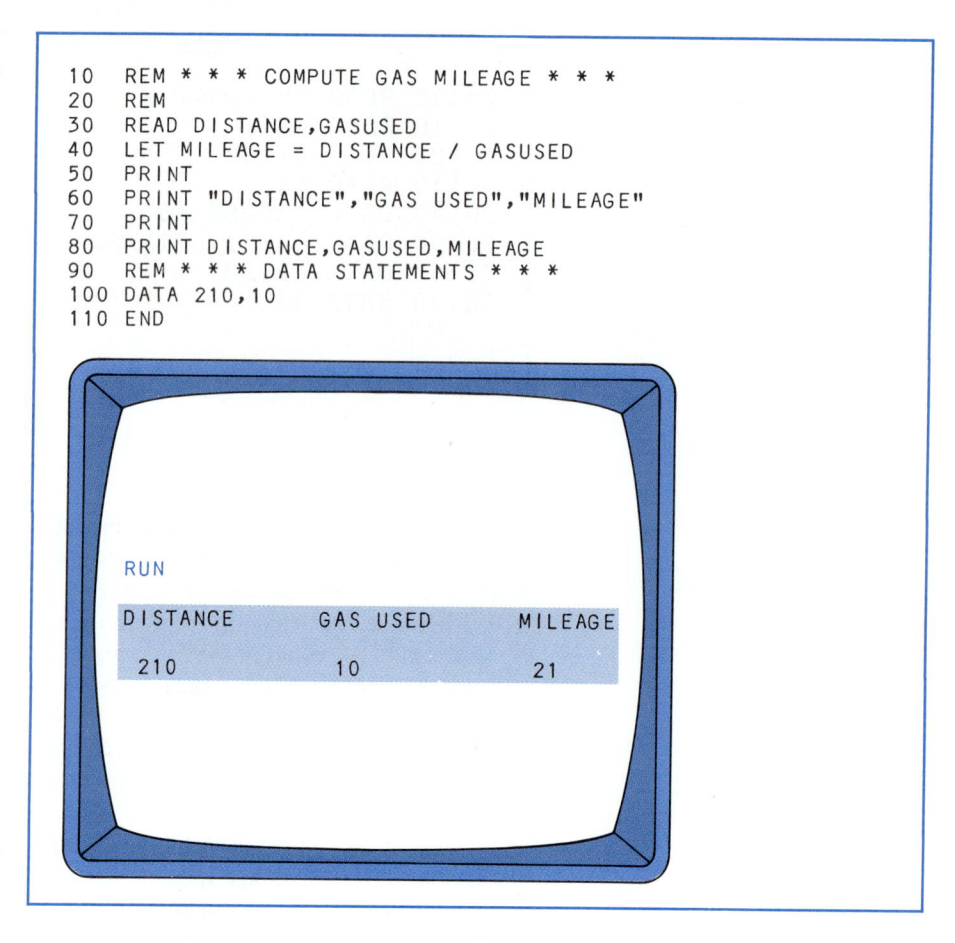

```
10   REM * * * COMPUTE GAS MILEAGE * * *
20   REM
30   READ DISTANCE,GASUSED
40   LET MILEAGE = DISTANCE / GASUSED
50   PRINT
60   PRINT "DISTANCE","GAS USED","MILEAGE"
70   PRINT
80   PRINT DISTANCE,GASUSED,MILEAGE
90   REM * * * DATA STATEMENTS * * *
100  DATA 210,10
110  END
```

```
RUN
DISTANCE        GAS USED         MILEAGE
  210              10               21
```

Comparison of the Two Data Entry Methods

The INPUT and the READ/DATA statements both can be used to enter data to BASIC programs. The relative advantages of the two methods depend on the application. Here are some general guidelines:

- The INPUT statement is ideal when data values change frequently, because it allows the data to be entered at the keyboard during program execution.
- The READ and DATA statements are well suited to programs that use large quantities of data, because the user does not have to enter a long list of data values during program execution, as would be necessary with the INPUT statement.
- The READ and DATA statements are most useful when data values are the same for each program execution. When the data values change, however, the program itself must be altered.

SECTION III: INPUT AND OUTPUT

> **Learning Check**
>
> 1. When data must be entered to a program while it is executing, a(n) _____ statement is used.
> 2. A(n) _____ is used to tell the user what kind of data to enter a program.
> 3. _____ statements contain the data values that will be assigned to the variables listed in a READ statement.
> 4. There must be a DATA statement immediately after each READ statement. True or false?
> 5. The _____ statement causes the next READ statement encountered to start at the beginning of the data list.
>
> **Answers**
>
> 1. INPUT 2. prompt 3. DATA 4. false. DATA statements can be anywhere within the program. 5. RESTORE

Clearing the Screen

User prompts and other program output should be as clear and attractive as possible. Before printing a user prompt, for example, you may want to clear the screen of any information previously displayed. On the IBM, the following statement clears the screen and places the cursor in the upper left corner of the screen:

    line# CLS

In a flowchart, the clear screen instruction is contained in an input/output symbol (▱).

Printing Results

As discussed in the previous chapter, the PRINT statement enables us to print the results of processing. When more than one item is to be printed on a line, a variety of methods can be used to control the spacing and format of the output.

Print Zones and Commas

The IBM screen consists of 2,000 print positions: 80 columns across and 25 rows down. The 80 columns are divided into five print zones, each containing 14 print positions (columns). The zones are divided as follows:

| Zone 1 | Zone 2 | Zone 3 | Zone 4 | Zone 5 |
| (1–14) | (15–28) | (29–42) | (43–56) | (57–80) |

Commas not only separate items within a PRINT statement, but also control the format of those items. A comma indicates that the next item to be printed will start at the beginning of the next empty print zone. The following example shows how this works:

```
10 READ NAM$,NUM,YEAR
20 PRINT NAM$,NUM,YEAR
30 DATA "JOHN",6,1968
```

The first item in the PRINT statement is printed at the beginning of the first print zone. The comma between NAM$ and NUM causes the computer to space over to the next unused print zone; then the value in NUM is printed. The second comma directs the computer to space over to the next zone (Zone 3) and print the value in YEAR. Thus the output is as follows:

```
JOHN          6             1968
```

If more items are listed in a PRINT statement than there are print zones in a line, the print zones of the next line also are used, starting with the first zone. Notice the output of the following example:

```
10 READ SEX$,AGE,CLASS$,MAJ$,HRS,GPA
20 PRINT SEX$,AGE,CLASS$,MAJ$,HRS,GPA
30 DATA M,19,JR,CS,18,2.5
```

RUN

```
M             19            JR            CS            18
2.5
```

If the value to be printed exceeds the width of the print zone, the entire value is printed, regardless of how many zones it occupies. The comma causes printing to continue in the next unused print zone, as shown in the following example:

```
10 LET SPOT$ = "BAGHDAD"
20 PRINT "YOUR NEXT DESTINATION WILL BE",SPOT$
```

ZONE 1   ZONE 2   ZONE 3

```
YOUR NEXT DESTINATION WILL BE           BAGHDAD
```

A print zone can be skipped by enclosing a space (the character blank) in quotation marks. This technique causes the entire zone to appear empty:

```
60 PRINT "NAME"," ","I.D.NUMBER"
```

SECTION III: INPUT AND OUTPUT

It is also possible to skip a zone by typing consecutive commas:

```
60 PRINT "NAME",,"I.D.NUMBER"
```

Both techniques cause the literal NAME to be printed in the first zone, the second zone to be blank, and the literal I.D. NUMBER to be printed in the third zone:

ZONE 1	ZONE 2	ZONE 3
NAME		I.D.NUMBER

If a comma appears after the last item in a PRINT statement, the output of the next PRINT statement encountered will begin at the next available print zone, as shown by the following statements and output:

```
10 READ NAM$,SEX$,VOICE$
20 PRINT NAM$,
30 PRINT SEX$,VOICE$
40 DATA "SHICOFF","M","TENOR"
99 END
```

RUN

| SHICOFF | M | TENOR |

Using Semicolons

Semicolons, like commas, can be used within a PRINT statement to control the format of printed output. The semicolon signals the computer to print the next item at the next available print *position*, rather than at the next print zone. In the following example, two strings in a PRINT statement are separated by a semicolon:

```
10 PRINT "JOHN";"DRAKE"
```

RUN

JOHNDRAKE

The first string is printed, and then the semicolon causes the next item to be printed in the next available print position, which is the next column.

To print these strings with a space between them, you can enclose a blank within the quotation marks of one of the strings:

```
10 PRINT "JOHN";" DRAKE"
```

RUN

JOHN DRAKE

A semicolon appearing after the *last* item in a PRINT statement prevents the output of the next PRINT statement from starting on a new line. Instead, the next item printed appears on the same line, at the next available print position:

```
10 PRINT "YVONNE DRAKE:";
20 PRINT 3567;" CHELSEA ST."

RUN

YVONNE DRAKE: 3567  CHELSEA ST.
```

The TAB Function

The comma and semicolon are easy to use, and many reports can be formatted in this fashion. There are times, however, when a report should be structured differently. The TAB function allows output to be printed in any column in an output line, thus providing the programmer greater flexibility in formatting printed output.

As with the comma and semicolon, one or more TAB functions are used within a PRINT statement. The general format of the TAB function is as follows:

TAB(expression)

The expression can be a numeric constant, a variable, or an arithmetic expression. When a TAB function is encountered in a PRINT statement, the computer spaces over to the column number indicated in the expression. The next variable value or literal found in the PRINT statement is printed starting in that column. The TAB prints blank spaces as it moves to the specified column, thereby erasing anything that was on the screen previously. The TAB function is separated from the items to be printed by semicolons. For example, the following statement causes the literal HELLO to be printed starting in column 10:

```
50 PRINT TAB(10);"HELLO";TAB(25);"GOODBYE"
```

Then, starting in column 25, the literal GOODBYE is printed.

The program in Figure III-6 illustrates the use of the TAB function. This program prints a simple table by using the TAB function to arrange the printed values in columns.

Note that the semicolon is used with the TAB function. If the comma is used instead, the computer uses the print zones by default, ignoring the columns specified in the parentheses. For example, if line 50 of the program in Figure III-6 had been

```
50 PRINT TAB(5),"ITEM";TAB(25),"GALLONS"
```

the output would have been as shown here:

SECTION III: INPUT AND OUTPUT

B-51

```
         INVENTORY REPORT
             ITEM
                              GALLONS

      ICE CREAM             50
      TOPPING               30
      CHERRIES              10
```

Figure III-6
Program Using the TAB Function

```
10   REM * * * INVENTORY REPORT * * *
20   REM
30   PRINT TAB (10);"INVENTORY REPORT"
40   PRINT
50   PRINT TAB(5);"ITEM";TAB(25);"GALLONS"
60   PRINT
70   READ ITEM$,QUANT
80   PRINT TAB(5);ITEM$;TAB(25);QUANT
90   READ ITEM$,QUANT
100  PRINT TAB(5);ITEM$;TAB(25);QUANT
110  READ ITEM$,QUANT
120  PRINT TAB(5);ITEM$;TAB(25);QUANT
130  REM
140  REM * * * DATA STATEMENTS * * *
150  DATA ICE CREAM,50,TOPPING,30,CHERRIES,10
999  END
```

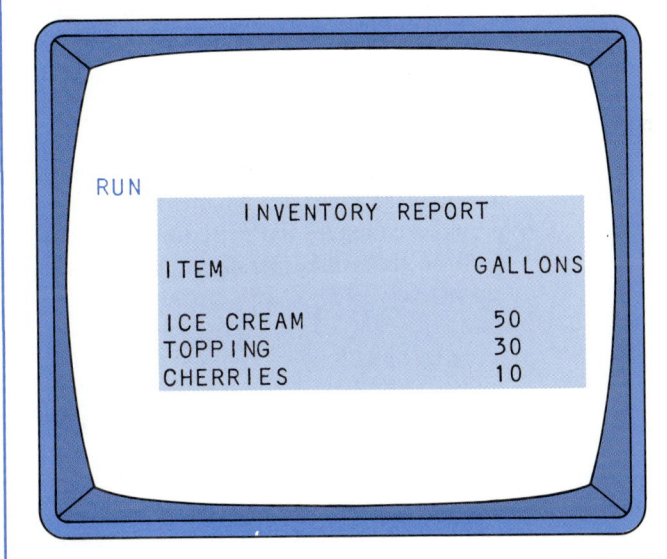

```
RUN
             INVENTORY REPORT

      ITEM                    GALLONS

      ICE CREAM                 50
      TOPPING                   30
      CHERRIES                  10
```

In this example, the computer spaced over five columns as indicated by the first TAB function, but when it found the comma following the parenthesis, it skipped over to the next print zone to print ITEM. The comma following the quotation marks after ITEM causes the computer to skip to the next available print zone, which begins at column 30. The next TAB function instructs it to skip to column 25, but it has already passed that column, so it goes to the *next* line and skips to column 25. Then it finds the comma after the parenthesis, which causes it to continue to column 30, where the next available print zone starts. It prints GAL-LONS starting in column 30. This is why the second heading, GALLONS, is not on the same line with ITEM in this output.

The TAB function can be used only to advance the print position from left to right; backspacing is not possible. Therefore, if more than one TAB function appears in a single PRINT statement, the column numbers specified should increase from left to right. When a TAB function specifies a column to the left of the current print position, the computer spaces to that column on the next line, as shown in the previous example. Another example will illustrate this point:

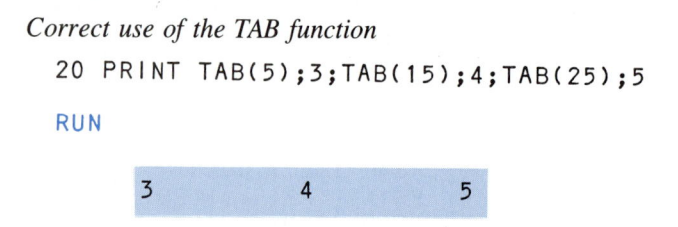

Correct use of the TAB function

```
20 PRINT TAB(5);3;TAB(15);4;TAB(25);5
```

RUN

```
    3         4         5
```

Incorrect use of the TAB function

```
20 PRINT TAB(25);3;TAB(15);4;TAB(5);5
```
RUN

```
                        3
              4
    5
```

As already mentioned, the column number of the TAB function can be expressed as a numeric constant, a numeric variable, or an arithmetic expression. All of our previous examples have used numeric constants. The following examples, which perform the same operations, use numeric variables and arithmetic expressions respectively.

```
10 Y = 25
20 X = 10
30 PRINT TAB(X);7;TAB(Y);"MONDAY"
```

RUN

```
    7              MONDAY
```

```
10 Y = 20
20 X = 15
30 PRINT TAB(X - 5);7;TAB(Y + 5);"MONDAY"
```
RUN

| 7 | MONDAY |

SPC

The SPC (space) function is similar to TAB in that it is used in controlling the printing of output. Instead of instructing the computer to print output in a specified column, however, it tells the computer how many spaces to advance beyond its current position before printing the output. Like the TAB function, the SPC function should be separated from other items in the PRINT statement by semicolons:

```
10 PRINT "WORD";SPC(10);"LETTER"
```
RUN

| WORD | LETTER |

When line 10 is executed, WORD is printed in columns 1 through 4. Then the computer leaves ten blank spaces between the end of WORD and the beginning of LETTER, so LETTER is printed starting in column 15.

Figure III-7 illustrates the difference between these two functions. When TAB is used, the output is printed in columns 5 and 10. With SPC, however, the output is printed in columns 5 and 15, because the SPC function spaces over ten columns from the last printed output (A) before printing B.

LOCATE

It is possible to specify where on the screen you want a message to be printed, or where you want to have an input value accepted. As we mentioned earlier, the display screen is divided into 2,000 positions, 80 columns across and 25 rows down. The LOCATE statement enables the user to specify the row and column in which to place the cursor.

The general format of the LOCATE statement is as follows:

line# LOCATE row,column

where the row is a number between 1 and 25, and the column is a number between 1 and 80. After a LOCATE statement has been executed, any subsequent input or output statement begins placing characters at the specified position.

Figure III-7
Program Segments Demonstrating the Difference Between TAB and SPC

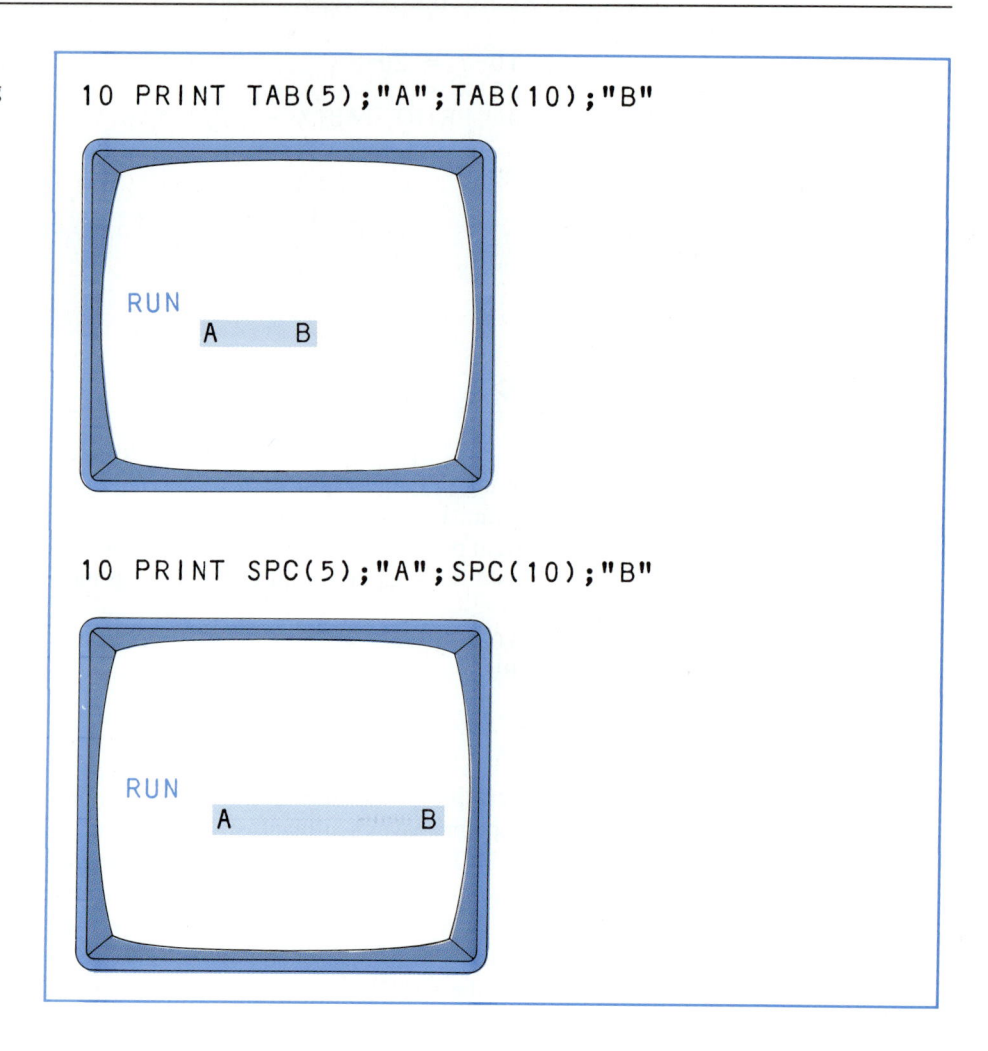

```
10 PRINT TAB(5);"A";TAB(10);"B"
```

```
RUN
    A    B
```

```
10 PRINT SPC(5);"A";SPC(10);"B"
```

```
RUN
     A          B
```

For example, suppose you want to print the message HAVE A NICE DAY in the center of the screen. The following statements would perform this task:

```
10 CLS
20 LOCATE 13,32
30 PRINT "HAVE A NICE DAY"
```

Line 10 clears the screen. Line 20 instructs the computer to move the cursor to row 13, column 32, thus causing the PRINT statement to begin printing in this specified position.

Normally, BASIC does not print text on line 25 because the KEY function display appears there. This display can be turned off by the command KEY OFF:

line# KEY OFF

This command enables you to print on line 25.

**Table III-1
Format Control Characters**

Character	Explanation
#	Numeric data; one symbol for each digit to be printed; zeroes are added to the left of the number to fill the field
$$	Two dollar signs cause the dollar sign to be floating, meaning that it will be in the first position before the number
\spaces\	This specifies the length of a string field to be 2 plus the number of spaces between the backslashes

The PRINT USING Statement

Another convenient feature for controlling output is the PRINT USING statement. This feature is especially useful when printing table headings or aligning columns of numbers. The general format of the PRINT USING statement is as follows:

line# PRINT USING ''format control characters''; expression list

The expression list consists of the string expressions or numeric expressions that are to be printed, separated by semicolons or commas. The format control characters are special formatting characters that determine the field and the format of the printed items. They must be enclosed by quotation marks. Table III-1 shows the most commonly used format control characters, which are explained in the remainder of this chapter.

String Expressions. When PRINT USING is used to print strings, the most commonly used formatting characters are as shown here:

\n spaces\

where n blank spaces are enclosed by the backslashes. This format specifies that 2+n characters from the string are to be printed. If the backslashes are types with no spaces, two characters are printed; if the backslashes are types with one space between them, three characters are printed, and so on. If the string is longer than the field, the extra characters are ignored. If the field is longer than the string, the string is left-justified in the field and padded with spaces on the right. For example:

```
10 A$ = "LOOK"
20 B$ = "OUT"
30 PRINT USING "\   \";A$;B$
40 PRINT USING "\  \";A$;B$
50 PRINT USING "\ \";A$;B$
RUN

LOOKOUT
LOOK OUT
LOOOUT
```

Line 30 creates a print field of four characters (the two backslashes plus the two spaces between). The string "LOOK" is four characters long, so it is printed in the field as is. The string "OUT" is only three characters long, however, so it is left-justified in the format field.

Line 40 creates a print field of five characters. Both strings are left-justified in the print field, but with this example you can see the padding at the end of the field. The string LOOK used only four characters, even though five characters were allotted in the format; thus it was left-justified and a blank was added at the right. This blank separates the string OUT from the string LOOK in the output.

The last example, line 50, allows only three characters to be printed. The string LOOK is longer, so when line 50 is executed, only the first three letters of LOOK are printed.

Numeric Expressions. When PRINT USING is used to print numbers, special characters can be used to format the numeric field. The most commonly used characters are the number sign and double dollar sign.

A number sign (#) is used to represent each digit position. Digit positions are always filled. If the number to be printed has fewer digits than the positions specified, the number is right-justified in the field and is preceded by spaces. A decimal point can be inserted at any position in the field. If the format string specifies that a digit is to precede the decimal point, a digit always is printed, even if it is 0. Numbers are rounded if necessary. The following examples illustrate these concepts:

Statement	Result	Reason
PRINT USING "####";78	78	More digit positions than digits.
PRINT USING "##.##";78	78.00	No decimal fraction specified.
PRINT USING "##.##";.78	0.78	No digits preceding the decimal.
PRINT USING "##.##";.788	0.79	Number rounded because there are more digits than specified positions following the decimal point.
PRINT USING "###";100.20	100	Number truncated because there are more digits than specified positions.

Another format character is the double dollar sign ($$), which causes a dollar sign to be printed to the immediate left of the formatted number. The $$ specifies two more digit positions, one of which is the dollar sign. Therefore, if you need to print a dollar value of four digits with a dollar sign, you would need only the double dollar sign and three number signs ($$###), as shown here:

Figure III-8
PRINT USING Example Program

```
10   REM * * * ILLUSTRATING PRINT USING * * *
20   REM
30   PRINT
40   PRINT USING "\        \             \      \";"ITEM","TOTAL"
50   PRINT USING "\       \            \        \";"PURCHASE","PRICE"
60   PRINT
70   READ A$,X
80   Y = X * .06
90   PRINT USING "\            \  $$##.##    $$#.##";A$,X
100  READ A$,X
110  Y = X * .06
120  PRINT USING "\            \  $$##.##    $$#.##";A$,X
130  READ A$,X
140  Y = X * .06
150  PRINT USING "\            \  $$##.##    $$#.##";A$,X
160  READ A$,X
170  Y = X * .06
180  PRINT USING "\            \  $$##.##    $$#.##";A$,X
190  READ A$,X
200  Y = X * .06
210  PRINT USING "\            \  $$##.##    $$#.##";A$,X
220  REM
230  REM * * * DATA STATEMENTS * * *
240  DATA TOASTER,27.50,BLENDER,18.45
250  DATA BLANKET,9.90,KNIVES,34.99,FAN,29.00
999  END
```

```
RUN

ITEM            TOTAL
PURCHASE        PRICE

TOASTER         $27.50
BLENDER         $18.45
BLANKET          $9.90
KNIVES          $34.99
FAN             $29.00
```

Statement	Result
PRINT USING "$$###.##";4563.78	$4563.78

Figure III-8 is a program that prints a table by implementing the PRINT USING statement.

Learning Check

1. The _____ function causes output to be printed in a column specified by the programmer.

2. A semicolon between items in a PRINT statement tells the computer to skip to the next available _____ to print the next item.

3. What output will the following statement produce? 110 PRINT "JOE IS";"NINETY".

4. When a PRINT statement ends with a comma or semicolon, the next value output begins _____.
   a. on the next line
   b. on the next page
   c. on the same line, if there is room

5. What would be the format used for printing a five-digit number, with a decimal point two positions to the left and with a dollar sign in front?

Answers

1. TAB 2. position 3. JOE ISNINETY 4. c 5. PRINT USING $$###.##

Comprehensive Programming Problem

Problem Definition

You are a loan officer for the local credit union. Your client, Ms. Rodgers, wants to borrow $70,000 to purchase a house. She wants to know how much her monthly payments will be. The annual interest rate for her loan will be 12 percent, and the term of the mortgage is 20 years. Because you must make this type of calculation often, you decide to write a program that reports the mortgage information and calculates payments for you.

The input for the problem consists of the given mortgage amount, interest rate, and term. The desired output is a report that lists this information along with the calculated monthly payment. To calculate the monthly payment from the given data, the program must determine the monthly interest rate, using the following formula:

Monthly interest rate = (Annual interest rate ÷ 100) ÷ 12.

The monthly interest rate then is used to calculate the mortgage multiplication factor:

SECTION III: INPUT AND OUTPUT   B-59

Mortgage multiplication factor = Monthly interest rate ÷
[(1 + Monthly interest rate) ^
(Years of term × 12) − 1] +
Monthly interest rate.

The monthly payments then can be calculated based on the following formula:

Monthly payment = Mortgage multiplication factor × Mortgage amount.

Solution Design

The general problem is to produce a mortgage loan report. The flow of data processing determines three smaller problems to solve:

1. Enter the given data.
2. Calculate the monthly payment.
3. Display the report.

Three formulas are involved in calculating the monthly payment, so the second step can be divided as follows:

2.A. Calculate the monthly interest rate.
2.B. Calculate the mortgage multiplication factor.
2.C. Calculate the monthly payment.

The display of the report also can be divided into smaller tasks:

3.A. Display a heading.
3.B. Display the report values.

The structure chart in Figure III-9 shows this refinement of the problem.
Next we decide what program steps are needed to perform these tasks, and the order in which the steps should be performed. Figure III-10 shows the flowchart for a possible solution. We will make this an interactive program, because it will be used with frequently changing values.
The first step is to clear the screen so that the user prompts can be seen clearly. Next, the input values are entered. The calculations are performed, and the screen is cleared again to place the report at the top of the screen. Finally the report is printed.

The Program

The program in Figure III-11 documents its major variables in lines 30 through 100. Line 120 clears the screen. Lines 130 through 150 ask the user for the needed

Figure III-9
Mortgage Program Structure Chart

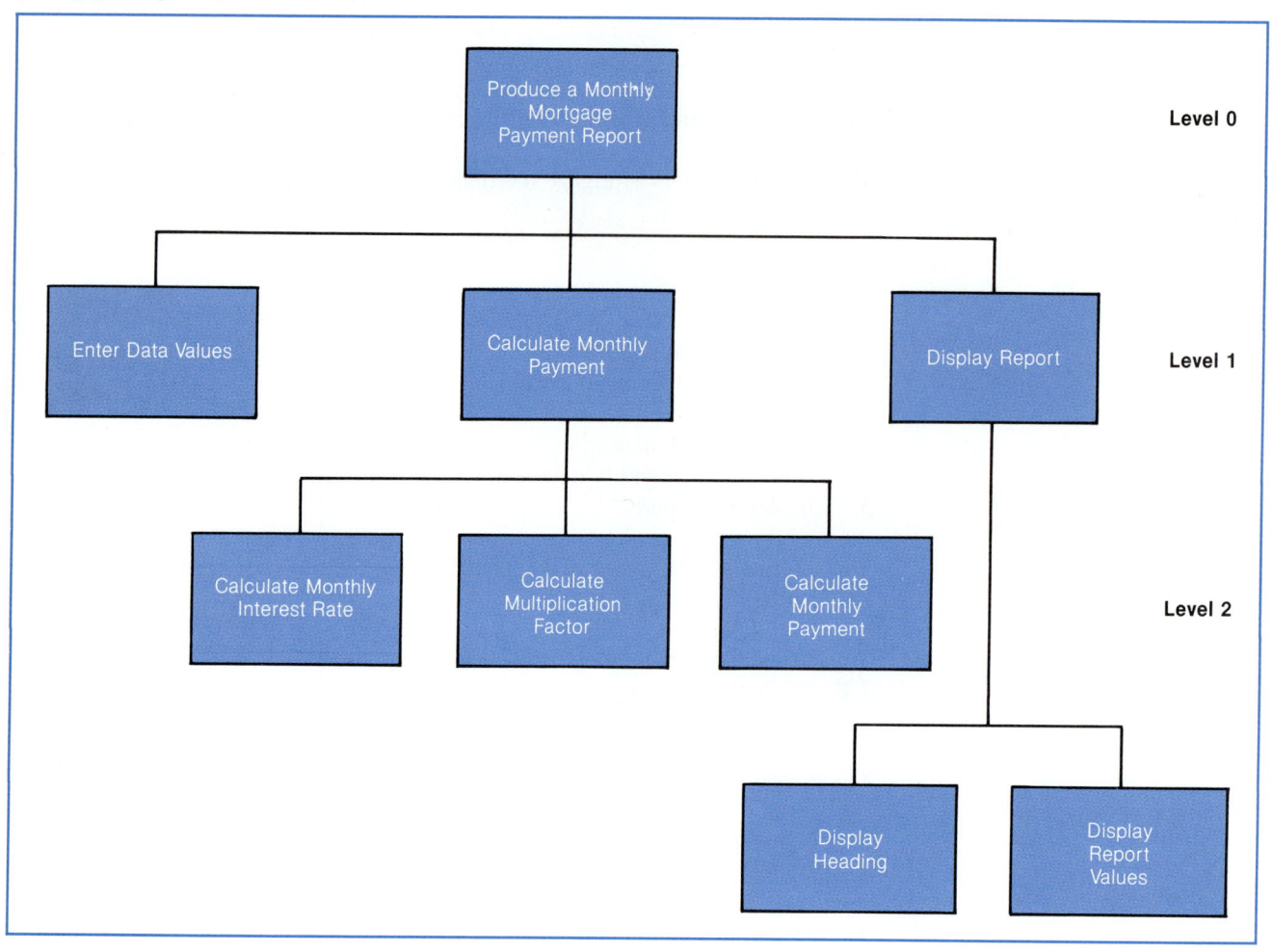

```
                    Produce a Monthly
                       Mortgage                                    Level 0
                    Payment Report
                           │
        ┌──────────────────┼──────────────────┐
        │                  │                  │
  Enter Data Values   Calculate Monthly   Display Report         Level 1
                         Payment
                            │
            ┌───────────────┼───────────────┐
            │               │               │
      Calculate Monthly  Calculate     Calculate                 Level 2
      Interest Rate    Multiplication   Monthly
                         Factor         Payment
                                           │
                                   ┌───────┴───────┐
                                   │               │
                                Display         Display
                                Heading         Report
                                                Values
```

data values, accept these values, and store them in the appropriate variables. The computer is then instructed to perform the calculations by lines 180 through 200. Line 230 again clears the screen to make room for the report. The heading and report information are indented to the second print zone by the commas in line 260 and lines 290 through 310.

Summary Points

■ The INPUT statement allows data to be entered at the keyboard during program execution. Each value entered is assigned to a corresponding variable in the INPUT statement. The variables must be separated by commas.

**Figure III-10
Mortgage Program Flowchart**

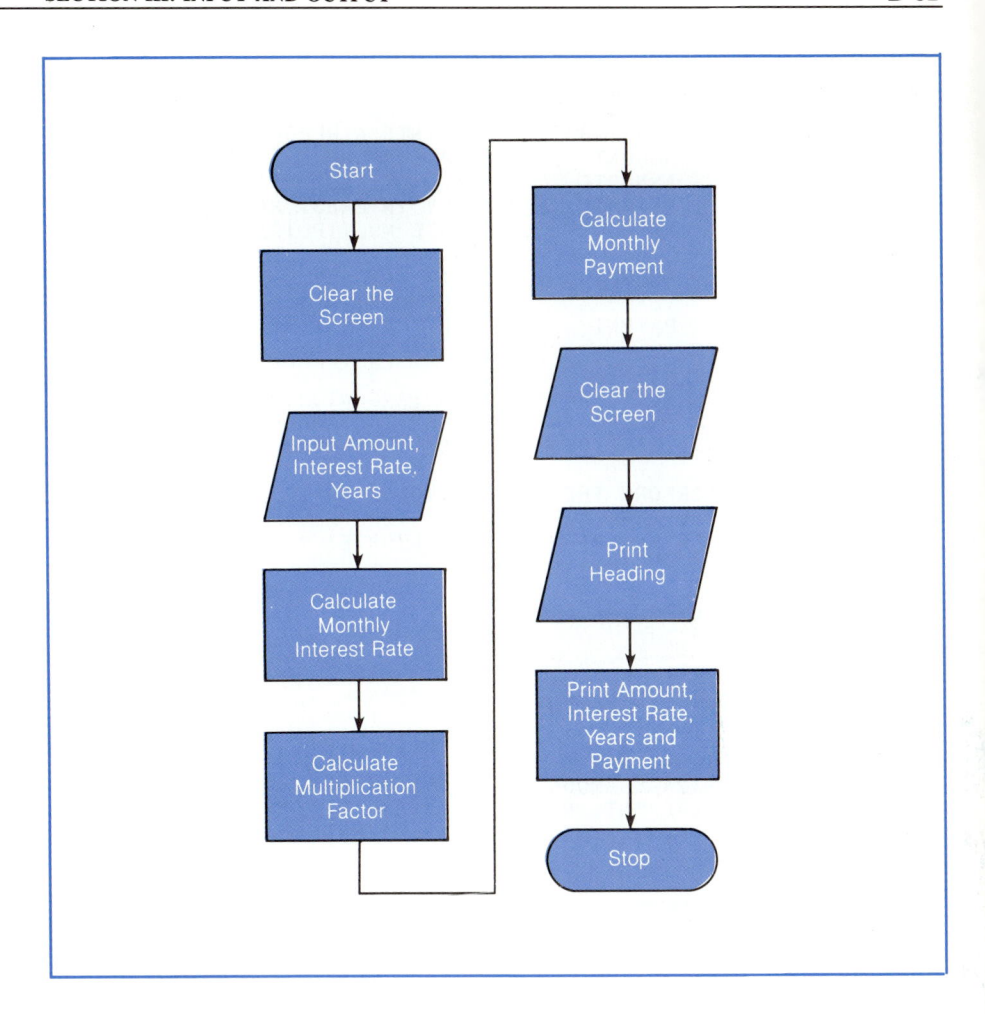

- Prompts should be used to tell the user what type of data to enter.
- Before prompts are printed on the monitor screen, it is good practice to clear the screen of any other printing. This can be done by using the CLS statement.
- The READ and DATA statements also can be used to read values to variables. In this case, the input is placed in DATA statements within the program. READ statements are used to read these values and assign them to variables.
- The INPUT statement is particularly well suited for situations in which data values change often. The READ and DATA statements are most useful when data values do not change often.
- The results of processing can be formatted by using commas in PRINT statement. A comma causes the next output to be printed in the next print zone. Using commas enables the programmer to print output in table form.
- A semicolon in a PRINT statement causes the next output to be printed in the next available print position.
- The PRINT USING statement allows string expressions and numeric values to be formatted for output. It is used primarily for printing tables.

Figure III-11
Mortgage Program

```
10   REM * * * THIS PROGRAM COMPUTES THE MONTHLY PAYMENTS * * *
20   REM * * * FOR MORTGAGES AND PRINTS A REPORT.          * * *
30   REM * * *     AMOUNT      MORTGAGE AMOUNT             * * *
40   REM * * *     ANNLRTE     ANNUAL INTEREST RATE        * * *
50   REM * * *     MNTHRTE     MONTHLY INTEREST RATE       * * *
60   REM * * *     MMFACTR     MORTGAGE MULTIPLICATION     * * *
70   REM * * *                 FACTOR                      * * *
80   REM * * *     AMOUNT      MORTGAGE AMOUNT             * * *
90   REM * * *     YEARS       TERM OF MORTGAGE            * * *
100  REM * * *     PAYMNT      MONTHLY PAYMENT             * * *
110  REM
120  CLS
130  INPUT "ENTER MORTGAGE AMOUNT $";AMOUNT
140  INPUT "ENTER ANNUAL INTEREST RATE: ";ANNLRTE
150  INPUT "ENTER YEARS OF MORTGAGE: ";YEARS
160  REM
170  REM * * * PERFORM THE CALCULATIONS. * * *
180  LET MNTHRTE = (ANNLRTE / 100) / 12
190  LET MMFACTR = MNTHRTE / ((1 + MNTHRTE) ^ (YEARS * 12) - 1) + MNTHRTE
200  LET PAYMNT = MMFACTR * AMOUNT
210  REM
220  REM * * * PRINT THE REPORT. * * *
230  CLS
240  PRINT
250  PRINT
260  PRINT ,"MORTGAGE REPORT"
270  PRINT
280  PRINT
290  PRINT ,"MORTGAGE AMOUNT      $";AMOUNT
300  PRINT ,"ANNUAL INT. RATE      ";ANNLRTE;"%"
310  PRINT ,"MONTHLY PAYMENT      $";PAYMNT
999  END
```

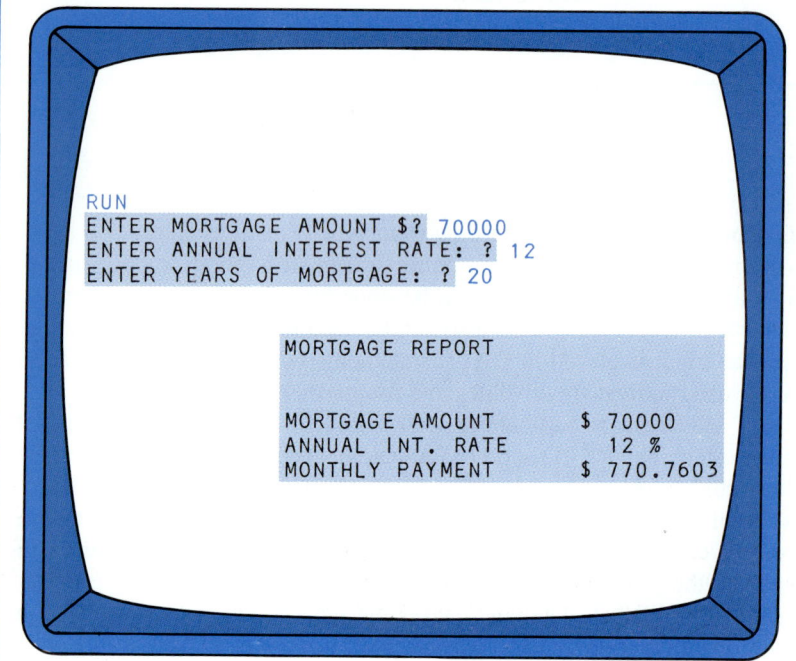

```
RUN
ENTER MORTGAGE AMOUNT $? 70000
ENTER ANNUAL INTEREST RATE: ? 12
ENTER YEARS OF MORTGAGE: ? 20


          MORTGAGE REPORT


          MORTGAGE AMOUNT     $ 70000
          ANNUAL INT. RATE      12 %
          MONTHLY PAYMENT     $ 770.7603
```

Review Questions

1. What is a data list, and how is it created?
2. Which statement should be used when there is an inquiry/response situation in a program?
3. What does the computer do when it comes to an INPUT statement?
4. What symbol separates the variables in an INPUT statement?
5. A _____ explains to the user what values are to be entered. It can be used either in an INPUT statement or in a PRINT statement that precedes an INPUT statement.
6. What happens if a program asks for a string value and the user enters a numeric value instead?
7. How does the RESTORE statement work?
8. The _____ statement is used with the READ statement, is nonexecutable, and can be located anywhere in a program.
9. What is the effect of a comma in a PRINT statement?
10. What is the difference between the TAB function and the SPC function?

Debugging Exercises

1.
```
10 INPUT "ENTER CITY AND STATE:",CITY$,ST
20 INPUT "AND ZIP CODE",ZIP$
30 PRINT TAB(5);CITY$;",";TAB(25);ST;TAB(35);ZIP$
```

2.
```
50 READ W1$,W2$,W3$
60 READ X,Y,Z
70 X = X - 10
80 Y = Y + 5
90 PRINT W1$;TAB(X);W2$;TAB(Y);W3$
100 DATA "WHAT","IS","LIFE?",8,5,15
```

Additional Programming Problems

1. Mrs. Mathey wants to know how much it would cost to fertilize her garden, which measures 15 by 20 feet. The economy fertilizer costs $1.75 per pound, and one pound covers 20 square feet. She also wants to know how much it would cost if she used the deluxe fertilizer, which is $2.00 per pound, and one pound covers 20 square feet. The program should output the cost of using each and the cost difference between the two.

2. Write a program that asks for a person's name and weight in pounds, and computes the weight in kilograms (1 pound = 0.453592 kilograms). The program

should print the name of the person, his/her weight in pounds, and weight in kilograms, each in a different print zone.

3. Write a program that will provide the user with an arithmetic quiz. The program should ask the user to enter two numbers. Then it should print a message telling the user to press any key when ready to see the sum, difference, product, and quotient of the two numbers. The program should then print the four results mentioned. Your output should be as follows:

```
ENTER ANY TWO NUMBERS
(SEPARATE THE NUMBERS WITH A COMMA) XXX, XXX
PRESS ANY KEY WHEN READY TO SEE THE ANSWERS: X
XXX + XXX = XXXX
XXX − XXX = XXX
XXX*XXX = XXXXXX
XXXX/XXX = XX
```

4. Tod Stiles has friends across the country, and would like to have a computerized address book. Write a program to read the following sample data and print it with the headings NAME, STREET, CITY, and STATE, using the TAB function:

Irene Bulas, 124 Columbia Hts, Brooklyn, NY
Monica Murdock, 778 Riverview Dr., New Orleans, LA
Link Case, 86 Eldorado Dr., Dallas, TX
Karen Milhoan, 799 Royal St. George, Naperville, IL

5. Write a program using READ/DATA statements to tally the cost of grocery list items. The program should calculate the total of the prices, a 6 percent tax on this amount, and the final total. Make use of the PRINT USING statement to print the prices and totals. Use the following data: 12.79, 9.99, 4.57, 3.99. The output should look like this:

```
                        12.79
                         9.99
                         4.57
                         3.99
         Subtotal       XX.XX
         Tax             X.XX
                        ─────
  Total                $XX.XX
```

SECTION IV

Control Statements and Subroutines

Outline

Introduction
The GOTO Statement:
    Unconditional Transfer
The IF Statement: Conditional
  Transfer
  Single Alternative: IF/THEN
  Double Alternative: IF/THEN/
    ELSE
  Nested IF Statements
AND/OR

The ON/GOTO Statement
  Menus
Learning Check
Subroutines: Structured
  Programming
  The GOSUB Statement
  The RETURN Statement
  Example of Subroutine Usage
  The STOP Statement
  The ON/GOSUB Statement

Learning Check
Comprehensive Programming
  Problem
  The Problem
  Solution Design
  The Program
Summary Points
Review Questions
Debugging Exercises
Additional Programming Problems

Introduction

CONTROL STATEMENT
A statement that enables the programmer to alter the order in which program statements are executed

SUBROUTINE
A module in a BASIC program containing a sequence of statements designed to perform a specific task; subroutines follow the main program

This section introduces the **control statement,** a powerful programming tool that will be used in all programs from this point on. Control statements enable the programmer to control the order in which program statements are executed. The GOTO, IF/THEN/ELSE, and ON/GOTO statements are control statements introduced in this section. The section also explains how programs are divided into subprograms or modules, which in BASIC are called **subroutines.** The GOSUB and ON/GOSUB statements are the two methods of executing a subroutine in BASIC.

The GOTO Statement: Unconditional Transfer

All of the programs we have written so far have been executed in a simple sequential manner. That is, they were executed from the lowest-numbered line to the highest-numbered line. To solve many programming problems, however, it is necessary to use control statements to alter the sequence in which statements are executed. One type of control statement is the GOTO statement. Its general format looks like this:

line# GOTO transfer line#

The transfer line number tells the computer the line number of the next statement to be executed, and control transfers to that program line regardless of its location in the program.

When a GOTO statement is executed, any of three possible actions may be taken:

1. If the statement indicated by the transfer line number is executable, it is executed, and program execution continues from that point.
2. If the statement indicated by the transfer line number is nonexecutable (such as a REM or DATA statement), control passes to the next executable statement after it.
3. If the transfer line number does not correspond to any statement in the program, an error message is displayed and execution is terminated.

The following is an example of a GOTO statement:

```
100 GOTO 60
```

This statement causes program execution to branch to line 60, execute if possible, and continue with the line following line 60.

Because control of the execution path *always* changes when the GOTO statement is encountered, such a statement is known as an **unconditional transfer.** The program segment in Figure IV–1 shows how execution paths are controlled with

Figure IV-1
GOTO Statement Execution Path

```
00030 X = 10
00040 Y = 20
00050 GOTO 70
00060 PRINT X
00070 PRINT Y
00080 -------
```

UNCONDITIONAL TRANSFER
Control is always passed to a specified line, regardless of any program conditions.

GOTO statements. The GOTO statement in line 50 causes control to pass to line 70. Therefore, only the value of Y is printed; line 60 is skipped.

At this point a word of caution is in order. Although the GOTO statement gives the programmer increased control over the logical flow of a program, unconditional transfers can produce an execution path so complex that the logic is virtually impossible to follow, and debugging becomes a nightmare. Later in this chapter and in the next chapter, you will be introduced to control statements that are preferable to the GOTO statement. The GOTO statement should be used only when it is not feasible to use another control statement.

The IF Statement: Conditional Transfer

CONDITIONAL TRANSFER
Program control is transferred to another point only if a stated condition is satisfied.

SINGLE-ALTERNATIVE DECISION STRUCTURE
A decision step in which a specific action is taken if a stated condition is true; otherwise, execution proceeds to the next statement.

DOUBLE-ALTERNATIVE DECISION STRUCTURE
A decision step in which a specific action is taken if a stated condition is true; otherwise, a different action is taken.

A second type of control statement is the **conditional transfer** or decision statement. A conditional transfer statement tells the computer that a decision must be made to determine which path of execution to take. This decision is based on the value of an expression. If the value meets a stated condition—that is, if the condition is true—then one path of execution is followed. If the condition is false, a different path is taken. Most program decisions fall into one of two categories:

1. **Single alternative:** A special set of one or more statements is executed if the condition is true. If the condition is false, these statements are ignored and the normal program flow continues. The flowchart for a single-alternative decision structure is shown in Figure IV–2.

2. **Double alternative:** There is a choice between two sets of statements or alternative paths. One path is executed if the condition is true, and the other is executed if the condition is false. Figure IV–3 shows the flowchart for a double-alternative decision structure.

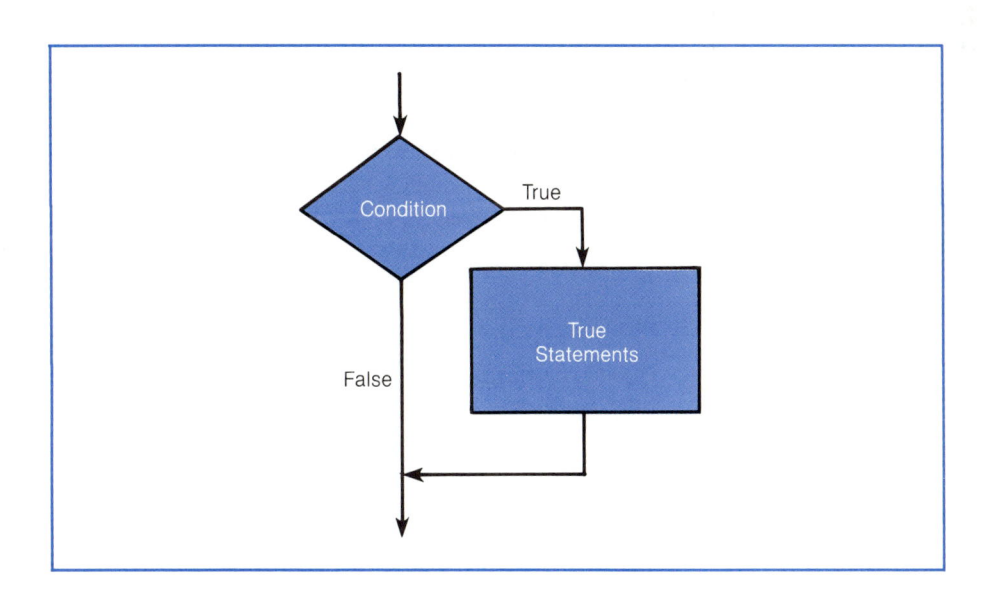

Figure IV-2
Single-Alternative Flowchart

**Figure IV-3
Double-Alternative Flowchart**

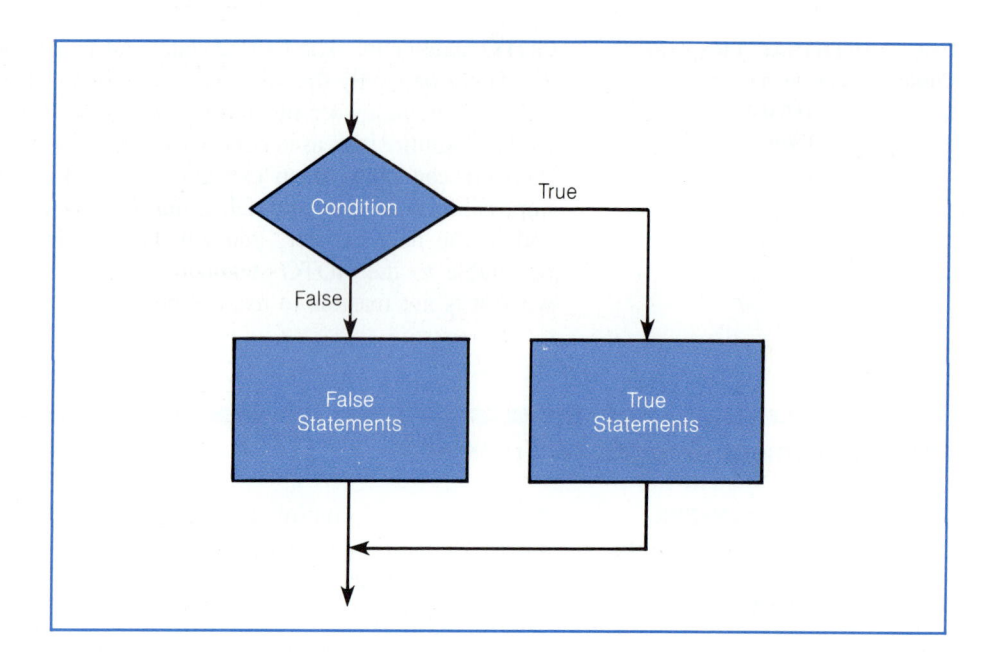

Single Alternative: IF/THEN

In BASIC, the IF/THEN statement is used for a single-alternative decision structure. The two general formats of the IF/THEN statement are as follows:

$$\text{line\# IF condition} \begin{Bmatrix} \text{THEN} \\ \text{GOTO} \end{Bmatrix} \text{transfer line\#}$$

$$\text{line\# IF condition THEN statement(s)} \begin{Bmatrix} \text{transfer line\#} \\ \text{statement(s)} \end{Bmatrix}$$

The brackets in the first statement indicate that one of the enclosed words is to be chosen when writing the statement. In other words, the first format of the IF/THEN can be worded in either of two ways:

line# IF condition THEN transfer line#
line# IF condition GOTO transfer line#

The execution of the IF/THEN statement follows these steps:

1. If the condition is true, the THEN or GOTO clause is executed. The program branches to the transfer line number and executes that statement (or the next executable statement).

**Table IV-1
Relational Operators**

Symbol	Meaning	Example
<	less than	small < BIG
<=	less than or equal to	1/2 <= .5
>	greater than	stock > 100
>=	greater than or equal to	X + 1 >= Y
=	equal to	NME$ = "BRUCE"
<>	not equal to	CODE$ <> "OK"

2. If the condition is false, the THEN or GOTO clause is ignored and execution continues with the next executable line following the IF/THEN statement.

The format of the condition looks like this:
expression1   relational symbol   expression2

RELATIONAL SYMBOL (relational operator) A symbol used to specify a relationship between two values.

The values of the expressions can be either numeric or character strings (both must be the same type). The expressions can be constants, variables, and/or arithmetic expressions. The condition compares the two expressions by means of **relational symbols,** as defined in Table IV–1. In Table IV–1 the equals sign (=) is used to show both relational operations and assignment.

Figure IV–4 shows examples of valid IF/THEN statements. Notice the various conditions that are possible and the types of statements that can be used.

Double Alternative: IF/THEN/ELSE

**Figure IV-4
Valid IF/THEN Statements**

An extension of the IF/THEN statement is the IF/THEN/ELSE statement. Like the IF/THEN statement, it has two forms:

```
40   IF A = 6 THEN 60              10   IF X = Y THEN PRINT "X = Y"

70   IF A >= 10 THEN 90            30   IF C > 2 * D THEN LET A = A + 1

30   IF A <= 4 + B THEN 65         80   IF C$ <> "CONTINUE" THEN END

60   IF A = B + C THEN 10          20   IF X = 5 THEN Y = X + 1

90   IF G$ = "YES" THEN 80         50   IF N$ = "M" THEN PRINT "MONDAY"

50   IF X = Y / X THEN 85          55   IF A = 5 * A ^ B THEN PRINT X$
```

$$\text{line\# IF condition} \begin{Bmatrix} \text{THEN} \\ \text{GOTO} \end{Bmatrix} \text{transfer line\# ELSE} \begin{Bmatrix} \text{transfer line\#} \\ \text{statement(s)} \end{Bmatrix}$$

$$\text{line\# IF condition THEN statement(s) ELSE} \begin{Bmatrix} \text{transfer line\#} \\ \text{statement(s)} \end{Bmatrix}$$

The entire IF/THEN/ELSE statement must appear on one physical line (a physical line ends with a carriage return). If a statement exceeds the width of the screen, the computer causes the statement to "wrap around" to the next line without the use of the carriage return; thus it is still one physical line. A line can be up to 255 characters long. For example, the following program segment is invalid:

```
10 IF X > Y THEN Y = 0
20 ELSE X = 0
```

The statement should be written as follows:

```
10 IF X > Y THEN Y = 0 ELSE X = 0
```

The IF/THEN/ELSE statement is an example of the double-alternative decision structure mentioned earlier in this chapter. It is executed in this way:

1. If the condition is true, the THEN clause is executed and the ELSE clause is ignored.
2. If the condition is false, the THEN clause is ignored and the ELSE clause is executed.

The following are examples of the IF/THEN/ELSE statement:

```
70 IF X > 100 THEN PRINT "BIG" ELSE PRINT "SMALL"
80 IF X > Y THEN Z = X - Y ELSE Z = X + Y
40 IF X > Y THEN BIG = X ELSE BIG = Y
```

Nested IF Statements

It is possible to nest two or more IF/THEN or IF/THEN/ELSE statements. This means that an IF/THEN or IF/THEN/ELSE statement can be placed within the THEN or ELSE clause of another IF/THEN/ELSE statement. The following is an example of an IF/THEN/ELSE statement nested within the ELSE clause of another IF/THEN/ELSE statement:

```
10 IF N > 0 THEN PRINT "POSITIVE" ELSE IF N < 0 THEN
   PRINT "NEGATIVE" ELSE PRINT "ZERO"
```

Nesting statements in this manner can make a program difficult to follow. To avoid errors in logic, make sure that the nested IF/THEN/ELSE statements contain the same number of ELSE and THEN clauses; on execution, each ELSE is matched with the closest unmatched THEN. The following line illustrates this fact:

```
10 IF R = S THEN IF S = T THEN PRINT "R = T" ELSE "R <> T"
```

If R equals S and S equals T, this statement prints "R = T". This statement should print "R <> T" when either R is not equal to S or when S is not equal to T. As it is written, the statement does not print "R <> T" when R does not equal S because the ELSE clause is matched to the second THEN clause and thus is executed only when R equals S. The statement could be written correctly as follows:

```
10 IF R = S THEN IF S = T THEN PRINT "R = T" ELSE PRINT "R <> T"
   ELSE PRINT "R <> T"
```

AND/OR

The IF/THEN statement can be expanded by adding the AND and OR clauses to it. The program in Figure IV–5 contains examples of both these clauses. The IF/AND/THEN statement requires that *both conditions be true* before the THEN clause is executed. The IF/OR/THEN statement requires that *at least one of the conditions* be true before the THEN clause is executed. (If both conditions are true, the THEN clause also is executed.)

For example, the IF/AND/THEN statement in line 50 (Figure IV–5) requires that both conditions be true before control is transferred to line 90. By contrast, with the IF/OR/THEN statement in line 60, only one of the conditions must be true. If either A = 1 or B = 2 (or both), the computer skips to line 130 and continues from there. If neither statement is true, the computer continues onto line 70. If the appropriate conditions are not met for the corresponding IF/THEN statements, control of the program always passes to the next line in sequence.

The AND/OR clause also can be used with the double-alternative structure. The IF/AND/THEN requires that *all* the conditions be true for the THEN clause to be executed; if at least one condition is false, the ELSE clause is executed. The IF/OR/THEN requires that *at least one* condition be true for the THEN clause to be executed; otherwise, the ELSE clause is executed.

The ON/GOTO Statement

The ON/GOTO statement transfers control to other statements in the program. Any one of several transfers may occur, depending on the value computed for a mathematical expression. Because transfer depends upon the value of the expression, the ON/GOTO is another conditional transfer statement. Its general format is this:

line# ON expression GOTO line#1[,line#2,...]

The arithmetic expression is evaluated as an integer value; the expression is rounded if necessary. The execution of the ON/GOTO statement is as follows:

**Figure IV-5
AND and OR Clauses**

```
10   CLS
20   PRINT "ENTER THE NUMBERS 1,2,3"
30   PRINT "IN ANY ORDER"
40   INPUT N1,N2,N3
50   IF N1 = 1 AND N2 = 2 THEN 90
60   IF N1 = 1 OR N2 = 2 THEN 130
70   IF N1 <> N2 + N3 THEN 170
80   GOTO 200
90   PRINT
100  PRINT "BOTH CONDITIONS ARE MET"
110  PRINT "N1 = 1 AND N2 = 2"
120  GOTO 70
130  PRINT
140  PRINT "ONE OF THE CONDITIONS IS MET"
150  PRINT "EITHER N1 = 1 OR N2 = 2"
160  GOTO 70
170  PRINT
180  PRINT "N1 <> N2 + N3"
190  GOTO 999
200  PRINT
210  PRINT "N1 = N2 + N3"
999  END
```

```
RUN
ENTER THE NUMBERS 1,2,3
IN ANY ORDER
? 5,2,3

ONE OF THE CONDITIONS IS MET
EITHER N1 = 1 OR N2 = 2

N1 = N2 + N3
```

1. The expression is rounded to an integer value.

2. Depending upon the value of the expression, control passes to the corresponding line number.

    a. If the value of the expression is 1, control passes to the first line number listed.

SECTION IV: CONTROL STATEMENTS AND SUBROUTINES

    b. If the value of the expression is 2, control passes to the second line number listed.
    c. If the value of the expression is *n,* control passes to the *n*th line number listed.

The following examples demonstrate the execution of the ON/GOTO statement.

Statement	Value of x	Execution
10 ON X GOTO 30,50,70	X = 1 X = 2 X = 3	Control passes to line 30 Control passes to line 50 Control passes to line 70
10 ON X − 2 GOTO 100,150	X = 3 X = 4	3 − 2 = 1; control passes to line 100 4 − 2 = 2; control passes to line 150
20 ON X/3 GOTO 40,60,80	X = 7	7/3 = 2.33; result rounded to 2; control passes to line 60

Three additional rules apply to the ON/GOTO statement:

1. If the value of the expression is zero, the rest of the ON/GOTO statement is ignored and control passes to the next statement in sequence.
2. If the value of the expression is greater than the number of transfer lines listed, control passes to the next statement in sequence.
3. If the value of the expression is negative, an error message is displayed and execution stops.

Learning Check

1. A statement that always alters the execution path when it is encountered is a(n) _____ transfer statement.
2. A control statement that makes a decision based on the value of an expression is called a(n) _____ transfer statement.
3. Must the condition of an IF/THEN statement be evaluated only as true or false?
4. The expression in the ON/GOTO statement always is evaluated as a(n) _____.
5. The _____ clause indicates that *both* conditions must be true for the THEN/GOTO clause to be executed.

Answers

1. unconditional 2. conditional 3. yes 4. integer 5. AND

Figure IV–6 shows how to use the ON/GOTO statement in a program. If the expression N / 2 in line 30 equals 1 or is rounded to 1, control is transferred to line 100. If N / 2 equals 2 or is rounded to 2, control is transferred to line 200, and so on. Line 40 is inserted to prevent an error if N / 2 exceeds the values in the ON/GOTO statement. That is, if N / 2 is greater than 5, the message requesting a number within bounds is repeated.

Menus

A **menu** is a displayed list of the functions that a program can perform. Just as a customer in a restaurant looks at the menu to choose a meal, so a program user looks at a menu displayed on the screen to choose a desired function. The user makes a selection by entering a code, usually a simple number or letter, at the keyboard. Figure IV–7 presents a simple example of a menu.

MENU
A screen display of a program's functions. The user enters a code at the keyboard to make a selection.

Figure IV-6
ON/GOTO Program

```
10 CLS
20  INPUT "ENTER A NUMBER FROM 1 TO 10";N
30  ON N / 2 GOTO 100,200,300,400,500
40  IF N / 2 > 5 THEN 20
100 PRINT "THE NUMBER WAS 1 OR 2"
110 GOTO 999
200 PRINT "THE NUMBER WAS 3 OR 4"
210 GOTO 999
300 PRINT "THE NUMBER WAS 5 OR 6"
310 GOTO 999
400 PRINT "THE NUMBER WAS 7 OR 8"
410 GOTO 999
500 PRINT "THE NUMBER WAS 9 OR 10"
999 END
```

```
RUN
ENTER A NUMBER FROM 1 TO 10? 12
ENTER A NUMBER FROM 1 TO 10? 10
THE NUMBER WAS 9 OR 10
```

SECTION IV: CONTROL STATEMENTS AND SUBROUTINES

Figure IV-7
Menu Program Using the ON/GOTO Statement

```
10   REM *** CONVERT DOLLARS TO FOREIGN CURRENCY ***
20   CLS
30   PRINT "        MONEY CONVERSION MENU"
40   PRINT
50   PRINT "ENTER NUMBER OF DOLLARS TO BE CONVERTED"
60   INPUT DOLLARS
70   PRINT
80   PRINT "PLEASE ENTER ONE OF THE FOLLOWING NUMBERS:"
90   PRINT "   1. TO CONVERT TO POUNDS"
100  PRINT "   2. TO CONVERT TO MARKS"
110  PRINT "   3. TO CONVERT TO FRANCS"
120  PRINT "   4. TO CONVERT TO LIRA"
130  PRINT
140  INPUT CODE
150  ON CODE GOTO 180,220,260,300
160  REM
170  REM *** POUNDS ***
180  RESULTS = DOLLARS * .94
190  GOTO 310
200  REM
210  REM *** MARKS ***
220  RESULTS = DOLLARS * 2.4
230  GOTO 310
240  REM
250  REM *** FRANCS ***
260  RESULTS = DOLLARS * 7.2
270  GOTO 310
280  REM
290  REM *** LIRA ***
300  RESULTS = DOLLARS * 1439!
310  PRINT "THE RESULT =";RESULTS
999  END
```

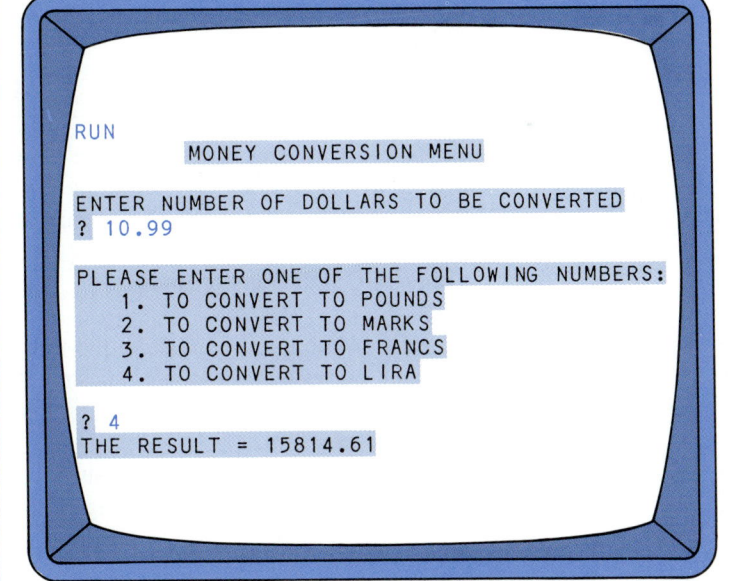

```
RUN
          MONEY CONVERSION MENU

ENTER NUMBER OF DOLLARS TO BE CONVERTED
? 10.99

PLEASE ENTER ONE OF THE FOLLOWING NUMBERS:
   1. TO CONVERT TO POUNDS
   2. TO CONVERT TO MARKS
   3. TO CONVERT TO FRANCS
   4. TO CONVERT TO LIRA

? 4
THE RESULT = 15814.61
```

The ON/GOTO statement often is used in menu programs such as the one in Figure IV–7. After entering the number of dollars to be converted, the user enters a 1, 2, 3, or 4 to indicate the currency desired. The ON/GOTO statement in line 150 then branches to the part of the program which performs the indicated conversion.

Subroutines: Structured Programming

STRUCTURED PROGRAMMING
A method of programming in which programs have easy-to-follow logic and are divided into subprograms, each designed to perform a specific task.

When computers were first developed, programming was extremely complex and programmers were happy just to get their programs to work. There was little concern about writing programs in a style that was easy for other people to understand. Gradually, however, programmers began to realize that working with such programs was very difficult, particularly when someone other than the original programmer had to alter an existing program.

Because of this problem, programmers began developing ways to make programs easier to understand and modify. These techniques, which have been developed over the past 20 years, are referred to as **structured programming.** Structured programming has two basic characteristics: (1) the program logic is easy to follow, and (2) the program is divided into smaller subprograms or modules, which in BASIC are referred to as subroutines.

Subroutines are modules in BASIC, each designed to perform a specific task. A subroutine is a sequence of statements which typically is located after the main body of the program. It can be executed any number of times in a given program.

The GOSUB Statement

The GOSUB statement transfers the flow of program control from the calling program to a subroutine. A subroutine can be called either from the main program or from another subroutine. The format of the GOSUB statement is as follows:

line# GOSUB transfer line#

The transfer line number must be the first number of the subroutine. This is very important, because the computer does not detect an error if it is instructed to branch to an incorrect line. It detects an error only if the transfer line number does not exist in the program.

The GOSUB statement causes an unconditional transfer to the specified line number. For example, the following statement causes a branch to the subroutine starting at line 1000:

```
100 GOSUB 1000
```

The RETURN Statement

After a subroutine is executed, the RETURN statement causes program control to return to the line following the one that contained the GOSUB statement. The format of the RETURN statement is as follows:

line# RETURN

Note that no transfer line number is needed in the RETURN statement. The computer automatically returns control to the statement immediately following the GOSUB statement that called the subroutine. If the line returned to is a nonexecutable statement, such as a REM statement, the computer simply skips it. Each subroutine must contain a RETURN statement as its last line; otherwise the program cannot branch back to the point from which the subroutine was called.

Example of Subroutine Usage

The program in Figure IV-8 prints a simple multiplication table. It contains a subroutine that prints a row of asterisks to divide the multiplication table into sections to make it more readable. The subroutine is called from three places in the main program: line 70, line 90, and line 210. Each time this subroutine is called, program control transfers to line 1000. Because lines 1000 through 1050 are nonexecutable statements, execution skips down to line 1060.

In this program, the subroutine is very short, so it would be easy to repeat the statements each time they are needed instead of using a subroutine. If the subroutine were longer, however, it would be tedious and wasteful to type it three times. Using subroutines simplifies program logic by organizing specific tasks into neat, orderly subsections.

The STOP Statement

When the STOP statement is executed, it causes the program to end. Sometimes a STOP statement is placed immediately before the subroutines of a program so that the subroutines are not executed after the last line of the main program is reached. The general format of the STOP statement is as follows:

line# STOP

In the program in Figure IV-8, the STOP statement in line 220 prevents the execution of the subroutines after the main program has been executed. Notice the message in the program output:

```
Break in 220
```

Figure IV-8
Multiplication Program Using a Subroutine

```
10    REM *** MULTIPLICATION PROGRAM ***
20    CLS
30    REM *** THE PURPOSE OF THIS PROGRAM IS TO SHOW ***
40    REM *** THE USE OF SUBROUTINES ***
50    REM
60    PRINT TAB(30);"MULTIPLICATION TABLE"
70    GOSUB 1000
80    PRINT TAB(5);"ONE";TAB(15);"TWO";TAB(25);"THREE"
90    GOSUB 1000
100   REM
110   REM *** PRINT TABLE ***
120   OUTER = 1
130   INNER = 1
140   PRINT OUTER;"*";INNER;"=";OUTER * INNER;
150   INNER = INNER + 1
160   IF INNER < 4 GOTO 140
170   PRINT
180   OUTER = OUTER + 1
190   IF OUTER < 11 THEN GOTO 130
200   PRINT
210   GOSUB 1000
220   STOP
1000  REM
1010  REM ************************
1020  REM ***SUBROUTINE ASTERISK***
1030  REM ************************
1040  REM *** PRINT ASTERISK ***
1050  REM
1060  COUNT = 1
1070  PRINT "*";
1080  COUNT = COUNT + 1
1090  IF COUNT <= 80 THEN 1070
1100  PRINT
1110  RETURN
9999  END
```

(Figure continued on the next page)

If an END statement were used in place of the STOP statement, this message would not be printed.

The ON/GOSUB Statement

Because the GOSUB statement is an unconditional transfer statement, it always transfers program control to the subroutine starting at the indicated line number. Sometimes, however, it is necessary to branch to one of several subroutines de-

**Figure IV-8
Continued**

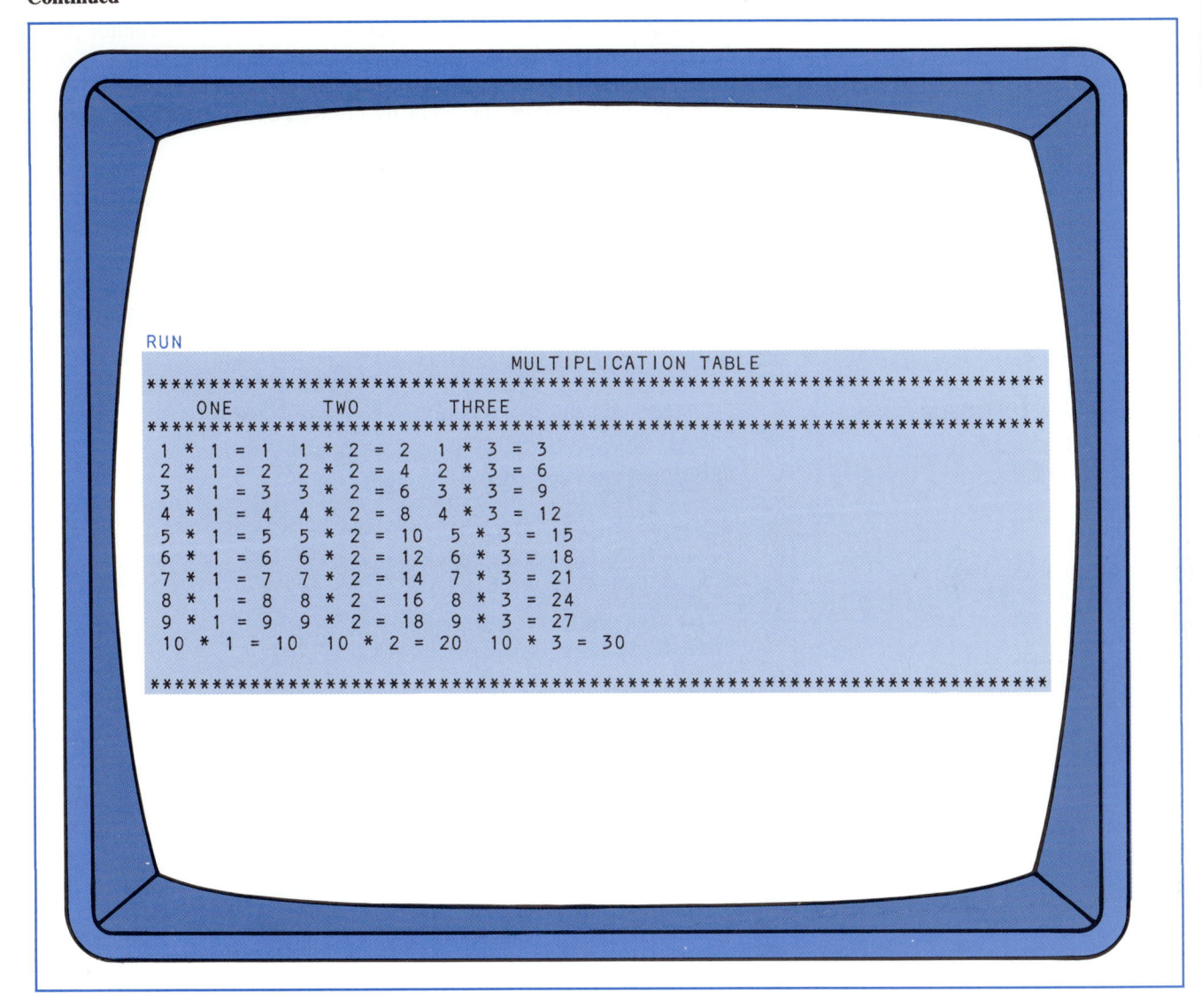

```
RUN
                         MULTIPLICATION TABLE
****************************************************************
     ONE         TWO          THREE
****************************************************************
 1 *  1 =  1    1 *  2 =  2    1 *  3 =  3
 2 *  1 =  2    2 *  2 =  4    2 *  3 =  6
 3 *  1 =  3    3 *  2 =  6    3 *  3 =  9
 4 *  1 =  4    4 *  2 =  8    4 *  3 = 12
 5 *  1 =  5    5 *  2 = 10    5 *  3 = 15
 6 *  1 =  6    6 *  2 = 12    6 *  3 = 18
 7 *  1 =  7    7 *  2 = 14    7 *  3 = 21
 8 *  1 =  8    8 *  2 = 16    8 *  3 = 24
 9 *  1 =  9    9 *  2 = 18    9 *  3 = 27
10 *  1 = 10   10 *  2 = 20   10 *  3 = 30

****************************************************************
```

pending on existing conditions. The ON/GOSUB statement is useful for this purpose. The format of the ON/GOSUB statement is as follows:

line# ON expression GOSUB transfer line#1[transfer lines#2,...]

The ON/GOSUB is similar to the ON/GOTO statement in that it uses an arithmetic expression to determine the line number to which program control will transfer. The transfer line numbers in the ON/GOSUB statement, however, are not within the main program. Each transfer line number indicates the beginning of a subroutine.

The execution of the ON/GOSUB statement proceeds as follows:

1. The expression is evaluated as an integer, and is truncated if necessary.
2. Control passes to the subroutine starting at the line number that corresponds to the value of the expression. If the value of the expression is *n*, control passes to the subroutine starting at the *n*th line number listed.
3. After the specified subroutine is executed, control is transferred back to the line following the ON/GOSUB statement by the RETURN statement at the end of the subroutine.

If the expression in an ON/GOSUB statement is evaluated as a number larger than the number of transfer lines indicated, control is passed to the next executable statement.

Figure IV–9 demonstrates a simple use of the ON/GOSUB statement. The user enters an integer value representing his or her year in college. This integer value

Figure IV-9
Program Using ON/GOSUB

```
10   REM *** GRADUATION PROGRAM ***
20   CLS
30   REM *** PRINTS YEAR OF GRADUATION ***
40   INPUT "ENTER THE STUDENT'S NAME";STUDENT$
50   INPUT "ENTER CURRENT YEAR";YR
60   ON YR GOSUB 100,200,300,400
70   STOP
100  REM *** SUBROUTINE FRESHMAN ***
110  PRINT STUDENT$;" WILL GRADUATE IN 1991"
120  RETURN
200  REM *** SUBROUTINE SOPHOMORE ***
210  PRINT STUDENT$;" WILL GRADUATE IN 1990"
220  RETURN
300  REM *** SUBROUTINE JUNIOR ***
310  PRINT STUDENT$;" WILL GRADUATE IN 1989"
320  RETURN
400  REM *** SUBROUTINE SENIOR ***
410  PRINT STUDENT$;" WILL GRADUATE IN 1988"
420  RETURN
999  END
```

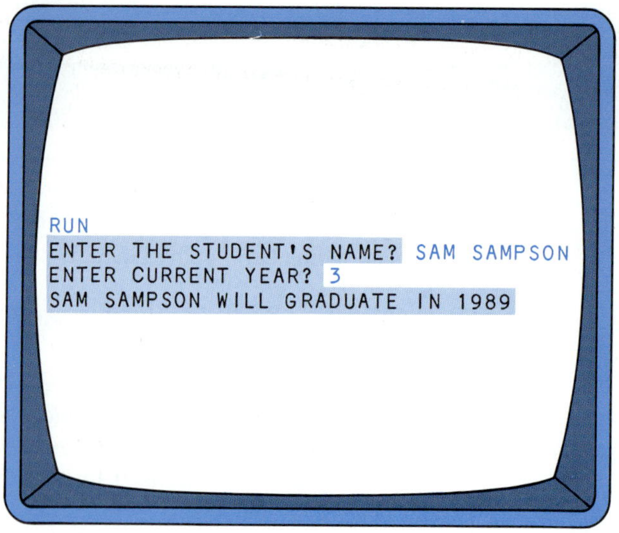

```
RUN
ENTER THE STUDENT'S NAME? SAM SAMPSON
ENTER CURRENT YEAR? 3
SAM SAMPSON WILL GRADUATE IN 1989
```

SECTION IV: CONTROL STATEMENTS AND SUBROUTINES   B-81

is assigned to the variable YR, which is used to determine which subroutine will be executed. After the appropriate subroutine is executed, control is returned to the main program, which then stops execution.

Learning Check

1. Subprograms in BASIC are called _____.
2. A(n) _____ statement causes an unconditional branch to a subroutine.
3. The _____ statement causes control to be transferred from a subroutine back to the calling program.
4. How many times can a given subroutine be called in a program?
5. The _____ statement is used to prevent unnecessary execution of subroutines or other statements.

Answers

1. subroutines 2. GOSUB 3. RETURN 4. There is no limit. 5. STOP

Comprehensive Programming Problem

The Problem

The math teachers at Stamm's Elementary school would like a program to help their students learn elementary arithmetic. The program should enable the user to enter a request to add, subtract, multiply, or divide two numbers (a menu can be used to display these options). After the operation is chosen, the program should ask for two numbers. Then it should use a subroutine to perform the computation and print the results.

Solution Design

The general problem we must solve is to calculate and print the results of a mathematical operation that is chosen by the user. The flow of data processing indicates that there are two smaller problems to solve:

1. Enter the necessary data.
2. Calculate the mathematical operation necessary.

Step 1 can be divided into two smaller units:

1.A. Display the menu of mathematical operations.
1.B. Enter the choice and the data values.

Because four mathematical operations are possible, the calculated results depend on a choice made by the user. Therefore, the second step can be divided into three steps:

2.A. Determine which operation to perform.
2.B. Calculate the results of the operation.
2.C. Print the results.

The structure chart in Figure IV–10 shows this refinement of the problem.

Next we decide what program steps are needed to perform these tasks and the order in which they should be performed. Figure IV–11 shows the flowchart for a possible solution. The program needs to be interactive, so that the user can select the operation and the numbers.

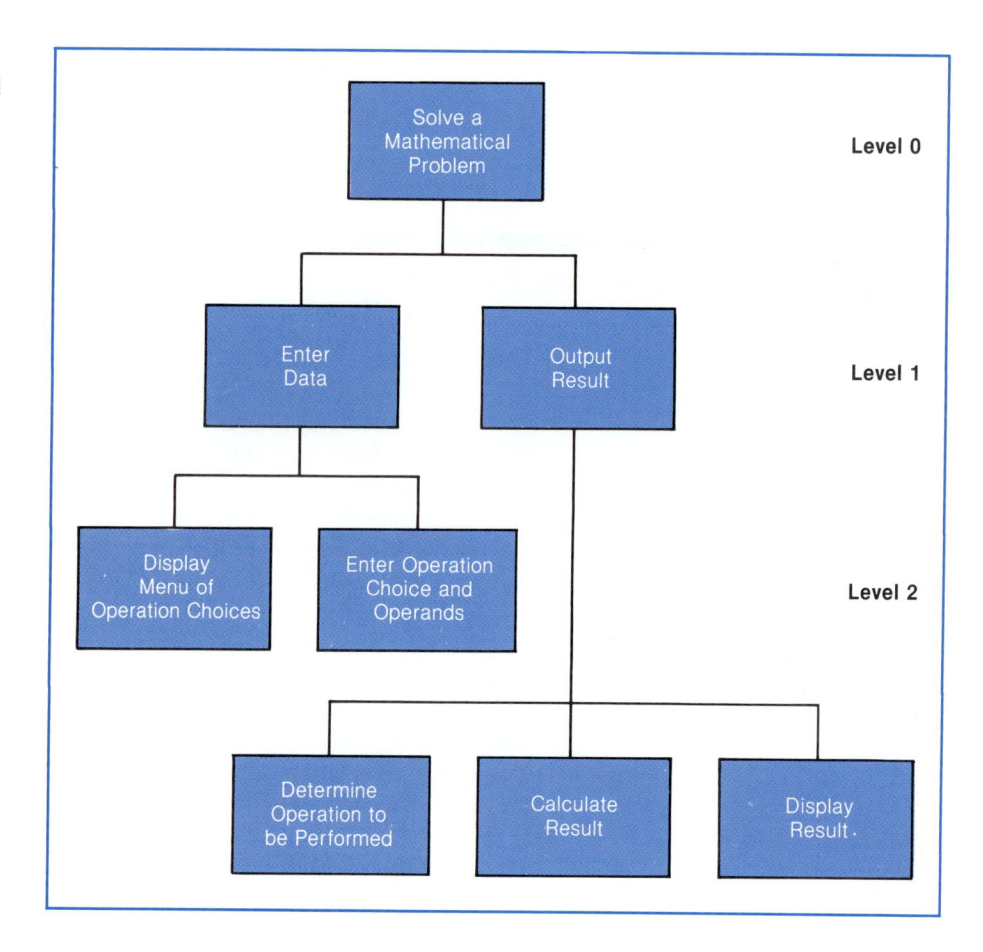

Figure IV-10
Structure Chart for Mathematical Operations Program

Figure IV-11
Flowchart for Mathematical Operations Program

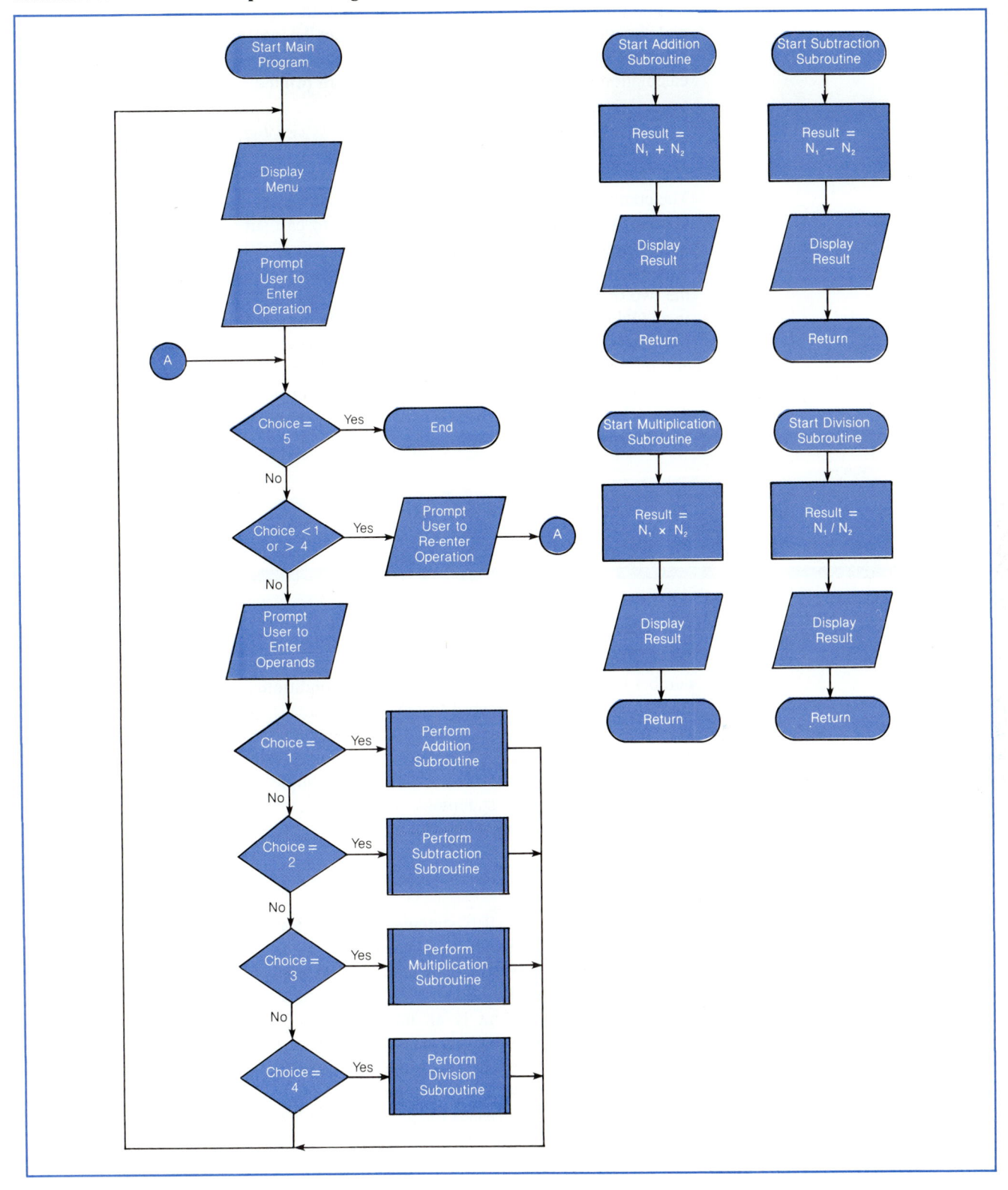

The first step is to clear the screen so that the operation menu can be displayed and the mathematical operation choice can be entered by the user. Next, the operands are entered. The subroutine of the chosen operation is called and the calculation is performed; then the results are printed.

The Program

The complete program is shown in Figure IV–12. The main body of this program is rather short, because its main purpose is to call subroutines.

The first subroutine displays the mathematical operations menu (lines 1000–1170) and enables the user to select the operation. In line 170 of the main program, the two operands are catered. The value that was entered for the operation is used in an ON/GOSUB statement in line 180 to determine which of the four subroutines will be executed. Each of the subroutines performs a different mathematical operation and prints the results. After the mathematical operation is executed and the result is printed, control returns to the main program (line 190), which calls the menu subroutine again and gives the user the option to perform another mathematical operation.

Summary Points

- The GOTO statement tells the computer to execute the statement whose line number follows the word GOTO. It is an unconditional transfer statement, because control is sent without regard to any condition.
- The IF/THEN evaluates a condition as true or false. If the condition is true, control passes to the THEN clause. If it is false, control passes to the next line.
- The IF/THEN statement is an example of a single-alternative decision structure.
- The IF/THEN/ELSE statement, an extension of the IF/THEN, passes control to the THEN clause if the condition is true and to the ELSE clause if the condition is false. IF/THEN and IF/THEN/ELSE statements can be nested.
- The IF/THEN/ELSE statement is an example of a double-alternative decision structure.
- When the IF/AND/THEN statement is used, both conditions specified must be true for the THEN clause to be executed.
- When the IF/OR/THEN statement is used, at least one (or both) of the conditions must be true for the THEN clause to be executed.
- The GOSUB statement is an unconditional branch that causes the flow of execution to be passed to the line number contained in the GOSUB statement.
- The RETURN statement causes control to be transferred back to the statement after the one that called the subroutine.
- The STOP statement causes the program to end at the point where it is executed. Usually it is placed immediately before the subroutines, to ensure that they are not executed when they are not needed.

Figure IV-12
Mathematical Operations Program

```
10    REM ***             MATHEMATICAL OPERATIONS             ***
20    CLS
30    REM *** THIS PROGRAM PERFORMS ADDITION, SUBTRACTION ***
40    REM *** MULTIPLICATION AND DIVISION OF TWO NUMBERS  ***
50    REM *** BASED ON THE USER'S CHOICE.                 ***
60    REM *** MAJOR VARIABLES:                            ***
70    REM *** CHOICE           MATHEMATICAL OPERATION     ***
80    REM *** N1,N2            TWO NUMBERS                ***
90    REM *** ADD              RESULT OF ADDITION         ***
100   REM *** SUBTRACT         RESULT OF SUBTRACTION      ***
110   REM *** MULTIPLY         RESULT OF MULTIPLICATION   ***
120   REM *** DIVIDE           RESULT OF DIVISION         ***
130   REM
140   REM *** CALL SUBROUTINE TO PRINT MENU ***
150   GOSUB 1000
160   IF CHOICE = 5 THEN STOP
170   INPUT "ENTER TWO NUMBERS (SEPARATED BY A COMMA)";N1,N2
180   ON CHOICE GOSUB 2000,3000,4000,5000
190   GOTO 150
1000  REM
1010  REM ************************
1020  REM *** SUBROUTINE MENU ***
1030  REM ************************
1040  REM *** PRINT MATHEMATICAL OPERATION ***
1050  REM
1060  REM
1070  PRINT
1080  PRINT TAB(30);"MATHEMATICAL OPERATIONS"
1090  PRINT
1100  PRINT TAB(30);"1. ADDITION"
1110  PRINT TAB(30);"2. SUBTRACTION"
1120  PRINT TAB(30);"3. MULTIPLICATION"
1130  PRINT TAB(30);"4. DIVISION"
1140  PRINT TAB(30);"5. QUIT"
1150  PRINT
1160  INPUT "ENTER THE NUMBER OF DESIRED OPERATION";CHOICE
1170  RETURN
2000  REM
2010  REM *****************************
2020  REM *** SUBROUTINE ADDITION ***
2030  REM *****************************
2040  REM *** ADD TWO NUMBERS ***
2050  REM
2060  ADD = N1 + N2
2070  PRINT
2080  PRINT N1;" + ";N2;" = ";ADD
2090  PRINT
2100  RETURN
3000  REM
3010  REM *******************************
3020  REM *** SUBROUTINE SUBTRACTION ***
3030  REM *******************************
3040  REM *** SUBTRACT TWO NUMBERS ***
3050  REM
3060  SUBTRACT = N1 - N2
3070  PRINT
3080  PRINT N1;" - ";N2;" = ";SUBTRACT
3090  PRINT
3100  RETURN
4000  REM
4010  REM ********************************
```

(Figure continued on the next page)

Figure IV-12 Continued

```
4020 REM *** SUBROUTINE MULTIPLICATION ***
4030 REM ********************************
4040 REM *** MULTIPLY TWO NUMBERS ***
4050 REM
4060 MULT = N1 * N2
4070 PRINT
4080 PRINT N1;" * ";N2;" = ";MULT
4090 PRINT
4100 RETURN
5000 REM
5010 REM ***************************
5020 REM *** SUBROUTINE DIVISION ***
5030 REM ***************************
5040 REM *** DIVIDE TWO NUMBERS ***
5050 REM
5060 DIVIDE = N1 / N2
5070 PRINT
5080 PRINT N1;" / ";N2;" = ";DIVIDE
5090 PRINT
5100 RETURN
9999 END
```

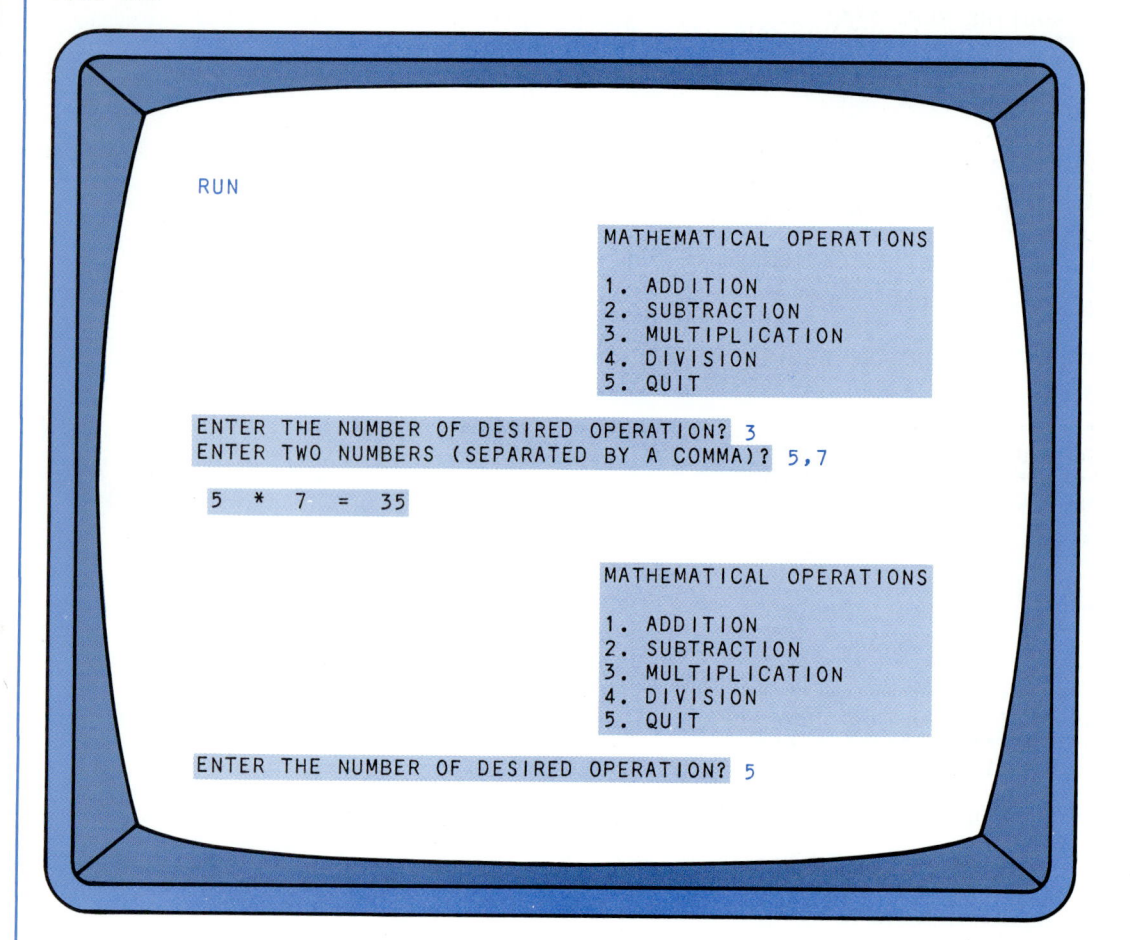

```
RUN

                              MATHEMATICAL OPERATIONS

                              1. ADDITION
                              2. SUBTRACTION
                              3. MULTIPLICATION
                              4. DIVISION
                              5. QUIT

ENTER THE NUMBER OF DESIRED OPERATION? 3
ENTER TWO NUMBERS (SEPARATED BY A COMMA)? 5,7

   5  *  7  =  35

                              MATHEMATICAL OPERATIONS

                              1. ADDITION
                              2. SUBTRACTION
                              3. MULTIPLICATION
                              4. DIVISION
                              5. QUIT

ENTER THE NUMBER OF DESIRED OPERATION? 5
```

Review Questions

1. What is a control statement?
2. Why is the GOTO statement an unconditional transfer statement?
3. Why is the IF statement a conditional transfer statement?
4. Which of the following are valid IF statements?

   a. 40 IF X$ = "FRANCO" THEN M = M + 1
   b. 50 IF Y$ <> "YES" THEN 40
   c. 20 IF Z = "NIENTE" THEN 100
   d. 70 IF Y THEN 20
   e. 60 IF "HOPELESS" >= "HOPEFUL" THEN 999

5. The expression of the ON/GOTO statement must be evaluated as an ___.
6. Control passes to what line when the following is executed, is SUM = 21?

   10 ON SUM/7 GOTO 50, 80, 110

7. What is a menu?
8. Where are RETURN statements placed in programs?
9. What happens if the transfer line number in a GOSUB statement is a non-executable statement?
10. Why is the GOSUB statement referred to as an unconditional branching statement?

Debugging Exercises

1.
```
10 READ A,B
20 X = A + B
30 IF X THEN 120
40 PRINT X
```

2.
```
10 REM *** CALCULATES THE AVERAGE OF FIVE TEST SCORES *
20 CNT = 1
30 IF CNT > 5 THEN 80
40   INPUT "ENTER SCORE";PTS
50   TT = TT + PTS
60 GOTO 30
70 AVG = TT / 5
80 PRINT "THE AVERAGE IS";PTS
99 END
```

Additional Programming Problems

1. World Travel wants a program that displays a menu with a list of countries to which the agency can send a customer at special discount rates. After the user enters the name of a particular country, the program should print all cities in that country in which the special rates are available. Use the following data:

Country	Cities
France	Nice
	Cannes
	Nantes
	Chamonix
Italy	Milan
	Verona
	Venice
	Naples
U.S.A.	Chicago
	San Francisco
	New York
	Miami

2. Budget Balloons provides hot-air balloon rides for fairs, parties, and other special occasions. The basic fee is $65.00 for the first hour and $45.00 for every additional hour. The company needs a program to help calculate its clients' bills. The program should call a subroutine to do the actual calculating, and use a loop to allow as many bills to be calculated as desired. The output of the program should include the name of the client and his or her total bill.

3. R & R Railways wants a program to determine the cost for passengers to various cities. The cost per person for the following cities is as follows:

Columbus	$ 39.00
Denver	142.00
New York	108.00
New Orleans	158.00

    A menu should display the names of the cities and ask how many people would like to purchase tickets. If a customer wants first-class tickets, there is an additional $30.00 flat fee. The cost of the needed tickets should be calculated in subroutines. Develop your own data to test the program.

4. As the manager of an apartment building, you need a program to help you keep track of the various apartments for rent. Write a program using subroutines which will give the user the choice of a studio, one-bedroom, or two-bedroom apartment. The monthly rent depends on the size of the apartment and whether it is to be furnished or unfurnished (this data should also be entered by the user). Use the following data:

| | | Rent | |
Type	Deposit	Furnished	Unfurnished
Studio	$ 75	$150	$135
One-bedroom	150	275	250
Two-bedroom	200	325	315

The program should print the apartment description, required deposit, and monthly rent according to the choices entered, using the following format:

Description:	One-bedroom furnished
Deposit:	$150
Rent:	$275

5. Write a program that will print current weather forecasts. A menu should be used to display the choices. Use the ON/GOTO statement and the following sample data:

Date	Forecast
9/01	Cloudy; 60% chance of afternoon showers; high 70–75°
9/02	Sunny and breezy; high 80–85°
9/03	Partly cloudy; 40% chance of rain; high 65–70°

SECTION V

Looping

Outline

Introduction
Looping Methods
   Trailer Values
   Counters
Elements of Looping
Learning Check

The FOR/NEXT Loop
   Rules for Using the FOR/NEXT Loop
   Flowcharting the FOR/NEXT Loop
   Advantages of Using the FOR/NEXT Loop
Learning Check
The WHILE/WEND Loop

Comprehensive Programming Problem
   Problem Definition
   Solution Design
   The Program
Summary Points
Review Questions
Debugging Exercises
Additional Programming Problems

Introduction

One of the most powerful features of the computer is its ability to perform repetitive tasks quickly and accurately. This process is referred to as looping. Two types of loops will be introduced in this section: the FOR/NEXT and the WHILE/WEND.

Looping Methods

Often a situation arises in which a single task must be performed several times. For example, a teacher may need a program to find the average test score of all the students in a given class. The job of processing a single student's data is simple enough:

    Read name, score
    Print name, score

Now consider the problem of repeating these steps for a class of thirty students:

    Read name, score
    Add score to total
    Print name, score
    Read name, score
    Add score to total
    Print name, score
        .
        .
        .
    Read name, score
    Add score to total
    Print name, score
    Divide total by 30
    Print class average

The same three statements to process a single student's data would have to be written thirty times, or they could be written once in a subroutine which the main program would call thirty times. The problem could be simplified greatly by writing the processing statements (or the subroutine call) just once, then executing those statements as many times as needed. This procedure, called looping, is flowcharted at the top of the next page.

One of the most important uses of control statements is the creation of loops. Control statements can determine which actions are to be repeated and the number of repetitions to be made. Some techniques for loop control include the use of trailer values, counters, and such looping statements as the FOR/NEXT statement.

SECTION V: LOOPING

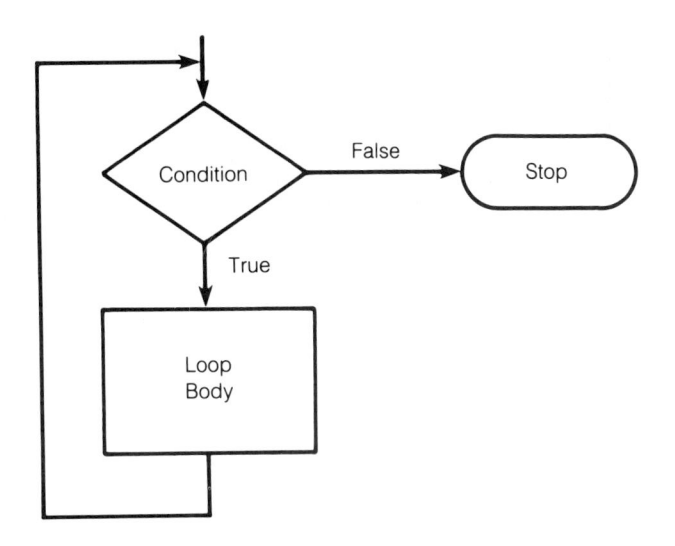

B-93

Trailer Values

TRAILER VALUE
A unique data value that signals the termination of a loop.

SENTINEL VALUE
See Trailer value.

A **trailer value** is a dummy value that follows or "trails" the data items to be processed. Sometimes it is referred to as a **sentinel value.** The trailer value signals the program that all the data has been read. The trailer can be either a numeric value or a character string, depending on the type of data being input, but it should always be a value outside the range of the actual data. For example, if a program reads people's ages, a good trailer value might be -1. If names are being read, an example of a good trailer value would be the string FINISHED.

A trailer value can control a loop in the following way. Before the loop begins, a READ or INPUT statement reads the first data item or group of data items to a certain variable or variables. The loop begins with an IF/THEN statement, which checks one of the variables to see if its value equals the trailer value. If so, then all the data items have been read, and program control passes to the first executable statement following the loop. If the variable's value is not equal to the trailer value, however, then the statements in the loop are executed. At the end of the loop, the next data item or group of data items is read, and a GOTO statement passes control back to the beginning of the loop.

Trailer values also must be given for the other data items read by the READ statement, so that an out-of-data error does not occur; the computer expects a value to be present for each variable in the READ statement. This same principle is true when the INPUT statement is used to read data until the trailer value is entered.

Figure V-1 shows an honor roll program with a loop controlled by a trailer value. Because names are being read, the string FINISHED is appropriate for the trailer value. Notice the actions performed between the IF/THEN statement in line 80 and the GOTO statement in line 130; this is the loop. This loop continues processing data until the trailer value has been read and the condition in the IF/THEN statement evaluates as true. This event causes the branch statement in the THEN clause to be executed, and control passes out of the loop to the end of the program.

Figure V-1
Example of a Loop Using a Trailer Value

```
10  CLS
20  PRINT "FRESHMAN HONOR ROLL"
30  PRINT
40  REM *** READ FIRST STUDENT ***
50  READ NME$,CLASS$,GPA
60  REM
70  REM *** BEGIN LOOP TO PROCESS ONE STUDENT PER PASS ***
80  IF NME$ = "FINISHED" THEN 999
90     IF CLASS$ <> "FR" THEN 120
100    IF GPA < 3.5 THEN 120
110    PRINT TAB(8);NME$
120    READ NME$,CLASS$,GPA
130 GOTO 80
140 REM
150 REM *** DATA STATEMENTS ***
160 DATA PAT LORD,FR,4.0,BRAD BUSCH,FR,3.7
170 DATA DERYL JONES,FR,2.9,IRENE DRAKE,SR,4.0
180 DATA CHLOE TULLY,JR,3.0,MONICA DYLAN,FR,3.8
190 DATA FINISHED,NONE,0
999 END
```

```
RUN
FRESHMAN HONOR ROLL

        PAT LORD
        BRAD BUSCH
        MONICA DYLAN
```

Care is needed when using GOTO statements in loops. An incorrect transfer line number can produce unexpected results. For example, study Figure V-1 and consider what would happen if the GOTO statement in line 130 were written like this:

```
220 GOTO 90
```

INFINITE LOOP (endless loop) A loop with no exit point.

In this case, control would always be passed to the line after the IF/THEN statement. The students' names would not be tested for the trailer value, and there would be no way to end the loop. A loop such as this, without an exit, is called an **infinite** (or **endless**) **loop.** An infinite loop can cause an error or can prevent the program from continuing to a normal termination. Careful checking of all program branches helps the programmer to avoid infinite loops.

Counters

A second method of controlling a loop is to create a special variable to keep track of the number of times the loop has been executed. Such a variable is called a

SECTION V: LOOPING

COUNTER
A variable used to control loop repetition. Each time the loop is executed, the counter is tested to determine if the desired number of repetitions has been performed.

counter. The counter is increased, or incremented, by a fixed amount (usually 1) each time the loop is executed. When the programmer knows in advance how many times the loop should be repeated the counter can be tested by an IF/THEN statement after each loop execution to see if the proper number has been reached.

To set up a counter for loop control, you should perform the following steps:

1. Initialize the counter (before entering the loop) by setting it to a beginning value.
2. Increment the counter each time the loop is executed.
3. Test the counter each time the loop is executed to see if the loop has been performed the desired number of times.

The program in Figure V-1 has been rewritten in Figure V-2 to use a counter rather than a trailer value. There are six students, so the loop must be executed exactly six times. The counter is initialized to 1 in line 40, before the loop starts. Line 70 tests the counter to see if it is greater than 6, and exits the loop if the condition is true. Otherwise, the loop is executed and the counter is incremented in line 120 before branching to the top of the loop again.

Figure V-2
Example of a Counter Loop

```
10   CLS
20   PRINT "FRESHMAN HONOR ROLL"
30   PRINT
40   COUNT = 1
50   REM
60   REM *** BEGIN LOOP TO PROCESS ONE STUDENT PER PASS ***
70   IF COUNT > 6 THEN 999
80      READ NME$,CLASS$,GPA
90      IF CLASS$ <> "FR" THEN 120
100     IF GPA < 3.5 THEN 120
110     PRINT TAB(8);NME$
120     COUNT = COUNT + 1
130  GOTO 70
140  REM
150  REM *** DATA STATEMENTS ***
160  DATA PAT LORD,FR,4.0,BRAD BUSCH,FR,3.7
170  DATA DERYL JONES,FR,2.9,IRENE DRAKE,SR,4.0
180  DATA CHLOE TULLY,JR,3.0,MONICA DYLAN,FR,3.8
999  END
```

```
RUN
FRESHMAN HONOR ROLL

       PAT LORD
       BRAD BUSCH
       MONICA DYLAN
```

Elements of Looping

LOOP CONTROL VARIABLE
A variable whose value is used to determine the number of loop repetitions.

LOOP BODY
The statements that constitute the action to be performed by the loop.

The loop is an extremely powerful and vital programming tool. Many looping methods exist in various programming languages, but all these methods share some basic components. A **loop control variable,** for example, is a variable whose value is used to determine the number of times a loop is repeated. The counter variable is an example of a loop control variable. All loops contain some action that may be performed repeatedly; the statements that perform such an action make up the **loop body.**

Execution of the basic loop structure consists of the following five steps:

1. The loop control variable is initialized to a particular value before loop execution begins.
2. The program tests the loop control variable to determine whether it should execute the loop body or exit the loop.
3. The loop body, which can consist of any number of statements, is executed.
4. At some point during loop execution, the value of the loop control variable must be modified to allow exit from the loop.
5. The loop is exited when the test in Step 2 determines that the right number of loop repetitions has been made. Execution continues with the next statement following the loop.

Research has determined that the first statement of a loop always should contain Step 2, the condition controlling loop repetition. Therefore, the branch at the bottom of the loop transfers program control to this statement. This structure makes the boundaries of the loop readily identifiable. Also, the execution path of the loop is tightly controlled, and therefore easy to follow, because no actions of the loop can be performed unless the controlling condition is satisfied.

As an example of this concept, consider the following loop:

```
10 READ AGE
20 IF AGE > 18 THEN 99
30 PRINT AGE
40 GOTO 10
99 END
```

This loop begins with a READ statement, because the GOTO statement at the end of the loop always branches to line 10. The READ statement initializes and modifies the value of the variable AGE, but does not test it. The same loop is better designed as follows:

```
10 READ AGE
20 IF AGE > 18 THEN 99
30 PRINT AGE
40 READ AGE
50 GOTO 20
99 END
```

The extra READ statement within the loop makes line 20 the first statement of the loop, a good programming principle. Remember this when setting up a loop.

The FOR/NEXT Loop

FOR/NEXT statements are used together to form a loop that is repeated a stated number of times. Figure V-3 contains a single program that uses a FOR/NEXT loop to add ten numbers together. In this program, the value of SUM is initially set to zero. The FOR/NEXT loop is then entered.

The variable I is referred to as a loop control variable; it is the variable that determines if the loop will be executed. When the FOR statement is executed, the loop control variable is set to an initial value (in this case 1). This value is tested against the terminal value (10). As long as the value of I is less than or equal to the terminal value, the loop is executed. Each time the loop is executed, the value of I is incremented by 1. When I is greater than 10, the loop is not executed again.

The statements in lines 30 and 40 constitute the body of this loop contains the actions that the loop performs. For each execution of the loop, the next number is read from the DATA statement and added to SUM. Notice that the loop body is indented. Indenting control statements makes no difference to the computer, but makes the program more readable for humans.

When the NEXT statement in line 50 is reached, the value of I is incremented by one and program control is transferred to the top of the loop. If the current value of I is less than or equal to the terminal value, the body of the loop is executed again; if I is greater than the terminal value, program control is transferred to the first statement following the NEXT statement. In this example, after the loop has executed ten times, control is transferred to line 60 and the sum of the ten numbers is printed.

In the loop in Figure V-3, both the initial and terminal values are numeric constants. These values could be numeric expressions or variables instead. In the

Figure V-3
Program to Add Ten Numbers

```
10 SUM = 0
20 FOR I = 1 TO 10
30    READ NMBR
40    SUM = SUM + NMBR
50 NEXT I
60 PRINT SUM
70 DATA 4,15,72,80,6,29,34,42,96,9
99 END
```

```
RUN
387
```

next example, the initial value is numeric expression and the terminal value is a numeric variable:

```
30 A = 8
40 FOR I = 2 + 4 TO A
50    PRINT I
60 NEXT I
```

This loop executes three times, and the output appears as follows:

```
6
7
8
```

It is possible to alter the value by which the loop control variable is incremented. This is done by placing a step value at the end of the FOR statement. The FOR statement in the program at the top of Figure V-4 has a step value of 2.

If a FOR statement contains no step value, a step value of +1 is assumed. The following FOR statements are equivalent, because the default step value is +1:

```
FOR I = 10 TO 20          FOR I = 10 TO 20 STEP 1
```

The FOR/NEXT loop in Figure V-4 executes 10 times, and the even numbers from 2 through 20 are printed. It is also possible to have a negative step value, as shown in the program at the bottom of Figure V-4. When a negative step value is used, the loop control variable is decremented each time through the loop. This program prints the even numbers from 20 through 2.

Rules for Using the FOR/NEXT Loop

To avoid errors in using the FOR and NEXT statements, it is important to be aware of the following rules:

■ The body of the loop is not executed if the initial value is greater than the terminal value when using a positive step, or if the initial value is less than the terminal value when using a negative step. For example, a loop containing either of the following statements would not be executed at all:

```
10 FOR X = 10 TO 5 STEP 2
20 FOR COUNT = 4 TO 6 STEP -1
```

■ The initial, terminal, and step values cannot be modified in the loop body.
■ It is possible to modify the loop control variable in the loop body, but this should *never* be done. Note how unpredictable the execution of the following loop would be, because the value of I is dependent on the integer entered by the user:

```
30 FOR I = 1 TO 10
40    INPUT "ENTER AN INTEGER";X
50    I = X
60 NEXT I
```

Figure V-4
FOR/NEXT Loops Using Positive and Negative Step Values

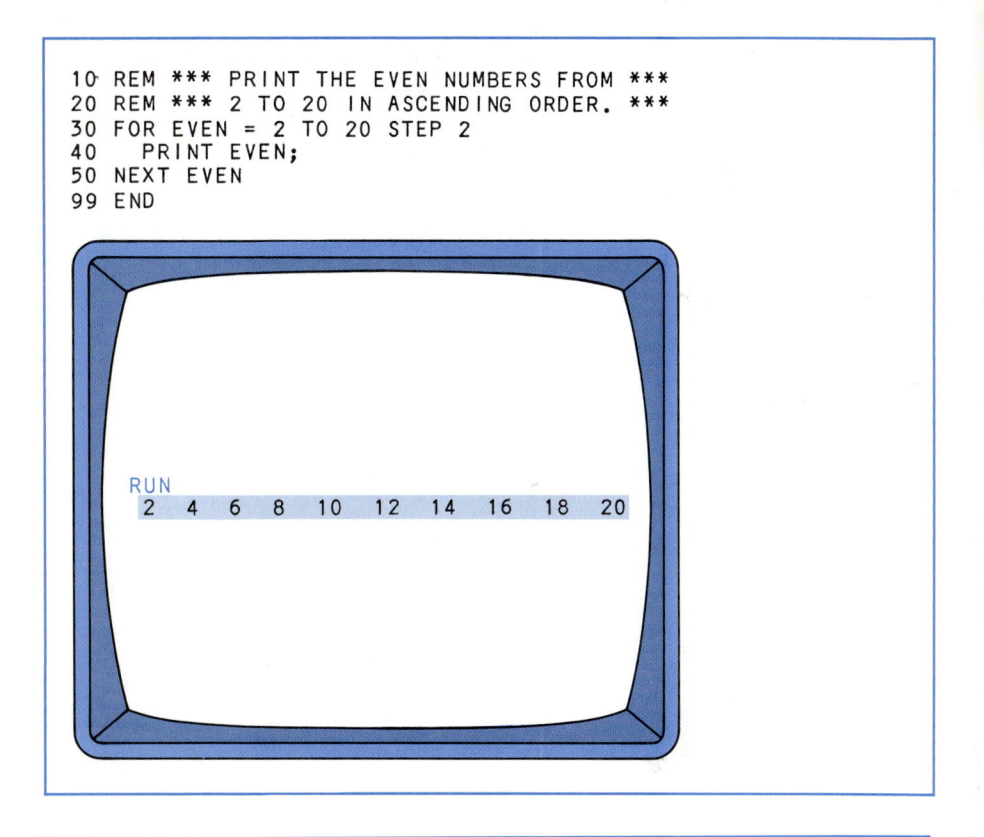

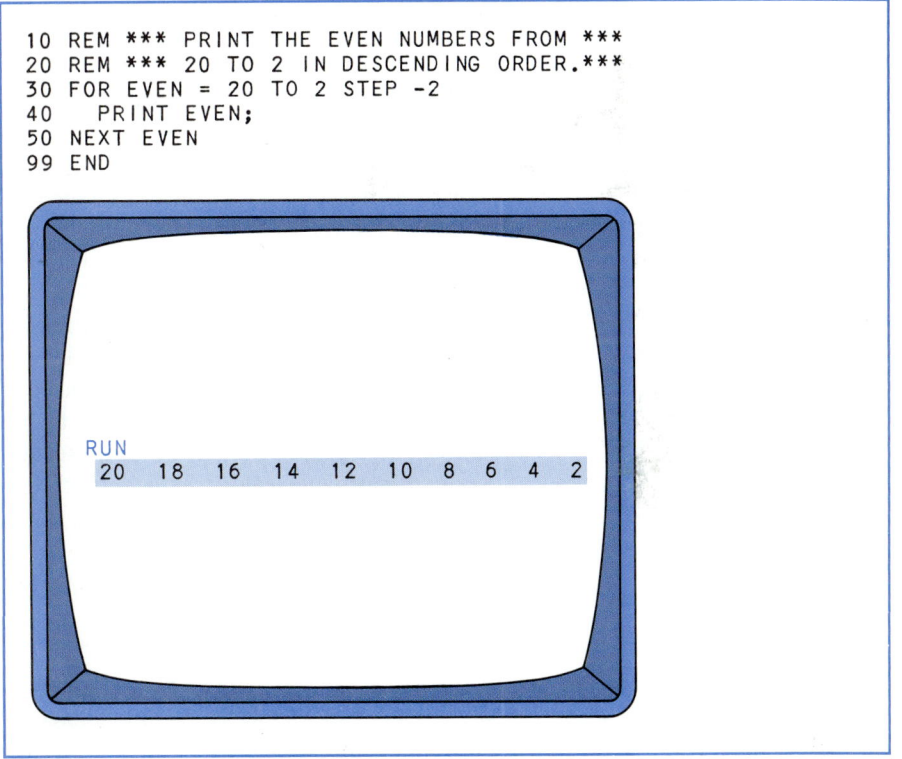

```
10 REM *** PRINT THE EVEN NUMBERS FROM ***
20 REM *** 2 TO 20 IN ASCENDING ORDER. ***
30 FOR EVEN = 2 TO 20 STEP 2
40   PRINT EVEN;
50 NEXT EVEN
99 END
```

```
RUN
 2   4   6   8   10   12   14   16   18   20
```

```
10 REM *** PRINT THE EVEN NUMBERS FROM ***
20 REM *** 20 TO 2 IN DESCENDING ORDER.***
30 FOR EVEN = 20 TO 2 STEP -2
40   PRINT EVEN;
50 NEXT EVEN
99 END
```

```
RUN
 20   18   16   14   12   10   8   6   4   2
```

- If the step value is zero, an infinite loop is created:

  `10 FOR X = 10 TO 20 STEP 0`

  This loop could be rewritten so that it would execute ten times, as follows:

  `10 FOR X = 10 TO 20 STEP 1`

- Each FOR statement must have a corresponding NEXT statement.

Flowcharting the FOR/NEXT Loop

Figure V-5a shows the common method of flowcharting a FOR/NEXT loop. An alternate method, shown in Figure V-5b, shows a convenient shorthand symbol that we have developed. This symbol provides a concise way to indicate the initial, terminal, and step values. The symbol represents the actions of both the FOR and NEXT statements. As long as the terminal condition (indicated on the right portion of the symbol) is false, the execution path containing the loop body is followed. The arrow from the last loop body action to the step value portion of the symbol indicates the action of the NEXT statement. When the terminal condition is true, the path containing the actions following the loop is taken.

Advantages of Using the FOR/NEXT Loop

The FOR/NEXT loop often is used in programs because it performs many tasks automatically. The loop control variable is incremented or decremented automatically. Also, the condition that controls loop repetition is checked automatically each time the FOR statement is executed. Therefore, the programmer does not need to perform these tasks.

The FOR/NEXT loop is very useful when writing programs that use **counting loops,** in which the exact number of loop repetitions is known before the loop is executed for the first time. The program in Figure V-6 is an example of a situation in which it is appropriate to use a counting loop. In this program, the user is asked to enter the number of paychecks that need to be calculated for a village payroll. Then this number, which is assigned to the variable NMBR, is used to control the number of times the FOR/NEXT loop executes. In this way, the user can determine the number of paychecks calculated each time the program is executed.

COUNTING LOOP
A type of loop in which repetition is controlled by a counter, which is a numeric variable that is tested each time the loop is executed to determine if the desired number of repetitions has been performed.

Nested FOR/NEXT Loops

It is possible to nest two or more FOR/NEXT loops. This means that a FOR/NEXT loop can be placed within another FOR/NEXT loop, as shown in the following example:

SECTION V: LOOPING

```
FOR I = X TO Y STEP 2
   FOR J = 1 TO 2
      .
      .
      .
   NEXT J
NEXT I
```

Figure V-5
Flowcharting the FOR/NEXT Statements

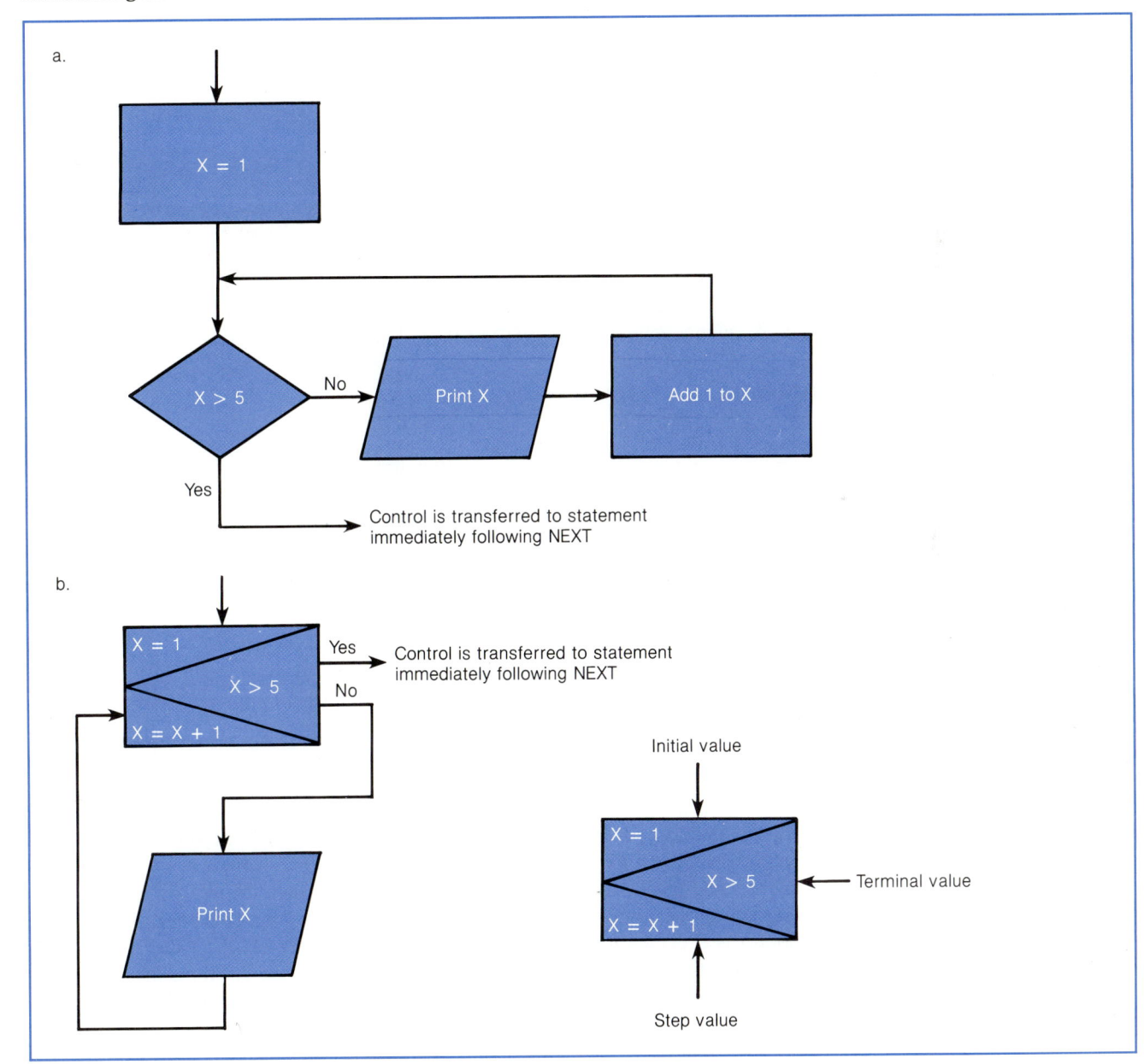

a.

- X = 1
- X > 5 ?
  - No → Print X → Add 1 to X → (loop back)
  - Yes → Control is transferred to statement immediately following NEXT

b.

Combined box containing: X = 1, X > 5, X = X + 1
- Yes → Control is transferred to statement immediately following NEXT
- No → Print X → (loop back)

Legend box:
- X = 1 ← Initial value
- X > 5 ← Terminal value
- X = X + 1 ← Step value

```
10  REM ***            THE VILLAGE PAYROLL            ***
20  REM
30  LET RTE = 4
40  REM
50  CLS
60  REM *** DETERMINE HOW MANY PAYCHECKS ARE TO BE CALCULATED ***
70  INPUT "HOW MANY PAYCHECKS NEED TO BE CALCULATED";NMBR
80  REM *** LOOP TO PROCESS EACH EMPLOYEE'S PAYCHECK ***
90  FOR I = 1 TO NMBR
100    INPUT "ENTER NAME AND NUMBER OF HOURS WORKED";NME$,HOURS
110    WAGE = RTE * HOURS
120    PRINT "NAME","WAGE"
130    PRINT NME$,WAGE
140 NEXT I
999 END
```

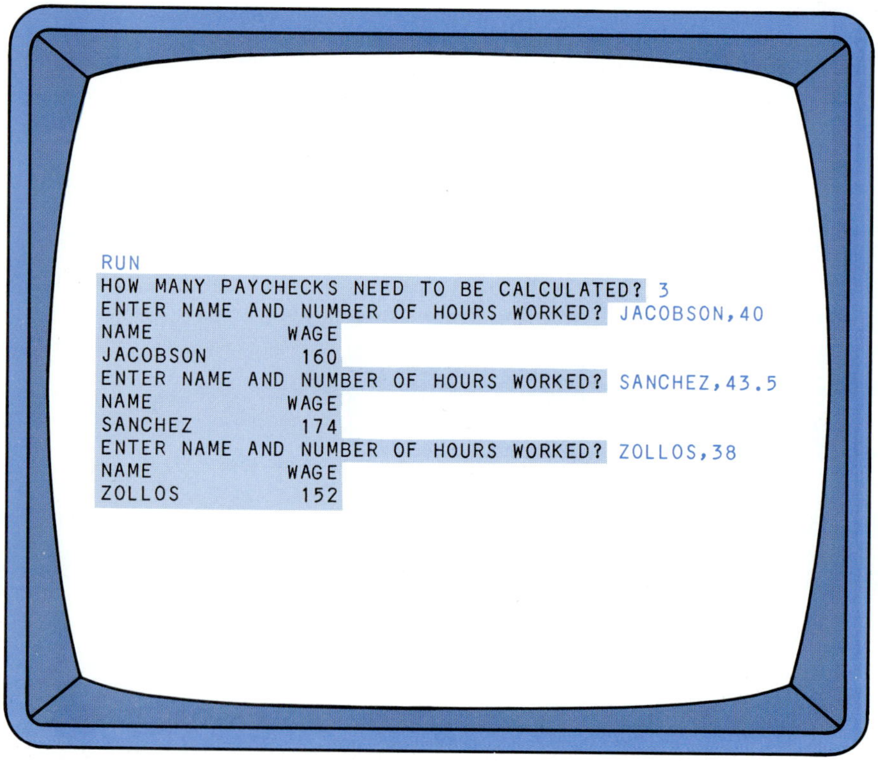

```
RUN
HOW MANY PAYCHECKS NEED TO BE CALCULATED? 3
ENTER NAME AND NUMBER OF HOURS WORKED? JACOBSON,40
NAME            WAGE
JACOBSON         160
ENTER NAME AND NUMBER OF HOURS WORKED? SANCHEZ,43.5
NAME            WAGE
SANCHEZ          174
ENTER NAME AND NUMBER OF HOURS WORKED? ZOLLOS,38
NAME            WAGE
ZOLLOS           152
```

Figure V-6
Program to Calculate a Payroll

Each time the outer loop (loop I) is executed once, the inner loop (loop J) is executed twice, because J varies from 1 to 2. When the inner loop has terminated, control passes to the first statement after the NEXT J, which in this case is the statement NEXT I. This statement causes I to be incremented by 1 and tested against the terminal value of 4. If I still is less than or equal to 4, the body of loop I is executed again. The loop J is again encountered, the value of J is reset to 1, and the inner loop is executed until J is greater than 2. Altogether, the outer loop is executed I times (4 times in this case) and the inner loop is executed I × J times (4 × 2 = 8 times).

The following rules should be remembered when using nested FOR/NEXT loops:

SECTION V: LOOPING

■ Each loop must have a unique loop control variable. The following example is invalid, because execution of the inner loop modifies the value of the outer loop control variable:

```
FOR I = X TO Y STEP 2
   FOR I = Q TO R
      .
      .
      .
   NEXT I
NEXT I
```

These nested loops should be rewritten so that each uses a unique loop control variable:

```
FOR I = X TO Y STEP 2
   FOR J = Q TO R
      .
      .
      .
   NEXT J
NEXT I
```

■ The NEXT statements for an inner loop must appear within the body of the outer loop, so that one loop is entirely contained within another.

Invalid	Valid
`FOR I = 1 TO 5`	`FOR I = 1 TO 5`
`   FOR J = 1 TO 10`	`   FOR J = 1 TO 10`
`      .`	`      .`
`      .`	`      .`
`      .`	`      .`
`   NEXT I`	`   NEXT J`
`NEXT J`	`NEXT I`

In the invalid example, the J loop is not entirely inside the I loop, but extends beyond the NEXT I statement.

■ It is possible to nest many loops within one another. Figure V-7 illustrates multiple nested loops.

Figure V-7
Multiple Nested FOR/NEXT Loops

```
10   FOR I = 1 TO 3
20      PRINT I
30      FOR J = 1 TO 4
40         PRINT J
50         FOR K = 1 TO 2
60            PRINT K        Loop 3  Loop 2  Loop 1
70         NEXT K
80      NEXT J
90   NEXT I
```

Loop 1 is executed 3 times, loop 2 is executed 3 × 4 = 12 times, and loop 3 is executed 3 × 4 × 2 = 24 times. Each loop is completely contained within its outer loop.

Figure V-8 shows an application of nested FOR/NEXT loops. The program prints the multiplication tables for the numbers 1, 2 and 3, with each table in a single column. The inner loop S controls the printing in each of the three columns, whereas the outer loop R controls the printing of rows. The first time the outer loop is executed, the first row is printed; the inner loop then prints three statements on that row. The first time the S loop is executed, R = 1 and S = 1, so the printed statement is 1 × 1 = 1. The comma at the end of line 90 causes a space to appear before the next output.

When the S loop has been completed (when three statements have been printed on the first 2 rows), the PRINT statement in line 110 causes the remainder of the line to remain blank; the next output starts at the left margin on the next line. As line 120 increments R and passes control back to the top of the R loop, this loop begins a second execution, during which a second row is printed. The program ends when the R loop has been executed ten times and ten rows have been printed.

Learning Check

1. When the terminal value is exceeded in a FOR/NEXT loop (using a positive step value), control passes to what statement?

2. When no step value is specified in a FOR statement, it is assumed to be _____.

3. A loop that is completely enclosed by another loop is called a(n) _____ loop.

4. Two or more nested loops can have the same loop control variable name. True or false?

5. The FOR statement serves to _____.
   a. initialize and test the loop control variable
   b. increment the loop control variable by the step value
   c. pass control to the NEXT statement

Answers

1. The first statement following the NEXT statement. 2. +1 3. nested 4. false 5. a

Figure V-8
Multiplication Table with Nested FOR/NEXT Loops

```
10   REM *** PRINT THREE MULTIPLICATION TABLES ***
20   CLS
30   REM *** MAJOR VARIABLES                      ***
40   REM ***    R          OUTER LOOP INDEX       ***
50   REM ***    S          INNER LOOP INDEX       ***
60   REM
70   FOR R = 1 TO 10
80     FOR S = 1 TO 3
90       PRINT S;" X ";R;" = ";S * R,
100    NEXT S
110    PRINT
120  NEXT R
999  END
```

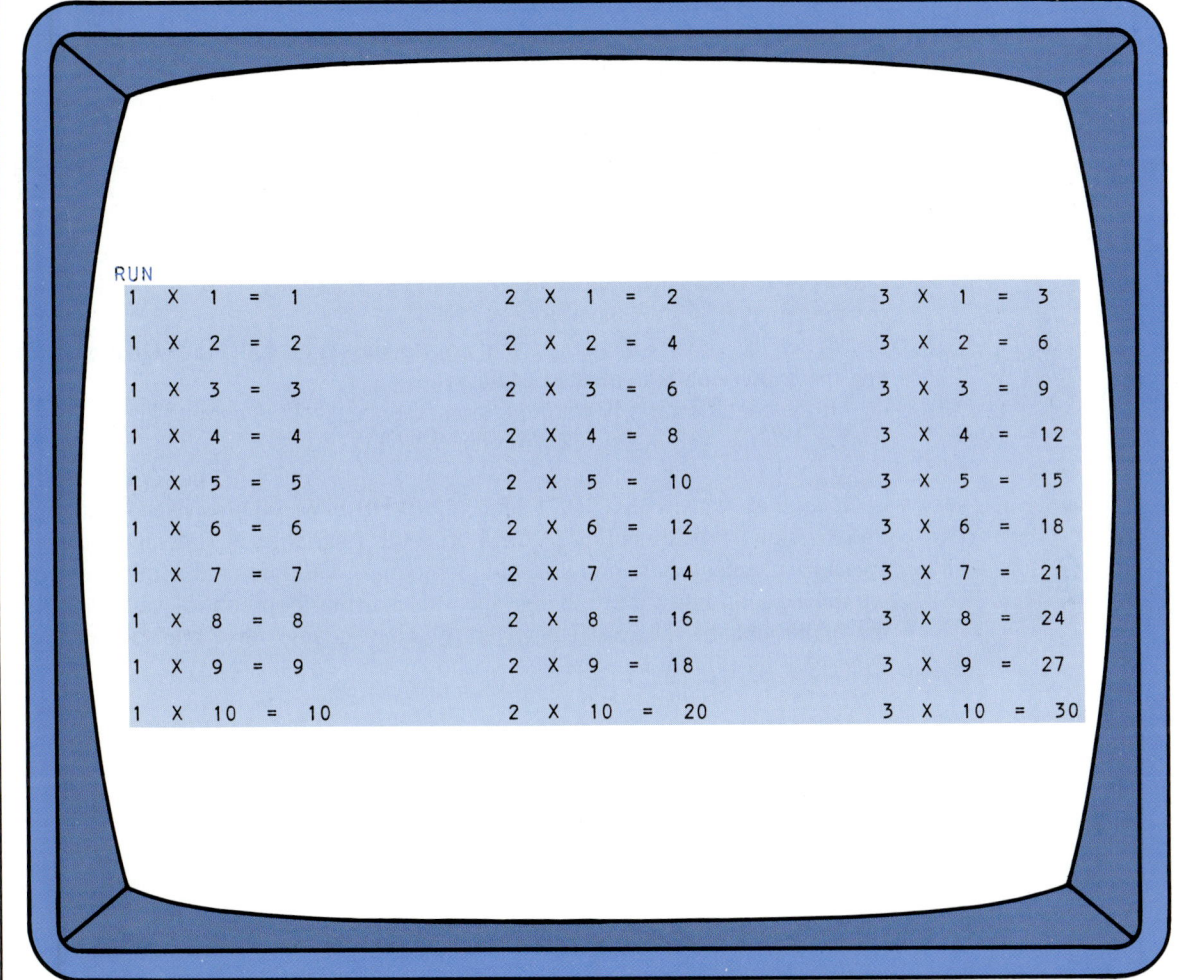

```
RUN
1 X 1  = 1      2 X 1  = 2       3 X 1  = 3
1 X 2  = 2      2 X 2  = 4       3 X 2  = 6
1 X 3  = 3      2 X 3  = 6       3 X 3  = 9
1 X 4  = 4      2 X 4  = 8       3 X 4  = 12
1 X 5  = 5      2 X 5  = 10      3 X 5  = 15
1 X 6  = 6      2 X 6  = 12      3 X 6  = 18
1 X 7  = 7      2 X 7  = 14      3 X 7  = 21
1 X 8  = 8      2 X 8  = 16      3 X 8  = 24
1 X 9  = 9      2 X 9  = 18      3 X 9  = 27
1 X 10 = 10     2 X 10 = 20      3 X 10 = 30
```

The WHILE/WEND Loop

Another type of loop available in BASIC is the WHILE/WEND. Unlike the FOR/NEXT, which executes a specified number of times, the WHILE/WEND continues to execute as long as a stated condition is true. The format of the WHILE/WEND loop is as follows:

    line# WHILE expression
        .
        .
        .
    line# WEND

The loop executes according to the following steps:

1. The expression, which can be a numeric expression or a numeric variable, is evaluated as true or false. If the expression is a variable, it is true if it is not equal to zero.
2. If the expression is true, the statements in the loop body are executed until the WEND statement is encountered. If the expression is false, control passes to the first statement after the WEND.
3. When the WEND is encountered, control passes back to the WHILE statement and the expression is evaluated again.
4. If the condition is still true, the loop body is executed again; if false, the loop is exited to the statement following the WEND.

In contrast to the FOR/NEXT loop, the WHILE/WEND involves no automatic initialization or incrementing of the loop control variable. A statement before the WHILE statement must initialize the loop control variable, and another statement within the loop body must change the value of the loop control variable so that the expression of the WHILE statement can become false and end the loop. Otherwise an infinite loop results, as shown here:

```
200 WHILE CNT < 50
210    PRINT CNT
220 WEND
```

This loop could be written correctly as follows:

```
190 CNT = 0
200 WHILE CNT < 50
210    PRINT CNT
220    CNT = CNT + 1
230 WEND
```

Figure V-9 implements the WHILE/WEND loop using an expression that consists of a single variable. The condition is true as long as the variable's value is not equal to XXX.

SECTION V: LOOPING

Figure V-9
Example of WHILE/WEND Loop

```
10  REM ***      LIBRARY LISTING OF NEW BOOKS        ***
20  CLS
30  REM *** THIS PROGRAM READS DATA FOR ALL NEW      ***
40  REM *** BOOKS AND PRINTS A LISTING OF THEM.      ***
50  REM
60  REM *** MAJOR VARIABLES                          ***
70  REM ***     TITLE$      BOOK'S TITLE             ***
80  REM ***     AUTHR$      BOOK'S AUTHOR            ***
90  REM ***     BNUM        NUMERIC RATING OF BOOK   ***
100 REM ***     INDEX       LIST NUMBER OF BOOK      ***
110 REM
120 REM *** PRINT HEADING ***
130 PRINT TAB(6);"TITLE";TAB(30);"AUTHOR";TAB(42);"RATING"
140 REM
150 REM *** INITIALIZE VARIABLES ***
160 INDEX = 0
170 READ TITLE$,AUTHR$,BNUM
180 REM
190 REM *** LOOP TO PROCESS ONE BOOK PER PASS ***
200 WHILE TITLE$ <> "XXX"
210    PRINT
220    INDEX = INDEX + 1
230    PRINT INDEX;". ";
240    PRINT TAB(6);TITLE$;TAB(30);AUTHR$;TAB(42);
250    FOR I = 1 TO BNUM
260       PRINT "*";
270    NEXT I
280    READ TITLE$,AUTHR$,BNUM
290 WEND
300 REM
310 REM *** DATA STATEMENTS ***
320 DATA "COMPETITIVE TANNING","HARRIS,Z.",1
330 DATA "BOMBAY","GOODTIME,C.",2
340 DATA "LEARNING TO LOVE C","LORD,P.",5
350 DATA "THE SURVIVOR","BULAS,I.",3
360 DATA "XXX","XXX",0
999 END
```

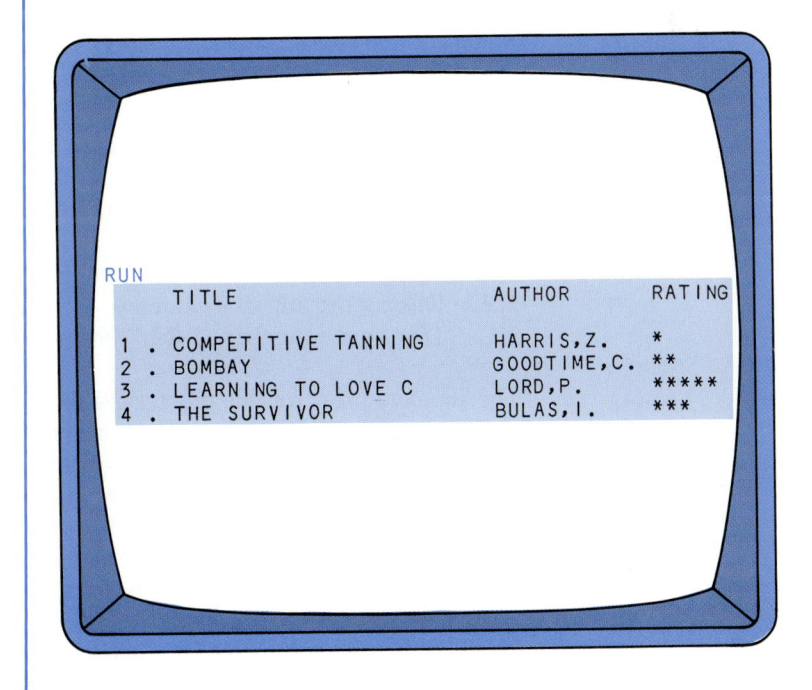

```
RUN
       TITLE                    AUTHOR          RATING

   1 . COMPETITIVE TANNING      HARRIS,Z.         *
   2 . BOMBAY                   GOODTIME,C.      **
   3 . LEARNING TO LOVE C       LORD,P.        *****
   4 . THE SURVIVOR             BULAS,I.        ***
```

Comprehensive Programming Problem

Problem Definition

The film critic of the *Wopekeneta Daily News* would like a program to create a chart indicating the title and rating for each movie she has reviewed in the past week. This chart is to be printed in her weekly column. She assigns each movie a rating from 1 through 5, and she wants to be able to enter the movie title and its corresponding rating at the keyboard. The program should display a chart similar to the following:

Films Reviewed the Week of 4/24/87

Title	Rating
Dinner on Grounds	*****
Escape from The Amazon	****
Return of the Canal Beast	**
Love's Fury	***

Solution Design

This program must perform three major tasks:

1. Enter the date.
2. Read the data for each movie.
3. Display the chart.

The second and third tasks can be subdivided as follows:

2.B. Read the rating (1–5) for each movie.
3.A. Display the heading.
3.B. Display the title of each movie.
3.B. Display the title of each movie.
3.C. Display the number of stars for each movie.

The structure chart for this program is shown in Figure V-10.

The program can use READ statements to read each movie title and rating. Because it is not known in advance how many films will be read, this is a perfect situation in which to use an IF/THEN loop with a trailer value. This means that the last movie title value in the DATA statements must be DONE. Each movie rating is an integer value; therefore, this value can be used to determine how many times a FOR/NEXT loop should be executed to print the necessary number of stars. Figure V-11 depicts the flowchart for this program.

Structure Chart

- **Level 0:** Create a Movie Review Chart
  - **Level 1:**
    - Read the Date
    - Read Title and Rating for Each Movie
      - **Level 2:**
        - Read Title of Each Movie
        - Read Rating for Movie
    - Display the Chart
      - Display Heading
      - Display Title
      - Display Rating Stars

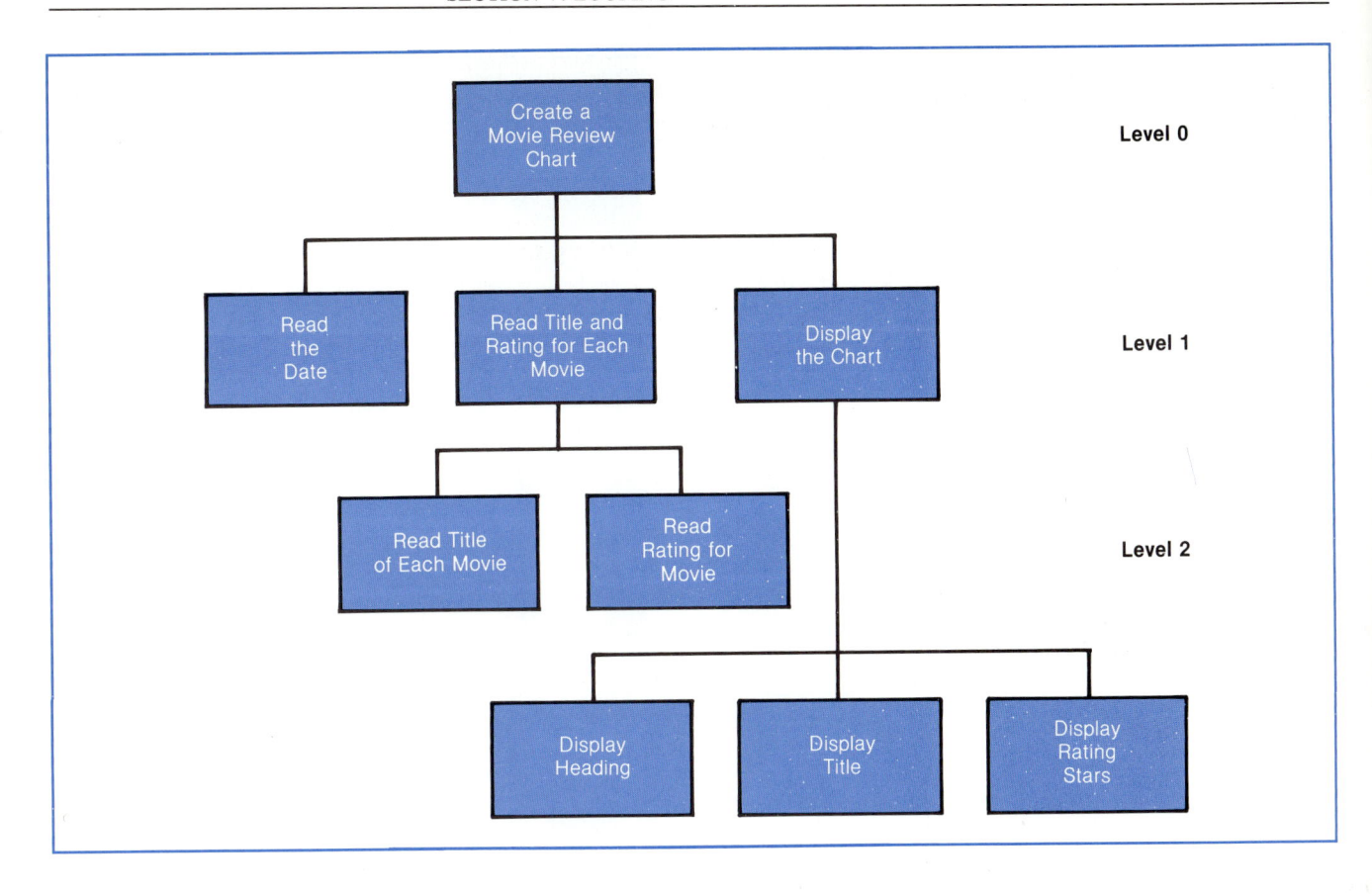

Figure V-10
Structure Chart for Movie Review Program

The Program

The complete program is shown in Figure V-12. First the date is entered and a table heading is printed. Notice that the data for the first movie is read before the IF/THEN loop is entered for the first time. The title of the movie is printed; then a FOR/NEXT loop, contained in lines 240–260, is used to print a horizontal bar graph indicating the movie's rating. Data on each subsequent movie is read at the bottom of the IF/THEN loop, and execution then transfers to the top of the loop to determine if the sentinel value DONE has been read. The loop continues to execute until the sentinel value is encountered; then program execution terminates.

Summary Points

■ Control statements enable the programmer to alter the sequence in which program statements are executed. Loops are control statements that allow a given portion of a program to be executed as many times as needed.

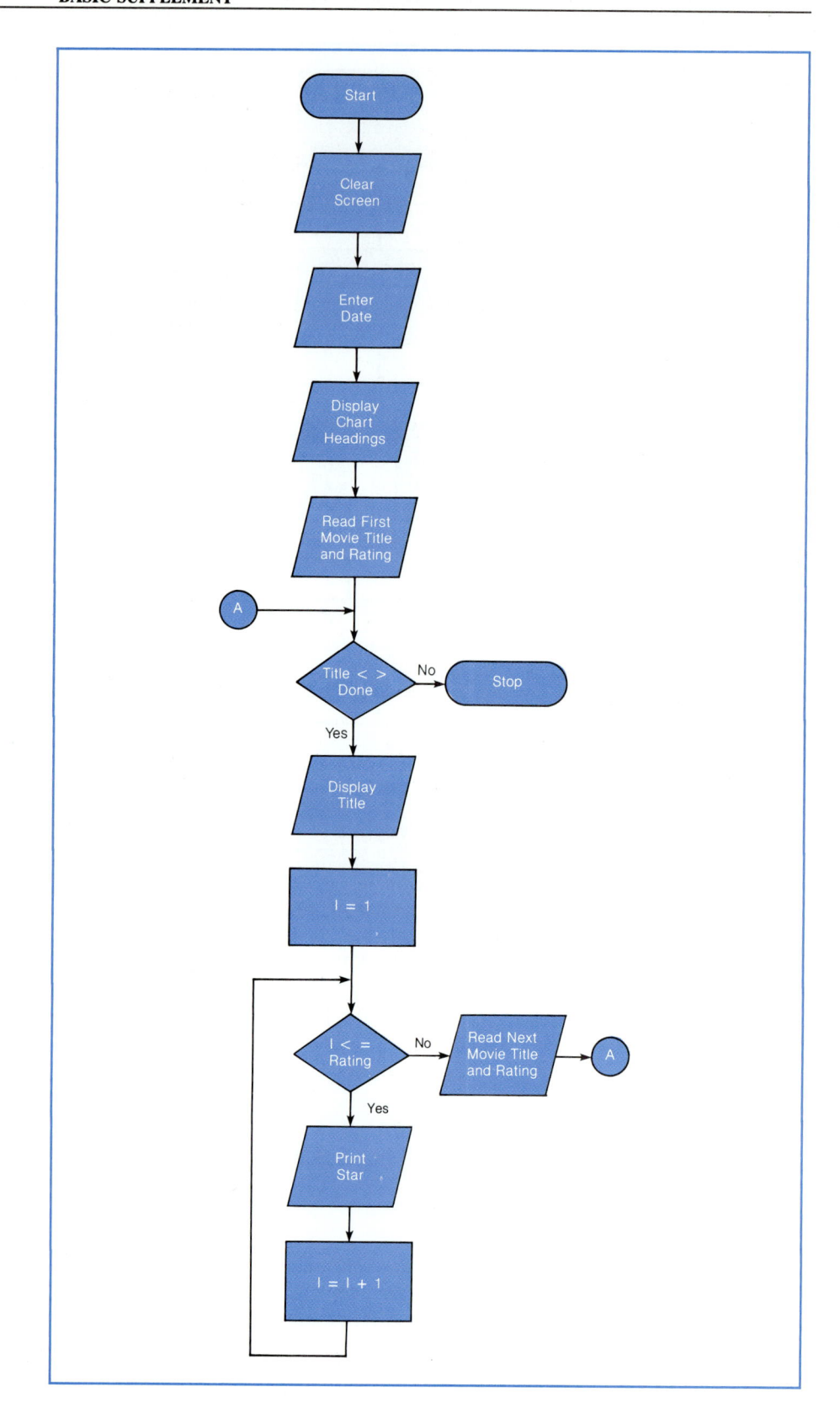

**Figure V-11
Flowchart of Movie Review
Program**

Figure V-12
Movie Review Program

```
10  REM ***                   MOVIE REVIEW                    ***
20  REM *** THIS PROGRAM READS THE TITLE AND RATING           ***
30  REM *** (1-5) FOR EACH MOVIE REVIEWED IN A GIVEN          ***
40  REM *** WEEK.  A CHART CONTAINING A BAR GRAPH FOR         ***
50  REM *** EACH MOVIE REVIEWED IS THEN PRINTED.              ***
60  REM *** MAJOR VARIABLES:                                  ***
70  REM ***      DTE$          DATE                           ***
80  REM ***      TTLE$         TITLE OF THE MOVIE             ***
90  REM ***      RTE           RATING (1-5) OF MOVIE          ***
100 REM
110 CLS
120 PRINT
130 INPUT "ENTER THE DATE";DTE$
140 PRINT "Films Reviewed the Week of ";DTE$
150 PRINT
160 PRINT "Title","Rating"
170 PRINT
180 REM *** READ DATA FOR THE FIRST MOVIE. ***
190 READ TTLE$,RTE
200 REM *** LOOP TO READ AND PRINT EACH TITLE AND RATING. ***
210 WHILE TTLE$ <> "DONE"
220    PRINT TTLE$,
230    REM *** LOOP TO PRINT STARS FOR RATING BAR GRAPH. ***
240    FOR I = 1 TO RTE
250       PRINT "*";
260    NEXT I
270    PRINT
280    PRINT
290    READ TTLE$,RTE
300 WEND
310 REM *** DATA STATEMENTS ***
320 DATA "COLOR PURPLE",5,"OUT OF AFRICA",4,"SPIES LIKE US",2
330 DATA "GHOST BUSTERS",3,"DONE",0
999 END
```

```
RUN

ENTER THE DATE? 2/24/87
Films Reviewed the Week of 2/24/87

Title           Rating

COLOR PURPLE    *****

OUT OF AFRICA   ****

SPIES LIKE US   **

GHOST BUSTERS   ***
```

- The basic steps in loop execution are as follows:
1. The loop control variable is initialized to a particular value before loop execution begins.
2. The loop control variable is tested to determine whether the loop body should be executed or the loop should be exited.
3. The loop body, consisting of any number of statements, is executed.
4. At some point during loop execution, the value of the loop control variable must be modified to allow exit from the loop.
5. The loop is exited when the stated condition determines that the right number of loop repetitions has been performed.
- The FOR/NEXT loop executes the number of times specified in the FOR statement. The NEXT statement increments the loop control variable, tests it against the terminal value, and returns control to the statement immediately following the FOR statement if another loop execution is required. Otherwise, execution continues with the statement following the NEXT statement.
- A step value can be placed in a FOR statement to determine the value by which the loop control variable should be incremented (or decremented) with each loop repetition. The default step value is +1.
- The FOR/NEXT loop is useful for counting loops, in which the number of repetitions needed can be determined before the loop is first executed.
- The major advantage of the FOR/NEXT loop is that the loop control variable is initialized, incremented, and tested automatically. The FOR/NEXT loop cannot be used when the number of loop repetitions needed cannot be determined ahead of time.
- The body of a loop, which contains the action that the loop performs, should be indented to make the program more readable.
- The WHILE/WEND statement repeats execution of its loop body as long as the condition in the WHILE statement is true.

Review Questions

1. When should a loop structure be used in a program?
2. What are the five elements of a controlled loop?
3. What tasks are performed automatically by the FOR/NEXT loop?
4. Which of the following are valid FOR statements?

   a. 20 FOR I = 8 TO 12 STEP 3
   b. 100 FOR K = 15 TO 20 STEP 6
   c. 80 for $N\$$ = 3 TO 5 STEP .5
   d. 400 FOR X = -2 TO -1
   e. FOR I = 1 TO 100 STEP 20

5. When the step value in the FOR/NEXT loop is negative, does a loop stop executing when the loop control variable is greater than or less than the terminal value?

SECTION V: LOOPING

6. What happens when the step value of a FOR statement is zero?
7. What is a counting loop?
8. What happens if no step value is specified in a FOR statement?
9. When is the WHILE/WEND loop a more appropriate choice than a FOR/NEXT loop?
10. How many times is each of the following loops executed?

```
FOR I = 50 TO 10 STEP -5
    FOR J = 1 TO 6 STEP 2
        FOR K = 5 TO 5
        NEXT K
    NEXT J
NEXT I
```

Debugging Exercises

1.
```
10 REM *** READ AND PRINT TEN NAMES. ***
20 FOR I = 1 TO 10
30    READ NME$
40 NEXT
50 PRINT NME$
60 DATA SAM,SARA,SUSAN,SALLY,SAMSON,SHAMERA,STEVEN
70 DATA STEPHANIE,SMILEY,SONIA
99 END
```

2.
```
10 FOR X = 1 TO 5
20    FOR Y = 1 TO 10
30       FOR Z = 1 TO 20
40          PRINT X,Y,Z
50          PRINT "*","*","*"
60          SUM = X + Y + Z
70          PRINT SUM
80       NEXT Y
90    PRINT "Z = ";Z
100   NEXT Z
110 PRINT "X = ";X
120 NEXT X
```

Additional Programming Problems

1. Your landlord is considering a raise in rent of 5 percent, 7 percent, or 10 percent. To determine how much additional money you and your fellow tenants may have to pay, write a program to show sample rents of $200 to $600 (by

increments of $50) and the three proposed increased rents for each. Create a table like the following:

RENT	+5%	+7%	+10%
200	XXX	XXX	XXX
250	XXX	XXX	XXX
.	.	.	.
.	.	.	.

2. Write a program to display a multiplication table. Allow the user to enter the upper and lower limits of the table, then print the appropriate values. Use the following format for the table:

X	3	4	5	6
3	9	12	15	18
4	12	16	20	24
5	15	20	25	30
6	18	24	30	36

3. The high school tennis team is holding its annual tryouts. The coach selects the team members on the basis of the results of a series of matches. Each player is placed on a first, second, or third string team depending on his or her number of wins:

Number of wins	Team
10 or more	First string
4 to 9	Second string
3 or less	Third string

You are to write a program using a WHILE loop that indicates the team on which each player belongs. Use the following data:

Name	Wins
Sanders, S.	7
Crosby, D.	5
Casey, E.	9
Case, L.	12
Sandoval, V.	10
Coles, S.	3
Schnur, R.	2

4. Write a program to calculate X^N. This value should be found by multiplying X times itself N number of times (e.g., $X^4 = X \cdot X \cdot X \cdot X$). Use the following values for X and N to test your program:

SECTION V: LOOPING   B-115

X	N
1	2
6	3
5	4
2	6

The output should have the following format:

X raised to the N = R.

A trailer value should be used to determine the end of the data.

5. The Happy Hedonist Health Spa has asked you to write a payroll program that will calculate the weekly net pay for each of its employees. The employees have the option of participating in a medical insurance plan that deducts $10 per week. The income tax rate is 25 percent. Use a FOR/NEXT loop in your program. The following is the company pay code key:

Code	Wage Rate
1	$5.00
2	6.75
3	9.50

Use the following data:

Name	Medical Plan	Hours	Wage Code
Cochran, K.	Yes	40	2
Batdorf, D.	Yes	45	1
Jones, S.	No	38	3
Goolsby, L.	Yes	30	2
Halas, G.	No	35	1

The output should appear as follows:

NAME	NET PAY
XXXXXXXX	$XXX.XX

SECTION VI

Arrays

Outline

Introduction
Subscripts
The DIM Statement
Learning Check
One-Dimensional Arrays
   Reading Data to an Array
   Displaying the Contents of an
     Array
   Computations on Array
     Elements
Learning Check

Two-Dimensional Arrays
   Reading and Displaying Two-
     Dimensional Arrays
   Computations on Array
     Elements
Learning Check
Manipulating Arrays
   Sorting Arrays—The Bubble
     Sort
   Merging
   Searching

Learning Check
Comprehensive Programming
   Problem
   Problem Definition
   Solution Design
   The Program
Summary Points
Review Questions
Debugging Exercises
Additional Programming Problems

Introduction

ARRAY
A collection of related data items. A single variable name is used to refer to the entire collection of items.

BASIC permits us to deal with many related data items as a group by means of a structure known as an **array**. The type of variable described in earlier chapters represented a single location in computer memory. For example, a variable B might represent the storage location of a numeric value, such as 500. An array, by contrast, is used to store a series of values in adjacent storage locations. When two or more related data items need to be entered, instead of giving each one a separate variable name, the programmer can give one variable name to the entire collection of data items. This capability is important when large quantities of data are needed in a program.

An array can be used to store integer, real, or string values, but the values in a given array must be of the same type. That is, if an array is given a numeric variable name, a string data item cannot be entered to it; only numeric values are allowed.

Subscripts

ELEMENT
An individual data item stored in an array.

Each individual data item within an array is called an **element**. An array consists of a group of consecutive storage locations, each containing a single value. The entire array is given one name; the programmer indicates an individual element in the array by referring to its position. For example, suppose that there are five test scores to be stored: 97, 85, 89, 95, and 100. The scores could be put in an array called TESTS, which we might visualize like this:

Array Tests

97	85	89	95	100

SUBSCRIPT
A value enclosed in parentheses which identifies an element's position in an array.

The array name TESTS now refers to all five storage locations containing the test scores. The gain acess to a single test score within the array, a **subscript** is used. A subscript is a value enclosed in parentheses which identifies the position of a given element in the array. For example, the first element of array TESTS (containing the value 97) is referred to as TESTS(1). The second test score is in TESTS(2), the third test score is in TESTS(3), and so on. Therefore, the following statements are true:

TESTS(1) = 97
TESTS(2) = 85
TESTS(3) = 89
TESTS(4) = 95
TESTS(5) = 100

The subscript enclosed in parentheses does not have to be an integer constant; it can be any legal numeric expression. When an array element subscript is an expression, the computer carries out the following steps:

SECTION VI: ARRAYS

- It evaluates the expression within the parentheses.
- It converts the result to an integer value, by truncation.
- It accesses the indicated element in the array.

SUBSCRIPTED VARIABLE
A variable that refers to a specific element of an array.

Variables that refer to specific elements of arrays, such as TEST(4), are called **subscripted variables**. A subscripted variable refers to one value in the array. It is possible to access a different value in the array by changing the subscript.

The same rules that apply to naming simple variables also apply to naming arrays. It is possible to use the same name for both a simple variable and an array in a program, but this is not good programming practice because it makes the logic of the program difficult to follow.

Assume that the array X and the variables A and B have the following values:

$$X(1) = 2 \quad X(2) = 15 \quad X(3) = 16 \quad X(4) = 17 \quad X(5) = 32$$

$$A = 3 \quad B = 5$$

The following examples show how the various forms of subscripts are used:

Example	Reference
X(3)	Third element of X, or 16
X(B)	B = 5; thus the fifth element of X, or 32
X(X(1))	X(1) = 2; thus the second element of X, or 15
X(B−A)	B = 5, A = 3; 5 − 3 = 2; thus the second element of X, or 15

The DIM Statement

When a program contains an array, the computer automatically sets aside eleven storage locations (0 through 10) for the elements in the array. The programmer does not have to fill all of the reserved array storage spaces with values; it is illegal, however, to refer to an array element for which space has not been reserved. For example, if only eleven storage spaces have been set aside, twelve data items cannot be entered to the array.

The DIM (dimension) statement enables the programmer to override this standard array space reservation and to reserve space for an array of any desired size. A DIM statement is not required for an array of eleven or fewer elements, but it is good programming practice to specify DIM statements for all arrays to help document the array usage.

The general format of the DIM Statement is as follows:

line# DIM variable1(limit1)[,variable2(limit2),...]

The variables are the names of the arrays. Each limit is an integer constant that supplies the maximum subscript value possible for that particular array. For example, if space is needed to store 25 elements in an array ITEM$, the following statement reserves the necessary storage locations:

```
10 DIM ITEM$(24)
```

Although it may seem that this statement sets aside only 24 positions, remember that array positions 0 through 24 are equal to 25 locations. For the sake of clarity and program logic, programmers often ignore the zero element. If we choose not to use the zero position, we dimension the array ITEM$ as follows:

```
10 DIM ITEM$(25)
```

As indicated in the statement format, more than one array can be declared in a single DIM statement. For example, the following statement declares the variables ACCNT, NME$, and OVERDRWN as arrays:

```
10 ACCNT(100),NME$(15),OVERDRWN(5)
```

ACCNT can contain up to 101 elements, NME$ up to 151 elements, and OVERDRWN up to 51 elements.

DIM statements must appear in a program before the first reference to the arrays they describe. A good practice is to place them at the beginning of the program. The following standard preparation symbol generally is used to flowchart the DIM statement:

Learning Check

1. A subscript can consist of any legal numeric or character expression. True or false?
2. If an array is dimensioned as follows, it must contain 20 elements. True or false? 20 DIM X(20)
3. _____ are used with variables to identify a particular storage location within an array.
4. One array can be used to store more than one type of variable (string, real, and integer). True or false?
5. If a DIM statement is not used for an array, _____ storage locations are set aside automatically for the data elements.

Answers

1. false 2. false 3. Subscripts 4. false 5. eleven

One-Dimensional Arrays

ONE-DIMENSIONAL ARRAY
An array that has only one row.

All the arrays we have discussed so far in this chapter have been **one-dimensional arrays**, that is, arrays with a single row of elements. One-dimensional arrays can be thought of as lists of values. The following is a one-dimensional array named X:

| 15 | 20 | 27 | 8 | 16 |

In the next part of this chapter, we will learn how to manipulate the elements of one-dimensional arrays.

Reading Data to an Array

A major advantage of using arrays is the ability to use a variable rather than a constant as a subscript. Because a single name such as TESTS(I) can refer to any element in the array TESTS, depending on the value of I, this name can be used in a loop that varies the value of the subscript I. A FOR/NEXT loop can be an efficient method of reading data to an array if the exact number of items to be read is known in advance. The following program segment reads a list of five numbers into the array TESTS:

```
10 FOR I = 1 TO 5
20    READ TESTS(I)
30 NEXT I
40 DATA 85,71,63,51,99
```

The first time this loop is executed, the loop variable I equals 1. Therefore, when line 20 is executed, the computer reads the first number from the data list (which is 85) and stores it in TESTS(1). The second time through the loop, I equals 2. The second number is read to TESTS(2), the second location in the array. The loop processing continues until all five numbers have been read and stored. This process is outlined as follows:

For I =	ACTION	Array TESTS:
1	READ TESTS(1)	85
2	READ TESTS(2)	85, 71
3	READ TESTS(3)	85, 71, 63
4	READ TESTS(4)	85, 71, 63, 51
5	READ TESTS(5)	85, 71, 63, 51, 99

An array also can be filled using an INPUT statement or an assignment statement within a loop. To initialize an array of ten elements to zero, for example, the following statements could be used:

```
50 FOR I = 1 TO 10
60    SCORES(I) = 0
70 NEXT I
```

It is possible to read data to several arrays within a single loop. In the following segment, each data line contains data for one element of each of three arrays:

```
10 DIM NME$(5),AGE(5),SSN$(5)
20 FOR I = 1 TO 5
30    READ NME$(I),AGE(I),SSN$(I)
40 NEXT I
50 DATA TOM BAKER,41,268-66-1071
60 DATA LALLA WARD,28,353-65-2861
70 DATA MASADA WILMOT,33,269-59-9064
80 DATA PATRICK JONES,52,269-84-2834
90 DATA BERYL JONES,49,234-34-9382
```

When the exact number of items to be read to an array is unknown, a loop with a trailer value can be used. This method is demonstrated in the following segment, where the data contains a trailer value of -1. The programmer must ensure that the number of items read does not exceed the size of the array.

```
10 DIM X(5)
20 I = 1
30 INPUT X(I)
40 WHILE X(I) <> -1
50    I = I + 1
60    INPUT X(I)
70 WEND
99 END
```

Displaying the Contents of an Array

The FOR/NEXT loop can be used to print the contents of the array TEST, as shown in the following segment.

```
70 FOR T = 1 TO 5
80    PRINT TESTS(T)
90 NEXT T
```

RUN

```
85
71
63
51
99
```

Because there is no punctuation at the end of the PRINT statement in line 80, each value is printed on a separate line. As the loop control variable T varies from

SECTION VI: ARRAYS

1 to 5, so does the value of the array subscript, and the computer prints elements 1 through 5 of the array TESTS.

Computations on Array Elements

Figure VI-1 illustrates a program that might be used by a small business. The total sales for the day are calculated using three different arrays: arrays A and B are

Figure VI-1
Total Sales Program

```
10  REM ***        SALES PROGRAM       ***
20  DIM A(10),B(10),C(10)
30  PRINT "COST","SOLD","SALES"
40  PRINT
50  REM
60  REM *** ENTER DATA TO ARRAYS A AND B ***
70  FOR K = 1 TO 10
80     READ A(K),B(K)
90  NEXT K
100 REM
110 REM *** COMPUTE ARRAY C FOR ITEM SALES ***
120 FOR M = 1 TO 10
130    LET C(M) = A(M) * B(M)
140    PRINT A(M),B(M),C(M)
150 NEXT M
160 REM
170 REM *** CALCULATE TOTAL SALES ***
180 FOR N = 1 TO 10
190    LET S = S + C(N)
200 NEXT N
210 REM *** END OF CALCULATIONS ***
220 PRINT
230 PRINT "THE TOTAL SALES IS $ ";S
240 REM
250 REM *** DATA STATEMENTS ***
260 DATA .99,10,1.39,3,.59,17,.19,15
270 DATA 2.49,12,1,23,1.98,40
280 DATA .43,4,.39,63,9.49,37
999 END
```

```
RUN
COST            SOLD            SALES

.99             10              9.899999
1.39            3               4.17
.59             17              10.03
.19             15              2.85
2.49            12              29.88
1               23              23
1.98            40              79.2
.43             4               1.72
.39             63              24.57
9.49            37              351.13

THE TOTAL SALES IS $  536.45
```

used to enter the unit cost and number sold respectively, and array C is used to hold the information obtained by multiplying the elements of arrays A and B together.

Line 20 dimensions the arrays to reserve storage space and to document the arrays used by the program. Lines 70 through 90 input the cost of the items and the number sold by using a FOR/NEXT loop. When the loop variable is set to 1, the first value entered is assigned to A(1) and the second value is assigned to B(1). As the loop continues to 2, the third and fourth pieces of data are input and assigned to A(2) and B(2) respectively. This process continues until the looping is completed. Control then passes to the next line.

The FOR/NEXT loop in lines 120–150 takes the information in arrays A and B, multiplies them together, and stores the results in array C. On the first pass through the loop, M = 1 and line 130 appears as follows:

LET C(1) = A(1)*B(1),

thus C(1) = .99*10 or 9.90.

This loop also contains a PRINT statement that displays what is contained in each array. The total sales for each item are stored in array C. Adding the contents of this array gives the total sales for all items (lines 180–200).

Learning Check

1. A(n) _____ array contains only one column.
2. What values are held in positions J(2) and J(3) in array J?

   ARRAY J

25	13	3	89	55

3. Write a loop that adds the corresponding elements of arrays A and B, each containing ten elements, and stores the results in array C.
4. Write a PRINT statement that displays the value 89 from array J in Question 2.

Answers

1. one-dimensional 2. 13 and 3, respectively 3. FOR I=1 TO 10 C(I) = A(I) + B(I) NEXT I 4. PRINT J(4)

Two-Dimensional Arrays

All the arrays shown so far in this chapter have been one-dimensional arrays; that is, arrays that store values in the form of a single list. A **two-dimensional array**,

SECTION VI: ARRAYS

TWO-DIMENSIONAL ARRAY
An array that can be compared to a table with both rows and columns.

by contrast, has both rows and columns. For example, suppose that a fast-food restaurant chain is running a four-day promotional T-shirt sale at each of its three store locations. It might keep the following table of data concerning shirts sold by each of the three restaurants:

STORE

DAY	1	2	3
1	12	14	15
2	10	16	12
3	11	18	13
4	9	9	10

Each row of the data refers to a specific day of the sale, and each column contains the sales for one store. Thus, the number of shirts sold by the second store on the third day of the sale (18) can be found in the third row, second column. A two-dimensional array named SHIRTS, containing the preceding data, can be pictured like this:

array SHIRTS

12	14	15
10	16	12
11	18	13
9	9	10

The array SHIRTS consists of twelve elements arranged as four rows and three columns. In order to reference a single element of a two-dimensional array such as this, two subscripts are needed: one to indicate the row and a second to indicate the column. For instance, the subscripted variable SHIRTS(4,1) contains the number of shirts (9) sold on the fourth day by the first store. In BASIC, the first subscript gives the row number and the second subscript gives the column number.

The rules regarding one-dimensional arrays also apply to two-dimensional arrays. A two-dimensional array is named in the same way as other variables and cannot use the same name as another array in the same program. A two-dimensional array can contain only one type of data; numeric and character string values cannot be mixed. As with one-dimensional arrays, two-dimensional array subscripts can be indicated by any legal numeric expression, as in the following examples:

```
SHIRTS(3,3)
SHIRTS(1,2)
SHIRTS(I,J)
SHIRTS(1,I + J)
```

Assume that I = 4 and J = 2, and that the array X contains the following 16 elements:

Array X

10	15	20	25
50	55	60	65
90	95	100	105
130	135	140	145

The following examples, based on this same array, show how the various forms of subscripts are used:

Example	**Refers to**
X(4,I)	X(4,4)—the element in the fourth row, fourth column of X, which is 145.
X(J,I)	X(2,4)—the element in the second row, fourth column of X, which is 65.
X(3,J + 1)	X(3,3)—the element in the third row, third column of X, which is 100.
X(I − 1,J − 1)	X(3,1)—the element in the third row, first column of X, which is 90.

As with one-dimensional arrays, the computer automatically reserves space for a two-dimensional array. By default, it reserves room for 11 rows and 11 columns, so the space for a two-dimensional array is 11 × 11 = 121 elements. As mentioned earlier, the 0 subscripted element often is ignored.

The DIM statement also can be used to set the dimensions of a two-dimensional array. The general format of such a DIM statement is as follows:

line# DIM variable1(limit1,limit2)[,variable2(limit3,limit4),...]

where the variable is the array name and the limits are the highest possible values of the subscripts for each dimension. For example, the following statement reserves space for the two-dimensional character array STDNT$, with up to 16 rows and 6 columns, for a total of 16 × 6 = 96 elements:

```
30 DIM STDNT$(15,5)
```

Reading and Displaying Two-Dimensional Arrays

As we explained in previous sections of this chapter, the FOR/NEXT loop is a convenient means of accessing all the elements of a one-dimensional array. The loop control variable of the FOR statement is used as the array subscript, as in the following example:

```
30 DIM X(5)
40 FOR I = 1 TO 5
50    READ X(I)
60 NEXT I
```

FOR/NEXT loops also can be used to read data to and print information from a two-dimensional array. It may be helpful to think of a two-dimensional array as a group of one-dimensional arrays, with each row making up a single one-dimensional array. A single FOR/NEXT loop can read values to one row. This process must be repeated for as many rows as the array contains; therefore, the FOR/NEXT loop that reads a single row is nested within a second FOR/NEXT loop that controls the number of rows being accessed.

The array SHIRTS of the previous example can be filled from the sales data table one row at a time, moving from left to right across the columns. The following segment shows the nested FOR/NEXT loops that do this:

```
30 FOR I = 1 TO 4
40   FOR J = 1 TO 3
50     READ SHIRTS(I,J)
60   NEXT J
70 NEXT I
80 DATA 12,14,15
90 DATA 10,16,12
100 DATA 11,18,13
110 DATA 9,9,10
```

Each time line 50 is executed, one value is read to a single element of the array; the element is determined by the current values of I and J. The outer loop (loop I) controls the rows, and loop J controls the columns. The READ statement is executed $I \times J = 4 \times 3 = 12$ times, which is the number of elements in the array.

Each time the outer loop is executed once, the inner loop is executed three times. While I = 1, J becomes 1, 2, and finally 3 as the inner loop is executed. Therefore, on the first pass through the outer loop, line 50 reads values to SHIRTS(1,1), SHIRTS(1,2), and SHIRTS(1,3), and the first row is filled:

	J = 1	2	3
I = 1	12	14	15

While I equals 2, J again varies from 1 to 3, and line 50 reads values to SHIRTS(2,1), SHIRTS(2,2), and SHIRTS(2,3) to fill the second row:

	J = 1	2	3
	12	14	15
I = 2	10	16	12

I is incremented to 3 and then to 4, and the third and fourth rows are filled in the same manner.

To print the contents of the entire array, the programmer can substitute a PRINT statement for the READ statement in the nested FOR/NEXT loop. The following segment prints the contents of the array SHIRTS, one row at a time:

```
40   BLANK = 10
50   FOR I = 1 TO 10
60     FOR J = 1 TO 3
70       PRINT TAB(BLANK * J);SHIRTS(I,J);
80     NEXT J
90     PRINT
100  NEXT I
```

The semicolon at the end of line 70 tells the computer to print the three values on the same line. After the inner loop is executed, the blank PRINT statement in line 90 causes a carriage return, so that the next row is printed on the next line. The program in Figure VI-2 shows how the data table for T-shirt sales results can be read to a two-dimensional array and printed in table form with appropriate headings.

Computations on Array Elements

Adding Rows Once data has been stored in an array, often it is necessary to manipulate certain array elements. For instance, the sales manager in charge of the T-shirt promotional sale might want to know how many shirts were sold on the last day of the sale.

Because the data for each day is contained in a row of the array, it is necessary to total the elements in one row of the array (the fourth row) to find the number of shirts sold on the fourth day. The fourth row can be thought of as a one-dimensional array, so one loop is required to access all the elements in this row:

```
30 DAY4SALES = 0
40 FOR J = 1 TO 3
50    DAY4SALES = DAY4SALES + SHIRTS(4,J)
60 NEXT J
```

Notice that the first subscript of SHIRTS(4,J) restricts the computations to the elements in row 4, whereas the column J, varies from 1 to 3.

Adding Columns To find the total number of T-shirts sold by the third store, for example, it is necessary to total the elements in the third column of the array. This time we can think of the column by itself as a one-dimensional array of four elements:

```
40 SALE3SHOP = 0
50 FOR I = 1 TO 4
60    SALE3SHOP = SALE3SHOP + SHIRTS(I,3)
70 NEXT I
```

Figure VI-2
Two-Dimensional Array Program

```
10  REM ***                 T-SHIRT SALES REPORT              ***
20  REM
30  REM ***    THIS PROGRAM PRINTS A REPORT ON THE NUMBER OF  ***
40  REM ***    T-SHIRTS SOLD PER STORE FOR 4 DIFFERENT DAYS.  ***
50  REM ***    MAJOR VARIABLES:                               ***
60  REM ***       SHIRTS         ARRAY OF T-SHIRTS SOLD       ***
70  REM ***       I,J            LOOP CONTROLS                ***
80  REM
90  REM *** DIMENSION ARRAY ***
100 DIM SHIRTS(4,3)
110 REM
120 REM *** READ THE DATA ***
130 FOR I = 1 TO 4
140    FOR J = 1 TO 3
150       READ SHIRTS(I,J)
160    NEXT J
170 NEXT I
180 REM
190 REM *** PRINT TABLE OF QUANTITIES SOLD ***
200 PRINT "DAY #";TAB(10);"STORE 1";TAB(20);"STORE 2";TAB(30);"STORE 3"
210 BLANK = 10
220 FOR I = 1 TO 4
230    PRINT I;
240    FOR J= 1 TO 3
250       PRINT TAB(BLANK * J);SHIRTS(I,J);
260    NEXT J
270    PRINT
280 NEXT I
290 REM
300 REM *** DATA STATEMENTS ***
310 DATA 12,4,15,10,6,12,11,8,13,9,9,10
999 END
```

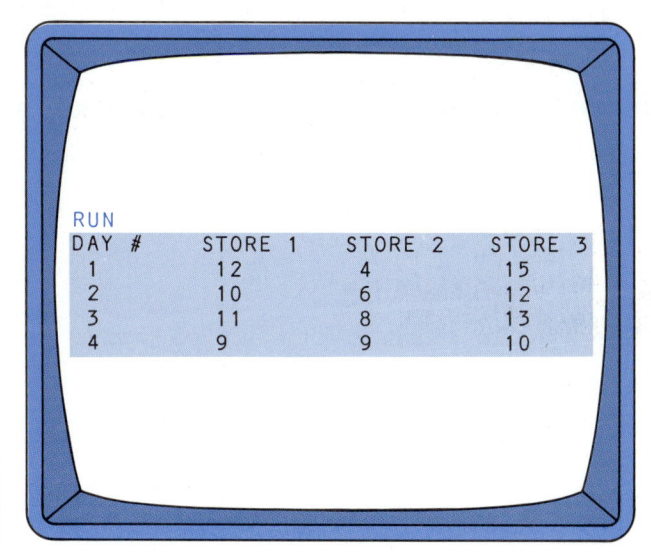

```
RUN
DAY #     STORE 1     STORE 2     STORE 3
 1          12           4          15
 2          10           6          12
 3          11           8          13
 4           9           9          10
```

In line 60, the second subscript (3) restricts the computations to the elements in the third column. The row, I, varies from 1 to 4.

Totaling a Two-Dimensional Array   Consider the problem of finding the grand total of all T-shirts sold during the entire four-day sale. The program must access all the elements of the array one at a time and add them to the grand total. Remember that nested FOR/NEXT loops were used to print or read values to a two-dimensional array. This same method can be used to total the elements of an array, by substituting an addition operation for the READ or PRINT statement:

```
50   TSHIRT = 0
60   FOR I = 1 TO 4
70     FOR J = 1 TO 3
80       TSHIRT = TSHIRT + SHIRTS(I,J)
90     NEXT J
100  NEXT I
```

This segment adds the elements in a row-by-row sequence. The same operation also can be performed in a column-by-column sequence:

```
50   TSHIRT = 0
60   FOR J = 1 TO 3
70     FOR I = 1 TO 4
80       TSHIRT = TSHIRT + SHIRTS(I,J)
90     NEXT I
100  NEXT J
```

Learning Check

1. What is the difference between a one-dimensional array and a two-dimensional array?

2. Given the statement
   10 DIM (20,10)
   how many elements could this array contain?

3. A(n) _____ stores values as a table consisting of rows and columns.

4. The first subscript of a two-dimensional array refers to the _____ of the elements, and the second subscript refers to the _____.

Answers

1. A one-dimensional array consists of only 1 row, whereas a two-dimensional array consists of rows and columns.   2. 231   3. two-dimensional array   4. row, column.

SECTION VI: ARRAYS

Manipulating Arrays

Sorting Arrays—The Bubble Sort

Many programming applications require data items stored in arrays to be sorted or ordered in some way. For example, names must be alphabetized, social security numbers must be arranged from lowest to highest, sports statistics must be arranged by numeric value, and so on. There are various methods the programmer can use to sort data items. We will examine only the **bubble sort**, as it is the easiest to understand.

The basic idea behind the bubble sort is to arrange the elements of an array in ascending or descending order by making a series of comparisons of the adjacent values in the array. If two adjacent values are out of sequence, they are exchanged.

When arranging an array in ascending order, the bubble sort "bubbles" the smallest value to the top of the array. The values of two adjacent array elements are compared, and the elements are switched if the value of the first is larger than that of the second. Then the next pair of adjacent elements is compared and switched if necessary.

This sequence of comparisons (called a pass) is then repeated, starting from the beginning of the array. After each complete pass through the array, the element moved to the end of the array need not be included in the comparisons of the next pass, because it is now in its proper position. Successive passes are performed until no elements are switched, indicating that the entire array is sorted.

As an illustration of this bubbling procedure, an array consisting of five integers is sorted into ascending order in Figure VI-3. Notice that, after each pass is completed, the largest of the numbers compared in that pass becomes the last of those numbers. After the first pass through the array, some of the numbers are close to their proper positions, but the array is not yet completely ordered. The largest value, 7, has been positioned successfully at the bottom of the array and therefore is not included in the comparisons in the following passes.

After each pass through the array, the program checks a flag variable which indicates whether the array is in final order. After a fourth pass through this array, the array is completely arranged in ascending order, but another pass is required to set the flag value to indicate this fact. The actual code for a bubble sort is shown in Figure VI-4. This program sorts the names of ten astronauts into alphabetical order. The subroutine called at line 140 reads the astronauts' names into an array ASTRO$ and prints them. The subroutine starting at line 2000 performs the bubble sort. Let us examine this code carefully.

Line 2050 refers to the variable FLAG, which is initialized to 0. Its value is checked later by the computer to determine if the entire array has been sorted.

Notice the terminal value of the FOR/NEXT loop that sorts the array. The terminal value is one less than the number of items to be sorted, because two items at a time are compared. J varies from 1 to 9, which means that the computer eventually compares item 9 with item 9 + 1. If the terminal value were 10, the computer would try to compare item 10 with item 11, which does not exist in the array.

BUBBLE SORT
A sort that progressively arranges the elements of an array in ascending or descending order, by making a series of comparisons of the adjacent array values and exchanging those pairs of values which are out of order.

**Figure VI-3
Bubble Sort Process**

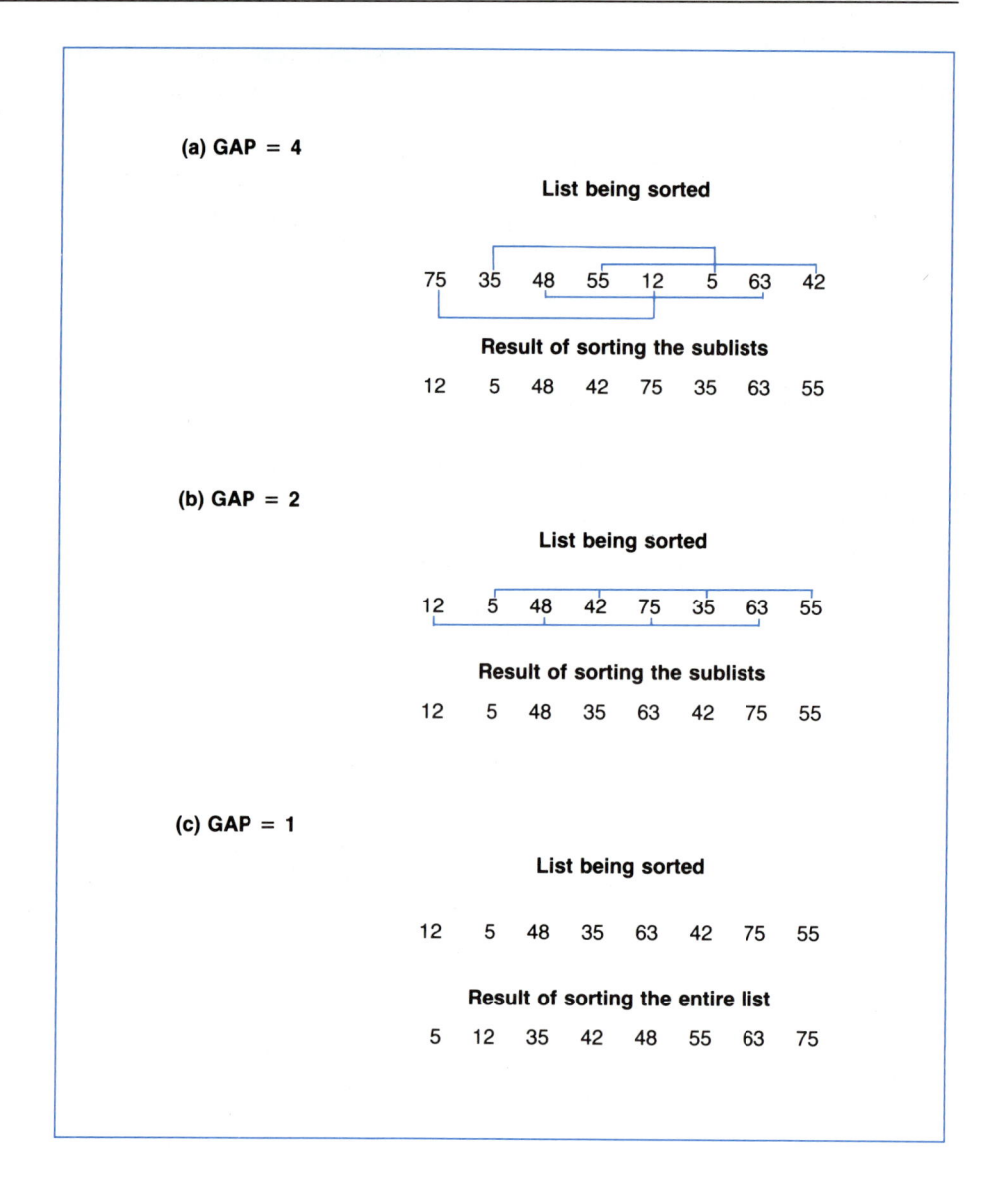

(a) GAP = 4

List being sorted

75 35 48 55 12 5 63 42

Result of sorting the sublists

12 5 48 42 75 35 63 55

(b) GAP = 2

List being sorted

12 5 48 42 75 35 63 55

Result of sorting the sublists

12 5 48 35 63 42 75 55

(c) GAP = 1

List being sorted

12 5 48 35 63 42 75 55

Result of sorting the entire list

5 12 35 42 48 55 63 75

The IF/THEN statement in line 2070 tells the computer whether to interchange two compared values. For example, when J = 1, the computer compares JETSON, G. with SOLONG, H. Because J (the first letter of JETSON) is less than S, there is no need to switch these two items. The J is incremented to 2, and SOLONG, H. is compared with QUIRK, J. These two must be interchanged; the switch is performed by lines 2080 through 2100. Note that we have created a holding area, TEMP$, so that the switch can be made. SOLONG, H. is moved to TEMP$, and QUIRK, L. is moved to SOLONG, H.'s previous position. Now SOLONG, H. is placed in the position previously occupied by QUIRK, J.

Whenever the computer interchanges two values, FLAG is set to 1 in line 2110. This loop continues until every item in the array has been examined. After one pass through this entire loop, the array ASTRO$ looks like this:

Figure VI-4
Bubble Sort Program

```
10   REM ***              ASTRONAUT'S MIX-UP                ***
20   REM
30   REM *** THIS PROGRAM SORTS THE ASTRONAUTS OF THE       ***
40   REM *** ASTRO AIR STATION INTO ALPHABETICAL ORDER.     ***
50   REM *** MAJOR VARIABLES:                               ***
60   REM ***     ASTRO         NAMES OF THE ASTRONAUTS      ***
70   REM ***     TEMP          TEMPORARY STORAGE OF NAME    ***
80   REM
90   REM *** SET-UP NAME ARRAY SIZE ***
100  DIM ASTRO$(10)
110  REM
120  REM
130  REM *** READ NAMES INTO ARRAY AND PRINT THEM OUT ***
140  GOSUB 1000
150  REM
160  REM *** BUBBLE SORT ***
170  GOSUB 2000
180  REM
190  REM *** PRINT LIST ***
200  GOSUB 3000
210  GOTO 9999
1000 REM
1010 REM ****************************************************
1020 REM ****             SUBROUTINE ORIGINAL LIST        ****
1030 REM ****************************************************
1040 REM ***     READ NAMES INTO ARRAY AND PRINT THEM     ***
1050 REM
1060 PRINT "ASTRO AIR STATION -- UNSORTED"
1070 PRINT
1080 FOR I = 1 TO 10
1090    READ ASTRO$(I)
1100    PRINT ASTRO$(I)
1110 NEXT I
1120 PRINT
1130 PRINT
1140 RETURN
2000 REM
2010 REM ****************************************************
2020 REM ***              SUBROUTINE BUBBLE SORT           ***
2030 REM ****************************************************
2040 REM
2050 FLAG = 0
2060 FOR J = 1 TO 9
2070    IF ASTRO$(J) <= ASTRO$(J + 1) THEN 2120
2080    TEMP$ = ASTRO$(J)
2090    ASTRO$(J) = ASTRO$(J + 1)
2100    ASTRO$(J + 1) = TEMP$
2110    FLAG = 1
2120 NEXT J
2130 IF FLAG = 1 THEN 2050
2140 RETURN
3000 REM
3010 REM ****************************************************
3020 REM ****             SUBROUTINE SORTED LIST          ****
3030 REM ****************************************************
3040 REM ***        PRINT HEADING AND SORTED NAMES        ****
3050 REM
3060 PRINT "ASTRO AIR STATION -- SORTED"
3070 PRINT
3080 FOR I = 1 TO 10
3090    PRINT ASTRO$(I)
3100 NEXT I
3110 RETURN
3120 REM
```

(Figure continued on the next page)

```
3130 REM *** DATA STATEMENTS ***
3140 DATA "JETSON,G.","SOLONG,H.","QUIRK,J."
3150 DATA "SKYWALTZER,L.","MADER,D.","MCSOY,D."
3160 DATA "KANOBI,B.","SPECK,M.","OHORROR,L."
3170 DATA "CHECKUP,V."
9999 END
```

```
RUN
ASTRO AIR STATION -- UNSORTED

JETSON,G.
SOLONG,H.
QUIRK,J.
SKYWALTZER,L.
MADER,D.
MCSOY,D.
KANOBI,B.
SPECK,M.
OHORROR,L.
CHECKUP,V.


ASTRO AIR STATION -- SORTED

CHECKUP,V.
JETSON,G.
KANOBI,B.
MADER,D.
MCSOY,D.
OHORROR,L.
QUIRK,J.
SKYWALTZER,L.
SOLONG,H.
SPECK,M.
```

Figure VI-4
Continued

JETSON, G.
QUIRK, J.
SKYWALTZER, L.
MADER, D.
MCSOY, D.
KANOBI, B.
SOLONG, H.
OHORROR, L.
CHECKUP, V.
SPECK, M.

Although several switches have been made, the list is not sorted completely. That is why we need line 2050. As long as FLAG equals 1, the computer knows that switches were made in the previous pass and that the sorting process must continue. When the loop is completed without setting FLAG to 1—that is, when

SECTION VI: ARRAYS

no switches are made—the computer finds FLAG equal to 0 and knows that the list is ordered. Numbers also can be sorted by this same method.

Merging

MERGE
A type of sort that combines two sorted arrays into a single sorted array.

It is possible to **merge**, or combine, two sorted arrays into one large sorted array. Suppose that two sorted integer arrays, A and B, need to be merged to form array C:

Array A
| 2 | 4 |

Array B
| 1 | 2 | 2 |

The first element in A is compared with the first element in array C, and the smaller of the two is placed in array C. Because 1 is less than 2, array C now looks like this:

Array C
| 1 | | | |

The integer placed in array C is not considered again. Next, the first element (2) in array A is compared with the second element (2) in array B. They are of equal value, so the array B is chosen arbitrarily to supply the next element of array C. The 2 in array B is no longer considered. Array C now appears this way:

Array C
| 1 | 2 | | |

The first element of array A and the last element of array B are now compared. Because 2 is less than 3, 2 is moved into array C.

Array C
| 1 | 2 | 2 | |

The 2 in array A is no longer considered. Now the last elements of the two arrays are compared, and 3 is moved into array C:

Array C
| 1 | 2 | 2 | 3 |

At this point, all of array B has been transfered into array C. The remaining element of array A is now moved into array C; if array A were larger, more than one integer would need to be moved. Array C now contains all the elements of both arrays A and B, in sorted order:

```
1000 REM *********************************************
1010 REM ***         SUBROUTINE MERGE SORT        ****
1020 REM *********************************************
1030 REM *** MERGE SORTED ARRAYS A AND B INTO C   ****
1040 REM
1050 REM ***        INITIALIZE ARRAY INDEXES       ***
1060 AINDX = 1
1070 BINDX = 1
1080 CINDX = 1
1090 REM
1100 REM *** MERGE UNTIL ALL OF ONE ARRAY IS READ ***
1110 WHILE (AINDX <= ASIZE) AND (BINDX <= BSIZE)
1120    IF A(AINDX) < B(BINDX) THEN C(CINDX) = A(AINDX):
        AINDX = AINDX + 1 ELSE C(CINDX) = B(BINDX):
        BINDX = BINDX + 1
1130    CINDX = CINDX + 1
1140 WEND
1150 REM
1160 REM *** ADD REMAINING ITEM TO END OF NEW ARRAY ***
1170 WHILE AINDX <= ASIZE
1180    C(CINDX) = A(AINDX)
1190    AINDX = AINDX + 1
1200    CINDX = CINDX + 1
1210 WEND
1220 REM
1230 WHILE BINDX <= BSIZE
1240    C(CINDX) = B(BINDX)
1250    BINDX = BINDX + 1
1260    CINDX = CINDX + 1
1270 WEND
1280 RETURN
```

**Figure VI-5
Merge Subroutine**

Array C

| 1 | 2 | 2 | 3 | 4 |

Figure VI-5 presents a subroutine that performs a merge sort. Is is assumed that the sizes of arrays A and B have been established in the main program, and that array C is large enough to hold the elements of both arrays. The loop of lines 1110 through 1140 places values into C until either A or B has no more elements left to be considered.

As indicated in the preceding example, if two compared integers are equal, this program places the integer from array B in array C. This comparison and the appropriate move into C are made in line 1120. The WHILE/WEND loop of lines 1170 through 1210 adds the remaining elements of array A (if any) to the end of C. If values of A run out before those of B, the loop of lines 1230 through 1270 adds the remaining values of B to C.

Searching

SEQUENTIAL SEARCH
A search that examines array elements from first to last, in the order in which they are stored. When the target element is located, the search terminates.

A given value in an array can be located by examining each array element until the desired value is found. This process is referred to as a **sequential search**. For example, you may want to know the number of scores greater than 89 in an array QUIZ, containing 40 test scores. The following segment performs this task:

```
50 CNT = 0
60 FOR I = 1 TO 40
70    IF QUIZ(I) > 89 THEN CNT = CNT + 1
80 NEXT I
```

The variable CNT holds a count of the scores greater than 89. The loop checks the value of each array element in numeric order, and the count is incremented only if the score being checked is greater than 89.

In another application, you might wish to locate a single value in an array. Suppose you wanted information regarding the August 19th concert at the local concert hall. The computer might prompt you to enter the date of the concert in which you are interested. It would then search an array of concert dates until it matched the given date. Finally, the computer would access the corresponding values from the arrays containing the rest of the concert information and display those values on the monitor screen.

If more than one array holds corresponding (related) data, the data must be contained in the same relative position in each array. In other words, if the desired date matches the third element of the date array, the third elements of the other arrays also are accessed. This process is shown in Figure VI-6.

**Figure VI-6
Concert Information Example**

	DAY$		ARTIST$		TIM$
(1)	0801	(1)	THE KINKS	(1)	7:30 PM
(2)	0810	(2)	THE WHO	(2)	7:30 PM
(3)	0819	(3)	THE RUTTLES	(3)	8:00 PM
(4)	0820	(4)	MOBY GRAPE	(4)	8:00 PM
(5)	0830	(5)	DETROIT WHEELS	(5)	7:00 PM

```
ENTER DATE: 0819

CONCERT DATE:  : 0819
ARTIST         : THE RUTTLES
TIME           : 8:00 PM
```

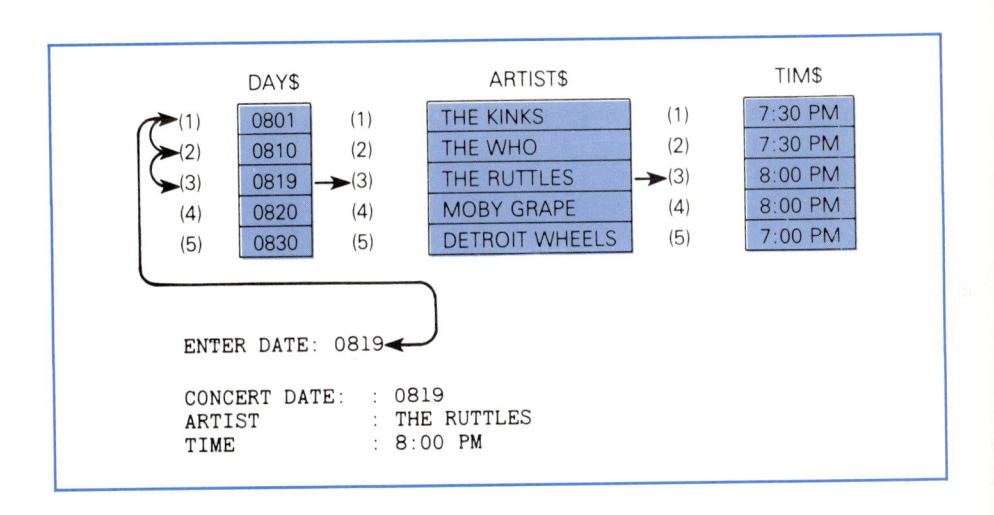

Learning Check

1. A(n) _____ consists of examining the elements of an array until the desired value or values are found.

2. In a sequential search of the following list, how many values will be examined before 236 is located?
   12   44   103   177   236   582   978   1235

3. What is indicated when a bubble sort makes an entire pass without making an exchange?

4. A(n) _____ combines two sorted lists into a single sorted list.

Answers

1. sequential search   2. 5   3. The array is sorted.   4. merge

Comprehensive Programming Problem

Problem Definition

The scorekeeper of the Centrovian Open Ice Skating Championships needs a program to determine the winner of the final round. Each competitor is given six scores, of which the highest and lowest are discarded. The remaining four scores then are averaged to obtain the final score. The maximum score for each event is 6.0. Write a program to read the names and scores of the ten finalists and produce a listing of the skaters' names and final scores in order of finish. Sample input and needed output are shown in the following table.

Input:

Name						
BALDUCCI, G.	5.7	5.3	5.1	5.0	4.7	4.8
CREED, A.	3.1	4.9	4.1	3.7	4.6	3.9
WILLIAMS, E.	4.1	5.3	4.9	4.4	3.9	5.4
HAMILTON, S.	5.1	5.7	5.6	5.5	4.4	5.3
LORD, P.	5.9	4.8	5.5	5.0	5.7	5.7
STRAVINSKY, I.	5.1	4.7	4.1	3.1	4.6	5.0
MONTALBAN, R.	5.1	5.1	4.9	3.4	5.5	5.3
SCHELL, M.	4.9	4.3	5.2	4.5	4.6	4.9
CRANSTON, T.	6.0	6.0	5.7	5.8	5.9	5.9
CROWLEY, S.	4.3	5.2	6.9	5.3	4.3	6.0

SECTION VI: ARRAYS

Needed Output

PLACE	NAME	SCORE
1	BALDUCCI, G.	5.7
•	•	•
•	•	•
•	•	•

Solution Design

The problem provides us with seven items of data for each skater—a name and six scores—and asks for a list of names, sorted by average. Once the data items have been read (the first step), two basic operations must be performed in order to produce the listing: the averages must be calculated, and these averages with their associated names must be sorted. Thus, the problem can be divided into four major tasks: (1) read the data, (2) calculate the averages, (3) sort the names and averages, and (4) print the sorted information. The structure chart is shown in Figure VI-7.

The input for this problem consists of two types of data, alphabetic and numeric, so two arrays must be used to store them. The output calls for the names already stored plus a new set of values, the averages; another array can be used to store these averages. In calculating the averages, variables also are needed to keep track of the high and low scores. These scores can be determined by means of a sequential search on the six scores of each skater.

A sort is required in the third step of our algorithm. A descending-order bubble sort could be used here. As the averages are rearranged, the corresponding skater's name must be carried with each average.

**Figure VI-7
Structure Chart for Skating Scores Problem**

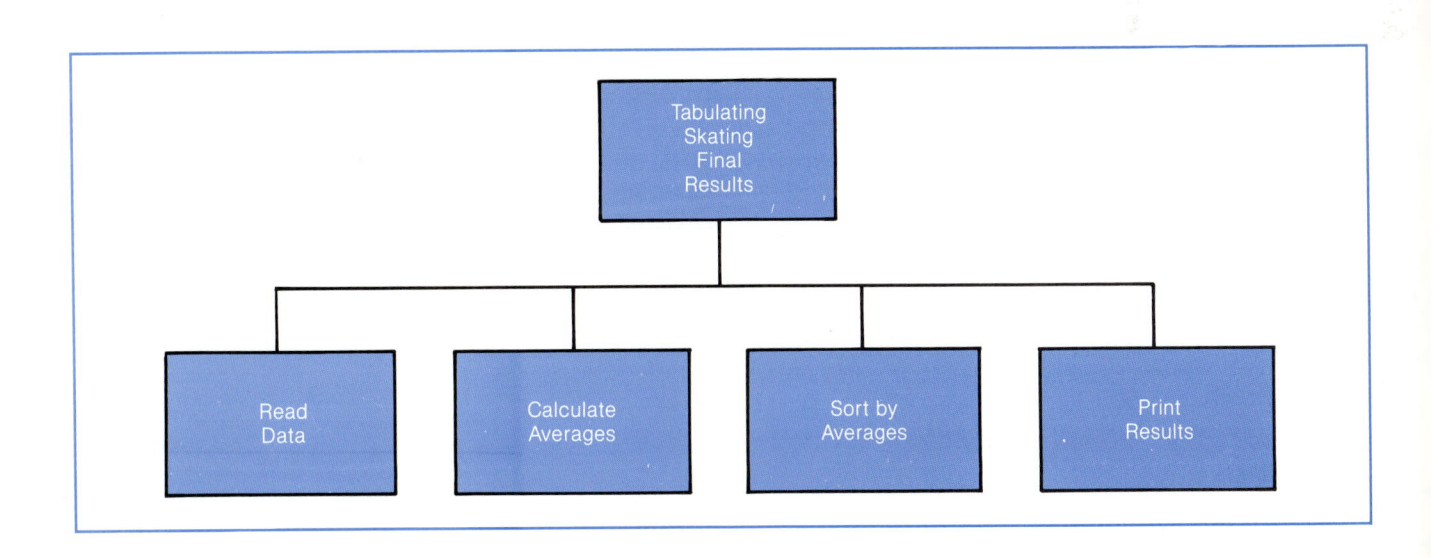

The Program

The program of Figure VI-8 shows the solution to the problem. Line 140 of the main program reserves space for a two-dimensional array of the scores, called PTS. Each row of array PTS contains the scores for one skater, so ten rows with six columns each are needed.

The first subroutine called by the main program reads the names and scores to their respective arrays. The second subroutine finds the average score for each skater, by performing a sequential search on each row of scores in PTS (lines 2050 through 2110). When the low and high scores for the row have been found, lines 2150 through 2170 add the scores for that row, except the low and high scores, to the total; then the average for that row is calculated.

The sorting of the final average is performed in the bubble sort in the third subroutine, lines 3000 through 3170. Notice that the flag, which indicates that a switch has been made, can be a string variable, as in line 3050. The actual value stored in the flag is unimportant; the critical factor is whether that value is changed during the sort.

The condition AVG(I) > AVG(I+1) in line 3070 causes the averages to be sorted from highest to lowest. Every time an average is moved, its corresponding name from the array SKNM$ also is moved. The sorted results are printed by the fourth subroutine in lines 4000 through 4100.

Summary Points

- An array is a collection of related values stored under a single variable name.
- Individual array elements can be accessed by using subscripts.
- A subscript of an array element can be any legal numeric expression.
- The DIM statement sets up storage for arrays, and must appear before the first reference to the array it describes.
- Array manipulation is carried out through the use of loops.
- A two-dimensional array stores values as a table, grouped into rows and columns.
- The first subscript of a two-dimensional array refers to the element's row, and the second subscript refers to the column.
- The bubble sort places elements of an array in ascending or descending order by comparing adjacent elements.
- The merge combines two sorted arrays into one sorted array.
- A sequential search of an array consists of examining each element in the array sequentially until the desired value is located.

Review Questions

1. What is an array?
2. Give two advantages of using arrays.

SECTION VI: ARRAYS

Figure VI-8
Skating Scores Program

```
10   REM ***                    SKATING FINAL RESULTS            ***
20   REM
30   REM *** THIS PROGRAM COMPUTES THE AVERAGES OF SKATING        ***
40   REM *** SCORES, USING SIX SCORES AND DROPPING THE LOW        ***
50   REM *** AND HIGH SCORES.  IT THEN SORTS ALL THE AVERAGE***
60   REM *** SCORES IN ASCENDING ORDER.                           ***
70   REM *** MAJOR VARIABLES:                                     ***
80   REM ***      SKNM$        ARRAY OF SKATERS' NAMES            ***
90   REM ***      PTS          ARRAY OF SCORES                    ***
100  REM ***      AVG          ARRAY OF AVERAGES                  ***
110  REM ***      HI,LO        HIGHEST/LOWEST SCORES              ***
120  REM
130  REM *** DIMENSION THE ARRAYS ***
140  DIM SKNM$(10),PTS(10,6),AVG(10)
150  REM
160  REM *** READ NAMES AND SCORES ***
170  GOSUB 1000
180  REM
190  REM *** CALCULATE FINAL AVERAGE ***
200  GOSUB 2000
210  REM
220  REM *** SORT BY AVERAGE ***
230  GOSUB 3000
240  REM
250  REM *** PRINT RESULTS ***
260  GOSUB 4000
270  GOTO 9999
1000 REM *******************************************************
1010 REM ***                SUBROUTINE READ                  ****
1020 REM *******************************************************
1030 REM ***       READS THE NAMES AND SIX SCORES             ***
1040 REM
1050 FOR I = 1 TO 10
1060    READ SKNM$(I)
1070    FOR J= 1 TO 6
1080       READ PTS(I,J)
1090    NEXT J
1100 NEXT I
1110 RETURN
2000 REM *******************************************************
2010 REM ***                SUBROUTINE AVERAGE                ***
2020 REM *******************************************************
2030 REM ***    DROP HIGH/LOW SCORES, THEN AVERAGE SCORE      ***
2040 REM
2050 FOR I = 1 TO 10
2060    HI = PTS(I,1)
2070    LO = PTS(I,1)
2080    FOR J= 2 TO 6
2090       IF PTS(I,J) < LO THEN LO = PTS(I,J)
2100       IF PTS(I,J) > HI THEN HI = PTS(I,J)
2110    NEXT J
2120    REM
2130    REM *** AVERAGE REMAINING SCORES ***
2140    TPTS = 0
2150    FOR J = 1 TO 6
2160       IF PTS(I,J) <> LO OR PTS(I,J) <> HI THEN
              TPTS = TPTS + PTS(I,J)
2170    NEXT J
2180    AVG(I) = TPTS / 4
2190 NEXT I
2200 RETURN
3000 REM *******************************************************
3010 REM ***              SUBROUTINE BUBBLE SORT              ***
3020 REM *******************************************************
3030 REM ***          SORT AVERAGES IN ASCENDING ORDER        ***
3040 REM
3050 SWITCH$ = "N"
```

(Figure continued on the next page)

**Figure VI-8
Continued**

```
3060 FOR I = 1 TO 9
3070   IF AVG(I) > AVG(I + 1) THEN 3150
3080   TEMP = AVG(I)
3090   STEMP$ = SKNM$(I)
3100   AVG(I) = AVG(I + 1)
3110   SKNM$(I) = SKNM$(I + 1)
3120   AVG(I + 1) = TEMP
3130   SKNM$(I + 1) = STEMP$
3140   SWITCH$ = "Y"
3150 NEXT I
3160 IF SWITCH$ = "Y" THEN 3050
3170 RETURN
4000 REM ************************************************************
4010 REM ***                  SUBROUTINE PRINT                    ***
4020 REM ************************************************************
4030 REM ***      PRINT THE HEADINGS AND THE RESULTS              ***
4040 CLS
4050 PRINT "PLACE";TAB(10);"NAME";TAB(30);"SCORE"
4060 PRINT
4070 FOR I = 1 TO 10
4080   PRINT I;TAB(10);SKNM$(I);TAB(30);AVG(I)
4090 NEXT I
4100 RETURN
4200 REM
4210 REM *** DATA STATEMENTS ***
4220 DATA "BALDUCCI,G",5.7,5.3,5.1,5.0,4.7,4.8
4230 DATA "CREED,A",3.1,4.9,4.1,3.7,4.6,3.9
4240 DATA "WILLIAMS,E",4.1,5.3,4.9,4.4,3.9,5.4
4250 DATA "HAMILTON,S",5.1,5.7,5.6,5.5,4.4,5.3
4260 DATA "LORD,P",5.9,4.8,5.5,5.0,5.7,5.7
4270 DATA "STRAVINSKY,I",5.1,4.7,4.1,3.1,4.6,5.0
4280 DATA "MONTALBAN,R",5.1,5.1,4.9,3.4,5.5,5.3
4290 DATA "SCHELL,M",4.9,4.3,5.2,4.5,4.6,4.9
4300 DATA "CRANSTON,T",6.0,6.0,5.7,5.8,5.9,5.9
4310 DATA "CROWLEY,S",4.3,5.2,6.9,5.3,4.3,6.0
9999 END
```

```
RUN
PLACE      NAME                SCORE

1          CRANSTON,T          8.825
2          LORD,P              8.150001
3          CROWLEY,S           8
4          HAMILTON,S          7.9
5          BALDUCCI,G          7.65
6          MONTALBAN,R         7.325
7          SCHELL,M            7.100001
8          WILLIAMS,E          7
9          STRAVINSKY,I        6.65
10         CREED,A             6.075
```

SECTION VI: ARRAYS

3. What is a subscript?
4. Where must the DIM statement appear in a program?
5. Write a segment to sum the 10 values of a one-dimensional array of 10 elements.
6. How is the terminal value of the FOR/NEXT loop of the bubble sort determined?
7. How is a sequential search performed?
8. The _____ combines two sorted lists into a single sorted list.
9. How many elements can a one-dimensional array and a two-dimensional array hold if they have not been dimensioned?
10. The _____ statements provide an efficient method for manipulating arrays.

Debugging Exercises

```
1.  10 REM *** READ DATA TO ARRAY A ***
    20 FOR I = 1 TO 20
    30    INPUT A(I)
    40 NEXT I
    99 END

2.  10  DIM X(26)
    20  REM *** ASCENDING BUBBLE SORT ***
    30  F = 0
    40  FOR I = 1 TO 26
    50     IF X(I) <= X(I + 1) THEN 90
    60     T = X(I)
    70     X(I) = X(I + 1)
    80     X(I + 1) = T
    90     F = 1
    100 NEXT I
    110 IF F = 1 THEN 40
```

Additional Programming Problems

1. A stereo equipment store is holding a sale. The manager needs a program that will place the prices of all sale items in one array and the corresponding rate of discount in a second array. A third array should be used to hold the sale price of each item (sale price z price w (rate * price)). Use the following data:

Price	Rate of Discount
$178.89	0.25
59.95	0.20
402.25	0.30
295.00	0.25
589.98	0.30
42.99	0.20

Print the original prices and their corresponding sales prices.

2. Read 12 numbers to array A and 12 numbers to array B. Compute the product of the corresponding elements of the two arrays, and place the results in array C. Print a table similar to the following:

A	B	C
2	3	6
7	2	14

3. Your teacher has a table of data concerning the semester test scores for your class:

Name	Test 1	Test 2	Test 3
Mathey, S.	88	83	80
Sandoval, V.	98	89	100
Haggerty, B.	75	65	79
Drake, J.	60	85	99
Jenkins, J.	75	89	89

Your teacher would like to know the test average for each student, and the class average for each test. The output should include the preceding table.

4. The following list of employee names and identification numbers is in alphabetical order. Use a bubble sort to print the list in ascending order by I.D. number (Remember that when you change the position of a number in the array, the position of the name also must be changed so that they correspond.)

Name	I.D. #
Altt, D.	467217
Calas, M.	624719
Corelli, F.	784609
Kanawa, K.	290013
Lamas, F.	502977
Lehman, B.	207827
Shicoff, N.	389662
Talvela, M.	443279
Tousteau, J.	302621
Wymer, E.	196325

5. The manager of the Epitome Books store would like a program that will generate a report regarding the sales of the various types of books the store carries. The program should use the following data:

Year	Pop. Fiction	Classics	Biography	Instruction
1982	4,561	549	973	3,702
1983	5,140	632	1,375	4,300
1984	5,487	581	1,798	4,345
1985	5,952	605	2,204	5,156

The report should indicate what percentage of each year's total sales consisted of each book type. The format for the report is as follows:

SALES PERCENTAGES FOR EACH YEAR:

YEAR	POP. FICTION	CLASSICS	BIOGRAPHY	INSTRUCT.
1982	XX.XX%	XX.XX%	XX.XX%	XX.XX%
1983				
1984				
1985				

SECTION VII

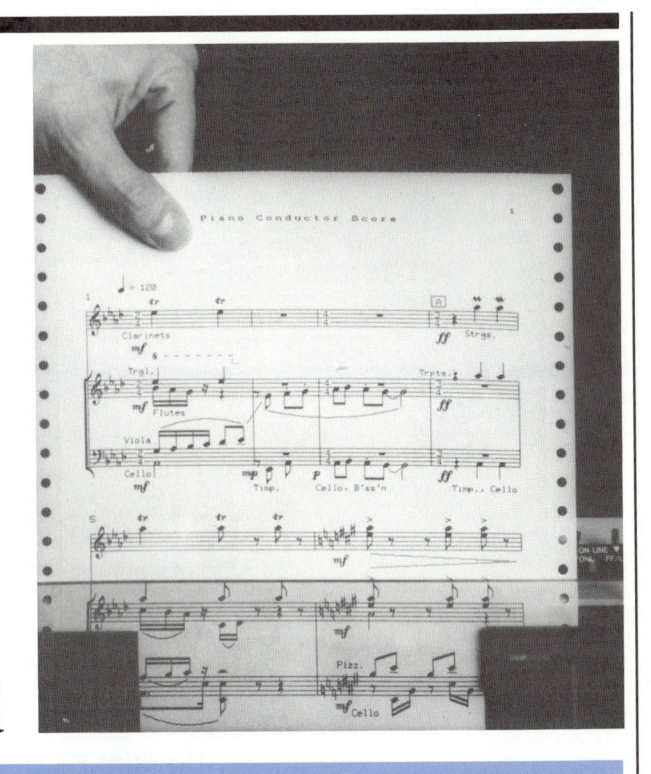

Graphics and Sound

Outline

Introduction
Display Modes
Medium-Resolution Graphics
    Mode
  Color Graphics
  The PSET and PRESET
    Statements
  The LINE Statement
Learning Check

High-Resolution Graphics Mode
  The CIRCLE Statement
Graphics and Text
Learning Check
Sound on the PC
  The BEEP Statement
  The SOUND Statement
  The PLAY Statement
Learning Check

Comprehensive Programming
    Problem
  The Problem
  Solution Design
  The Program
Summary Points
Review Questions
Debugging Exercises
Additional Programming Problems

Introduction

Programming a computer for graphics and sound is enjoyable. Graphics can be used to enhance programs, making otherwise dull material interesting and readable. Sounds produced by the computer can be used to attract attention to specific prompts or displays, or to play music.

Display Modes

The IBM PC screen operates in three display modes: text, medium-resolution graphics, and high-resolution graphics. In previous chapters of this book, only the text mode has been used; however, graphics programming must be performed in the medium- and high-resolution graphics modes. In order to use these modes, you must equip your IBM PC with a special circuit board called a color/graphics interface and a color graphics monitor. The interface circuit board enables you to design detailed graphics that include a variety of colors. A monochrome graphics monitor allows you to design graphics, too, but the graphics will not appear in color.

The SCREEN command switches the format of the screen from one display mode to another. Its format is as follows:

line #SCREEN mode-number

The mode-number must be an integer between 0 and 2. The command SCREEN 0 activates the text mode, SCREEN 1 activates the medium-resolution graphics mode, and SCREEN 2 activates the high-resolution graphics mode. The screen is set automatically to the text mode when it is turned on.

In order to produce graphics displays that are clear and easy to read, you should first clear the screen of any existing characters through the use of the CLS command. Then you should remove the key functions displayed at the bottom of the screen by using the statement KEY OFF.

Medium-Resolution Graphics Mode

MEDIUM-RESOLUTION GRAPHICS
The graphics mode that divides the screen into 64,000 image points (320 across and 200 down).

PIXEL
An image point.

The **medium-resolution graphics** mode divides the screen into 320 image points across and 200 down, for a total of 64,000 image points. Each image point is referred to as a **picture element** or **pixel**. A pixel is specified by a pair of coordinates consisting of a column number (0 through 319) and a row number (0 through 199). In either the medium- or the high-resolution graphics mode, the column number must be specified *before* the row number. Notice also that the column and row numbers begin with 0, not 1 as in the case of the text mode.

Color Graphics

Of the three display modes for the IBM PC, the medium-resolution graphics mode is the only one that allows for color graphics. In order to use the available colors in your display, you must use the SCREEN statement to turn on the color switch for medium-resolution graphics mode:

    line# SCREEN 1,0

The number 1 puts you in the medium-resolution graphics mode, and the number 0 initiates the color capabilities. To turn the color off, you need to execute the following statement:

    line# SCREEN 1,1

Once the color capabilities have been turned on, you must select a background color and a foreground color. For the background color (the color of all 64,000 pixels *before* any pixels are lit up), there are 16 possible options, numbered 0 through 15. The foreground colors (the color that lights up as you specify particular pixels), however, are limited to only three options. These three colors are chosen from one of two groups of colors, or palettes. Palette 0 consists of the colors green, red, and brown, whereas palette 1 is made up of the colors cyan, magenta, and white. Table VII-1 lists the 16 background colors and defines the palettes of foreground colors.

**Table VII-1
Colors Used in Medium-Resolution Graphics Mode**

Background Colors			
Color	Number	Color	Number
Black	0	Gray	8
Blue	1	Light blue	9
Green	2	Light green	10
Cyan	3	Light cyan	11
Red	4	Light red	12
Magenta	5	Light magenta	13
Brown	6	Yellow	14
White	7	Bright white	15

Foreground Colors			
Palette 0		Palette 1	
Color	Number	Color	Number
Green	1	Cyan	1
Red	2	Magenta	2
Brown	3	White	3

The COLOR statement is used to set both the background and foreground colors. Its format is as follows:

line # COLOR background color, foreground palette number

With the COLOR statement, you specify the number that corresponds to the color of the desired background. The foreground color, however, is not chosen directly using the COLOR statement. Instead, the palette of colors is designated. For example, the following statement sets the background color as blue (1) and selects palette 0 for the foreground:

```
10 COLOR 1,0
```

The PSET and PRESET statements are used to select the specific foreground color from the available options—in this case green, red, and brown (Table VII-1).

The PSET and PRESET Statements

The PSET statement is used to light up a specified pixel. Its format is as follows:

line # PSET (column, row),color-number

The column and row number are the coordinates of the specific pixel you wish to color, and the color-number is one of the available colors in the palette that was chosen in the COLOR statement.

To see how the PSET statement is used, look at the following program segment:

```
10 CLS
20 KEY OFF
30 SCREEN 1,0
40 COLOR 7,0
50 PSET(100,100),2
```

Line 30 switches the display mode to medium-resolution graphics. It also turns on the color capabilities. Line 40 selects white as the background color, and selects the foreground colors offered by palette 0. Line 50 causes the color of the pixel at column 100 and row 100 to be changed to red.

The PRESET statement is used to return a specific pixel to the background color. Its format is as follows:

line # PRESET (column,row)

The following statement returns the pixel at coordinate (100,100) to the background color. (It was colored red by the previous segment.)

```
60 PRESET(100,100)
```

The LINE Statement

Graphics displays often require the use of lines. It is possible to draw a line by using the PSET statement within a FOR/NEXT loop. Figure VII–1 is an example of a program that connects four lines to form a rectangle. The rows and columns are variables whose values depend on the value of the loop control variable of the FOR/NEXT loop. Notice that the GOTO statement in line 260 forms an infinite loop, which keeps the graphics display on the screen. (To terminate the program, hold down the <Ctrl> key and then press the <Break> key.)

Drawing in this manner is effective but not efficient. If you execute the program shown in Figure VII–1, you will notice that the lines are produced rather slowly. IBM BASIC offers the LINE statement as a more efficient alternative. Its format is as follows:

line # LINE$(x_1,y_1) - (x_2,y_2)$,color number

Figure VII–1
Rectangle Program Using the PSET Statement

```
10   REM *** PROGRAM RECTANGLE ***
20   REM *** X = COLUMN COORDINATE ***
30   REM *** Y = ROW COORDINATE ***
40   REM
50   REM *** PREPARE MEDIUM-RESOLUTION GRAPHICS SCREEN ***
60   CLS
70   KEY OFF
80   SCREEN 1,0
90   COLOR 7,0
100  REM *** DRAW TOP SIDE OF RECTANGLE ***
110  FOR X = 100 TO 200
120      PSET(X,75),2
130  NEXT X
140  REM *** DRAW RIGHT SIDE OF RECTANGLE ***
150  FOR Y = 75 TO 125
160      PSET(X,Y),2
170  NEXT Y
180  REM *** DRAW BOTTOM SIDE OF RECTANGLE ***
190  FOR X = X TO 100 STEP -1
200      PSET (X,Y),2
210  NEXT X
220  REM *** DRAW LEFT SIDE OF RECTANGLE ***
230  FOR Y = Y TO 75 STEP -1
240      PSET(X,Y),2
250  NEXT Y
260  REM *** INFINITE LOOP TO KEEP DISPLAY ON SCREEN ***
270  GOTO 270
999  END
```

```
10   REM *** PROGRAM RECTANGLE ***
20   REM *** X = COLUMN COORDINATE ***
30   REM *** Y = ROW COORDINATE ***
40   REM
50   REM *** PREPARE MEDIUM-RESOLUTION GRAPHICS SCREEN ***
60   CLS
70   KEY OFF
80   SCREEN 1,0
90   COLOR 7,0
100  REM *** DRAW TOP SIDE OF RECTANGLE ***
110  LINE (100,75)-(200,75),2
120  REM *** DRAW RIGHT SIDE OF RECTANGLE ***
130  LINE (200,75)-(200,125),2
140  REM *** DRAW BOTTOM SIDE OF RECTANGLE ***
150  LINE (200,125)-(100,125),2
160  REM *** DRAW LEFT SIDE OF RECTANGLE ***
170  LINE (100,125)-(100,75),2
180  REM *** INFINITE LOOP TO KEEP DISPLAY ON SCREEN ***
190  GOTO 190
999  END
```

**Figure VII-2
Rectangle Program Using the LINE Statement**

This statement is used to draw a line that connects the pixel at character position (x_1,y_1) to the pixel at (x_2,y_2). Specifying the color of the line is optional; if the color is not specified, the line is drawn in color 3 of the active palette. Using the LINE statement decreases the complexity of drawing lines and greatly increases the speed at which they are drawn. Figure VII-2 is a modified version of the rectangle program of Figure VII-1. It uses the LINE statement instead of the PSET statement inside a FOR/NEXT loop.

The LINE function has an extended format just for drawing rectangles. Before explaining its use, however, let's examine the rectangle diagrammed in Figure VII-3. This rectangle has corner A opposite corner C, and corner B opposite corner D. The sides meet at right angles (90°).

**Figure VII-3
Drawing a Rectangle**

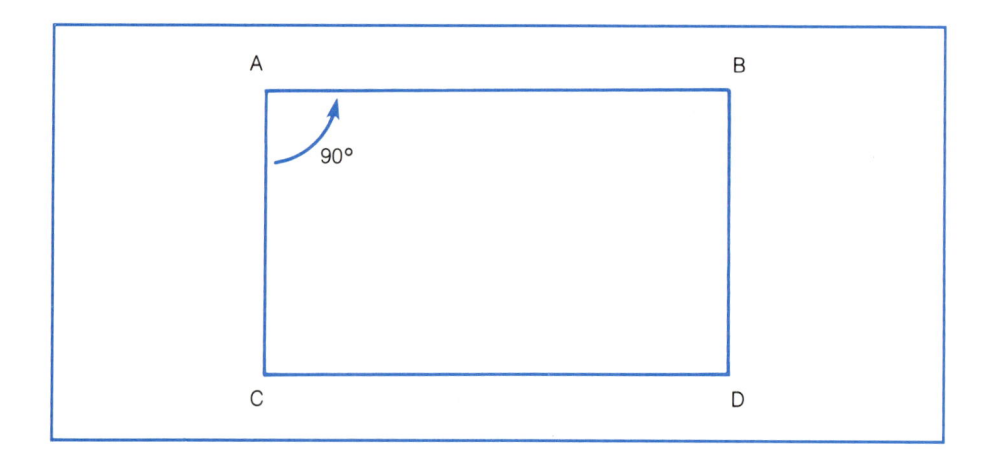

```
10   REM *** PROGRAM RECTANGLE ***
20   REM *** X = COLUMN COORDINATE ***
30   REM *** Y = ROW COORDINATE ***
40   REM
50   REM ** PREPARE MEDIUM-RESOLUTION GRAPHICS SCREEN ***
60   CLS
70   KEY OFF
80   SCREEN 1,0
90   COLOR 7,0
100  REM *** DRAW RECTANGLE ***
110  LINE (100,75)-(200,125),2,B
120  REM *** INFINITE LOOP TO KEEP DISPLAY ON SCREEN ***
130  GOTO 130
999  END
```

Figure VII–4
Rectangle Program Using the LINE Statement and Box Parameter

One LINE statement can be used to draw this rectangle by specifying the coordinates of opposite corners, such as A and C.

The color number is followed by the letter B, which tells the computer to box in the two corners:

```
110 LINE (100,75) - (200,125),2,B
```

This statement draws the same rectangle that is produced by the four LINE statements in Figure VII–2. That is, it draws a 100 × 50 rectangle, with the top left corner at pixel (100,75) and the bottom right corner at pixel (200,125).

Using this form of the LINE statement greatly decreases the complexity of designing graphics displays. For example, the program shown in Figure VII–4 draws the same 100 × 50 rectangle produced by the program in Figures VII–1 and VII–2 with only a fraction of the statements.

Learning Check

1. The screen of the medium-resolution graphics mode is divided into ____ columns and ____ rows.
2. Each character position is called a(n) ____ and is specified by a pair of ____.
3. The ____ statement is used to illuminate a specified pixel.
4. A statement that draws a line connecting two pixels is a(n) ____ statement.

Answers

1. 320,200   2. pixel, coordinates   3. PSET   4. LINE

High-Resolution Graphics Mode

The **high-resolution graphics** mode divides the screen into 640 columns and 200 rows. Each of the 128,000 pixels can be controlled by any of the statements presented in the previous section. Although the high-resolution mode allows for sharper, more detailed graphics displays, each pixel can be only one of two colors: white(1) or black(0). The high-resolution graphics mode is activated by the statement SCREEN 2. There are no color capabilities to activate, because only two colors are available.

Although only two colors are available in this mode, it is possible to create different shades of white by turning on different combinations of pixels. For example, consider the rectangle position of the graphics screen shown in Figure VII–5. It is possible to color the rectangle pure white by lighting up all the pixels in the rectangle with the statement

```
10 LINE (X1,Y1) - (X2 - Y2),1,BF
```

where the letters BF (box fill) cause the entire box to be filled with the color specified (in this case white).

To fill the rectangle with a darker shade, the LINE statement could be used within a FOR/NEXT loop to color in every other column of pixels. The following program segment fills in the rectangle shown in Figure VII–5:

```
40 FOR X1 = X1 TO X2 STEP 2
50     LINE (X1,Y1) - (X1,Y2),1
60 NEXT X1
```

If the STEP value in line 40 is increased to 3, the program segment lights up every third column, thereby creating a still darker shade.

The program shown in Figure VII–6 divides the high-resolution screen into six 213 × 100 rectangles, each shaded differently. Study the algorithms used to shade each rectangle in order to understand how to create different shades of white.

Figure VII–5
Creating Different Shades of White

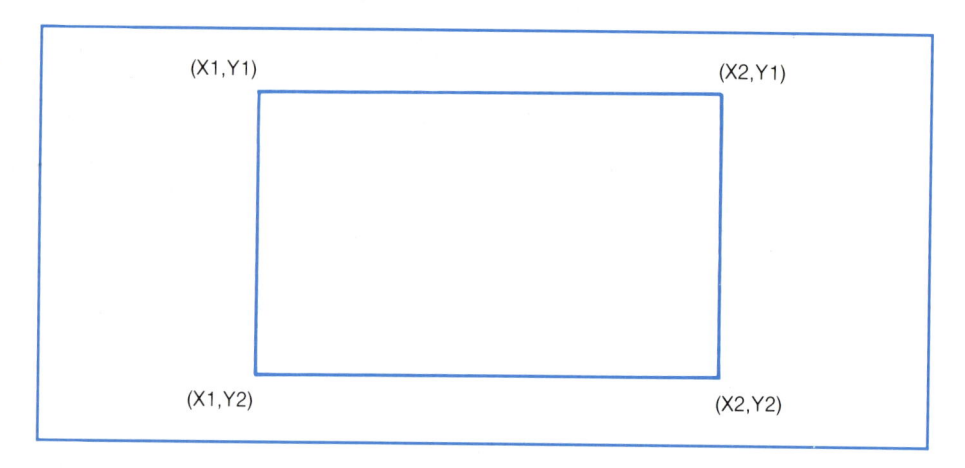

Figure VII-6
Program to Shade

```
10  REM *** PROGRAM SHADES ***
20  REM *** THIS PROGRAM DIVIDES THE SCREEN INTO SIX RECTANGLES ***
30  CLS
40  KEY OFF
50  SCREEN 2
60  REM *** BEGIN DRAWING IN TOP LEFT CORNER AT 0,0 ***
70  REM *** COLOR RECTANGLE I ***
80  LINE (0,0)-(212,99),1,BF
90  REM *** COLOR RECTANGLE II HORIZONTAL LIGHT GRAY ***
100 FOR Y = 0 TO 99 STEP 2
110     LINE (213,Y)-(425,Y),1
120 NEXT Y
130 REM *** COLOR RECTANGLE III VERTICAL LIGHT GRAY ***
140 FOR X = 426 TO 639 STEP 2
150     LINE (X,0)-(X,99),1
160 NEXT X
170 REM *** COLOR RECTANGLE IV VERTICAL DARK GRAY ***
180 FOR X = 0 TO 212 STEP 3
190     LINE (X,100)-(X,199),1
200 NEXT X
210 REM *** COLOR RECTANGLE V HORIZONTAL DARK GRAY ***
220 FOR Y = 100 TO 199 STEP 3
230     LINE (213,Y)-(425,Y),1
240 NEXT Y
250 REM *** INFINITE LOOP TO KEEP DISPLAY ON SCREEN ***
260 GOTO 260
999 END
```

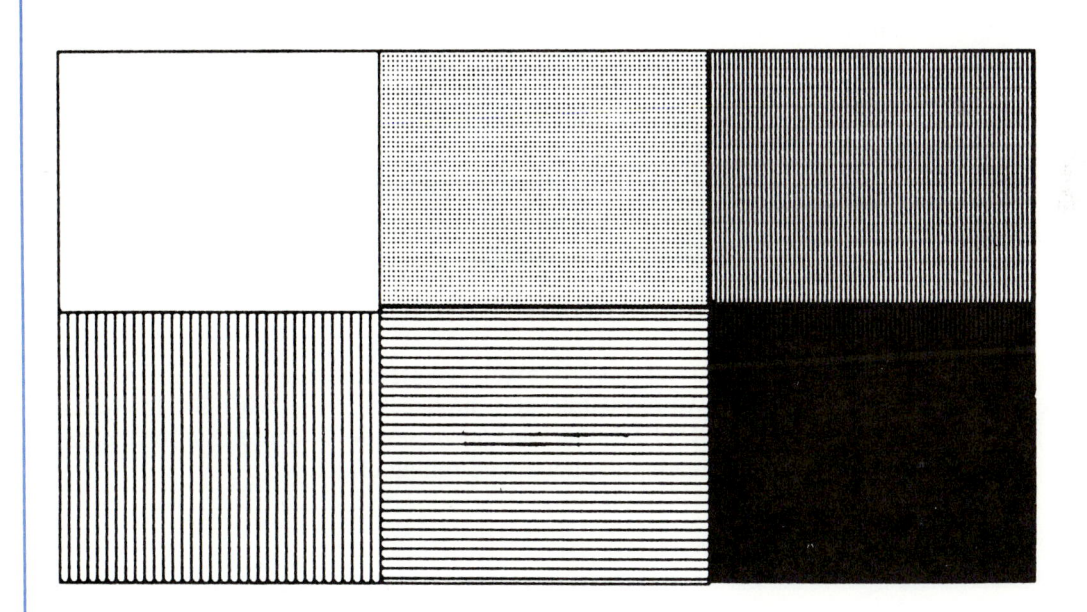

```
10  REM *** PROGRAM ROLLING BALL ***
20  CLS
30  KEY OFF
40  SCREEN 2
45  REM *** DRAW THE GROUND LINE ***
47  LINE (0,199)-(639,199),1
50  FOR X = 63 TO 574
60      CIRCLE (X+1,170),64,1
65      CIRCLE (X,170),64,0
70  NEXT X
80  REM *** INFINITE LOOP TO KEEP DISPLAY ON SCREEN ***
90  GOTO 90
99  END
```

Figure VII–7
Program for Rolling a Ball

The CIRCLE Statement

IBM BASICA also features a statement that enables you to create circles. This statement can be used in both medium- and high-resolution graphics mode, but because of the limited resolution of the medium-resolution mode, the circles produced in this mode are not smooth and often are unclear. For this reason, only a high-resolution example of the CIRCLE statement is provided here.

The format of this statement is as follows:

line # CIRCLE (column,row),radius,color

The column and row positions specify the coordinates of the center of the circle, and the radius specifies the distance from the center to any coordinate on the curve of the circle. For example, the statement

```
40 CIRCLE (100,75),40,1
```

draws a circle with a radius of 40 pixels, centered at column 100 and row 75.

The program shown in Figure VII–7 produces a circle that rolls slowly across the screen. The FOR/NEXT statement increases the X coordinate for the center of the circle, thus creating the horizontal rolling effect.

Graphics and Text

Many graphics displays require character string messages to clarify or explain their purpose. For this reason, BASIC enables you to include text with graphics displays. The PRINT and PRINT USING statements perform exactly as they would in the text mode, except that the cursor is hidden while in the graphics mode.

SECTION VII: GRAPHICS AND SOUND

To print text within a graphics display, we suggest using the LOCATE statement (refer to Section III). A common mistake made by many beginning programmers is to specify the coordinates for the LOCATE statement in the sequence (column,row), as with the graphics statements. Remember that the LOCATE coordinates must be specified in the sequence (row, column) even while in the graphics modes. In the medium-resolution mode, text can be printed only within the first 40 columns and is displayed in color 3 of the active palette.

Learning Check

1. The high-resolution graphics mode divides the screen into ____ columns and ____ rows.
2. There are ____ possible colors for any high-resolution pixel.
3. The high-resolution graphics mode is activated by the statement ____.
4. The distance from the center of a circle to any point on the curve is called the ____ of a circle.

Answers

1. 640,200   2. two   3. SCREEN   4. radius

Sound on the PC

The BEEP Statement

Sounds can be produced on the IBM PC with any of three statements: BEEP, SOUND, and PLAY. The easiest and most often used is the BEEP statement. The BEEP does exactly what it says: when executed, it produces a single sound at 800 Hertz (cycles per second) which lasts for 1/4 of a second. (This frequency and duration cannot be changed when using the BEEP statement.) It is used most commonly in application programs when it is necessary to call attention to error messages or to request user input. Its format is as follows:

　　line# BEEP

Figure VII–8 shows how this command can be used to indicate user input.

The SOUND Statement

The SOUND statement enables the user to specify the frequency and length of tones. Its format is as follows:

Figure VII-8
Program Using the BEEP Statement

```
10   CLS
20   PRINT "PRESS Y FOR BEEP"
30   PRINT "PRESS N TO END PROGRAM"
40   INPUT "BEEP?",A$
50   IF A$ = "N" THEN 99
60      BEEP
70      GOTO 40
99   END
```

line# SOUND frequency, duration

Changing the frequency produces a beep at a higher or lower tone. The frequency can be set to any number between 37 and 32767 Hertz. The duration specifies how long the sound is to last. The duration actually is the number of clock ticks (remember that BASIC/BASICA features an internal clock), which can range between 0 and 65535; there are approximately 18.2 clock ticks per second.

The ability to change frequency and duration enables you to create a large variety of interesting sounds. The program in Figure VII-9 produces a series of increasingly high-pitched tones and a siren.

The PLAY Statement

The PLAY statement enables the user to program music. The sounds produced are sophisticated, yet the program is not difficult to use. Some background in

Figure VII-9
Program Using the SOUND Statement

```
10   REM *** TONES ***
20   FOR I = 300 TO 1200 STEP 100
30      SOUND I,8
40      FOR T = 1 TO 500
50      NEXT T
60   NEXT I
70   FOR T = 1 TO 600
80   NEXT T
90   REM *** SIREN ***
100  FOR I = 1 TO 3
110     FOR F = 450 TO 1200
120        SOUND F,.1
130     NEXT F
140     FOR F = 1200 TO 450 STEP -1
150        SOUND F,.1
160     NEXT F
170  NEXT I
999  END
```

SECTION VII: GRAPHICS AND SOUND   B-159

10 PLAY "O3L4CEL2G"   20 PLAY "O3L8GABGL4AL8GB"

Figure VII–10
Coded Music Strings

music is helpful; however, beginners also can create music easily. The format of the PLAY statement is as follows:

line# PLAY string

The string is a series of letters, numbers, and symbols which indicates a variety of musical information the computer needs in order to produce music. These combinations of letters and numbers are referred to as commands, and each command serves a specific purpose.

Figure VII–10 gives two examples of what coded music strings might be like. Although they may look difficult to code, actually they are quite simple. The following paragraphs contain an overview of how to code music on the IBM PC.

Octave   The octave is specified with the letter O followed by the octave number. There are seven possible octaves, from 0 to 6, with each octave ranging from C to B (octave 3 starts at middle C). For example: O3 means that all notes come from the third octave until another octave is specified. If no octave is specified, the notes are assumed to come from the fourth octave. Figure VII–11 shows octaves 1 through 4.

Notes   Just as with sheet music, notes are specified with the letters A through G, and each octave starts with C. A sharp is indicated by the symbol # or + following the note; a flat is indicated by the symbol − following the note. For a note to be sharp or flat, the note must correspond to a black key on the piano keyboard. For example, the notes B# and F− are invalid, whereas C# and B− are allowable.

Figure VII–11
Octaves 1 Through 4

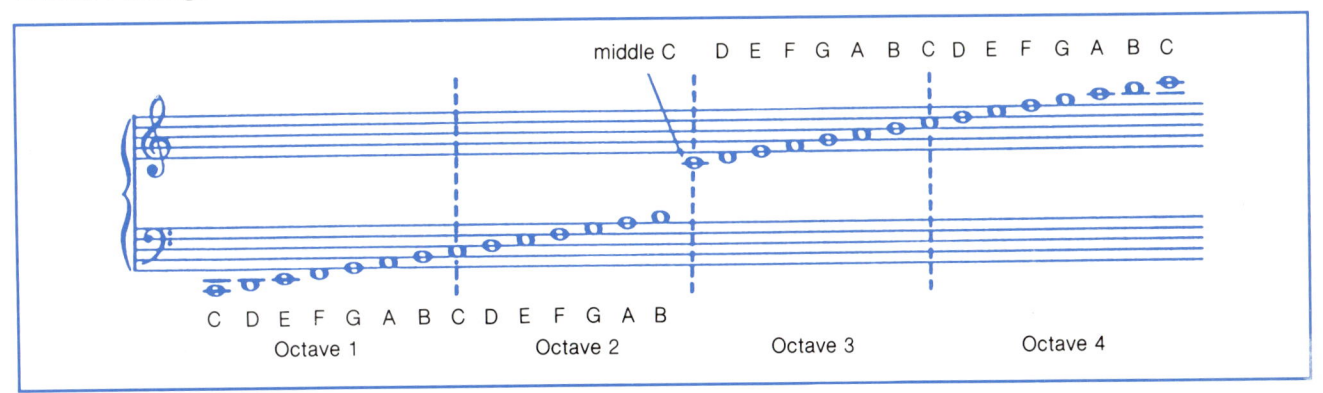

Length The length is set in the same way as the octave. It is coded by the letter L, followed by a number that indicates the length of all subsequent notes until another length is specified. The length of the notes ranges from 1 to 64, where 1 indicates a whole note, 2 a half note, 4 a quarter note, and so on.

Pause A pause, or rest, note is indicated with the letter P. It is set in the same manner as the length, that is, with the letter P followed by a number in the range 1 to 64. Therefore, P1 indicates a whole note rest, P2 a half note rest, and so on.

Tempo The speed at which the music is played is called the tempo. Setting tempo is much like setting length. The user sets the number of quarter notes per minute, ranging from 32 to 255. For example, T60 sets the tempo at 60 quarter notes per minute. That tempo remains in effect until another tempo command is given.

Style The IBM PC allows three styles of music to be played: staccato, legato, and normal. *Staccato* is indicated by the character MS; each note plays for three-quarters of the time specified by the L (length) command. *Legato* is indicated by the characters ML; each note plays for the full period set by the L command. *Normal* is indicated by the characters MN; each note plays for seven-eighths of the time specified by the L command. As with the other settings, the style remains in effect until the user changes it.

Repeating Strings Almost all musical compositions contain sections that are repeated. Instead of recoding the same piece of music each time it is to be played, the IBM PC enables you to assign a string of coded music to a string variable:

```
100 M$ = "L4CEL2G"
```

To include this string with the string in the PLAY statement, the user types the letter X followed by the string variable name and semicolon. Thus, if M$ is defined as previously indicated, the following two statements are equivalent:

```
200 PLAY "O3L4CEL2GL4CEL2GL4GFED"
200 PLAY "O3XM$;XM$;L4GFED"
```

Comprehensive Programming Problem

The Problem

Your calculus professor wants you to produce a graph of the function $f(X) = 199 - \sqrt{X}$. X should range from 0 to 600.

SECTION VII: GRAPHICS AND SOUND

B-161

Learning Check

1. The three commands on the IBM PC that produce sounds are ___, ___, and ___.
2. Music can be programmed by using the ___ statement.
3. If no octave is specified, all notes come from the ___ octave.
4. A sharp is indicated by following a note with a ___ or a ___.

Answers

1. BEEP, SOUND, PLAY 2. PLAY 3. fourth 4. number sign (#), plus sign (+)

Solution Design

The X axis must lie at the bottom of the screen, and the Y axis must lie on the left edge. Therefore, the dimensions of the graph will be 600 × 180. The input will be the value of X, between 0 and 600. The Y value will be the result of the calculation of the function. The output will be the plot of the coordinates (X,Y); therefore, a bottom and left edge of the graph should be displayed. The graph will appear the same whether in medium or high resolution, but with a high resolution, the graph will be crisper and clearer.

The Program

Figure VII–12
Comprehensive Program—Function Plotting

Figure VII–12 shows the program that graphs the function f(X) = 199 − sqr(X), with X ranging from 0 to 600. The first thing necessary is to be in the graphics

```
10   REM *** PROGRAM PLOTTER ***
20   KEY OFF
30   CLS
40   SCREEN 2
50   REM *** DRAW X AXIS AT THE BOTTOM OF THE SCREEN ***
60   LINE (0,0)-(600,0),1
70   REM *** DRAW Y AXIS AT LEFT EDGE OF THE SCREEN ***
80   LINE (0,0)-(0,199),1
90   REM *** PLOT POINTS OF FUNCTION F(X) = X - 1 ***
100  FOR X = 0 TO 600
110      PSET(X,199-SQR(X)),1
120  NEXT X
999  END
```

mode, with a clear screen. Lines 20 through 40 perform this task. The LINE statements in lines 60 and 80 draw the border for the graph, across the bottom and down the left-hand side. Lines 100–120 use a FOR/NEXT loop to assign a value to X (from 0 to 600), calculate a value for Y, and light up the pixel indicated by the coordinate (X,Y).

Summary Points

- The IBM PC has three display modes: text, medium-resolution graphics, and high-resolution graphics.
- The medium-resolution graphics mode divides the screen into 320 pixels across and 200 down.
- The medium-resolution graphics mode has 16 possible background colors (0–15) and two palettes (0–1), each with three foreground colors (0–2).
- The PSET statement is used to illuminate a specific pixel.
- The PRESET statement returns a specific pixel to the background color.
- The LINE statement draws a straight line from one pixel to another.
- The high-resolution graphics mode divides the screen into 640 pixels across and 200 down.
- The high-resolution graphics mode has only two possible colors: white (1) and black (0).
- The CIRCLE statement draws a circle of a specified radius, centered at a specified pixel.
- Sounds can be produced by using the BEEP, SOUND, and PLAY statements.

Review Questions

1. Which display mode allows for the sharpest detail?
2. How many background colors are available in the medium-resolution graphics mode?
3. Which statement is used to program musical compositions?
4. Write the statement that lights up the pixel at column 80 and row 40 in the color green, assuming palette 0 is active.
5. What single statement draws a line from pixel (10,20) to pixel (40,80) in color 1 of the active palette?
6. What single statement draws a 50 × 40 rectangle whose top left corner is at (2,30) and whose color is option 2 of the active palette?
7. What statement draws a circle of radius 60 with its center at (100,100) in color 1?
8. When is the BEEP statement most commonly used?
9. How does the SOUND statement differ from the BEEP statement?
10. What does the *string* in the PLAY statement consist of?

SECTION VII: GRAPHICS AND SOUND

B-163

Debugging Exercises

1.  ```
    10 CLS
    20 KEY OFF
    30 COLOR 7,0
    40 SCREEN ,1,0
    50 LINE (100,75) + (200,75),2
    60 LINE (200,125) - (100,125),2
    99 END
    ```

2.  ```
    100 PLAY "O3L4CE"
    110 M = "L4CEL2G"
    120 PLAY "O3XM$XM$L4GFED"
    ```

Additional Programming Problems

1. Write a program that produces the following graphics displays with the LINE statement:
    - *a.* A straight line that connects pixels (10,40) and (100,90).
    - *b.* A rectangle with corners at (30,50); (150,50); (150,100); (30,100).
    - *c.* The rectangle described in b, colored in with color 2.
2. Write a program that creates a rectangle in the middle of the terminal screen and then enlarges it to twice its original size. Have the computer beep once after it has drawn the original rectangle, and twice after it has drawn the enlarged rectangle.
3. Write a program that produces the following graphics displays with the CIRCLE statement:
    - *a.* A circle with radius 64 and center at pixel (100,71).
    - *b.* A circle with radius 25 and center at pixel (100,100) in color 1.
4. Write a program that causes the computer to BEEP 25 times with a pause between each beep, and which enables the user to enter a certain frequency parameter and to hear the resulting sound for 1 second.
5. Use the PLAY statement to program the following four measures of Beethoven's Ninth Symphony:

BASIC Glossary

Algorithm The sequence of instructions arranged in a specific, logical order that are needed to solve a problem.

Array An ordered collection of related data items. A single variable name is used to refer to the entire collection of items.

Assignment statement A statement that causes a value to be stored in a variable.

Bubble sort A sort that progressively arranges the elements of an array in ascending or descending order by making a series of comparisons of the adjacent array values and exchanging those values that are out of order.

Conditional transfer Program control is transferred to another point only if a stated condition is satisfied.

Constant A value that cannot change during program execution.

Control statement A statement that allows the programmer to alter the order in which program statements are executed.

Conversational mode See **Inquiry-and-response mode.**

Counter A variable used to control loop repetition; each time the loop is executed, the counter is tested to determine if the desired number of repetitions has been performed.

Counting loop A type of loop in which repetition is controlled by a counter, which is a numeric variable that is tested each time the loop is executed to determine if the desired number of repetitions has been performed.

Data list A single list containing the values in all of the data statements in a program; the values appear in the list in the order in which they occur in the program.

Debug To locate and correct program errors.

Documentation Comments that explain a program to people; documentation is ignored by the computer.

Double-alternative decision structure A decision structure in which a specific action is taken if a stated condition is true; otherwise, a different action is taken.

Element An individual data item stored in an array.

Execute When the computer carries out the instructions submitted to it.

Flowchart A graphic representation of the solution to a programming problem.

Hierarchy of operations The order in which arithmetic operations are performed. In BASIC the order is (1) anything in parentheses; (2) exponentiation; (3) multiplication and division; (4) addition and subtraction.

High-resolution graphics The graphics mode that divides the screen into a total of 128,000 image points (640 across and 200 down).

Immediate mode The mode in which commands are executed as soon as the RETURN key is pressed; it is used without line numbers.

Indirect mode The mode in which statements are not executed until the RUN command is given. The statements must have line numbers.

Infinite loop A loop with no exit point.

Input The data needed to solve a problem.

Inquiry-and-response mode A mode of operation in which the program asks a question and the user enters a response.

Line number A number preceding a BASIC statement that is used to reference the statement and determine its order of execution.

Literal An expression in a PRINT statement that contains any combination of letters, numbers, and/or special characters.

Logic error A flaw in an algorithm developed to solve a programming problem; this results in the program's output being incorrect.

Loop body The statement(s) that constitutes the action to be performed by the loop.

Loop control variable A variable of which the value is used to determine the number of loop repetitions.

Medium-resolution graphics The graphics mode that divides the screen into a total of 64,000 image points (320 across and 200 down).

Menu A screen display of a program's functions. The user enters a code at the keyboard to make a selection.

Merge A type of sort that combines two sorted arrays into a single sorted array.

One-dimensional array An array that has only one column.

Output Information that is the result of processing.

Picture element See **Pixel.**

Pixel The smallest graphic point addressable by a computer, pixels are turned on or off to form characters and graphics images on a computer screen.

Processing The producing of output or information from the input or data.

Prompt A message telling the user that data should be entered at this point.

Relational symbol A symbol used to specify a relationship between two values.

Reserved word A word that has a specific meaning to the BASIC system and therefore cannot be used as a variable name.

Run-time error An error that causes program execution to stop prematurely.

Scroll To have lines move vertically off the top of the monitor screen.

Sentinel value See **Trailer value.**

Sequential search A search that examines array elements from the first to last in the order in which they are stored. When the target element is located, the search terminates.

Single-alternative decision structure A decision structure in which a specific action is taken if a stated condition is true; otherwise, execution proceeds to the next statement.

Structure chart A diagram that visually illustrates how a problem solution has been developed using stepwise refinement.

Structured programming A method of programming in which programs have easy-to-follow logic and are divided into subprograms, each designed to perform a specific task.

Subroutine A module in a BASIC program containing a sequence of statements designed to perform a specific task; it follows the main program.

Subscript A value enclosed in parentheses which identifies the position in an array of a particular element.

Subscripted variable A variable that refers to a specific element of an array.

Syntax error A violation of the grammatical rules of a language.

Top-down design A method of solving a problem that proceeds from the general to the specific.

Trailer value A method of controlling a loop in which a unique value signals the termination of the loop.

Two-dimensional array An array that can be compared to a table with both rows and columns.

Unconditional transfer Control is always passed elsewhere, regardless of any program condition.

Variable A storage location the contents of which can change during program execution.

BASIC INDEX

Arithmetic expressions, B-28–29
  printing values of, B-31
Arithmetic operations, hierarchy, B-28–29
Algorithm, B-5
Alphanumeric characters, B-21
AND, B-71
Arrays, B-118–137
  dimensioning
    one-dimensional, B-119–120
    two-dimensional, B-126
  naming, B-119
  one-dimensional, B-121–124
    computations on elements, B-123–124
    displaying contents, B-122–123
    reading data to, B-121–122
  searching, B-137
  sorting, B-131–137
    bubble sort, B-131–135
    merge, B-135–137
  two-dimensional, B-124–130
    adding columns, B-128–130
    adding rows, B-128
    computations on elements, B-128–130
    displaying contents, B-127–128
    reading data to, B-126–128
    subscripts, B-125–126
    totaling, B-130
Assignment statement, B-26–29
Asterisk
  in multiplication, B-28
  with REM statement, B-26

BASIC
  background, B-4

BASICA, B-9
  commands, B-11–15
  disk BASIC, B-9
  Microsoft BASIC, B-8–10
  statements, B-25–31
BASIC mode, B-11
BEEP, B-157
Boot, B-10
Bubble sort, B-131–135

CIRCLE, B-156
Clearing the screen, B-47
COLOR, B-150
Commas
  in printing, B-47–49
  with TAB, B-50–52
Conditional transfer, B-67
  with IF statement, B-67
  with ON/GOSUB statement, B-78–81
Constants, B-20–21
  numeric, B-20–21
    integer, B-20–21
    real, B-20
  string, B-21
Control statement, B-66
  see also: Conditional transfer
           Unconditional transfer
Conversational mode, B-44
Copying a disk, B-11
Counter, B-94–95

DATA, see READ and DATA
Data list, B-44

Data processing, basic steps, B-5
Data types, B-20
  numeric, B-20–22
  string, B-20–22
Debugging, B-7–8
DIM, B-119–120
DIR, B-11
Display modes, B-148
Documentation, B-25–26
DOS, B-10
  commands, B-10–11
Double-alternative decision structure, B-67–70

Editing, line, B-24–25
Element (of arrays), B-118
END, B-31
Error message
  OUT OF DATA, B-44
Errors
  logic, B-8
  program, B-8
  run-time, B-8
  syntax, B-8
Execute a program, B-12
Exponential notation, B-20

File, removing from disk, B-11, B-15
File name, B-13
FILES, B-15
Flowchart, B-5–6
Format control characters, printing, B-55–56
Formatting a disk, B-10–11
FOR/NEXT, B-97–104

GOSUB, B-76
GOTO, B-66–67
Graphics, B-148–157
   color, B-149–150
   drawing circles, B-156
   drawing lines, B-151–153
   drawing rectangles, B-152–153
   high-resolution, B-154–156
   medium-resolution, B-148–153
   with text, B-156–157

Hierarchy of operations, B-28–29
High-resolution graphics mode, B-154–156

IBM PC, B-8–10
   graphics, B-148–157
   sound, B-157–160
IF, B-67
   nested, B-70–71
IF/THEN, B-68–71
IF/THEN/ELSE, B-69–70
Image points, B-148
Immediate-mode commands, B-11
Indirect mode, B-22–23
Infinite loop, B-94
Input, B-5
INPUT, B-40–43
   printing prompts, B-42–43
   vs. READ and DATA, B-46
Inquiry-and-response mode, B-44
Interactive mode, B-44
Interface, color/graphics, B-148

Kemeny, John, B-4
Key functions, removing, B-148
KEY OFF, B-148
KILL, B-15
Kurtz, Thomas, B-4

LET, B-26–28
LINE, B-151–153
Line, editing, B-24–25
Line numbers, B-22–25
   END statement, B-31
LIST, B-14–15
Literals, B-30
   printing value of, B-30
LOAD, B-14
LOCATE, B-53–54
Loop control variable, B-96
   incrementing, B-97–100
   step value, B-98
Looping, B-92–106
   methods, B-92–95

Loops
   body, B-96
   controlling, B-92–95
   counting, B-100
   FOR/NEXT, B-97–104
     advantages, B-100
     flowcharting, B-100
     nested, B-100–104
     rules for using, B-98–100
     rules for using (nested), B-103
   infinite (endless), B-94
   inner, B-102
   outer, B-102
   WHILE/WEND, B-106

Mantissa, B-20
Medium-resolution graphics mode, B-148–153
Menus, B-74–76
Merge, B-135–137
Monitor, color graphics, B-148
Music, programming, B-158–160

Naming a file, B-13
NEW, B-12
Nonexecutable statement, B-25
Numbers, rules for using in BASIC, B-21

ON/GOSUB, B-78–81
ON/GOTO, B-71–74
OR, B-71
Output, B-5

Parentheses, in arithmetic operations, B-28–29
Picture element, B-148
Pixel, B-148
   lighting individual pixels, B-150
PLAY, B-158–160
PRESET, B-150
PRINT, B-29–31
   in prompts, B-42
PRINT TAB, B-50–52
PRINT USING, B-55–57
Print zones, B-47–49
Printing, B-47–57
   arithmetic expressions, B-31
   arrays, B-122–123, B-127–128
   blank lines, B-31
   character strings, B-55–56
   formatting, B-47–57
     format control characters, B-55–56
     with commas, B-47–49
     with LOCATE, B-53–54
     with PRINT USING, B-55–57
     with semicolons, B-49–50

     with SPC, B-53
     with tabs, B-50–52
   headings, B-30
   literals, B-30
   numeric data, B-56
   variables, B-30
Processing, B-5
Programming process, B-4–8
Prompts, B-42–43
PSET, B-150

READ and DATA, B-44–46
   rules for using, B-44
   vs. INPUT, B-46
Readability of program, B-31, B-97
Relational symbols, B-69
REM, B-25–26
Renaming a file, B-11
Reserved words, B-22
RESTORE, B-45
Retrieving a program, B-13
RETURN, B-77
RUN, B-12

SAVE, B-13
Scientific notation, B-20
SCREEN, B-149
Scroll, B-14
   controlling, B-15
Searching, B-137
Semicolons
   in printing, B-49–50
   with SPC, B-53
   with TAB, B-50
Sentinel value, B-93
Sequential search, B-137
Single-alternative decision structure, B-67–69
Sorting, B-131–137
SOUND, B-157–158
   music, B-158–160
SPC, B-53
STEP, B-98
STOP, B-77–78
Structure chart, B-5
Structured programming, B-76
Subroutine, B-66, B-76–81
   returning from, B-77
Subscripts, B-118

TAB, B-50–52
Top-down design, B-5
Trailer value, B-93

Unconditional transfer
   with GOSUB statement, B-76

BASIC INDEX

with GOTO statement, B-66–67

Variable names, B-21–22
Variables, B-21–22

assigning values to, B-26–29
flag, B-131
inputting values, B-40–43
numeric, B-22
printing values of, B-30

string, B-22
subscripted, B-119

WHILE/WEND, B-106

GLOSSARY

Access To get or retrieve data from a computer system.
Active cell The cell on a spreadsheet currently available for use; the active cell is indicated by the cell pointer.
Ada A high-level structured programming language developed for use by the Department of Defense and named for the "first programmer," Augusta Ada Byron, Countess of Lovelace and daughter of the poet Lord Byron.
Algorithm A set of well-defined instructions that outline the solution of a problem in a finite number of steps.
American Standard Code for Information Interchange (ASCII) A 7-bit standard code used for information interchange among data-processing systems, communications systems and associated equipment.
Analog computer A computer that measures the change in continuous electrical or physical conditions rather than counting data; contrast with digital computer.
Analytical Graphs Charts and graphics used for financial analysis and other types of numerical comparison.
Application program A sequence of instructions written for solving a specific user problem.
Arithmetic/logic unit The section of the processor, or CPU, that handles arithmetic computations and logical operations.
Artificial intelligence (AI) Intelligence exhibited by a machine or software; field of research currently developing techniques whereby computers can be used for solving problems that appear to require imagination, intuition, or intelligence.

Assembler program The translator program for an assembly language program; produces a machine language program (object program) that can then be executed.
Assembly language A low-level, symbolic programming language that uses convenient abbreviations called mnemonics rather than the groupings of 0s and 1s used in machine language. Because instructions in assembly language generally have a one-to-one correspondence with machine language instructions, assembly language is easier to translate into machine language than are high-level language statements.

Bandwidth Range, or width, of the frequencies available for transmission on a given channel; also known as grade.
Bar code A machine-readable code made up of bars and spaces of varying widths; often used on packaging of retail merchandise and read by wand readers or scanners.
BASIC (Beginners' All-purpose Symbolic Instruction Code) A high-level programming language commonly available with interpreter programs; widely implemented on microcomputers and often taught to beginning programmers.
Batch processing A method of processing data in which data items are collected and forwarded to the computer in a group; normally uses punched cards or magnetic tape for generating periodic output, e.g. payroll.
Baud Unit that describes transmission speeds.

Binary number system Base 2 number system that uses the digits 0 and 1; convenient for use in computer coding because it corresponds to the two possible states in machine circuitry, on and off.

Binary representation Use of a two-state, or binary, system for representing data, as in setting or resetting the electrical state of semiconductor memory to either 1 or 0.

Biomechanics Application of engineering methodologies to biological systems.

Bit Acronym for BInary digiT; the smallest unit of data that the computer can handle and that can be represented in the digits (0 and 1) of binary notation.

Block movement A feature that enables the user to define a block of text and then perform a specific operation on the entire block. Common block operations include block move, block copy, block save, and block delete.

Boot To load an operating system into a computer's main memory.

Branch Program logic used to bypass or alter the normal flow of program execution.

Bubble memory A memory medium in which data is represented by magnetized spots (magnetic domains, or "bubbles") resting on a thin film of semiconductor material.

Byte A fixed number of adjacent bits, usually eight, operated on as a unit.

C A high-level structured programming language that includes low-level language instructions; C is popular because it is portable and is implemented on a wide variety of computer systems.

Cell A storage location within a spreadsheet.

Cell pointer The highlight that indicates the active cell in a spreadsheet.

Central processing unit (CPU) Acts as the "brain" of the computer; composed of three sections—arithmetic/logic unit (ALU), control unit, and primary storage unit.

Character A single letter, digit, or special sign (like $, #, or ★).

Character enhancement A special printing effect such as underlining, boldfacing, subscripting, or superscripting.

Chief programmer team (CPT) A method of organization used in developing software systems in industry in which a chief programmer supervises the development and testing of software; programmer productivity and software reliability are increased.

Clock speed The number of electronic pulses a microprocessor can produce each second.

COBOL (COmmon Business-Oriented Language) A high-level programming language generally used for business applications; well-suited for manipulating large data files.

Coding The process of writing a programming problem solution in a programming language.

Communication channel Pathway along which data is transmitted between sending and receiving devices.

Compatible Descriptive of hardware and/or software that can work together.

Compiler program The translator program for a high-level language such as FORTRAN or COBOL; translates the entire source program into machine language at once, creating an object program that is then executed.

Composite color monitor A color monitor that displays a composite of colors received in a single video signal.

Computer General-purpose electronic machine with applications limited only by the creativity of the humans who use it; its power is derived from its speed, accuracy, and memory.

Computer literacy General knowledge about computers; may include the ability to use computers for solving problems, technical knowledge about hardware and software, and awareness of how computers affect society.

Computer-aided design (CAD) Process of designing, drafting, and analyzing a prospective product using computer graphics on a video terminal.

Computer-aided manufacturing (CAM) Use of a computer to simulate or monitor the steps of a manufacturing process.

Computer-assisted instruction (CAI) Use of a computer to instruct or drill a student on an individual or small-group basis.

Computer-integrated manufacturing (CIM) Arrangement that links various departments within an organization to a central data base for the purpose of improving the efficiency of the manufacturing process.

Computerized axial tomography (CT or CAT) Form of noninvasive physical testing that combines x-ray techniques and computers to aid diagnosis.

Computer output microfilm (COM) A form of computer output in which information from a printer or magnetic tape is placed on microfilm or microfiche.

Control panel The portion of the spreadsheet which provides status and help information. The control panel is composed of a status line, an entry line, and a prompt line.

Control unit The section of the CPU that directs the sequence of operations by electrical signals and governs the actions of the various units that make up the computer.

Coordinate The location of a cell within a spreadsheet.

Coprocessor A microprocessor that can be plugged into a microcomputer to replace or work with the microcomputer's original microprocessor.

Cursor A character, such as a square, vertical bar, or arrow (>), on a computer display screen that shows where the next typed character will appear; the cursor may flash.

Daisy-wheel printer An output device resembling a daisy-wheel electronic typewriter; it has a removable flat wheel of petals or spokes, each having a character embossed at its tip; it is an impact printer and printing occurs one character at a time.

Data Facts; the raw material of information.

Data base A grouping of independent files that are commonly defined, consistently organized, and can be accessed through one central point; designed to fit the information needs of a wide variety of users in an organization.

Data manager A data management software package that consolidates data files into an integrated whole, allowing access to more than one data file at a time.

Data processing A systematic set of procedures for collecting, manipulating, and disseminating data to achieve specified objectives.

Data redundancy The repetition of the same data in several different files.

Debugging The process of locating, isolating, and resolving errors in a program.

Dedicated system A computer equipped to handle only one function, such as word processing.

Default setting The setting that a program automatically assumes when no other setting is designated by the user.

Deletion A word processing feature in which a character, word, sentence, or larger block of text can be removed from the existing text.

Demodulation Process of retrieving data from a modulated carrier wave.

Digital computer The type of computer that relies on counting for its operations and operates on distinct data (for example, binary digits) by performing arithmetic and logic processes on specific data units; commonly used in business and education.

Direct-access storage Secondary storage from which data can be retrieved at random; an example is a magnetic disk.

Directory A special kind of file that organizes the other files stored on a disk.

Disk drive The mechanical device used to rotate a disk, floppy disk, or disk pack past a read/write head during data transmission.

Documentation Written material that accompanies a program and includes definitions, explanations, charts, tests, and changes to the program.

Dot-matrix printer Impact printer that forms characters from a matrix of pins arranged in a rectangular shape. The matrix may consist of seven rows of five pins each and only the pins necessary for forming a particular character are selected from the matrix. (The dot-matrix formation may also be used in nonimpact printers.)

Editing window The area on a computer screen that contains the typed words in a document; also, the area in which changes can be made in a document.

Electronic bulletin board Smaller, user-run version of the commercial information services, offered at little or no cost to users.

Electronic data processing (EDP) Data processing performed largely by electronic equipment, such as computers, rather than by manual or mechanical means.

Electronic mail Transmission of messages at high speeds over communication channels.

Electronic spreadsheet A large computerized grid, or table, divided into rows and columns, which uses computer storage and capabilities for financial analysis.

Encryption The process of encoding data or programs to disguise them from unauthorized personnel.

Erasable programmable read-only memory (EPROM) A form of read-only memory that can be erased and reprogrammed, but only by being submitted to a special process such as exposure to ultraviolet light.

Expert system Software program that uses a base of knowledge in a particular field of study for decision-making and evaluation processes that result in suggestions for actions similar to those of human experts in that field.

Extended Binary Coded Decimal Interchange Code (EBCDIC) An 8-bit code for character representation.

Feedback A check within a system to see whether predetermined goals are being met.

Field A subdivision of a record that holds a meaningful item of data, such as an employee number.

File A group of related records stored together; a specific unit of data stored on a disk or tape such as a program or text file.

Filename A meaningful name given to a file.

Floppy disk A low-cost, direct-access form of secondary storage made of flexible plastic; a flexible magnetic disk currently made in 3 1/2-, 5 1/4-, and 8-inch diameters; also called flexible disk or diskette.

Flowchart A graphic representation in which symbols represent the flow of operations, logic, data, and equipment of a program or system.

Footer A piece of text that is stored separately from the main text and printed at the bottom of each page.

Format See Initialize.

Formatting The function of a word processor which communicates with the printer to tell it how to print the text on paper.

Formula A mathematical expression used in a spreadsheet.

FORTH A high-level programming language that includes low-level language instructions; FORTH is the standard language used at astronomical observatories around the world.

FORTRAN (FORmula Translator) The oldest surviving high-level programming language; used primarily in performing mathematical or scientific operations.

Function A built-in formula or process included in a spreadsheet program. When a function is used in a formula, a calculation is automatically performed. For example, a sum function automatically adds a range of numbers.

Global search and replace A search and replace operation that is carried out throughout the entire document, without user intervention.

Hard copy Printed output.

Hardware Physical components that make up a computer system.

Header A piece of text that is stored separately from the main text and printed at the top of each page.

High-level language Languages that are oriented more toward the user than the computer system (contrast with low-level languages). High-level languages generally contain English words such as READ and PRINT and must be translated into machine language before execution. A single high-level language statement may translate into several machine language statements.

Impact printer A printer that forms characters by physically striking ribbon, paper, and embossed characters together.

Information Data that has been organized and processed so it is meaningful.

Information service Commercial service that offers information over communication lines to paying subscribers; also called information utility, information network, and commercial data base.

Initialize To prepare a disk so that data and programs can be stored on it.

Input Data submitted to the computer for processing.

Insertion A word processing feature in which a character, word, sentence, or larger block of text can be added to the existing text.

Instruction set The fundamental logical and arithmetic procedures that the computer can perform, such as addition and comparison, designed into the electronic circuitry of the CPU; the basic set of instructions built into a computer that tells it what to do.

Integrated circuit An electronic circuit etched on a small silicon chip less than 1/4-inch square, permitting much faster processing than with transistors and at a greatly reduced price.

Integrated software Two or more application programs that work together, allowing easy movement of data between the applications; they also use a common group of commands between the applications.

Interactive processing A data-processing method where the user enters input via a keyboard during processing.

Interactive video Multimedia learning concept that merges computer text, sound, and graphics by using a videodisk, videodisk player, microcomputer with monitor and disk drive, and computer software; allows the user to respond to questions from the system and input inquiries into the system.

Interpreter program A high-level language translator that evaluates and translates a program one statement at a time; used extensively on microcomputer systems because it takes less primary storage than a compiler.

Justification A feature for making lines of text even at the margins.

Kilobyte (K) 1,024 (2^{10}) storage units (1024 bytes); often rounded to 1,000; K is the symbol used for representing kilobytes.

Label Information used for describing some aspect of a spreadsheet.

Language translator program System program that

GLOSSARY

translates programming languages other than machine language (the source programs) into machine-executable code.

Large-scale integration (LSI) Method by which circuits containing thousands of electronic components are densely packed in a single chip.

LISP (LISt Processing) A high-level programming language commonly used in artificial intelligence research and in the processing of lists of elements.

Load To put a program into a computer's primary memory from a disk or tape.

Local area network Specialized network of computers and peripherals that operates within a limited geographic area, such as a building or complex of buildings, with the stations being linked by communications cables; requires special software and allows the sharing of data and hardware.

Logo An education-oriented programming language designed to allow anyone quickly to begin programming and communicating with computers; it commonly uses an object such as a turtle for tracing the formation of images on the screen.

Loop Program logic that allows a specified sequence of instructions to be executed repeatedly as long as stated conditions are met.

Low-level language A machine-oriented language; machine language and assembly languages are low-level languages.

Machine language The only type of instructions that a computer can execute directly; a code that designates the proper electrical states in the computer as combinations of 0s and 1s.

Magnetic disk A direct-access storage medium consisting of a metal or plastic platter coated with a magnetic recording material upon which data can be stored as magnetized spots.

Magnetic-ink character recognition (MICR) The process that allows characters printed with ink containing magnetized particles to be read by a magnetic-ink character reader; used for sorting checks.

Magnetic tape A sequential storage medium consisting of a narrow strip of material treated with a magnetizable coating upon which spots are magnetized to represent data.

Mainframe A type of large, full-scale computer capable of supporting many peripheral devices.

Management information system (MIS) A formal network that uses computers to provide information that supports structured managerial decision making; its goal is to get the correct information to the appropriate manager at the right time.

Mass storage A type of storage developed for recording huge quantities of data; typically each unit of storage medium is retrieved mechanically and mounted on a drive for reading or writing.

Materials Requirement Planning (MRP) Computerized method of inventory control that involves entering data into a computer and receiving a report based on the data.

Megahertz (MHz) One million times per second; the unit of measurement for clock speed.

Menu A list of choices or options shown on the display screen from which the user selects a command or data for entry into the computer.

Microcomputer A small, low-priced computer used in homes, schools, and businesses; also called a personal, or home, computer.

Microprocessor A programmable processing unit, placed on a chip made of silicon or similar material, containing arithmetic, logic, and control circuitry; used in microcomputers, calculators, and microwave ovens and for many other applications.

Minicomputer A type of computer with the components of a full-sized system but with smaller primary memory.

Mnemonics Symbolic names or memory aids; used in assembly and high-level programming languages.

Model A numeric representation of a real-world situation.

Modeling Process of making a prototype of an idea or object in order to design and test it.

Modem An acronym for modulator/demodulator; a device that modulates and demodulates signals transmitted over communication lines; allows linkage with another computer.

Modula-2 A high-level structured programming language that is a descendant of Pascal and is based on the concept of modules that are nested within one another. Modula-2 incorporates low-level language commands.

Modular approach A method of simplifying a programming project by breaking it into segments or subunits referred to as modules.

Modulation Technology used in modems to make data processing signals compatible with communication facilities.

GLOSSARY

Module Part of a whole; a program segment or subsystem; a set of logically related program statements that perform one specified task in a program.

Monitor A video display device or screen used for showing output.

Monochrome monitor A monitor that displays a single color, such as white, green, or amber, against a black background; used primarily for displaying text.

Natural language A language designed primarily for novice computer users that allows use of statements very much like everyday speech, usually for the purpose of accessing data in a data base.

Nondestructive read/destructive write The feature of computer memory that permits data to be read and retained in its original state, allowing repeated reference during processing; new data written over the old, however, destroys (replaces) the old.

Nonimpact printer Printer in which the printing process involves heat, laser, or photographic methods of producing images; since no hammering or striking is involved, it is a quiet means of printing.

Nuclear magnetic resonance (NMR) scanning Computerized diagnostic tool that involves sending magnetic pulses through the body in order to identify medical problems.

Object program A sequence of machine-executable instructions generated by a language translator program from source-program statements.

Office automation Integration of computer and communication technology with traditional office procedures in order to increase productivity and efficiency in the office.

Offline Not in direct communication with the central computer.

Online In direct communication with the computer.

Operating system (OS) A collection of system programs used by the computer to manage its own operations; provides an interface between the user, application program, and computer hardware.

Optical character recognition (OCR) Method of electronic scanning that reads numbers, letters, bars, or other characters and then converts the optical images into appropriate electrical signals; some OCR scanners can read only certain fonts, while others can read fairly well-formed handwritten characters.

Output Information that comes from the computer as a result of processing into a form that can be used by people.

Overtype To type directly over an existing character, replacing it with a new character.

Parallel processing A type of processing in which instructions and data are handled simultaneously by two or more processing units.

Parity bit A bit added to detect incorrect transmission of data within a computer system; used in conducting internal checks to determine whether the correct number of bits are present.

Pascal A high-level structured programming language originally developed for instructional purposes and now commonly used in a wide variety of applications; named in honor of the French mathematician Blaise Pascal.

Peripheral device Device that attaches to the central processing unit, such as secondary storage device, input device, or output device.

Plotter An output device that converts data emitted from the CPU into graphic forms; typically uses pens in producing hard copy graphic output such as drawings, charts, maps, and other picture images.

Point-of-sale (POS) terminal Computer terminal that serves as a cash register but also records data for such tasks as inventory control and accounting at the location where goods are sold; connected to a central computer.

Portable Describing a program that can be run on many different computers with minimal changes.

Portable computer A small microcomputer that is light enough to be carried easily and does not need an external source of power; may be divided further by size into briefcase and notebook.

Precedence In a spreadsheet program, the order in which calculations are executed in a formula containing several operators.

Primary memory Also known as internal storage, main storage, or primary storage; the section of the computer that holds instructions, data, and intermediate and final results during processing.

Print formatting The function of a word processor which communicates with the printer to tell it how to print the text on paper.

Printer A machine that prints characters or other images on paper; may be categorized as impact and nonimpact, depending on whether printing occurs by the striking action of print elements against paper and ribbon or by laser, chemical, thermal, or other means.

GLOSSARY

Privacy The right of an individual to be left alone; as related to data processing, the right of an individual to control the collection, processing, storage, dissemination, and use of data about personal attributes and activities.

Process To transform data into useful information by classifying, sorting, calculating, summarizing, or storing.

Program A series of step-by-step instructions that tells the computer exactly what to do; of two types, application and system.

Programmable read-only memory (PROM) Read-only memory that can be programmed by the manufacturer or user for special functions in order to meet the unique needs of the user; can be programmed once.

Programmer The person who writes the step-by-step instructions that tell a computer exactly what to do.

Programming The process of writing the step-by-step instructions that direct a computer in performing a task.

Prompt A message or cue that guides the user during computer processing—it indicates to the user what type of input is needed, what might be wrong in case of error, or how the user can ask for help; in BASIC programming, the PRINT statement written before an INPUT statement is used for printing an explanation of what data are to be entered next.

Proper program A structured program in which each individual segment or module has only one entrance and one exit.

Pseudocode An informal, narrative language used for representing the logic of a programming problem solution.

Punched cards Heavy paper storage medium in which data is represented by holes punched according to a coding scheme much like that used on Hollerith's cards.

Query language See Natural language.

RGB monitor A monitor that receives three separate color signals, one for each of three colors—red, green, and blue.

RPG (Report Program Generator) A high-level language designed for producing business reports. RPG requires the programmer to record data and operations on specification forms; the generator program then builds the needed program. RPG requires little skill on the part of the programmer for use.

RAM disk A portion of RAM memory that is temporarily acting as a disk drive, but approximating the speed of the microprocessor; often used for holding utility programs that may be needed while the user is working with an application program; it appears like a disk to the computer but is not actually a disk.

Random-access memory (RAM) Form of primary memory into which instructions and data can be read, written, and erased; the contents may be changed many times during processing; directly accessed by the computer; volatile, or temporary, memory that is erased when the computer is turned off.

Range A rectangular block of one or more cells in the worksheet, which is treated as one unit.

Read-only memory (ROM) The part of computer hardware containing items (circuitry patterns) that cannot be deleted or altered by stored-program instructions.

Read/write head The electromagnet of a tape or disk drive; in reading, it detects magnetized spots and translates them into electrical pulses; in writing, it magnetizes appropriate areas, thereby erasing any previously recorded data.

Real time Descriptive of a system's capability to receive and process data, providing output fast enough to control the outcome of an activity.

Record A collection of related data fields that comprise a single unit, such as an employee record.

Register An internal computer component used as a temporary holding area for an instruction or data item during processing; capable of accepting, holding, and transferring that instruction or datum very rapidly.

Remote terminal A terminal that is placed at a location distant from the central computer.

Robotics Science dealing with the construction, capabilities, and applications of robots.

Scrolling Moving a line or lines of text onto or off the screen.

Search and find A routine that searches for a specific string of characters and places the cursor at that location.

Search and replace A routine that searches for a specified character string and replaces it with a specified replacement string.

Secondary storage Also known as external or auxiliary storage; supplements primary memory and is external to the computer; data is accessed at slower speeds.

Selection Program logic that requires the computer to make a comparison; the result of the comparison determines which execution path will be taken next.

Semiconductor A substance (for example, silicon) whose conductivity is less that that of metals, but greater than

... insulators; conductivity is improved by the addition of certain substances or by the application of heat, light, or voltage.

Sequential-access storage Secondary storage from which data must be read one after another in a fixed sequence from the beginning until the needed data is located; an example is magnetic tape.

Silicon chip Solid-logic circuitry on a small piece of silicon.

Simple sequence Program logic in which one statement is executed after another, in the order in which they occur in the program.

Simulation A computer program that imitates conditions in a real-world situation; it can show what happens when variables are changed.

Soft copy A temporary, or nonpermanent, record of machine output, for example, a display that appears on a screen or monitor.

Software Program or programs used to direct the computer in solving problems and overseeing operations.

Software package A set of standardized computer programs, procedures, and related documentation needed for a particular application.

Software piracy The unauthorized copying of a copyrighted computer program.

Source program A sequence of instructions written in a language other than machine language that must be translated into machine language before the computer can execute the instructions.

Source-data automation Approach to data collection in which data is gathered in computer-readable form at its point of origin.

Spatial digitizer An input device that can graphically reconstruct a three-dimensional object on a computer's display screen.

Spreadsheet A ledger or table used in a business environment for financial calculations and for the recording of transactions.

Spreadsheet analysis A mental process of evaluating information contained in an electronic spreadsheet; also called what-if analysis.

Spreadsheet program A set of computer instructions which generates and operates an electronic spreadsheet.

Status line A message line above or below the text area on a display screen which gives format and system information.

Stored program A program held in primary memory in electronic form so that no human intervention is required during processing; can be executed repeatedly during processing.

Stored-program concept The idea that program instructions can be stored in primary memory in electronic form so that no human intervention is required during processing; allows the computer to process the instructions at its own speed.

Structure chart A graphic representation of the results of the top-down design process, displaying the modules of the solution and their relationships to one another.

Structured programming A collection of techniques that encourage the development of well-designed, less error-prone programs with easy-to-follow logic. Structured programming techniques include top-down design and extensive documentation and program testing.

Supercomputer The largest, fastest, most expensive type of computer in existence, capable of performing millions of calculations per second and processing enormous amounts of data; also called maxicomputer or monster computer.

Supermicrocomputer A microcomputer powerful enough to compete with low-end microcomputers; usually built around 32-bit microprocessors.

Syntax The structure that must be followed when writing program instructions; the grammatical rules of a language; in dBase, the structure of the commands.

System analyst The person who is the communication link or interface between users and technical persons (such as programmers and operators); responsible for system analysis, design, and implementation of computer-based information systems.

System program Instructions written for coordinating the operation of computer circuitry and helping the computer run quickly and efficiently.

Tape drive A drive that moves tape past a read/write head.

Telecommunications The combined use of communication facilities, such as telephone systems and data-processing equipment.

Telecommute To work at home and communicate with the office or send data to the office via electronic machines and telecommunications facilities.

Teleconference Meeting that occurs via telephone, electronic and/or image-producing facilities, thereby eliminating the need for travel.

Text editing The function of a word processor which enables the user to enter and edit text.

GLOSSARY

Timesharing An arrangement in which two or more users can access the same central computer resources and receive what seems to be simultaneous results.

Top-down design A method of defining a solution in terms of major functions to be performed, and further breaking down the major functions into subfunctions; the further the breakdown, the greater the detail.

Touch screen A computer screen equipped for detecting the point at which it is touched by the user; it allows the user to bypass the keyboard.

Track One of a series of concentric circles on the surface of a magnetic disk.

Transportable A class of microcomputer smaller than the desktop models for easier carrying, but larger than the portables and therefore bulkier to carry.

Users group An informal group of owners of a particular brand of microcomputer or software who meet to exchange information about hardware, software, service, and support.

Value A single piece of numeric data used in the calculations of a spreadsheet.

Very-large-scale integration (VLSI) Method by which circuits containing hundreds of thousands of electronic components are densely packed on a single chip, packed even more densely than with LSI.

Voice recognition The ability of electronic equipment to recognize speech and voice patterns.

Voice recognition system An input system that recognizes certain speech and voice patterns; the user must follow only the patterns the system is programmed to recognize.

Voice response unit A device through which the computer ''speaks'' by arranging half-second records of phonemes, or voice sounds.

Voice synthesizer The output portion of a voice communication system; used to provide verbal output from the computer system to the user.

Window The portion of an electronic spreadsheet which can be seen on the computer display screen.

Word size The number of bits that can be manipulated at one time, for instance, an 8-bit microprocessor can manipulate 8 bits (one byte) of data at a time.

Word processing The act of composing and manipulating text electronically.

Word processing system The hardware and software used for word processing.

Word processor A program or set of programs designed to enable you to enter, manipulate, format, print, store, and retrieve text.

Word wrap The feature by which a word is automatically moved to the beginning of the next line if it goes past the right margin.

Worksheet The grid of rows and columns created using a spreadsheet software package. The worksheet falls within the row and column borders.

INDEX

Abacus, 17
Ada, 122–123
Aiken, Howard, 20
Algorithm, 101
American National Standards Institute (ANSI), 102
Analytical engine, 9
ANSI, 102
Arithmetic/Logic Unit (ALU), 68–69
Artificial Intelligence (AI), 203–205
ASCII, 93
Assembly language, 25–26
Atanasoff, John Vincent, 22
Atanasoff-Berry Computer (ABC), 22
Automatic Teller Machine (ATM), 6–7
Automation, 158–164, 204–205
   home, 168–170
   manufacturing, 161–164
   office, 158–161

Babbage, Charles, 19
Bandwidth, 154
Bar codes, 83
BASIC, 115–118
   True BASIC, 117
Batch processing, 16
Baud, 154
Binary number system, 91
Binary representation, 91
Biochips, 30–31
Biomechanics, 176
Bit, 10, 130
   parity, 93
Block movement, 231, 299

Boot, 137, 216, 284, 426
Branch pattern, 101
Bubble memory, 78–80
Bugs, 28, 44
Business forecasting, 172
Byte, 93

C, 120
CAD/CAM, 175
Calculations of numbers, 170–172
CAT scan, 174
Cell, active (spreadsheet), 349
Cell, spreadsheet, 347
Cell pointer, spreadsheet, 349
Central Processing Unit (CPU), 13, 68–73
Character enhancement, 246, 314
   with WordStar 2000, 255–256
Characters, storage, 10
Chief programmer team (CPT), 109
Chip, silicon, 27
Clock speed, 136
COBOL, 114–115
CODASYL, 114
Code checking, 93–94
Coding (writing a program), 102
Codes, computer, 93
   ASCII, 93
   EBCDIC, 93
Communication channel, 152
Communication networks, 156–157
Compatible, 138
Compiler, 102
Comprehensive Crime Control Act of 1984, 195

Computer crime, 192–195
   categories, 193–194
Computer ethics, 199–210
Computer literacy, 178
Computer mistakes, 197–199
   causes of, 197–198
   responsibility for, 198–199
Computer needs, 201–203
Computers, 5
   accuracy, 12
   advantages, 10–12
   analog, 10
   applications, 4–9
   at home, 4–5
   basic functions, 11
   classifications, 64–68
      mainframe, 64–65
      microcomputer, 66
      minicomputer, 65–66
      supercomputer, 66–67
   digital, 10
   history, 4, 17–31
      first generation, 24–26
      second generation, 26–27
      third generation, 27–29
      fourth generation, 29–31
   families, 64
   in business, 6
   in colleges, 181–182
   in education, 8, 177–182
   in government, 6–7
   in manufacturing, 6
   in science and medicine, 7–8
   in sports, 8
   speed, 11–12

I-1

Computer-aided design (CAD), 175
Computer-aided manufacturing (CAM), 175
Computer-assisted instruction (CAI), 179–180
Computer-integrated manufacturing (CIM), 162
Computer-output microfilm (COM), 89–90
Connection machine, 70
Control panel, spreadsheet, 349
Control unit, 68–69
Coordinate, spreadsheet, 349
Coprocessor, 138
Copyright Act of 1978, 200
CorrectStar, 232–235
    spelling correction menu, 233
CPT, 109
Cray, Seymour, 205
Cursor, 35
Cursor-control keys, with WordStar 2000, 220–221

Data, accessing, 13
Data and information, 9
Data manager, 422
    uses, 424
Data processing, 9
    electronic, 9
    stages, 13–16
Data redundancy, 423
Data representation, 91–94
    binary, 91–92
    computer codes, 93
Databases, 125, 152, 423
    commercial, 4
    government, 188–190
    privacy concerns, 188–190
Database management system (DBMS), 422
dBase, 425
dBase III, 425–456, 462–491
    accessing a record, 469
    adding numeric fields, 454
    adding records, 446
    averaging values of numeric fields, 455
    commands, 435–452, 462–491
        APPEND, 445
        AVERAGE, 455
        BROWSE, 445–446
        COUNT, 453
        CREATE REPORT, 471
        DELETE, 450
        DIR, 436
        DISPLAY, 438–442
        EDIT, 448–449
        FIND, 469
        GOTO, 452
        GO TOP and GO BOTTOM, 452
        HELP, 437
        INDEX ON, 465–468
        JOIN WITH, 485
        LIST, 443–444
        MODIFY REPORT, 477–478
        MODIFY STRUCTURE, 442
        PACK, 447–448
        PRINT REPORT, 479
        QUIT, 436
        RECALL, 450–451
        SELECT, 480
        SORT TO, 462–464
        SUM, 454
        summary commands, 453–455
        summary of, 487–491
        syntax, 436
        USE, 436
        using, 435–436
    counting records, 453
    creating a file, 427–434
    data structure, 442
    deleting records, 450, 446–448
    deleting fields, 446–448
    displaying a record, 452
    dot prompt, 427
    editing records, 448
    entering records, 433–434
    exiting, 436
    field definition, 428–430
    file names, 428
    files
        indexing, 465–468
        joining, 484–485
    getting started, 426–427
    help messages, 437
    logical operators, 440
    multiple files, 480–485
        joining, 484–485
        opening, 480
    printing files, 455–456
    relational operators, 440
    reports, 471–479
        creating, 471–475
        defining columns, 474–475
        formatting, 472–473
        modifying, 477–478
        printing, 479
    searching files, 440
    sorting records, 462–464
        conditional sorts, 464
Debugging, 102–104
Default settings, 271, 288, 356, 428
Deletion, 226, 294
Demodulation, 152
Difference Engine, 19
Directory, 356
Disks
    disk pack, 75
    floppy, 37, 78
    hard, 135–136
    magnetic, 74
Disk drive, 34, 37–38, 78
Disk operating system (DOS), 41–44
Disk operating system (DOS) commands, 47–48
Documentation, 107–108

EBCDIC (Extended binary coded decimal interchange code), 93
Eckert, J. Presper, 21–22, 24
Edison, Thomas, 44
Editing window, 288
EDSAC, 98
EDVAC (Electronic Discrete Variable Automatic Computer), 23, 24
Electronic bulletin boards, 157
Electronic data processing (EDP), 9
Electronic mail, 159–160
Encryption, 195
ENIAC (Electronic Numerical Integrator and Calculator), 21–22, 98
EPROM, 73
Erasable programmable read-only memory (EPROM), 73
Error checking
    codes, 93–94
Errors, program, 104
    logic, 102
    run-time, 102
    syntax, 104
Expert system, 170–171, 203
Extended binary coded decimal interchange code (EBCDIC), 93

Feedback, 16
Field, 422
File, 47, 422
Firmware, 137
Floating-point operations per second (FLOPS), 66
Flowchart, 101
Footer, 262, 331
Formatting, 45–46
    documents, 314
Formulas, spreadsheets, 347
FORTH, 124
FORTRAN, 114
Full-duplex transmission, 154
Function, spreadsheet, 392

Garbage in-garbage out, 12
Global search and replace, 265
GOTO, 101
Graphs, analytical, 401–402
    with Lotus 1-2-3, 401–405
Graphics, 172–177
    analyzing motion, 176
    business, 176

INDEX

Half-duplex transmission, 154
Hard copy, 16
Hardware, 10
   for input and output, 80–90
   IBM, 34–39
Header, 262, 331
Hillis, Daniel, 70
Hoff, Ted, 29
Hollerith, Herman, 19–20
Hopper, Grace, 26, 44

IBM, 20
Information and data, 9
Information retrieval, 161
Information service, 156–157
Initialize, 45–46
Input, 13
   methods, 81–86
      key-to-magnetic media, 82
      punched cards, 81
      source-data automation, 82
      specialized devices, 83–86
Input devices
   for microcomputers, 139–140
   special, 141
Insertion, 226, 294
Instruction set, 11, 130
Integrated circuit, 27
Interactive processing, 16
Interpreter, 102

Jacquard, Joseph, 18
Jacquard's loom, 18–19
Justification, 220, 314

Kemeny, John, 117
Keyboard, 36–37, 139
Keypunch, 81
Kilby, Jack, 27
Kilobyte, 34
Kurtz, Thomas, 117
Kurzweil, Ray, 90
Kurzweil Reading Machine, 90

Labels, spreadsheets, 347
Languages
   see Programming languages
Language-translator program, 102
Large-scale integration (LSI), 27
Ledger sheets, 346
Leibniz, Gottfried von, 18
LISP, 124
Load, 40
Local Area Networks (LAN), 157
Liquid Crystal Displays (LCD), 143

Logic patterns, 100–101, 107
Logo, 124–125
Loop, 19, 101
Lotus 1-2-3, 349–380, 388–409
   Access System, 352
   calculations, order of precedence, 397
   cell addresses, in formulas, 369
   cell width, 363
   charts, pie, 403
      creating, 405
   column widths, adjusting, 376
   control panel, 349
   copy and move, 388–389
   creating a worksheet, 362–374
   cursor movement, 353
   deleting rows and columns, 377–378
   editing data, 363
   erasing a cell, 374
   ERROR message, 359–360
   error message area, 349
   formatting cells, 372
   formulas, entering, 369
   functions
      built-in, 391–392
      copying, 393–394
   getting started, 351–352
   global commands, 390
   GOTO, 353
   graphics, 401–409
   graphs, 402–403
      creating, 403–405
      printing, 408–409
   Help facility, 359–360
   indicators, 349–350
   inserting rows and columns, 377–378
   labels
      aligning, 375
      entering, 363
   mathematical operators, 369
   menus and menu options, 354
   mode indicator, 349
   moving around the worksheet, 352–353
      freezing titles, 394–395
   parts of the worksheet, 349–350
   pointer movement keys, 353
   printer options, 379
   PrintGraph, 408–409
   printing graphs, 408–409
   printing worksheets, 378–380
   quitting files and access system, 361–362
   range, 366–367
      printing, 379
   retrieving files, 356–358
   saving files, 356–358
      amended files, 358–359
   spreadsheet analysis, 400
   submenus, 354
   values, entering, 365–366
   window, 352–353

   worksheet, changing appearance, 375–ɔ
Lovelace, Ada, 19

Machine language, 25
Magnetic-ink character recognition (MICR), 82–83
Management Information System (MIS), 202
Mark I, 20
Mark II, 44
Materials Requirement Planning (MRP), 162
Mauchly, John, 20–22, 24
McCarthy, John, 124
Medical diagnosis, 173–174
Megahertz, 136
Memory, in microcomputers, 136–137
Menu, 48
Message transmission, 152–154
   modes, 154
   speeds, 154
MICR (Magneteic-ink character recognition), 82
Microcomputers, 29
   add-ons, 145
   compatibility, 138
   overview, 130–135
   using, 139–148
Microcomputers, IBM, 34
   care of, 39–40
   getting started, 40–44
Microfilm, computer-output (COM), 89–90
Microprocessor, 29, 130–131, 136
   speed, 136
Minicomputers, 28
Mnemonics, 113
Model, 388
Modeling, 170
Modem, 48, 132, 153
Modula-2, 123
Modular approach, 106
Modules, 106
Modulation, 152
Monitoring, electronic, 164–170
   earth, 172–173
   home, 168–170
   human body, 166–168
   in science laboratories, 164–166
   of workers, 193
Monitors, 34
   composite color, 140
   microcomputer, 140–142
   monochrome, 140
   RGB (Red, green, and blue), 140–142
Moore, Charles, 124
Motherboard, 131

Nanoseconds, 11
Napier, John, 17

INDEX

...tive write, 72
Nuclear Magnetic Resonance (NMR), 174

Object program, 102
Offline data entry, 13
Online data entry, 13
Oppenheimer, Peter, 110
Operating system, 41, 110–111
   control program, 111
   microcomputers, 137–138
   processing program, 111
Optical Character Recognition (OCR), 159
Optical recognition, 83
Output, 16
   specialized devices, 89–90
   voice, 90
Output devices, 86–90
   flat panel displays, 142–143
   for microcomputers, 140–143
Overtype, 229, 297

Papert, Seymour, 124
Pascal, 118–120
   TURBO, 120
Pascal, Blaise, 18
Pascaline, 18
Peripheral devices, 64, 131
Plotters, 89
Point-Of-Sale (POS) terminals, 83
Portable microcomputer, 132
Precedence, spreadsheet, 397
Primary memory, 12, 34, 69–70, 72–73
Print formatting, 246
Printers, 34, 86–88
   dot-matrix, 87
   daisy-wheel, 87
   electrostatic, 87
   impact, 86–87
   ink-jet, 88
   laser, 88
   nonimpact, 86–88
   thermal, 87–88
   xerographic, 88
Printing
   character enhancements, 246, 255–256, 324
   formatting, 246–261
      WordPerfect, 314–330
   with dBase III, 455–456
Privacy, 188–191
   legislation, 190–191
Privacy Act of 1974, 190–191
Processing, 16
   batch, 16
   interactive, 16
   parallel, 30, 70
Processing data, 13–16
Processor, 68
Programs, 10
   application, 109–110
   assembler, 102
   characteristics, 102
   compiler, 102
   control, 111
   interpreter, 102
   language translator, 111
   library, 111
   portable, 120
   processing, 111
   proper, 107
   spreadsheet, 346
   stored, 69
   system, 109–110
   types, 109–110
   utility, 111
Programmable Implantable Medicine System (PIMS), 168
Programmable Read-Only Memory (PROM), 72–73
Programmer, 98
Programming, 98
   education, 178–179
   structured, 104–109
      goals, 106
Programming languages, 112–125
   high-level, 102, 113–125
   low-level, 112–113
      assembly, 102, 113
      machine, 91, 102, 112
   natural, 125
   query, 125
Programming process, 98–104
PROM (Programmable Read-Only Memory), 72
Prompt, 36
   dot (with dBase III), 427
Pseudocode, 101
Publishing, desktop, 162
Punched cards, 18–20

RAM (Random-Access Memory), 72
   microcomputers, 137
RAM disk, 148
Random-Access Memory (RAM), 72
Range, spreadsheet, 366–367
Read-Only Memory (ROM), 72–73
Read/write head, 74
Real-time processing, 16
Record, 422
Registers, 70–71
Remote terminals, 83
Report Program Generator (RPG), 120
Reports, with dBase III, 471–479
Risk analysis, 6
Ritchie, Dennis, 120
Robotics, 163–164
ROM (Read-Only Memory), 72
   microcomputers, 137

Scanner, 83
Screen width, IBM, 36
Scrolling, 228, 288
Search and find, 265, 333
Search and replace, 265
Secondary storage, 13
   see also Storage, secondary
Security, 195–197
   common measures, 195–196
   needs, 201–203
Selection pattern, 101
Simple sequence, 100
Simplex transmission, 154
Simulation, 48, 170
Slide rule, 17
Soft copy, 16
Software, 10, 28–29
   for transmission, 154–156
   integrated, 147
   packages, 146–148
   piracy, 199–201
   utilities, 147–148
Source-data automation, 82–83
Source program, 102
Spatial digitizer, 85
Speller, with WordPerfect, 301–303
Spreadsheet analysis, 388
   with Lotus 1-2-3, 400
Spreadsheets, 146, 346
Spreadsheets, electronic, 29, 172, 347
   see also Lotus 1-2-3
   terms, 347
   uses, 347–349
Status line, 226, 285
Stepped reckoner, 18
Storage, primary, 12
   microcomputers, 143–145
Storage, secondary, 13, 73–80
   cassette tapes, 143
   direct access, 73
      media, 74–78
   disk, 26–27
   floppy disks, 144
   hard disks, 144
   media, 78–80
      bubble memory, 78–80
      laser, 80
      mass storage, 78
   optical disks, 144–145
   sequential-access, 73
      media, 73–74
   tape, 26–27

INDEX

Stored-program concept, 22, 70
Structure chart, 107
Supercomputers, 29–30
Supermicrocomputers, 133–135
Syntax, 112, 436
Synthesizers, voice, 90
System analyst, 99–100, 201
System approach, 201

Tabulating machine, 19–20
Tape, magnetic, 73–74
Tape drive, 74
Telecommunications, 152–157
Telecommuting, 160–161
Teleconferencing, 160
Text editing, 226, 294
Timesharing, 181
Testing a program, 108–109
Top-down design, 106–107
Touch screen, 85–86
Tracks, on disks, 74
Transistor, 26
Transmission software, 154–156
Transportable microcomputers, 133
Typewriter Voice-Activated (VAT), 90

UNIVAC I, 24
Users' groups, 148

Values, spreadsheets, 347
Very Large-Scale Integration (VLSI), 29
Video, interactive, 180–181
Voice recognition, 203–204
Voice recognition systems, 86
Voice response units, 90

Weather forecasting, 171–172
WestSoft 1.0, 48–57
  loading, 49
  simulations
    Dental Office Manager, 57
    Home Banking System, 49–50
    Information Network, 55–56
    Personality Traits Program, 52
    Ticket Office Manager, 53
Whirlwind, 26
White-collar crime, 193
Window, spreadsheet, 352
Wirth, Niklaus, 118, 123
Word processing, 5, 158–159, 212, 278
  terms, 214–215, 280–281
Word processing system, 212, 278
  dedicated, 212, 278
Word processor, 212–215, 278–279
  uses, 213–215, 279
Word size, 136
WordPerfect, 279–308, 314–333
  advanced features, 331–333
  character enhancements, 324
  command codes, 324–325
  correcting spelling mistakes, 301–303
    saving corrections, 303
  creating a document, 288–292
  cursor movement, 294–295
  editing a document, 294–303
  entering text, 288
  footnotes and endnotes, 333
  getting started, 284–285
  help messages, 286
  indenting paragraphs, 318
  line format, 315–318
  moving blocks of text, 299–300
  page format, 331–333
  print format, 314
  printing, 306–307
  removing text, 296–297
  retrieving a document, 292
  saving a document, 290–292
  search, 333
WordStar 2000, 216–241, 246–271
  advanced features, 262–271
  blocks menu, 231
  changing format design, 270–271
  command tags, 248–250
  copying a document, 227
  correcting spelling mistakes, 232–235
  creating a document, 218–225
  cursor menu, 227
  editing a document, 226–235
  editing menu, 223
  entering text, 222–223
  footnotes, 264
  formatting a document, 220–221
  getting started, 216–217
  headers and footers, 262–264
  help messages, 217–218
  History Screen, 221
  locate and replace, 265–266
  moving text, 231
  moving the cursor, 227–228
  naming a file, 219
  opening menu, 217–218
  options menu, 233, 248
  print enhancements, 255–256
  printing, 235–236
  recording a document's history, 221
  remove menu, 228–229
  removing text, 228–230
  saving a document, 224–225
  setting tabs and margins, 246–248
  summary of menus, 237–242
  undo command, 230
Word wrap, 223, 288
Worksheet (spreadsheet), 347

of 1632 from NCR Corp., **Fig. 5-7** Courtesy of ... Computer, Inc., **Fig. 5-8a** Courtesy of Apple Computer, Inc., **Fig. 5-8b** Courtesy of The Mouse House, Inc., **Fig. 5-8c** Photo courtesy of Hewlett-Packard Company, **Fig. 5-9** Courtesy of Amdek Corporation, **Fig. 5-10** Zenith Data Systems, subsidiary of Zenith Electronics Corp., **Fig. 5-11** Courtesy of Verbatim Corporation, **Fig. 5-12a** Photos courtesy of 3M, **Fig. 5-12b** Photos courtesy of 3M, **Fig. 5-13** Courtesy of Maxtor Corporation, **Fig. 5-14** Courtesy of Interstate Voice Products, **Fig. 5-15a** Photos courtesy of Microsoft Corporation, **Fig. 5-15b** Reprint permission granted by Computer Associates, Micro Products Division, Oct. 1985, **Fig. 5-15c** Courtesy of SAS Institute, Inc., Cary, N.C., **Fig. 5-15d** Smart Software photos by permission of Innovative Software, Inc., **Fig. 6-2a** Jay Freis, Courtesy of Planning Research Corporation, **Fig. 6-2b** Photo courtesy of Anderson Jacobson, Inc., **Fig. 6-5** Courtesy of International Business Machines Corporation, **Fig. 6-6** Courtesy of International Business Machines Corporation, **Fig. 6-7** Courtesy of Oberon International, **Fig. 6-8** Compression Labs, Incorporated, **Fig. 6-9** Courtesy of Apple Computer, Inc., **Fig. 6-10** Courtesy of Cincinnati Milacron, **Fig. 6-11a** Courtesy of SAFER Emergency Systems, **Fig. 6-11b** Courtesy of SAFER Emergency Systems, **Fig. 6-12** Courtesy of AT&T Bell Laboratories, **Fig. 6-13** Reproduced with permission of Medtronic, Inc., **Fig. 6-14** Reproduced with permission of Medtronic, Inc., **Fig. 6-15** Courtesy of National Severe Storms Forecast Center, **Fig. 6-16** Optronics International, Inc., **Fig. 6-17** Courtesy of Parkland Memorial Hospital, **Fig. 6-18** Photos courtesy of Rockwell International, **Fig. 6-19a** Courtesy of Visual Communications Network, Inc., **Fig. 6-19b** 1985 Time Arts Inc. *Artist:* John Dorry, **Fig. 6-20** Photograph by John Morgan, **Fig. 6-21** Courtesy of Blyth Software, **Fig. 6-22** Courtesy of Apple Computer, Inc., **Fig. 7-2** Courtesy of the F.B.I., **Fig. 7-7** Honeywell Inc., Building Services Division, **Fig. 7-8** Photo courtesy INTERMEC.

IMPORTANT: PLEASE READ BEFORE OPENING DISKETTE PACKAGE
THIS TEXT IS NOT RETURNABLE IF SEAL IS BROKEN.

INTRODUCTION TO COMPUTERS USING IBM/MS-DOS
POPULAR COMMERCIAL SOFTWARE VERSION LIMITED USE LICENSE

READ THE FOLLOWING TERMS AND CONDITIONS CAREFULLY BEFORE OPENING THIS DISKETTE PACKAGE. OPENING THE DISKETTE PACKAGE INDICATES YOUR AGREEMENT TO THE LICENSE TERMS. IF YOU DO NOT AGREE, PROMPTLY RETURN THIS PACKAGE UNOPENED TO WEST SERVICES FOR A FULL REFUND.

BY ACCEPTING THIS LICENSE, YOU HAVE THE RIGHT TO USE THE STUDENT FILES, WESTSOFT AND THE ACCOMPANYING DOCUMENTATION, BUT YOU DO NOT BECOME THE OWNER OF THESE MATERIALS.

THIS COPY IS LICENSED TO YOU FOR USE ONLY UNDER THE FOLLOWING CONDITIONS:

1. PERMITTED USES
You are granted a non-exclusive limited license to use the STUDENT FILES and WESTSOFT under the terms and conditions stated in this License. You may:
   a. Use the disk on a single computer.
   b. Make a single copy in machine-readable form solely for backup purposes in support of your use on a single machine. You must reproduce and include the copyright notice on any copy you make.
   c. Transfer this copy and the License to another user if the other user agrees to accept the terms and conditions of this License. If you transfer this copy, you must also transfer or destroy the backup copy you made. Transfer of this copy and the License automatically terminates this License as to you.

2. PROHIBITED USES
YOU MAY NOT USE, COPY, MODIFY, DISTRIBUTE OR TRANSFER THE STUDENT FILES AND WESTSOFT OR ANY COPY, IN WHOLE OR IN PART, EXCEPT AS EXPRESSLY PERMITTED IN THIS LICENSE.

3. TERM
This License is effective when you open the diskette package and remains in effect until terminated. You may terminate this License at any time by ceasing all use and destroying this copy and any copy you have made. It will also terminate automatically if you fail to comply with the terms of this License. Upon termination, you agree to cease all use and destroy all copies.

4. DISCLAIMER OF WARRANTY
EXCEPT AS STATED HEREIN, THE STUDENT FILES AND WESTSOFT ARE LICENSED "AS IS" WITHOUT WARRANTY OF ANY KIND, EXPRESS OR IMPLIED, INCLUDING WARRANTIES OF MERCHANTABILITY OR FITNESS FOR A PARTICULAR PURPOSE. YOU ASSUME THE ENTIRE RISK AS TO THE QUALITY AND PERFORMANCE. YOU ARE RESPONSIBLE FOR THE SELECTION TO ACHIEVE YOUR INTENDED RESULTS AND FOR THE INSTALLATION, USE AND RESULTS OBTAINED FROM IT. WEST PUBLISHING AND WEST SERVICES DO NOT WARRANT THE PERFORMANCE OF NOR RESULTS THAT MAY BE OBTAINED. West Services does warrant that the diskette upon which the STUDENT FILES and WESTSOFT are provided will be free from defects in materials and workmanship under normal use for a period of 30 days from the date of delivery to you as evidenced by a receipt.

SOME STATES DO NOT ALLOW THE EXCLUSION OF IMPLIED WARRANTIES SO THE ABOVE EXCLUSION MAY NOT APPLY TO YOU. THIS WARRANTY GIVES YOU SPECIFIC LEGAL RIGHTS. YOU MAY ALSO HAVE OTHER RIGHTS WHICH VARY FROM STATE TO STATE.

5. LIMITATION OF LIABILITY
Your exclusive remedy for breach by West Services of its limited warranty shall be replacement of any defective diskette upon its return to West at the above address, together with a copy of the receipt, within the warranty period. If West Services is unable to provide you with a replacement diskette which is free of defects in material and workmanship, you may terminate this License by returning the disk, and the license fee paid hereunder will be refunded to you. IN NO EVENT WILL WEST BE LIABLE FOR ANY LOST PROFITS OR OTHER DAMAGES INCLUDING DIRECT, INDIRECT, INCIDENTAL, SPECIAL, CONSEQUENTIAL OR ANY OTHER TYPE OF DAMAGES ARISING OUT OF THE USE OR INABILITY TO USE THE DISK EVEN IF WEST SERVICES HAS BEEN ADVISED OF THE POSSIBILITY OF SUCH DAMAGES.

6. GOVERNING LAW
This Agreement will be governed by the laws of the State of Minnesota.

YOU ACKNOWLEDGE THAT YOU HAVE READ THIS LICENSE AND AGREE TO ITS TERMS AND CONDITIONS. YOU ALSO AGREE THAT THIS LICENSE IS THE ENTIRE AND EXCLUSIVE AGREEMENT BETWEEN YOU AND WEST AND SUPERSEDES ANY PRIOR UNDERSTANDING OR AGREEMENT, ORAL OR WRITTEN, RELATING TO THE SUBJECT MATTER OF THIS AGREEMENT.